Initiatives by Subsidiaries of Multinational Corporations

Lars R. Dzedek

Initiatives by Subsidiaries of Multinational Corporations

An Empirical Study on the Influence of Subsidiary Role Context

With a foreword by Prof. Dr. Stefan Schmid

Springer Gabler

Lars R. Dzedek
Fort Lauderdale, USA

Dissertation ESCP Europe Wirtschaftshochschule Berlin, 2017

Original Title: "Role-Specific Subsidiary Initiative-Taking in Multinational Corporations – A Contingent and Dynamic Resource-Based Perspective"

ISBN 978-3-658-20949-0   ISBN 978-3-658-20950-6 (eBook)
https://doi.org/10.1007/978-3-658-20950-6

Library of Congress Control Number: 2018932035

Springer Gabler
© Springer Fachmedien Wiesbaden GmbH, part of Springer Nature 2018
This work is subject to copyright. All rights are reserved by the Publisher, whether the whole or part of the material is concerned, specifically the rights of translation, reprinting, reuse of illustrations, recitation, broadcasting, reproduction on microfilms or in any other physical way, and transmission or information storage and retrieval, electronic adaptation, computer software, or by similar or dissimilar methodology now known or hereafter developed.
The use of general descriptive names, registered names, trademarks, service marks, etc. in this publication does not imply, even in the absence of a specific statement, that such names are exempt from the relevant protective laws and regulations and therefore free for general use.
The publisher, the authors and the editors are safe to assume that the advice and information in this book are believed to be true and accurate at the date of publication. Neither the publisher nor the authors or the editors give a warranty, express or implied, with respect to the material contained herein or for any errors or omissions that may have been made. The publisher remains neutral with regard to jurisdictional claims in published maps and institutional affiliations.

Printed on acid-free paper

This Springer Gabler imprint is published by the registered company Springer Fachmedien Wiesbaden GmbH part of Springer Nature
The registered company address is: Abraham-Lincoln-Str. 46, 65189 Wiesbaden, Germany

Foreword

For 20 years, the phenomenon of subsidiary initatives has received considerable attention in International Business (IB) and International Management (IM) literature. While Julian Birkinshaw's 1997 article in Strategic Management Journal was certainly breaking the ground, many other authors have provided us with valuable and insightful research on subsidiaries being proactive, risk-taking and autonomous or semi-autonomous.

The present thesis has several merits: First of all, the thesis contains an excellent literature review on subsidiary initiatives in Multinational Corporations (MNCs). The literature review fosters our understanding of subsidiariy initiatives, various types of subsidiary initiatives, their antecedents and consequences. The literature review provides us with the state-of-the art of the literature, identifies gaps to be closed, and comes up with avenues for research to be continued. Second, the thesis links the „subsidiary initative field" to the „role typology field" in IB and IM literature. It is in the empirical part of this thesis that Lars Dzedek investigates the influence of subsidiary roles on subsidiary initiatives. Based on two case study companies, one from the automotive industry, the other from the telecommunications industry, Lars Dzedek is able to shed light on the subsidiary initiative phenomenon, in particular on the link between the subsidiary role in question and initative processes and initiative outcomes. Third, the thesis implicitly calls for future research that is even more processual and longitudinal in nature as well as moving from the functionalist towards the interpretative paradigm so as to better understand the variety of factors shaping subsidiary initiatives (and their manifold consequences) over time.

The thesis in hand is logically structured, very well-written and easy to read despite its length. It shifts the view from the typical headquarters-centred MNC towards an MNC in which subsidiaries can have not only a voice, but can trigger important new developments. If you are convinced that in MNCs it is not only headquarters, but also subsidiaries abroad that matter, you will benefit from the present thesis. You will learn under which conditions subsidiaries have a greater likelihood to become influential in their parent companies and their sister subsidiaries as well as in the environment in which they are embedded. I wish you new and useful insights!

Berlin, November 2017   Stefan Schmid

Preface

This doctoral thesis was initiated during my time at ESCP Europe Wirtschaftshochschule Berlin where I was working as a research assistant at the Chair of International Management and Strategic Management. Completing this academic endeavor has only been made possible through the support of many people who I owe much appreciation.

First, I would like to express my deep gratitude to my advisor Prof. Dr. Stefan Schmid who encouraged and continuously supported this dissertation over the past years. He gave me the opportunity to choose this highly interesting research topic and promoted many fruitful discussions, for example, at various research colloquia and international conferences. His academic rigor, critical guidance and valuable advice have helped to successfully complete this dissertation.

Second, much appreciation also goes to my second supervisor Prof. Dr. Mark Lehrer who not only acted as a second reviewer but who also helped to critically shape this dissertation from its beginning. Thank you so much for many great discussions and valuable feedback at research meetings, over lunches or even during long walks together.

An essential part of this dissertation is the empirical study. I am very grateful for the trust and support from the two multinational firms and the participating managers both at headquarters and in the many subsidiaries abroad. This research would not have been possible without their important input on how subsidiary initiatives develop and unfold in various settings.

I would also like to thank my colleagues from ESCP Europe who supported me in many ways and of which many have become close friends over the years. They were always open for discussions, shared ideas and provided moral support when needed. Many thanks go to Dr. Joern Basel, Prof. Dr. Tobias Dauth, Dr. Ruben Dost, Dr. Holger Endrös, Dr. Swantje Hartmann, Prof. Dr. Lena Knappert, Dr. Thomas Kotulla, Dr. Max Kury, Dr. Martina Maletzky, Renate Ramlau, Esther Rödel, Dr. Timo Runge, Carsten Schiefelbein, Jens Sievert, Dr. Sven Seehausen and Dr. Dennis Wurster.

Most of all I am deeply indebted to my wife Anna-Kathrin for her continuous support, endless encouragement and great patience. I also sincerely thank my parents, my family and close friends for all their help and trust throughout this challenging journey. Thank you all for helping to make this possible.

Fort Lauderdale, November 2017   Lars R. Dzedek

Brief Contents

1	**INTRODUCTION**	**1**
1.1	Subsidiary Initiative-Taking in Foreign Subsidiaries	1
1.2	Research Background and Research Questions	2
1.3	Objectives and Structure of the Study	4
2	**REVIEW OF THE LITERATURE ON SUBSIDIARY INITIATIVES**	**9**
2.1	Roots of Subsidiary Initiative Research	9
2.2	Findings from the Literature Review and Analysis	10
2.3	Summary of Findings and Implications for Research Project	38
3	**RESEARCH FRAMEWORK**	**45**
3.1	Overview of the Research Framework	45
3.2	Elements of the Research Framework	48
3.3	Theoretical Perspectives	71
3.4	Contingent and Dynamic Resource-Based Framework	151
3.5	Predictions for Role-Specific Initiative-Taking	192
4	**EMPIRICAL STUDY**	**259**
4.1	Research Philosophy	259
4.2	Research Design	267
4.3	Operationalization of the Research Framework	280
4.4	Collection of Data	313
4.5	Data Analysis	323
4.6	Scientific Quality Criteria	329
5	**EMPIRICAL FINDINGS**	**333**
5.1	Company A: Strategic Business Unit Autocomp	333
5.2	Company B: Strategic Business Unit Telecomp	404
5.3	Overview of Findings at Autocomp and Telecomp	469
6	**CONTRIBUTIONS, LIMITATIONS AND THE ROAD AHEAD**	**511**
6.1	Implications for International Business Research	511
6.2	Implications for Management Practice	515
6.3	Limitations	520
6.4	Avenues for Further Research	523

Contents

1 INTRODUCTION.. 1
1.1 Subsidiary Initiative-Taking in Foreign Subsidiaries 1
1.2 Research Background and Research Questions 2
1.3 Objectives and Structure of the Study.. 4

2 REVIEW OF THE LITERATURE ON SUBSIDIARY INITIATIVES 9
2.1 Roots of Subsidiary Initiative Research.. 9
2.2 Findings from the Literature Review and Analysis 10
   2.2.1 Overview of the Publication Activity in the Field 10
   2.2.2 Framework for the Literature Review and Analysis 12
   2.2.3 Concept of Subsidiary Initiatives 13
      2.2.3.1 Types of Subsidiary Initiatives 13
      2.2.3.2 Objectives of Subsidiary Initiatives 16
      2.2.3.3 Process of Subsidiary Initiatives 17
   2.2.4 Antecedents of Subsidiary Initiatives 22
      2.2.4.1 Environmental Level Context 22
      2.2.4.2 Organizational Level Context 23
      2.2.4.3 Individual Level Context... 27
   2.2.5 Consequences of Subsidiary Initiatives 29
      2.2.5.1 Environmental Level Consequences.. 29
      2.2.5.2 Organizational Level Consequences 30
   2.2.6 Theoretical Approaches in the Subsidiary Initiative Field 32
   2.2.7 Research Methodologies in the Subsidiary Initiative Field 35
2.3 Summary of Findings and Implications for Research Project 38

3 RESEARCH FRAMEWORK 45
3.1 Overview of the Research Framework.. 45
3.2 Elements of the Research Framework 48
   3.2.1 Subsidiary Role Types 48
      3.2.1.1 Introduction to Subsidiary Role Typologies 48
      3.2.1.2 Subsidiary Role Determination and Development......................... 53
      3.2.1.3 Subsidiary Roles and Entrepreneurial Behavior............................ 56
      3.2.1.4 Selection of Subsidiary Role Typologies for the Research............ 59
      3.2.1.5 Overview of Selected Role Typologies 62
   3.2.2 Subsidiary Initiative-Taking Behavior 67
      3.2.2.1 Initiative-Related Resource Management 67
      3.2.2.2 Headquarters-Subsidiary Alignment 68
   3.2.3 Subsidiary Initiative Outcomes 69

3.3		Theoretical Perspectives	71
	3.3.1	Selection of Theoretical Perspectives for the Study	72
		3.3.1.1 Excluded Theories	72
		3.3.1.2 Selected Theories	83
	3.3.2	Resource-Based View of the Firm	87
		3.3.2.1 Overview of the Resource-Based View	87
		3.3.2.2 Advancements of the Resource-Based View	93
		3.3.2.3 Resource-Based View in International Business Literature	108
		3.3.2.4 Resource-Based View in Entrepreneurship Literature	123
	3.3.3	Resource Dependence Theory	126
		3.3.3.1 Overview of Resource Dependence Theory	126
		3.3.3.2 Resource Dependence Theory in International Business Literature	129
	3.3.4	Contingency Theory	135
		3.3.4.1 Overview of Contingency Theory	135
		3.3.4.2 Contingency Theory in International Business Literature	139
	3.3.5	Linking the Theoretical Perspectives	143
		3.3.5.1 Relationship Between RBV and RDT	144
		3.3.5.2 Relationship Between Contingency Theory and RBV	146
		3.3.5.3 Relationship Between Contingency Theory and RDT	147
		3.3.5.4 Application of Theoretical Lenses	149
3.4		Contingent and Dynamic Resource-Based Framework	151
	3.4.1	Introduction and Basic Assumptions	151
	3.4.2	Entrepreneurial Resource Management	153
		3.4.2.1 Initiative-Related Opportunity Identification	155
		3.4.2.2 Initiative-Related Resource Structuring	156
		3.4.2.3 Initiative-Related Resource Bundling	160
	3.4.3	Headquarters-Subsidiary Alignment	162
		3.4.3.1 Headquarters Involvement	166
		3.4.3.2 Corporate Resistance	168
		3.4.3.3 Subsidiary Initiative Selling	170
		3.4.3.4 Summary of Subsidiary Initiative-Taking Behavior	173
	3.4.4	Subsidiary Initiative-Taking Outcomes	175
		3.4.4.1 Realized Subsidiary Initiatives	176
		3.4.4.2 Resource-Based Outcomes	177
		3.4.4.3 Subsidiary Evolution	182
	3.4.5	Subsidiary Roles as Contingency Factors	184
	3.4.6	Conclusion	190
3.5		Predictions for Role-Specific Initiative-Taking	192
	3.5.1	Role Typology by Bartlett and Ghoshal	192
		3.5.1.1 Strategic Importance of the Subsidiary Environment	192

3.5.1.2	Subsidiary Resources and Capabilities	200
3.5.1.3	Role-Specific Predictions	208
3.5.2	Role Typology by Jarillo and Martinez	224
3.5.2.1	Subsidiary's Localization and Local Responsiveness	224
3.5.2.2	Subsidiary Integration	231
3.5.2.3	Role-Specific Predictions	238

4 EMPIRICAL STUDY ... 259

4.1	Research Philosophy		259
4.2	Research Design		267
	4.2.1	Rationale for Case Study Design	268
	4.2.2	Description of the Multiple Case Study Design	272
	4.2.2.1	Selection of the Case Study Design	272
	4.2.2.2	Determination of Units of Analysis and Units of Observation	273
	4.2.2.3	Case Selection	273
	4.2.2.4	Types of Data	279
4.3	Operationalization of the Research Framework		280
	4.3.1	Subsidiary Role Dimensions	280
	4.3.1.1	Strategic Importance of the Subsidiary Environment	280
	4.3.1.2	Subsidiary Resources and Capabilities	282
	4.3.1.3	Subsidiary's Localization and Local Responsiveness	284
	4.3.1.4	Subsidiary Integration and Subsidiary Autonomy	286
	4.3.2	Subsidiary Initiative-Taking	289
	4.3.2.1	Subsidiary Initiative Opportunity Identification	289
	4.3.2.2	Resource Structuring	292
	4.3.2.3	Resource Bundling	299
	4.3.2.4	Headquarters-Subsidiary Alignment	302
	4.3.3	Subsidiary Initiative-Taking Outcome	304
	4.3.3.1	Extent and Types of Subsidiary Initiatives	305
	4.3.3.2	Specialized Subsidiary Resources and Capabilities for MNC Application	307
	4.3.4	Additional Measures	309
	4.3.4.1	Subsidiary Role and Position in the MNC	309
	4.3.4.2	Subsidiary Performance	311
	4.3.4.3	Control Measures	312
4.4	Collection of Data		313
	4.4.1	Questionnaire	314
	4.4.1.1	Objectives	314
	4.4.1.2	Approach	315
	4.4.2	Interviews	318
	4.4.2.1	Objectives	318

    4.4.2.2   Approach 319
  4.4.3   Archival and Secondary data 323
    4.4.3.1   Objectives 323
    4.4.3.2   Approach 323
4.5   Data Analysis 323
  4.5.1   Questionnaire 323
  4.5.2   Interviews and Secondary Data 325
4.6   Scientific Quality Criteria 329

5 EMPIRICAL FINDINGS 333

5.1   Company A: Strategic Business Unit Autocomp 333
  5.1.1   German Subsidiary 334
    5.1.1.1   Subsidiary Roles 335
    5.1.1.2   Subsidiary Initiative-Taking 338
    5.1.1.3   Subsidiary Initiative-Taking Outcome 342
  5.1.2   Mexican Subsidiary 344
    5.1.2.1   Subsidiary Roles 344
    5.1.2.2   Subsidiary Initiative-Taking 347
    5.1.2.3   Subsidiary Initiative-Taking Outcome 352
  5.1.3   South Korean Subsidiary 355
    5.1.3.1   Subsidiary Roles 355
    5.1.3.2   Subsidiary Initiative-Taking 358
    5.1.3.3   Subsidiary Initiative-Taking Outcome 362
  5.1.4   Australian Subsidiary 364
    5.1.4.1   Subsidiary Roles 365
    5.1.4.2   Subsidiary Initiative-Taking 368
    5.1.4.3   Subsidiary Initiative-Taking Outcome 371
  5.1.5   Chinese Subsidiary 374
    5.1.5.1   Subsidiary Roles 374
    5.1.5.2   Subsidiary Initiative-Taking 377
    5.1.5.3   Subsidiary Initiative-Taking Outcome 381
  5.1.6   Romanian Subsidiary 383
    5.1.6.1   Subsidiary Roles 384
    5.1.6.2   Subsidiary Initiative-Taking 387
    5.1.6.3   Subsidiary Initiative-Taking Outcome 390
  5.1.7   Indian Subsidiary 393
    5.1.7.1   Subsidiary Roles 394
    5.1.7.2   Subsidiary Initiative-Taking 397
    5.1.7.3   Subsidiary Initiative-Taking Outcome 400
5.2   Company B: Strategic Business Unit Telecomp 404

- 5.2.1 Hungarian Subsidiary 405
  - 5.2.1.1 Subsidiary Roles 406
  - 5.2.1.2 Subsidiary Initiative-Taking 408
  - 5.2.1.3 Subsidiary Initiative-Taking Outcome 411
- 5.2.2 Polish Subsidiary 413
  - 5.2.2.1 Subsidiary Roles 414
  - 5.2.2.2 Subsidiary Initiative-Taking 416
  - 5.2.2.3 Subsidiary Initiative-Taking Outcome 419
- 5.2.3 Croatian Subsidiary 422
  - 5.2.3.1 Subsidiary Roles 423
  - 5.2.3.2 Subsidiary Initiative-Taking 425
  - 5.2.3.3 Subsidiary Initiative-Taking Outcome 428
- 5.2.4 Slovakian Subsidiary 431
  - 5.2.4.1 Subsidiary Roles 431
  - 5.2.4.2 Subsidiary Initiative-Taking 434
  - 5.2.4.3 Subsidiary Initiative-Taking Outcome 437
- 5.2.5 Greek Subsidiary 440
  - 5.2.5.1 Subsidiary Roles 440
  - 5.2.5.2 Subsidiary Initiative-Taking 443
  - 5.2.5.3 Subsidiary Initiative-Taking Outcome 447
- 5.2.6 Romanian Subsidiary 449
  - 5.2.6.1 Subsidiary Roles 450
  - 5.2.6.2 Subsidiary Initiative-Taking 452
  - 5.2.6.3 Subsidiary Initiative-Taking Outcome 456
- 5.2.7 Montenegrin Subsidiary 459
  - 5.2.7.1 Subsidiary Roles 460
  - 5.2.7.2 Subsidiary Initiative-Taking 462
  - 5.2.7.3 Subsidiary Initiative-Taking Outcome 465
- 5.3 Overview of Findings at Autocomp and Telecomp 469
  - 5.3.1 Subsidiary Roles 469
    - 5.3.1.1 Strategic Leader and Active Subsidiary 469
    - 5.3.1.2 Contributor and Receptive Subsidiary 470
    - 5.3.1.3 Black Hole and Autonomous Subsidiary 471
    - 5.3.1.4 Implementer and Quiescent Subsidiary 472
  - 5.3.2 Subsidiary Initiative-Taking 472
    - 5.3.2.1 Entrepreneurial Resource Management 472
    - 5.3.2.2 Headquarter-Subsidiary Alignment 477
  - 5.3.3 Subsidiary Initiative Outcome 479
    - 5.3.3.1 Extent of Subsidiary Initiative-Taking 479
    - 5.3.3.2 Resource-Related Outcomes 482

      5.3.3.3   Further Outcomes 483
   5.3.4   Summary on Role-Specific Initiative-Taking 485
   5.3.5   Additional Findings on Subsidiary Initiatives 489
      5.3.5.1   Objectives of Subsidiary Initiatives 489
      5.3.5.2   Antecedents of Subsidiary Initiatives 491
      5.3.5.3   Subsidiary Initiative Process 498
      5.3.5.4   Subsidiary Initiative Outcomes 504
   5.3.6   Conclusion 507

6   CONTRIBUTIONS, LIMITATIONS AND THE ROAD AHEAD 511
6.1   Implications for International Business Research 511
6.2   Implications for Management Practice 515
6.3   Limitations 520
6.4   Avenues for Further Research 523

APPENDIX 527

REFERENCES 551

List of Figures

Figure 1.1:	Structure of the thesis	6
Figure 2.1:	Publication dates of the literature on subsidiary initiatives	12
Figure 2.2:	Framework for the literature review and analysis	13
Figure 2.3:	Classification of subsidiary initiative types	15
Figure 2.4:	Simplified process view on subsidiary initiative development	21
Figure 2.5:	Overview of research approaches for the investigation of subsidiary initiatives	35
Figure 2.6:	Subsidiary initiatives, their antecedents and consequences – research areas and methodologies in previous publications	41
Figure 3.1:	Overview of the basic research framework	48
Figure 3.2:	Factors influencing subsidiary roles and role development	55
Figure 3.3:	Subsidiary role typology by Bartlett and Ghoshal	62
Figure 3.4:	Subsidiary role typology by Jarillo and Martinez	65
Figure 3.5:	Subsidiary role typology by Taggart	66
Figure 3.6:	Overview of the extended research framework	70
Figure 3.7:	Theoretical perspectives and their application in the research framework	87
Figure 3.8:	Overview of the resource-based framework	90
Figure 3.9:	Components and underlying activities of resource management processes from existing literature	103
Figure 3.10:	Key contingency factors outlined in resource management literature	106
Figure 3.11:	Sample resources and capabilities at different levels of the MNC	111
Figure 3.12:	Development of specialized subsidiary resources and capabilities	113
Figure 3.13:	FSA- and SSA-based competitive advantage through subsidiary resources	117
Figure 3.14:	Simplified resource-based perspective on subsidiary resource and capability development and potential firm-level advantage	122
Figure 3.15:	Extended version of the contingency model	136
Figure 3.16:	Theoretical perspectives and their application in the research framework	150
Figure 3.17:	Mechanisms and sources for subsidiary initiative-related resource	157
Figure 3.18:	Key elements of subsidiary initiative-taking behavior	175
Figure 3.19:	Subsidiary initiative types and the associated resource and capability characteristics	182
Figure 3.20:	Outcomes of subsidiary initiatives	184
Figure 3.21:	Overview of final research framework on role-specific subsidiary initiative-taking	188
Figure 4.1:	Four paradigms for the analysis of organizations	264

Figure 4.2:	Research Methodologies and related philosophical paradigms	266
Figure 4.3:	The environment of MNCs	275
Figure 4.4:	Overview of applied selection criteria	278
Figure 4.5:	Proposed research framework	280
Figure 4.6:	Overview of data collection approaches used in this study	314
Figure 4.7:	Section of headquarters questionnaire on subsidiary roles	315
Figure 4.8:	General structure of the subsidiary interview guide	322
Figure 4.9:	Sample graph chart on subsidiary role dimensions	324
Figure 4.10:	Initial coding scheme used for the analysis	328
Figure 5.1:	Organizational structure of Company A and its Autocomp division	333
Figure 5.2:	Survey Results – Subsidiary roles at Autocomp	334
Figure 5.3:	Survey Results Germany – Strategic importance and subsidiary resources/ capabilities	335
Figure 5.4:	Survey Results Germany – Subsidiary localization/local responsiveness and subsidiary integration	337
Figure 5.5:	Survey Results Germany – Subsidiary decision-making autonomy	338
Figure 5.6:	Survey Results Germany – Identification and innovativeness of initiative opportunities	339
Figure 5.7:	Survey Results Germany – Initiative-related resource structuring activities	340
Figure 5.8:	Survey Results Germany – Headquarters-subsidiary alignment and interaction	341
Figure 5.9:	Survey Results Germany – Types and extent of subsidiary initiatives	342
Figure 5.10:	Survey Results Germany – New subsidiary resources and impact on MNC capabilities	343
Figure 5.11:	Survey Results Germany – Performance outcomes and subsidiary role and position	344
Figure 5.12:	Survey Results Mexico – Strategic importance and subsidiary resources/ capabilities	345
Figure 5.13:	Survey Results Mexico – Subsidiary localization/local responsiveness and subsidiary integration	346
Figure 5.14:	Survey Results Mexico – Subsidiary decision-making autonomy	347
Figure 5.15:	Survey Results Mexico – Identification and innovativeness of initiative opportunities	349
Figure 5.16:	Survey Results Mexico – Initiative-related resource structuring activities	350
Figure 5.17:	Survey Results Mexico – Headquarters-subsidiary alignment and interaction	351
Figure 5.18:	Survey Results Mexico – Types and extent of subsidiary initiatives	352
Figure 5.19:	Survey Results Mexico – New subsidiary resources and impact on MNC capabilities	353

Figure 5.20: Survey Results Mexico – Performance outcomes and subsidiary role and position 354

Figure 5.21: Survey Results SK – Strategic importance and subsidiary resources/ capabilities 356

Figure 5.22: Survey Results SK – Subsidiary localization/local responsiveness and subsidiary integration 357

Figure 5.23: Survey Results SK – Subsidiary decision-making autonomy 358

Figure 5.24: Survey Results SK – Identification and innovativeness of initiative opportunities 359

Figure 5.25: Survey Results SK – Initiative-related resource structuring activities 360

Figure 5.26: Survey Results SK – Headquarters-subsidiary alignment and interaction 361

Figure 5.27: Survey Results SK – Types and extent of subsidiary initiatives 362

Figure 5.28: Survey Results SK – New subsidiary resources and impact on MNC capabilities 363

Figure 5.29: Survey Results SK – Performance outcomes and changes to subsidiary role and position 364

Figure 5.30: Survey Results AUS – Strategic importance and subsidiary resources/ capabilities 366

Figure 5.31: Survey Results AUS – Subsidiary localization/local responsiveness and subsidiary integration 367

Figure 5.32: Survey Results AUS – Subsidiary decision-making autonomy 368

Figure 5.33: Survey Results AUS – Identification and innovativeness of initiative opportunities 369

Figure 5.34: Survey Results AUS – Initiative-related resource structuring activities 370

Figure 5.35: Survey Results AUS – Headquarters-subsidiary alignment and interaction 371

Figure 5.36: Survey Results AUS – Types and extent of subsidiary initiatives 372

Figure 5.37: Survey Results AUS – New subsidiary resources and impact on MNC capabilities 373

Figure 5.38: Survey Results AUS – Performance outcomes and changes to subsidiary role and position 374

Figure 5.39: Survey Results China – Strategic importance and subsidiary resources/ capabilities 375

Figure 5.40: Survey Results China – Subsidiary localization/local responsiveness and subsidiary integration 376

Figure 5.41: Survey Results China – Subsidiary decision-making autonomy 377

Figure 5.42: Survey Results China – Identification and innovativeness of initiative opportunities 378

Figure 5.43: Survey Results China – Initiative-related resource structuring activities 379

Figure 5.44: Survey Results China – Headquarters-subsidiary alignment and interaction 380

Figure 5.45: Survey Results China – Types and extent of subsidiary initiatives 381
Figure 5.46: Survey Results China – New subsidiary resources and impact on MNC capabilities 382
Figure 5.47: Survey Results China – Performance outcomes and changes to subsidiary role and position 383
Figure 5.48: Survey Results ROM – Strategic importance and subsidiary resources/ capabilities 384
Figure 5.49: Survey Results ROM – Subsidiary localization/local responsiveness and subsidiary integration 386
Figure 5.50: Survey Results ROM – Subsidiary decision-making autonomy 387
Figure 5.51: Survey Results ROM – Identification and innovativeness of initiative opportunities 388
Figure 5.52: Survey Results ROM – Initiative-related resource structuring activities 388
Figure 5.53: Survey Results ROM – Headquarters-subsidiary alignment and interaction 390
Figure 5.54: Survey Results ROM – Types and extent of subsidiary initiatives 391
Figure 5.55: Survey Results ROM – New subsidiary resources and impact on MNC capabilities 392
Figure 5.56: Survey Results ROM – Performance outcomes and changes to subsidiary role and position 393
Figure 5.57: Survey Results India – Strategic importance and subsidiary resources/ capabilities 395
Figure 5.58: Survey Results India – Subsidiary localization/local responsiveness and subsidiary integration 396
Figure 5.59: Survey Results India – Subsidiary decision-making autonomy 397
Figure 5.60: Survey Results India – Identification and innovativeness of initiative opportunities 398
Figure 5.61: Survey Results India – Initiative-related resource structuring activities 399
Figure 5.62: Survey Results India – Headquarters-subsidiary alignment and interaction 400
Figure 5.63: Survey Results India – Types and extent of subsidiary initiatives 401
Figure 5.64: Survey Results India – New subsidiary resources and impact on MNC capabilities 402
Figure 5.65: Survey Results India – Performance outcomes and changes to subsidiary role and position 403
Figure 5.66: Organizational structure of Company B and its Telecomp Division 404
Figure 5.67: Survey Results – Subsidiary roles at Telecomp 405
Figure 5.68: Survey Results HUN – Strategic importance and subsidiary resources/ capabilities 406
Figure 5.69: Survey Results HUN – Subsidiary localization/local responsiveness and subsidiary integration 407

Figure 5.70:	Survey Results HUN – Subsidiary decision-making autonomy	407
Figure 5.71:	Survey Results HUN – Identification and innovativeness of initiative opportunities	409
Figure 5.72:	Survey Results HUN – Initiative-related resource structuring activities	409
Figure 5.73:	Survey Results HUN – HQ-S alignment and interaction	410
Figure 5.74:	Survey Results HUN – Types and extent of subsidiary initiatives	411
Figure 5.75:	Survey Results HUN – New subsidiary resources and impact on MNC capabilities	412
Figure 5.76:	Survey Results HUN – Performance outcomes and subsidiary role and position	413
Figure 5.77:	Survey Results PL – Strategic importance and subsidiary resources/capabilities	414
Figure 5.78:	Survey Results PL – Subsidiary localization/local responsiveness and subsidiary integration	415
Figure 5.79:	Survey Results PL – Subsidiary decision-making autonomy	416
Figure 5.80:	Survey Results PL – Identification and innovativeness of initiative opportunities	417
Figure 5.81:	Survey Results PL – Initiative-related resource structuring activities	417
Figure 5.82:	Survey Results PL – HQ-S alignment and interaction	419
Figure 5.83:	Survey Results PL – Types and extent of subsidiary initiatives	420
Figure 5.84:	Survey Results PL – New subsidiary resources and impact on MNC capabilities	421
Figure 5.85:	Survey Results PL – Performance outcomes and subsidiary role and position	422
Figure 5.86:	Survey Results CR – Strategic importance and subsidiary resources/capabilities	423
Figure 5.87:	Survey Results CR – Subsidiary localization/local responsiveness and subsidiary integration	424
Figure 5.88:	Survey Results CR – Subsidiary decision-making autonomy	425
Figure 5.89:	Survey Results CR – Identification and innovativeness of initiative opportunities	426
Figure 5.90:	Survey Results CR – Initiative-related resource structuring activities	427
Figure 5.91:	Survey Results CR – HQ-S alignment and interaction	428
Figure 5.92:	Survey Results CR – Types and extent of subsidiary initiatives	429
Figure 5.93:	Survey Results CR – New subsidiary resources and impact on MNC capabilities	430
Figure 5.94:	Survey Results CR – Performance outcomes and subsidiary role and position	431
Figure 5.95:	Survey Results SL – Strategic importance and subsidiary resources/capabilities	432

Figure 5.96: Survey Results SL – Subsidiary localization/local responsiveness and subsidiary integration 433

Figure 5.97: Survey Results SL – Subsidiary decision-making autonomy 434

Figure 5.98: Survey Results SL – Identification and innovativeness of initiative opportunities 435

Figure 5.99: Survey Results SL – Initiative-related resource structuring activities 436

Figure 5.100: Survey Results SL – HQ-S alignment and interaction 437

Figure 5.101: Survey Results SL – Types and extent of subsidiary initiatives 438

Figure 5.102: Survey Results SL – New subsidiary resources and impact on MNC capabilities 439

Figure 5.103: Survey Results SL – Performance outcomes and subsidiary role and position .. 440

Figure 5.104: Survey Results Greece – Strategic importance and subsidiary resources/ capabilities 441

Figure 5.105: Survey Results Greece – Subsidiary localization/local responsiveness and subsidiary integration 442

Figure 5.106: Survey Results Greece – Subsidiary decision-making autonomy 443

Figure 5.107: Survey Results Greece – Identification and innovativeness of initiative opportunities 444

Figure 5.108: Survey Results Greece – Initiative-related resource structuring activities 445

Figure 5.109: Survey Results Greece – HQ-S alignment and interaction 446

Figure 5.110: Survey Results Greece – Types and extent of subsidiary initiatives 447

Figure 5.111: Survey Results Greece – New subsidiary resources and impact on MNC capabilities 448

Figure 5.112: Survey Results Greece – Performance outcomes and subsidiary role and position 449

Figure 5.113: Survey Results ROM– Strategic importance and subsidiary resources/ capabilities 450

Figure 5.114: Survey Results ROM – Subsidiary localization/local responsiveness and subsidiary integration 451

Figure 5.115: Survey Results ROM – Subsidiary decision-making autonomy 452

Figure 5.116: Survey Results ROM – Identification and innovativeness of initiative opportunities 453

Figure 5.117: Survey Results ROM – Initiative-related resource structuring activities 454

Figure 5.118: Survey Results ROM – HQ-S alignment and interaction 456

Figure 5.119: Survey Results ROM – Types and extent of subsidiary initiatives 457

Figure 5.120: Survey Results ROM – New subsidiary resources and impact on MNC capabilities 459

Figure 5.121: Survey Results ROM – Performance outcomes and subsidiary role and position 459

Figure 5.122: Survey Results MON – Strategic importance and subsidiary resources/ capabilities 460

Figure 5.123: Survey Results MON – Subsidiary localization/local responsiveness and subsidiary integration 461

Figure 5.124: Survey Results MON – Subsidiary decision-making autonomy 462

Figure 5.125: Survey Results MON – Identification and innovativeness of initiative opportunities 463

Figure 5.126: Survey Results ROM – Initiative-related resource structuring activities..............464

Figure 5.127: Survey Results MON – Headquarters-subsidiary alignment and interaction 465

Figure 5.128: Survey Results MON – Types and extent of subsidiary initiatives 466

Figure 5.129: Survey Results MON – New subsidiary resources and impact on MNC capabilities 467

Figure 5.130: Survey Results MON – Performance outcomes and changes to subsidiary role and position..468

Figure 5.131: Main antecedents of subsidiary initiatives by role types 497

Figure 5.132: Additional findings on subsidiary initiative sub-processes 501

Figure 5.133: Key antecedents of entrepreneurial subsidiary initiatives 508

List of Tables

Table 3.1:	Comparison of subsidiary role typologies	49
Table 3.2:	Subsidiary role types with entrepreneurial potential.	58
Table 3.3:	Selection of suitable subsidiary role typologies for study	61
Table 3.4:	Contingency factors impacting organizational structure and behavior	137
Table 3.5:	Summary of predictions for the subsidiary role typology by Bartlett/ Ghoshal	223
Table 3.6:	Summary of predictions for the subsidiary role typology by Jarillo/Martinez	257
Table 4.1:	Comparison of different research philosophies	262
Table 4.2:	Comparison of objectivist and subjectivist approach	263
Table 4.3:	Overview of Autocomp and Telecomp cases	276
Table 4.4:	Sample of subsidiaries included in research	279
Table 4.5:	Measurement of the strategic importance of the subsidiary's market environment	282
Table 4.6:	Measurement of subsidiary resources and capabilities	283
Table 4.7:	Measurement of the subsidiary's localization and local responsiveness	285
Table 4.8:	Measurement of subsidiary integration	287
Table 4.9:	Measurement of subsidiary decision-making autonomy	288
Table 4.10:	Measurement of subsidiary initiative opportunity identification	291
Table 4.11:	Measurement of the innovativeness of subsidiary initiative opportunities	292
Table 4.12:	Measurement of initiative-related resource structuring	298
Table 4.13:	Measurement of initiative-related resource bundling	302
Table 4.14:	Measurement of headquarters-subsidiary alignment	304
Table 4.15:	Measurement of subsidiary initiative-taking per initiative type	306
Table 4.16:	Measurement of the enhancement of distinctive subsidiary resources and capabilities through subsidiary initiatives	308
Table 4.17:	Measurement of the subsidiary initiative impact on MNC capability development	309
Table 4.18:	Measurement of changes in subsidiary role, influence and credibility	311
Table 4.19:	Measurement of change in subsidiary performance	312
Table 4.20:	Elements of subsidiary-level questionnaire	317
Table 5.1:	Strategic Leader and Active Subsidiary: Subsidiary role dimensions and other information	470
Table 5.2:	Contributor and Receptive Subsidiary: Subsidiary role dimensions and other information	470
Table 5.3:	Black Hole and Autonomous Subsidiary: Subsidiary role dimensions and other information	471

Table 5.4:	Implementer and Quiescent Subsidiary: Subsidiary role dimensions and other information	472
Table 5.5:	Case Comparison: Identification and innovativeness of initiative opportunities	474
Table 5.6:	Case Comparison: Initiative-related resource structuring activities	476
Table 5.7:	Case Comparison: Initiative-related resource bundling activities	477
Table 5.8:	Case Comparison: Headquarters-subsidiary alignment and interaction	479
Table 5.9:	Case Comparison: Types and extent of subsidiary initiatives	482
Table 5.10:	Case Comparison: New subsidiary resources and impact on MNC capabilities	483
Table 5.11:	Case Comparison: Further outcomes of subsidiary initiatives	484
Table 5.12:	Summary of findings on role-specific subsidiary initiative-taking	488
Table 5.13:	Identified objectives of subsidiary initiatives	491
Table 5.14:	Perceived risks and benefits of subsidiary initiatives	506

1 Introduction[1]

1.1 Subsidiary Initiative-Taking in Foreign Subsidiaries

Traditional concepts in International Business (IB) literature have generally taken a hierarchical and center-dominated perspective of the Multinational Corporation (MNC) in which competitive advantage is generated at the corporate center for subsequent implementation by foreign subsidiaries located at the MNC periphery (Hymer 1976, pp. 41-43, Kutschker/Schmid 2011, p. 340). In contrast, more advanced concepts – such as the geocentric company, the transnational organization or the heterarchy – acknowledge the growing relevance of subsidiaries for the competitiveness of the entire corporation (Schmid et al. 2002, Kutschker/Schmid 2011, pp. 286-31523). More specifically, it has been shown that subsidiary units can contribute to the development of the MNC by, for instance, obtaining locally acquired knowledge (Almeida/Phene 2004, Mu et al. 2007) or more generally by developing unique resources and capabilities (Birkinshaw et al. 1998, Schmid/Schurig 2003, Cantwell/Mudambi 2005) which are then transferred to other units of the MNC, such as headquarters or sister subsidiaries (Ambos et al. 2006, Schotter/Bontis 2009, Schmid/Hartmann 2011).There is also a growing body of IB literature demonstrating that subsidiaries pursue innovative and entrepreneurial opportunities for local and global application – often even independently of the parent organization (e.g. Ghoshal/Bartlett 1988, Birkinshaw 1997, Scott/Gibbons 2009). Examples presented in scholarly literature of such dispersed innovative and entrepreneurial endeavors undertaken by foreign subsidiaries in MNCs include, for example, the introduction of the teletext technology by the UK subsidiary of Philips (Bartlett/Ghoshal 1986, p. 90, Birkinshaw 1997, p. 212), the development of an advanced automatic teller machine by the Scottish subsidiary of NCR (Ambos et al. 2010, p. 1099), or innovation activities in the area of wireless technologies by the US subsidiary of T-Mobile (Ambos/Schlegelmilch 2005, pp. 23-24).

Evidently, the identification and development of new business opportunities and the creation of new resources and capabilities do not necessarily have to take place at corporate headquarters. Instead, subsidiaries, as geographically dispersed entities within the MNC network (Bartlett/Ghoshal 1989), may benefit from their exposure to the various stimuli and resources immanent in their heterogeneous host environments (Frost 2001), thereby enhancing the MNC's accessibility to valuable knowledge and locally dispersed entrepreneurial opportunities (Mahnke et al. 2007). The identification, evaluation and exploitation of such entrepreneurial opportunities in the MNC host countries can either be coordinated by corporate headquarters or driven through subsidiaries' own initiative (Burgelman 1983, Birkinshaw 1997, Birkinshaw et al. 1998, Birkinshaw/

---

[1] Certain elements of this text have been previously published as parts of a working paper (Schmid/Dzedek 2011) and a journal article (Schmid et al. 2014).

Ridderstråle 1999). However, following the conceptualization of the MNC as a differentiated network of semi-autonomous entities and given the considerable size and complexity of many MNCs, it cannot be assumed that headquarters managers – in all cases – are able to foresee potential sources of opportunity and initiative across the wider MNC network (Birkinshaw 1998). These bounded rationality constraints therefore may force headquarters to grant the independent development of autonomous subsidiaries entrepreneurial undertakings, hoping that "profitable opportunities will be captured well beyond the headquarters' own *ex ante* capabilities to understand or even to identify such opportunities themselves" (Rugman/Verbeke 2003, p. 134).

Within the wider IB literature, these entrepreneurial subsidiary activities have been researched and brought together under the larger umbrella termed "subsidiary initiatives". This phenomenon is commonly understood as proactive, risk-taking and innovative behavior that takes place outside the home country in a foreign subsidiary of an MNC and which is typically started by actors in the unit abroad. The underlying initiative process commonly unfolds over several stages, beginning with the identification of an opportunity and finishing with the commitment of resources for the specific opportunity in the end. Subsidiary initiatives may take various forms, ranging from e.g. smaller internal business improvement efforts to extensive new product development activities for the external market. They do not only provide an important means by which foreign units can grow their own resource base but – in the longer term – they also allow the subsidiary to maintain or improve its standing within the corporate network (see e.g. Birkinshaw 1997, p. 207, 1999, p. 9, Birkinshaw/Ridderstråle 1999, Ambos et al. 2010, p. 1099, Ambos/Birkinshaw 2010, p. 456).

Although the potential benefits of subsidiaries engaging in entrepreneurial initiatives for subsequent exploitation across the MNC are increasingly acknowledged, not all subsidiaries exhibit such autonomous behavior (Birkinshaw et al. 1998, p. 235). Apparently, the phenomenon of subsidiary initiatives only materializes in a subset of MNC subsidiaries and empirical evidence – at least at first sight – seems to remain rare (Birkinshaw et al. 1998, p. 224, Birkinshaw/Ridderstråle 1999, p. 149, Birkinshaw 2000, p. 16, Borini et al. 2009, p. 260, Keupp/Gassmann 2009a, p. 194).

1.2 Research Background and Research Questions

A growing body of research has been dealing with entrepreneurial subsidiary initiatives over the past two decades. Despite the increasing interest from IB scholars, however, this subject still appears to have only received limited attention and remains an underexplored topic (Birkinshaw 1997, Birkinshaw et al. 2005). Accordingly, the concept of subsidiary initiatives is still labeled a "troublesome and little-understood concept" (Ambos et al. 2010, p. 1100). In line with these statements, the systematic literature review and critical analysis that was conducted as part of this research, revealed a number of different research gaps which inspired and guided the present study.[2] Three of the identified research gaps were particularly relevant when determining the focus of and the guiding questions for this research. (1) First, it was derived that the effect of subsidiary context – in the form of subsidiary roles – on entrepreneurial initiatives remains underexplored. (2) Second, it was noted that the initiative process has not yet been systematically and purposefully investigated yet. (3) Third, it was identified that in future research more attention needs to be paid to outcomes of subsidiary initiatives at subsidiary and corporate level.

(1) Concerning the firm as a whole it has already been stated earlier that it is "the principal challenge to management researchers ... to identify the entrepreneurial processes that lead to various forms of corporate entrepreneurship, and then to theoretically predict and empirically verify the forms of this phenomenon that produce the best results for firms in various business and industry contexts" (Covin/Miles 1999, p. 60). The same seems to hold true for subsidiary initiative-taking as a specific form of corporate entrepreneurship. Here, it has been requested that future research needs to strive towards developing a better understanding of subsidiary entrepreneurial initiatives in different contextual settings, as a single structural context is unlikely to facilitate all different forms of initiatives. Although it has been, rather generally, articulated earlier that the role a foreign subsidiary holds should potentially impact its innovative and entrepreneurial behavior, comprehensive and systematic research appears lacking (e.g. Birkinshaw 1997, p. 227, Young et al. 2003, p. 39, Mahnke et al. 2007, p. 1294).

(2) Various scholars have acknowledged that – in general – more process related research is needed in the subsidiary entrepreneurship arena. More specifically, research is warranted in relation to initiative opportunity identification, the physical realization of initiatives as well as headquarters-subsidiary interaction and alignment. Here, it is believed that further investigation of these particular process facets should generate valuable new insights (e.g. Boojihawon et al. 2007, p. 568, Mahnke et al. 2007, p. 1293, De Clercq et al. 2011, p. 1271, Hoskisson et al. 2011, p. 1149).

(3) Previous research has largely focused on antecedents of subsidiary initiatives. However, outcomes of entrepreneurial subsidiary activities have been analyzed less frequently and in less depth. Accordingly it has been recommended that more attentions is to be paid on the potential link between initiatives and resulting outcome at both subsidiary and corporate level (e.g. Rugman/Verbeke 2001, p. 239, Boojihawon et al. 2007, p. 569, Liouka 2007, p. 7, Verbeke et al. 2007, p. 596, Williams/Lee 2009, p. 297).

---

[2] See also Sections 2.3 and 3.1 of this publication for further details on research gaps in the field of subsidiary initiatives.

In addition, previous research often deals with specific aspects of subsidiary initiatives only. Work integrating the different pieces into a "larger picture" and taking a more holistic perspective appears to be missing. Thus, scholars have highlighted the need to adopt a more holistic perspective and conceptualization on subsidiary entrepreneurial initiatives (Birkinshaw et al. 2005, p. 246, Scott et al. 2010, p. 336, Strutzenberger/Ambos 2014, p. 315).

Based on these research gaps, it is this key objective of this dissertation to more holistically examine the potential relations between (a) the role a foreign subsidiary holds in the MNC, (b) its entrepreneurial initiative-taking behavior and (c) the resulting outcomes. Altogether, this leads to the following overarching research question: (How) do subsidiary initiative-taking behavior and initiative outcomes differ with regard to the specific role a subsidiary holds within the MNC? This research question can be further broken down into three sub-questions as follows:

[1] *(How) do the* **amount and types of initiatives** *of a subsidiary differ with regard to a specific role it holds within the MNC?*

[2] *(How) does the* **initiative-taking behavior** *differ with regard to a specific role a subsidiary holds within the MNC?*

[3] *(How) do the subsidiary* **initiative outcomes** *differ with regard to a specific role a subsidiary holds within the MNC?*

1.3   Objectives and Structure of the Study

The present dissertation aims – in general – at enhancing the understanding of the complex and multilevel phenomenon of subsidiary initiatives for both academia and management practice. More specifically, the present research has three main objectives.

First, this work intends to *contribute to IB literature* and, more precisely, to research streams relating to subsidiary role and subsidiary entrepreneurship. As to subsidiary role research, this dissertation plans to advance knowledge on subsidiary role typologies by empirically investigating how and why different subsidiary roles potentially pursue entrepreneurial initiatives, perhaps even in different ways. Furthermore, it is to enrich our understanding of how and why different role types might contribute in distinct ways to subsidiary or even firm-level advantages in the MNC. Concerning subsidiary entrepreneurship, the present research aims at deriving new insights into the "process black box" of subsidiary initiatives by empirically investigating different process aspects and linking them to the subsidiary role context. Moreover, by involving both headquarter and subsidiary level in this research, a more holistic and comprehensive approach is to be applied than typically used in the field so far.

Second, it is the objective of this dissertation to *contribute to theory* as well. Currently, a wider range of theoretical perspectives is used in the subsidiary initiative field. Oftentimes, theoretical considerations are not at the center of contributions and discussions do not take place at great depth. Hence, one further goal is to develop and empirically test a holistic research framework on role-specific initiative-taking that is more strongly grounded in theory than commonly done in the field. Among the theories employed, this dissertation will draw from newer strands of the Resource-Based View (RBV) which represent more dynamic and process-oriented approaches as they are deemed particularly fit for this research endeavor. As no other empirical study could be identified that has previously applied and empirically tested this particular theoretical approach in the subsidiary initiative field, it is hoped to contribute to theory-testing and theory-extending of these rather novel RBV strands.

Third, it is the goal of this work to provide *new knowledge for management* practice. The present work aims not only at enhancing awareness and understanding of different role types among managers in multinational firms but also intends to provide guidance as what entrepreneurial activities to potentially expect from different subsidiary roles. Furthermore, it is expected to obtain additional clarity on which particular context factors either support or impede entrepreneurial subsidiary efforts. This should help managers at the corporate or subsidiary level to better understand how they can possibly influence or steer dispersed entrepreneurial efforts in the wider corporation and how the MNC as a whole can benefit from these activities.

In order to achieve these objectives, the dissertation involves the execution of a comprehensive literature review and analysis of publications in the subsidiary initiative field (Chapter 2), the development of a theoretically derived research framework (Chapter 3), the design and execution of an empirical study (Chapter 4), the presentation and discussion of empirical findings (Chapter 5), and lastly, the assessment of contributions and limitations of this work (Chapter 6). Accordingly, the document is structured as shown in Figure 1.1 and described in more details as follows.

Following the introduction into the topic of subsidiary initiatives in Chapter 1, the results and findings of the systematically derived literature review will be presented in Chapter 2. Following a brief overview of the roots of subsidiary initiative research in Section 2.1, the detailed findings of the critical review are presented including, for example, the concept of subsidiary initiatives, antecedents and consequences, or theoretical approaches applied in the field (2.2). The last section of Chapter 2 then summarizes the findings and outlines research gaps and avenues for further research (2.3) which, in part, also form the foundation for the present research.

Chapter 3 starts with a short overview of the proposed research framework and explains how it links to some of the previously described research gaps (3.1). In Section 3.2, the three core elements of the research framework will be introduced: subsidiary role context, subsidiary initiative-taking behavior and subsidiary initiative outcomes. Afterwards, the theoretical foundations employed for the present research are introduced (3.3): the resource-based view, resource dependency theory and contingency theory. In Section 3.4 the final contingent and resource-oriented framework is presented before, in Section 3.5, predictions are derived for role-specific subsidiary initiative-taking and outcomes.

1	Introduction					
2	Review of the Literature on Subsidiary Initiatives					
	2.1 Roots	2.2 Findings	2.3 Conclusions			
3	Research Framework					
	3.1 Overview	3.2 Elements	3.3 Theoretical Perspectives	3.4 Research Framework	3.5 Role-Specific Predictions	
4	Empirical Study					
	4.1 Research Philosophy	4.2 Research Design	4.3 Operationalization	4.4 Data Collection	4.5 Data Analysis	4.6 Scientific Qual. Criteria
5	Empirical Findings					
	5.1 Findings on Autocomp	5.2 Findings on Telecomp	5.3 Summary of Findings			
6	Contributions, Limitations and the Road Ahead					

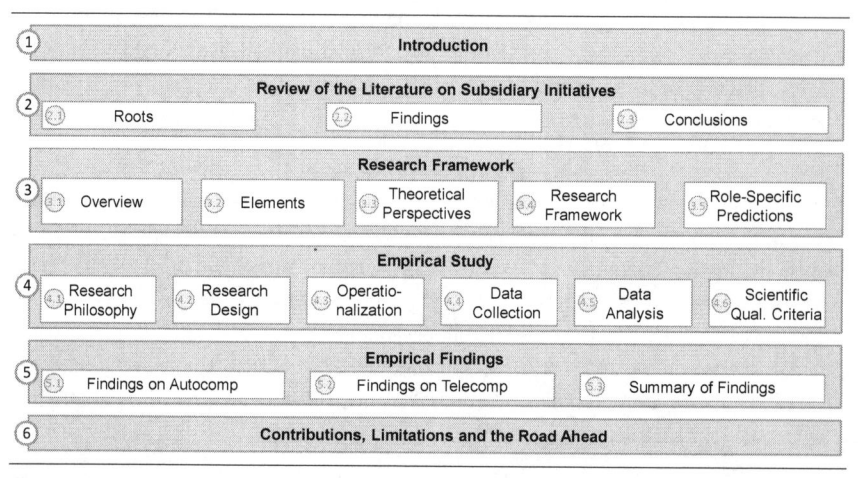

Figure 1.1: Structure of the thesis

Following the conceptual and theoretical part of the study, Chapter 4 describes in detail how the empirical research was designed, conducted and analyzed. In Section 4.1, the realist research philosophy adopted in the present work is described and explained why it is deemed particularly fit for this research endeavor. In the next Section (4.2), the applied multiple case study design is presented which utilizes both quantitative and qualitative data. Here, it is further explained why and how this particular research methodology was chosen, or, why and how the two cases were selected. Section 4.3 then deals with operationalizing the different elements of the research framework while Section 4.4 explains the data collection approaches applied in this work. As is described in detail, data was obtained through questionnaires, interviews as well as secondary and archival data and collected both at the corporate and the subsidiary level. Chapter 4 ends with a discussion on scientific quality criteria and an assessment how they apply to the current research (4.6).

Chapter 5 presents the findings from the empirical study. In Sections 5.1 and 5.2, each case is thoroughly described and data gained through questionnaires, interviews and secondary sources is displayed in a systematic manner. Each case description entails, for instance, the subsidiary role categorization, the detailed presentation of subsidiary initiative-taking behavior and the outcomes of altogether 14 foreign units in two MNC. Individual case summaries (within-case analyses) are presented at the end of Sections 5.1 and 5.2 and the findings are contrasted with the previously derived predictions. At the end of Chapter 5, findings are compared across the two cases (cross-case analyses), similarities and differences are identified and contrasted with the theoretically derived predictions (5.3). Moreover, additional findings relating to subsidiary role typologies, subsidiary initiative-taking behavior and outcomes are presented.

In Chapter 6, the dissertation concludes with discussions on the contributions of this study to IB research and management practice and links it to the research objectives conveyed in the beginning of this publication (6.1 and 6.2). As all research, this dissertation does not come without limitations and these are outlined and discussed in Section 6.3. Finally, avenues for future research on subsidiary roles, subsidiary entrepreneurship and other areas are presented in Section 6.4.

2 Review of the Literature on Subsidiary Initiatives[3]

2.1 Roots of Subsidiary Initiative Research

Julian Birkinshaw, in his article 'Entrepreneurship in Multinational Corporations: The Characteristics of Subsidiary Initiatives', originally defines the phenomenon of subsidiary initiative as "a discrete, proactive undertaking that advances a new way for the corporation to use or expand its resources." He further describes it as "essentially an entrepreneurial process, beginning with the identification of an opportunity and culminating in the commitment of resources to that opportunity" (Birkinshaw 1997, p. 207). Although many subsequent publications refer to Birkinshaw's definition,[4] various authors state that the phenomenon remains somewhat vague and is not yet fully understood (Dörrenbächer/Geppert 2009, p. 100, Ambos et al. 2010, p. 1100, Grohmann 2010, p. 7).

Apparently, the research on subsidiary initiatives – essentially concerned with entrepreneurial behavior in foreign subsidiaries of MNCs – has, to some extent, been shaped by findings from both the field of (international) corporate entrepreneurship as well as by research in international business on headquarters-subsidiary relationships, subsidiary roles and subsidiary behavior (Birkinshaw 1998a, Paterson/Brock 2002). The corporate entrepreneurship literature deals – from a *firm-level perspective* – with the entrepreneurial efforts within the context of existing organizations. Here, entrepreneurial behavior implies the existence of (1) product or process innovation, (2) a risk-taking propensity by the firm's key decision makers, and (3) evidence of pro-activeness regarding product-market introductions or the early adoption of new administrative techniques or process technologies (Miller 1983, p. 771, Covin/Miles 1999, p. 49). Within this field of research, different areas provide useful insights for the concept of subsidiary entrepreneurial activities. Among those contributions is, for instance, the work of Burgelman (1983a, 1984) who recognizes that autonomous entrepreneurial actions and behavior often occur at different levels of large and complex organizations. Furthermore, it is stated that entrepreneurial behavior in the MNC does not have to reside at one specific location, but instead might be dispersed throughout the organization with various individuals possessing the capacity for entrepreneurial activities more or less simultaneously (e.g. Burgelman 1984, p. 156, Birkinshaw 1997, p. 213).

In addition to the firm-level view, pro-active and risk-taking entrepreneurial behavior has also been investigated from a *subsidiary-level perspective*. Within the broader field of

---

[3] Different versions of this critical review and analysis of the subsidiary initiative literature have also been published as a working paper (Schmid/Dzedek 2011) and as a journal article (Schmid et al. 2014).
[4] Out of the 52 relevant publications that were reviewed and analyzed in this paper, more than 20 contributions directly refer to the definition by Birkinshaw (1997).

international business and international management literature,[5] the management of international subsidiaries has developed as a distinct research area over the past three decades (Paterson/Brock 2002). More specifically, the research stream of subsidiary roles and subsidiary (role) development (Birkinshaw/Hood 1998b, Schmid et al. 1998, Schmid 2003, Schmid/Kutschker 2003, Schmid 2004, Dörrenbächer/Gammelgaard 2006) makes valuable contributions to the notion of subsidiary entrepreneurial initiatives. Scholars determined that subsidiary roles can – besides environmental determinism and headquarters assignment – be changed by subsidiaries themselves through autonomous entrepreneurial behavior (Birkinshaw 1997). Such autonomous activity at the subsidiary level can lead to the planned and discrete development of subsidiary resources and capabilities, which in turn may result in the reinforcement or extension of the subsidiary charter over time (Birkinshaw/Hood 1998d).[6]

Given the important influences from the field of corporate entrepreneurship and from research on subsidiary roles and subsidiary (role) development, it could be argued that the topic of subsidiary initiatives lies at the interface of these two areas (see also Boojihawon et al. 2007, p. 550, Grohmann 2010, p. 7).[7] However, different perspectives also lead to variations in definitions, ascribed characteristics and other features of subsidiary initiatives, leaving it a rather ambiguous concept and research area. Since a clear understanding is crucial for future research on this topic, further light will be shed on its various facets through the systematic literature review and critical analysis.

2.2 Findings from the Literature Review and Analysis

2.2.1 Overview of the Publication Activity in the Field

Altogether 52 different publications on the topic of subsidiary initiatives were identified throughout a systematic literature identification and selection process.[8] A first look at the publication dates of the literature reveals that the subject of subsidiary initiatives can be considered a relatively "young" research area with the first publications dating back to the mid-1990s (see Figure 2.1). Although earlier publications exist which address this

---

[5] For a discussion on how far international business and international management are linked, see Schmid (1996, pp. 51-71) or Schmid and Oesterle (2009, pp. 10-13).
[6] Birkinshaw and Hood (1998b, p. 782) refer to Galunic and Eisenhardt's definition of charter as "the business – or elements of the business – in which the subsidiary participates and for which it is recognized to have responsibility in the MNC" (Galunic/Eisenhardt 1996, p. 256).
[7] It may be argued that there are also other research areas which provide useful insights into the concept of subsidiary initiatives. For instance, literature related to corporate venturing (e.g. Burgelman 1983a), entrepreneurial orientation (e.g. Covin 1991), subsidiary embeddedness (e.g. Andersson et al. 2001), knowledge development and transfer within the MNC (e.g. Gupta/Govindarajan 1994) or subsidiary contribution and value creation (e.g. Rugman/Verbeke 2001). However, as these research areas have not yet developed into specific research streams, they will not be considered in more detail for the present contribution.
[8] Reference date is December 31st, 2010. For a detailed overview of the identification and selection process, see Schmid and Dzedek (2010, pp. 4-6).

topic to some extent,[9] two articles by Julian Birkinshaw (1995, 1997) can most likely be viewed as the general starting point of this field. Whereas the first article deals with the topic of subsidiary initiative as one of many mechanisms for subsidiary role development (Birkinshaw 1995), the second article concentrates on the subject of subsidiary initiatives itself (Birkinshaw 1997) and can be viewed as one of two "key contributions" by this author. In the first key contribution, Birkinshaw not only provides his definition, but moreover identifies different types, examines facilitators and outlines the underlying processes and intended outcomes of subsidiary initiatives.

Following this "ground-laying" period, one can see a first peak of publications with six journal articles and book chapters in the year 1998 which primarily deal with subsidiary initiatives as drivers in the development process of foreign subsidiaries (Birkinshaw/ Hood 1998c, Delany 1998), various aspects of the subsidiary initiative concept – such as the initiative process or different initiative types (Birkinshaw 1998a, Birkinshaw/Fry 1998) – as well as antecedents and consequences of initiative-taking (Birkinshaw 1998b, Birkinshaw et al. 1998). As can be clearly seen, Birkinshaw is identified as a scholar who strongly influenced the field from the beginning (see also Young/Tavares 2004, p. 224).

Between the years 1999 and 2004 ten contributions were published. The majority of the literature within this timeframe focuses on the examination of various drivers and consequences of initiative-taking.[10] Among these ten publications is also – what can be considered – the second "key contribution" by Birkinshaw on this matter. In his book "Entrepreneurship in the Global Firm" the author summarizes previous findings in the field and covers various aspects of the subsidiary initiative phenomenon, ranging from different initiative types to underlying development processes, drivers and consequences as well as some theoretical considerations (Birkinshaw 2000).

A phase of higher publication activity can again be seen between 2005 and 2010 with more than 60% of all literature (33 contributions) having appeared in this period. When compared to previous phases, it can be noticed that the publications throughout this period often deal with more specific aspects of the phenomenon, such as various forms of initiatives,[11] or the behavior and influence of different actors in the initiative develop-

---

[9] Through the analysis, earlier publications which deal with the topic of autonomous subsidiary initiatives were identified as well. However, as they did not fulfill all inclusion criteria, they were not considered in the systematic review and analysis. Among those are, for instance, Ghoshal and Bartlett's research on local and global innovations in MNCs (Ghoshal/Bartlett 1988), Gupta and Govindarajan's contribution on knowledge flows within MNCs (Gupta/Govindarajan 1994) or Burgelman's work on entrepreneurial processes in large, complex organizations (Burgelman 1983a,b).
[10] See e.g. Birkinshaw 1999, Delany 2000, Zahra et al. 2000, Yamin 2002, Lee/Chen 2003, Tseng et al. 2004, Sohail/Ayadurai 2004.
[11] For example, within this period, antecedents for specific initiatives have been studied, such as marketing initiatives (Couto et al. 2005), technology initiatives (Boojihawon et al. 2007, Medcof 2007) or proactive environmental strategies (Raţiu/Molz 2010).

ment process.[12] In addition, the topic is increasingly investigated in specific subsidiary and/or industry settings (e.g. software and electronics) and country settings (e.g. less developed regions).[13]

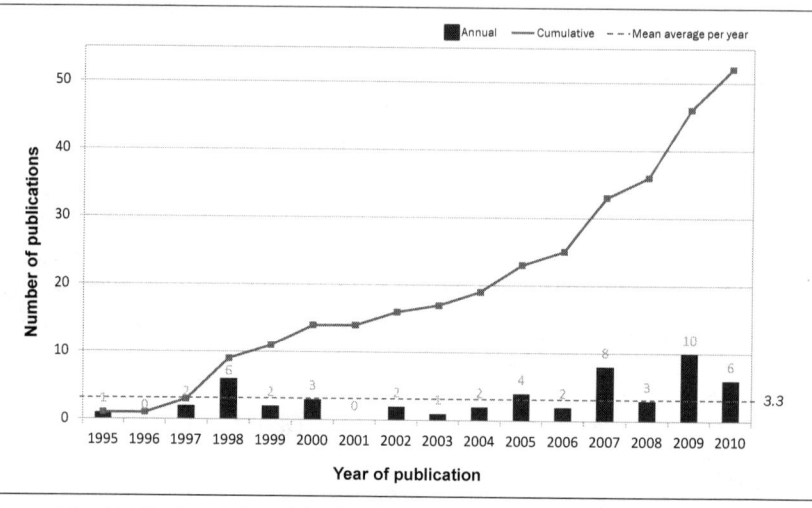

Figure 2.1: Publication dates of the literature on subsidiary initiatives

2.2.2 Framework for the Literature Review and Analysis

In order to better structure the findings and the contents of previous research, a structural framework is applied for the presentation of the literature review and analysis. Based on the investigation, existing studies on subsidiary initiatives can be generally grouped into three categories, namely (1) literature dealing with the subsidiary initiative concept, (2) literature focusing on antecedents, and (3) literature investigating the consequences of subsidiary initiatives. As antecedents from different context levels were identified, they were further subdivided into components relating to the environmental, the organizational and the individual level. Similarly, the consequences were grouped into environmental, organizational and individual level outcomes. Moreover, the theoretical foundations and research approaches of previous work were examined. Figure 2.2 illustrates the framework.

---

[12] For instance, Dörrenbächer/Geppert (2009, 2010) examine the personal motivations of subsidiary managers to undertake initiatives and Lyly-Yrjänäinen et al. (2008) investigate the role of global key accounts in the diffusion of subsidiary initiatives in the MNC.

[13] Research in particular contexts was conducted e.g. in software subsidiaries of MNCs in India (Krishnan 2006), in Maquiladoras of the automotive and electronics industry in Mexico (Sargent/Matthews 2006) or in advertising agencies in the UK (Boojihawon et al. 2007).

2 – Review of the Literature on Subsidiary Initiatives

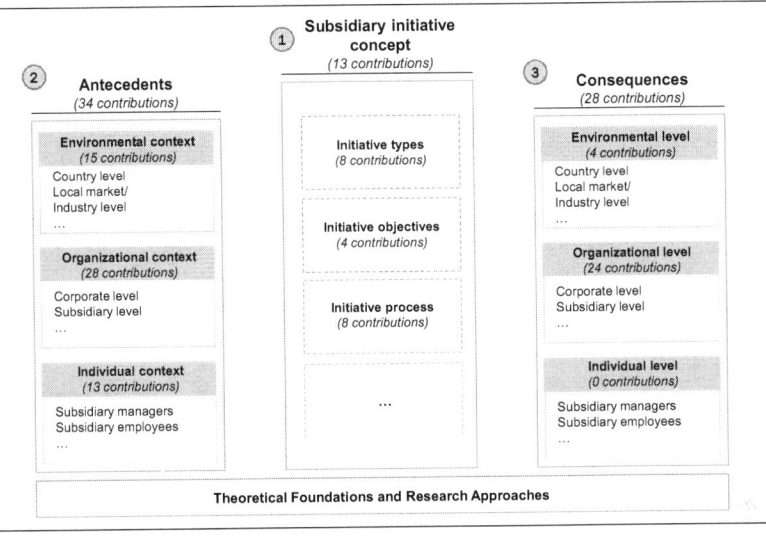

```
                    ① Subsidiary initiative
                       concept
                       (13 contributions)
② Antecedents                                    ③ Consequences
  (34 contributions)                               (28 contributions)

Environmental context        Initiative types     Environmental level
(15 contributions)           (8 contributions)    (4 contributions)
Country level                                     Country level
Local market/                                     Local market/
Industry level                                    Industry level
...                          Initiative objectives ...
                             (4 contributions)
Organizational context                            Organizational level
(28 contributions)                                (24 contributions)
Corporate level                                   Corporate level
Subsidiary level             Initiative process   Subsidiary level
...                          (8 contributions)    ...

Individual context                                Individual level
(13 contributions)                                (0 contributions)
Subsidiary managers                               Subsidiary managers
Subsidiary employees         ...                  Subsidiary employees
...                                               ...

              Theoretical Foundations and Research Approaches
```

Figure 2.2: Framework for the literature review and analysis[14]

2.2.3 Concept of Subsidiary Initiatives

2.2.3.1 Types of Subsidiary Initiatives

Eight of the 52 publications cover different subsidiary initiative types. When analyzing these eight publications, three different typologies of subsidiary initiatives were identified. In addition, wit was discovered that the three typologies use, in total, four different criteria for characterizing and classifying initiatives, i.e. the locus of origin, the locus of pursuit, the end objective and the relatedness to existing business. The locus of origin refers to the location or the market in which the opportunity for subsidiary initiative-taking emerges (e.g. internal or external market), whereas the locus of pursuit corresponds to the location or market in which the opportunity is finally realized (Birkinshaw 2000). The end objective indicates which subsidiary goal is to be achieved (Delany 2000) and the relatedness to existing business specifies to what extent the initiative causes changes to the present business activities (Verbeke et al. 2007).

(1) The first typology is presented by Birkinshaw and his co-authors. In five contributions (Birkinshaw 1997, 1998a, Birkinshaw/Fry 1998, Birkinshaw/Ridderstråle 1999, Birkinshaw 2000), the authors describe two principal forms of subsidiary initiatives, namely (a) internal and (b) external initiatives.[15] (a) *External initiatives* – with an external **locus of**

---

[14] As many publications address more than one aspect of subsidiary initiatives, the number of contributions in each single field does not add up to the total of 52.
[15] In addition, slightly different terms have also been used, such as internally/externally-oriented initiatives (Birkinshaw 1998a) or internally/externally-focused initiatives (Birkinshaw 1997).

origin – refer to initiative opportunities that are identified outside the boundaries of the corporation and which develop through interactions with local customers, suppliers or other stakeholders and entities.[16] *Internal initiatives* – with an internal locus of origin – represent opportunities that are recognized within the boundaries of the corporation and which emerge through interactions of subsidiary managers with other actors from the internal, corporate system (Birkinshaw 1998a, p. 359, 2000, pp. 27, 73). In three of the above mentioned publications (i.e. Birkinshaw 1997, 1998a, 2000), the authors refine the basic types of external and internal initiatives. *Local* and *global market initiatives* are described as specific forms of external market initiatives. Both sub-types stem from opportunities that are recognized outside the boundaries of the MNC (external locus of origin), but more specifically in either the subsidiary's local or global market environment. They aim at developing e.g. products or services for customers in local or global markets and are therefore additionally characterized by an external **locus of pursuit**.[17] In contrast, *internal market* and *global-internal hybrid initiatives* are identified and described as sub-types of internal initiatives. Internal market initiatives are internally focused towards e.g. efficiency improvement and rationalization activities within the MNC network, and they usually depend upon corporate approval or support (internal locus of origin and internal locus of pursuit). In the case of global-internal hybrid initiatives, however, the locus of origin is outside the subsidiary's home market, but the actual locus of pursuit is internal. This type represents activities in which the subsidiary identifies global opportunities and subsequently engages in the internal process of convincing headquarters to relocate these internationally focused activities to its location or to provide global investments for its implementation (Birkinshaw 1997, p. 216, 2000, pp. 28-30). In addition, Birkinshaw classifies and describes four sub-types of internal initiatives as a result of his research on US-owned subsidiaries in Canada, i.e. *bid initiatives*, *leap-of-faith initiatives*, *reconfiguration initiatives* and *maverick initiatives* (Birkinshaw 1998a, pp. 357-361). Figure 2.3 summarizes the researcher's understanding of the classification of the different subsidiary initiatives types.

---

[16] Many other publications have also stressed that the activities of foreign subsidiaries in local host country networks and their relationships and interactions with local stakeholders expose MNCs to new knowledge, opportunities and ideas (e.g. Andersson et al. 2002, Schmid/Schurig 2003, Schmid/Hartmann 2011).

[17] In earlier publications, Birkinshaw does not clearly differentiate between the locus of origin and the locus of pursuit. He finally clarifies this issue in his book publication (Birkinshaw 2000, p. 22).

```
                        Subsidiary
                        initiatives
           ┌───────────────┴───────────────┐
        External                        Internal
       initiatives                     initiatives
       ┌────┴────┐                 ┌───────┴───────┐
   Global market Local market  Internal market  Global-internal
    initiatives   initiatives   initiatives     hybrid initiatives
                              ┌────┬────┬────┬────┐
                           Reconfi- Maverick  Bid   Leap-of-
                           guration initiatives initiatives faith
                           initiatives               initiatives
```

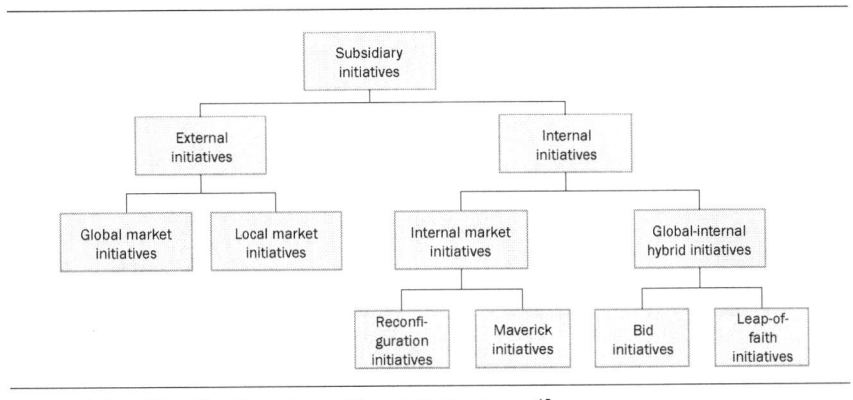

Figure 2.3: Classification of subsidiary initiative types[18]

(2) Another attempt to characterize different types of subsidiary initiatives is undertaken by Delany (1998, 2000) who introduces three subsidiary initiative types based on their **end objective**, i.e.: *domain developing initiatives*, *domain consolidating initiatives* and *domain defending initiatives*.[19] According to Delany, *domain developing initiatives*, as the first form, aim at the extension of a subsidiary mandate; they include activities such as the pursuit of new business opportunities in the local market, a bid for corporate investments, a mandate extension as well as a reconfiguration of existing operations (Delany 1998, p. 254, 2000, p. 234). *Domain consolidating initiatives*, as a second form, generally seek to stabilize or strengthen the current subsidiary position, whereas *domain defending initiatives* have the objective of securing the position or even justifying the existence of the subsidiary (Delany 1998, p. 252, 2000, pp. 234-235).

(3) Verbeke et al. (2007) differentiate between *subsidiary renewal* and *subsidiary venturing* as two forms of subsidiary entrepreneurship based on what herein is interpreted as "**relatedness to the existing business**".[20] *Subsidiary renewal initiatives* imply significant changes to a subsidiary's existing business strategy, structure, systems and processes. In contrast, *subsidiary venturing initiatives* refer to the "creation of new business", either within the existing organization or outside of the subsidiary in a separate venture unit (Verbeke et al. 2007, p. 588). Similarly, various other authors state that subsidiary initiatives can be characterized with regard to the extent or the scale of changes they cause (Birkinshaw 2000, Liouka 2007, Dimitratos et al. 2009a). It is

---

[18] The categorization of different sub-types of internal market and global-internal hybrid initiatives is based on our interpretation of Birkinshaw's writings (Birkinshaw 1998a, pp. 358-361).
[19] According to Delany (1998, p. 250, 2000, p. 233), Birkinshaw's typology only includes all those types that relate to the end objective of domain building. Delany identifies two additional forms (domain consolidating and domain defending) through a qualitative study of MNC subsidiaries in Ireland.
[20] Verbeke et al. do not explicitly refer to the differentiating attribute as "relatedness to the existing business". Instead, this term was derived based on the definition and description of the two forms of subsidiary entrepreneurship as given by the authors (see Verbeke et al. 2007, p. 588).

argued that subsidiary initiatives may not only consist of radical change challenging the "existing fabric of the MNC" (Dimitratos et al. 2009a, p. 411), but they also include incremental innovations which "stay within the existing parameters of the business" (Birkinshaw 2000, pp. 76-77).

2.2.3.2 Objectives of Subsidiary Initiatives

It is self-evident that subsidiaries pursue distinct objectives through initiative-taking. Surprisingly, however, only four out of the 52 publications are truly interested in the objectives subsidiary initiatives have or may have (i.e. Birkinshaw 1997, Delany 1998, 2000, Ambos et al. 2010). Through the review and analysis it was possible to distinguish between five – more or less interdependent – objectives that are typically associated with subsidiary initiatives.

(1) Subsidiary initiatives might be pursued by individuals with the intention of satisfying their own *personal needs*. This could, for instance, relate to subsidiary managers' personal motivations and objectives to further develop the local subsidiary. Moreover, initiative-taking has been associated with the objective of improving individuals' career perspectives and with the goals of achieving more personal autonomy or the possibility of collaborating with others in the MNC (Dörrenbächer/Geppert 2009, p. 106, Ambos et al. 2010, p. 1102).

(2) Initiatives have also been linked to the objective of realizing *new business opportunities* which present themselves in the local and global market. This is especially the case for external initiatives which commonly aim at generating new business, improving the market position and increasing the revenues for the firm. This business improvement may take place through several means, such as the identification of new customer needs, the development of new suppliers or the forging of new alliance relationships (Birkinshaw 1997, p. 224, 1998a, p. 356, Birkinshaw/Ridderstråle 1999, p. 171).

(3) Besides the generation of new external business, initiative-taking has also been associated with the objective of *improving internal business* operations. Internal initiatives frequently have the objective of improving the efficiency and performance of existing operations, of enhancing resource allocation and/or achieving cost reduction for the firm (Birkinshaw 1997, p. 224, 2000, p. 27).

(4) Initiatives may also be set off with the intention of growing the subsidiary's *resource base* or with the goal of leveraging existing capabilities into related areas. This may allow the subsidiary to enhance its bargaining power within the organization – which then can be used to increase the subsidiaries' autonomy and influence within the MNC network (e.g. Birkinshaw 1997, pp. 207, 214, Birkinshaw/Fry 1998, p. 58, Ambos et al. 2010, p. 1102, Dörrenbächer/Geppert 2010, p. 612).

(5) In the relevant publications it has also been proposed that subsidiaries ultimately seek to enhance their *position*,[21] their *scope of responsibility* and/or their *degrees of freedom* within the MNC through initiative-taking (e.g. Birkinshaw/Fry 1998, p. 52, Birkinshaw 2000, p. 8, Delany 2000, Ambos et al. 2010, p. 1100, Ambos/Birkinshaw 2010, p. 453).

2.2.3.3 Process of Subsidiary Initiatives

Altogether eight publications were identified that examine – in more or less detail – the **subsidiary initiative process**.[22] In addition to these eight contributions, more insight into the initiative process could be obtained from descriptive elements of outlined case studies (e.g. Birkinshaw 1995, Krishnan 2006, Boojihawon et al. 2007) or from conceptual arguments and considerations (e.g. Birkinshaw/Hood 1998d, Lee/Williams 2005, Verbeke/Yuan 2005, Mahnke et al. 2007, Grohmann 2010). It appears that – in contrast to other aspects of the subsidiary initiative phenomenon – the initiative process has not yet been systematically and purposefully investigated in detail. Consequently, as none of these studies provides a thorough and complete view on the subsidiary initiative development process, it was necessary to tie the identified "bits and pieces" together to obtain a more comprehensive understanding of the initiative process.

What was derived with regard to the overall development process? Birkinshaw, viewing subsidiary initiative as a key manifestation of corporate entrepreneurship, defines it as "essentially an entrepreneurial process, beginning with the identification of an opportunity and culminating in the commitment of resources to that opportunity" (Birkinshaw 1997, p. 207).[23] In between the process cornerstones of "identification" and "commitment of resources", the subsidiary typically undertakes activities to obtain and utilize needed resources and to sell the initiative to headquarters in order to gain corporate approval (Birkinshaw 1997, p. 224, Birkinshaw et al. 2005, p. 233). Concluding from previous literature – and in line with the view on "general" entrepreneurship processes in MNCs (e.g. Shane/Venkataraman 2000, p. 218) – it may be argued that the initiative process could be further subdivided into the phases of (1) *opportunity identification*, (2) *resource attainment and utilization*, (3) *initiative selling, evaluation and approval* as well as (4) *commitment of resources and implementation*.[24] However, it needs to be noted that such a technocratic process view on entrepreneurial initiative-taking has its limita-

---

[21] Different terms are applied in various publications. For instance, Birkinshaw and Ridderstråle (1999, p. 155) refer to changes in the charter of a subsidiary unit; Ambos et al. (2010, p. 1100) speak of the enhancement of the subsidiary standing within the MNC network. It also has to be noted that, besides charter enhancement, charter or domain consolidating and defending objectives fall into this category (see Delany 2000, p. 234).

[22] See Birkinshaw 1997, Birkinshaw/Fry 1998, Birkinshaw/Ridderstråle 1999, Birkinshaw 2000, Lyly-Yrjänäinen et al. 2008, Dörrenbächer/Geppert 2009, Keupp/Gassmann 2009a, Dörrenbächer/Geppert 2010.

[23] See also Chapter 2 of this paper.

[24] Likewise, Ardichvili et al. (2003, p. 106) argue that between the identification of an opportunity and its exploitation lies the decisive opportunity evaluation and development stage.

tions.[25] For instance, the initiative process might take a variety of forms, the outlined phases may not always take place in a sequential order and they may also overlap. Nevertheless, a process perspective and the separation into distinct phases might help to better structure the complex and manifold activities throughout the subsidiary initiative development and allow a more systematic analysis of the phenomenon (see also Baron 2007, p. 21). What insights could be gained into the activities during the different phases of the initiative process?

(1) From the publications that were reviewed and analyzed, only a small share addresses the *initiative opportunity identification* and recognition phase of the initiative process. However, some conclusions can be drawn from case examples that are illustrated. It can be considered as commonly accepted that the starting point of this entrepreneurial process is the MNC subsidiary – rather than the parent company (e.g. Birkinshaw 1999, p. 10, Johnson/Medcof 2002, p. 188, Tseng et al. 2004, p. 94, Verbeke/ Yuan 2005, p. 32, Liouka 2007, p. 284). Entrepreneurial opportunities may be identified either externally through interactions with actors such as suppliers, customers or other local market players (external initiatives) or internally through interactions with actors from within the corporate system (internal initiatives; Birkinshaw/Hood 1998d, pp. 785-786). During the phase of opportunity identification, the local subsidiary management obviously plays a crucial role in the scanning and detection of opportunities and in finding innovative solutions (Boojihawon et al. 2007, p. 563, Zucchella et al. 2007, p. 320). Middle managers often function as project or initiative champions who further develop the identified ideas into more concrete proposals and then approach subsidiary executive management to gain their backing. If convinced of the proposed opportunity, these subsidiary executives may take the role of sponsors, using their contacts in the parent company to build support with headquarters' management (Birkinshaw 1995, p. 35, Birkinshaw/Fry 1998, p. 54).

(2) Different publications depict activities related to the *attainment and utilization of resources and capabilities* in order to realize subsidiary initiatives. For example, Birkinshaw and colleagues describe subsidiary initiative-taking as a process that "advances a new way for the corporation to use or expand its resources" (e.g. Birkinshaw 1997, p. 207, 1999, p. 9, Birkinshaw/Ridderstråle 1999, p. 151) or that represents the "pursuit of a specific market opportunity and the development of the appropriate capabilities to fulfill it" (Birkinshaw/Hood 1998d, p. 786). Similarly, Birkinshaw et al. (2005, p. 233) state that "subsidiaries may engage in entrepreneurial activities to overcome the limitation of their resources, to make their resources valuable, or to leverage their resources in unique ways previously unknown in their firm or industry." Likewise, other authors see

---

[25] This technocratic view is linked to Mintzberg's planning view in the strategy literature (see Mintzberg/Waters 1985). It is partially neglecting the emergent character of subsidiary initiatives.

initiative-taking as a process which involves resource management activities such as the acquisition, accumulation, integration or renewal of resources in order to respond to new opportunities (Manolopoulos 2008, p. 4, Lee/Chen 2003, p. 64, Tseng et al. 2004, p. 94, Liouka 2007, p. 75).

(3) The larger portion of the relevant publications deals with the interaction between headquarters and subsidiaries throughout the *initiative selling, evaluation and approval* stage. Specifically, the works of Birkinshaw and his co-authors (Birkinshaw 1997, Birkinshaw/Fry 1998, Birkinshaw/Ridderstråle 1999) and the publications of Dörrenbächer and Geppert (2009, 2010) provide useful insights. It may be concluded that most initiatives – at some point in time – require some form of corporate approval or additional resources from headquarters to allow subsidiaries to continue with their entrepreneurial efforts (Birkinshaw 1997, p. 221). In those cases, corporate managers will likely assess and evaluate the proposed initiatives in order to select the most promising and attractive ones for further development (Birkinshaw 1995, p. 36, 2000, p. 39, Verbeke/Yuan 2005, p. 32). When determining the initiative attractiveness, that is, broadly, the potential of the opportunities to generate competitive advantage and entrepreneurial returns to the firm (Shane/Venkataraman 2000, p. 218, Haynie et al. 2009, p. 338, Williams/Lee 2009, p. 296), numerous aspects may come into play.[26]

(4) In the publications which were subject to review, only sporadic information can be found on how the process stage of *resource commitment and implementation* takes place. Summarizing the findings from portrayed case examples, it can be concluded that, once an initiative has passed through one or several rounds of evaluation and refinements, headquarters' managers eventually will decide upon the (preliminary) implementation of the initiative. In the case that an initiative is approved, it can be expected that the subsidiary receives an official implementation mandate and is provided with the required resources to launch or further progress with the initiative (Keupp 2008, p. 33). Headquarters' support may then come in the form of e.g. political support, official endorsement or rights and budgets for the subsidiary (Keupp/Gassmann 2009a, p. 197).

Moreover, existing research suggests that, throughout the development process, subsidiary initiatives face various forms of **resistance and uncertainties**. Birkinshaw terms *resistance* that initiatives face from various actors in the MNC "corporate immune sys-

---

[26] Evaluations are likely to be conducted several times at different stages of the initiative development (see e.g. Ardichvili et al. 2003, p. 106). Also, it is to be assumed that the evaluation of initiatives does not only occur at headquarters but also earlier in the process, e.g. within the subsidiary. Typical indicators for the initiative assessment are, for instance, the business potential or economic viability (Krishnan 2006, p. 66, Mahnke et al. 2007, p. 1285), the fit with the MNC strategy (Birkinshaw 2000, p. 39), the cost reduction potential (Lyly-Yrjänäinen et al. 2008, p. 8), the technological feasibility (Keupp 2008, p. 33), the perceived risk of the initiative (Johnson/Medcof 2002, p. 197) or the expected contribution to the firm's competitive advantage (Verbeke/Yuan 2005, p. 36). Yet, in line with the overall variations in the initiative process, the initiative evaluation may again take diverse forms, depending on many factors, such as the firm type and firm characteristics (Keupp 2008), initiative characteristics (Mahnke et al. 2007) or headquarters orientation towards external stakeholders (Dörrenbächer/Geppert 2010).

tem" and defines it as "the set of organizational forces that suppress the advancement of creation-oriented activities such as initiatives" (Birkinshaw/Ridderstråle 1999, p. 153, Birkinshaw 2000, p. 39). It is characterized as a complex, multi-level phenomenon with (a) visible manifestations at the top and (b) underlying interpreted predispositions of individuals in the corporate system at the bottom. Resistance may stem from different MNC actors, such as individuals in the vertical line of command, (potentially) competing divisions or other corporate actors. It may manifest itself as (1) delay, rejection or request for greater justification by corporate managers, (2) lobbying and rival initiatives by competing divisions and as (3) a lack of legitimacy of the initiative in other MNC units. Furthermore, with regard to the underlying predispositions, the authors identify ethnocentrism of corporate managers,[27] headquarters' suspicion of the unknown as well as resistance to change (Birkinshaw/Ridderstråle 1999, pp. 159-166, Birkinshaw 2000, pp. 40-43).[28] In addition to the corporate immune system which acts as a corporate resistor to subsidiary initiatives, Mahnke et al. (2007) identify three types of *uncertainties* which influence all stages of the initiative process. It is argued that the level of communicative, behavioral and value uncertainty negatively affects the recognition and acceptance of a subsidiary initiative at headquarters (Mahnke et al. 2007, pp. 1282-1284).

In summary, what can we learn from previous research on the subsidiary initiative process? *First*, subsidiary initiatives – in line with general entrepreneurship processes in MNCs – represent a complex set of activities which unfold over several stages. Assuming a rather technocratic view, the initiative development process typically starts with the identification of an opportunity, then involves resource attainment and utilization, initiative selling, evaluation and approval-seeking activities and finishes with the commitment of resources for the specific opportunity (see Figure 2.4). *Second*, within the MNC, various actors from different organizational levels are involved, such as employees from the subsidiary who identify and nurture the opportunity or managers from MNC headquarters who are engaged in negotiation, evaluation and central decision-making activities. *Third*, given the focus on the subsidiary as the unit of analysis, more attention has, naturally, been given to what occurs inside the subsidiary. Yet, the role headquarters play in this entire process remains largely underexplored.

---

[27] Ethnocentrism, in essence, refers to the corporate managers' belief in the superiority over foreign nationals in headquarters or subsidiaries (Perlmutter 1969, p. 11). A more thorough presentation and discussion on the concept of ethnocentrism can be found in Schmid and Machulik (2006, pp. 31-35) or Machulik (2010, pp. 42-49).
[28] Lyly-Yrjänäinen et al.'s (2008, p. 6-9) empirical research shows that global key accounts may support the diffusion of subsidiary initiatives and help with reducing the effects of the corporate immune system.

Simplified process view	Identification of initiative opportunity	Attainment and utilization of resources	Selling, evaluation and approval of initiative	Commitment/ implementation of initiative
Possible impediments	← Resistance through corporate immune system →			
	← Various uncertainties →			

Figure 2.4: Simplified process view on subsidiary initiative development

Fourth, although previous literature – in general – provides support for the outlined process stages, the specific activities and interaction patterns between headquarters and subsidiaries are likely to vary from case to case. It has to be noted that the initiative process may take a variety of forms, the outlined stages do not always have to take place in a sequential order and they may also overlap (see also Birkinshaw/Ridderstråle 1999, p. 151, Birkinshaw 2000, p. 37). Numerous aspects which impact the way this process takes place were identified previously, such as e.g. initiative types and characteristics or factors from the organizational and the individual context. Although the outlined process view might be valuable for identifying and allocating the various entrepreneurial activities and actors involved in the different stages of the process, it does not come without limitations. *Fifth*, it could be shown that subsidiary initiatives face different forms of corporate resistance and different types of uncertainties as they move through the process and develop from an idea to an approved and funded business activity. These impediments may possibly provide some explanation for the low number of subsidiary initiatives that has been observed in previous studies (e.g. Birkinshaw et al. 1998, Birkinshaw/Ridderstråle 1999, Borini et al. 2009a), as these obstacles hinder the advancement of initiatives if no countermeasures or precautionary actions are taken by subsidiary managers. *Sixth*, it can be concluded that very few of the selected studies have yet fully examined the entire initiative development process from recognition to approval and resource commitment. Instead, the larger portion of the relevant literature investigates aspects predominantly related to initiative selling, evaluation and approval. Only a smaller number addresses the stages of (1) initiative opportunity identification, (2) resource attainment and utilization or (4) commitment of resources and initiative implementation. *Finally*, despite certain limitations, the application of the process view on subsidiary initiatives in this paper underlines its potential usefulness; it might provide an additional structure or framework for subsequent investigation and research on this phenomenon.

2.2.4 Antecedents of Subsidiary Initiatives

Out of the 52 publications in the field, 34 are concerned with antecedents of subsidiary initiatives, that is, all those factors which (positively or negatively) affect initiative-taking in the MNC subsidiary. In total, these contributions examine more than 50 different factors which impact subsidiary initiative-taking. It was decided to group these various factors based on the similarity of their contents and meaning, resulting in 26 different "antecedent groups".[29] The number of antecedents examined in each of the relevant contributions varies. Some studies focus on one specific variable, while others consider a broad range of variables. For instance, Lyly-Yrjänäinen et al. (2008) specifically investigate the facilitating role of global key accounts in the diffusion of subsidiary initiatives, whereas one of the journal articles by Birkinshaw empirically examines seven different influencing factors from both the environmental level and the organizational level (see Birkinshaw 1999).[30] Most of the literature investigates the influence of antecedents on the overall existence, amount or level of subsidiary initiatives. However, few studies focus on specific aspects, such as the recognition of initiatives (e.g. Liouka 2007, Mahnke et al. 2007), initiative survival (e.g. Keupp 2008, Keupp/Gassmann 2009a) or subsidiary evolution through initiative-taking (e.g. Birkinshaw/Hood 1998d, Delany 2000). While it is not the objective here to discuss the findings on each identified influencing factor in detail, an overview of the main results of the analysis for the environmental, organizational and individual level will be provided.

2.2.4.1 Environmental Level Context

The environmental context, also referred to as the local market context (Birkinshaw 1999), as country and industry-level factors (Birkinshaw et al. 1998) or as host country factors (Birkinshaw/Hood 1998c), concerns all host country elements outside the foreign subsidiary and outside its relationships within the MNC organization. It includes, for instance, economic, technological, legal and regulatory, customer, supplier, competitor as well as social dimensions which affect initiative-taking in the subsidiary (see e.g. Birkinshaw 1999, Sohail/Ayadurai 2007). 15 publications were found which address six different factors from the environmental level context. Numerous studies have identified *local market dynamism* as one crucial factor within the **local market and industry context** (Birkinshaw/Hood 1998d, Birkinshaw 1999, Zahra et al. 2000, Verbeke et al. 2007, Zucchella et al. 2007, Borini et al. 2009b, Keupp/Gassmann 2009a, Raţiu/Molz 2010). Apparently, a dynamic local market characterized by, for instance, strong compe-

---

[29] For instance, strategic control systems (Zahra et al. 2000), strategically focused incentive systems (Scott et al. 2010) as well as financial incentives and performance credits (Johnson/Medcof 2002, Mahnke et al. 2007) were summarized in the antecedent group "strategic incentives and controls".

[30] These factors are: local market dynamism (from the environmental context) and centralization of subsidiary decision-making, corporate-subsidiary communication, subsidiary credibility at the head office, subsidiary leadership, supportive behavioral context as well as distinctive subsidiary capabilities (from the organizational context; see Birkinshaw 1999, pp. 16-18).

tition, demanding customers or a strong presence of related and supporting industries, encourages or even necessitates that subsidiaries respond to the growing pressures through entrepreneurial behavior (Birkinshaw 1999, p. 18, Zahra et al. 2000, pp. 12-13, Borini et al. 2009b, p. 258).[31] Furthermore, other industry characteristics have been shown to positively influence subsidiary initiative-taking. Birkinshaw et al. (1998) find confirmation for the positive effect of the *level of industry globalization* on subsidiary initiative-taking. Grohmann discovers that MNCs in a *transnational or multinational environment* encounter a higher degree of subsidiary entrepreneurship than firms in the international and global environment (Grohmann 2010, p. 200; see also Westney/ Zaheer 2003, p. 361, Kutschker/Schmid 2011, p. 300). Finally, certain **country-specific characteristics** have been recognized to positively influence subsidiary initiatives. Birkinshaw and Hood (1998c) argue in a conceptual way that the *strategic importance of the host country*, the *relative cost of factor inputs* in the host country as well as *host government support* will have a positive effect on subsidiary charter extension through initiative-taking (Birkinshaw 1997, Raţiu/Molz 2010).

2.2.4.2 Organizational Level Context

The organizational context, as the "set of administrative and social mechanisms ... over which top management have some control" (Birkinshaw 2000, p. 52), embodies all factors that influence the behavior of actors within the organization. Frequently, it is further subdivided into the corporate and the subsidiary context, whereof the first involves the structural and behavioral components which are controlled by the parent and the latter is typically represented by the characteristics of the subsidiary's organizational structure and behavior that can be managed by the subsidiary itself (see e.g. Birkinshaw/Hood 1998d, Birkinshaw et al. 1998, Birkinshaw 1999, Verbeke et al. 2007).

In total, 28 publications address 17 different antecedent groups from the organizational context which affect initiative-taking in the MNC subsidiary. By further subdividing these organizational level determinants into either the corporate or the subsidiary level context, the predominant logic of previous publications was deliberately followed (e.g. Birkinshaw 1999, 2000, Verbeke et al. 2007, Dörrenbächer/Geppert 2009, Williams/Lee 2009, Dörrenbächer/Geppert 2010, Grohmann 2010). Nevertheless, it needs to be pointed out that this grouping of the organizational antecedents comes with certain ambiguities. Some factors can be evidently influenced by both headquarters and the subsidiary (e.g. subsidiary autonomy, subsidiary charter/mandate) while others relate to headquarters-subsidiary relationship characteristics (e.g. headquarters-subsidiary

---

[31] All studies – except for Birkinshaw (1999) – come to the conclusion that a high level of local market dynamism promotes subsidiary initiative. Furthermore, it has to be acknowledged, however, that similar to related concepts such as industry dynamics, local market dynamism itself is a fuzzy and often inconsistently defined concept (see e.g. Hauschild et al. 2011).

communication). Hence, this allocation – although in line with existing publications – can be seen as somewhat arbitrary. As not all findings on influencing factors from these 28 publications can be presented and discussed in detail, some examples on variables will be provided (1) that, based on previous studies, may be considered "more important" than others, (2) for which contradictory findings were obtained, (3) that affect distinct initiative types in a different manner and (4) that appear particularly relevant for specific initiative development stages.

(1) Within the **corporate context**, numerous publications identify *subsidiary autonomy* as a highly relevant factor. This factor refers to the subsidiary's ability to pursue innovative and entrepreneurial activities independently from headquarters, such as the development of new products or markets (e.g. Birkinshaw 1995, p. 35, Birkinshaw/Hood 1997, p. 355, Zahra et al. 2000, p. 9) or – more generally – the pursuit of opportunities that are identified. The majority of studies supports the notion that high levels of autonomy promote entrepreneurship and initiative-taking in the MNC subsidiary (Birkinshaw 1995, p. 35, Birkinshaw/Hood 1997, p. 354, Birkinshaw et al. 1998, p. 235, Zahra et al. 2000, p. 10, Johnson/Medcof 2002, p. 196, Couto et al. 2005, p. 308, Krishnan 2006, p. 66, Boojihawon et al. 2007, p. 566, Liouka 2007, p. 259, Mahnke et al. 2007, p. 1288, Keupp 2008, p. 86, Raţiu/Molz 2010, p. 185).[32] However, some publications in the field propose a more differentiated view, arguing that different types of subsidiary initiatives are facilitated by different degrees of autonomy (Birkinshaw 1997, p. 224, Birkinshaw/Fry 1998, pp. 53-55, Birkinshaw 2000, pp. 22-30).

With regard to the **subsidiary context**, several publications have stressed the high relevance of *subsidiary resources and capabilities* for the entrepreneurial behavior in MNC subsidiaries.[33] Distinctive subsidiary capabilities may be understood as the "extent to which the subsidiary has value-adding capabilities that they believe to be superior to those in sister units around the world" (Birkinshaw 1999, p. 17). They provide the necessary technical and market-based expertise required for initiative-taking. In addition, they may help to overcome corporate resistance through demonstrating to headquarters that the subsidiary has the necessary capabilities for a particular initiative. The assumption that subsidiary resources and capabilities are crucial for initiative-taking is empirically and conceptually supported in various publications by Birkinshaw and his co-authors (Birkinshaw 1997, p. 224, Birkinshaw et al. 1998, p. 223, Birkinshaw 1999, p. 24, 2000, pp. 22-30) and by other authors (Tseng et al. 2004, Zucchella et al. 2007, Dörren-

---

[32] When investigating the impact of subsidiary autonomy, some authors only consider specific aspects of subsidiary initiative-taking. For instance, Keupp (2008) relates particularly to subsidiary initiative survival. Liouka (2007) and Mahnke et al. (2007) focus on the phase of opportunity recognition.

[33] In line with Amit and Schoemaker (1993, p. 35), resources are understood as "stocks of available factors that are owned or controlled by the firm", whereas capabilities represent "a firm's capacity to deploy resources, usually in combination, using organizational processes ... that are firm-specific and are developed over time through complex interactions among the firm's resources."

bächer/Geppert 2010). Likewise, the findings of several studies highlight the positive effect of *credibility, reputation and track record* of a subsidiary vis-à-vis headquarters on subsidiary initiatives (Birkinshaw 1997, Birkinshaw/Fry 1998, Birkinshaw/Hood 1998d, Birkinshaw 1999, Krishnan 2006).

(2) Contradictory findings are obtained for some variables regarding their potential impact on initiative taking. Concerning the **corporate context**, a few studies address the impact of *subsidiary integration* into the corporate system (e.g. Birkinshaw/Fry 1998, Tseng et al. 2004, Krishnan 2006, Borini et al. 2009b) with partially inconsistent findings. While Birkinshaw and Fry (1998) observe that a tight subsidiary integration into the corporate system facilitates initiatives, other publications provide dissimilar conclusions. For instance, Krishnan et al.'s (2006) qualitative research on MNC subsidiaries in India reveals that the level of subsidiary initiatives was highest in those units with low levels of integration. Also, in the study of Borini et al. (2009a), the proposition that initiatives are associated with a high degree of headquarters-subsidiary integration has not been validated. Instead, the authors find that the level of integration has an inverse relation with the presence of initiatives in Brazilian subsidiaries. According to the authors, possible explanations could be that (a) the "appropriate" level of integration depends on the type of initiative, (b) a high integration only indirectly impacts initiatives though fostering an entrepreneurial culture or (c) beyond a certain level, a high integration could actually impede initiatives (see Birkinshaw/Fry 1998, Borini et al. 2009b). Thus, further investigations have to provide additional insights and clarify the relationship between integration and subsidiary initiatives.

Similarly, within the range of variables covering the **subsidiary context**, some conflicting results are published as well. For example, Keupp's empirical study shows that certain *subsidiary characteristics*, such as age, experience and specific subsidiary roles (e.g. centers of excellence) positively affect initiative survival. It is suggested that older and established subsidiaries typically move beyond the status of knowledge recipients toward knowledge providers, thus enhancing the chance of initiatives originating in these types of subsidiaries. Also, age, experience and specific roles may signal competence and trustworthiness of the subsidiary, increasing the likelihood that proposed initiatives are accepted and survive (Keupp 2008, pp. 26-27). In comparison, research by Sohail and Ayadurai indicates that subsidiaries that are in operation for a shorter period of time are more entrepreneurial (Sohail/Ayadurai 2004, p. 50).

(3) Apparently, some of the antecedents from the organizational level impact the various initiative types (see Subsection 2.1.1) in different manners. For example, regarding once again the degree of autonomy as one important variable from the **corporate context**, it can be concluded that different degrees of *subsidiary autonomy* seem to be beneficial for distinct initiative types. While external initiatives (local market and global

market initiatives) are supported by a high degree of subsidiary autonomy, internal initiatives (internal market and global-internal hybrid initiatives) are obviously driven by low(er) degrees of autonomy (Birkinshaw 1997, Birkinshaw/Fry 1998, Birkinshaw 2000). A similar logic applies for different antecedents from the **subsidiary context**, such as subsidiary *resources and capabilities* or *subsidiary credibility, reputation and track record*. For example, Birkinshaw observes that both global market and internal initiatives are facilitated by a high level of proven resources which are recognized by headquarters.[34] Local and global-internal hybrid initiatives, however, only require a rather moderate to high level of proven resources (Birkinshaw 1997, 2000).

(4) Furthermore, a number of antecedents appear to be particularly relevant for one or more specific phases of the subsidiary initiative development process outlined in Subsection 2.1.3 of this dissertation. Certain aspects of the **corporate context**, such as *predispositions and attitudes of headquarters managers* may primarily impact the initiative selling, evaluation and approval stage. Once an initiative is identified, various aspects of the corporate immune system – i.e. ethnocentrism, a suspicion of the unknown and a general resistance to change on the side of headquarters' managers – may suppress the advancement of subsidiary initiatives (Birkinshaw/Fry 1998, Birkinshaw/Hood 1998d, Birkinshaw/Ridderstråle 1999, Birkinshaw 2000; see also Subsection 2.1.3 of this publication). From the **subsidiary context**, *headquarters-subsidiary relationships* may specifically impact the initiative opportunity identification stage. Zucchella et al. conclude from their qualitative study of MNC subsidiaries in Italy that – specifically for this stage – it is beneficial when "managers of the group are well networked and in frequent contact", thereby generating and combining new knowledge for local innovations (Zucchella et al. 2007, p. 320). Also, Liouka (2007, p. 173) finds some support for the positive effect of intra-MNC networking on subsidiary initiative through promoting idea generation and idea sharing across sites. In addition to the positive effect during the identification phase, good and trusting headquarters-subsidiary relationships may also enhance the recognition and acceptance of a proposed initiative at headquarters (Birkinshaw/Hood 1998d, Delany 2000, Dörrenbächer/Geppert 2009, Keupp/Gassmann 2009a). As proposals are often also evaluated based on the qualities of the individuals bringing them forward, a good knowledge of the individual and a trustful relationship prove beneficial (Birkinshaw/Hood 1998d, p. 789, Keupp/Gassmann 2009a, p. 201).

---

[34] Birkinshaw does not clearly differentiate between resources and capabilities. Also, the author applies both the term resources and capabilities for the same type of initiatives in different publications (see Birkinshaw 1997, 2000).

2.2.4.3 Individual Level Context

Few publications study antecedents from the individual context which relates to, for instance, characteristics and behaviors of individual actors within the MNC subsidiary.[35] In sum, 13 contributions were identified which propose various influencing factors that were summarized in three "antecedent groups".

First, a number of publications examine and discuss different aspects related to the subsidiary management's *personal motivation and drive*. For example, the subsidiary management's high need for achievement, power and personal fulfillment might act as a driver for subsidiary development through initiative-taking (Delany 2000, p. 237). Furthermore, the subsidiary management's desire to decrease the dependence on the parent and to achieve more autonomy seems to positively impact the initiative-taking activities (Delany 2000, p. 238, Boojihawon et al. 2007, p. 561, Ambos et al. 2010, p. 1103). Other personal motivations relate to subsidiary managers' ambitions to protect their vested rights or to enhance their career prospects (e.g. Krishnan 2006, p. 65, Mahnke et al. 2007, p. 1290, Dörrenbächer/Geppert 2009, p. 106, 2010, p. 604). Second, the *entrepreneurial attitude and orientation* of subsidiary managers has also been shown to be an important factor (Birkinshaw/Hood 1998d, p. 789). Third, certain *personal abilities and skills* appear to be positively linked to initiatives. Subsidiary executives need to be able to provide an appropriate environment and setting in the subsidiary for initiatives to occur and advance (Birkinshaw 1995, Boojihawon et al. 2007). Additionally, a subsidiary manager's ability to build relationships with headquarters and to form internal coalitions may facilitate initiative-taking (Birkinshaw 1995, p. 35, Birkinshaw/Hood 1998d, p. 786, Birkinshaw/Ridderstråle 1999, p. 175, Keupp/Gassmann 2009a, p. 201, Dörrenbächer/Geppert 2010, p. 616). Entrepreneurial competencies of subsidiary management may also be of relevance. It is argued that, in order to respond to local customer needs, subsidiary managers should possess entrepreneurial skills related to activities such as opportunity scanning and the development of innovative value propositions through global and local networking (Zucchella et al. 2007, p. 316; see also Delany 2000, p. 240, Dörrenbächer/Geppert 2010, p. 616).

What are the major outcomes of this analysis concerning the antecedents of subsidiary initiatives? *First*, well beyond 50 different antecedents of subsidiary initiatives have been examined and discussed in previous publications which were summarized into 26 antecedent groups (see also Figure 2.6). The majority of variables concern the organizational level. Antecedents from the environmental and especially from the individual

---

[35] One could also subsume the individual context under the subsidiary context (see e.g. Birkinshaw et al. 1998). However, it has been shown that individual actors can have a strong and direct influence on the entrepreneurial posture of a firm and they have been frequently seen as the key component in theories and models of entrepreneurial behavior (Covin/Slevin 1991). It was therefore decided to introduce the individual context as a separate category.

level have been investigated to a lesser extent – leaving ample room for additional research. For instance, as certain characteristics and attributes of subsidiary managers may have a significant influence on initiative-taking behavior, further investigations on individual motivations, aspirations and orientations might be beneficial. *Second*, it appears likely that various aspects from the individual, organizational and environmental context need to be "in place" in order for subsidiary initiatives to arise and endure in the MNC. For instance, it appears critical (a) that subsidiary managers are motivated and possess the right skills to undertake and support the progress of initiatives, (b) that there exists the appropriate organizational setting to enable subsidiaries to undertake initiatives and (c) that certain environmental conditions support or even necessitate initiatives. *Third*, considering the numerous antecedents which have been previously identified, it is not entirely clear which ones exert the largest influence on subsidiary initiative-taking. It can only be presumed that certain variables from the individual, organizational and environmental context play a (more) significant role, as they have been repeatedly supported by a number of empirical studies performed by different researchers. For instance, it may therefore be tentatively stated that (1) local market dynamism, (2) subsidiary autonomy, (3) subsidiary specialized resources and distinctive capabilities, (4) headquarters-subsidiary communication and relationship, (5) subsidiary external engagement and orientation as well as (6) the motivation and entrepreneurial orientation of subsidiary managers are of high relevance for subsidiary initiative-taking. *Fourth*, in how far specific antecedents influence the level of initiative-taking also depends on the type of initiative. This again demonstrates how important it is not just to speak of subsidiary initiatives in general, but to distinguish between various forms and to consider particular influencing factors. *Fifth*, it could be further shown that not each influencing factor is equally relevant throughout the different phases of the initiative development process. Instead, certain antecedents appear crucial for the identification of initiatives (e.g. subsidiary external market orientation) and others for the selling, evaluation and approval stage (e.g. subsidiary credibility, reputation and track record). However, to the best of knowledge, a clear investigation of the various drivers in the different stages of the initiative development process has not yet been undertaken.

2.2.5 Consequences of Subsidiary Initiatives

Out of the 52 contributions in the field, 28 address consequences and outcomes of subsidiary initiatives. This review and analysis came across 15 different outcomes which are described as the result of subsidiary initiative-taking. Similar to the work on antecedents, the number of outcomes studied in the literature varies considerably. For example, Delany (1998, 2000) primarily focuses on the particular consequences of subsidiary development, while Birkinshaw (1999) and Ambos et al. (2010) empirically research a broad range of initiative outcomes. Similar to the procedure within the field of antecedents, the different consequences were grouped into outcomes at the environmental level and outcomes at the organizational level. As no research was identified that addresses outcomes related to the individual level, such as consequences for subsidiary managers' careers, the individual level did not become a separate part of the paper.

2.2.5.1 Environmental Level Consequences

Overall, only four studies have investigated the environmental outcomes of subsidiary initiatives (i.e. Zucchella et al. 2007, Dimitratos et al. 2009a, Dimitratos et al. 2009b, Jindra et al. 2009). For example, Dimitratos et al. find a positive and highly significant effect of subsidiary entrepreneurial output on the *economic development* in the host country.[36] It is argued that the MNC entrepreneurial output, for instance in the form of new economic activity, market development, technological solutions or novel administrative and work practices, can have significant spillover effects in the local economy (Dimitratos et al. 2009b, p. 182). Jindra et al.'s research provides evidence for the hypothesis that subsidiaries taking initiatives have a higher share of *forward and backward vertical linkages* with local customers and suppliers.[37] The extent and intensity of these linkages may then again influence the potential for a developmental impact of the subsidiary in the host economy (Jindra et al. 2009, p. 177). Zucchella et al. examine the possible impact of subsidiary entrepreneurship on local industry conditions. The cases analyzed suggest that MNC subsidiaries' entrepreneurial undertakings may also shape the *industry offer and structure*. It is observed that especially those subsidiaries that are capable of radically innovating their offers and value systems can induce changes within their industry, in related industries, or in the relationships with customers (Zucchella et al. 2007, p. 314).

---

[36] The economic development contribution was assessed by the subsidiary managers' perceptions linked to the contribution of the subsidiary to the economic welfare of the country (Dimitratos et al. 2009b, p. 184).
[37] The impact of initiative-taking on the extent of vertical linkages was found significant and positive only for forward linkages.

2.2.5.2 Organizational Level Consequences

The larger share of literature in the field addresses outcomes of subsidiary initiatives at the organizational level. 24 publications could be identified which altogether studied twelve main consequences of subsidiary initiatives of which a condensed overview is provided below.

It has been repeatedly stated that subsidiary entrepreneurship is beneficial and important for the performance of the MNC (e.g. Zahra et al. 2000, p. 2, Yamin 2002, p. 133). However, empirical evidence seems rare. Only three contributions were found which investigate the direct and indirect relationship of subsidiary entrepreneurial initiative-taking and *improved subsidiary performance* (Birkinshaw et al. 2005, Liouka 2007, Ambos/Birkinshaw 2010). For instance, research by Liouka (2007) empirically confirms that subsidiary initiative identification is positively related to subsidiary entrepreneurial performance, which again directly and positively influences the overall subsidiary performance.[38] Also, the study by Ambos and Birkinshaw (2010) substantiates empirically that subsidiaries undertaking entrepreneurial initiatives perform better, both financially and managerially, when compared to other units of the MNC.[39] Other empirical work outlines more direct outcomes, such as the development of new and innovative offers and hence increased business, sales and/or revenues. This is typically the case for external initiatives whereas internal initiatives usually lead to an improved efficiency of operations, cost reductions or increased investments from headquarters (Birkinshaw 1997, pp. 223-224, Birkinshaw/Fry 1998, pp. 54-56, Birkinshaw 2000, pp. 22-30, Lyly-Yrjänäinen et al. 2008, p. 8).

Besides the performance improvement potential, subsidiary initiatives have also been shown to lead to *enhanced subsidiary resources and capabilities*. For example, Birkinshaw's case study research reveals a high impact of subsidiary initiatives on the development of distinctive subsidiary capabilities, for instance in the form of specific manufacturing capabilities or distinct expertise (Birkinshaw 1999). Likewise, a number of other contributions underline the finding that initiatives will lead to the acquisition of resources and capabilities in the subsidiary (Birkinshaw 2000, p. 60, Johnson/Medcof 2002, p. 198, Bouquet/Birkinshaw 2008, p. 581, Dörrenbächer/Geppert 2010, p. 602, Raţiu/Molz 2010, p. 179). These enhanced resources and capabilities might be shared throughout the corporate network (Birkinshaw 1997, p. 223, Ambos/Birkinshaw 2010, p. 456), enhancing the *learning of the entire MNC* (Birkinshaw 1997, p. 208, 2000, p. 62).

---

[38] Subsidiary performance was measured by subsidiary managers' subjective perception of their subsidiary performance relative to the subsidiary's objectives, to main competitors, to other sister subsidiaries and to MNC headquarters expectations (see Liouka 2007, p. 221). A comprehensive overview of different approaches towards performance and performance evaluation of foreign subsidiaries is given by Schmid and Kretschmer (2010).

[39] In the study, subsidiary performance is also based on subjective assessments of subsidiary managers on how their units performed relative to other subsidiary units of the MNC (see Ambos/Birkinshaw 2010, p. 458).

A large number of publications propose that subsidiary initiatives are undertaken with the ultimate objective of expanding the subsidiary's *scope of responsibility, charter or mandate*.[40] This notion could be supported by several empirical studies (e.g. Birkinshaw/Hood 1997, Birkinshaw 1998b, Delany 1998, 2000, Krishnan 2006, Sargent/ Matthews 2006). Evidently, initiatives provide an important means through which subsidiaries can maintain and improve their position in the MNC network. Finally, besides positive and beneficial consequences, subsidiary initiatives also imply *significant costs* for the MNC. Birkinshaw (1998a, pp. 361-363) observes through his empirical research four principal costs that might arise: (1) costs related to empire-building, (2) costs related to a lack of focus, (3) costs associated with the administration of the internal market and (4) costs resulting from internal unemployment and personnel changes.

What can be learned from this review and analysis of the different outcomes that have been proposed in previous writings? *First*, compared to the vast literature dealing with antecedents of subsidiary initiatives, apparently fewer contributions have examined the actual consequences and outcomes. *Second*, subsidiary entrepreneurial initiatives have been shown to result in environmental and organizational level consequences. Although it can be assumed that they also lead to individual level outcomes (e.g. individual career progression), existing research has not yet covered this area sufficiently. *Third*, more specifically at the organizational level, initiatives evidently do have the potential to provide numerous benefits for both the subsidiary and the MNC in the form of, for instance, improved subsidiary performance or worldwide learning in the MNC. However, all these potential positive effects have not been studied in a very systematic and structured way so far. *Fourth*, it needs to be noted that the results of initiative-taking have been mostly viewed from a positive angle. In other words: the outcomes are seen as potentially beneficial to the MNC. Some research has, however, at least mentioned that initiatives also imply certain costs. It is therefore important to consider the overall "balance" when evaluating the total benefits, which – to our knowledge – has not yet been undertaken in detail. Considering the balance between costs and benefits is even more important if we take into account that, in many cases, various subsidiaries may compete against each other with subsidiary initiatives (see on competition between subsidiaries also Maurer 2011 and Schmid/Maurer 2011). *Fifth*, it can be concluded that different outcomes are interlinked and possibly influence each other. We can also assume that there is no direct link between subsidiary initiative-taking and the "final" outcome of an improved subsidiary charter or mandate. Instead, it seems more likely that the various "intermediate" outcomes (e.g. improved subsidiary resources and capabilities) help to put the subsidiary in a better position vis-à-vis headquarters to eventually obtain an enhanced

---

[40] See, for instance, Birkinshaw/Fry 1998, p. 52, Birkinshaw 2000, p. 8, Delany 2000, Ambos et al. 2010, p. 1100, Ambos/Birkinshaw 2010, p. 453. For all identified objectives of subsidiary initiatives, see again Subsection 2.2.3.2 of this paper.

charter, higher degrees of autonomy or additional resources. *Finally*, certain consequences may again function as antecedents of subsidiary initiatives (e.g. subsidiary charter/mandate, subsidiary autonomy, subsidiary resources and capabilities). Apparently, there exists a reciprocal relationship between certain context factors and subsidiary initiative-taking (see also Birkinshaw 1999, p. 29, Raţiu/Molz 2010, p. 187), resulting in a dynamic subsidiary development process – in which repeated successful initiatives may help to sustain or gradually improve the subsidiary endowment, standing and position in the MNC.

2.2.6 Theoretical Approaches in the Subsidiary Initiative Field

So far, the focus was on findings related to the contents within the research field. But what about the theoretical lenses which have been used? The analysis reveals that researchers apply a very broad range of theoretical perspectives when investigating the phenomenon of subsidiary initiatives. Overall, 19 different theoretical approaches and frameworks could be identified that have been employed in the respective field. Whereas a few contributions are entirely based on one single theoretical perspective (e.g. Johnson/Medcof 2002, Williams/Lee 2009), many others apply a range of theories – but often in a rather superficial manner. Of the 19 theoretical approaches, ten were recognized that have been repeatedly applied and/or discussed at more length within the 52 contributions in the field.[41] What are these ten approaches and for which facets of the initiative phenomenon have they been applied for?

For Birkinshaw and Hood (1998c), the main theoretical underpinnings of the subsidiary initiative concept are *network theory* (Ghoshal/Bartlett 1990) and the *resource-based view* (Wernerfelt 1984, Barney 1991, Grant 1991).[42] According to Birkinshaw and Hood, the network perspective and the resource-based view provide insights into the subsidiary as a semi-autonomous entity with links to both internal and external networks and which possesses specialized capabilities on which the rest of the MNC is dependent. In addition to these more dominant theories, Birkinshaw and Hood also apply the *decision process perspective* (Bower 1970, Burgelman 1983a; see also Dimitratos et al. 2009a, p. 420) which then helps to shed light on autonomous behavior at various levels of a

---

[41] These ten theoretical perspectives are network theory (Bartlett/Ghoshal 1989, Ghoshal/Bartlett 1990), resource-based view (Wernerfelt 1984, Barney 1991, Grant 1991), resource dependence theory (Pfeffer/Salancik 1978), agency theory (Jensen/Meckling 1976), the concept of bounded rationality (March/Simon 1958), the transaction cost perspective (Williamson 1975), organizational politics/micropolitics (Burns 1961, March 1962, Mintzberg 1985), Porter's concept of competitive advantage (Porter 1980), the integration/responsiveness framework (Prahalad/Doz 1987) and self-determination theory (Deci/Ryan 1985). Their applicability for the present thesis is discussed – in more detail – in Section 3.3 of this publication.

[42] The authors also use elements from the product life cycle model (Vernon 1966) and the internationalization process approach (Johanson/Vahlne 1977) in their attempt to theoretically ground their approach.

large and complex organization, which is not necessarily promoted by top management in headquarters (Birkinshaw/Hood 1998d, p. 778).[43]

From a firm-level perspective, the concept of *bounded rationality* (March/Simon 1958) also gives reasons as to why subsidiary initiatives might actually arise. It is argued that headquarters are probably not in full control of all decisions in the MNC network and that they do not have sufficient insight into various opportunities and stimuli that subsidiaries are exposed to. Hence bounded rationality constraints may force headquarters to allow autonomous initiatives of subsidiaries (e.g. Birkinshaw 1998a, p. 356, Ambos et al. 2010, p. 1101). Rather from a subsidiary-level perspective, *self-determination theory* (Deci/Ryan 1985) has recently been applied to provide arguments as to why individuals in subsidiaries are motivated to pursue subsidiary initiatives. For instance, it is suggested that, once subsidiary managers have achieved the basic performance objectives set by headquarters, they will likely take initiatives which help them with fulfilling their own personal needs, such as autonomy and affiliation with others (e.g. Ambos et al. 2010, p. 1102).

Both *resource dependence theory* (Pfeffer/Salancik 1978) and *organizational politics perspective* (Mintzberg 1985) have also been used in previous writings since they provide insights into initiative-taking as a particular aspect of headquarters-subsidiary relationships. Some authors argue that subsidiaries pursue initiatives in order to develop unique resources and capabilities on which the MNC depends. This, in turn, may help to strengthen the subsidiary's bargaining power vis-à-vis headquarters when negotiating for an enhanced subsidiary charter, mandate or position (e.g. Williams/Lee 2009, Ambos et al. 2010).

Agency theory (Jensen/Meckling 1976) and *transaction cost perspective* (Williamson 1975) can also be found in some of the 52 publications; these approaches are cited in order to depict and discuss potential intra-organizational impediments to initiative-taking. Furthermore, some authors derive insights from these new institutional economics approaches that suggest specific governance mechanisms and incentives which may help facilitating subsidiary initiatives (Johnson/Medcof 2002, Verbeke/Yuan 2005).

Finally, for some other authors in the field, *Porter's concept of competitive* strategy (Porter 1980) and Prahalad and Doz's *integration-responsiveness framework* (Prahalad/Doz 1987) indicate that both the external and internal environment of the subsidiary can influence entrepreneurial behavior and possibly vice versa (Birkinshaw et al. 2005, Grohmann 2010).

---

[43] As the decision process perspective is only used briefly, it is not considered to be among the ten more dominant theoretical approaches.

What can be derived from this brief overview? *First*, there is no major theoretical perspective which could be claimed as being dominant in the field. While it seems that the network perspective and the resource-based view may be the most extensively cited approaches, this can also be linked to the widespread recurrence of these approaches by Birkinshaw who has been identified as the dominant author in the field. A holistic and overarching theoretical perspective can be considered largely absent. However, due to the numerous facets of the research field and due to the various levels that were identified, a call for one overarching theory may certainly pose a challenge or even be inappropriate.[44] *Second*, although many of the publications use some theoretical arguments, it can be concluded that the existing theoretical base for the phenomenon of subsidiary initiatives, including its antecedents and consequences, appears to remain rather weak. In most of the publications, the theoretical discussion is not at the center of the relevant contribution. *Third*, the large number of theories, often being cited in a rather superficial manner, possibly also reflects the "infant" or early developmental stage of the field (Boojihawon et al. 2007, p. 554). It has already been acknowledged by other scholars that such challenges are not unusual for emergent fields of management research (Dimitratos/Jones 2005, p. 119). Since existing research on subsidiary initiatives and subsidiary entrepreneurship has been mostly inductive, it is not surprising that only minor theoretical development has been made so far (see also Johnson/ Medcof 2002, p. 187). Moreover, authors in the field have so far not discussed in detail to what extent specific theoretical approaches can be applied to specific aspects of this topic. For instance, thorough discussions on the applicability of theories for the subject in general and for specific propositions or hypotheses are lacking. Likewise, debates about the ontological, epistemological, methodological and anthropological applicability of the respective theories to the field and its sub-questions are missing (see e.g. Burrell/ Morgan 1979).

---

[44] For a similar argumentation in the field of internationalization theory in general, see Kutschker/Schmid (2011, pp. 473-481).

2.2.7 Research Methodologies in the Subsidiary Initiative Field

When analyzing the research methodologies that have been used, it becomes evident that the majority of contributions apply empirical approaches (78%); purely conceptual work accounts for less than one quarter of the contributions (22%). This result is also illustrated in Figure 2.5. With regard to changes over time, no clear pattern can be observed. The different research methodologies, i.e. empirically-quantitative, empirically-qualitative and conceptual approaches, were used rather consistently in the time period between 1995 and 2010.

Reviewing the research methodologies in more detail, it can be noticed that the empirically-quantitative work mostly applies surveys in the form of direct mail or electronic questionnaires, frequently directed at (top) managers of foreign subsidiaries. Naturally, quantitative designs often seem to come into play when the focus is on the investigation of antecedents or consequences of initiative-taking or on the examination of relationships between different variables (e.g. Birkinshaw et al. 1998, Birkinshaw 1999, Zahra et al. 2000, Sohail/Ayadurai 2004, Tseng et al. 2004).

		All Contents		Research Contents		
				Specific Contents[45] (Classified according to our research framework)		
				Subsidiary Initiative Concept	Antecedents	Consequences
Research Methodologies	Empirically-quantitative[46]	21	(42%)	1 (8%)	13 (39%)	12 (46%)
	Empirically-qualitative	18	(36%)	8 (67%)	13 (39%)	11 (42%)
	Purely conceptual	11	(22%)	3 (25%)	7 (22%)	3 (12%)
	Total No. of Publications	50[47]	(100%)	12 (100%)	33 (100%)	26 (100%)

Figure 2.5: Overview of research approaches for the investigation of subsidiary initiatives

---

[45] As some publications address more than one specific content area (i.e. subsidiary initiative concept, antecedents, and consequences) at the same time, the total number of contributions adds up to more than 50. For example, Ambos et al. (2010) investigate contents related to both the subsidiary initiative concept and consequences.
[46] In the event that a study applies both empirically-quantitative and empirically-qualitative methodologies (as for example often done in case study design) the "dominant" research approach was selected. Overall, ten studies employed both quantitative and qualitative designs. Thereof, the following studies were allocated to the empirically-qualitative work: Birkinshaw 1997, Birkinshaw/Hood 1997, Zucchella et al. 2007.
[47] Out of the 52 contributions in the field, two provide only summaries of literature (i.e. Birkinshaw 2000 and Medcof 2007). Therefore, the total number of contributions analyzed with regard to research methodologies is 50.

Furthermore, frequently applied for the investigation and exploration of the subsidiary initiative phenomenon is a case study approach. From the 39 empirical studies, 18 employ a case study design – often incorporating data collection through multiple sources, such as semi-structured interviews, questionnaires and other secondary or archival data (e.g. Birkinshaw 1997, 1999, Lee/Chen 2003, Boojihawon et al. 2007). As research on the initiative phenomenon can still be considered at an early stage of development (Boojihawon et al. 2007, p. 554) and with only a limited amount of existing research, case studies might – for the time being – provide an adequate way to further develop new and useful insights that are otherwise difficult to obtain through more remote forms of data collection (Birkinshaw et al. 2005, p. 236, see also Eisenhardt 1989b, Yin 2009). Accordingly, (qualitative) case study design appears to be often used when e.g. investigating activities and interactions of the various actors throughout the subsidiary initiative process (e.g. Birkinshaw/Ridderstråle 1999, Lyly-Yrjänäinen et al. 2008, Dörrenbächer/Geppert 2009, 2010) or when examining the subsidiary development process (e.g. Birkinshaw/Hood 1997, Sargent/Matthews 2006). Other forms of research approaches appear to be used only in fewer instances. Among them are, for example, observation and plant visits (Sargent/Matthews 2006), long term interventionists action research (Lyly-Yrjänäinen et al. 2008) or the qualitative analysis of previously portrayed case studies (Krishnan 2006, Raţiu/Molz 2010).

Regarding the timeframe, it appears that the majority of studies collect and analyze data for a single point in time only. With regard to the dynamic research questions in the field, such as the investigation of the initiative development process or the subsidiary evolution over time, such a practice may not be without problems. For instance, using retrospective accounts – as often done in initiative-related research – might lead to difficulties linked to personal recollection, such as interpretative issues, possible memory failure or attribution bias (see e.g. Schwenk 1988, Dougherty 1992, Golden 1992). Not surprisingly, numerous contributions on subsidiary initiatives argue that longitudinal research might be a superior approach and propose its use for future studies (e.g. Birkinshaw 1997, p. 226, Birkinshaw 1999, p. 30, Tseng et al. 2004, Couto et al. 2005, p. 310, Dörrenbächer/Geppert 2009, p. 109, Jindra et al. 2009, p. 178); yet very few authors seem to have taken full advantage of this opportunity (e.g. Sargent/ Matthews 2006).

When taking a closer look at the unit(s) of analysis of the selected contributions, it becomes apparent that the larger part of the 39 empirical studies focuses on the subsidiary only (30 studies). Here, data is collected mostly from subsidiary (top) managers and only in very few cases from other respondents, such as middle managers (Lee/Williams 2005) or functional heads (Birkinshaw et al. 2005). This comes somewhat surprising, as middle managers often function as project or initiative champions that further develop and nurture the identified opportunities and hence seem to also play a key role in the initiative process. From the remaining nine empirical studies, eight obtain and analyze data from both the subsidiary and headquarters and one study solely relies on the headquarters' perspective (i.e. Grohmann 2010). As the large majority of the selected publications focus on one side of the picture only (i.e. the subsidiary's or the headquarters' perspective), this might lead to a biased picture of the initiative phenomenon (Birkinshaw et al. 1998, p. 236, Sargent/Matthews 2006, p. 245). Previous research has already shown that certain initiative-related aspects or variables might be perceived differently from headquarters' and subsidiary's point of view, such as the subsidiary's role (Daniel 2010, Schmid/Daniel 2010) resulting from procedural justice or subsidiary's integration within the MNC (Tseng et al. 2004, p. 99). Accordingly, a number of researchers suggest including both the subsidiary's and headquarters' perspective in future research (Birkinshaw et al. 1998, p. 236, Tseng et al. 2004, p. 109, Boojihawon et al. 2007, p. 569, Bouquet/Birkinshaw 2008, p. 595, Ambos/Birkinshaw 2010, p. 1115) and also investigating the phenomenon at headquarters more thoroughly (Dörrenbächer/Geppert 2009, p. 109, Jindra et al. 2009, p. 178).

This analysis also examined the countries and industries that were involved in previous empirical research. Whereas early studies between 1995 and 2003 largely concentrated on MNC subsidiaries in Canada, Scotland, Sweden, Ireland and the USA,[48] later work extended the regional scope and included various other regions and countries, such as South-East Asia (e.g. Lee/Chen 2003, Sohail/Ayadurai 2004, Tseng et al. 2004), South America (Sargent/Matthews 2006), Eastern Europe (Jindra et al. 2009) or Australia (Jindra et al. 2009, Ambos et al. 2010, Ambos/Birkinshaw 2010). Nevertheless, empirical studies are still predominantly conducted in peripheral countries. It is therefore suggested to examine subsidiaries in other host country settings, such as in large developed countries (such as Germany or France) or in less developed regions (Birkinshaw et al. 1998, p. 236, Bouquet/Birkinshaw 2008, p. 595). Concerning the industries under investigation, it appears that, to a large extent, MNCs from the manufacturing industry were studied – and only in few cases from the service industry (for exceptions on service industries see Sohail/Ayadurai 2004, Tseng et al. 2004, Boojihawon et al. 2007, Dimitratos et al. 2009a). Thus, it could prove fruitful to also cover MNCs and subsidiaries from service industries or to use samples of firms with both service and manufacturing subsidiaries.

Which conclusions can be drawn from the analysis of the previously applied research approaches? *First*, in order to appropriately study subsidiary initiative-taking, research methodologies are needed that are suitable for such a complex and multi-level phe-

---

[48] See e.g. Birkinshaw 1995, 1997, Birkinshaw/Hood 1997, Birkinshaw 1998a, 1998b, Birkinshaw/Fry 1998, Delany 1998, Birkinshaw/Ridderstråle 1999, Delany 2000, Zahra et al. 2000.

nomenon that unfolds over several process phases and involves numerous actors from different levels of the organization. When, for instance, attempting to capture the socially complex interactions between various actors across multiple levels, a combination of quantitative and qualitative research approaches could be helpful to obtain a deeper and richer understanding of the phenomenon. *Second*, there is further room for qualitative studies on this relatively young and still poorly understood topic. As qualitative research is particularly suited to investigate the black box of organizational processes and for studying the various facets of individual and collective action as it takes place over time (Doz 2011, p. 583), it should be applicable for many aspects of the subsidiary initiative phenomenon. *Third*, in line with the requests expressed in existing publications, future studies could more often incorporate a longitudinal dimension to their research. This could, for example, allow for a more comprehensive analysis of the initiative process as it unfolds over time, to better examine in which manner it is linked to certain contingencies and in how far the context affects the subsidiary initiative outcomes, such as subsidiary development (see e.g. Burgelman 2011, p. 599). *Fourth*, in order to gain a more complete and "balanced" view, the subsidiary initiative phenomenon could ideally be examined both at the parent company and the subsidiary level at the same time. *Lastly*, it could be fruitful to conduct empirical research in other subsidiary's settings. Comparative research designs could possibly be adopted in the future in order to contrast subsidiary initiative-taking in different countries, industries or concerning other organizational and environmental settings.

2.3 Summary of Findings and Implications for Research Project

In this chapter, it was intended to provide a systematically derived overview of the state-of-the-art on the topic of subsidiary initiatives. It was the aim to go beyond a "mere accumulation" of writings and to also systematically review and critically analyze previous findings. Moreover, by applying a structural framework and by categorizing numerous aspects of the initiative phenomenon, it was attempted to obtain a more clear-cut picture on the status quo of the field. What can be summarized as the key findings of this review and analysis?

(1) First, the major "building blocks" of the subsidiary initiative phenomenon were identified, categorized and briefly discussed. It could be shown that scholars in this field have already developed some understanding on many facets of initiative-taking, including different initiative types and characteristics, initiative objectives and certain parts of the underlying development process. Also, more than 50 antecedents had been addressed and examined in earlier work, which were summarized into 26 antecedent groups. Based on the analysis of the existing literature, it can be presumed that local market dynamism, subsidiary autonomy, specialized subsidiary resources and capabil-

ities, headquarters-subsidiary communication and relationship as well as the motivation and entrepreneurial orientation of subsidiary managers play an essential role for subsidiary initiative-taking. However, given the traditional research approaches, it cannot be ruled out that other factors have an important (or even more important role) to play. Moreover, 15 different consequences materialized through our analysis of past contributions. Evidently, subsidiary initiatives do have the potential to provide a number of benefits at both the subsidiary and the MNC level, for instance in the form of subsidiary development, improved subsidiary and MNC performance as well as worldwide learning within the MNC. Yet, initiative-taking might come with certain costs for the MNC. Hence, it is critical to consider "both sides of the coin" when evaluating the overall outcome of subsidiary initiatives. Figure 2.6 gives an overview and includes all major research areas identified from the analysis of past writings. When having a closer look at Figure 2.6 and its contents, one can discover that previous research has been quite fragmentary. It appears that many scholars have merely taken some variables in their studies without placing them in the broader context of all potential variables.

(2) When taking the different findings on the subsidiary initiative phenomenon into consideration, it can be best summarized and described as a complex, multi-level and multifaceted phenomenon. It represents a set of (entrepreneurial) activities which unfold over several stages. Initiative-taking is associated with different objectives and it can also materialize as different types and forms. Within the MNC, it usually involves actors from different hierarchical levels. Various factors from the environmental, organizational and individual level context influence the subsidiary initiative-taking behavior. Likewise, its outcomes can again be seen at the environmental, organizational and, although not yet researched in detail, most likely at the individual level. Overall, initiative-taking has the potential to provide benefits for the subsidiary, the MNC and the host country as well.

(3) As stated at the beginning of this chapter, Birkinshaw's original definition of subsidiary initiatives was used. Based on this comprehensive analysis, which included a review of the definitions used in the field,[49] it is suggested to amend Birkinshaw's original definition. Consequently, subsidiary initiatives should be understood as proactive, risk-taking and innovative – and as such entrepreneurial – activities which originate outside the home country in a foreign subsidiary of an MNC and which are typically initiated by actors in the subsidiary. The underlying initiative process unfolds

---

[49] In addition to the review and analysis of the 52 publications, an examination of the definitions that were given/applied took place. Overall, 33 contributions contained (more or less explicit) definitions concerning subsidiary initiatives. These 33 definitions were compared and reviewed for similarities/deviations of contents and meaning (e.g. regarding overall subsidiary initiative definition, process development, types and objectives, involved actors etc.) as well as the origins and the sources which were indicated.

over several stages, beginning with the identification of an opportunity, involving resource attainment and utilization as well as selling, evaluation and approval seeking activities, and finishing with the commitment of resources for the specific opportunity in the end. Subsidiary initiatives may take various forms, ranging from e.g. smaller internal business improvement efforts to extensive new product development activities for the external market. In the shorter term, they are to provide the MNC with new or improved business activities and – in the longer term – allow the subsidiary to maintain or improve its standing within the corporate network.

Although this is still quite close to Birkinshaw's original definition, some deliberate modifications were made. *First*, herein initiative-taking is viewed as a broader concept which involves numerous forms of entrepreneurial activities in the MNC subsidiary – rather than autonomous actions "merely" aiming at improving the subsidiary's scope of responsibility (as e.g. mentioned by Birkinshaw 1997, p. 211, Birkinshaw/Fry 1998, p. 52, Birkinshaw et al. 1998, p. 223, Birkinshaw 2000, p. 8). *Second*, in line with Birkinshaw, initiative-taking is viewed as an entrepreneurial process (e.g. Birkinshaw 1997, p. 207, 1998a, p. 356, Birkinshaw et al. 2005, p. 228). However, the researcher explicitly acknowledges the resource attainment and utilization as well as the selling, evaluation and approval seeking activities which typically occur between the identification of an opportunity and the commitment of resources in the end. *Third*, additionally included are the various types and forms which were discussed in previous work (e.g. internal, global internal, local as well as global market initiatives) and it is recognized that initiatives might imply consequences ranging from smaller and incremental to larger and more radical changes in the MNC. *Finally*, although initiative-taking might come with certain costs, a generally positive stance is taken on the phenomenon and the potential benefits for the MNC are highlighted, such as improved performance or worldwide learning.

Antecedents

Environmental level context

	QN	QL	C
Country characteristics			
• Strategic importance of host country	✓		
• Relative cost of factor inputs	✓		
• Host government support	✓	✓	
Local market/industry characteristics			
• Local market dynamism	✓		
• Transnational/multinational environment	✓		
• Industry characteristics and globalization	✓	✓	

Organizational level context

	QN	QL	C
Corporate context			
• Subsidiary autonomy	✓	✓	
• Subsidiary charter/mandate	✓	✓	
• MNC organizational structure	✓	✓	
• Strategic incentives and controls	✓	✓	
• Subsidiary integration	✓	✓	
• Competitiveness of int. resource allocation	✓	✓	
• Procedural justice	✓		
• Predispositions/attitudes of HQ managers	✓		
Subsidiary context			
• Subsidiary resources and capabilities	✓	✓	
• HQ-S communication and relationship	✓	✓	
• External engagement and orientation	✓	✓	
• Subsidiary credibility, reputation and track record	✓	✓	

Individual level context

	QN	QL	C
Subsidiary managers/employees			
• Personal motivation and drive	✓	✓	✓
• Personal abilities and skills	✓	✓	✓
• Entrepreneurial attitude/orientation	✓	✓	✓

Subsidiary initiative concept

Subsidiary initiative types

- Locus of origin/locus of pursuit
  - Internal market initiatives ⎤ internal
  - Global-internal hybrid initiatives ⎦ initiatives
  - Local market initiatives ⎤ external
  - Global market initiatives ⎦ initiatives
- End objective
  - Domain developing initiatives
  - Domain consolidating initiatives
  - Domain defending initiatives
- Relatedness to existing business
  - Subsidiary renewal initiatives
  - Subsidiary venturing initiatives

Subsidiary initiative objectives

- Fulfillment of subsidiary employees personal needs
- Generation of new external business
- Improvement of internal business operations
- Development of capabilities and resources
- Enhancement of the subsidiary charter/mandate

Subsidiary initiative process

- Process stages
  - Initiative opportunity identification
  - Initiative selling, evaluation and approval
  - Resource commitment and implementation

Consequences

Environmental level consequences

	QN	QL	C
Country level consequences			
• Host country economic development	✓		
Local market/industry level consequences			
• Industry offer and structure	✓		
• Forward and backward vertical linkages	✓		

Organizational level consequences

	QN	QL	C
Corporate level consequences			
• MNC learning	✓	✓	
• Costs associated with SI (e.g. for lack of focus, administration of internal market)		✓	
• Subsidiary charter/mandate	✓	✓	
• Subsidiary autonomy	✓	✓	
• Intrafirm competition		✓	
Subsidiary level consequences			
• Subsidiary performance	✓	✓	
• Subsidiary resources and capabilities	✓	✓	
• Subsidiary value added scope	✓	✓	
• HQ-S relationship (trust, credibility)	✓	✓	
• HQ attention and visibility	✓	✓	
• HQ monitoring	✓		
• Subsidiary position, power and influence	✓	✓	

Individual level consequences

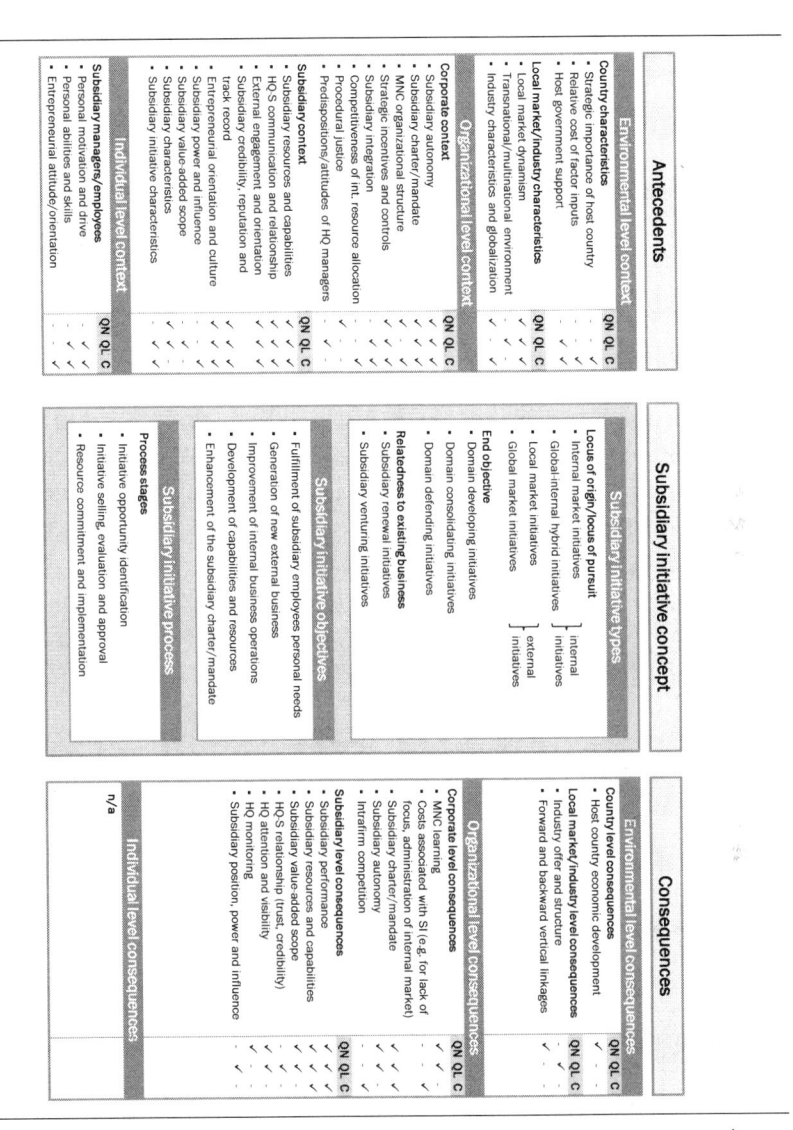

n/a

Figure 2.6: Subsidiary initiatives, their antecedents and consequences – research areas and methodologies in previous publications[50]

---

[50] Figure 2.6 also outlines which research methodologies have been used to study antecedents and consequences. The research approaches are denoted as follows: QN = empirically-quantitative, QL = empirically-qualitative and C = conceptual studies. A check mark (✓) indicates that the given research approach was used for the respective antecedent/consequence.

What remains open for future research in the subsidiary initiative field? Following the systematic review and analysis of the relevant literature, potential for further work is seen in the following areas which also provides guidance for the present doctoral thesis.

(1) As outlined, previous work has already led to some basic understanding of the different facets of the subsidiary initiative phenomenon. Yet, the majority of existing contributions largely focus on specific aspects of the subsidiary initiative phenomenon; work integrating the different pieces into a "larger picture" appears to be lacking. Therefore, there is need for a more comprehensive conceptualization of the field (see also Birkinshaw et al. 2005, p. 246). Future work should, even when only dealing with specific aspects of the phenomenon (i.e. certain "pieces of the puzzle"), be conscious about its place and its possible integration within the "larger picture" of the subsidiary initiative concept. Furthermore, more comprehensive research approaches are envisioned which entail a combination of different research methodologies or which include and link various initiative aspects (e.g. certain antecedents, initiative types, processes and specific outcomes) when investigating the field.

(2) There also remains ample room for research related to each single "building block". Concerning the initiative concept, both the initiative process and the initiative typologies have not been adequately investigated so far. In general, taking a more thorough and comprehensive process view could yield valuable insights. Relating to specific process phases, the initiative opportunity identification at subsidiary level and the subsequent recognition of the initiative at headquarters also require greater attention (see also Mahnke et al. 2007, p. 1294). Moreover, the existing initiative typologies should be used by authors in the field and be further refined and extended. As the findings indicate that the various initiative types are impacted differently by antecedents (e.g. subsidiary autonomy, subsidiary resources and capabilities), future studies should more often attempt to incorporate different forms into their research. This could also help to better assess the validity and applicability of the existing types.

(3) Previous literature has – to a large extent – focused on antecedents of subsidiary initiatives, especially those associated with the environmental and organizational level context. However, earlier work has mostly neglected the individual entrepreneur and the entrepreneurial team in the subsidiary as the unit of analysis. Although some publications have begun to address these issues, it is, for instance, largely unclear what stimulates subsidiary managers and employees to act in an entrepreneurial manner or how different roles and characteristics of subsidiary managers may impact initiative-taking (see also Young/Tavares 2004, p. 232, Dörrenbächer/Geppert 2009, p. 101). Therefore, it is suggested that further research should be carried out in order to determine the importance of individual level factors.

(4) Compared to the rather extensive investigation of antecedents, the actual consequences of subsidiary initiative-taking have only been examined in less depth. In particular, the outcomes at the environmental and the individual level have been rarely studied. Similarly, at the organizational level, only a limited number of studies have explored the linkages between subsidiary initiatives and the subsidiary and corporate level performance (see also Boojihawon et al. 2007, p. 569, Verbeke et al. 2007, p. 596). Furthermore, it remains partially unclear, in how far the different outcomes are interlinked and to what extent they will eventually lead to an enhanced subsidiary charter or mandate.

(5) It has been shown that a larger part of the relevant literature deals with the effect of subsidiary initiative-taking on the subsidiary role or mandate development. Yet, research in the "opposite direction", i.e. the investigation of the relationship between different subsidiary roles and the subsidiary initiative-taking behavior and outcomes has not been undertaken yet in detail (see also Liouka 2007, p. 34). Although different subsidiary contexts are likely to lead to different subsidiary entrepreneurial behavior (e.g. Ghoshal/Bartlett 1994, pp. 104-105, Gupta/Govindarajan 1994, p. 446), to the best of the researcher's knowledge, no existing study has investigated in depth the link between different subsidiary context settings in the form of subsidiary strategic roles and initiative-taking behavior. Future work could, for instance, explore in more detail if and in how far different subsidiary roles impact the type and amount of initiatives that emerge, to what extent they shape the initiative development process or influence the initiative outcomes.

(6) Most of the subsidiary initiative research has – naturally – been undertaken from a subsidiary perspective. Yet, despite the importance of subsidiaries, the role headquarters play throughout the initiative development process should be further explored. For instance, it remains largely unclear how corporate entrepreneurship at the parent level and initiative-taking at the subsidiary level are interlinked. Also, the headquarters' role in all facets of subsidiary initiative-taking, for instance in the opportunity recognition process and the involvement of various headquarters' actors) have not been systematically analyzed so far (see also Birkinshaw/Hood 1998d, p. 792, Birkinshaw et al. 2005, p. 246, Mahnke et al. 2007, p. 1294).

(7) Finally, it was noted that the theoretical development of the phenomenon remains at a rather early stage and does not appear to be very solid yet. Although numerous theoretical perspectives have been employed in the field, no dominant theory seems to prevail. In the case of future work being of theory-testing nature, more thorough discussions on the applicability of existing theories for the specific aspects in question are needed. For theory-developing work, there is also ample room for further improvement. As recently suggested by Doz, (inductive) theory building requires first rich

(qualitative) data which covers e.g. the various activities and interactions of organizational actors, actual processes, antecedents and consequences of activities. Second, an appropriate aggregation of findings, categorization and definitions may then help to develop conceptual maps and frameworks which structure and relate existing results, representing the foundation on which to build future theories (see Doz 2011, p. 586).

Overall, this examination and analysis of the literature on subsidiary initiatives indicates that, despite the growing interest and the increasing number of publications in this topic area, several aspects are still unexplored or not sufficiently explored. In how far some of these research gaps are addressed in this research endeavor is explained in the following chapter of this publication in more detail.

3 Research Framework

This chapter first introduces the basic research framework for role-specific subsidiary initiative-taking in Section 3.1. Next, Section 3.2 describes the key elements of the framework, which are subsidiary roles (Subsection 3.2.1), subsidiary initiative-taking behavior (Subsection 3.2.2) and subsidiary initiative outcomes (Subsection 3.2.3). Subsequently, in Section 3.3, the theoretical foundations are introduced and then, in Section 3.4, the contingent and dynamic resource-based framework is described in detail. The framework links the conceptual and theoretical considerations and provides the basis for the development of the propositions that are derived in the last Section of this Chapter (3.5).

3.1 Overview of the Research Framework

As described in Section 2.3, the analysis of the relevant subsidiary initiative literature led to the identification of different areas that deserve further investigation and research. Since the present research cannot address all identified gaps in the subsidiary initiative field, it was decided to focus primarily on three aspects, which are described in more detail below: (1) the influence of the subsidiary role setting on (2) aspects of the subsidiary initiative process and (3) on selected outcomes.[51]

(1) The detailed review and analysis of the subsidiary initiative antecedents revealed more than 50 factors from the environmental, organizational and individual context levels that have been shown to impact initiative-taking and entrepreneurial behavior in MNC subsidiaries (see Subsection 2.2.4). Among the numerous antecedents from the organizational and environmental level that have been investigated, several represent or are closely related to the dimensions of different subsidiary role typologies that have been portrayed in the IB literature over the past two and a half decades.[52] Apparently, different factors from the environmental and organizational context relating to certain dimensions of specific subsidiary role typologies seem to have a considerable effect on initiative-taking behavior in MNC subsidiaries. This assumption has been articulated, albeit rather generally, in the literature before. For instance, it has been suggested that subsidiaries in the roles of "Global Innovators" and "Integrated Players" possess supe-

---

[51] The eventual selection of the research focus was also inspired by, for instance, internal discussions with my PhD advisor and colleagues as well as by comments and feedback obtained at national and international conferences and research colloquia where different research directions on subsidiary initiatives were presented and discussed.
[52] For example, subsidiary resources and capabilities (e.g. Birkinshaw 1997, Birkinshaw et al. 1998, Birkinshaw 1999, Tseng et al. 2004) or aspects of the subsidiary's market environment such as dynamism, sophistication or competitive intensity (e.g. Birkinshaw/Hood 1998d, Birkinshaw 1999, Zahra et al. 2000, Sargent/Matthews 2006, Borini et al. 2009a) have been shown to impact subsidiary initiatives – factors that can be seen as closely related to the dimensions of Bartlett and Ghoshal's role typology (Bartlett/Ghoshal 1986, 1989). In addition, subsidiary integration (e.g. Birkinshaw/Ridderstråle 1999, Krishnan 2006) and subsidiary local orientation and responsiveness (e.g. Tseng et al. 2004, Boojihawon et al. 2007, Scott et al. 2010) represent antecedents that can be connected to the dimensions of the role typology presented by Jarillo/Martinez (1990) or Taggart (1997b).

rior capabilities and therefore potentially take a more innovative and entrepreneurial role within the MNC system (Boojihawon et al. 2007, p. 553, see also Gupta/Govindarajan 1994, p. 455). Similarly, entrepreneurial initiatives are said to be more likely to emerge from subsidiaries that hold the role of a "Strategic Leader" or a "Contributor" (Verbeke et al. 2007, p. 586; see also Bartlett/Ghoshal 1986, p. 90). Likewise, it has been stated that only subsidiaries with more advanced roles, such as strategic centers, should undertake initiatives since they have "the capabilities necessary on which to build further development and the management expertise necessary to drive initiatives to completion" (Birkinshaw/Fry 1998, p. 58). Although the potential impact of the subsidiary (role) setting for subsidiary initiatives appears to be generally recognized, research evidently has not yet examined the relationship between distinct subsidiary (role) settings and the subsidiary initiative-taking process and outcomes in detail (Liouka 2007, p. 34), and the area is even said to remain "in its infancy" (Johnson/Medcof 2007, p. 473). Therefore, it has been suggested that future research should investigate the specific contextual characteristics of subsidiaries that exhibit entrepreneurial initiatives in more detail (see e.g. Birkinshaw 1997, p. 227, Young et al. 2003, p. 39, Mahnke et al. 2007, p. 1294).[53]

(2) A second research gap addressed in the present study concerns the initiative process. As seen in Subsection 2.2.3, the initiative process has not yet been systematically and purposefully investigated in detail. In line with this view, it has been stated that "little is known about what occurs inside the subsidiary and how its activities and processes generate firm-level capabilities" (Boojihawon et al. 2007, p. 568) and more process research in the subsidiary entrepreneurship arena has been called for (Hoskisson et al. 2011, p. 1149). In particular, the process phases and activities related to initiative opportunity identification, initiative realization and headquarters-subsidiary alignment may benefit from further investigation. For example, concerning initiative opportunity identification, Mahnke et al. call for further research on "the nature and phases of opportunity recognition ... within MNEs" (2007, p. 1293), while Dimitratos and Jones highlight the theme of opportunity search and identification as an emergent research area that could generate valuable new insights (2005, p. 120). With regard to the realization phase, many contributions in the field acknowledge that subsidiary initiatives involve the use and expansion of resources and capabilities in order to "physically" realize an opportunity (e.g. Birkinshaw 1997, Birkinshaw/Hood 1998d, Birkinshaw 1999).[54] Nevertheless, the existing literature remains largely silent on how these process activities actually take place and how subsidiaries use and enhance their resources and capabilities through initiative-taking. As a result, it has been stated that "much more attention needs to be paid in future [research] to the ways that capabilities

---

[53] Birkinshaw states that "a single structural context cannot facilitate all ... types of subsidiary initiatives." Therefore, different subsidiary (role) settings may be linked to specific types of initiatives (see Birkinshaw 1997, p. 225).
[54] See Subsection 2.2.3.3 herein for additional details.

are developed at a subfirm level and then disseminated or transferred within the firm" (Birkinshaw/Hood 1998d, p. 791).[55] Finally, a further research need has been identified with regard to the interactions between headquarters and the subsidiary throughout the initiative process, such as the involvement of headquarters in general (Mahnke et al. 2007, p. 1294), headquarters resistance against initiatives (Schotter/Beamish 2011, p. 243), or selling efforts undertaken by the subsidiary to attract headquarters attention and to further promote initiatives at the corporate center (Birkinshaw 1997, p. 222, Gammelgaard 2009, p. 215, De Clercq et al. 2011, p. 1271).

(3) A third research gap that will be taken into account concerns the outcomes of subsidiary initiative-taking. Many contributions to the field focus on the investigation of antecedents to subsidiary initiatives while the actual outcomes have been examined in less depth. Although different subsidiary initiative outcomes have been presented in earlier work,[56] it remains largely unclear how they relate to different subsidiary (role) settings, or to what extent they result from different initiative process activities. It therefore has been recommended that more attention be paid to the linkages between subsidiary initiatives and the resulting outcomes at both the subsidiary level and the corporate level (see e.g. Boojihawon et al. 2007, p. 569, Liouka 2007, p. 7, Verbeke et al. 2007, p. 596, Williams/Lee 2009, p. 297).

In addressing these three areas in need of further research in the subsidiary initiative field, the present thesis aims to investigate how distinct subsidiary role settings influence aspects of the subsidiary initiative process and, eventually, key subsidiary initiative outcomes. This contribution therefore not only explicitly deals with some of the identified research gaps in the field, but also responds to calls for a more holistic perspective and conceptualization of subsidiary initiatives in order to achieve a more thorough understanding of this complex phenomenon, as it links antecedent with the initiative-taking process and outcomes. Figure 3.1 presents the basic elements of the research framework for this thesis, which are described in more detail in the following Section.

---

[55] For a similar line of reasoning on subsidiary resource and capability development in more general terms, see, for example, Andersson et al. (2002, p. 991) or Schmid and Schurig (2003, p. 757).
[56] See Subsection 2.2.5 herein for additional details.

```
┌─────────────┐     ┌───────────────────┐     ┌─────────────┐
│  Subsidiary │ ──▶ │ Subsidiary        │ ──▶ │ Subsidiary  │
│    Role     │     │ Initiative-       │     │ Initiative  │
│             │     │ Taking Behavior   │     │ Outcome     │
└─────────────┘     └───────────────────┘     └─────────────┘
```

Figure 3.1: Overview of the basic research framework

3.2 Elements of the Research Framework

3.2.1 Subsidiary Role Types

3.2.1.1 Introduction to Subsidiary Role Typologies

In line with the changing view on multinational corporations, from hierarchical and center-dominated firms towards alternative conceptions such as geocentric companies, transnational organizations or heterarchies (e.g. Perlmutter 1969, Hedlund 1986, Bartlett/Ghoshal 1989), scholars have also begun to pay more attention to the varying roles that foreign subsidiary units can play in the MNC. Researchers have recognized that individual subsidiaries, especially in network MNCs,[57] may perform distinctive tasks and take on different roles, which gave rise to a line of research inquiry concerned with subsidiary role typologies (Schmid 2004, p. 237). In contrast to earlier research streams on MNC and subsidiary management (e.g. the strategy-structure stream or the headquarters-subsidiary relationship stream; see Paterson/Brock 2002), research on subsidiary roles shifted the emphasis towards the subsidiary as the unit of analysis (Birkinshaw/Hood 1998a, p. 7, Paterson/Brock 2002, p. 142). This allowed for the more detailed investigation and thus a better understanding of many subsidiary facets such as subsidiary strategies, subsidiary tasks or the development of subsidiary roles over time (Schmid 2004, pp. 245-246, Manolopoulos 2008, p. 24).

Following the early works by, for example, White and Poynter (1984) or D'Cruz (1986), scholars have presented a multitude of subsidiary role typologies over the past two and a half decades (for overviews see e.g. Birkinshaw/Morrison 1995, pp. 732-733, Schmid et al. 1998, Paterson/Brock 2002, pp. 144-147, Schmid/Kutschker 2003, Enright/Subramanian 2007, pp. 897-900, Manolopoulos 2008, pp. 44-46). Typically, most role typologies consist of two or three classifying dimensions that determine or characterize the specific role of a subsidiary. The role dimensions may include attributes relating to environmental characteristics such as the strategic importance of the local environment

---

[57] Subsidiary role differentiation may very well be present in MNCs that cannot be characterized as "network MNCs" in the sense of, for instance, Bartlett and Ghoshal or Perlmutter. Nevertheless, it can be assumed that differentiation is not as developed or it may be less relevant from a management perspective (see also Schmid 2004, p. 238).

(Bartlett/Ghoshal 1986) or to organizational characteristics such as the subsidiary's market scope and value-added scope (White/Poynter 1984), the subsidiary's decision-making autonomy (D'Cruz 1986), or the subsidiary's degree of localization and local responsiveness (Jarillo/Martinez 1990, Taggart 1997b). Among the numerous role typologies that have been developed, some are repeatedly mentioned and appear to be more established in the IB domain. Table 3.1 provides an overview and comparison of these well-recognized typologies.[58]

Publication	Role Dimensions[59]	Subsidiary Roles	Empirical Basis	Geographic Scope
White/Poynter (1984)	• Market scope • Product scope • Value added scope	• Miniature Replica • Marketing Satellite • Rationalized Manufacturer • Product Specialist • Strategic Independent	• More qualitative empirical basis • Approx. 35 subsidiaries, approx. 7 in depth	Subsidiaries from Canada (HQ probably in the U.S.)
D'Cruz I (1986)	• (Annual business plans) • (Strategic plans)	• Truncated Business • Miniature Replica • Mature Non-Strategic Subsidiary	• Personal interviews • 47 subsidiaries	Subsidiaries from Canada (HQ probably in the U.S.)
D'Cruz II (1986)	• Decision-making autonomy • Extent of market involvement	• Importer • Satellite Business • Local Service Business • Branch Plant • World Product Mandate • Globally Rationalized Business	• Case study • 1 subsidiary	Subsidiary from Canada (HQ in the U.S.)
Bartlett/Ghoshal (1986, 1989)	• Strategic importance of local environment • Competence of the local organization	• Strategic Leader • Contributor • Implementer • Black Hole	• Questionnaire • 618 subsidiaries of 66 companies	Localization of subsidiaries not indicated (HQ in North America and Europe)
Marcati (1989)	• (Level of coordination) • (Dependence from HQs)	• Bridgehead Subsidiary • Fragmented Subsidiary • Connected Subsidiary • Loose Subsidiary	• Questionnaire • 14 subsidiaries	Subsidiaries from the U.S. (HQ in Italy)

Table 3.1: Comparison of subsidiary role typologies (1/3)

---

[58] The subsidiary role typologies outlined in Table 3.1 are those that have been repeatedly presented in publications that provide overviews and summaries on the topic (i.e. Birkinshaw/Morrison 1995, Schmid et al. 1998, Paterson/Brock 2002, Schmid/Kutschker 2003, Enright/Subramanian 2007, Manolopoulos 2008). Certainly, many other typologies can be found in the literature (e.g. Medcof 1997, Mudambi 1999, Pearce 1999, Delany 2000). However, for the purpose of this thesis, it was decided to limit the overview to the most prominent and well-established ones.

[59] The majority of subsidiary role dimensions are explicitly referred to within the publications. However, some role dimensions can only be deduced implicitly through, for instance, the descriptions of different role types as presented by the authors. The latter dimensions are in parentheses to indicate their implicit nature.

Publication	Role Dimensions	Subsidiary Roles	Empirical Basis	Geographic Scope
Ferdows (1989, 1997)	• Primary strategic reason for the site • Extent of technical activities at the site/Site competence	• Off-Shore • Source • Server • Contributor • Outpost • Lead	• Case studies • First 8, then 10 international firms in the electronics industry with their subsidiaries	Subsidiaries mainly from Europe (HQ in north America, Europe and Japan)
Jarillo/Martinez (1990)	• Degree of localization • Degree of integration	• Autonomous Subsidiary • Receptive Subsidiary • Active Subsidiary	• Structured personal interviews • 50 subsidiaries	Subsidiaries from Spain (HQ in North America, Japan and Europe)
Gupta/Govindarajan (1991, 1994)	• Outflow of knowledge • Inflow of knowledge	• Local Innovator • Global Innovator • Implementor • Integrated Player	• Questionnaire • 359 subsidiaries of 79 parent companies	Localization of subsidiaries not indicated (HQ in the U.S., Japan and Europe)
Hoffmann (1994)	• MNC strategy • Subsidiary capabilities • Local environment of the subsidiary	• Partner • Contributor • Specialist • Satellite • Independent • Interdependent • Implementer • Isolate	• Empirical (secondary) cases only for illustrative purposes • 8 subsidiaries	Subsidiaries from countries all over the world (HQ in the U.S., Europe and Japan)
Birkinshaw/Morrison (1995)	• (Market scope) • (Product scope) • (Value added scope)[60]	• Local Implementer • Specialized Contributor • World Mandate	• Questionnaire • 115 subsidiaries	Subsidiaries from the U.S., Canada, UK, Germany, France and Japan (localization of HQ not indicated)
Forsgren/Pedersen (1997, 1998)	• Corporate embeddedness • External embeddedness	• Independent Centre • External Centre • Internal/Corporate Centre • Strategic Centre	• Questionnaire • 60 subsidiaries	Subsidiaries from Denmark (HQ worldwide)
Taggart I (1997b)	• Degree of local responsiveness • Degree of integration	• Autonomous Subsidiary • Receptive Subsidiary • Constrained Independent • Quiescent Subsidiary	• Questionnaire • 171 subsidiaries	Subsidiaries from the UK (location of HQ not indicated)
Taggart II (1997a)	• Autonomy • Procedural justice	• Vassal Subsidiary • Militant Subsidiary • Collaborator Subsidiary • Partner Subsidiary	• Questionnaire • 171 subsidiaries	Subsidiaries from the UK (location of HQ not indicated)
Taggart III (1998)	• Coordination of activities • Configuration of activities	• Autarchic Subsidiary • Detached Subsidiary • Confederate Subsidiary • Strategic Auxiliary	• Questionnaire • 171 subsidiaries	Subsidiaries from the UK (location of HQ not indicated)
Nobel/Birkinshaw (1998)	• Nature of activities • Geographic scope • Linkages to other entities	• Local Adaptor • International Adaptor • International Creator	• Questionnaire • 110 subsidiaries of 15 companies	Subsidiaries from Sweden and outside of Sweden (HQ in Sweden)

Table 3.1: Comparison of subsidiary role typologies (2/3)

---

[60] In addition to these three dimensions, Birkinshaw and Morrison also characterize their role types through other attributes, such as the degree of subsidiary autonomy, subsidiary integration, or interdependencies (see Birkinshaw/Morrison 1995, pp. 742-743).

Publication	Role Dimensions	Subsidiary Roles	Empirical Basis	Geographic Scope
Randøy/Li (1998)	• Outflow of resources • Inflow of resources	• Resource Independent • Resource Provider • Resource User • Resource Networker	• Questionnaire • Aggregated data from 25 industries	Direct investments in the U.S. from all over the world
Surlemont (1998)	• Domain of influence • Scope of influence	• Dormant Centre • Administrative Centre • Strategic Centre of Excellence • Global Headquarters	• Questionnaire • Number of subsidies not indicated	Subsidiaries from Belgium (HQ worldwide)
Benito et al. (2003)	• Scope of activities • Level of competence	• Miniature Replica • Single-Activity Unit • Multi-Activity Unit • Highly Specialized Unit • Strategic Center	• Questionnaire • 728 subsidiaries	Subsidiaries from Denmark, Finland, Norway (HQ worldwide)
Schmid/Daub (2005), Daub (2009)	• Network integration • Strategic relevance	• Service Factory • Internal Competence Center • Support Center • Specialized Contributor	• Case studies • 4 subsidiaries	Subsidiaries from Eastern Europe (HQ from Germany)
Tavares/Young (2006)	• Market scope • Product scope • Value-added scope	• Miniature Replica • Rationalized Manufacturer • Product Mandate	• Questionnaire • 233 subsidiaries	Subsidiaries from Ireland, Portugal, Spain and UK (HQ from Japan and EU)

Table 3.1: Comparison of subsidiary role typologies (3/3)
Source: Adapted and expanded from Schmid (2004, pp. 242-244)

Overall, the subsidiary role stream has made important contributions to IB literature.[61] First, it has led to a change in perspectives in the IB domain as it more strongly emphasized the relevance of subsidiary units and the differing roles they can play within the MNC (Schmid et al. 1998, p. 94, Schmid/Kutschker 2003, p. 173, Manolopoulos 2008, p. 50). It has also supported the development of richer descriptions and conceptualizations of MNCs as it provides greater clarity on what happens inside MNCs, for instance with regard to relationships between headquarters and different subsidiaries from a network perspective (Schmid 2004, p. 245). Second, the distinction among various subsidiary roles also provides the grounds for works that deal with the differentiated management of distinct role types within intra-organizational networks (Schmid et al. 1998, p. 95, Schmid 2004, p. 246). These contributions show that different types of subsidiaries need to be managed differently in terms of, for example, centralization, formalization or integration (see e.g. Ghoshal/Nohria 1989). Third, findings in this research field also indicate that a differentiated and appropriately managed portfolio of subsidiary units may also have positive performance implications for the wider MNC. This requires, however, that a multinational firm is able to effectively leverage the distinct potentials inherent to the different types of units. Fourth, the subsidiary role stream has inspired

---

[61] As it is not the intention of this thesis to provide a detailed summary on the achievements and weaknesses of the subsidiary role typology stream, only key aspects are outlined. For a more thorough overview and discussion see, for example, Schmid et al. (1998, pp. 93-100) or Schmid (2004, pp. 245-248).

and influenced subsequent research in other fields, such as research on subsidiary role development (e.g. Birkinshaw 1996, Birkinshaw/Hood 1998c, Delany 2000), or on subsidiary capability-building in foreign markets (e.g. Andersson et al. 2001a, Schmid/ Schurig 2003, Holm et al. 2005).

Despite the many contributions of the subsidiary role literature, certain shortcomings and critical aspects are also pointed out by different scholars. First, the grouping of subsidiary units along only two or three dimensions into a limited number of roles naturally leads to an oversimplification of reality. It can be expected that foreign subsidiaries do not only differ in just two or three dimensions but vary with regard to numerous characteristics. Furthermore, the frequent division of the dimensions in a dichotomous manner (e.g. distinction between low or high value) is to be questioned as subsidiaries should be rather seen on a continuum of these dimensions (Schmid 2004, p. 247). Hence, such a simplification and the neglect of the multiple dimensions in which subsidiaries may differ can result in researchers only obtaining a partial picture of reality, and possibly even in neglecting role types that do not fit neatly into the predetermined role categories (Enright/Subramanian 2007, p. 900). Second, the selection of the subsidiary role dimensions has been seen as somewhat arbitrary. It remains somewhat unclear why specific dimensions are considered important and which theoretical considerations, if any at all, have guided their selection and use (Schmid 2004, p. 247). Third, subsidiary role typologies imply that a clear allocation of certain roles is an easy and straightforward task. However, subsidiary roles may not necessarily apply for an entire subsidiary unit, but can vary substantially, for example, across value chain activities (Rugman et al. 2011b, p. 253). Moreover, subsidiaries may, depending on the dimensions applied, take on different roles of different typologies simultaneously (Schmid/Kutschker 2003, p. 174). Lastly, different actors, such as headquarters and subsidiary managers, may perceive the subsidiary's role in different ways, making a clear and unambiguous role determination a challenging or even impossible task. Consequently, it may well be the case that subsidiary units take on multiple roles simultaneously depending on, for instance, the role dimensions, the business units or the value chain activities under consideration (Daniel 2010, p. 1, Schmid/Daniel 2010, p. 259). Fourth, the empirical basis of most research on subsidiary roles is considered a critical issue. Although one would expect researchers to consider the intra-organizational network of an MNC as the unit of analysis when investigating subsidiary role differentiation in one company (or in a few select companies), empirical studies frequently study subsidiaries from many different MNCs. This makes it difficult to determine, for example, how subsidiary roles are arranged within one single company, why such a differentiation has occurred and how the interdependencies play out in selected MNC settings (Schmid et al. 1998, p. 98). Fifth, the question of how subsidiaries actually obtain (and change) their role is only partially addressed in the field. While most contributions assume that headquarters determines and assigns subsidiary roles, and therefore still imply a somewhat hierarchical orientation in MNCs (Schmid 2004, pp. 247-248), this perspective has not gone unchallenged and alternative, more dynamic views have been offered by, for instance, Birkinshaw and colleagues (e.g. Birkinshaw/ Hood 1997, 1998d).

3.2.1.2 Subsidiary Role Determination and Development

Different views exist as to how subsidiaries actually obtain their particular role. In essence, three contrasting perspectives can be found in the subsidiary role literature. The first perspective assumes that the role of a subsidiary is assigned to it (or at least influenced) by headquarters. In this parent-centric view, corporate management is responsible for defining the overall strategic directions of the entire MNC and thus assigns roles to its foreign subsidiaries that best allow for meeting their strategic objectives. A second perspective more directly focuses on the subsidiary level and argues that the role is to a large extent determined by subsidiary management itself. It is assumed that local subsidiary managers are better positioned to judge their local market and local capabilities than headquarters and hence can best decide on the appropriate role for their subsidiary themselves. Although somewhat constrained by their local context, subsidiaries are thus seen as having sufficient latitude to shape their own role (or strategy) within the MNC. The third perspective emphasizes the function of the subsidiary's environment with regard to role determination. Presuming that the MNC's foreign units are active in different environments with unique characteristics, the subsidiary's role is considered largely the result of the distinct opportunities and constraints that exist in the local market (Birkinshaw 1997, p. 210, Birkinshaw et al. 1998, pp. 222-223).

The matter of subsidiary role development is closely linked to the mechanisms of role determination and may also be termed subsidiary evolution. Within the field of research on subsidiary roles, scholars have also recognized that the given role of a subsidiary is in fact not static, but may change over time. Different researchers have investigated the underlying process and the factors that influence role changes of foreign subsidiaries (e.g. Birkinshaw 1996, Birkinshaw/Hood 1997, 1998d, Delany 1998, 2000, Dörrenbächer/Gammelgaard 2006). In order to shed light on the different mechanisms and processes that drive subsidiary role changes, Birkinshaw and Hood (1997, 1998c) offer a resource-based model of subsidiary evolution.[62] The scholars argue that subsidiary role development results from the growth or decline of valuable and distinctive resources in the subsidiary (Birkinshaw/Hood 1997, p. 340, 1998d, p. 778, see also

---

[62] More precisely, Birkinshaw and Hood take a dynamic capabilities approach to subsidiary evolution. Correspondingly, the authors draw on more dynamic resource-based works, such as Dierickx/Cool (1989) or Teece et al. (1997) that are concerned with the mechanisms through which firms accumulate and develop new resources and capabilities (see Birkinshaw/Hood 1998d, p. 781).

Delany 2000, p. 239, Dörrenbächer/Gammelgaard 2006, p. 270). As the subsidiary increases its stock of distinctive resources, it can reduce its dependence on other MNC units and gain more control over its own behavior. In particular, three different mechanisms are brought forward that influence the level of distinctive resources in the subsidiary and hence drive its development: (1) headquarters assignment, (2) subsidiary choice and (3) environmental determinism.[63]

(1) Based on the notion that headquarters assigns distinct roles to subsidiary units, it is also expected that changes in the subsidiary role are the result of headquarters decisions and actions. In this view, headquarters can drive subsidiary development though direct investment in the form of, for example, a new plant or a transfer of new technology – activities which will directly lead to an enhanced resource base of the subsidiary.[64] In addition, headquarters may influence the development of subsidiary resources and capabilities more indirectly by making use of their legitimate authority and by shaping the structural context of the subsidiary including, for instance, administrative or cultural control mechanisms (Birkinshaw/Hood 1997, pp. 341-342, 1998d, pp. 775-777).

(2) Despite the constraints and the influence exerted by headquarters, subsidiary units are also seen as having the ability to influence their own development over time by developing resources that are critical for the wider MNC. In addition to the more gradual resource and capability development that comes with their regular business activities and that is in line with their assigned responsibilities, subsidiaries may also engage in more entrepreneurial resource development efforts in the form of subsidiary initiatives. It is expected that such entrepreneurial subsidiary initiatives, as activities that lie outside the accepted responsibilities of the subsidiary, lead to the planned and directed development of new subsidiary resources and capabilities and hence of the subsidiary role over time (Birkinshaw/Hood 1997, pp. 342-343, 1998d, pp. 778-779, Birkinshaw 2000, p. 84).

(3) Lastly, the local environment in which a subsidiary operates may impact its role development as well. The unique nature of the local conditions shaped by, for instance, customers, competitors, suppliers or governmental institutions, constrains and determines the subsidiary's capacity to obtain new resources and capabilities and consequently its ability to develop its role. For example, the dynamism of the local market environment or the quality of customers and suppliers may contribute to evolution or development of the subsidiary (Birkinshaw/Hood 1997, pp. 343-345, 1998d, pp. 779-780, Birkinshaw 2000, pp. 84-85).

---

[63] These three mechanisms underlying subsidiary evolution directly relate to the three perspectives on role determination described previously in this paragraph.
[64] Although not explicitly mentioned here, headquarters can also disinvest or sanction investments leading to a decline of the subsidiary resource base.

It must be noted, however, that these three mechanisms, as seen in Figure 3.2, are not to be viewed as distinct and separate ways to change the subsidiary role. Instead, they should rather be seen as interdependent and complementary factors. For instance, autonomous subsidiary resource creation processes depend, at least in part, on the structural context set by the parent company. Likewise, the resource profile of a subsidiary may also influence headquarters' resource allocation decisions or even influence the standing of the subsidiary in the local environment (Birkinshaw/Hood 1997, p. 343, 1998d, p. 775).

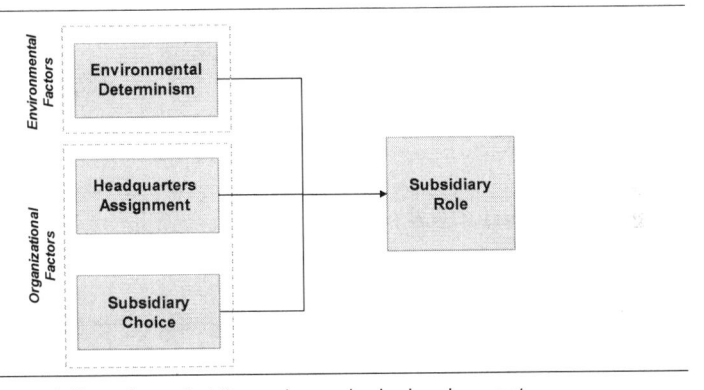

Figure 3.2: Factors influencing subsidiary roles and role development
Source: Broadly based on Birkinshaw/Hood 1998c, p. 775.

As a result, Birkinshaw and Hood integrate these three mechanisms of subsidiary development, arriving at five generic processes that may result in subsidiary evolution (or decline) over time.[65] The process termed "subsidiary-driven charter extension" is of particular relevance for this study as it is concerned with subsidiary-driven role development through subsidiary initiatives. It is argued that the initiative-driven development process represents "a conscious effort by the subsidiary to seek out and develop new business opportunities" (Birkinshaw/Hood 1998d, p. 784). It involves, first, the search for new market opportunities locally and within the MNC, second, the realization of the opportunities through the development of appropriate capabilities to fulfill it and, third,

---

[65] These five processes are (1) parent-driven investment, (2) parent-driven divestment, (3) subsidiary-driven charter extension, (4) subsidiary-driven charter reinforcement and (5) atrophy through subsidiary neglect. (1) Parent-driven investment involves, in most cases, a considerable resource commitment and allocation to the subsidiary, followed or preceded by the decision to enhance the subsidiary's charter by headquarters. (2) In the case of parent-driven divestment, the subsidiary loses a mandate for, e.g., a certain market or product and the related capabilities subsequently decline. (3) Subsidiary-driven charter extension is described in more detail in the text section. (4) Subsidiary-driven charter reinforcement refers to the enhancement of subsidiary capabilities through the subsidiary itself in order to maintain or stabilize its charter. Finally, (5) atrophy through subsidiary neglect relates to the gradual decline of subsidiary capabilities so that the performance under the particular charter deteriorates and headquarters eventually withdraws it. As the focus of this thesis is on the topic of subsidiary initiatives in distinct subsidiary role settings, the matter of subsidiary role development is addressed only briefly at this point. For more details see Birkinshaw/Hood (1998d, pp. 783-787) and Birkinshaw (2000, pp. 89-93).

the alignment and interaction with headquarters aimed at gaining headquarters approval for the initiative and the enhancement of the respective subsidiary mandate (Birkinshaw/ Hood 1998d, pp. 785-786).[66] Furthermore, the scholars propose that the subsidiary-initiative-driven development process is influenced by the different environmental and organizational conditions in which the subsidiary operates. Examples include environmental factors such as the dynamism of the local environment or the strategic importance of the host country, or organizational factors such as the decentralization of decision-making, a strong track record of the subsidiary or a good headquarters-subsidiary relationship (Birkinshaw/Hood 1998d, pp. 787-791).[67]

In sum, it can be concluded that subsidiary role development is seen by certain scholars as the result of the accumulation or depletion of subsidiary resources and capabilities over time. In this context, subsidiary initiative-taking represents one central means through which the subsidiary can grow and enhance its own distinctive resource base. The cumulative effects of these resource and capability development efforts, in the form of entrepreneurial initiatives that the foreign subsidiary undertakes over time, will then drive the gradual and evolutionary process of subsidiary development (Delany 2000, p. 227). However, findings suggest that this link between subsidiary initiatives and subsidiary role development is not necessarily unidirectional. Instead, it can be assumed that relationship is reciprocal with certain subsidiary (role) characteristics impacting initiatives, which in turn influence the subsidiary role setting in the long run (Birkinshaw/Hood 1997, p. 343, Birkinshaw 1999, p. 29). However, as already outlined, the possible link between subsidiary roles and subsidiary initiative-taking behavior has been identified as a research gap in the field and is further addressed in the present thesis.

3.2.1.3 Subsidiary Roles and Entrepreneurial Behavior

As already described briefly in Section 3.2.1.1, it can be assumed that the role a foreign subsidiary holds also influences its capacity for innovative and entrepreneurial activities and hence its potential to generate new resources and capabilities for local or even global application (Bartlett/Ghoshal 2002, p. 153, Almeida/Phene 2004, p. 850, Jindra et al. 2009, p. 169). Typically, subsidiaries with more advanced roles (e.g. Strategic Leaders, Global Innovators, Active Subsidiaries) are expected to show higher levels of innovative and entrepreneurial behavior, as they should possess the resources, capabilities and/or autonomy that are needed to realize such efforts (Birkinshaw/Fry 1998, p. 58, Birkinshaw et al. 1998, p. 222, Young/Tavares 2004, pp. 220-221).

---

[66] See also Subsection 2.2.3 of this publication for further details.
[67] Birkinshaw and Hood point out that the relationship between a subsidiary's role (or charter) and the subsidiary's distinctive resource base is not "a simple one". It is not to be expected that the subsidiary's role precisely reflects the subsidiary's current resource profile. Instead, changes in the resource profile may "lead or lag the charter change" (Birkinshaw/Hood 1998d, pp. 782-783).

For example, with regard to the typology offered by Gupta and Govindarajan, the authors suggest that the greater the (knowledge) resource creation expected from a subsidiary, "the greater should be the need for the exercise of autonomous initiative by the subsidiary." Therefore, it is expected that the need for autonomous subsidiary initiative is highest for "Global Innovators" and lowest for "Implementors" (Gupta/Govindarajan 1994, p. 448). Similarly, Boojihawon et al. state that subsidiaries in the roles of "Global Innovators" and "Integrated Players" possess superior capabilities and therefore potentially take a more innovative and entrepreneurial role within the MNC (2007, p. 553). Likewise, for the role typology presented by Bartlett and Ghoshal (1986, 1989), it is presumed that innovative and entrepreneurial activities are more likely to emerge from subsidiaries that hold the role of a "Strategic Leader" or a "Contributor" (Verbeke et al. 2007, p. 586). Bartlett and Ghoshal note that "subsidiaries with the strategic leader role are ... innovative spark plugs" and "many of the local innovations they create are subsequently diffused throughout the organization". In contrast, subsidiaries at the other end of the spectrum, those "assigned an implementer role ... are not expected to create significant innovations from which the company as a whole can benefit" (2002, p. 153). Lastly, with regard to the role typology developed by Jarillo and Martinez (1990), it is suggested that "Active Subsidiaries" often engage in innovative activities that even go beyond the local market needs because of, for example, their high network responsiveness and relatively high decision-making autonomy. "Quiescent Subsidiaries" at the opposite end of the spectrum, possess fewer internal linkages within the MNC and are less locally responsive, thereby making innovative activities and the creation of new resources less likely (Manolopoulos 2008, pp. 37-38).

Although these contributions already generally indicate that certain subsidiary role types are more likely to engage in innovative and entrepreneurial activities, detailed studies that link subsidiary role typologies to subsidiary entrepreneurial initiatives are lacking. However, some further conclusions may be drawn by looking at previously identified factors that have been shown to positively impact entrepreneurial subsidiary activities that are, at the same time, also related to single subsidiary role dimensions. For example, internally oriented characteristics, such as unique subsidiary resources and capabilities (e.g. Ghoshal/Bartlett 1988, p. 370, Birkinshaw et al. 1998, p. 226, Birkinshaw 1999, p. 24, Bartlett/Ghoshal 2002, p. 152, Tseng et al. 2004, p. 99), subsidiary autonomy (e.g. Birkinshaw et al. 1998, Birkinshaw 1999, Zahra et al. 2000) or subsidiary integration (e.g. Birkinshaw/Fry 1998) have been identified as important drivers of subsidiary innovation and entrepreneurial initiatives. Similarly, externally oriented factors, such as certain market characteristics (e.g. market dynamism, competitive intensity, market sophistication), the strategic importance of the host country, or the subsidiary local orientation and local responsiveness have been recognized as important antecedents to subsidiary initiative (e.g. Birkinshaw et al. 1998, Birkinshaw/ Hood 1998d, Birkinshaw 1999, Borini et al. 2009).

Therefore, in summarizing these arguments on the relationship between certain subsidiary roles (and related role dimensions) and subsidiary entrepreneurial and innovative behavior, it can be initially concluded that some of the more advanced subsidiary role types may have a higher potential or propensity to engage in entrepreneurial initiatives than their less advanced counterparts (see Table 3.2).

Role Typology	Focus	Role Dimensions Related to Subsidiary Entrepreneurship	Role(s) with Entrepreneurial Potential
Bartlett/Ghoshal (1986, 1989)	All subsidiaries	• Competence of local organization • Strategic importance of the local organization • (Subsidiary autonomy)[66]	Strategic Leader
D'Cruz II (1986)	Strategic business units of subsidiaries[68]	• Decision-making autonomy • Extent of market involvement	World Product Mandate
Jarillo/Martinez (1990)	All subsidiaries	• Degree of localization • Degree of integration • (Subsidiary autonomy)[66]	Active Subsidiary
Gupta/Govindarajan (1991, 1994)	All subsidiaries	• Knowledge outflow • (Subsidiary autonomy)[66]	Global Innovator and Integrated Player
Hoffman (1994)	All subsidiaries	• Subsidiary capabilities • Local environment • (Subsidiary autonomy)[69]	Independent
Birkinshaw/Morrison (1995)	All subsidiaries	• Subsidiary autonomy • Subsidiary integration	World Mandate
Taggart (1997b)	All subsidiaries	• Degree of local responsiveness • Degree of integration	Constrained Independent

Table 3.2: Subsidiary role types with entrepreneurial potential

Although these role types could be expected to show a higher likelihood for entrepreneurial initiatives in general, the linkages between different subsidiary roles and subsidiary initiatives may be more complex. Existing research shows that different types of subsidiary initiatives are facilitated by different contextual settings. For example, while external initiatives (i.e. local and global market initiatives) are driven by high(er) levels of subsidiary autonomy, internal initiatives are typically associated with low(er) levels of subsidiary autonomy (Birkinshaw 1997, p. 224). Likewise, Bartlett and Ghoshal argue that differences in the subsidiary context "imply significant differences in the contributions that subsidiaries can potentially make to the innovation processes"

---

[68] Although not explicitly referred to in the different role dimensions, the degree of subsidiary autonomy is implicitly incorporated in the typology (see e.g. Young/Tavares 2004, p. 222).
[69] The degree of subsidiary autonomy is implicitly incorporated in the role typology. In particular within MNCs that follow a multidomestic strategy (versus a global strategy) it can be expected that subsidiaries can act rather autonomously in their own market (see Hoffman 1994, p. 75).

(Bartlett/Ghoshal 2002, p. 153). Thus, as a single subsidiary role context is unlikely to facilitate all forms of entrepreneurial subsidiary initiatives, the present thesis will investigate initiative-taking behavior and the resulting outcomes not only for potentially entrepreneurial subsidiary role types but for all roles belonging to selected typologies in order to gain a more complete picture for the wider MNC.

3.2.1.4 Selection of Subsidiary Role Typologies for the Research

As not all of the subsidiary role typologies presented in the previous subsections can be incorporated into the present research, it is necessary to systematically select the most appropriate ones that will serve as contingency factors in the research framework. Four criteria are used to select from the broad range of role typologies outlined above those that will be applied in this dissertation. Suitable role typologies must meet the following standards: (1) they must be applicable to all types of subsidiaries, (2) their role dimensions must be linked to "important" influencing factors as identified in previous studies, (3) the typologies should possess both externally and internally oriented role dimensions and (4) the typologies should be measureable and empirically tested.

(1) The research objectives and the research questions relate to initiatives that emerge from foreign subsidiary units in general and are not restricted to particular types. Therefore, a given role typology should be relevant for all types of subsidiary units, ranging from, for example, more specialized subsidiaries such as R&D or sales units to "full-fledged" subsidiaries that carry out many or even all value-adding activities and functions locally. This eliminates seven out of the 20 role typologies presented earlier as they focus only on special types of subsidiaries, such as manufacturing units (Ferdows 1989, Marcati 1989, Ferdows 1997), R&D units (Nobel/Birkinshaw 1998), coordination centers (Surlemont 1998), product mandates (Forsgren/Pedersen 1997, 1998), offshoring subsidiaries (Schmid/Daub 2005, Daub 2009) or subunits within subsidiaries (D'Cruz 1986).[70]

(2) Existing research in the field has already identified numerous antecedents to subsidiary initiatives. Among them are certain influencing factors that could potentially play a more critical role than others as they have been repeatedly supported by a number of empirical studies performed by different scholars.[71] Therefore, in order to take these existing findings into account, the subsidiary role typologies selected for this study must have role dimensions that are ideally (closely) linked to these factors. This results in the exclusion of another seven typologies offered by White and Poynter

---
[70] The second role typology by D'Cruz (see Table 3.1 in Subsection 3.2.1.1) more specifically refers to strategic business units within subsidiaries themselves (D'Cruz 1986, p. 80; see also Schmid et al. 1998, pp. 25-26).
[71] These factors are: subsidiary (specialized) resources and capabilities, subsidiary autonomy, headquarters-subsidiary relationship and communication, local market characteristics as well as the subsidiary's external engagement and orientation (see Subsection 2.2.4).

(1984), D'Cruz (1986), Gupta and Govindarajan (1991, 1994), Birkinshaw and Morrison (1995), Randøy and Li (1998), Taggart (1998) and Tavares and Young (2006), since their role dimensions cannot be linked directly to the potentially more critical variables.

(3) Previous research has shown that both external and internal contingencies largely determine the entrepreneurial and innovative behavior of a subsidiary. Correspondingly, Bartlett and Ghoshal state that subsidiary innovation "requires both external stimuli and internal response capabilities" (Bartlett/Ghoshal 2002, p. 153), while Birkinshaw and colleagues highlight the importance of both external and internal subsidiary settings "in which players fight – through their own proactive entrepreneurial initiatives – to establish and defend advantageous positions and ultimately secure competitive advantage" (Birkinshaw et al. 2005, p. 228).[72] Hence, in order to better account for the existing research and the role of both external and internal factors, subsidiary role typologies for this study must have both externally and internally oriented role dimensions. As a result, two further role typologies by Taggart (1997a) and Benito et al. (2003) are excluded, leaving four potentially relevant typologies.[73]

(4) Finally, suitable role typologies for this study should both be measurable and have been previously tested empirically, as the aim is to link (empirically determined) role types to initiative behavior and outcomes. This requirement leads to the elimination of the typology identified by Hoffmann (1994) since the three-factor role typology is derived from prior literature and only validated by illustrative case studies for each role type (see Hoffman 1994, pp. 77-81).

Consequently, applying all four selection criteria leads to three remaining subsidiary role typologies that are not only suitable for this study but are also "particularly well recognized" (Birkinshaw et al. 2005, p. 233), namely those of Bartlett and Ghoshal (1986, 1989), Jarillo and Martinez (1990) and Taggart (1997b). Table 3.3 illustrates the application of the four selection criteria and the final selection of the three typologies for this study.

---

[72] More precisely, Birkinshaw et al. refer to the external and internal setting as "internal and external competitive forces" or "internal and external competitive arena" (Birkinshaw et al. 2005, pp. 227-228). In addition, other works on subsidiary initiatives offer models and concepts that explicitly incorporate both the external and internal context as influencing factors (e.g. Birkinshaw 1999, Zahra et al. 2000, Verbeke et al. 2007, Rațiu/Molz 2010).

[73] Both role typologies have only internally oriented role dimensions, such as autonomy and procedural justice (Taggart 1997a) and level of competence and scope of activities (Benito et al. 2003) and lack an externally oriented dimension.

3 – Research Framework

Role Typology	Selection Criteria				Selection
	Applicable for all Subsidiary Types	Related to Important SI Drivers	Includes Int./Ext. Dimension	Empirically Tested Typology	
White/Poynter (1984)	✓	✗	✗	✓	✗
D'Cruz I (1986)	✓	✗	✗	✓	✗
D'Cruz II (1986)	✗	✓	✓	✗	✗
Bartlett/Ghoshal (1986, 1989)	✓	✓	✓	✓	✓
Marcati (1989)	✗	✗	✗	✓	✗
Ferdows (1989, 1997)	✗	✗	✗	✓	✗
Jarillo/Martinez (1990)	✓	✓	✓	✓	✓
Gupta/Govindarajan (1991, 1994)	✓	✗	✗	✓	✗
Hoffmann (1994)	✓	✓	✓	✗	✗
Birkinshaw/Morrison (1995)	✓	✗	✗	✓	✗
Forsgren/Pedersen (1996, 1997)	✗	✗	✓	✓	✗
Taggart I (1997b)	✓	✓	✓	✓	✓
Taggart II (1997a)	✓	(✓)	✗	✓	✗
Taggart III (1998)	✓	✗	✗	✓	✗
Nobel/Birkinshaw (1998)	✗	✗	✗	✓	✗
Randoy/Li (1998)	✓	✗	✗	✓	✗
Surlemont (1998)	✗	✗	✗	✓	✗
Benito et al. (2003)	✓	(✓)	✗	✓	✗
Daub/Schmid (2005), Daub (2009)	✗	✗	✗	✓	✗
Tavares/Young (2006)	✓	✗	✗	✓	✗

Table 3.3: Selection of suitable subsidiary role typologies for study

As Taggart's work represents an evaluation and expansion of the role typology put forth by Jarillo and Martinez (see Taggart 1997b, p. 296), both typologies will be viewed jointly in this thesis, thus resulting in two typologies being applied for the present study. Although both role typologies are at first glance quite similar or even identical, there are nevertheless important differences, for instance with regard to measures and scales for the operationalization and assessment of the subsidiary role dimensions (Schmid et al. 1998, pp. 56-57; see also Subsections 4.2.1.3 and 4.2.1.4 for further details). The differences are explicitly acknowledged and accounted for in the course of this study.

3.2.1.5 Overview of Selected Role Typologies

(1) Role Typology of Bartlett and Ghoshal

Bartlett and Ghoshal's contributions are among the earlier works on the varying roles and responsibilities of foreign subsidiaries in MNCs (Bartlett/Ghoshal 1986, 1989) and produced one of the most prominent role typologies in IB literature (Schmid 2004, p. 240, Birkinshaw et al. 2005, p. 233). Based on their observations within different MNCs, the scholars conclude that a subsidiary's role is the function of both its local environment and of the competence of the subsidiary. Accordingly, their typology classifies subsidiaries in four types based on the two dimensions "strategic importance of the local environment" and "competence of the local organization" (Bartlett/Ghoshal 1986, p. 90). Figure 3.3 shows the typology and how the four different roles relate to the two dimensions used to characterize them.

	Low Strategic importance of the local environment High	
Competence of local organization High	Contributor	Strategic Leader
	Implementer	Black Hole

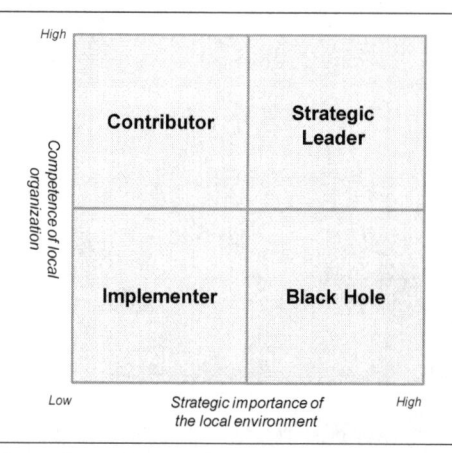

Figure 3.3: Subsidiary role typology by Bartlett and Ghoshal
Source: Adapted from Bartlett/Ghoshal 1986, p. 90.

The first dimension, "strategic importance of the local environment," broadly reflects the significance of the subsidiary's national environment for the larger MNC.[74] More specifically, the strategic importance is considered dependent on the size of subsidiary's market, the competitive intensity, the sophistication of customer demand and the level of technological dynamism (Bartlett/Ghoshal 1986, p. 90). Therefore, subsidiaries in large markets that are also characterized by high levels of competitive intensity, highly sophisticated customer demand, and a high degree of technological dynamism can be

---
[74] In addition to the term "strategic importance of the local environment," somewhat different labels are also used in other publications for this dimension, such as "environmental complexity" (e.g. Ghoshal/Nohria 1989, p. 326, Nohria/Ghoshal 1994, p. 493) or "learning opportunities in the local environment" (Ghoshal 1986, p. 419, Ghoshal/Nohria 1986, p. 13). For more details on the operationalization and measurement of this role dimension for this thesis, see Subsection 4.3.1 herein.

considered to operate in environments that are strategically important for the MNC. The second dimension, "competence of local organization," does not focus on a particular local environment but refers to the organizational competencies of a single subsidiary.[75] Although predominantly representing the competencies and capabilities of a subsidiary, this dimension more broadly refers to the resources and capabilities a subsidiary possesses in different areas such as "... in technology, production, marketing, or any other area" (Bartlett/Ghoshal 1986, p. 90).

Based on these two dimensions, Bartlett and Ghoshal distinguish between four subsidiary role types: Strategic Leader, Contributor, Implementer and Black Hole. *Strategic Leaders* are those foreign units that operate in a strategically important market for the MNC and that, at the same time, possess a high level of competency in one or even all functions. In this role, subsidiaries typically function as legitimate partners of headquarters and play a critical role in developing and implementing strategy applicable for the wider MNC (Bartlett/Ghoshal 1986, p. 90, 2002, pp. 121-122). *Contributor* subsidiaries, like Strategic Leaders, possess a high level of competency but are located in less strategically important market environments. This subsidiary type is important for the corporation because of its high level of competency, often in specific areas. These are commonly not only applicable locally but also globally, thereby contributing important resources and capabilities to the wider MNC (Bartlett/Ghoshal 1986, pp. 90-91, 2002, pp. 123-124). In contrast to these first two types, subsidiaries in the roles of Implementers and Black Holes possess only a low level of competency. *Implementers* typically only have the competencies necessary for their local operations and are situated in markets of little strategic relevance. It is expected that in many companies this is the predominant subsidiary type, with its primary purpose of serving the local market and implementing the strategies that are put forward by headquarters or more advanced subsidiary types (e.g. Strategic Leaders or Contributors; see Bartlett/Ghoshal 1986, pp. 90-91, 2002, pp. 125-126). Finally, subsidiaries in the role of *Black Holes* are located in strategically important markets, yet they do not have extensive competencies and thus are unable to leverage the potentials that exist in such munificent environments. Therefore, this role is only deemed acceptable for a limited period of time when, for example, building up a strong local presence in such markets (Bartlett/Ghoshal 1986, p. 91, 2002, pp. 126-128).[76]

---

[75] As is the case for the first dimension, Bartlett and Ghoshal do not use consisting wording or terminology with regard to the second role dimension. Instead, they refer to the dimension in different publications as "subsidiary capabilities" (Bartlett/Ghoshal 2002, p. 72), subsidiary competencies (Bartlett/Ghoshal 2002, p. 72) or subsidiary resources (Nohria/Ghoshal 1994, p. 500). For more details on the operationalization and measurement of this role dimension for this thesis, see Subsection 4.2.1.2 of this publication.

[76] Additional details on these four subsidiary role types can be found in Subsection 3.5.1 herein.

(2) Role Typology of Jarillo and Martinez

At the beginning of the 1990s, Jarillo and Martinez (1990) presented their empirically-derived role typology, which is conceptually rooted in the configuration-coordination framework developed by Porter (1986) and the integration-responsiveness framework in line with the thinking of Bartlett (1986) and Prahalad and Doz (1987). Since Porter's model primarily deals with the strategic characteristics of industries and Bartlett's framework mainly focuses on strategic orientation at the firm level, Jarillo and Martinez argue that a third step is needed "to analyze the strategy at the subsidiary level" (Jarillo/Martinez 1990, p. 503). Extending the thinking of the integration-responsiveness framework to the subsidiary level, the authors propose that foreign subsidiary units can be characterized through their "degree of subsidiary localization" and "degree of subsidiary integration".[77] Based on these two dimensions, a two-by-two matrix is used to differentiate the four subsidiary role types illustrated in Figure 3.4.

The first dimension, "the degree of localization," expresses the extent to which different value chain activities of the subsidiary (e.g. manufacturing, purchasing, marketing or R&D) are performed locally. According to Jarillo and Martinez, a subsidiary that performs many or even all value-adding activities at the subsidiary location is considered to have a high degree of localization.[78] The second dimension, "degree of integration," reflects the extent to which the value-adding activities of the subsidiary are integrated and coordinated with the same activities in other parts of the MNC.[79] Thus, a subsidiary is viewed as highly integrated if many or even all of its value-adding activities are highly linked to and coordinated with the rest of the group (Jarillo/Martinez 1990, p. 503).[80] On the basis of these two dimensions, the researchers empirically identify three types of subsidiaries: Active Subsidiary, Receptive Subsidiary and Autonomous Subsidiary.[81]

Active Subsidiaries execute many value-adding activities in the host country that are, at the same time, closely coordinated with the rest of the firm. As a result of their high interconnectedness, they function as an active node in the intra-organizational network. This type is expected to be more frequently found in firms with a transnational orientation. Foreign units in the role of *Receptive Subsidiaries* perform only a few value-

---

[77] When transferring the integration-responsiveness concept to the subsidiary level, Jarillo and Martinez substitute "responsiveness" with "localization" (see also Schmid et al. 1998, p. 49-50).
[78] For more detail on this role dimension, including the operationalization and measurement for this thesis, see Subsection 4.3.1.3 herein.
[79] This dimension ranges from "very autonomous" to "highly integrated" with headquarters or other MNC units and therefore implicitly relates to the notion of subsidiary autonomy as well (Jarillo/Martinez 1990, p. 503; see also Manolopoulos 2008, p. 36).
[80] For more detail on this role dimension, including the operationalization and measurement for this thesis, see Subsection 4.3.1.4 herein.
[81] In order to empirically test their framework, Jarillo and Martinez use a sample of 50 Spanish manufacturing subsidiaries of foreign MNCs from eight industrial sectors. Data from these subsidiaries was gathered in personal and structured interviews with top managers (Jarillo/Martinez 1990, pp. 503-504).

adding functions locally and typically represent subsidiaries with only marketing and sales activities or pure manufacturing units. Nevertheless, the few functions are highly integrated with the rest of the firm. The receptive subsidiary strategy is presumed to be appropriate for subsidiaries of global firms that compete in global industries. Finally, *Autonomous Subsidiaries* carry out most value-adding functions themselves, but they are integrated to little or no extent with the rest of the MNC. According to Jarillo and Martinez this type is found predominantly in subsidiaries of multinational firms.[82] Although the authors acknowledge that subsidiaries may occupy any of the four quadrants of their matrix, they do not describe a fourth subsidiary role (or strategy) for the "low localization" and "low integration" field.[83]

		High		
Degree of integration		Receptive Subsidiary	Active Subsidiary	
		Autonomous Subsidiary		
	Low		Degree of localization	High

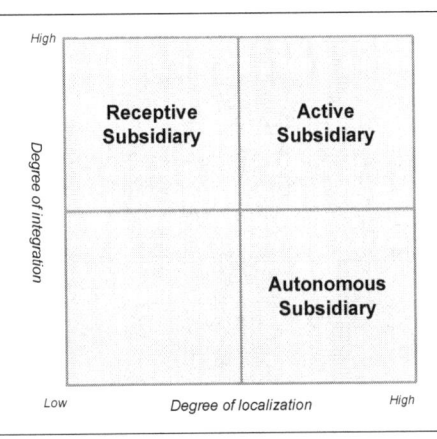

Figure 3.4: Subsidiary role typology by Jarillo and Martinez
Source: Adapted from Jarillo/Martinez 1990, p. 503.

In an attempt to evaluate and extend the role typology by Jarillo and Martinez, Taggart later adds the fourth role type to this classification, which he terms a *Quiescent Subsidiary*, arguing that "there seems no *prima facie* reason why an MNC subsidiary should not adopt a low integration-low responsiveness strategy, either proactively or due to the negligence on the part of the parent corporation" (Taggart 1997b, p. 301).[84] As a result of their low integration, many decisions in such subsidiaries (concerning e.g.

---

[82] Additional details on these three subsidiary role types can be found in Subsection 3.5.2 of this publication.
[83] Jarillo and Martinez do not further specify the reasons for why they did not find empirical evidence for the fourth subsidiary role type. Taggart (1997b, pp. 313-314) suggests that this was not possible due to the inappropriate environment of the study, the non-probabilistic nature of their sample and the operationalization and measurement of the constructs used for the two dimensions (see also Manolopoulos 2008, p. 36).
[84] Although one would expect Taggart's work to represent a replication of Jarillo and Martinez's efforts in order to evaluate and further test their role typology, Taggart's study differs in many respects. For example, he uses different constructs for the operationalization and measurement of the role dimension, thereby making a direct comparison or even integration of the two typologies somewhat difficult. For further details on the different empirical constructs, see Subsections 4.3.1.3 and 4.3.1.4 herein.

manufacturing, product or quality) are made without the intention to serve the MNC's customers in other markets. Furthermore, local conditions, such as easily identifiable customer needs, stable technology, relatively mature products and advanced manufacturing processes, make only a low degree of local responsiveness necessary (Taggart 1997b, p. 307). Figure 3.5 outlines the full role typology as proposed by Taggart, including the fourth role type in the form of the Quiescent Subsidiary.[85]

	Low — Local Responsiveness — High	
High *Integration* **Low**	Receptive Subsidiary	Constrained Independent
	Quiescent Subsidiary	Autonomous Subsidiary

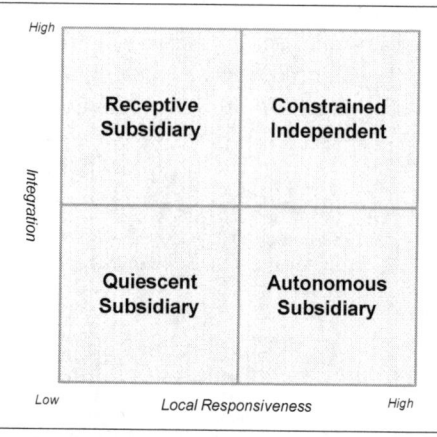

Figure 3.5: Subsidiary role typology by Taggart
Source: Adapted from Taggart 1997b, p. 310.

Having specified and broadly described the two (or three) subsidiary role typologies that are incorporated in the research framework as contingency factors,[86] the following section now focuses on broadly outlining the key aspects of the subsidiary initiative-taking behavior that will serve as the independent variable in the research framework.

---

[85] As can be seen, Taggart decided to rename the "Active Subsidiary" type as "Constrained Independent." He argues that, although it bears many similarities to the Active Subsidiary as proposed by Jarillo and Martinez, the Constrained Independent is somewhat closer to, e.g., the Product Specialist of White and Poynter (1984) and as such a revised role name for this type is considered appropriate (Taggart 1997b, p. 310).

[86] Due to the close connection and the sequential nature of the two role typologies, both will be viewed jointly in the remainder of this publication. Since the typology developed by Jarillo and Martinez can be viewed as the "initial" one, Taggart's extensions will be incorporated under the larger umbrella of the initial typology. Nevertheless, the consideration and inclusion of constructs for both typologies will allow the analysis of the empirical findings for both typologies in the end. Furthermore, despite certain differences between the two typologies, it seems fairly common in IB literature to analyze them jointly (see e.g. Jindra 2005, Enright/Subramanian 2007, Manolopoulos 2008, Lin/Hsieh 2010).

3.2.2 Subsidiary Initiative-Taking Behavior

The subsidiary initiative process has already been described in some detail in the literature review section above.[87] As was shown, subsidiary initiative-taking is viewed as an entrepreneurial process that leads to new ways for the corporation to use and expand its resources. The initiative process typically unfolds over several stages and involves activities such as the identification of new initiative opportunities or the acquisition, development and use of appropriate resources and capabilities in order to realize an opportunity. In addition to these activities concerned with the management of resources and capabilities, subsidiary initiative-taking is also seen to involve more "political" activities related to the alignment and the interactions between headquarters and subsidiaries in order to gather support for initiatives and help them move through the socio-political system of the MNC (e.g. Birkinshaw/Hood 1998d, p. 786). Although the initiative process might take a variety of forms and involve further stages and activities,[88] the present thesis will focus on the two central elements of the subsidiary initiative process that deal with (a) the management of resources and capabilities and (b) the alignment and interaction between headquarters and subsidiaries. These two core elements are introduced briefly in Subsections 3.2.2.1 and 3.2.2.2 and are discussed at greater length in Section 3.5, which presents the theoretical framework for this research study.

3.2.2.1 Initiative-Related Resource Management

In line with entrepreneurship contributions more generally (e.g. Schumpeter 1934, Penrose 1959, Shane 2003), subsidiary initiative-taking has been viewed as an entrepreneurial process at the subsidiary level which pivots around the use and expansion of subsidiary resources and capabilities when pursuing (internal and external) market opportunities in order to derive subsidiary-level and firm-level advantages. Accordingly, Birkinshaw and colleagues describe subsidiary initiative-taking as a process that "advances a new way for the corporation to use or expand its resources" (e.g. Birkinshaw 1997, p. 207, 1999, p. 9, Birkinshaw/Ridderstråle 1999, p. 151) or that represents the "pursuit of a specific market opportunity and the development of the appropriate capabilities to fulfill it" (Birkinshaw/Hood 1998c, p. 786). Similarly, Birkinshaw et al. (2005, p. 233) state that "subsidiaries may engage in entrepreneurial activities to overcome the limitation of their resources, to make their resources valuable, or to leverage their resources in unique ways previously unknown in their firm or industry." Many other works have also emphasized the role of resources and capabilities and described entrepreneurial initiatives as "important means by which the subsidiary grows its own resource base" (Ambos et al. 2010, p. 1099) and as a "process in which a subsidiary

---

[87] For more details, see Subsection 2.2.3.3 of this publication.
[88] For example, other possible activities in subsidiary initiative process concern the evaluation and approval of initiatives at headquarters or the implementation of initiatives in the end.

exhibits, exploits and explores resources in order to respond to opportunities" (Tseng et al. 2004, p. 94).[89] Some publications go even a step further and provide details on the resource development and deployment activities related to initiative-taking, proposing that it involves "resource utilization, integration and renewal" (Lee/Chen 2003, p. 64) or the "identification, acquisition and accumulation of resources to take advantage of perceived opportunities" (Liouka 2007, p. 75).[90] Yet, although research in the field is beginning to recognize more specific activities associated with the development and deployment of new resources and capabilities in the initiative process, a more complete and theoretically-grounded picture is lacking. Hence, given the importance of these resource management activities in the subsidiary initiative process and the identified research need, the present thesis will incorporate this particular aspect into the conceptual framework.

3.2.2.2 Headquarters-Subsidiary Alignment

In addition to the activities related to the development and deployment of resources and capabilities, the subsidiary initiative process also strongly depends on the appropriate alignment and interaction between headquarters and the foreign subsidiary. Although affiliates abroad are frequently viewed as semi-autonomous units in the MNC that can, at least in part, follow their own interests and pursue entrepreneurial opportunities in the local market more or less independently, they are often still dependent on the strategic decisions of headquarters when it comes to, for instance, the approval or allocation of resources for subsidiary initiatives (Birkinshaw/Ridderstråle 1999, p. 151, Andersson et al. 2001b, p. 6). Previous research frequently describes three important aspects of the alignment and interaction between headquarters and the subsidiary: headquarters involvement in the initiative process,[91] corporate resistance and subsidiary initiative selling (see e.g. Birkinshaw 1997, pp. 221-222, Birkinshaw/Fry 1998, pp. 53-56, Birkinshaw/Ridderstråle 1999, pp. 151-152). Headquarters involvement broadly refers to the extent to which the corporate center is engaged in the initiative process. For example, while in some cases subsidiaries may enjoy a large degree of autonomy and have little or no contact with headquarters at all, in other cases they may face a higher degree of decision-making centralization and intensive communication with headquarters (Birkin-

---

[89] Similarly, Manolopoulos states that a "subsidiary initiative represents an entrepreneurial process in which a subsidiary exploits and explores distinctive resources to respond to local or wider opportunities" (Manolopoulos 2008, p. 47).
[90] Referring to both strategic initiatives in general and subsidiary initiatives in particular, Lechner and Kreutzer argue that "initiatives require the alteration of an organization's resource base (i.e. leveraging existing resources, creating new resources, accessing external resources and releasing resources) in order to refresh existing capabilities or add new capabilities" (Lechner/Kreutzer 2010, p. 286).
[91] Headquarters involvement in the initiative process relates to aspects of (a) the centralization of initiative-related decision-making and (b) the extent of headquarters-subsidiary communication (e.g. Birkinshaw 1997, p. 224, Birkinshaw et al. 1998, p. 231, Birkinshaw 1999, p. 34, 2000, pp. 22-30; see also Subsection 4.3.2.4 of this publication for further details).

shaw 1997, p. 224).[92] Furthermore, subsidiaries may be confronted more or less strongly with corporate resistance (or the corporate immune system) "as the set of organizational forces that suppress the advancement of ... initiatives" (Birkinshaw/ Ridderstråle 1999, p. 153). This typically takes the form of rejection, delay or a request from headquarters for greater justification, of lobbying and rival initiatives by other divisions or of a lack of recognition of subsidiary initiatives in the MNC (Birkinshaw/ Ridderstråle 1999, pp. 162-166). Lastly, subsidiaries might engage in active initiative selling to differing degrees to push initiatives forward in the corporate system. For example, in instances where formal corporate approval is required, subsidiaries should more often engage in active initiative selling, which could involve "several rounds of credibility building with parent management and refining of proposals," while in other cases selling may be more implicit with headquarters being informed but not directly intervening in the process (Birkinshaw 1997, p. 221). Consequently, these findings underline that the initiative process is not necessarily a "straightforward" resource development and deployment process, but that it is also driven by the interactions between headquarters and subsidiaries and the degree of subsidiary power that enables it to gather support and gain traction for initiatives in the corporate system (Birkinshaw/Ridderstråle 1999, p. 152). In view of the importance of these activities in the initiative process and the identified research need, they will also be included in the present research framework.

3.2.3 Subsidiary Initiative Outcomes

The systematic literature review revealed that a number of different consequences of subsidiary initiatives have been identified in previous research, ranging from the subsidiary level (e.g. subsidiary performance) to the firm level (e.g. MNC learning) or even the environmental level (e.g. host country economic development).[93] However, it would appear that many of the identified consequences represent secondary or "downstream" outcomes of successfully approved and/or implemented subsidiary initiatives. For example, subsidiary autonomy, subsidiary influence in the MNC, intrafirm competition and headquarters attention have been shown to result from past subsidiary initiatives (e.g. Bouquet/Birkinshaw 2008, Becker-Ritterspach/Dörrenbächer 2009, Ambos et al. 2010). In order to capture the more immediate outcome of subsidiary initiative-taking behavior, the present study will focus primarily on the level of realized subsidiary initiatives, an approach that conforms with many previous empirical studies (e.g. Birkinshaw 1997, 1999, Tseng et al. 2004, Borini et al. 2009a, Borini et al. 2009b,

---

[92] As shown by Birkinshaw, the first setting typically facilitates external initiatives (i.e. local and global market initiatives) while the latter supports internal initiatives (internal market and global-internal hybrid initiatives) (Birkinshaw 1997, p. 224).
[93] See Subsection 2.2.5 herein for further detail on the consequences of subsidiary initiatives.

Williams/Lee 2011b).[94] However, as the level of realized or successful subsidiary initiatives by itself says little about the potential value added or the benefits for the subsidiary or even the wider MNC, an additional outcome measure is incorporated in the model. As was shown, subsidiary initiatives are also directly linked to the development of specialized resources and capabilities which, if further leveraged in the MNC, may contribute to a firm-level advantage (Peng 2001, p. 811, Rugman/Verbeke 2001, p. 245, Birkinshaw/Pedersen 2009, p. 379).[95] Hence, in line with existing writings that recognize specialized subsidiary resources and capabilities as important outcomes of subsidiary initiatives (e.g. Birkinshaw 1998, Birkinshaw/Hood 1998c, Birkinshaw 1999, 2000, Rugman/Verbeke 2001), resource-related consequences are also included in the present research framework, as shown in Figure 3.6 below.[96]

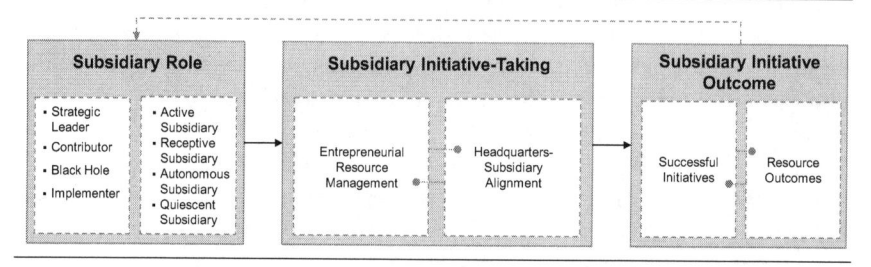

Subsidiary Role	Subsidiary Initiative-Taking	Subsidiary Initiative Outcome
• Strategic Leader • Contributor • Black Hole • Implementer	• Active Subsidiary • Receptive Subsidiary • Autonomous Subsidiary • Quiescent Subsidiary	Entrepreneurial Resource Management ↔ Headquarters-Subsidiary Alignment	Successful Initiatives ↔ Resource Outcomes

Figure 3.6: Overview of the extended research framework

---

[94] More specifically, the intent is not to investigate the general level or degree of realized subsidiary initiatives but rather the different types of subsidiary initiatives (e.g. global, local, internal and global-internal market initiatives; see Subsection 4.2.3.1 for more detail).
[95] See Subsections 3.2.2.1 and 3.4.2 herein for further detail on the development and acquisition of new subsidiary resources and capabilities through initiative-taking. See also Subsection 3.4.4 herein for more detail on the link between subsidiary resources and firm-level advantages.
[96] As is explained later in more detail, the present study incorporates (a) the level of specialized resources and capabilities resulting from subsidiary initiatives that (b) can be further applied throughout the MNC as an outcome measure. This is also partly the consequence of the underlying theoretical perspectives that are applied for the research framework, which are presented in the following section.

3.3 Theoretical Perspectives

As all research endeavors, this dissertation is also confronted with the task of selecting one or more appropriate theoretical perspectives that can help guide the research. In organizational science, numerous theoretical approaches exist that aim at helping to better understand, explain and predict the functioning of organizations and their actors. As organizations represent highly complex social constructs, single theories can often only illuminate certain aspects of organizational problems, so research frequently needs to draw from different theories when investigating complex organizational phenomena (Hoskisson et al. 1999, p. 446, Scherer 2006, pp. 20-21). The same holds true for the topic of subsidiary initiative-taking, which has been described as a complex, multifaceted and multilevel phenomenon. Accordingly, scholars have drawn from many different theoretical perspectives when conducting research in this field and when addressing the manifold facets of this matter.[97]

As outlined previously, this thesis focuses on selected aspects of initiative-taking, namely the links between subsidiary roles, initiative-taking behavior and initiative outcomes. For this purpose, three particular theoretical perspectives have been chosen. The first two, Resource-Based View (RBV) and Resource Dependence Theory (RDT), provide the theoretical foundations for the initiative-taking process, which represents the central part of the research framework. More specifically, RBV helps to explain the resource-management aspects of the initiative process that lead to the development of new specialized resource bundles or capabilities at the subsidiary level, which in turn may subsequently even be leveraged in the wider MNC. RDT then provides theoretical guidance with regard to the alignment and interactions between the subsidiary and headquarters or other MNC units. However, these aspects of the subsidiary initiative process and the outcomes are expected to be contingent upon the specific contextual setting in which a subsidiary operates. Consequently, contingency theory will be used as a third theoretical pillar to integrate the subsidiary setting, in the form of subsidiary roles, into the research framework.

This section aims to explicate the three theoretical foundations selected for the research framework outlined. First, Subsection 3.3.1 explains why these theoretical foundations in particular have been chosen for this study. Subsection 3.3.2 then presents RBV and its advancements towards more dynamic and process-oriented versions, followed by the presentation of RDT and contingency theory in Subsections 3.3.3 and 3.3.4. Finally, the different theoretical elements are integrated into a contingent and dynamic resource-oriented framework regarding role-specific subsidiary initiative-taking that is illustrated in Section 3.4.

---

[97] See Subsection 2.2.6 for details on theoretical lenses applied in the subsidiary initiative field.

3.3.1 Selection of Theoretical Perspectives for the Study

To evaluate and select appropriate organizational theories for this research, emphasis is placed on ten theoretical perspectives that have been repeatedly applied and/or discussed at greater length in previous contributions in the subsidiary initiative field.[98] From among these, theoretical perspectives are deemed appropriate that can help to adequately address the inner workings of subsidiary units with regard to (1) the (entrepreneurial) development and deployment of resources and capabilities and (2) the complex alignment and interactions that take place between headquarters and subsidiaries. Furthermore, theories are deemed well-suited that (3) allow for the consideration of the subsidiary context and are compatible with the notion of subsidiary roles. The following two subsections discuss the applicability of these ten theories. Subsection 3.3.1.1 presents the theories that are not considered suitable and explains why they have not been selected. Subsection 3.3.1.2 then briefly introduces the three theoretical pillars that have been chosen for the present research before these are discussed in more detail in Subsection 3.3.2.

3.3.1.1 Excluded Theories

(1) **Agency theory** (e.g. Jensen/Meckling 1976, Fama/Jensen 1983, Eisenhardt 1989a) focuses on the contractual relationship between one party (the principal) that engages another party (the agent) to perform some service on its behalf. In such a situation, the principal delegates certain tasks and decision-making authority to the agent, which receives some form of compensation for its efforts. Agency theory formulates certain behavioral assumptions such as divergent interests, risk attitudes and information asymmetries between the two parties, as well as self-interest seeking behavior.[99] Based on these general assumptions, the focus of the theory is on the determination of appropriate contractual governing mechanisms (e.g. incentive, control and information systems) to efficiently handle these problems (Jensen/Meckling 1976, pp. 308-309, Ebers/Gotsch 2006, pp. 258-259).[100] In addition to the broader literature on headquarters-subsidiary relationships (e.g. Roth/O'Donnell 1996, Chang/Taylor 1999, Mudambi/Pedersen 2007), agency theory has also been applied in four publications that deal with subsidiary initiatives (i.e. Johnson/Medcof 2002, 2007, Mahnke et al. 2007, Medcof 2007). In this

---

[98] As presented in Subsection 2.2.6, these are network theory (Bartlett/Ghoshal 1989, Ghoshal/Bartlett 1990), resource-based view (Wernerfelt 1984, Barney 1991, Grant 1991), resource dependence theory (Pfeffer/Salancik 1978), agency theory (Jensen/Meckling 1976), the concept of bounded rationality (March/Simon 1958), the transaction cost perspective (Williamson 1975), organizational politics/micropolitics (Burns 1961, March 1962, Mintzberg 1985), Porter's concept of competitive advantage (Porter 1980), the integration/responsiveness framework (Prahalad/Doz 1987), and self-determination theory (Deci/Ryan 1985).

[99] For example, is expected that the agent has much more intimate knowledge pertaining to the service she/he is to deliver, resulting in information asymmetries which, due to self-interest seeking behavior, may be used by the agent to her/his benefits (Schreyögg 2012, p. 164).

[100] As agency theory is not further used in this publication, an extensive overview and discussion is not provided at this point. For a more detailed summary see e.g. Ebers and Gotsch (2006, pp. 258-277) or Scherm and Pietsch (2007, pp. 55-63).

context, agency theory may be useful in determining the contractual and governance structures that help facilitate subsidiary initiatives (e.g. outcome-based contracts).

However, for the purpose of this study and the specified research framework, agency theory is not considered applicable for the following reasons. First, the theory assumes a hierarchical relationship between headquarters as the principal and the subsidiary as the agent. This view neglects other subsidiary relationships which cannot be described solely in a hierarchical manner with, for instance, sister subsidiaries or external partners that may also be of relevance for initiative-taking (Doz/Prahalad 1991, p. 149, O'Donnell 2000, p. 541). Second, agency theory is not fully compatible with the notion of subsidiary roles. In particular the "subsidiary choice" view, which recognizes that subsidiaries may also define and influence their roles themselves, conflicts to some degree with the hierarchical perspective assumed in agency theory.[101] Third, self-interest seeking or even opportunistic behavior as proposed in the theory only applies in part to the subsidiary initiative phenomenon. Although in certain instances initiative-taking may be motivated opportunistically, in most cases entrepreneurial initiatives by subsidiaries are expected to be consistent with the overall strategic goals of the MNC (Birkinshaw/Fry 1998, p. 52, Yamin 2002, p. 135).[102] Furthermore, through an agency theory lens it is presumed to be difficult for headquarters to "encourage entrepreneurial subsidiary manager behavior while simultaneously expecting and guarding against opportunistic behavior" (O'Donnell 2000, p. 542). Fourth, given only the dichotomous choice between monitoring and incentives as suggested by agency theory, this perspective may be too simplistic to explain the complex relationships and interactions between headquarters and subsidiaries in the initiative process (O'Donnell 2000, p. 541). Fifth, while agency theory may help describe certain hierarchically-oriented aspects of headquarters-subsidiary alignment and interactions throughout the initiative process, it does not appear well suited to explain the initiative-related resource management process that deals with the development and deployment of resources in order to realize identified initiative opportunities.

(2) **Transaction cost theory** (Williamson 1975, Buckley/Casson 1976) attempts to explain why certain transactions take place through institutional arrangements characterized as "market" or as "organization" on the basis of the comparative costs that are associated with these two solutions.[103] It is expected that as long as the costs for the market solution are lower, transactions take place externally in the market. However, if

---

[101] See Subsection 3.2.1.2 herein for details on subsidiary role determination and development.
[102] Similarly, Rugman and Verbeke argue that the propensity to engage in opportunistic behavior in established MNCs is rather low and "opportunistic' managers in the Williamsonian sense seldom continue to work in large, modern MNEs over prolonged periods of time" (Rugman/Verbeke 2003, p. 136, see also Verbeke/Yuan 2005, pp. 5-6).
[103] In between the two poles of "market" and "hierarchy" various hybrid modes can be found, such as longer term contracts or partial ownership arrangements (see e.g. Shelanski/Klein 1995, p. 337 or Ebers/Gotsch 2006, pp. 284-288).

the market costs are higher than the organizational costs, the transaction is internalized and executed within the organization. Transaction costs for a market solution result from, for instance, searching and planning costs, adaptation costs, or monitoring costs that occur when goods or services are transferred. Moreover, the theory is based on two key behavioral assumptions that explain why these costs in fact arise: the bounded rationality and opportunistic behavior of the transaction partners.[104] Transaction cost theory has been previously applied in IB literature to topics such as the management of MNCs (e.g. Rugman/Verbeke 1992, 2003), foreign market entry (e.g. Anderson/ Gatignon 1986, Anderson/Coughlan 1987), and international staffing (e.g. Benito et al. 2005, Tan/Mahoney 2006). This theoretical lens is also mentioned in three publications dealing with subsidiary initiatives (i.e. Birkinshaw 2000, Verbeke/Yuan 2005, Mahnke et al. 2007).

However, for the present research, transaction cost theory is not suitable for the following reasons. First, the underlying behavioral assumptions of the theory, generally speaking, make it difficult or even impossible to address managerial issues in the MNC (Doz/Prahalad 1991, p. 148). For example, transaction cost thinking, as with agency theory, implies opportunistic behavior by the involved actors. This is similarly too restrictive and not fully compatible with the behavior exhibited in initiative-taking (Doz/Prahalad 1991, p. 148). Second, the "very stylized" or mechanistic way in which the internal functioning of MNCs is handled in transaction cost theory neglects the complexity of the organizational context and interactions that may take place during the initiative process (Rugman/Verbeke 2001, p. 239).[105] Third, subsidiary-driven investment in the form of initiatives cannot be easily connected to this theory as initiatives represent gradual and path-dependent capability-building efforts within the subsidiary itself (Birkinshaw 2000, p. 102). Here, transaction cost theory is said to lack "a dynamic component with regard to learning within the organizational structure," and as such can only insufficiently address the entrepreneurial resource- and capability-building process related to subsidiary initiatives (Ghoshal/Moran 1996, p. 35, Rugman/Verbeke 2001, p. 239).

(3) **The concept of bounded rationality** (e.g. March/Simon 1958, Simon 1976) deals with the cognitive limitations of humans in decision-making processes. Although individuals are expected to have the intention to behave rationally, various constraints related to information processing prohibit them from doing so. In particular, three aspects are highlighted that lead to bounded rationality. First, actors are viewed as having only

---

[104] As transaction cost theory is not further utilized in this publication, an extensive overview and discussion is not provided at this point. For a more detailed summary see e.g. Ebers and Gotsch (2006, pp. 277-305) or Scherm and Pietsch (2007, pp. 46-57).
[105] For example, Rugman and Verbeke (2001, p. 239) argue that aspects such as credibility, experience and reputation of individuals and groups is only insufficiently addressed. Similarly, Scherm and Pietsch (2007, p. 54) state that transaction cost theory is frequently criticized for neglecting power, culture, society and (macro-)political influences on institutional arrangements.

incomplete knowledge of the exact consequences of various decision alternatives. Second, even if individuals were to predict outcomes precisely, they are seen as being limited in their ability to evaluate the future valences of their decisions, as anticipated and actual results often differ noticeably. Third, it is assumed that individuals are unable to consider the full range of all possible alternatives when making decisions.[106] The concept of bounded rationality has been repeatedly applied in IB literature concerned with, for instance, subsidiaries' value-creating and innovative activities (e.g. Forsgren/ Holm 2010, Ciabuschi et al. 2012) and has also been mentioned in connection with subsidiary initiatives (Birkinshaw/Hood 1998d, Birkinshaw/Ridderstråle 1999, Verbeke/ Yuan 2005, Ambos et al. 2010).

Although this theoretical lens may help to explain why autonomous actions in the form of subsidiary initiatives may actually come to exist in MNCs, it is not suitable for the present study for several reasons. First, the concept of bounded rationality has been criticized for not representing a systematically integrated theoretical perspective; it has even been stated that it "does not constitute a necessary part of theorizing on economic organization." Instead, it is rather viewed as a "background assumption" in other concepts and theories and therefore is said to play a more rhetorical than substantive role (Foss 2003, pp. 246, 256, Scherm/Pietsch 2007, p. 33).[107] Second, with regard to the topic of subsidiary initiatives, the concept of bounded rationality typically serves as a supporting view or underlying assumption when more generally describing or conceptualizing headquarter-subsidiary relationships (Birkinshaw/Ridderstråle 1999, Ambos et al. 2010) or when applying other overarching theories (Birkinshaw/Hood 1998d, Verbeke/ Yuan 2005).[108] Therefore, it does not constitute a theoretical lens through which the subsidiary initiative phenomenon can be comprehensively described and explained. Third, the concept aims at explaining individual rather than organizational decision-making. Hence, when applied at the organizational level, the multiple and possibly divergent interests that need to be considered make it very difficult or even impossible to predict organizational decision-making through this theoretical lens (Scherm/Pietsch 2007, p. 33). In particular, for the topic of subsidiary initiative-taking as a multi-level phenomenon where the many differing or even conflicting interests of subsidiary and headquarters actors collide (Mahnke et al. 2007, p. 1279), it is expected that the con-

---

[106] As the concept of bounded rationality is not further used in this publication, an extensive overview and discussion is not provided at this point. For a more detailed summary see e.g. Berger and Bernhard-Mehlich (2006, pp. 177-179) or Scherm and Pietsch (2007, pp. 26-28).
[107] For example, bounded rationality assumptions are incorporated in different other theoretical perspectives that are used in the subsidiary initiative field and beyond, such as transaction cost theory (Williamson 1975, Buckley/Casson 1976), decision process perspective (e.g. Bower 1970, Burgelman 1983a, 1983b), or organizational capability approach (Nelson/Winter 1982).
[108] For example, Birkinshaw and Hood mention it in connection with decision process perspective or Verbeke and Yuan use it in the context of transaction cost theory.

cept of bounded rationality alone cannot provide clear and unambiguous theoretical guidance.

(4) **Self-determination theory** (Deci/Ryan 1985, 2002a) articulates key principles that form the basis for sustainable motivation in organizations. The theory views human beings as proactive and growth-oriented actors that inherently seek challenges in their environments to use and demonstrate their current or potential capabilities. However, the intrinsic motivation of individuals is expected to be facilitated or impeded by the social context in which they are active. In particular, three basic psychological needs are deemed central to the motivation of organizational actors: competence, relatedness and autonomy. Consequently, creating social environments that allow the satisfaction of these three needs is predicted to support sustainable intrinsic motivation.[109] Self-determination theory has been used in IB literature in connection with, for example, subsidiary innovation (e.g. Mudambi et al. 2007), MNC knowledge transfer (e.g. Minbaeva 2008), and subsidiary motivation (Foss et al. 2012). In addition, it has also been applied in connection with the topic of subsidiary initiatives (i.e. Ambos et al. 2010) when discussing the motivation of subsidiary managers to undertake initiatives.

However, for the present study, self-determination is not considered applicable. First, this theoretical perspective was originally used to explain individual-level rather than organizational-level or subsidiary-level motivation. It thus leaves open the question of how to aggregate or connect the multiple individual motives of, for example, subsidiary managers to the level of the overall subsidiary company. Second, linked to initiative-taking, self-determination theory is only applied as a complementary perspective when discussing what motivates individuals in foreign subsidiaries (see Ambos et al. 2010, p. 1102). Although it may be helpful as a theoretical supplement, it does not constitute a strong theoretical basis on which to ground the complex phenomenon of subsidiary initiatives. Third, self-determination theory focuses too narrowly on individual motivation and thus neglects other aspects that are also (or even more) critical for initiative-taking. For example, existing work shows that it not only depends on the motivation of individual managers, but perhaps more so on the subsidiary's overall ability to pursue initiatives or on the prevalence of initiative opportunities in internal or external markets – aspects that cannot be directly linked to this perspective. Fourth, empirical support for self-determination theory has come primarily from laboratory experiments and field studies in areas outside of work organizations (Gagné/Deci 2005, p. 356). It therefore remains unclear to what extent this theoretical framework can also help to explain the emergence and patterns of subsidiary initiatives in MNCs.

---

[109] As self-determination theory is not further used in this publication, an extensive overview and discussion is not provided at this point. For a more detailed summary see e.g. Deci and Ryan (2002b, pp. 3-33) or Stone et al. (2009, pp. 75-79).

3 – Research Framework

(5) **Organizational politics approaches** (e.g. Burns 1961, March 1962, Mintzberg 1985), in essence, view organizations as political systems in which individuals or groups exert influence and power when attempting to achieve their own goals or to secure their own interests.[110] Therefore, the notion of organizational politics is often linked to aspects such as differing interests, power and power struggles, or conflicts over sources of power and influence (Vigoda 2003, p. 5, Vigoda-Gadot/Drory 2006, p. 9). Although studies often view organizational politics negatively as, for example, indications of illegitimate or dysfunctional managerial behavior or the result of activities concerned with the advancement of self-interest (Burns 1961, p. 278, March 1962, p. 663, Mintzberg 1985, p. 134), more balanced approaches are advised that also acknowledge the positive facets of political maneuvering in organizations (Vigoda 2003, pp. 9-10, Vigoda-Gadot/Drory 2006). Organizational politics approaches may be further subdivided into macro- and micro-politics. While macro-political approaches typically focus on an entire organization or its central units, micro-politics centers on power and influence relations within work organizations and among their members. Micro-political approaches thus more strongly emphasize the standing, perceptions and behaviors of individual powerful actors or small groups within organizations (Vigoda-Gadot/Drory 2006, pp. 5-7, Geppert/Dörrenbächer 2011, pp. 5-6).[111] Overall, IB contributions dealing with politics, power and conflicts in MNCs remain relatively scarce and narrow in their focus (Dörrenbächer/Geppert 2006, p. 262, Geppert/Dörrenbächer 2011, p. 4). For example, scholars have used organizational politics approaches in connection with topics such as control mechanisms in MNCs (Blazejewski 2009), intrafirm competition (Becker-Ritterspach/Dörrenbächer 2011) and subsidiary role development (Dörrenbächer/Gammelgaard 2006).[112] Furthermore, the literature review and analysis identified five publications on subsidiary initiatives that employed organizational politics approaches (i.e. Lee/Williams 2005, Becker-Ritterspach/Dörrenbächer 2009, Dörrenbächer/Geppert 2009, Williams/Lee 2009, Dörrenbächer/Geppert 2010).

However, organizational politics approaches, in the broader sense as portrayed here, are not suitable for the present study for the following reasons.[113] First, the field of organizational politics does not represent a single and coherent school of thought, but is

---

[110] In addition, resource dependence theory (Pfeffer/Salancik 1978) is viewed by some authors as a theory related to organizational politics (see e.g. Dörrenbächer/Gammelgaard 2006, p. 267, Geppert/Dörrenbächer 2011, p. 4). However, resource dependence theory as one important theoretical pillar of this study will be discussed separately at more length in Subsection 3.3.3 of this publication and is therefore not included here.
[111] As the organizational politics approaches portrayed here are not further utilized in this publication, an extensive overview and discussion is not provided at this point. For a more detailed summary see e.g. Vigoda-Gadot and Drory (2006).
[112] For further works related to organizational politics in MNCs see, for example, the special issue of the Journal of International Management (Vol. 12, No. 3, 2006) on socio-political underpinnings of the management and organization of the MNC or the edited book publication on politics and power in the MNC by Dörrenbächer and Geppert (2011).
[113] The critical comments specifically refer to the three organizational politics approaches that were identified in the subsidiary initiative field (i.e. Burns 1961, March 1962, Mintzberg 1985).

instead associated with a diverse body of literature.[114] This has not only resulted in a multitude of definitions and conceptualizations, but also led to a rather fragmented understanding in the field with only scarce attempts to link these different research efforts (Lepisto/Pratt 2012, p. 68). Consequently, it is difficult to derive clear theoretical guidance from these numerous contributions and concepts for the present research framework per se.[115] Second, the often negative view of organizational politics as a phenomenon involving conflict, illegitimate behavior and actions driven by individual self-interest (Schreyögg 1999, pp. 434-444, Ferris/Treadway 2012, p. 13) is not fully compatible with subsidiary initiative-taking. As argued previously, although initiatives by foreign subsidiaries may sometimes be motivated opportunistically, in most cases they are expected to be consistent with the overall strategic objectives of the MNC (Birkinshaw/Fry 1998, p. 52, Yamin 2002, p. 135). Therefore, rather than necessitating the political maneuvers and games that take place "behind the scenes" (Mintzberg 1985, p. 134, Schreyögg 1999, p. 422), the initiative process predominantly involves less political activities such as initiative-selling and credibility-building, often even following established approval processes in MNCs (Birkinshaw 1997, pp. 221-222). Third, (micro-) political approaches are mostly concerned with interests, strategies and behavior of individual actors or small groups (Dörrenbächer/Geppert 2006, p. 255, Becker-Ritterspach/Dörrenbächer 2009, p. 204). The present thesis is, however, interested in investigating the alignment and interactions that take place between corporate headquarters and subsidiary units. Hence, theoretical approaches are deemed more suitable if they take an organizational-level perspective.

(6) The **integration-responsiveness framework** (Prahalad/Doz 1987) represents an important conceptualization for the examination of strategy in a global context that has a long tradition in international business (Roth/Morrison 1990, p. 541, Haugland 2010, p. 94). The integration-responsiveness (IR) framework proposes that companies competing internationally are confronted with two salient needs simultaneously. On the one hand, they need to be responsive to local market demands in each location where the firm is active. Such pressures for local responsiveness arise from, for instance, differences in market structures, distribution channels, or customer needs, which require firms to adapt to these local circumstances. On the other hand, internationally operating companies are also faced with the pressure for global integration as a result of, for example, the needs for economies of scale, universal products or the presence of global

---

[114] Political approaches are, for instance, linked to contributions viewing organizations as political coalitions (March 1962, Cyert/March 1963), to power dependence and resource dependence theories (Emerson 1962, Pfeffer/Salancik 1978), to concepts of power in and around organizations (Pfeffer 1981, Mintzberg 1983), to institutional theory (Selznick 1957), or to more micro-political concepts (Burns 1961). For comprehensive overviews on the origins and the evolution of organizational politics see, for instance, Ferris and Treadway (2012) or Lepisto and Pratt (2012).

[115] As a result, the present thesis more specifically incorporates resource dependence considerations (Pfeffer/ Salancik 1978) as described in more detail in Subsection 3.3.3 of this publication.

customers and global competitors (Doz/Prahalad 1991, pp. 158-159). As a response to these multiple and often conflicting challenges, companies may decide to react to them individually or jointly at the same time through three basic strategies: integrated, locally responsive, or multifocal (Roth/Morrison 1990, pp. 543-544, Johnson 1995, p. 621, Luo 2002, p. 192). Following contingency thinking, which suggests that there is no single best organizational orientation (Lawrence/Lorsch 1967, Thompson 1967), the IR framework thus allows for the conceptualization of international strategy in different contextual settings (Roth/Morrison 1990, p. 542, Haugland 2010, p. 94).[116] Within the domain of IB, scholars have used the IR framework when, for example, studying MNC strategies across multiple industries (e.g. Roth/Morrison 1990, Martinez/Jarillo 1991) or within single industry contexts (e.g. Johnson 1995). Furthermore, it has been applied in connection with the strategies, roles and activities of foreign subsidiaries in MNCs (e.g. Jarillo/Martinez 1990, Taggart 1997b, Luo 2001, 2002) and with subsidiary initiatives when investigating headquarters' strategies toward subsidiary entrepreneurship (Grohmann 2010).

Despite its strengths and frequent use, the IR framework as originally proposed by Prahalad and Doz is not directly applicable to the present study for the following reasons. First, the IR framework originally represented a contingency approach to international strategy at the firm level (Jarillo/Martinez 1990, p. 502). However, as this thesis is interested in entrepreneurial behavior at the subsidiary level, the theory does not correspond to the purpose of this study. Second, the IR framework provides little specification and description of the content of the different strategies. Moreover, it remains somewhat unclear how the particular industry forces and different strategies interact (Roth/Morrison 1990, p. 545). Therefore, the lack of details on the inner workings of firms makes it difficult to apply the framework to this research, which is interested in investigating the entrepreneurial behavior, and as such the inner workings, of subsidiaries in different contextual settings. Third, the IR framework has also been criticized for lacking theoretical backing. Although the two dimensions of local responsiveness and global integration appear widely acknowledged and have been used extensively over time, it remains unclear from which theoretical domain they originate (Haugland 2010, p. 95). Fourth, there seems to be no consistent approach in the literature to operationalizing and measuring the two dimensions. For example, the dimensions have been measured as both pressures and responses and scholars have taken different approaches towards their operationalization (Venaik et al. 2002, pp. 8-13).

(7) Porter's influential work on **competitive strategy** (Porter 1980, 1985) produced a theoretical framework that can be applied in understanding the nature and structure of

---

[116] As the integration-responsiveness framework portrayed here is not further used in this publication, an extensive overview and discussion is not provided. For a more detailed overview see e.g. Prahalad and Doz (1987).

an industry which has quickly become a dominant paradigm of competitive strategy and competitive positioning. It extended the earlier, more general view in industrial organization economics and more clearly specified the forces that drive competition in an industry. Porter's five forces model – highlighting the threat of new entrants, the bargaining power of suppliers, the threat of substitute products, the power of buyers and rivalry among businesses in an industry – provides an analytical tool to assess an industry's attractiveness and to determine a firm's competitive position within its industry (Hoskisson et al. 1999, pp. 425-426, Stonehouse/Snowdown 2007, p. 257). Based on the structural analysis of these five external forces, Porter argues, firms can identify their strengths and weaknesses relative to the industry and then develop (separately or in combination) a generic competitive strategy to outperform other firms in the form of a cost leadership, differentiation, or focus strategy (Porter 1980, pp. 29, 35).[117] Porter follows the "structure-conduct-performance" paradigm of industrial organization economics, which assumes that industry and market structure determines the conduct (or strategy) and, ultimately, the performance of firms in an industry (Kutschker/Schmid 2011, p. 840).[118] His work on competitive strategy has not only deeply influenced the domain of strategic management, but has also found its way into IB literature (Bartlett/Ghoshal 1991, p. 10). IB scholars have applied Porter's framework on industry structure in connection with topics such as MNCs' foreign direct investments (Luo/Tan 1997), multinational alliances (Luo 1999), global integration strategies (Birkinshaw et al. 1995), subsidiary competence development in competitive environments (Holm et al. 2005) and industry structure and subsidiary performance (Christmann et al. 1999). Furthermore, the literature review found one publication by Birkinshaw, Hood and Young that incorporates Porter's competitive strategy framework when investigating the interplay between subsidiary entrepreneurial initiatives and the external competitive arena (e.g. local customers, local suppliers or local competitors) and the internal competitive arena (e.g. internal customers, internal suppliers or internal competitors) of a subsidiary (Birkinshaw et al. 2005).[119]

However, despite the prominence of Porter's work in strategic management, it is not directly applicable for the present research. First, the analytical framework centers on the industry as the unit of analysis rather than on the individual firm (Stone-

---

[117] As Porter's analytical framework as portrayed here is not further used in this publication, an extensive overview and discussion is not provided. For a more detailed overview see, for instance, Porter (1980, pp. 3-33).
[118] The structure-conduct-performance paradigm is rooted in the works of, for instance, Bain (1956) and Mason (1939). For Porter's view on the relation and the contribution of industrial organization and its structure-conduct-performance paradigm for strategic management see, for instance, Porter (1981).
[119] Birkinshaw et al. (2005, p. 233) point out that the emphasis of their contribution on the competitive environment does not lessen the importance of other theoretical lenses for the concept of subsidiary initiatives – and in particular not of the resource-based view (Wernerfelt 1984, Barney 1991).

house/Snowdown 2007, p. 258).[120] It aims to explain differences in performance outcomes as a result of the industry structure and the relative positioning of firms within an industry (Porter 1991, pp. 99-100). As this research pivots around the examination of entrepreneurial behavior at the subsidiary level and views the entrepreneurial process as the main unit of analysis, it is not interested in investigating the detailed industry structure as a determinant of subsidiary initiatives. Second, as a result of its strong emphasis on the external environment, the industry structure framework largely neglects the effects of internal organizational characteristics and idiosyncratic firm attributes such as distinctive resources or capabilities (Barney 1991, p. 100, Bartlett/ Ghoshal 1991, p. 11, Zou/Cavusgil 1996, p. 56). Porter's approach is thus not fully compatible with the notion of subsidiary roles as applied in the research framework of this dissertation, as it is unable to fully capture both the external and the internal contextual dimensions that are expected to impact initiative-taking behavior in foreign subsidiaries. Third, Porter's work has been criticized for the generic character of the proposed strategies, which suggests that firms need to choose between cost leadership, differentiation or focus strategy. However, there is mounting evidence that firms may also follow hybrid strategies that combine elements of cost leadership, differentiation and possibly even of focus strategy (Stonehouse/Snowdown 2007, p. 258, Kutschker/Schmid 2011, p. 841), raising questions about the "exclusiveness" of these three generic strategies. More importantly, the realization of these strategies also necessitates that appropriate resources and capabilities exist or can be developed by the firm – an aspect that is not only largely neglected in Porter's framework but that is also central to the present research study (Wright 1987, pp. 94-95, Stonehouse/Snowdown 2007, p. 258). In addition, the three strategy types are not regarded as suitable for the given research since they cannot provide clear theoretical guidance on either the resource management or the headquarters-subsidiary alignment aspects that are part of the research framework of this study. Fourth and finally, Porter's framework is considered too static, thereby making it difficult to link it to dynamic aspects such as changing environmental conditions, processes of internal environmental adaption or even entrepreneurial activities in firms (Bartlett/Ghoshal 1991, p. 11, Spanos/Lioukas 2001, p. 924, Stonehouse/Snowdown 2007, p. 259).

(8) **Network Approaches to the MNC** essentially view multinational firms not as unitary and strictly hierarchical organizations but as intra- and inter-organizational networks of exchange relationships.[121] While the intra-organizational perspective (e.g. Hedlund

---

[120] It needs to be noted, however, that Porter argues that the industry structure framework can not only be applied at the level of the industry and the level of strategic groups, but even at the level of the individual firm (Porter 1991, p. 100).
[121] In IB research a differentiation between three levels of networks can be also found which outlines: (a) the intra-organizational network, (b) the inter-organizational network between different organizations in general and (c) the local network which represents the linkages of MNC units, such as headquarters or subsidiaries, to local entities,

1986, Bartlett/Ghoshal 1989) emphasizes the web of relationships within the boundaries of the firm, the inter-organizational perspective (e.g. Håkansson/Snehota 1989, Ghoshal/Bartlett 1990, Håkansson/Snehota 1995) focuses on the multiple linkages between the MNC (and its subunits) and external entities, such as customers, suppliers, competitors or governments (Schmid et al. 2002, p. 45). Within IB literature, numerous MNC network models have presented. Among the most prominent ones are, for example, Bartlett and Ghoshal's Transnational Solution (Bartlett/Ghoshal 1989), Hedlund's Heterarchy (Hedlund 1986) and White and Poynter's Horizontal Organization (White/ Poynter 1989). Bartlett and Ghoshal view the transnational firm as a network organization in which specialized resources and capabilities are dispersed throughout the firm but are still integrated through strong interdependencies. The dispersed, specialized and interdependent capabilities are also reflected in the different roles and responsibilities that foreign units have and in the different contributions they make to the MNC. While some subsidiaries may lead certain parts of the company and develop distinct resources and capabilities for global applications, others may function as Implementers that deliver the value-add of the company. The differentiation of capabilities and organizational roles in the MNC not only results in reciprocal interdependencies between the different MNC units, but it also requires mutual cooperation and knowledge-sharing in order to create innovative products or processes (see Bartlett/Ghoshal 2002, pp. 68-76).[122] Network approaches to the MNC have been applied when dealing with topics such as the creation and transfer of subsidiary capabilities (e.g. Andersson et al. 2002, Andersson 2003, Andersson et al. 2005, Holm et al. 2005) and subsidiary innovation (e.g. Almeida/Phene 2004, Hartmann 2011). Also, four contributions on subsidiary initiatives have employed network approaches to help explain, for example, why subsidiaries have the ability to pursue initiatives or to outline the sources of initiative opportunities (i.e. Birkinshaw 1997, 2000).

Although the network view of the multinational firm is fully compatible with the perspective taken in this thesis, it does not constitute a theoretical lens through which the topic under investigation can be thoroughly captured. First, network approaches typically view the multinational firm as embedded in a network of inter- and intra-organizational relationships. Thus, their emphasis is on analyzing the structure of networks (e.g. network density) and the characteristics of linkages between different actors (e.g. activity structures, resource ties).[123] However, as the present study is not interested solely in specific

---

such as local customers, suppliers or governments in particular (see e.g. Schmid et al. 2002, Andersson et al. 2005, Schmid 2005).

[122] As network approaches to the MNC as portrayed here are not explicitly further utilized in this publication, an extensive overview and discussion is not provided. For a more detailed overview see e.g. Renz (1998), Rall (2002), Schmid (2002, 2005), or Forsgren (2008, pp. 101-124).

[123] See, for instance, the publication by Bartlett and Ghoshal (1990) which discusses the effects of density in the external network or the contribution by Håkansson and Snehota (1995) which addresses the characteristics of business relationships.

network or relationship characteristics of MNCs but intends to account more broadly for different internal and external contingency factors, an emphasis on network approaches is not considered appropriate. As is clear, this theoretical view is not suitable to holistically capture environmental or organizational characteristics of firms (Macharzina 2003, p. 29). Although generally useful for the topic of subsidiary initiative-taking, it simply does not go far enough to constitute a strong theoretical basis for this research (see also Birkinshaw 2000, pp. 108-109).[124] Second, network approaches do not sufficiently address how inter-organizational relationships and network characteristics impact structures and processes within organizations and they are also not well-suited to address change processes within firms (Macharzina 2003, p. 29, Sydow 2006, p. 435). Hence, it is assumed that they are not well equipped to provide theoretical direction on the internal initiative-taking processes of foreign subsidiary units in MNCs. Third, in connection with subsidiary initiatives, these network conceptualizations of MNCs are only used as supplementary perspectives for certain facets of the phenomenon, such as to explain the general ability of subsidiaries to pursue initiatives (Birkinshaw/Hood 1998d, Birkinshaw 2000) or to discuss the different origins of initiative opportunities in internal and external markets (Birkinshaw 1997, 1998a). Therefore, rather than constituting a broad theoretical foundation on which multiple aspects of the complex initiative phenomenon can be grounded, network approaches have mostly fulfilled a supporting function. Fourth and finally, the network perspective often remains largely descriptive "which makes it unfalsifiable, and therefore detracts from its power as a theory" (Birkinshaw 2001, p. 387). Furthermore, the complete capturing of the complex relations within and between organizations is viewed as problematic, as are the operationalization and measurement of many central network characteristics (e.g. density, distance or centrality; see Macharzina 2003, p. 29).

3.3.1.2 Selected Theories

(1) One central pillar for the present research is represented by the **resource-based view** (e.g. Wernerfelt 1984, Barney 1991) which focuses on unique internal resources of firms as the source of competitive advantage. As will be described in more detail later, the recently flourishing dynamic and process-oriented approaches to RBV (e.g. Bowman/Collier 2006, Helfat et al. 2007, Sirmon et al. 2007, Hitt et al. 2011, Sirmon et al. 2011) are particularly suitable for the resource management process of subsidiary initiatives for the reasons outlined below.[125] First, the RBV in general takes an "inside-out" perspective and focuses on the inner workings of organizations. It is therefore well-suited to deal with (micro-)organizational processes and organizational behavior and

---
[124] For instance, network theory could help to explain from which sources of the network needed resources for the realization of subsidiary initiatives are obtained. Yet, how these resources are further utilized within the subsidiary cannot be adequately addressed through this theory.
[125] See Subsections 3.3.2.2 herein for details on dynamic and process-oriented approaches of RBV.

their links to the success or failure of firms (Barney et al. 2001, p. 635, Spanos/Lioukas 2001, p. 924). Second, the more dynamic and process-related branches of the theory, which focus on the managerial processes concerned with the development and deployment of resources in firms, are easily applicable when studying entrepreneurial phenomena from a processual viewpoint (Mahoney/Pandian 1992, p. 369, Alvarez/Barney 2002, p. 90, Young et al. 2003, p. 39, Helfat et al. 2007, p. 120, Kraaijenbrink et al. 2010, p. 366). More specifically, these theoretical strands deal with the process and activities through which firms acquire, bundle and deploy resources in order to exploit marketplace opportunities – aspects which are also central to subsidiary initiative-taking.[126] Accordingly, it has been stated that not only is the RBV in general well-suited for investigating the phenomenon of subsidiary entrepreneurial initiatives (Birkinshaw et al. 2005, p. 247, see also Birkinshaw 2000, pp. 102-108), but it appears that the more dynamic resource-based versions are particularly promising for this field (Birkinshaw/ Hood 1998d, p. 781, Liouka 2007, p. 25).[127] Third, although the RBV devotes more attention to internal firm attributes, it does not ignore the external context of firms, but rather explicitly acknowledges its relevance for resource acquisition, creation and deployment as well as for the generation of firm-level advantages (see e.g. Barney 1986b, p. 1240, Amit/Schoemaker 1993, pp. 37-39, Teece et al. 1997, p. 515). It has even been argued that the RBV "may, in fact, act as a bridge between firm-based and industry-based perspectives on advantage" (Fahy 2000, p. 100, for similar arguments see e.g. Mahoney/Pandian 1992, p. 375, Hoskisson et al. 1999, p. 440). Consistent with such an understanding, scholars have subsequently developed contingency approaches to RBV that deliberately incorporate environmental and organizational contexts and discuss their effects on the development and deployment of unique resources and the generation of competitive advantage (e.g. Godfrey/Gregersen 1999, Aragón-Correa/ Sharma 2003, Bowman/Collier 2006, Sirmon et al. 2007).[128] Consequently, the "openness" of the RBV and the possibility of accounting for the influence of environmental and organizational contexts makes the theory highly applicable for the present research. Fourth, more generally, the RBV is considered a theoretical lens which can be easily linked to other theories. Its "permeable, eclectic and permissive nature" (Lockett et al. 2009, p. 25) allows for dialogue among scholars from different schools of thought,

---

[126] See Subsection 3.2.2.3 herein for details on the importance of resource management activities in the subsidiary initiative process.

[127] As will be shown in detail in Subsection 3.3.2.3 herein, the resource-based view has already been repeatedly applied for the investigation and discussion of subsidiary initiative-taking. However, it appears that this theoretical perspective has not yet been "wholeheartedly embraced" for this phenomenon. Part of the neglect could be attributed to some of the weaknesses of the more traditional RBV. For instance, Birkinshaw and Hood criticize two aspects that have made its application for the topic somewhat difficult so far: first, its focus on explaining performance heterogeneity at firm level and, second, its limitations concerning dynamic aspects and process orientation. Hence, they propose that "more attention needs to be paid in the future to the ways that capabilities are developed at subfirm level" and consequently suggest using more dynamic resource-based approaches (Birkinshaw/Hood 1998d, p. 791).

[128] See Subsection 3.3.2.2 herein for further detail on contingency approaches towards the RBV.

with some authors suggesting that it may even "form the kernel of a unifying paradigm for strategic management research" (Hoskisson et al. 1999, p. 440). Finally, although the RBV was originally intended to explain performance heterogeneity at firm level, it has also been usefully applied for the investigation of subsidiary-level issues such as subsidiary role development or the development and transfer of specialized resources by foreign units of MNCs.[129] In sum, the focus on internal resource management activities, the opportunity of incorporating the contextual setting and the possibility to apply the theory at the subsidiary level provide compelling arguments for the selection of the contingent and dynamic RBV for the entrepreneurial resource management activities of the subsidiary initiative process.

(2) **Resource dependence theory** (Pfeffer/Salancik 1978), which deals with resource-based power in inter- and intra-organizational relations, has been chosen as a second theoretical pillar for this research. As is explicated in more detail below, this theory is deemed particularly relevant for the investigation of headquarters-subsidiary alignment activities in the subsidiary initiative process for the following reasons. First, RDT represents an applicable theory for the discussion of intra-organizational relationships in general and for power dynamics and interactions between different units of MNCs in particular (Medcof 2001, p. 1002, Pfeffer/Salancik 2003, p. 71, Johnston/Menguc 2007, p. 790). The theoretical lens therefore can and has been usefully applied to explain headquarters-subsidiary relationships, in connection with, for instance, subsidiary innovations (Ambos/Schlegelmilch 2007) or subsidiary entrepreneurial initiatives (e.g. Birkinshaw/Ridderstråle 1999, Liouka 2007, Ambos et al. 2010).[130] Furthermore, RDT is expected to be especially appropriate when dealing with initiative-taking subsidiaries that create new resources and capabilities. In this context, the theory should better reflect the mutual dependencies and power relations within MNCs rather than assuming that it is solely headquarters that exerts influence on subsidiaries unidirectionally (Mudambi/Pedersen 2007, pp. 10-11). Second, RDT also acknowledges the importance of external and internal contingencies on the organizational structure and the distribution of power and control within organizations (Astley/Sachdeva 1984, p. 104, Pfeffer/Salancik 2003, p. 231). As such, it has been previously applied to link subsidiary roles, as proxies for the contextual setting of subsidiaries, to headquarters-subsidiary relations (see e.g. Ghoshal/Nohria 1989) and it should therefore also be well-suited to address the alignment and interactions between headquarters and subsidiaries in the initiative process. Third and finally, RDT is considered compatible with many other schools of thought and has demonstrated a long history of integration with other theoretical perspectives (Hillman et al. 2009, p. 1416). Specifically with regard to the other

---

[129] See Subsection 3.3.2.3 herein for details on the application of the RBV in connection with MNC subsidiaries and the possible challenges.
[130] See Subsections 3.3.3.2 herein for details on the application of RDT in IB research.

two theoretical pillars of this research, RDT can be viewed as highly complementary to the RBV and even closely related to contingency theory, thereby allowing for their joint application in this study.[131]

(3) **Contingency theory** (e.g. Lawrence/Lorsch 1967, Thompson 1967), which in essence argues that the organizational context influences the structure, behavior and efficiency of organizations, is used as a third and overarching theoretical perspective for the research framework. This theoretical lens is considered suitable because it, first, places emphasis on the link between the contextual setting of a firm and its "internal life" (Forsgren 2008, p. 78) concerning matters such as firm's structures (e.g. Stopford/Wells 1972, Egelhoff 1988), strategies (e.g. Ginsberg/Venkatraman 1985) and innovative and entrepreneurial behavior (Burns/Stalker 1961, Lorsch/Lawrence 1965, Utterback/Abernathy 1975, Damanpour 1991, 1996). Second, contingency theory provides a somewhat flexible and open framework which allows for the consideration of various contingency factors and of different aspects concerning the structure and behavior of organizations (Kieser/Kubicek 1992, p. 62, Kieser 2006, p. 218). It therefore permits, in one comprehensive framework, the inclusion of (i) subsidiary roles as contingencies, (ii) subsidiary initiative-taking as the behavioral component and (iii) subsidiary initiative outcomes as the performance variable. Third, contingency theory is compatible with diversified multinational firms (e.g. Doz/Prahalad 1991) and has even provided the theoretical roots for many subsidiary role typologies (e.g. Ghoshal/Nohria 1989, Gupta/Govindarajan 1991, Nohria/Ghoshal 1994). As such, it is applicable to the research objectives and the underlying basic assumptions of this research framework. Fourth, contingency theory in general offers the possibility to integrate other theoretical lenses to better explain, for example, the structure and behavior of organizations (Kieser/Walgenbach 2010, p. 42).[132] More specifically with regard to the two further theoretical approaches used in this study, contingency theory can be linked to the RBV in order to model and explain context-specific entrepreneurial resource and deployment activities more precisely (see e.g. Godfrey/Gregersen 1999, Hitt et al. 2011). Furthermore, it can be used in connection with RDT to illuminate how the contextual setting is linked to organizational actions and structures through the distribution of power and control in an organization (Pfeffer/Salancik 2003, pp. 226-228).

In summary, both the RBV and RDT provide the theoretical foundations for the two central aspects of the subsidiary initiative-taking behavior under investigation. While the

---

[131] See Subsection 3.3.5 for a discussion on the potential linkage between RBV, RDT and contingency theory.
[132] Among other aspects, contingency theory has been criticized for not specifying the processes of internal change and adaptation (Doz/Prahalad 1991, p. 151, Kieser 2006, p. 235) and for lacking theoretical grounding (Schmid 1994, p. 16, Scherm/Pietsch 2007, p. 41, Höhne 2009, p. 94). The present research attempts to – at least in part – address these shortcomings by integrating resource-based and resource dependence considerations. These efforts aim at better specifying and theoretically substantiating entrepreneurial resource management and headquarters-subsidiary alignment activities as central aspects of subsidiary initiative-taking behavior.

3 – Research Framework

RBV comes into play to explain the entrepreneurial resource management activities necessary to realize initiative opportunities, RDT gives theoretical guidance with regard to the alignment and interactions between headquarters and the subsidiary. As both these aspects of subsidiary initiative-taking behavior and the outcomes are expected to be contingent on the subsidiary's role setting, a contingency perspective is also applied as an overarching theoretical link to combine these different elements within one comprehensive framework (see Figure 3.7).

```
                            Subsidiary Initiative-Taking
General      Subsidiary    ┌──────────────┬──────────────┐   Subsidiary
Framework    Role       →  │ Entrepreneurial │ Headquarters- │ → Initiative
                            │ Resource      │ Subsidiary   │   Outcome
                            │ Management    │ Alignment    │
                            └──────────────┴──────────────┘

Theoretical               Resource-Based      Resource-Dependence
Considerations            Considerations      Considerations

                                    Contingency
                                    Perspective
```

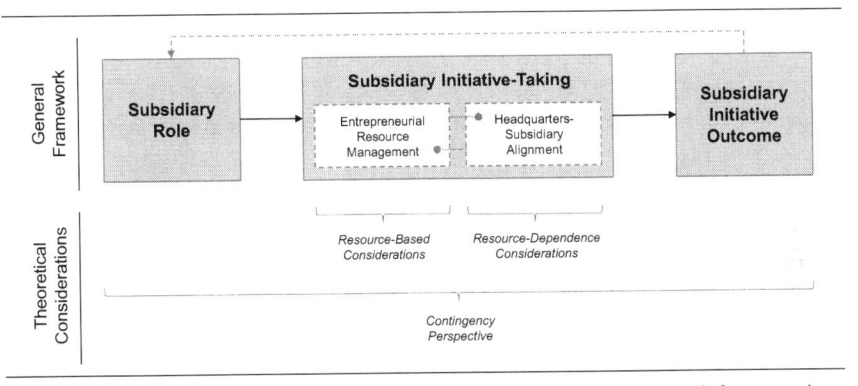

Figure 3.7: Theoretical perspectives and their application in the research framework

3.3.2 Resource-Based View of the Firm

3.3.2.1 Overview of the Resource-Based View

(1) Introduction to the Resource-Based View

Within the field of strategic management and international business, the resource-based view has emerged as one of many different approaches attempting to explain sustained differences in firm performance. The RBV, focusing on internal firm sources of competitive advantage, can be viewed as a complement to the industrial organization (IO) view (e.g. Porter 1980, p. 224, 1990). Whereas the IO view focuses on the industry and market structure as external determinants of firms' performance differences, the RBV takes a more internal view and argues that performance heterogeneity is based on the unique resources a firm possesses or controls (see e.g. Kraaijenbrink et al. 2010, p. 350, Kutschker/Schmid 2011, pp. 840-843). Although the development of the RBV has been largely influenced by the works of Wernerfelt (1984) and Barney (1991), prior important theoretical input stems from economic theory, and particularly from contributions by Penrose (1959). Following a period of substantial theoretical development in the early 1990s, it has in the meantime established itself as an influential theoretical perspective in the fields of strategic management and international management (Barney/Arikan 2001, p. 124, Peng 2001, p. 803, Crook et al. 2008, p. 1141).

In essence, the RBV views firms as historically determined bundles of resources and capabilities which provide the potential to generate competitive advantage. Resources refer to all tangible and intangible factors that a firm controls and that it uses to conceive of and implement its strategies. Tangible resources relate, for instance, to a firm's physical capital assets such as plant equipment and machines or its financial assets in the form of equity capital and retained earnings. Intangible resources include, for example, a firm's human capital (such as training, experience, relationships and insights of individual employees), or its organizational capital in the form of a formal reporting structure, its brand name and reputation in the market, or informal internal and external relationships of groups (Wernerfelt 1984, pp. 172-174, Barney 1991, pp. 101-102, Barney/Arikan 2001, pp. 138-139, Barney et al. 2001, p. 625).[133]

Based on the fundamental assumption that a firm's resources and capabilities may be heterogeneous and immobile, the RBV argues that they must have four different characteristics in order to hold the potential for sustained competitive advantage: they need to be valuable, rare, imperfectly imitable and not substitutable. Resources are considered (a) valuable "when they enable a firm to conceive of or implement strategies that improve its efficiency and effectiveness" and as such allow it to "exploit opportunities or neutralize threats in a firm's environment" (Barney 1991, p. 106, Barney/Clark 2007, pp. 57-58). Hence, the value of a resource is also linked to environmental and market characteristics that help determine the attributes through which firms can exploit opportunities or neutralize threats. In addition to being valuable, resources also need to be (b) rare, meaning that they are solely possessed or controlled by one or very few potentially competing firms. It is expected that only when a firm implements a value-creating strategy that is not simultaneously used by many other competitors can it achieve a competitive advantage. Furthermore, resources are required to be (c) imperfectly imitable, which implies that there are no alternative sources or possibilities to duplicate them. More specifically, imperfect imitability may result from the unique historical conditions of firms, causal ambiguity or social complexity.[134] Lastly, in order for a resource to poten-

---

[133] Although Barney and Wernerfelt originally do not further differentiate between resources and capabilities, other authors suggest that, while resources represent a firm's fundamental tangible and intangible factors, capabilities refer to those attributes that enable the firm to actually utilize and exploit its resources in an integrated manner (Hitt et al. 2007, p. 17).

[134] The unique historical conditions essentially reflect the path-dependent perspective of the RBV which assumes that the ability of a firm to acquire and exploit resources and hence to obtain a competitive edge is also determined by the unique path a firm took over time. Therefore, due to the path-dependent nature of many resources they cannot be duplicated by other firms. Causal ambiguity refers to the imperfect understanding of firms with regard to the link between resources they control and a firm's competitive advantage. It is argued that because of causal ambiguity, imitating firms do not understand which actions they need to take to duplicate the strategies of firms that possess a competitive advantage. Social complexity entails that firms' resources often are very complex social phenomena that cannot be managed and influenced in a systematic manner which makes it

tially lead to sustained competitive advantage, (d) other firms cannot be able to replace it through a similar or alternative resource that can serve as strategic substitute. It is expected that only when there is no strategically equivalent resource that other firms can apply to implement the same strategy can a resource be a source of competitive advantage. A firm is considered to have a competitive advantage when it exploits its resources or capabilities and realizes a "value creating strategy not simultaneously being implemented by any current or potential competitors *and* when these other firms are unable to duplicate the benefits of this strategy" (Barney 1991, p. 102).[135] For example, if a firm exploits a resource or capability that is merely valuable, it can only generate competitive parity. If a resource, in addition, is also rare, it may help the firm to achieve a temporary competitive advantage and, if furthermore is hard and/or costly to imitate may even lead to sustained competitive advantage (Barney/Clark 2007, p. 71).[136]

Nevertheless, such unique resources and capabilities cannot be a source of competitive advantage in and of themselves. Instead, a further critical aspect concerns the firm's ability to effectively and efficiently assemble and exploit them in organizational processes to eventually realize the competitive advantage (Grant 1991, p. 115, Eisenhardt/ Martin 2000, p. 1116, Barney/Clark 2007, p. 67). Thus, a firm that is well-endowed with valuable, rare, imperfectly imitable and non-substitutable (VRIN) resources, but that does not effectively and efficiently utilize them, will not be able to generate a competitive edge. Furthermore, the exploitation of VRIN resources' full competitive advantage is also said to be influenced by further firm resources or capabilities that are often more common and/or complementary (e.g. reporting structures, control systems or compensation policies). Hence it is the combination of the two types that enables firms to attain their full potential for competitive advantages (Barney/Clark 2007, p. 67). The assumed linkage between a firm's resource portfolio, resource exploitation activities and sustainable competitive advantage as portrayed here is presented in Figure 3.8.

---

very difficult or even impossible for other firms to imitate them (Barney 1991, pp. 107-111, Barney/Clark 2007, pp. 59-65).
[135] Competitive advantage can also be expressed as a firm's ability to create more economic value relative to other marginal competitors in a particular product market through superior differentiation and/or lower costs (Barney/ Clark 2007, p. 26).
[136] It needs to be noted that, in contrast to Barney's contribution in 1991, Barney and Clark (2007, pp. 65-67) slightly revise some aspects of the RBV and subsume the fourth resource characteristics of "imperfect substitutability" under "imperfectly imitable resource. Hence, the effects of "imperfect substitutability" on competitive advantage are not explicitly mentioned.

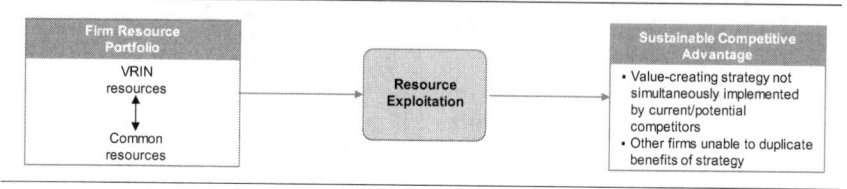

Figure 3.8: Overview of the resource-based framework

(2) Criticism of the Resource-Based View

The RBV has been subject to various criticisms over time. As the present thesis cannot thoroughly discuss every single critical point, particular attention will be given to those aspects that are especially relevant for this research. Therefore, the following critical points will briefly presented: (1) the static nature of the theory, (2) the insufficient consideration of a process perspective, (3) its strong internal focus, (4) the lack of managerial implications, (5) its tautological reasoning, (6) the danger of infinite regress and finally (7) certain definitional and methodological issues.

(1) It has been repeatedly noted that the theoretical core of the traditional RBV, as proposed by Barney (1991) for instance, is essentially static and equilibrium-based (e.g. Foss 1998, p. 138, Barney 2001b, pp. 644-646, Priem/Butler 2001, p. 33, Easterby-Smith et al. 2009, p. S1). Central to this static view is the assumption that firms differ in their resource positions, and these heterogeneous resource stocks then provide firms with different potentials for competitive advantage (Barney 1991, p. 101). Yet how these heterogeneous resource positions come to exist or how they might change over time is considered largely neglected in the existing RBV literature (Godfrey/Gregersen 1999, p. 39, Ahuja/Katila 2004, p. 887, Barney/Clark 2007, p. 257, Maritan/Peteraf 2011, p. 1375). The emphasis of the static approach on the possession and the control of unique resources also makes it difficult for the theory to address dynamic issues such as innovation and entrepreneurship (Foss/Ishikawa 2006, p. 9, Kraaijenbrink et al. 2010, p. 366), as these topics deal with the creation of new resources or the recombination of existing ones (Hitt et al. 2001, p. 480). Not surprisingly, it has been repeatedly stated that the static RBV has to this point insufficiently addressed the questions of how resources are obtained (e.g. Schmid/Schurig 2003, p. 757, Bowman/Collier 2006, p. 192, Foss/Ishikawa 2006, p. 3) and effectively developed and managed (Eisenhardt/Martin 2000, p. 1117, Barney et al. 2001, p. 635). This led to requests to embrace dynamic aspects and to adopt a more evolutionary point of view within the RBV (Foss 1998, p. 145, Barney 2001b, p. 647, Helfat/Peteraf 2003, p. 998, Kraaijenbrink et al. 2010, p. 366).

(2) Closely linked to the previous argument, it has been stated that a comprehensive process perspective in the RBV remains underdeveloped (Barney et al. 2011, p. 1306, Maritan/Peteraf 2011, p. 1383). The processes and mechanics through which different resource and capability endowments of firms come into existence, through which they change and develop, and through which competitive advantage is generated, seem to remain a "black box" (Priem/Butler 2001, p. 33) and not well understood (Bowman/Ambrosini 2003, p. 293, Sirmon et al. 2007, p. 274, Wernerfelt 2011, p. 1369). Accordingly, it is claimed that more attention should be paid in the RBV to process issues and to questions concerning the "how," such as how resources are obtained or how they may contribute to competitive advantage. A process perspective on the development of resources and capabilities should also "examine the paths and sequences of their evolution" (Barney et al. 2011, p. 1307) and include social dynamics or behavioral components (Priem/Butler 2001, p. 35, Maritan/Peteraf 2011, p. 1383). Although RBV scholars have for some time recognized the value of a process perspective that considers the distinct phases of resource development (Amit/Schoemaker 1993, p. 39), this aspect of the RBV has only very recently begun to attract more attention (see e.g. Sirmon et al. 2007, Garbuio et al. 2011, Hitt et al. 2011, Sirmon et al. 2011, Wernerfelt 2011).

(3) Another point of criticism is the RBV's strong focus on internal firm attributes and its (partial) neglect of the environment and the business setting in which a firm operates (Porter 1991, p. 108, Foss 1998, p. 143, Boccardelli/Magnusson 2006, p. 162, Sirmon et al. 2007, p. 274, Freiling 2008, p. 39). Since the theory focuses more on the characteristics of existing rent-generating resources rather than on differing situations or contexts (Priem/Butler 2001, p. 33), external effects on resource endowment and development have only been considered to a limited degree. However, there seems to be increasing recognition that external factors such as the behavior and preferences of customers, the activities of competitors, or the firm's ownership context have an impact on the creation, development and utilization of unique resources. Thus it is requested to examine and integrate external contingencies and firms' contexts in the RBV more thoroughly (Bowman/Collier 2006, p. 192, Wang/Chen 2010, p. 142, Barney et al. 2011, p. 1306).

(4) Some scholars have criticized the RBV for having no "prescriptive ability" and thus not offering clear managerial implications (Foss 1998, Priem/Butler 2001, Bowman/Collier 2006, Kraaijenbrink et al. 2010). Following the authors' line of reasoning, it is argued that the underdeveloped process understanding (Foss 1998, p. 145) and the limited consideration of context and contingencies in the process (Bowman/Collier 2006, p. 192; see also critiques 2 and 3 above) make it difficult to derive meaningful managerial implications for issues such as resource development or organizational learning. In its traditional sense, the RBV seems to suggest merely that managers should obtain or

develop unique resources, and it offers little guidance on how this should take place in general or even in different settings and contexts.

(5) The RBV has also been accused of implying tautological or circular reasoning (e.g. Porter 1991, Fahy 2000, Priem/Butler 2001, Lado et al. 2006, Brühl et al. 2008, Lockett et al. 2009, Kraaijenbrink et al. 2010).[137] The nature of the criticism is that, within the RBV, the creation of value and competitive advantage is considered the result of valuable resources, which by definition already imply value (Lockett et al. 2009, p. 11). Thus, the inherent problem is that "competitive advantage is defined in terms of value and rarity, and the resource characteristics argued to lead to competitive advantage are value and rarity" (Priem/Butler 2001, p. 28).[138]

(6) In addition, the RBV has been criticized for possibly leading to an infinite regress (Collis 1994, Fahy 2000, Priem/Butler 2001, Kraaijenbrink et al. 2010). It is argued that this danger arises when the RBV logic is extended to "second-order issues or beyond" (Priem/Butler 2001, p. 34). This implies that not only unique resources by themselves (as a first-order issue) are considered in the RBV, but furthermore the ability to learn how to develop unique resources (as a second-order issue) is again viewed as a unique resource by itself. This could initiate an infinite process of "learning to learn to learn" (Collis 1994, p. 144) and lead firms to go on never-ending quests for higher-order capabilities (Kraaijenbrink et al. 2010, p. 352). Hence, it has been stated that this problem of infinite regress may undermine the theoretical value of the RBV in explaining how competitive advantage can be achieved (Lado et al. 2006, p. 119).[139]

(7) Finally, the RBV has also been confronted with concerns about definitional issues (e.g. Priem/Butler 2001, Kraaijenbrink et al. 2010) and methodological challenges (e.g. Barney et al. 2001, Lockett et al. 2009, Barney et al. 2011). For instance, it has been complained that the definition of resources may be too broad and overly inclusive, driving it "toward tautology" (Kraaijenbrink et al. 2010, p. 358) and making it difficult to establish "contextual and prescriptive boundaries" for the RBV as a perspective on strategy research (Priem/Butler 2001, p. 34). Concerning the methodological and measurement issues within the RBV, it has been stated that measuring resources appears to be an ongoing struggle for researchers (Barney et al. 2001, p. 636, Barney et al. 2011, p. 1311). As critical resources are often intangible and unobservable, identifying and

---

[137] This issue has also been extensively discussed by Barney (2001a) as a response to the critique brought forward by Priem and Butler (2001).
[138] However, it is argued that in order to evade this circular reasoning, it is necessary to view the relationship between resources and advantage as a longitudinal process (Fahy 2000, p. 100), or as "routines ... to altering the resource base" (Eisenhardt/Martin 2000, p. 1108). Hence, taking a more process-oriented approach could help to address this concern.
[139] In order to overcome this problem, numerous suggestions have been brought forward. For instance, it has been proposed to take more dynamic approaches to resource development (e.g. Priem/Butler 2001, p. 34, Lado et al. 2006, p. 119), to incorporate temporal components (Priem/Butler 2001, p. 35), or to recognize that valuable resources and capabilities also depend on "the context of the industry and the time" (Collis 1994, p. 150).

measuring them often proves problematic. This, together with the complexity of large organizations, also leads to the problem of how to isolate the performance impact of specific resources (Lockett et al. 2009, p. 17). Lastly, the same seems to hold true for the concept of "competitive advantage." It is argued that not only does the definition remain controversial, but it also is a "slippery construct to operationalize and measure" (Lado et al. 2006, p. 124).

Although the RBV has clearly developed into an influential theoretical perspective over the past two and a half decades, it can also be concluded that the theory as originally proposed has not been without controversy. The extent to which the "traditional" RBV has reacted to some of the critiques is outlined below in Subsection 3.3.2.2, focusing particularly on the development of the theory in areas that are of relevance for this thesis. These include progress towards more dynamic approaches which recognize that resources and capabilities change over time (Paragraph 1), advances towards better understanding the process of how resources and capabilities actually develop and generate competitive advantage (Paragraph 2) and the recognition of environmental and organizational contingencies on the development and exploitation of resources and capabilities (Paragraph 3). Following the description of these developments in the RBV, a process and contingency perspective on resource management is presented that summarizes and brings together the different advancements in this theoretical domain (Paragraph 4).

3.3.2.2 Advancements of the Resource-Based View

(1) Dynamic Approaches

As outlined previously, as the theoretical core of the traditional RBV is essentially static and equilibrium-based (e.g. Foss 1998, p. 138, Barney 2001b, pp. 644-646, Priem/ Butler 2001, p. 33, Easterby-Smith et al. 2009, p. S1), much of the resource-based literature takes the resource stock of firms as given and only insufficiently addresses the entrepreneurial process of resource and capability accumulation and development (Fahy 2000, p. 100, Foss/Ishikawa 2006, p. 3). Yet certain strands of the resource-based literature take a more evolutionary and dynamic approach, incorporating the development of resources and capabilities over time. Important theoretical work in this area includes, for example, Dierickx and Cool's contribution on asset stock accumulation (Dierickx/Cool 1989), Teece at al.'s dynamic capabilities framework (Teece et al. 1997) and Helfat and Peteraf's concept of the capability lifecycle (Helfat/Peteraf 2003).[140]

---

[140] Further contributions on dynamic capabilities and dynamic approaches to the RBV are made by e.g. Amit and Schoemaker (1993), Helfat (1997), Eisenhardt and Martin (2000), or Makadok (2001). However, as this part of the

(1) Dierickx and Cool (1989), building on the notion of a dynamic resource-based perspective, do not view the firm's resources as given and static, but address the issue of resource growth and decay over time in their journal article (Boccardelli/Magnusson 2006, p. 164, Lockett et al. 2009, p. 15). The authors differentiate between two possibilities to obtain resources: external resource acquisition in strategic factor markets or internal resource accumulation. However, it is argued that only those resources that are developed internally should have the potential to generate competitive advantage, as all assets based on resources acquired externally can be (too) easily imitated or replicated by competitors.[141] Furthermore, the authors distinguish between resource stocks and resources flows, the former representing the given assets that a firm has accumulated over time and the latter being the process through which the existing resource stock is "refreshed" (Dierickx/Cool 1989, pp. 1506-1507). A continuous accumulation of firm-specific resources is deemed necessary, as each resource is considered subject to deterioration over time, depending on, for instance, the characteristics of the resource itself or the innovation pace of the industry. As a result, firms need to engage in the process of continuous internal resource accumulation to ensure a sustainable competitive advantage is maintained relative to competition, and possibly even more so in rapidly changing environments (Boccardelli/Magnusson 2006, p. 164).

(2) The topic of how firms can achieve and maintain competitive advantage specifically in highly dynamic business environments is dealt with, for example, in the work of Teece et al. (1997). It is suggested that in rapidly and unpredictably changing markets, the gradual accumulation of resources "is often not enough to support a significant competitive advantage." Instead, it is the firm management's ability to "integrate, build, and reconfigure internal and external competences" that actually becomes the source of competitive advantage (Teece et al. 1997, p. 515). Dynamic capabilities are seen as firm's processes related to the creation, extension or modification of resources in order to match or adapt to market changes (e.g. Eisenhardt/Martin 2000, p. 1107, Ambrosini/ Bowman 2009, pp. 32-33). Dynamic capabilities therefore seem to go beyond the standard RBV since they not only focus on the existence and consequences of unique resource bundles but also include "the mechanisms by which firms learn and accumulate new skills and capabilities, and the forces that limit the rate and direction of this process" (Teece et al. 1990, p. 11).[142]

---

thesis only aims at highlighting some of the important theoretical developments towards a more "dynamic" resource-based perspective, only select contributions are outlined in this subsection.

[141] More specifically, it is argued that imitability depends on how far the asset accumulation process meets the criteria of time compression diseconomies, asset mass efficiencies, interconnectedness, asset erosion, and causal ambiguity (see Dierickx/Cool 1989, pp. 1507-1509).

[142] More concrete examples of dynamic capabilities that are mentioned in the related literature are product development processes, product innovations, research and development activities, or entrepreneurial undertakings in firms (see e.g. Teece et al. 1997, Eisenhardt/Martin 2000, Boccardelli/Magnusson 2006 and Ambrosini/Bowman 2009).

(3) Further work concerned with the changes and evolution of resources and capabilities over time has been undertaken by Helfat and Peteraf (2003), who present their perspective on the dynamic RBV in general and capability life cycles in particular. The authors intend to fill the "dynamism gap" of the RBV by offering a "framework for understanding the evolution of capabilities over time" (Helfat/Peteraf 2003, p. 998). The capability life cycle (CLC) framework is described as being derived from evolutionary economics and aiming to link together different strands of the RBV literature, thus providing "a comprehensive approach to dynamic resource-based theory" (Helfat/ Peteraf 2003, p. 997).[143] The CLC outlines different stages of capability evolution: three initial stages of capability founding, development and maturity, followed by possible splitting into six additional stages. With regard to the initial stages, it is proposed that the founding stage is concerned with the (deliberate) creation of a new capability for the firm by an individual or team. The subsequent development stage involves the gradual building and improvement of the capability through, for instance, organizational learning, problem-solving, or investment over time. At some point, however, it is expected that development will come to an end with the capability reaching the maturity stage. This phase then involves the upkeep and maintenance of the capability. From this point on, the capability lifecycle might go into retirement (death), retrenchment (gradual decline), renewal (improvement), replication (reproduction in other geographic markets), redeployment (application in different product market) or recombination (combination with other capabilities; see Helfat/Peteraf 2003, pp. 1000-1003).

Although the body of literature outlined above has begun to better understand resource evolution and resource changes from a process perspective, it remains somewhat vague in regard to precisely how the process takes place, and the "mechanisms by which ... capabilities operate remain somewhat less clear" (Moliterno/Wiersema 2007, p. 1065). While the environmental setting is increasingly recognized as an important factor in the process, theoretical development often remains so general that it is unable to explain the details of how resources and capabilities will evolve in particular settings (Helfat/Peteraf 2003, p. 1000). A detailed process view and possible contingencies affecting this process have not been sufficiently addressed by the cited publications. Having presented some of the theoretical developments towards more dynamic and evolutionary approaches to the RBV in general, the next subsections therefore focus more thoroughly on recent theoretical discussions related to (a) the resource creation and resource management process and (b) the possible impact of the environment and business setting on this process.

---

[143] The approach apparently attempts to link different streams of RBV literature, such as the more traditional work (e.g. Wernerfelt 1984), dynamic capabilities (Teece et al. 1997), or the knowledge-based view (Kogut/Zander 1992).

(2) Process Perspectives

As stated earlier, it cannot be assumed that the mere possession of resources necessarily leads to competitive advantage. Instead, it is increasingly recognized among RBV scholars that resources have to be accumulated, bundled and exploited in order to create competitive advantage and value for the firm (Eisenhardt/Martin 2000, p. 1116, Fahy 2000, p. 98, Sirmon et al. 2007, p. 273, Hitt et al. 2011, p. 58, Sirmon et al. 2011, p. 1391). A process perspective might represent an important element of a more comprehensive RBV, since "a complete resource-based theory of firm performance would have to include a more general theory of this resource-development process" (Barney/Clark 2007, p. 258). Although it has been recognized that this is an area for further theoretical work (e.g. Priem/Butler 2001, p. 33, Spanos/Lioukas 2001, p. 924), scholars have only recently again called for further investigation and theoretical development on the process of resource acquisition, development and management in the resource-based theory (Barney et al. 2011, p. 1306-1308, Peteraf 2011, p. 1383-1384). As the present thesis intends to take a resource-based process perspective on subsidiary initiative-taking, it is important to understand what progress the RBV has made in this area over time.

Earlier writings have already recognized that, in order for firms to achieve a competitive advantage, appropriate resource acquisition, accumulation and application activities are needed (e.g. Dierickx/Cool 1989, Amit/Schoemaker 1993, Teece et al. 1997). However, these writings do not discuss in detail the process of how resources and capabilities are created, accumulated or deployed in order to generate competitive advantage. Subsequent to these early, more dynamic RBV contributions, various scholars have made attempts to help fill this gap concerning the "process black box" in the RBV. Among them are Godfrey and Gregersen's model of resource generation (Godfrey/Gregersen 1999), Lichtenstein and Brush's dynamic model of resource acquisition, development and effects in new ventures (Lichtenstein/Brush 2001), Bowman and Ambrosini's discussion on resource creation possibilities between strategic business units and the corporate level (Bowman/Ambrosini 2003), Bowman and Collier's contingency approach to resource creation processes (Bowman/Collier 2006), Helfat et al.'s asset orchestration framework (Helfat et al. 2007), Sirmon et al.'s resource management framework (Sirmon et al. 2007) and Sirmon et al.'s resource orchestration framework (Sirmon et al. 2011). These contributions are briefly discussed below. In the end, conclusions are drawn concerning the current understanding of the resource management process in the RBV literature as one important theoretical pillar for the present research.[144]

---

[144] It is not attempted to provide a "full-fledged" overview of the development on process aspects of the RBV. Thus, the portrayed literature only represents a selection, and it is important to note that also other contributions have dealt with (selected) aspects of the resource management process. Further examples include publications by Mahoney (1995), Fahy (2000), Brush et al. (2001), Makadok (2001), or Bowman/Ambrosini (2003).

(1) In order to shed further light on the question of where resources come from in the RBV, Godfrey and Gregersen (1999) provide a causal model of resource generation that builds on three central constructs: entrepreneurial ability, market context and organizational context. The authors' intention is to "generate a coherent, non-tautological model of resource generation that advances theorizing and research within the RBV" (Godfrey/Gregersen 1999, p. 38). The proposed model involves a resource generation process that entails the elements of rent creation and rent preservation. Entrepreneurial ability, as the "capacity to identify, develop, and complete new combinations of existing asset bundles or new asset configurations," is viewed as a central component of the resource generation process that can lead to rent creation (Godfrey/Gregersen 1999, p. 41). It is argued that firms, in order to generate entrepreneurial output, can build on both internally held credit sources and externally available credit markets when identifying and creating new asset combinations. Therefore, entrepreneurial output most often represents a combination of already (internally or externally) existing assets and skills that, when appropriately combined, result in new and unique output capable of delivering economic rents. Once valuable and unique asset combinations are generated, the (external) market structure and (internal) organizational path dependence are expected to influence rent preservation, since they may act as barriers to imitation.[145]

(2) Lichtenstein and Brush (2001), attempting to explain how resource bundles change over time, present a dynamic model of resource acquisition and development and its effects in new venture units. Their model suggests that the resources or resource bundles are (a) identified and acquired, and then later (b) developed and transformed before they may result in an improved competitive advantage, which in the end can improve the new venture unit's performance and its chances of survival. It is assumed that resource bundles develop and change over time as new venture units grow. Therefore the new venture development depends on "certain combinations and re-combinations of organizational resources, and the prudent sequencing of these resources over time" (Lichtenstein/Brush 2001, p. 41). Repeated resource acquisition and resource combination "loops" might be required before a new venture unit eventually becomes self-sustaining. (a) The authors state that, specifically throughout the early phases of new venture development, the *identification and acquisition* of resources are important. During this phase, entrepreneurs apparently must make judgments and decide which resources are relevant for the firm based on their future expectations. (b) In later development stages, it is deemed necessary to *develop*, transform or even

---

[145] With regard to the market structure, Godfrey and Gregersen outline property rights (e.g. patent or trademark law) and imperfect markets (e.g. resource owners withholding critical information) that can help to preserve a new asset's value. Organizational path dependence then implies that characteristics of either the resources or the resource generation process makes resource untradeable in open markets.

divest the resources in order to maintain "the right fit of resources to changes in product/market strategy and in the environment" (Lichtenstein/Brush 2001, p. 37).[146]

(3) Bowman and Ambrosini (2003) take an extended resource-based perspective by integrating certain resource creation arguments from dynamic resource-based approaches (e.g. Teece et al. 1997, Eisenhardt/Martin 2000) into the more traditional RBV (e.g. Wernerfelt 1984, Barney 1991). The authors outline four possibilities (or processes) for resource creation: *reconfiguration, leveraging, learning and integration*. Reconfiguration is described as the transformation and recombination of assets and resources, such as the centralization and consolidation of support activities as the result of acquisitions or mergers. Leveraging refers to the utilization or replication of existing resources in other settings (e.g. other business units or market domain), for instance by extending an existing brand to a wider range of products. Resource creation through learning is illustrated as a process that involves repetition and experimentation and that leads to the more effective and efficient execution of tasks. Finally, integration is viewed as the coordination and integration of the firm's resources to obtain new resource configurations. According to the authors, the process of integration can also include external resources originating from, for example, customers or suppliers, enabling the integration of external resources (e.g. customers' experiences) with internal resources (e.g. product design). Hence, coordination and integration of resources are viewed as "the main sources of process and product innovation" (Bowman/Ambrosini 2003, p. 295).

(4) Bowman and Collier (2006) take a contingency approach to the resource creation process. Their objective is to help clarify which resource creation processes are appropriate for different tasks and environmental contexts. In order to do so, the authors first present different process theories and apply the process thinking to the resource creation process in firms. Subsequently, various resource creation processes are discussed in relation to particular combinations of environmental and organizational factors. With regard to the resource creation process, Bowman and Collier largely draw from teleological process theory (Van De Ven/Poole 1995), which assumes that "the strategy process acts via adaptation and with purpose ... and is driven by creativity as it takes action to reach its envisioned end state" (Bowman/Collier 2006, p. 193). Thus, they claim that the resource creation process should be viewed as a directed process to obtain an end objective (e.g. reaching a firm's profit goal) that can be achieved through appropriate resource management actions taken by the firm's decision makers. Endogenous and exogenous shifts may also lead to changes of the desired end objective or may result in resource changes (e.g. decaying or degraded resources), requiring resource management actions (Bowman/Collier 2006, p. 195). Based on earlier publica-

---

[146] In addition, the authors derive from their empirical study that changes in resources and resource bundles over time may come in different forms. Thus, they differentiate between resource changes in the form of incremental alterations, evolutionary resource development, and discontinuous change.

tions, the authors identify four modes through which resources can be created and changed by firms: resource acquisition, internal resource development and through luck and alliances.[147] (a) According to Bowman and Collier, firms can (purposefully) *acquire* resources from strategic factor markets. This requires that firms be able to identify undervalued resources in the market better than their competitors, because of, for instance, superior foresight about the future resource value or through better market intelligence.[148] (b) As a second resource creation mode, firms may rely on the *internal development* of resources. This is viewed as an idiosyncratic resource creation process that involves, for example, a unique starting position, specific environmental conditions or other particular circumstances of a firm, thus potentially leading to the creation of unique resources. Also, it is seen as a path-dependent process which implies that a firm's "future resource-creation processes are influenced by its past resource-creation process" (Bowman/Collier 2006, pp. 198-199).

(5) Helfat et al. (2007) also take a process perspective in their asset orchestration framework, which is theoretically rooted in the dynamic capabilities literature (e.g. Teece et al. 1997, Eisenhardt/Martin 2000). It is stated that "taking a process perspective can clarify the dynamic interrelationships among actions taken, processes employed, and outcomes achieved in the dynamic capabilities domain" (Helfat et al. 2007, p. 38). Asset orchestration is viewed as a fundamental management function that involves assembling and orchestrating configurations of complementary and co-specialized assets – a function that is particularly critical in dynamic settings (Helfat et al. 2007, p. 25).[149] The scholars argue that asset orchestration consists of two main process: search/selection of resources and configuration and deployment of resources (Helfat et al. 2007, p. 8, Sirmon et al. 2011, p. 1393). (a) The *search and selection* process involves management actions related to the search and identification of assets, the selection of appropriate configurations of co-specialized assets, investment decisions on which resources are to be created, developed or divested, as well as the selection and design of appropriate organizational and governance structures (Helfat et al. 2007, pp. 23-28).[150] (b) The *configuration and deployment* process then entails the actions of orchestrating and

---

[147] As the resource creation modes of luck and alliances are also based on the mechanisms of resource acquisition and resource development, they are not separately discussed here.
[148] In addition to resource acquisition, the authors briefly address resource combination activities by acknowledging that acquired resources (possibly even less unique ones) may be combined with other existing resources to create more unique resource bundles in the end (Bowman/Collier 2006, p. 197).
[149] In line with other RBV writings it is suggested that, in order to create resources, firms can either acquire resources externally or develop resources internally. Internal resource development can substitute or complement external resource acquisition in the case that markets for specific assets are difficult to access. Internally assembling and orchestrating specific constellations of assets can form the basis for "highly differentiated and innovative goods and services that customers want" (Helfat et al. 2007, p. 23).
[150] For instance, firms may search for new resource creation prospects in the form of new product development opportunities, potential partners for strategic alliances, or other possible avenues for further business growth (Helfat et al. 2007, p. 6). The search and selection process may also involve decisions on when to use an acquisition approach or rather use other options for creating, extending or altering the resource base (Helfat et al. 2007, p. 117).

coordinating co-specialized assets, of implementing assets and of nurturing innovation activities (Helfat et al. 2007, p. 28, Sirmon et al. 2011, p. 1393). Deployment includes means by which "bundles of often co-specialized assets are configured and coordinated, by managers as well as by teams and organizational units more generally" (Helfat et al. 2007, p. 116).[151]

(6) Parallel to the theoretical work on "asset orchestration" by Helfat et al. (2007), Sirmon et al. (2007) produced their process framework on "resource management." It follows resource-based logic and focuses on the actions and activities of managers throughout the resource management process.[152] Resource management is understood as the "comprehensive process of structuring the firm's resource portfolio, bundling the resources to build capabilities, and leveraging those capabilities with the purpose of creating and maintaining value" (Sirmon et al. 2007, p. 273). The resource management process thus consists of three sequential process steps: structuring of the resource portfolio, bundling of resources and leveraging capabilities.

(a) *Structuring* of the resource portfolio involves decisions and actions regarding which resources are to be included in the firm's portfolio. In order to structure and modify their resource base, firms have different options: they can acquire (purchase) resources, they can accumulate (internally develop) resources, or they can divest (shed) resources that are under their control. The external acquisition of resources from strategic factor markets can include tangible commodity resources, such as equipment or machinery, more intangible resources such as intellectual capital or brand assets or even complex combinations of tangible and intangible resources through, for instance, mergers and acquisitions (Sirmon et al. 2007, p. 278, Maritan/Peteraf 2011, p. 1375).[153] Furthermore, firms can internally develop and accumulate resources. This might be necessary, as not all required resources are likely available in strategic factor markets. In addition, the idiosyncratic process of internal resource development also leads to improved isolating mechanisms, which in turn can reduce the likelihood of imitation by competitors. Internal resource accumulation often involves learning and thus the growth of the tacit

---

[151] In addition to taking a process perspective, Helfat et al. also point to the relevance of internal and external context. The authors argue that the benefits a firm can generate from dynamic capabilities not only depend on the efficacy of the underlying processes but also on the internal and external setting in which the processes take place (Helfat et al. 2007, p. 2). For instance, environmental needs, stability or constraints may influence how well the processes "fit" the external environment (Helfat et al. 2007, p. 7). Similarly, aspects from the internal setting, such as how a capability is managed or how unique the process is in comparison to competing organizations, may codetermine to what extent competitive advantage can be obtained and how sustainable it will be (Helfat et al. 2007, pp. 14, 45).
[152] Although the RBV appears to be the dominant theoretical perspectives, the work also incorporates elements from contingency theory (Lawrence/Lorsch 1967, Thompson 1967) and organizational learning theory (March 1991).
[153] The concept of resource acquisition in strategic factor markets apparently goes back to earlier research on the traditional, more static RBV by Barney who described factor markets as "where firms buy and sell the resources necessary to implement their strategies" (Barney 1986a, p. 1232).

knowledge base.[154] The accumulation of resources may take place through purely internal development (e.g. inexperienced employees learning new skills from more experienced employees) or through interactions with other market actors (e.g. learning through strategic alliances with companies that possess the desired resources; Sirmon et al. 2007, p. 279, Maritan/Peteraf 2011, p. 1376).[155]

(b) Using their resource portfolio, firms can also undertake *bundling actions*, which involve the integration and combination of resources in order to create or alter capabilities. Bundling activities may range from the more incremental form of stabilizing (maintaining) to enriching (extending) and all the way to the more extensive form of pioneering (radically extending) resources. Stabilizing resources is understood as "minor incremental improvements in existing capabilities" to maintain a competitive advantage by continuously adapting to slowly changing environments.[156] Resource enrichment appears to go somewhat further than stabilizing, as it refers to the augmentation of existing capabilities by learning new skills or by adding complementary resources to current resource bundles.[157] Pioneering reflects a more radical extension of a firm's resource portfolio. Although it may include the "mere" recombination of existing resources, it frequently appears to involve the integration of completely new (and externally acquired) resources with existing ones in order to create new capabilities.[158]

(c) *Leveraging* is understood as process activities related to the application and exploitation of a firm's capabilities in order to take advantage of market opportunities; it entails the actions of mobilizing, coordinating and deploying resources. It is argued that capabilities must be first mobilized before they can be coordinated and deployed. Mobilizing is described as activities related to the design of the leveraging strategy. It involves the identification of the required capabilities and the determination of appropriate capability configurations to exploit market opportunities.[159] Once the required capability configura-

---

[154] The concept of resource accumulation is closely related to the more dynamic RBV approaches (e.g. Dierickx/Cool 1989, Teece et al. 1997).
[155] Here, it becomes clear that resource accumulation, although described as internal development by the authors, can also include more "external" forms of resource development. The accumulation of resources often accompanies the acquisition activities, thereby leading to more unique resource portfolios (Hitt et al. 2011, p. 65). Furthermore, firms can strategically divest or discard resources. This allows them to get rid of no longer required resources or those that do not (sufficiently) contribute to the generation or maintenance of competitive advantage. This could, for example, occur through layoffs of human capital, selling of equipment and machinery or spin-off of business units.
[156] Stabilizing could entail activities such as regular training sessions to "keep employees knowledge and skills up to date" (Sirmon et al. 2007, p. 281).
[157] Complementary resources may have already existed within the firm's resource portfolio, or they may have just been recently acquired with the intention to enrich a specific capability that already exists. It is suggested that, in more uncertain environments, more extensive enriching is frequently required to create or maintain value in those environments (Sirmon et al. 2007, pp. 281-282).
[158] Continuous pioneering may be particularly relevant in highly uncertain markets where new capabilities are frequently needed to gain or maintain competitive advantage (Sirmon et al. 2007, p. 282).
[159] Mobilizing may take place in more or less "proactive" ways. It is proposed that firms can design leveraging strategies to build on the reconfiguration of existing capabilities to provide (additional) value to customers in existing markets. Firms may also more proactively analyze and scan their environment for potential opportunities

tions are identified and a leveraging strategy has been defined, the mobilized capabilities can be coordinated, i.e. efficiently and effectively integrated. Ideally, capabilities are integrated in a way that is difficult for competitors to observe and imitate, thereby enhancing the likelihood of producing more unique value for customers (Sirmon et al. 2007, p. 285, Hitt et al. 2011, p. 65). Finally, after the capabilities have been coordinated the capability configurations can be deployed in the marketplace. This involves the physical application of the capability configurations and, if successfully deployed, creates value for customers and generates a competitive advantage for the firm (Sirmon et al. 2007, pp. 285-286).[160]

(7) Sirmon et al. (2011) subsequently combine Helfat et al.'s asset orchestration framework (Helfat et al. 2007) and Sirmon et al.'s resource management framework (Sirmon et al. 2007) into what they term a "resource orchestration" framework. The authors argue that "similarities and complementarities allow the integration of the frameworks as the foundation to enhance our understanding of manager's actions within the context of the resource-based theory" (Sirmon et al. 2011, p. 1407). Hence, frameworks rooted in the dynamic capabilities literature (i.e. Helfat et al. 2007) and in the more traditional RBV literature (i.e. Sirmon et al. 2007) are integrated and theoretically linked. More specifically, the article discusses how the sub-processes of resource management may apply across the scope of the firm (e.g. functional, divisional or regional scope), across the life cycle of the firm (e.g. start-up, growth, mature or decline stage) and across hierarchical levels (e.g. top, middle and operational level managers). With regard to the resource management process, the authors once again outline activities relating to (a) resource structuring, (b) resource bundling, and (c) resource leveraging, as described in the previous paragraphs. Figure 3.9 provides an overview of the key components of the resource-related processes and the underlying activities as described in the cited literature.

---

related to capabilities (that can be enriched, pioneered or newly created) to provide value to customers in existing, adjacent or even new markets.

[160] In addition to the detailed description of actions and activities in the resource management process, Sirmon et al. discuss the potential impact that the external environment may have on the different phases of the resource management process. Therefore, they include environmental contingencies, such as dynamics of industry structure, stability of market demand, probability of environmental shocks, and environmental munificence into their framework. The authors propose that under conditions of high environmental uncertainty and low environmental munificence, the acquisition of resources that "allow preferential access to future opportunities" will increase the firm's potential for value creation (Sirmon et al. 2007, p. 279).

3 – Research Framework

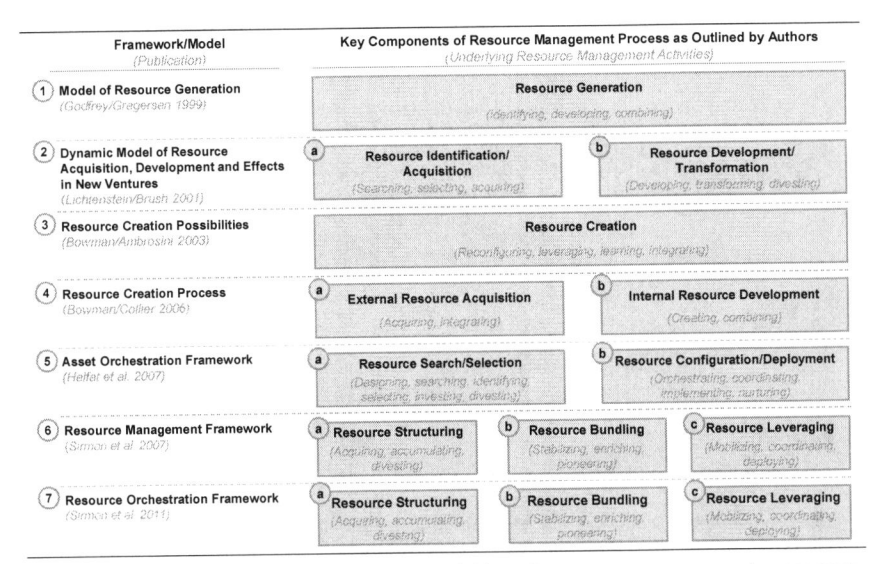

Framework/Model (Publication)	Key Components of Resource Management Process as Outlined by Authors (Underlying Resource Management Activities)		
(1) Model of Resource Generation (Godfrey/Gregersen 1999)	Resource Generation (Identifying, developing, combining)		
(2) Dynamic Model of Resource Acquisition, Development and Effects in New Ventures (Lichtenstein/Brush 2001)	a) Resource Identification/ Acquisition (Searching, selecting, acquiring)	b) Resource Development/ Transformation (Developing, transforming, divesting)	
(3) Resource Creation Possibilities (Bowman/Ambrosini 2003)	Resource Creation (Reconfiguring, leveraging, learning, integrating)		
(4) Resource Creation Process (Bowman/Collier 2006)	a) External Resource Acquisition (Acquiring, integrating)	b) Internal Resource Development (Creating, combining)	
(5) Asset Orchestration Framework (Helfat et al. 2007)	a) Resource Search/Selection (Designing, searching, identifying, selecting, investing, divesting)	b) Resource Configuration/Deployment (Orchestrating, coordinating, implementing, nurturing)	
(6) Resource Management Framework (Sirmon et al. 2007)	a) Resource Structuring (Acquiring, accumulating, divesting)	b) Resource Bundling (Stabilizing, enriching, pioneering)	c) Resource Leveraging (Mobilizing, coordinating, deploying)
(7) Resource Orchestration Framework (Sirmon et al. 2011)	a) Resource Structuring (Acquiring, accumulating, divesting)	b) Resource Bundling (Stabilizing, enriching, pioneering)	c) Resource Leveraging (Mobilizing, coordinating, deploying)

Figure 3.9: Components and underlying activities of resource management processes from existing literature

(3) Contingency Approaches

As described in Subsection 3.3.2.1, the RBV has been criticized for often being too strongly focused on internal firm attributes and thus frequently seems to neglect the environment and the business setting in which a firm operates. As the present thesis is interested in examining the effects of selected environmental and organizational contingencies (in the form of subsidiary roles) on the subsidiary initiative process (which will be viewed as a resource management process), it is necessary to briefly review what the resource-based literature has to say on this matter.

Since the RBV was originally developed as a complement to the "outside-in" perspective of the IO school (e.g. Porter 1980), the resource-based research naturally takes a more "inside-out" view by arguing that it is the heterogeneity in firms' resources that leads to performance differences (Kraaijenbrink et al. 2010, p. 350, Kutschker/Schmid 2011, pp. 840-843). Although the RBV predominantly takes an internal perspective to explain heterogeneity in firm performance, the external setting has not been neglected in all cases. For instance, Amit and Shoemaker recognize that the "applicability of the firm's bundle of resources and capabilities to a particular industry setting ... will determine the available rents" (Amit/Schoemaker 1993, p. 39). Similarly, Teece et al. argue that firms need to renew their resources and capabilities "so as to achieve congruence with the changing business environment," particularly in rapidly changing environments when future market and competitive moves are difficult to predict (Teece et al. 1997, p. 515). Despite acknowledging the relevance of the contextual setting, few insights are provided into how resource-based advantages can be built up in particular circumstances. Yet, achieving a better understanding of how they are created requires a detailed understanding not only of the resource management processes and activities, but also of how the process is linked to internal and external contextual settings (Bowman/Collier 2006, p. 192, Helfat et al. 2007, p. 43, Sirmon/Hitt 2009, p. 1392). Accordingly, it has been stated that resource-based "theory building about and empirical inquiry into the processes through which strategic resources lead to high performance, how value is appropriated and how resources interact with the environment and strategy is essential" (Crook et al. 2008, p. 1153).[161] As a result, it can be presumed that linking contingency approaches (e.g. Lawrence/Lorsch 1967) to the RBV, and more specifically to a resource-based process perspective, may be valuable for resource-based theoretical advancement and empirical research.

Certain conclusions on the relationship between the process of resource management and certain contingency factors can already be drawn from the literature presented in this subsection. All of the seven (process-oriented) publications acknowledge and include, in more or less detail, different internal and external contingencies that impact the process of resource management. Among the external contingency factors that have been mentioned are, for instance, environmental stability (Bowman/Collier 2006, Helfat et al. 2007), stability of market demand, probability of environmental shocks, environmental munificence (Sirmon et al. 2007), market structure (Godfrey/Gregersen 1999) and, more generally, environmental needs and constraints (Helfat et al. 2007). Examples of organizational context factors that may impact the resource management process include a firm's product and market strategy (Lichtenstein/Brush 2001), organizational structure, governance and incentive systems (Bowman/Ambrosini 2003, Sirmon et al. 2011), developmental stage (Sirmon et al. 2011) and task complexity (Bowman/Collier 2006).[162]

---

[161] Similarly, Freiling argues that "the RBV can stand to benefit considerably from an extension that takes the embeddedness of the firm in markets, industries, and the business environment into account" (Freiling 2008, p. 34).

[162] Among them, different publications already present rather sophisticated frameworks which explicitly link resource management processes to contingency theory (i.e. Godfrey/Gregersen 1999, Bowman/Collier 2006, Helfat et al. 2007 and Sirmon et al. 2007). For example, Godfrey and Gregersen (1999) – in addition to examining the entrepreneurial resource creation processes – link the RBV with contingency theory to investigate what possible impact the market and organizational contexts may have. Applying a contingency approach to resource creation processes, Bowman and Collier (2006) argue that different contingent circumstances will require different resource creation pathways and process. The authors introduce task complexity and environmental dynamism as contingency factors in order to discuss in more detail what resource-creation processes could be congruent with specific combinations of the contingency variables. Helfat et al. (2007) stress the context dependence of the asset orchestration processes. They suggest that different environmental and organizational factors influence the resource-oriented processes and thus impact the generation of competitive advantage and its sustainability. Similarly, Sirmon et al. (2007) provide a theoretical framework in which environmental uncertainty as the only contingency variable is modeled to impact the processes of resource structuring, bundling and leveraging.

In addition to these process-related contingency works in the resource-based literature, a number of other publications have taken more general contingency approaches, highlighting the impact of contingent factors on the likelihood of resource-based advantages (rather than on resource-related processes). For instance, Miller and Shamsie (1996) present a contingency resource-based framework and empirically demonstrate that property-based resources are more valuable in stable and predictable environments, whereas knowledge-based resources are more valuable in changing and unpredictable environments. Another contingent resource-based approach is presented by Brush and Artz (1999), who investigate the contingencies between resources, capabilities and performance in the medical service industry. Their empirical study reveals that the value of resources and capabilities is contingent on the context in which they are applied, and more specifically on the information asymmetry characteristics of the product market. Moreover, Fahy and Hooley (2002) adopt a contingency perspective on the RBV when examining the value of resources and the patterns of resource development and accumulation in different business settings. Research by Aragón-Correa and Sharma (2003) also integrates aspects from contingency theory and dynamic capabilities when discussing how a firm's general competitive environment may influence the development of the specific dynamic capability of "proactive environmental strategy building." More specifically, the authors examine the possible influence of environmental uncertainty, complexity and munificence as moderators between the specific dynamic capability and competitive advantage.

In addition to the literature outlined above, three more recent publications also take contingency approaches to resource-related processes and thus provide additional relevant insights. Sirmon and Hitt (2009) examine the contingent nature of resource investment and resource deployment decisions and activities. Ambrosini and Bowman's (2009) journal contribution attempts to review and synthesize the existing literature on dynamic capabilities. The scholars identify the underlying processes of dynamic capabilities and also summarize the internal and external factors that enable or inhibit these processes as outlined in previous literature. Largely in line with the conclusions drawn here, the external contingency factors presented in the paper are environmental complexity, uncertainty, munificence and home country characteristics.[163] As internal factors, the authors present managerial behavior, perceptions, proactivity, leadership, complementary organizational resources and social capital. Lastly, Hitt et al. (2011) provide an input-output model of the resource orchestration process underlying the concept of strategic entrepreneurship.[164] More specifically, the paper argues that the entrepre-

---

[163] The authors largely draw from the same literature that was outlined previously in this thesis: Teece et al. (1997), Eisenhardt and Martin (2000) and Aragon-Correa and Sharma (2003).
[164] Strategic entrepreneurship is defined as involving "both entrepreneurship's opportunity-seeking behaviors and strategic management's advantage-seeking behaviors" and therefore addresses both the issue of exploiting existing competitive advantages and exploring for new opportunities in the current environmental context (Hitt et

neurial process of structuring, bundling and leveraging resources is context-specific and influenced by factors at the environmental, organizational and individual levels. Among the environmental factors mentioned are environmental munificence, environmental dynamism and interconnectedness, such as a firm's network relationships. Organizational factors examined include top management's leadership abilities and skills to develop and grow the firm and to promote an entrepreneurial culture in the firm. Lastly, financial capital and human capital are proposed as individual-level factors that influence the resource orchestration process (Hitt et al. 2011, pp. 60-64). Figure 3.10 summarizes the different environmental and organizational contingency factors as outlined in the literature.

Environmental (External) Contingency Factors *(Publications)*	Organizational (Internal) Contingency Factors *(Publications)*
• **Environmental stability/dynamism** *(Miller/Shamsie 1996, Aragón-Correa/Sharma 2003, Bowman/Collier 2006, Helfat et al. 2007, Sirmon et al. 2007)*	• **Product and market strategy** *(Lichtenstein/Brush 2001)*
• **Environmental complexity** *(Aragón-Correa/Sharma 2003, Ambrosini/Bowman 2009)*	• **Organizational structure** *(Bowman/Ambrosini 2003, Sirmon et al. 2011)*
• **Stability of market demand** *(Sirmon et al. 2007)*	• **Governance and incentive systems** *(Bowman/Ambrosini 2003, Sirmon et al. 2011)*
• **Probability of environmental shocks** *(Sirmon et al. 2007)*	• **Firm's developmental stage** *(Sirmon et al. 2011)*
• **Environmental munificence** *(Aragón-Correa/Sharma 2003, Sirmon et al. 2007)*	• **Task complexity** *(Bowman/Collier 2006)*
• **Environmental needs and constraints** *(Helfat et al. 2007)*	• **Complementary organizational resources** *(Ambrosini/Bowman 2009)*
• **Market structure** *(Godfrey/Gregersen 1999)*	• **Managerial behavior, perceptions, proactivity and leadership** *(Ambrosini/Bowman 2009)*
• **Characteristics of product markets** *(Brush/Artz 1999)*	
• **Home country characteristics** *(Ambrosini/Bowman 2009)*	
• **Resource investment by competitors** *(Sirmon/Hitt 2009)*	

Figure 3.10: Key contingency factors outlined in resource management literature

al. 2011, pp. 59, 69). Although Hitt et al.'s model does not directly represent a contingency approach, the article draws on numerous factors that have been previously applied as contingency factors (e.g. environmental munificence, environmental dynamism). Moreover, the authors argue that strategic entrepreneurship and the underlying resource orchestration process are context-specific (Hitt et al. 2011, pp. 59, 64, 65, 69).

(4) Conclusions from Advancements of the Resource-Based View

The different contributions presented here show that the resource-based creation of value and competitive advantage is clearly much more complex and multifaceted than originally described by, for instance, Wernerfelt (1984) or Barney (1991). The generation of competitive advantage not only requires an effective and efficient resource management process, but also necessitates the consideration of and adaptation to environmental, organizational and possibly even individual context factors. But what conclusions can be drawn from the theoretical advancements of the RBV towards a more dynamic, process-oriented and contingency perspective with regards to the present research?

First, it can be concluded that theoretical sub-streams have developed that take a more dynamic approach to the RBV, recognizing that long-term competitive advantage is often unrealistic and that resources and capabilities are not necessarily static, but might change and develop over time. Especially in dynamic environments, competitive advantage is frequently short-lived, forcing firms to quickly adapt their resource stock to the changing requirements of the market.[165] In line with these considerations, it has been suggested that a dynamic resource-based approach can be seen as a complement or an extension to the more traditional RBV (see Zucchella/Scabini 2007, p. 86, Ambrosini/ Bowman 2009, p. 29, Lockett et al. 2009, p. 14) or that it should even be subsumed under the more general RBV (Barney et al. 2001, p. 630, Helfat/Peteraf 2011, p. 1386).

Second, it can be concluded that the resource-based theory has made progress towards developing a more comprehensive process perspective. The focus of theoretical development in the RBV seems to have shifted somewhat from discussions regarding the possession and control of specific resources towards managerial and organizational processes concerned with the structuring and leveraging of resources to generate sustained competitive advantage. Thus, the previously criticized process "black box" (see e.g. Priem/Butler 2001, p. 33) may already have become more transparent. It seems as if firms may take different (synchronized) actions to acquire, accumulate, bundle and exploit resources in order to achieve resource configurations that provide the potential for sustained competitive advantage.

Third, the clear dichotomy between the traditional thinking of the IO school and the RBV as proposed by some scholars may indeed be too "artificial." Rather than relying on "unitary explanations" that emphasize either resources or environment, more complementary views seem appropriate that acknowledge that both the contextual setting in which a firm operates and resource-based aspects should be viewed jointly when

---

[165] For instance, Ahokangas et al. (2010) discuss the notion of "temporary competitive advantage" from a dynamic resource-based view at more length.

attempting to explain how sustained competitive advantage is obtained. Hence, contingent approaches to the resource management process may better reflect the understanding that both resources and the internal and external contextual setting play a critical role when it comes to the performance and success of a firm. Such a combined theoretical view could provide a more complete picture on the rent creation process, and consequently may help to better explain how and under what circumstances resources and resource management activities will lead to sustained competitive advantage in firms (Mahoney/Pandian 1992, p. 375, Spanos/Lioukas 2001, p. 912, Makadok 2001, p. 391, Fahy/Hooley 2002, p. 251, Kutschker/Schmid 2011, p. 844).

Fourth, the theoretical advancement in the resource-based literature further underlines the critical role that managers play in the resource management process. The process is, in most cases, assumed to be a sequence of deliberate and purposeful actions by the firm's decision makers (Bowman/Collier 2006, p. 196, Helfat et al. 2007, p. 5) that are often based on strategic resource designs (Helfat et al. 2007, p. 46, Sirmon et al. 2007, p. 285). For instance, managers must analyze and assess their current internal resource situation and their external environment (Bowman/Collier 2006, p. 196) or they have to make strategic decisions on what resources to acquire, develop or divest (Lichtenstein/Brush 2001, p. 37). Thus, it is not only the unique resources held by a firm that may explain heterogeneity in performance, but also the strategic choices and the abilities of management related to the structuring, bundling and leveraging of these resources that influence the extent to which competitive advantage can be achieved (Fahy 2000, p. 99, Sirmon et al. 2007, p. 275, Sirmon et al. 2008, p. 922).[166]

3.3.2.3 Resource-Based View in International Business Literature

(1) Application in International Business Research

This research is positioned in the field of international business research, and specifically within the domains of subsidiary entrepreneurship and subsidiary roles. Hence, it must be clarified to what extent the RBV represents an appropriate approach for the investigation of phenomena within this domain. Although the RBV initially was not viewed with an international scope (Fladmoe-Lindquist/Tallman 1994, p. 56), it has grown to become an influential theoretical perspective in international business research (e.g. Peng 2001, p. 803, Fahy 2002, p. 62) and is considered to "offer great potential to the study of the MNE" (Birkinshaw/Pedersen 2009, p. 374). Given the rapid diffusion of the theory in the IB field as the result of its relative advantages, its compatibility with other theoretically perspectives, its simplicity, its trialability and its visibility,

---

[166] Additional contributions that underline the importance of managers and their activities concerning resource management are, for instance, Mahoney 1995, Fahy 2000, Adner and Helfat 2003, Garbuio et al. 2011, or Maritan/Peteraf 2011.

Peng (2001, p. 806) argues that the RBV represents a "theoretical innovation." Between the years 1992 and 2000 alone, Peng identified 61 articles in leading IB journals that cited the two key RBV papers by Barney (1991) and Wernerfelt (1984). As areas of central interest for the application of the RBV in IB research, Peng highlights the management of MNCs, strategic alliances, foreign market entries, international entrepreneurship and emerging market strategies.

Traditionally, the RBV has focused on the parent organization and the home country as the main points of origin for unique resources and capabilities and hence of potential competitive advantage (e.g. Dunning 2008, p. 120). However, it is increasingly acknowledged that foreign subsidiaries of multinational corporations might also serve as important providers of strategic resources and capabilities (e.g. Gupta/Govindarajan 1994, Birkinshaw et al. 1998, Schmid/Schurig 2003, Cantwell/Mudambi 2005, Holm et al. 2005). These units therefore represent channels through which MNCs can obtain access to geographically dispersed resources and capabilities that can then be transferred to other units of the MNC, such as headquarters or sister subsidiaries (e.g. Ambos et al. 2006, Schotter/Bontis 2009, Schmid/Hartmann 2011). Hence, they are seen as critical to the generation of competitive advantage for the entire MNC (Bartlett/ Ghoshal 1986, p. 94). In line with resourced-based thinking, contributions have looked at topics such as the development of subsidiary capabilities (e.g. Fahy 2002, Schmid/ Schurig 2003), the transfer of knowledge, resources and capabilities between subsidiary units and headquarters or *vice versa* (e.g. Gupta/Govindarajan 2000, Rugman/Verbeke 2001, Ambos et al. 2006) and subsidiary development and subsidiary initiative-taking (e.g. Birkinshaw 1996, Birkinshaw/Hood 1998d, Birkinshaw et al. 1998).

Although the RBV is considered a rich theory that offers much potential to generate new insights about MNC subsidiaries (Birkinshaw/Pedersen 2009, p. 375), utilizing a resource-based perspective to examine this does not come without challenges. Since the resource-based perspective originally aimed at explaining performance heterogeneity at the firm level, it assumes that unique resources and capabilities are developed and held at the firm level (Barney 1991, pp. 101-103, Birkinshaw 2001, p. 387). Consequently, as the relevant level of analysis for the RBV is originally the firm as a whole, certain adaptions or translations are necessary when applying the theory to the MNC subsidiary (Birkinshaw 2001, p. 386). However, few contributions appear to explicitly address the modifications that are necessary when taking a resource-based perspective at the subsidiary level. Among those contributions are the writings by Birkinshaw and colleagues (Birkinshaw/Hood 1998d, Birkinshaw et al. 1998, Birkinshaw 2000, Birkinshaw/Pedersen 2009) and by Rugman and Verbeke (2001). Within these publications, two central "translation issues" seem to prevail. First, it must be acknowledged that unique resources and capabilities can, in addition to the firm level, also be held and developed at the subsidiary level. Second, these subsidiary-level resources and capabilities must be combined and effectively utilized on a global level in order to provide potential competitive advantage for the firm as a whole (Birkinshaw/Hood 1998d, p. 791, Birkinshaw et al. 1998, pp. 224-225, Birkinshaw 2000, p. 103, Birkinshaw/Pedersen 2009, p. 374, Rugman et al. 2011a). This again requires that subsidiary resources and capabilities can be transferred to other locations in the MNC and that they be complementary to other resources and capabilities elsewhere in the corporation (Birkinshaw 2001, pp. 387-394). As the present thesis also intends to apply the RBV at the subsidiary level, the necessary adaptions to the theory are reviewed below.

(2) Subsidiary-Level Resources and Capabilities

Possession of subsidiary resources and capabilities: Numerous publications have recognized that unique resources and capabilities can exist within foreign subsidiary units (e.g. Gupta/Govindarajan 1994, Birkinshaw et al. 1998, Schmid/Schurig 2003, Cantwell/Mudambi 2005, Holm et al. 2005). However, clearly distinguishing between firm-level and subsidiary-level resources and capabilities is not always an easy undertaking. Although many tangible resources (e.g. plant, equipment or human capital) seem to be frequently held at the subsidiary level and intangible resources (e.g. financial resources, global brand names) are predominantly located at the firm level, a clear differentiation for capabilities is often more difficult (Birkinshaw/Pedersen 2009, p. 378).[167] Whereas certain capabilities might be easily attributable to the subsidiary level (e.g. local labor or supplier relations), others may reside somewhere in between the firm and subsidiary level. To illustrate this point, Birkinshaw (2000, p. 104) provides the hypothetical example of a "total quality management capability" that is dispersed throughout an MNC. Such a capability might have its origin in one location, but it is subsequently often transferred and applied in numerous locations of the MNC. Despite such "allocation challenges," the current literature clearly shows that subsidiaries can be in possession or control of subsidiary-specific resources and capabilities (Birkinshaw 2000, p. 104, Birkinshaw/Pedersen 2009, p. 379). Figure 3.11 gives an overview of resources and capabilities that can be held at different levels of the MNC.

---

[167] Birkinshaw and Pedersen (2009, p. 378) note that there certainly are numerous exceptions. For instance, certain employees or plant equipment may be relocated from on level to the other, or reputation or brand names may be specific to a local subsidiary. However, the authors attempt to make the point that resources and capabilities – in general – can be split between the two levels of analysis.

	Subsidiary Level	Firm Level
Resources	• Physical resources (e.g. plant, equipment, locally sourced raw materials) • Human resources employed in the subsidiary • Reputation with local customers and suppliers	• Financial resources (e.g. borrowing capacity) • Organizational resources (e.g. formal reporting system) • Centrally controlled access to suppliers • Patents and trademarks
Capabilities	• Rapid product innovation • Lean production systems • Effective distribution • Customer-focused marketing • Data processing skills	• Firm-specific capabilities (e.g. organizational culture supporting innovation, quality) • Ability to leverage subsidiary resources and capabilities on a firm-wide basis

Figure 3.11: Sample resources and capabilities at different levels of the MNC
Sources: Birkinshaw 2000, p. 104 and Birkinshaw/Pedersen 2009, p. 379.

Development of subsidiary resources and capabilities: In addition to the resource-based literature dealing with the differentiation between firm-level and subsidiary-level resources and capabilities, other work has concentrated on the creation and development of critical or specialized resources and capabilities at the subsidiary level (e.g. Birkinshaw et al. 1998, Andersson et al. 2001a, Frost 2001, Andersson et al. 2002, Özsomer/Gençtürk 2003, Schmid/Schurig 2003, Holm et al. 2005). However, literature dealing with how resources and capabilities are actually created and developed in foreign subsidiaries seems to remain limited (Andersson et al. 2002, p. 991, Schmid/ Schurig 2003, p. 757). Resource-based work on subsidiary resource and capability development particularly highlights three different aspects that may impact the extent to which subsidiary units may actually acquire and develop critical or specialized resources and capabilities: (a) the local subsidiary environment and local business relationships characteristics, (b) corporate and intra-firm relationship characteristics and (c) subsidiary activities and characteristics (in particular, see Birkinshaw/Hood 1997, p. 341, 1998d, p. 781, Andersson et al. 2001a, p. 1014, Peng 2001, p. 811, Rugman/Verbeke 2001, pp. 243-244, Özsomer/Gençtürk 2003, p. 3, Schmid/Schurig 2003, p. 762).

(a) While more traditional thinking has considered the home country of the MNC a main source of strategically important resources and capabilities (Birkinshaw/Hood 1998d, p. 773, Birkinshaw et al. 1998, p. 221), more recent writings argue that the geographical dispersion of activities gives the MNC better chances to benefit from the different resources that exist in the diverse environments in which it operates (Schmid/Schurig 2003, p. 756). More specifically, the activities of foreign subsidiaries in their local host country networks and their relationships and interactions with local actors expose MNCs to new knowledge, opportunities and ideas (e.g. McEvily/Zaheer 1999, p. 1135, Frost 2001, p. 101, Andersson et al. 2002, p. 979, Foss/Pedersen 2002, p. 55, Almeida/ Phene 2004, p. 848). For instance, well established relations with local institutions such as suppliers, customers or universities permit the subsidiary to gain access more easily to unique resources and knowledge, which represent potent foundations for subsidiary innovations and hence for MNC competitive advantage (Frost 2001, p. 101, Mu et al. 2007, p. 81, Williams 2009, p. 95). It is assumed that, particularly in dynamic local business environments, subsidiaries are encouraged more to develop and upgrade their resources and capabilities (Birkinshaw/Hood 1998d, p. 790). Finally, foreign subsidiaries may obtain additional resources through direct and indirect government support or investments (Birkinshaw/Hood 1997, p. 344, 1998c, p. 790).

(b) The development of critical subsidiary resources and capabilities is also influenced by intra-firm relationships between a subsidiary unit and other MNC units. It is suggested (e.g. in Hedlund 1986 and Bartlett/Ghoshal 1989) that the subsidiary's embeddedness in the intra-organizational network might provide access to unique resources or spur the development of critical capabilities (Schmid/Schurig 2003, p. 761). For example, close and frequent relationships between the subsidiary and other internal MNC units such as headquarters, internal suppliers or internal customers expose the subsidiary to the vast information resources and entrepreneurial opportunities that exist within the MNC network (e.g. Tsai/Ghoshal 1998, p. 465, Tseng et al. 2004, p. 99). Also, the corporate parent might directly provide unique and valuable resources to the subsidiary in the form of, for example, new plant, proprietary technology or other direct investments. In addition, headquarters can exert influence on the resource and capability efforts of subsidiaries by defining the structural context in which the subsidiary operates. This context, in the form of administrative or cultural mechanisms, for instance, can impact the extent to which resources and capabilities can be obtained at the subsidiary level (Birkinshaw/Hood 1997, p. 341, 1998d, p. 787).

(c) Finally, changes to the stock of subsidiary resources can be influenced by the subsidiary itself. Subsidiaries can pursue different pathways to resource creation and development. They may gradually grow their resources and capabilities in line with their current scope of responsibilities as assigned by headquarters, or they may more independently and proactively seek out opportunities to create and develop new resources or capabilities, for instance in the form of entrepreneurial activities (Birkinshaw/Hood 1997, p. 343, 1998d, p. 786). These resource creation processes are again affected by the set of resources and capabilities the subsidiary currently possesses, thus leading to a path-dependent resource development cycle (Birkinshaw/Hood 1997, p. 343, Birkinshaw et al. 1998, p. 224). Further examples of subsidiary-specific factors that may influence the resource creation and development process are the subsidiary management's entrepreneurial orientation (Birkinshaw/Hood 1998d, p. 789) or the subsidiary entrepreneurial culture (Birkinshaw et al. 1998, p. 227).[168]

It must be noted, however, that these environmental and organizational factors that influence the creation and development of subsidiary resources and capabilities are not to be seen as separate resource creation mechanisms. Instead, they should be viewed as interdependent and complementary means. For instance, autonomous subsidiary resource creation processes in the form of initiatives depend, at least in part, on the structural context established by the parent company (Birkinshaw/Hood 1997, p. 343). In addition, the given resource profile of a subsidiary may not only impact subsequent resource creation but also influence the decisions made at headquarters or even influence the standing of the subsidiary in the local environment (Birkinshaw/Hood 1998d, p. 775). Figure 3.12 broadly summarizes these relationships.

The literature examined above demonstrates the increasing awareness that, within the MNC network, foreign subsidiaries can possess, create and develop strategically important resources and capabilities. Particularly with the RBV as a firm-level theory, a question that needs to be addressed is under which circumstances can these resources and capabilities at the subsidiary level help to generate competitive advantage for the entire firm. However, it appears that little research has investigated how these resources are further transferred, bundled and leveraged in the wider MNC in order to contribute to competitive advantage at the firm-level (Birkinshaw/Hood 1998d, p. 791, Birkinshaw et al. 1998, p. 225, Schmid/Schurig 2003, p. 775).

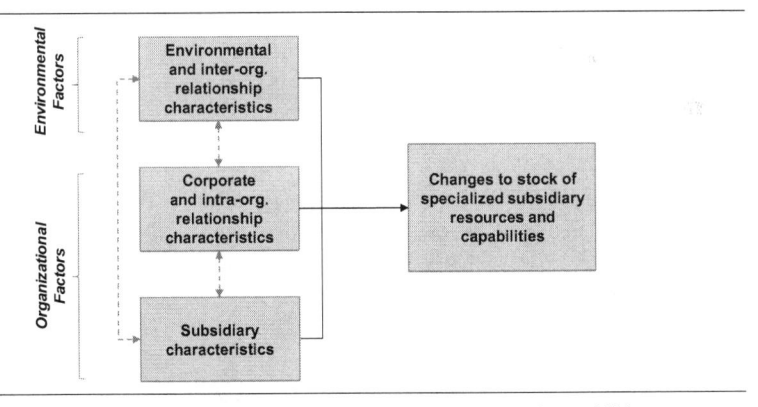

Figure 3.12: Development of specialized subsidiary resources and capabilities
Sources: Based on Birkinshaw/Hood 1997, p. 342; 1998c, p. 775

---

[168] As shown in Subsection 2.2.4, more than 50 factors have been shown to impact subsidiary initiative-taking. However, here only factors that explicitly impact resources and capability development are portrayed. While not explicitly mentioned, resources at subsidiary level may also be depleted (Birkinshaw/Hood 1998d, p. 786).

Dissemination of subsidiary-level resources and capabilities: A particular challenge for the MNC is to harvest the potential benefits that reside in the geographically dispersed resources and capabilities. It has been observed that if the subsidiary-specific resources and capabilities remain locally focused and are not further leveraged within the MNC, they cannot contribute to competitive advantage of the firm (Luo/Peng 1999, p. 289). This implies that resources and capabilities that are held in the foreign subsidiary need to be transferred and utilized in other parts of the MNC network (Peng 2001, p. 811, Birkinshaw/Pedersen 2009, p. 379). It has furthermore been stated that the integration of the dispersed subsidiary resources and capabilities in fact represents the particular advantage of the multinational corporation (Madhok/Phene 2001, p. 253, Andersson 2003, p. 426). However, resource "stickiness" and path-dependent development processes may cause resources and capabilities to be largely bound to the local subsidiary and difficult to disentangle from the local context (Birkinshaw/Hood 1998d, p. 781, Birkinshaw et al. 1998, p. 224).

Overall, only a limited number of publications have investigated the particular topic of resource and capability transfer from foreign subsidiaries to other units of the MNC (Ambos et al. 2006, p. 295, Schotter/Bontis 2009, p. 150). Among these, aside from the contributions of Birkinshaw and colleagues (Birkinshaw et al. 1998, Birkinshaw 2000), are the works of Frost (2001), Hakanson and Nobel (2000, 2001), Rugman and Verbeke (2001), Ambos et al. (2006) and Schotter and Bontis (2009). While most of these publications focus on the antecedents of resource transfer, only the contributions by (a) Birkinshaw and co-authors and (b) Rugman and Verbeke seem to explicitly address the conditions necessary for subsidiary-specific resources and capabilities to lead to firm-level competitive advantage.[169] These are reviewed briefly and the implications summarized below.

(a) Birkinshaw and his co-authors deliberately follow a resource-based perspective and accordingly conceptualize subsidiaries as heterogeneous bundles of resources. Furthermore, the authors formulate four necessary criteria for subsidiary resources and capabilities to lead to firm-specific advantages (FSAs).[170] It is argued that, first, resources and capabilities must be transferable from the subsidiary to the other parts of the MNC. Only those resources that are not (entirely) bound to the location of the subsidiary can be potentially leveraged by the wider MNC and provide the grounds for

---

[169] On the related manner of subsidiary knowledge resource transfer, Ciabuschi et al. argue that "literature focusing on knowledge flows seldom addresses the question of whether or not such flows actually benefit the organization" and "... it is often implicitly assumed that the more knowledge that flows inside the organization, the better" (Ciabuschi et al. 2010, p. 473).

[170] Although firm-specific advantage and competitive advantage are often used interchangeably (Erramilli et al. 1997, p. 736), there are subtle differences. Firm-specific advantages (FSA), for instance in the form of core skills or unique know-how, merely provide the grounds for competitive advantage. According to Birkinshaw et al. (1998, p. 224) FSA refers to "the MNC's ability to overcome its liability of foreignness." It hence can be expected that further activities are required to translate FSAs into actual competitive advantage (Aharoni 1993, p. 38) which represents "a sustainable low-cost or differentiated position against competitors" (Birkinshaw et al. 1998, p. 224).

potential FSAs. Second, subsidiary resources need to specialized, which is defined as "superior to those elsewhere in the corporation" (Birkinshaw et al. 1998, p. 224). The authors thereby use a less strict requirement than the classic RBV (e.g. Barney 1991), which entails that resources need to be valuable, rare, imperfectly imitable and not substitutable. It is argued that subsidiary resources and capabilities "only" need to be specialized, as the MNC's ability to effectively assemble and combine them in a unique and non-imitable way is the source of competitive advantage (Birkinshaw et al. 1998, p. 224, Birkinshaw 2000, p. 106, Birkinshaw/Pedersen 2009, p. 380). Third, headquarters must recognize that the subsidiary is in control of specialized resources and capabilities, denoting the "widespread understanding and acceptance ... in other parts of the MNC" (Birkinshaw et al. 1998, p. 224). This might occur through either a top-down process in which headquarters identifies leading subsidiaries, or in a bottom-up manner whereby subsidiary management demonstrates its expertise and abilities. Fourth, the non-location-bound, specialized and recognized subsidiary resources and capabilities need to be effectively utilized by the MNC to become part of firm-specific advantages. This again requires that they be complimentary with other resources within the MNC. The authors maintain that it is, in particular, the MNC's (firm-level) ability to effectively combine the various resources in the firm in a unique and non-imitable way that provides the grounds for competitive advantage (Birkinshaw et al. 1998, p. 225, Birkinshaw 2000, p. 106, Birkinshaw/Pedersen 2009, p. 380).

(b) Rugman and Verbeke (2001) also apply a resource-based perspective when introducing their concept of subsidiary-specific advantages (SSAs).[171] The notion of SSAs reflects resources and capabilities that are developed within foreign subsidiaries but that can lead to value creation for the wider MNC. However, although SSAs can be exploited globally (e.g. embodied in internationally marketed products or services), it is proposed that the underlying subsidiary-specific bundles of resources and capabilities do not necessarily have to be easily transferable (Rugman/Verbeke 2001, p. 244).[172] It is argued that the development of SSAs is dependent upon four criteria. First, the bundles of subsidiary-specific resources and capabilities must contain tacit and context-specific elements, and they must also be dispersed across several individuals within the subsidiary. This is presumed to result in mobility barriers that make the transfer of these bundles within the MNC somewhat difficult and may therefore require the transformation

---

[171] In addition, Moore and Heeler also discuss the construct of subsidiary-specific advantages (Moore/Heeler 1998, Moore 2001). However, they apply it in a different context and view it as an extension of Dunning's eclectic paradigm that entails firm-specific (or ownership) advantages, country-specific (or location) advantages and internationalization advantages – also known as the OLI framework (Dunning 1977, see also Kutschker/Schmid 2011, pp. 460-465). Moreover, Moore and Heeler argue that subsidiary-specific advantages are entirely location-bound and thus not shared across the MNC (Moore/Heeler 1998, p. 7, Moore 2001, p. 281), whereas Rugman and Verbeke propose that subsidiary-specific advantages can, although with difficulties, be diffused throughout the MNC (Rugman/Verbeke 2001, p. 244).

[172] Subsidiary-specific advantages therefore combine characteristics of both non-location-bound FSAs (i.e. global exploitation) and location-bound FSAs (i.e. difficult transferability within MNC; Rugman/Verbeke 2001, p. 248).

into non-location-bound resources by the subsidiary or possibly even the parent company. Second, it is stated that SSAs have to represent a "capability gap" within the MNC. This requirement seems to be analogous to the one put forward by Birkinshaw et al. (1998) concerning "specialized resources," which implies that the subsidiary resources must be superior to others in the MNC network. Third, SSA development necessitates the "perceived absence of negative externalities on other MNC operations," such as self-serving or empire-building behavior. Fourth, there must be synergies or "interest interdependence" between the rent creation potential of the non-location-bound FSAs at firm-level and SSAs at the subsidiary level (Rugman/Verbeke 2001, pp. 243-244). The authors identify three patterns of SSA development that directly relate to the four different subsidiary initiative types as defined by Birkinshaw (1997, 1998a, 2000) and described in more detail in Subsection 3.4.4 herein.[173]

Based on the contributions by Birkinshaw and colleagues as well as by Rugman et al., it can be concluded that two different pathways are possible for subsidiary resources and capabilities to potentially contribute to firm-level competitive advantage, as outlined below in Figure 3.13. First, advantage-creating resources at the subsidiary level can be either (a) entirely non-location-bound and easily transferable or (b) less easily transferable, thus requiring additional resource transformations inside the foreign subsidiary. In both cases, the transferability within the MNC in general can be viewed as a first key requirement that often does not represent an easy and straightforward task.[174] Second, these resources and capabilities need to be specialized, which is understood as superior to those available elsewhere in the MNC. Compared to the resource requirements found in the RBV, which postulates that rent-generating resources need to be valuable, rare, imperfectly imitable and not substitutable, this represents a less strict condition. This appears sufficient, as it is not only the specialized and superior resources alone that are the source of competitive advantage, but rather the firm-level ability to effectively assemble and combine these specialized resources in a unique and non-imitable way. Third, these transferable and specialized resources must also be recognized and accepted (or positively perceived) within the MNC. Only if the subsidiary resources are

---

[173] Global market initiatives are viewed as a pattern in which non-location-bound FSAs are generated autonomously in the subsidiary and which can then be directly transferred to other MNC units or which are embodied in internationally marketed products. Internal market and global-internal hybrid initiatives reflect patterns in which non-location-bound FSAs are created in the subsidiary, but with the process being largely influenced by decisions and guidelines of headquarters. Local market initiatives represent patterns through which location-bound FSAs are developed within the foreign subsidiary and, at a later point in time, are transformed into non-location-bound FSAs by the subsidiary itself. Therefore, subsidiary initiatives can result in either non-location-bound FSAs or partially location-bound SSAs that need to be transformed into non-location-bound FSAs before they can be leveraged globally (Rugman/Verbeke 2001; see also Rugman et al. 2011a).

[174] Among the factors that are believed to impact the resource and capability transfer within organizations are, for instance, resource characteristics such as resource stickiness (e.g. Szulanski 1996, 2000), ability and willingness of recipients (e.g. Cohen/Levinthal 1990) or context specificity, time and cost problems (e.g. Forsgren et al. 2000, Andersson 2003). As the primary focus of this thesis is on the process of resource development and deployment at the subsidiary level, the issue of transferability (e.g. facilitating or impeding conditions) will not be further discussed here.

widely understood and recognized in other parts of the firm will they be further considered and leveraged. Fourth, the subsidiary resources need to be complementary with other resources in the MNC and provide the potential for firm-level synergies. Fifth, in order to fully realize the potential for competitive advantage in the FSAs and SSAs as "building blocks of competitive advantage," they must be further combined and utilized in a unique and non-imitable way. It has thus been argued that FSAs and SSAs "reflect specialized competencies and capabilities, the bundling of which leads to greater performance potential than if they were exploited separately" (Rugman/Verbeke 2001, p. 245).

These extended resource-based considerations are indicative of the changing view of the MNC as they further underline the important role that foreign subsidiaries play within the MNC network as contributors to competitive advantage. It highlights the progression from headquarters-based advantage to advantage-creating elements that are embedded and dispersed throughout the MNC network. The "distributed" development of competitive advantage, however, requires resource management activities at both the subsidiary level (e.g. development of specialized or superior resources) and at the firm level (e.g. transfer, bundling and leveraging of these resources). It also involves the "dual challenge" for the MNC of enabling subsidiaries to create and develop new specialized resources (e.g. through interactions with local customers and suppliers) and at the same time ensuring that these (often sticky and context-specific) resources can still be integrated and leveraged globally.

(a) Nonlocation-Bound Subsidiary Resources and Capabilities	(b) Partially-Bound Subsidiary Resources and Capabilities
1. Nonlocation-bound and easily transferable	1. Tacit, context-specific and difficult to transfer
2. Specialized/superior	2. Specialized/superior (representative of capability gap)
3. Recognized and accepted within MNC	3. Positively perceived within MNC (absence of negative externalities)
4. Complementary to other firm resources	4. Synergies and interest interdependence
↓	↓
Contribution to FSA	Contribution to SSA

5. Firm-level structuring, bundling and leveraging

Contribution to Competitive Advantage at Firm Level

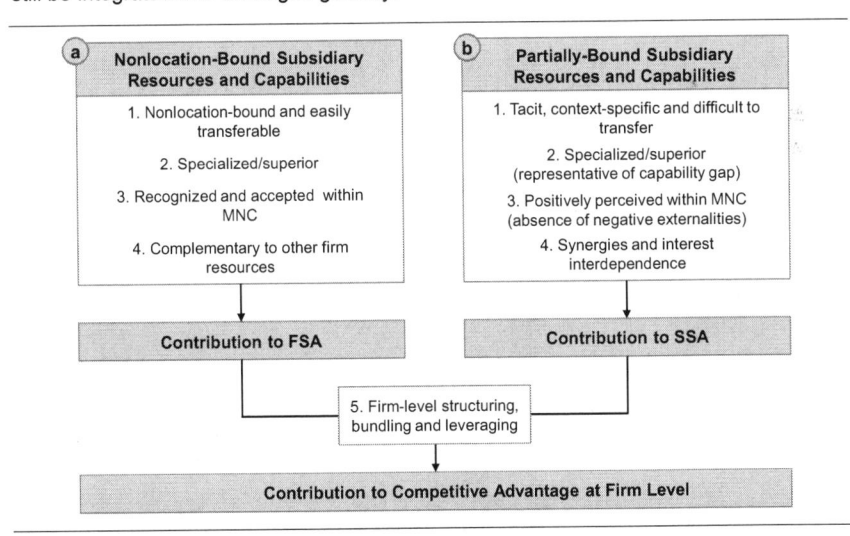

Figure 3.13: FSA- and SSA-based competitive advantage through subsidiary resources

(3) Resource-Based View and Subsidiary Initiatives

As already briefly addressed in Subsection 2.2.6, the RBV has been applied not only for research on MNC subsidiaries in general, but also for subsidiary initiatives in particular. Overall, eight publications were identified in the literature review that apply a resource-based perspective when investigating aspects of the topic.[175] These works apply the RBV for (1) examination and discussion of subsidiary evolution and development through changes in the subsidiary's resource and capability setting (Birkinshaw/Hood 1997, 1998d, Delany 2000), (2) the subsidiary's contribution to the competitive advantage of the firm (Birkinshaw et al. 1998, Birkinshaw 2000), (3) the opportunity identification phase of subsidiary entrepreneurship (Liouka 2007) and (4) initiative-related knowledge creation and transfer within the MNC (Mahnke et al. 2007, Williams 2009).[176]

(1) From a resourced-based perspective, subsidiary evolution or development is viewed as the result of the accumulation or depletion of subsidiary resources and capabilities over time (Birkinshaw/Hood 1997, p. 340, 1998d, p. 774, Delany 2000, p. 239). It is stated that subsidiaries possess and control, at least to some extent, unique resource and capability profiles as a consequence of, for example, the specific geographical setting in which they operate and as an outcome of their particular historic development paths. These specific subsidiary resource profiles can be regarded as the "reflection of [subsidiary] charter," which is understood as the business elements for which the subsidiary holds responsibility (Birkinshaw/Hood 1998d, p. 782).[177] Changes to the stock of subsidiary resources and thus to the subsidiary charter or mandate may occur through host country, parent company and subsidiary-related factors. More specifically, at the subsidiary level, development may be driven through induced or autonomous actions of subsidiary management. Induced development represents the gradual growth of resources through regular activities within the scope of the subsidiary's responsibilities. Autonomous development, however, is accomplished through entrepreneurial initiatives of subsidiary management that go beyond the assigned responsibilities and which result in the creation of new resources. Therefore, subsidiary initiative-taking, through a resource-based lens, might be broadly seen as a process through which specialized resources and capabilities are applied and developed. Accordingly, this process is assumed to be driven by the current subsidiary resource profile and ultimately to result in the enhancement of the profile (Birkinshaw/Hood 1997, pp. 343, 355).

---

[175] These publications are Birkinshaw and Hood (1997, 1998c), Birkinshaw et al. (1998), Birkinshaw (2000), Delany (2000), Liouka (2007), Mahnke et al. (2007) and Williams (2009).

[176] Mahnke (2007) and Williams (2009) refer to the knowledge-based view (Kogut/Zander 1992, 1993).

[177] It is assumed unlikely that the subsidiary's charter will precisely reflect the current subsidiary resource profile; capability changes will rather lead or follow charter change (Birkinshaw/Hood 1998d, p. 783).

(2) In addition to subsidiary development through initiative-taking, resources and capabilities at the subsidiary level have, in line with resource-based thinking, been shown to potentially contribute to the development of competitive advantage at firm level. As the RBV represents a firm-level theory in which the firm is viewed as a single entity, Birkinshaw and his co-authors (Birkinshaw et al. 1998, Birkinshaw 2000) propose certain modifications and additional assumptions in order to apply the theory at the level of the MNC subsidiary. As already outlined in the previous paragraphs, Birkinshaw et al. conceptualize the subsidiary as a heterogeneous bundle of resources. Subsidiary units are viewed as "building blocks" from which competitive advantage at firm level can potentially arise. However, according to the authors this requires that the corporate center be capable of managing the scattered resource and capability building efforts in the MNC and of effectively utilizing the dispersed resources and capabilities in order to generate firm level advantages (Birkinshaw 2000, p. 107). As outlined, the requirements are that the resources be specialized, transferable (non-location-bound), complementary, recognized, and understood by the corporate organization. However, resources with these characterristics do not *per se* result in the subsidiary's contribution to competitive advantage. Birkinshaw et al.'s findings suggest that only if these resources are applied through entrepreneurial initiatives can they enhance the subsidiary contributory role. Initiative-taking can hence be seen as a process of resource utilization that also leads to the recognition of the subsidiary's specialized resources at the head office, which is a precondition for the effective utilization at firm level. (Birkinshaw et al. 1998, pp. 232-234).

(3) Liouka (2007) takes a resource-based perspective on the MNC subsidiary and applies the RBV as an overarching theoretical perspective to examine antecedents and outcomes of entrepreneurial opportunity identification at the subsidiary level.[178] In line with previous reasoning (e.g. Birkinshaw 1997, Birkinshaw/Hood 1998b, Rugman/Verbeke 2001), the author acknowledges that strategic resources and capabilities might be dispersed in the MNC and also exist within foreign subsidiaries of MNCs (Liouka 2007, p. 39). It is argued that a resource-based approach to subsidiary entrepreneurship "essentially considers it as a process of identification, acquisition and accumulation of resources to take advantage of perceived opportunities" (Liouka 2007, p. 75). Within the proposed resource-based framework, subsidiary entrepreneurship is modeled to be influenced by (a) characteristics of the subsidiary's external environment, (b) subsidiary specific resources and capabilities and (c) aspects of the corporate setting in which the subsidiary is active. The author outlines, for instance, traditional factor endowments or accumulated knowledge in a specific location as characteristics of the external environ-

---

[178] The author also draws upon elements from resource dependence theory (Pfeffer/Salancik 1978) and location theory (Dunning 1977). However, these two additional theories are linked under a resource-based logic to develop a theoretical framework on subsidiary entrepreneurship (Liouka 2007, p. 47).

ment that may be of relevance for the development of firm-specific learning and innovating capabilities. Moreover, she highlights different subsidiary-specific resources and capabilities that are of strategic importance: the subsidiary's internal and external network-embeddedness and the subsidiary's knowledge base representing strategic resources, as well as the subsidiary's networking and learning orientation representing critical capabilities. Lastly, concerning the corporate setting, the impact of intra-organizational relationships and subsidiary power are also proposed to influence subsidiary entrepreneurship (Liouka 2007, pp. 40-49).

(4) Based on the knowledge-based view (Kogut/Zander 1993), Williams proposes a model of subsidiary-level determinants of global initiatives in MNCs (Williams 2009). Global initiatives are defined as "a new allocation of resources to meet an identified (but untapped) opportunity that spans many, if not all, of the countries in which the MNC operates." Thus they entail identified opportunities across countries and the new allocation of a firm's resources in order to exploit them (Williams 2009, p. 94). They are viewed as entrepreneurial processes in the MNC that involve the identification, selection and exploitation of opportunities. From a knowledge-based perspective, global initiatives are seen as knowledge creation and application activities which might be driven either by headquarters (centrally-driven initiatives) or subsidiaries (decentrally-driven initiatives). The process of knowledge creation at the subsidiary level and the subsequent knowledge transfer within the MNC network are considered particularly important.[179] Consequently, the proposed model incorporates three subsidiary-level factors that are suggested to drive knowledge flows relating to global initiatives in the MNC: inter-unit networking within the MNC, subsidiary learning from internal and external sources and shared goals between subsidiary and headquarters managers. It is suggested that global initiatives are more likely to arise if there is a high level of inter-subsidiary networking, leading to the sharing and discussion of ideas, opportunities and solutions to problems encountered. Moreover, subsidiaries' willingness to learn from the external business network (e.g. suppliers or customers) or from the intra-organizational network (e.g. HQ or sister subsidiaries) is assumed to enhance the acquisition of new knowledge, making it more likely that the MNC will pursue global initiatives. Lastly, it is argued that shared and common goals of both subsidiary and headquarters managers should, first, result in more open sharing, comprehensive discussions and evaluations of opportunities and, second, enhance the subsidiary's willingness to provide local resources for global initiatives (Williams 2009, p. 96).[180]

---

[179] According to Williams, knowledge transfer goes beyond the mere sending of knowledge from sender to recipient but also involves the critical activities of effective integration and application, which are "likely to determine the success of the initiative" (Williams 2009, p. 94).

[180] Although the overall model is based on the knowledge-based view, this reasoning draws from the shared valued approach (see Nohria/Ghoshal 1994).

In a similar vein, Mahnke et al. (2007) provide knowledge-based arguments on possible communicative uncertainties throughout the entrepreneurial process in MNCs. The authors state that entrepreneurial knowledge within the network MNC is dispersed across locations and hierarchical levels. This implies that entrepreneurial knowledge has to be shared among the different MNC units, leading to intra-organizational knowledge flows within the network. However, certain knowledge characteristics make an effective transfer or communication more or less difficult. For instance, local entrepreneurial knowledge may be co-specialized and socially complex. Entrepreneurial opportunities might arise through interactions with local actors (e.g. suppliers or research institutions) or they may be strongly linked to other local activities. Furthermore, local entrepreneurial knowledge might come in a rather tacit form, as it is often "embedded within individuals in a non-codified manner" (Mahnke et al. 2007, p. 1283). These characteristics can make entrepreneurial knowledge more specific and thus more difficult to communicate across the network. Consequently, the transfer from, for instance, subsidiaries to headquarters, can be impeded by communicative uncertainties, which are likely to lower the acceptance of the entrepreneurial opportunity at headquarters.

(4) Conclusions from Application of the Resource-Based View in IB Literature

Several conclusions can be drawn from previous applications of the resource-based perspective to subsidiary units and subsidiary initiative-taking. First, it seems increasingly acknowledged that unique resources and capabilities are dispersed within the MNC and that foreign subsidiaries can indeed be in possession and in control of such resources. Nevertheless, a clear "allocation" of particular resources and capabilities to either the subsidiary or firm level is not always easy, and capabilities may often reside somewhere between the two levels. However, it appears plausible and reasonable to extend the RBV to include the various resources and capabilities that are dispersed throughout the MNC network and that may reside at (or in between) the different organizational levels of the multinational firm.

Second, subsidiary resources and capabilities are not necessarily static, but instead may change and evolve over time. More specifically, they can also be created, developed and leveraged at the subsidiary level. In this context, subsidiary initiatives play a critical role, as they can be broadly viewed as an entrepreneurial process of resource development and deployment (e.g. Birkinshaw/Hood 1997, Liouka 2007, Williams 2009). Yet how precisely this process takes place and which actions subsidiaries take to acquire, develop and further leverage their resources to obtain more specialized and superior bundles of resources and capabilities is still largely unknown.

Here, the recent process-related developments in the RBV can serve as an important theoretical element concerning the process of subsidiary initiative-taking.

Third, under certain circumstances, subsidiary resources and capabilities can contribute to the development of competitive advantage at the firm level. As described, they must be specialized, generally transferable within the MNC and recognized and accepted by other MNC units, and they also must be further bundled and leveraged at the firm level. This view also puts a stronger emphasis on the role of headquarters and its managers as orchestrators of the distributed resources and capabilities within the MNC (Forsgren et al. 1999, Ambos/Birkinshaw 2010).

Fourth, characteristics of the subsidiary's local environment (including inter-organizational relationships), corporate characteristics (including intra-organizational relationships) and characteristics of the subsidiary itself can impact the development and deployment process of subsidiary resources and capabilities. However, the way in which the different environmental and organizational factors impact this process and the underlying resource-related activities in particular remains largely unclear. Thus, further investigation is needed to better understand which resource management activities in different subsidiary contexts can lead to better advantages at the subsidiary and firm levels. Figure 3.14 broadly summarizes the conclusions drawn from the previous applications of the RBV in IB literature.

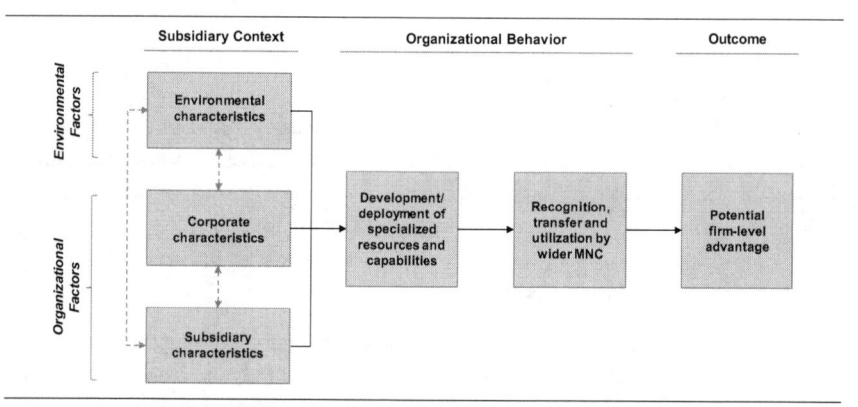

Figure 3.14: Simplified resource-based perspective on subsidiary resource and capability development and potential firm-level advantage

3.3.2.4 Resource-Based View in Entrepreneurship Literature

As previously argued, the topic of subsidiary initiatives can be viewed as lying somewhere at the intersection of research related to corporate entrepreneurship and subsidiary role development (see Section 2.1). The applicability of the RBV for research in IB in general and for foreign subsidiaries in particular has been articulated in the previous subsection. This section briefly reviews the extent to which the RBV is applicable to entrepreneurship in general and to entrepreneurial processes in particular.

Early resource-based works already considered entrepreneurship and entrepreneurial actions as important elements (Alvarez/Busenitz 2001, p. 755). For instance, the contributions of Wernerfelt (1984), Barney (1991) and Teece et al. (1997) also draw from the works of Schumpeter (1934) or Penrose (1959).[181] Related to this, it has been expressed that the RBV and entrepreneurship have many underlying commonalities. For instance, the RBV and entrepreneurship adopt the same unit of analysis – the resource. Furthermore, both consider heterogeneous resources and address the transformation of internal and external resources leading to superior returns (Alvarez/Busenitz 2001, p. 756, Alvarez/Barney 2002, p. 90). Not surprisingly, many definitions of entrepreneurship focus on the aspects of resources and resource transformation. For example, Ireland et al. define entrepreneurship as a "context-dependent process through which individuals and teams create wealth by bringing together unique packages of resources to exploit marketplace opportunities" (Ireland et al. 2001, p. 51; see also Hitt et al. 2001, p. 480). Similarly, Shane views entrepreneurial opportunities as "resource combinations that result in new products or services" (Shane 2003, p. 33), and Burgelman describes corporate entrepreneurship as "a process ... [which] requires new resource combinations" (Burgelman 1983a, p. 1350).[182] Overall, there appears to be a potential fit between the RBV and entrepreneurship. Thus it has been proposed that the RBV should not only be generally applicable for entrepreneurship, but should also be well positioned to provide a better understanding of the topic and to provide new insights into entrepreneurial processes and decision-making (Hitt/Ireland 2002, p. 4, Haynie et al. 2009, p. 339). Moreover, it has even be suggested that the RBV "may be the unifying theory that the field of entrepreneurship has lacked" (Alvarez/Barney 2002, p. 90).

Despite these recognizable similarities and the potential value of the RBV, connections between resource-based approaches and the topic of entrepreneurship remain limited

---

[181] More detailed discussions on Penrose's contribution to the RBV can be found in, for example, Rugman and Verbeke (2002) and Kor and Mahoney (2004).
[182] Further definitions of corporate entrepreneurship that include "resource-related aspects" have been brought forward by, for example, Burgelman (1984, p. 154), Covin and Slevin (1991, p. 7), Zahra (1995, p. 227, 1996, p. 1715), or Alvarez and Barney (2002, p. 89). Bartlett and Ghoshal (2002, p. 147), relating to the topic of innovation, state that "innovations are created by applying resources to exploit an opportunity, or to overcome a threat."

(Alvarez/Busenitz 2001, p. 756, Boccardelli/Magnusson 2006, p. 163). The potential of the RBV for entrepreneurship research, and *vice versa*, has seemingly not been fully utilized so far (Young et al. 2003, p. 33, Teng 2007, p. 120, Foss et al. 2008, p. 74). Part of this neglect may perhaps be attributed to the somewhat static and equilibrium-based nature of many earlier resource-based writings. As stated previously, the emphasis of these more static RBV approaches on the possession and control of unique resources makes it difficult to address the dynamic issue of entrepreneurship that essentially deals with the creation of new resources or the novel combination of existing ones. Here, the more dynamic and process-oriented resource-based thinking that has been presented above and has been developed rather recently (e.g. Helfat et al. 2007, Sirmon et al. 2007, Sirmon et al. 2011) should offer better theoretical guidance. These approaches not only acknowledge that resources and capabilities change over time, but they are explicitly concerned with resource structuring, bundling and leveraging – activities that are also central to entrepreneurial processes.

Nonetheless, the RBV has been repeatedly applied in the field of entrepreneurship in general (Barney et al. 2001, p. 634, Barney/Clark 2007, p. 240) and the subfields of corporate entrepreneurship (Teng 2007, p. 120) and international entrepreneurship in particular (Peng 2001, p. 815, Young et al. 2003, pp. 32-33). For example, within the more "general" entrepreneurship literature, Chandler and Hanks (1994) investigate the relationships of market attractiveness and resource-based capabilities with new venture performance. Brush et al. (2001) apply the RBV to explore how entrepreneurs in emerging organizations assemble and combine resources to build a resource portfolio that may yield distinctive capabilities. Likewise, Alvarez and Busenitz (2001) link the RBV and entrepreneurship in a theoretical discussion of the role of entrepreneurial resources (e.g. the cognitive ability of individual entrepreneurs) in the creation of heterogeneous outputs.

Within the domain of corporate entrepreneurship, for instance, Greene et al. (1999) draw from a resource-based framework when studying the role of corporate champions in the process of acquiring and assembling resources. Furthermore, Teng (2007) applies the RBV when examining how corporate entrepreneurship activities can benefit from needed resources through strategic alliances that may otherwise not be available. Concerning the literature on international entrepreneurship, it appears that resource-based research still "remain in its infancy" (Peng 2001, p. 815).[183] Nevertheless, here the RBV is also assumed to be of great potential for future studies (Young et al. 2003, p. 39), and obviously some work attempts to utilize this potential "more wholeheartedly." For instance, in their book publication, Zucchella and Scabini (2007, pp. 99-136) pre-

---

[183] In addition, Keupp and Gassmann (2009b) examined 179 journal contributions which deal with international entrepreneurship. Thereof, 82 articles did not specify any theoretical framework. Of the remaining 97 articles, only eight were (at least in part) grounded in the RBV.

sent their theoretical model for international entrepreneurship, which is largely grounded in the resource-based view and dynamic capability framework. Similarly, Ireland and Webb (2006, pp. 48-50) use the RBV as a central theoretical pillar of international entrepreneurship, which is then applied to build arguments relating to the management of resources in the unique environmental conditions associated with emerging economies.[184]

In addition to these publications, three of the process-oriented resource-based contributions described in Section 3.3.2.4 herein also link the RBV to entrepreneurial aspects. First, Godfrey and Gregersen provide a causal model of resource generation and give entrepreneurial ability a central place in their framework as the "capacity to identify, develop, and complete new combinations of existing asset bundles or new asset configurations" (Godfrey/Gregersen 1999, p. 41). Second, Lichtenstein and Brush present a resource-based and dynamic model of resource acquisition and development in entrepreneurial firms (Lichtenstein/Brush 2001) and, third, Hitt et al (2011) put forth a resource-based process model of strategic entrepreneurship that involves the activities of resource structuring, bundling and leveraging.

These findings can be summarized as follows: First, although not yet extensively utilized, the RBV appears to be a promising theory for entrepreneurship research. Particularly, the more dynamic and process-oriented strands will likely be of value when investigating the entrepreneurship processes of internationally active firms (Young et al. 2003, p. 39). Second, the RBV can likely be extended by the element of entrepreneurial recognition, which is defined as the "recognition of opportunities and opportunity-seeking behavior as a resource" (Alvarez/Busenitz 2001, p. 756; see also Boccardelli/ Magnusson 2006, p. 171). Such an extended RBV would thereby not only address the underlying activities of the resource management process, but also incorporate the recognition of opportunities and opportunity seeking behavior. Accordingly, it has been stated that entrepreneurship "generally involves the founder's unique awareness of opportunities, the ability to acquire the resources needed to exploit the opportunity, and the organizational ability to recombine homogenous inputs into heterogeneous outputs" (Alvarez/Busenitz 2001, p. 771). Third, concluding from the contributions and findings, subsidiary initiative-taking can be viewed as an resource-oriented entrepreneurial process involving the identification, structuring, bundling and leveraging of resources and capabilities in order to respond to perceived business opportunities in the market (e.g. Birkinshaw 1997, p. 207, Liouka 2007, p. 75).

---

[184] Other contributions which use a resource-based approach to entrepreneurship are, for instance, Boccardelli and Magnusson (2006), Zahra et al. (2006), and Haynie et al. (2009).

3.3.3 Resource Dependence Theory

3.3.3.1 Overview of Resource Dependence Theory

Another theoretical perspective in addition to RBV that centers on the control of critical resources is resource dependence theory (RDT), which has established itself as an influential view in the domain of organizational theory and strategic management (Hillman et al. 2009, p. 1404) and has also gained some standing in IB literature (Bouquet/ Birkinshaw 2008a, p. 482). Important theoretical contributions on RDT have been put forward by, for example, Pfeffer and Salancik (1978, 2003), Pfeffer (1992) and Astley and colleagues (Astley/Sachdeva 1984, Astley/Zajac 1991).

In essence, RDT characterizes the links between and within organizations as a set of power relationships based on the exchange of resources (Ulrich/Barney 1984, p. 472, Zaefarian et al. 2011, p. 863). While the RBV emphasizes the importance of the control over critical resources for competitive advantage, RDT argues that organizations or organizational subunits that are in control of critical resources possess power which can then be used to influence the behavior of other organizations or organizational subunits that depend on these resources (Pfeffer/Salancik 2003, p. 53, Nienhüser 2008, p. 10).

RDT is based on a number of key assumptions that help explain how organizations and their subunits can acquire resource-based power. First, resource dependence theorists view organizations as open social systems that require a supply of resources from the environment in order to survive and function. Organizations are therefore not entirely autonomous but are constrained by interdependencies with the larger environment in general or with other organizations in particular that can provide the needed resources (Pfeffer/Salancik 2003, p. 43, Hillman et al. 2009, pp. 1404-1405). The environment is seen as the central source of uncertainty for the organization. As organizations require a stable supply of resources, uncertainty or instability of resource supply threatens their existence. Thus, it is the management's responsibility to ensure the organization's survival by minimizing the likelihood of resources becoming scarce or uncertain (Pfeffer/ Salancik 2003, p. 47). Second, organizations are viewed as consisting of internal and external coalitions that engage in the exchange of resources and capabilities (Ulrich/ Barney 1984, p. 472, Pfeffer/Salancik 2003, pp. 24-27). Such resource exchanges may involve, for instance, financial or physical resources, information, human talent, technological skills, or specific reputations that are obtained from interactions with customers, suppliers or alliance partners, for example (Astley/Sachdeva 1984, p. 106, Pfeffer/ Salancik 2003, p. 43; see also Bouquet/Birkinshaw 2008a, p. 482). Third, the resource exchange patterns between organizations or organizational subunits influence inter-organizational and intra-organizational power. Drawing from exchange theory (e.g. Blau 1964) and power dependency theory (e.g. Emerson 1962), RDT argues that organizations that control resources have power over those that need these resources. In particular, three factors determine the power (or conversely dependence) of one organization on another: (1) resource importance, (2) discretion over the resource allocation and resource use and (3) concentration of resource control (Pfeffer/Salancik 2003, pp. 44-45).

First, a resource is considered important if it is critical for an organization's functioning and survival.[185] The more important are the resources controlled by one organization for another, the more power the former will have. Second, the extent to which an organization has control over resources needed by others is considered an important factor. The greater the unrestricted discretion one organization has in the allocation and application of a resource, the greater the dependence of others, and hence its power. Third, the fewer alternatives or substitutes that exist for resources controlled by an organization that others depend on, the greater its ability to gain power. Hence, when viewing these three factors combined, maximum resource dependence and thus maximum power emerges when organizations or their subunits have full control of scarce resources that cannot be substituted and that are of high importance to other organizations or organizational subunits (Pfeffer/Salancik 2003, p. 231).

Although RDT was predominantly formulated to explain relationships between organizations, the theoretical perspective also explicitly refers to subunits within organizations and acknowledges that they can also be in control of important resources (Pfeffer/Salancik 2003, p. 71, Nienhüser 2008, p. 15).[186] It is further argued that the organizational environment not only influences the external distribution of power, but also impacts organizational actions partly by altering the distribution of power and influence within the organization. The authors state that "those subunits most able to cope with the organization's critical problems acquire power in the organization."[187] In addition to their ability to solve problems facing the organization, organizational subunits can further enhance their power if their problem-solving capabilities or resources are not substitutable, and if the problem or contingency that the subunits can solve affects a larger area of organizational activity (Pfeffer/Salancik 2003, pp. 230-231). It is further proposed that, as environmental changes occur, subunits may not necessarily make other units aware of such changes if they could endanger the current power structure of the organization. Subunits may therefore attempt to influence the information seeking of other units in order to, for example, change resource allocation decisions in their favor (Pfeffer/Salancik 2003, p. 234, Nienhüser 2008, p. 16).

---

[185] More precisely, Pfeffer and Salancik refer to both magnitude of resource exchange and criticality of resources as the underlying dimensions of resources importance (see Pfeffer/Salancik 2003, p. 46).

[186] As described, resource dependence theory is largely rooted in exchange theory and power dependence concepts (e.g. Emerson 1962, Blau 1964) and works concerned with intraorganizational power (e.g. Hickson et al. 1971) which explicitly deal with power constellations within organizations. Yet, while social exchange theories focus on individual actors, RDT uses an organizational-level perspective.

[187] Pfeffer and Salancik acknowledge that, although problems often stem from the external environment, critical uncertainties can both "arise from within or from outside the organization" (Pfeffer/Salancik 2003, p. 231).

Following the works by Pfeffer and Salancik, other authors have further developed and employed resource dependence logic to explain intra-organizational relationships and power constellations. For instance, Astley and Sachdeva use a resource dependence perspective to highlight a subunit's ability to control the supply of resources to others as an important source of power arguing that "organizational actors that obtain the most critical and difficult to secure resources consequently acquire power because of the dependencies that are generated" (Astley/Sachdeva 1984, p. 106). In a later publication, the same scholars use resource dependence theory to describe power constellations in a coalition model of organizations. Coalitions are described as "loose networks of semiautonomous subunits" characterized by interdependent activities. Within these coalitions, semiautonomous subunits "may enhance their power by creating resource dependencies in others," but other subunits can counter these activities through "reciprocal resource contributions" (Astley/Zajac 1991, p. 402). In addition to these works, a number of other scholars have employed resource dependence theory for research on intra-organizational power (e.g. Harpaz/Meshoulam 1997, Medcof 2001, Mudambi/ Pedersen 2007), showing that RDT is also applicable when investigating relationships among units within organizations (Medcof 2001, p. 1002, Johnston/Menguc 2007, p. 790).

However, RDT has also not remained without controversy, as the theoretical view has been confronted with certain criticisms concerning both its conceptual aspects and its empirical testing. For instance, relating to conceptual aspects, it has been criticized that many of the underlying central concepts remain too general and ambiguous, making it "virtually impossible to refute" the theory (Astley/Zammuto 1992, p. 466; see also Nienhüser 2008, p. 28). Also, the theoretical foundations on which RDT rests are said to be too fragmented and the linkages to systems theory or power approaches, for instance, remain somewhat unclear (Schreyögg 1997, p. 483). A further conceptual critique has been put forward by Donaldson, who maintains that RDT focuses too strongly on the relevance of power structures and power processes for the explanation of organizational behavior. It is argued that organizations are as much technical and economic systems as they are political systems, yet RDT largely ignores such factors (Donaldson 1995, p. 152, see also Schreyögg 1999, p. 373, Nienhüser 2004, p. 108, 2008, p. 26). With regard to empirical testing, it has been further stated that there are relatively few systematic studies of RDT predictions and only a limited amount of empirical work overall (Pfeffer/Salancik 2003, p. xx). Moreover, the empirical support of RDT remains somewhat scarce, with studies often only finding weak effects and low proportions of explained variance (Nienhüser 2008, p. 25).

3.3.3.2 Resource Dependence Theory in International Business Literature

(1) Application in International Business Research

Some time after the publications by Pfeffer and Salancik (1978), work in the IB domain also highlighted the importance of resource dependence situations for MNCs (e.g. Doz/Prahalad 1981, 1984, 1986, Ghoshal/Nohria 1986). For instance, Doz and Prahalad take a resource dependence approach in their works on headquarters influence and control over MNC subsidiaries. The scholars argue that headquarters may use resource dependency as a strategic tool to secure power over its subsidiaries, as – at least in some cases – subsidiaries' dependence on headquarters for key resources allows the former to secure considerable influence. However, as subsidiaries mature and grow, it is suggested that they can afford a larger resource base of their own, thereby reducing their dependence on resources from headquarters (Doz/Prahalad 1981, p. 15, 1986, p. 60). Yet, despite this "early" resource dependence-based thinking in IB literature, it has been stated that resource dependence theory, although both applicable and useful for research on MNCs (Medcof 2001, p. 1002, Johnston/Menguc 2007, p. 790), "has only been sporadically applied" to this point (Ambos/Schlegelmilch 2007, p. 476).

While a number of subsequent contributions in IB research have used the resource dependence perspective when investigating and explaining the relationships of MNCs with external actors such as global customers (e.g. Birkinshaw et al. 2001), host country governments (e.g. Blumentritt/Nigh 2002), other groups and organizations (e.g. Inkpen/Beamish 1997), or the environment at large (e.g. Rosenzweig/Singh 1991), further publications have applied this theoretical view for the examination of power dynamics within MNCs. Among these works, a large fraction takes a resource dependence perspective when dealing with the topics of headquarters-subsidiary relationships and subsidiary power (e.g. Ghoshal/Nohria 1989, Andersson/Forsgren 1996, Andersson/Pahlberg 1997, Andersson et al. 2001a, Medcof 2001, Luo 2003, Mudambi/Navarra 2004, Forsgren et al. 2005, Yamin 2005, Dörrenbächer/Gammelgaard 2006, Ambos/Schlegelmilch 2007, Johnston/Menguc 2007, Mudambi et al. 2007, Mudambi/Pedersen 2007, Bouquet/Birkinshaw 2008a, Yamin/Sinkovics 2010, Dörrenbächer/Gammelgaard 2011, Chen et al. 2012).

For instance, Ghoshal and Nohria draw from resource dependence theory (e.g. Pfeffer/Salancik 2003), exchange theories (e.g. Emerson 1962), and contingency theory (e.g. Lawrence/Lorsch 1967). In their paper on internal differentiation within multinational corporations they argue that headquarters-subsidiary exchange relations are contingent upon the environmental and resource conditions that the subsidiaries face.[188] Accord-

---

[188] Ghoshal and Nohria classify the different environmental and resource contingencies into four generic subsidiary situations reflecting the subsidiary role typologies presented in other publications (e.g. Bartlett/Ghoshal 1986, 1989), and which are also outlined in Subsection 3.2.1 of this dissertation.

ingly, the authors state that internal power relationships in MNCs are, in addition to environmental complexity, dependent upon the internal distribution of organizational resources, suggesting that "resource dependency is the key determinant of the structure of internal exchange relationships within complex organizations" (Ghoshal/Nohria 1989, p. 324). For example, as resources levels of the subsidiary grow, chances increase that the subsidiary's independent interests become stronger and that these interests deviate more strongly from those of headquarters. Since the subsidiary represents an important pool of rich resources for the MNC, this results in increased headquarters dependency on the subsidiary (Ghoshal/Nohria 1989, p. 325).

Similarly, the contributions by Andersson and colleagues adopt a resource dependence perspective when investigating subsidiary influence in the MNC (Andersson/Forsgren 1996, Andersson/Pahlberg 1997, Andersson et al. 2007). Subsidiaries are viewed as entities that are embedded in a network of business relationships with internal and external actors with which they exchange important resources. The authors particularly highlight the importance of resources obtained from external network partners such as customers or suppliers for the resource-based power of subsidiary units. It is argued that, especially if those resources are important and cannot be accessed or secured by headquarters itself, this situation will lead to a strong power position of the subsidiary vis-à-vis headquarters (Andersson/Forsgren 1996, p. 488, Andersson/Pahlberg 1997, p. 321). Such resource-based power can then be used by subsidiaries for two purposes. They may apply it to become more autonomous in the MNC and essentially help subsidiaries to avoid control from headquarters (Andersson/Pahlberg 1997, p. 322). Alternatively, they can use their power to influence headquarters decisions and promote their particular interests (Andersson/Forsgren 1996, Andersson/Pahlberg 1997, p. 331, Andersson et al. 2007).[189] However, resource-based power not only applies to subsidiary units. It is also proposed that the efficiency of headquarters control mechanisms increases if the corporate parent is in control of resources needed by the subsidiary, such as financial assets or technology (Andersson/Forsgren 1996, p. 490).

Medcof, arguing that RDT has been "found to be readily applicable to relationships among units within organizations" (2001, p. 1002), uses the theory when discussing aspects of subsidiary power in MNCs. Drawing from the propositions of RDT, Medcof suggests that the higher the value (i.e. the importance) and the uniqueness (i.e. the fewer alternatives there are) of resources controlled by a foreign subsidiary unit, the greater headquarters dependency on it will be and the more powerful the subsidiary will be. The level of subsidiary power is also said to have implications concerning the extent

---

[189] For example, Andersson and Forsgren (2000, pp. 335-336) mention MNC's investments in R&D, changes in the organizational structure, (re)location of production facilities, or M&A activities as examples of headquarters decisions that can be influenced by subsidiaries controlling critical resources – such as its external relationships in the local market.

to which subsidiary managers should be included in headquarters decisions on strategy and resource allocation. It is suggested that subsidiary units that possess important and non-substitutable resources should also be more actively included in such decision-making processes (Medcof 2001, p. 1004).

In addition, Mudambi and Pedersen utilize RDT and agency theory as complementary explanations for subsidiary power in MNCs. While agency theory (Jensen/Meckling 1976) is said to be more appropriate for the traditional and hierarchical view of the MNC, in which the subsidiary exploits competencies developed at the home base, RDT is considered to be "a better basis upon which to understand the relationships between competence creating subsidiaries and their parents MNCs" (Mudambi/Pedersen 2007, p. 3). In particular when taking a network perspective on the MNC, RDT is suggested as the more appropriate theory for explaining subsidiary power. Following resource dependency thinking, the two scholars thus predict that subsidiary units that are in control of resources of strategic relevance for the MNC in dealing with its external environment will be able to exert influence on decision-making of headquarters (Mudambi/Pedersen 2007, p. 9).

In their journal article, Bouquet and Birkinshaw (2008a) summarize and integrate a range of literature on the power and influence in MNCs. The authors also highlight the importance of RDT in IB literature for explaining inter-organizational and intra-organizational relationships of MNCs. It is stated that, according to the resource dependence perspective, in order for subsidiaries to obtain power in the MNC, they need to find ways to control critical resources that are strongly needed by the other units that they intend to influence. It is proposed that, although subsidiaries may gain some power and influence by meeting targets and objectives set by the parent company, more complex and tacit resources can provide a more potent foundation for subsidiary power. Among these critical resources are, for example, specific knowledge and information on local market or competitive developments that have strategic implications for the larger company, or innovative ideas and practices that can be leveraged by other units of the firm (Bouquet/Birkinshaw 2008a, p. 482).

Finally, Dörrenbächer and Gammelgaard (2011) depict resource dependence power as a critical source of power that subsidiaries can apply when, for example, pursuing lucrative business opportunities in their local environment or when attempting to improve the subsidiary's position in the MNC. Among the various sources of subsidiary power, resource dependence power is said to be "the most frequently cited type." It is also deemed "to be quite sustainable" and "... is assessed to be strong, as subsidiaries' control over critical resources ... might be important or even key to the performance of the MNC as a whole." In line with resource dependence thinking, headquarters resource dependence on subsidiaries is said to be linked to the subsidiary's ability to solve critical problems stemming from the environment. More specifically, headquarters resource dependence may be associated with the subsidiary's ability to make use of economic opportunities that exist in its local environment or with the subsidiary developing "specialized knowledge, expertise or technologies by forging close external relationships with local business partners" that can be transferred and used by other units of the MNC (Dörrenbächer/Gammelgaard 2011, pp. 33-34).

(2) Resource Dependence Theory and Subsidiary Initiatives

From the literature review and critical analysis, five contributions were identified that take a resource dependence perspective when dealing with the topic of subsidiary initiatives, and these will be presented briefly below (i.e. Birkinshaw/Ridderstråle 1999, Liouka 2007, Lyly-Yrjänäinen et al. 2008, Jindra et al. 2009, Ambos et al. 2010).

In their journal article, Birkinshaw and Ridderstråle (1999) examine the process of subsidiary initiatives and the corporate forces that exert resistance based on case study analyses of 44 initiatives. The authors maintain that the "initiative process is driven to a large degree by the relative power the subsidiary unit vis-à-vis the corporate headquarters." In particular, two forms of subsidiary power that are considered relevant for the initiative process are presented: structural power as "legally granted authority" and resource-based power resulting from "control over valuable assets" (Birkinshaw/Ridderstråle 1999, p. 152). From a resource dependence perspective, it is proposed that subsidiaries that have control over valuable resources on which others depend will accumulate resource-based power that can be utilized to overcome corporate resistance and push initiatives forward in the MNC. Specifically, the subsidiary's external network is seen as an important source of resource-based power, especially if it can only be accessed through the subsidiary (Birkinshaw/Ridderstråle 1999, pp. 152, 176).

Liouka (2007) employs RDT when investigating the impact from certain aspects of headquarters-subsidiary relations on subsidiary entrepreneurial initiatives. Resource dependence thinking implies that a subsidiary in possession of critical resources on which other MNC units rely may be able to acquire a position of power. In general, the subsidiary may then apply this power to influence decisions and promote its interests in the MNC (Liouka 2007, p. 31). With regard to the initiative process, it is stated that critical resources controlled by the subsidiary can enhance its ability to pursue new entrepreneurial opportunities and to build up resources and capabilities beyond the control of headquarters (Liouka 2007, p. 95).

Ambos et al. (2010), in line with Ghoshal and Nohria's work (Ghoshal/Nohria 1989), view headquarters-subsidiary relationships as a mixed-motive dyad in which both sides follow somewhat different objectives. Accordingly, they also use RDT and adopt a resource-based power perspective when attempting to explain the consequences of subsidiary initiative-taking. It is claimed that, through such entrepreneurial activities, subsidiaries are able to create or develop valuable resources for the MNC even without the explicit approval of headquarters. This situation may result in stronger headquarters dependence on the subsidiary so that "a relationship of mutual dependence between headquarters and subsidiaries transpires" (Ambos et al. 2010, p. 1101). The increased resource dependence of headquarters allows a foreign unit to enhance its bargaining power, which can be applied to increase its autonomy or influence on other parts of the MNC (Ambos et al. 2010, p. 1103).

Furthermore, Jindra et al. (2009) apply RDT to suggest that subsidiary evolution and development not only result from headquarters assignment but can also be the product of independent and innovative activities (i.e. initiatives) by subsidiaries. Such initiatives allow the subsidiaries to develop unique resources and capabilities that are also of critical importance to the wider MNC and hence can help to improve the subsidiary role over time (Jindra et al. 2009, p. 169).

Finally, Lyly-Yrjänäinen et al. (2008), in their paper on the global key accounts role of the diffusion of subsidiary initiatives, propose that resource-based power be seen as critical for diffusing initiatives in the wider MNC. It is stated that small and peripheral subsidiaries in particular may be low in power and may face greater difficulties in overcoming corporate resistance to subsidiary initiatives (Lyly-Yrjänäinen et al. 2008, p. 4).

(3) Conclusions from Application of Resource Dependence in IB Literature

From the outlined IB publications it can be concluded that, first, RDT is applicable not only for inter- but also for intra-organizational relationships (see also Medcof 2001, p. 1002, Johnston/Menguc 2007, p. 791).[190] Given the growing number of publications on headquarters-subsidiary relationships and subsidiary power that take a resource dependence perspective, it appears that the theory is receiving increasing recognition in this area. Especially when taking a network view of the MNC, in which subsidiaries are viewed as semiautonomous entities with their own distinctive environments and resources (e.g. Bartlett/Ghoshal 1989, Nohria/Ghoshal 1994) and in which MNCs cannot solely rely on hierarchical control, RDT may indeed be an appropriate theoretical perspective when dealing with aspects such as subsidiary power (Bouquet/Birkinshaw 2008, p. 478; Mudambi/Pedersen 2007, Dörrenbächer/Gammelgaard 2011, p. 33).

Second, concerning the means, the literature illustrates, corresponding to the arguments brought forward by Pfeffer and Salancik (2003, p. 230), that subsidiary power in

---

[190] This IB-related statement is consistent with arguments that have been made concerning the applicability of RDT for both intraorganizational and interorganizational behavior of organizations in general (see e.g. Nienhüser 2008, p. 15, Brunner 2009, p. 31).

the MNC can in general result from its ability to solve critical problems stemming from the environment (e.g. Dörrenbächer/Gammelgaard 2011, p. 33). More precisely, subsidiaries may acquire power by controlling resources that are important or critical to other units in the MNC and unique or scarce with few or no alternatives existing (e.g. Medcof 2001, Ambos/Schlegelmilch 2007, p. 477, Bouquet/Birkinshaw 2008a, p. 482).[191] A number of different sources for subsidiary resource-power are presented in these contributions. Among them are, for instance, subsidiary embeddedness in local networks (Andersson/Forsgren 1996, Andersson et al. 2001a), the subsidiary's market access (Dörrenbächer/Gammelgaard 2011), knowledge of the local market and competitive developments (Bouquet/Birkinshaw 2008a), the subsidiary's role in the MNC with regard to product and process innovations (Andersson/Pahlberg 1997), and innovative ideas and practices that can be leveraged by others in the firm (Bouquet/Birkinshaw 2008a).

Third, regarding the ends, the outlined contributions argue that the subsidiary's control of such critical and unique resources should subsequently lead to increased power that can be used by the subsidiary for two purposes. On the one hand, it can apply (negative) power to become more autonomous and to avoid hierarchical control exerted by headquarters or another unit. On the other hand, the subsidiary may use its (positive) resource-based power to influence decisions made by headquarters or other units on, for example, the location and the investment in production or R&D (Andersson/Pahlberg 1997, Forsgren/Pedersen 2000, Andersson et al. 2007, Yamin/Sinkovics 2010), or the progression of subsidiary initiatives (Birkinshaw/Ridderstråle 1999).

Fourth and finally, RDT can be viewed as a useful theoretical lens to help explain resource and power relationships between different units of the MNC when engaging in entrepreneurial initiatives. However, RDT alone appears to be insufficient to cover the various facets of subsidiary initiatives, and hence it is frequently integrated with other theoretical perspectives such as network theory, resource-based view, or dynamic capability approach.

---

[191] It appears feasible that these conditions can be met. First, subsidiary control over important resources implies that they cannot be accessed or secured by headquarters directly. In many instances, critical subsidiary resources are tacit in nature and/or (partially) bound to the subsidiary location or local business networks. Hence, headquarters access to them is difficult or even impossible (e.g. Rugman/Verbeke 2001, Dörrenbächer/Gammelgaard 2011). Second, the importance of subsidiary resources refers to its ability to solve critical problems of the MNC which eventually impacts its chances for proper functioning, survival and success (Medcof 2001, Mudambi/Pedersen 2007). Previous literature shows that subsidiaries may provide critical resources that are important for the competitive advantage and survival of firms (Rugman/Verbeke 2001, Schmid/Schurig 2003). Third, it can be expected that some subsidiary resources are also difficult to imitate. In particular location-bound and business network knowledge is often co-specialized, tacit and complex and as such difficult or impossible to imitate or substitute (e.g. Andersson et al. 2001b, Mahnke et al. 2007, Dörrenbächer/Gammelgaard 2011).

3.3.4 Contingency Theory

3.3.4.1 Overview of Contingency Theory

Among the major theoretical areas related to the thinking about organizations is contingency theory, also sometimes referred to as situational approaches (e.g. Burns/Stalker 1961, Lawrence/Lorsch 1967, Thompson 1967). The theory in essence postulates that the situation or context of an organization impacts its structure, behavior and processes and consequently its efficiency (e.g. Schmid 1994, pp. 11-12, Scherm/Pietsch 2007, p. 36). This theoretical perspective developed mainly in the 1960s and dominated the scholarly work on organizational design and performance in the 1960s and 1970s (Doz/Prahalad 1991, p. 124, Birkinshaw et al. 2002, p. 275). Contingency approaches have their roots in different theories such as Weber's bureaucracy model (Kieser/Walgenbach 2010, p. 40). Particularly important contributions to the theory have been made by researchers belonging to the Comparative Organization Analysis Program (e.g. Blau 1970, Blau/Schoenherr 1971) and to the Aston-Group (e.g. Pugh et al. 1968, Pugh et al. 1969, Pugh/Hickson 1976).

Contingency theory is considered among the most widely used organization theories (Welge 1987, p. 78, Kieser/Kubicek 1992, p. 47). Within the broader domain of management, contingency theories have been used for numerous research topics such as the investigation of the contingent nature of organizational design (e.g. Lawrence/Lorsch 1967), organizational and business strategies (e.g. Hofer 1975, Beach/Mitchell 1978),[192] organizational processes (e.g. Lindsay/Rue 1980, Bryson/Bromiley 1993), leadership styles (e.g. Kerr et al. 1974) and innovation and entrepreneurship (e.g. Burns/Stalker 1961, Damanpour 1996, Dess et al. 1997).

The theory proposes that (a) the external and internal context or the situation in which firms operate influences (b) the structure of organizations and (c) the behavior of its actors. Moreover, the situation of the organization and the structure and behavior in turn influence (d) the efficiency of the organization. Based on these notions, it is argued that there is no single best way of organizing. Instead, organizations need to adapt their organizational structures and their behavior to the given external and internal situation in order to be efficient (Kieser/Kubicek 1992, pp. 56-58, Kieser 2006, p. 219, Forsgren 2008, p. 74). These basic premises of the contingency theory are summarized in Figure 3.15 and are described in more detail below.

---

[192] For a more comprehensive overview of contributions on organizational strategy that employ contingency theory see Ginsberg/Venkatraman (1985).

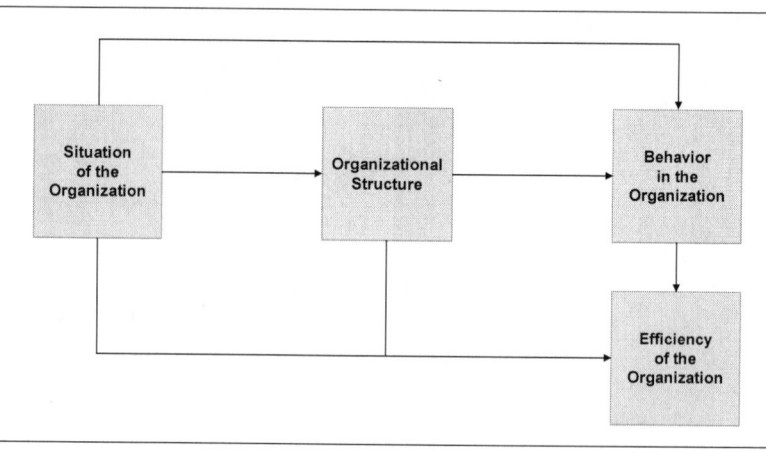

Figure 3.15: Extended version of the contingency model
Source: Kieser/Kubicek 1992, p. 57

(a) The situation or the organizational context, as the independent variable, can be described as the combination of situational factors that help to explain differences in organizational structure and organizational behavior. The "situation" can therefore be understood as a collective term that represents all possible explanatory factors. This allows the inclusion of a wide range of contextual factors and also enhances the possibility of integrating other theoretical lenses that focus on organizational structure and organizational behavior (Kieser/Walgenbach 2010, p. 42). A wide range of external and internal contextual factors has been investigated to this point. Whereas earlier empirical studies often focused on the particular effect of only one factor (i.e. single factor studies), later work incorporated two or more factors (i.e. multiple factor studies). As it can be assumed that organizations are, in reality, confronted with numerous influencing factors simultaneously, such multiple factor studies or multivariate configurations can offer more useful or complete explanations of complex organizations (see Dess et al. 1997, p. 682). Among contingency variables that have been previously identified (in single factor studies) are environmental complexity (Lawrence/Lorsch 1967), organization strategy (Chandler 1962), technology (Woodward 1965), and the size of the organization (Child 1975). As can be seen, contingency factors can include both external (e.g. environmental complexity) and internal factors (e.g. size of the organization). External contingencies are understood as all contextual factors that can explain differences in organizational structure and behavior and that cannot be influenced by the organization alone. Instead, they also result from the behavior of other (external) organizations. External contingencies have been further broken down into factors relating to the global environment (i.e. macro-environment) and the more immediate task-specific environment. In contrast, internal contingencies include all factors that represent characteristics of organizations and can be more directly influenced by organizations themselves. With regard to internal contingencies, one can further differentiate between factors concerning the present and factors related to the past of the organization (Kieser/Ebers 2006, p. 222). Table 3.4 provides an overview of external and internal contingency factors that impact organizational structure and behavior and have been repeatedly investigated in previous research.

Environmental (External) Contingency Factors	Organizational (Internal) Contingency Factors
Task-specific environment • Competitive situation • Customer structure • Dynamics of technical developments **Global environment** • Societal conditions • Cultural conditions	**Factors concerning the present** • Spectrum of products and services • Size • Manufacturing techniques • Information technique • Legal form and ownership structure **Factors concerning the past** • Age of the organization • Form of foundation • Developmental stage of the organization

Table 3.4: Contingency factors impacting organizational structure and behavior
Source: Adapted and translated from Kieser 2006, p. 222

(b) As articulated, contingency theory asserts that the context or situation of the organization first of all determines the formal organizational structure that can be described and operationalized through different dimensions. Although it has been stated that no standardized catalog of these structural dimensions exists, different book contributions on organizations and organization theory (i.e. Schreyögg 1999, p. 57, Kieser/Ebers 2006, p. 219, Scherm/Pietsch 2007, p. 37) rely on five dimensions that were identified by the Aston group (e.g. Pugh/Hickson 1968, Pugh et al. 1968): specialization, standardization, centralization, formalization and configuration. Newer conceptions of contingency theory have added further variables related to the coordination in organizations, such as personal directions, self-coordination, rules, programs and plans (Kieser/ Ebers 2006, p. 220).[193]

(c) The effects of the structure on the efficiency of the organization are conveyed indirectly through the actions of the organizational actors. It is assumed that the "opportunity space" for organizational activities is largely influenced by the organizational structure. For instance, formal rules frequently stipulate in a binding manner how organizational members need to behave in specific situations, thereby linking structure

---

[193] For a more comprehensive overview on different coordinating mechanisms within the MNC see also Kutschker/ Schmid (2011, pp. 1025-1065).

and behavior. However, the behavior and the characteristics of organizational actors are often neglected in empirical studies since organizational behavior is considered difficult to operationalize and to assess (Kieser 2006, p. 223, Höhne 2009, p. 91).

(d) Finally, contingency theory suggests that a high fit between the organizational context and the organizational structure (and thus behavior) should result in a high performance of the organization. Although the dependent variable of organizational performance often relates to measures such as revenue or profitability, it still remains somewhat unclear what constitutes the success of an organization from a contingency perspective. As a result of its broad meaning, further performance measures have been employed in previous research, including efficiency, innovation rate, employee satisfaction and patient well-being (Donaldson 2001, p. 10, Scherm/Pietsch 2007, p. 38).

Despite its wide use and acceptance, contingency theory has not remained without controversy. For instance, with regard to conceptual aspects it has been noted that the approach lacks a theoretical foundation. Apparently, much of the early work focused first on potentially plausible statistical causalities and developed explanations for significant findings afterwards, which were then summarized as "contingency theory" (Scherm/Pietsch 2007, p. 41, Höhne 2009, p. 94). Scholars also point to the overly deterministic view the theory takes. Contingency thinking argues in a unidirectional manner that the organizational context determines structure, behavior and consequently performance. It thereby reduces structural and behavioral decisions to "mere adaptive (re)actions" and ignores the fact that organizations can also, at least in part, influence their situation (Schmid 1994, p. 14, Donaldson 2001, p. 132, Kieser 2006, p. 234). Moreover, contingency approaches disregard aspects relating to organizational politics, such as individual interests, conflicts and power and their impact on structure, behavior and performance. Instead of assuming pluralistic values and interests and divergent decision-making, it is implied that organizations have fixed objectives on which all actors agree (Schmid 1994, p. 14, Scherm/Pietsch 2007, p. 41). Contingency theory also presumes there is only one "fitting" or best structure for a specific situation and that a certain amount of efficiency or a certain level of (economic) performance is required. However, it has been countered that the identification of an "optimal" organizational structure is likely impossible. Thus it cannot be ruled out *a priori* that, given a specific situation, different structures may provide equally good solutions. Furthermore, organizations with suboptimal structures and behavior are not necessarily eliminated. Instead, it is suggested that markets will tolerate such suboptimal structures to a certain degree and, even more, organizations can compensate for a suboptimal solution in one area by above average ones in other areas (Schmid 1994, p. 15, Schreyögg 1999, p. 360, Kieser 2006, p. 234). Finally, the contingency perspective has been criticized for leaving the issue of "organizational change and adaption to new environmental demands unanswered" (Doz/Prahalad 1991, p. 151). Thus, it remains largely unclear which processes and actions organizations can or must take to adapt to new situations (Schmid 1994, p. 15, Kieser 2006, pp. 235-236).

In addition to these conceptual critiques, contingency theory has also raised methodological concerns. For instance, it has been complained that not all potentially relevant contingency factors are included or even can be included in empirical research. While, over the course of time, many new contingency factors have been added, it is assumed that this process is far from being completed (Kieser 2006, p. 231, Scherm/Pietsch 2007, p. 41). Moreover, the operationalization and measurement of central constructs (e.g. situation or structure) are criticized and seen as problematic. For example, Kieser states that not only is the operationalization of these central elements extraordinarily complex, but researchers often neglect to appropriately assess the validity and reliability of their measures (Kieser 2006, p. 231). Lastly, contingency theory lacks clear and unambiguous empirical support (Schreyögg 1999, p. 349, Fahy 2002, p. 59). For instance, empirical results concerning the relationship between situation and structure vary widely, making it difficult to draw clear conclusions for the theory (Scherm/Pietsch 2007, p. 41). This has, at least in part, been attributed to the complexities inherent in the operationalization of constructs and inappropriate statistical samples and methods applied in earlier research (Kieser 2006, p. 231).

3.3.4.2 Contingency Theory in International Business Literature

(1) Application in International Business Research

Contingency theory can be viewed as widely accepted and applied in the domain of international business (Doz/Prahalad 1991, p. 151, Schmid 1994, p. 13, Banalieva/ Sarathy 2011, p. 600). In support of this view it has been stated that "much of international business and international management research is concerned with contingency effects [...]. Therefore the differences in national cultures, political systems, economies, institutions tend to be examined as determinants of variations in firm structure, processes, and performance, or the behavior of individual managers" (Collinson/Pettigrew 2009, p. 770). For instance, different models concerned with MNCs' structural adaptations to factors such as geographic or product diversity clearly represent contingency approaches (e.g. Stopford/Wells 1972, Egelhoff 1988; see Kutschker/Schmid 2011, pp. 551-558 for further details). Various publications that focus on foreign subsidiaries of MNCs also draw from contingency theory. Among them are works that relate to topics such as patterns and modes of headquarters control over foreign subsidiaries (e.g. Doz/Prahalad 1984, Ghoshal/Nohria 1989, Nohria/Ghoshal

1994, Ambos/Schlegelmilch 2007),[194] local responsiveness of subsidiaries (e.g. Luo 2001), performance evaluation of foreign subsidiaries (e.g. Kretschmer 2008, Schmid/ Kretschmer 2010), subsidiary competence development and management (e.g. Cui et al. 2005, Holm et al. 2005) and knowledge transfer between headquarters and subsidiaries (e.g. Cui et al. 2006, Rabbiosi 2011).[195]

For instance, among the publications concerned with headquarters control, Ghoshal and Nohria investigate the impact of environmental and organizational contingencies on the internal structure (or differentiation) of MNCs. The authors use "environmental complexity" and "local subsidiary resources" as contingencies and argue that, depending on the characteristics of these contingencies, there are particular "fit structures" of headquarters-subsidiary relations that will lead to enhanced subsidiary performance (Ghoshal/Nohria 1989, p. 333).[196] It is theoretically argued that, for example, subsidiaries possessing a high level of local resources and facing high environmental complexity should best fit with an "integrative" headquarters-subsidiary relationship model. According to Ghoshal and Nohria, this refers to a structure in which centralization of decision-making is low, formalization is moderate and normative integration is high (Bartlett/ Ghoshal 1986, 1989). In addition to the "integrated structure," the authors also present "hierarchical," "federative" and "clan-like" structure for the remaining three configurations of the two dimensions (Ghoshal/Nohria 1989, pp. 327-329).

Furthermore, Ambos and Schlegelmilch's journal article on innovation and control in the MNC focuses on control mechanisms used by firms to manage their foreign R&D subsidiaries (Ambos/Schlegelmilch 2007). The authors focus in particular on the two contingency factors they term the "interdependence of MNC units" and the "R&D mandate" of foreign units. While the factor "interdependence" is drawn from more "traditional" contingency literature (e.g. Lawrence/Lorsch 1967, Thompson 1967), the subsidiary's mandate as an important factor for shaping control is based on different contingency-oriented works on subsidiary role typologies (e.g. Bartlett/Ghoshal 1989, Ghoshal/ Nohria 1989, Gupta/Govindarajan 1991, Martinez/Jarillo 1991, Nobel/Birkinshaw 1998). With regard to the first contingency factors, it is claimed that increasing interdependencies in MNCs will lead to higher levels of centralization, formalization and socialization. Concerning the R&D mandates, researchers suggest that different mandates will also

---

[194] For further details on contingency approaches to headquarters-subsidiary relations see Blazejewski/Becker-Ritterspach 2011, pp. 147-153.
[195] Additionally, contingency theory is considered closely related to many other topics in the IB field, such as different subsidiary role typologies (e.g. Bartlett/Ghoshal 1986, Gupta/Govindarajan 1991), Bartlett and Ghoshal's typology of internationally active companies (e.g. Bartlett/Ghoshal 1989), or the integration-responsiveness framework by Prahalad and Doz (see Doz/Prahalad 1991, p. 151, Taggart 1997b, p. 297 and Kutschker/Schmid 2011, p. 362).
[196] The two contingencies represent dimensions that are used in other publications to differentiate between four different subsidiary role types (see e.g. Bartlett/Ghoshal 1986, 1989). In addition, as outlined in Section 3.3.4.2, the publication also draws from other theoretical strands, such as exchange theories (Emerson 1962) and resource dependence theory (Pfeffer/Salancik 1978).

require specific control mechanisms. For instance, foreign units in the role of "international creators" that augment or create new technological competences and capabilities abroad should require a high level of centralization, lower levels of formalization and high levels of socialization (Ambos/Schlegelmilch 2007, pp. 475-476).

In addition, works concerned with (knowledge) resource creation and management in foreign subsidiaries recognize the importance of contingency factors. For example, Holm et al. (2005) utilize a contingency perspective when discussing the impact of the competitive environment on competence development in foreign subsidiaries of MNCs.[197] In general it is argued that "the level of competition in the environment pressures MNC units to be innovative and to upgrade their competencies." More specifically, the authors suggest that the higher the competitive intensity in a subsidiary's market environment, the more likely it is to engage in competence development activities (e.g. via product or process innovations) through external business relationships (Holm et al. 2005, pp. 201, 204). Similarly, Cui et al. (2005) take a contingency approach to the knowledge management capabilities of MNC subsidiaries. Knowledge management is defined as "processes in an organization that develop and use knowledge within the firm" and, according to the author, consists of the interrelated processes of knowledge acquisition, knowledge conversion and knowledge application (Cui et al. 2005, p. 34). Following a contingent perspective, it is argued that the two contextual factors "competitive intensity" and "market dynamism" positively influence knowledge management capabilities, which are also seen as being positively correlated with the subsidiary's performance.

(2) Contingency Theory and Subsidiary Initiatives

With regard to the topic of subsidiary initiatives, publications have investigated numerous contingency factors relating to the context at the environmental, organizational and individual levels (see Subsection 2.2.4 for a detailed discussion). These studies clearly show that different contextual variables influence subsidiary initiative-taking behavior and its outcomes. For instance, empirical research indicates that, from the environmental context, situational factors such as the dynamism of the subsidiary's market environment (e.g. Zahra et al. 2000, Borini et al. 2009b, Keupp/Gassmann 2009a), competitive pressures (e.g. Sargent/Matthews 2006) and the complexity of the local environment (e.g. Zahra et al. 2000) influence initiative behavior of foreign subsidiaries.[198] Likewise, different situational factors from the organizational context, such as subsidiary resources and capabilities, subsidiary integration and autonomy (e.g. Birkinshaw et al. 1998, Birkinshaw 1999) and local orientation and responsiveness of the subsidiary (e.g.

---

[197] In addition to contingency theory, the authors apply the relation view in their contribution (i.e. Dyer/Singh 1998).
[198] The environmental-level context factors are also well-established in the general contingency literature (see e.g. Kieser 2006, p. 222).

Tseng et al. 2004, Liouka 2007) have been shown to impact subsidiary initiative-taking.[199]

Although these studies provide broad conceptual and/or empirical support for the contingent nature of subsidiary initiative-taking, very few contributions explicitly link their work to contingency theory. For instance, Birkinshaw et al. (1998) investigate the effect of subsidiary-level, corporate-level and country- and industry-level factors on subsidiary initiatives and the subsidiary's contributory role. Many of the arguments and the contingency factors under investigation are derived from previous work employing contingency thinking (e.g. Prahalad/Doz 1981, Bartlett/Ghoshal 1986, Ghoshal/Nohria 1989), yet an explicit link to contingency theory is not made. Similarly, Birkinshaw's contribution on the determinants and consequences of subsidiary initiatives in MNCs (Birkinshaw 1999) acknowledges the important effect of the environmental and organizational context on initiatives and draws from various contingency-oriented works (e.g. Burns/Stalker 1961, Doz/Prahalad 1981, Prahalad/Doz 1987, Bartlett/Ghoshal 1989, Covin/Slevin 1991). However, it does so without directly referring to the theoretical perspective. Aside from Birkinshaw and his colleagues, other scholars also highlight the importance of contextual factors for subsidiary initiative-taking. For example, Verbeke et al. state that "entrepreneurial initiatives are expected to originate in the subsidiary itself, aided by a favorable corporate context." The authors summarize various determinants from the environmental, the corporate and the subsidiary context that have been shown in earlier work to impact subsidiary initiatives (Verbeke et al. 2007, p. 586). Likewise, Scott et al. (2010, p. 329) argue that the subsidiaries' "levels of entrepreneurship will vary according to their individual contexts." In particular, the scholars investigate the effects of three contextual factors on the subsidiary's entrepreneurial orientation and on subsidiary contribution: subsidiary autonomy, the subsidiary's external focus and the strategic reward system. The findings indicate that subsidiaries operating in more favorable contexts and showing a high level of entrepreneurial orientation will also contribute more strongly to the MNC (in terms of strategic creativity, initiative generation and performance; see Scott et al. 2010, p. 337).[200]

(3) Conclusions from Application of Contingency Theory in IB Research

First, given the wide application of contingency theory in the IB domain over the past four decades, it can be presumed that the theoretical perspective is well-established in this area. The theory has widely influenced research on MNCs and helped explain how,

---

[199] The organizational-level context factors are also well-established in contingency-oriented works from the IB domain (e.g. Doz/Prahalad 1984, Bartlett/Ghoshal 1986, Prahalad/Doz 1987, Nohria/Ghoshal 1994).
[200] In addition, many other publications emphasize the significance of context for subsidiary initiative (e.g. Birkinshaw 1997, Zahra et al. 2000, Dörrenbächer/Geppert 2010, Rațiu/Molz 2010, Williams/Lee 2011a).

for instance, differences in cultures, economies, or institutions can lead to variations in multinational firms' structures, processes or performance.

Second, a large number of publications on foreign subsidiaries have employed contingency theory as well. Related literature highlights the importance of the contextual setting on various subsidiary aspects, such as role, strategy, performance and resource and capability development. Existing research suggests that, for example, contingency factors such as the competitive environment or market dynamism can positively influence capability development and management in foreign units of MNCs (e.g. Cui et al. 2005, Holm et al. 2005).

Third, with regard to subsidiary initiatives, numerous contributions indicate that the subsidiary's environmental and organizational context plays a critical role for the process as well. These writings support the assumption that subsidiary initiative-taking behavior should vary systematically with different contextual settings. As was shown both in the literature review (Subsection 2.2.4) and this subsection, more than 50 environmental-level and organizational-level contingency factors have been identified in the relevant literature on subsidiary initiatives. Among those are several that relate to certain dimensions of specific subsidiary role typologies suggesting that contingency factors from the subsidiary role context should impact the process of initiative-taking in foreign units of MNCs.

3.3.5 Linking the Theoretical Perspectives

As stated in the previous subsections, the present thesis draws from three theoretical perspectives: RBV, RDT and contingency theory. As was described, these three theories can and have been applied individually for the topic of subsidiary initiatives. However, since they will be employed together in a single research framework, it is important to discuss, at least briefly, the link between these three theoretical lenses. As explained in more detail below, this thesis applies a contingent and resource-oriented perspective for its framework on subsidiary initiative-taking. To this end, it makes use of the complementary potential between RBV and RDT and employs an overall resource-oriented view for the two sub-processes of subsidiary initiatives (see Subsection 3.3.5.1).[201] Moreover, an overall contingency perspective is applied to both sub-processes, assuming that they vary systematically with different subsidiary role contexts. Consequently, Subsections 3.3.5.2 and 3.3.5.3 discuss the potential relationships between RBV and RDT, respectively, and contingency theory.

---

[201] These two sub-processes are (1) initiative-related resource management and (2) headquarters-subsidiary alignment. See Subsections 3.2.2.1 and 3.2.2.2 for additional details.

3.3.5.1 Relationship Between RBV and RDT

Due to many alleged similarities, it is repeatedly claimed that RDT and RBV can and should be theoretically linked to each other (zu Knyphausen-Aufseß 1997, p. 479, Medcof 2001, p. 1002, Luo 2003, p. 291, Liouka 2007, p. 31, Hillman et al. 2009, p. 1417). For instance, Medcof argues that "RDT can be theoretically connected to the RBV because of the nearly identical meanings of certain of their fundamental concepts" (2001, p. 1002), while Hillman et al. state that "integrating RDT with the resource-based view may be particularly productive" (2009, p. 1417).

Among the similarities is, first and foremost, the terminological connection between RDT and RBV, as both theoretical perspectives center on the control of critical resources as the key determining factor of organizational behavior (Nienhüser 2008, p. 17). Moreover, it has been maintained that the two theories are also closely related with regard to many of their underlying theoretical assumptions. Besides the analogy concerning "resource control," it has also been claimed that the resource characteristics related to "value" and "uniqueness" as postulated by the RBV are closely linked to "importance" and "alternatives" as proposed by the RDT (Medcof 2001, p. 1002, Liouka 2007, p. 48).[202] For example, the notion of "value" in the RBV implies that resources enable a firm to be successful in a market and allow it to gain competitive advantage. As such, a valuable resource could be viewed "important" to a firm, as it allows it to improve its performance. In a somewhat similar vein the RDT proposes that an important resource helps the organization to function and survive. Also, both RBV and RDT acknowledge that the value and importance of a resource are, at least in part, dependent upon the environmental conditions of the firm. Furthermore, the concept of "uniqueness" in the RBV suggests that certain resources are only possessed or controlled by very few or even only one among (potentially) competing firms. Likewise, the RDT underlines the importance of the concentration of resources, referring to the limited availability or even the exclusive control over resources or potential alternatives (see Pfeffer/Salancik 2003, pp. 46-47, Barney/Clark 2007, pp. 57-58).

In addition to the analogies concerning resource characteristics offered by the two theoretical perspectives, further parallels have been drawn for the organizational outcomes of valuable (important) and unique resources. While the RBV stresses a firm's performance or competitive advantage as consequences, the RDT highlights organizational functioning and survival as outcome measures. Although these two outcomes appear somewhat divergent, it has been stated that they may in fact not be so different after all. For example, zu Knyphausen-Aufseß argues that if a firm is unable to deliver a sufficient value-add or above-normal rents (as implied by the RBV), it will also risk its

---

[202] The term "alternatives" refers to what Pfeffer and Salancik describe as "concentration of resource control" (see Pfeffer/Salancik 2003, p. 50).

survival as it may lose the support of important stakeholders over time (as implied by RDT). Consequently, not only being profitable, but also producing above-normal rents may be necessary for a firm's survival in the long run, thereby bringing the outcome measures of RBV and RDT closer together or even making them the same (see zu Knyphausen-Aufseß 1997, p. 462).

Not surprisingly, many of the proponents recommending such an integration of RBV and RDT in the IB field have indeed done so in their publications (e.g. Medcof 2001, Luo 2003, Liouka 2007).[203] For instance, Medcof links the two theoretical perspectives when conceptually investigating how important technical resources residing in internationally dispersed technology units in MNCs can develop resource-based power. While resource-based considerations are applied to help explain how unique and valuable resources located in the foreign units may contribute to the firm's competitive advantage (e.g. by developing market-leading products), RDT is used to explain how such resources may then lead to subsidiary power (Medcof 2001, pp. 1001-1002).[204] Luo also uses resource dependence theory and the dynamic capability framework when attempting to explain how parent-subsidiary links in MNCs influence the success and performance of foreign subsidiaries. Here, RDT comes into play when explaining how intra-corporate links within the MNC may help to reduce external dependence, while the dynamic capabilities framework sheds light on how these links can help subsidiaries strategically adapt to the to the host country environment in order to reap benefits for the company as a whole (Luo 2003, pp. 291-293).[205]

Despite these similarities between RBV and RDT, there are at least two important differences that one should consider when linking the two theoretical perspectives. *First*, while the RDT stresses the influence of the external environment on organizational functioning and survival, the RBV takes a more internal perspective and focuses on the relationship between internal resources and firm performance (Nienhüser 2008, p. 17).[206] *Second*, the RDT views organizations primarily as political phenomena that achieve their objectives through the acquisition and execution of power and influence, whereas the RBV takes a more economic and strategic approach to the internal func-

---

[203] Also a number of other publications from the fields of IB (e.g. Taylor et al. 1996), innovation and entrepreneurship (e.g. Lichtenstein/Brush 2001, Parhankangas/Arenius 2003, Teng 2007, Geh 2011), or the management domain at large (Morgan/Hunt 1999, Zaefarian et al. 2011) have used both RDT and RBV together in their works.
[204] In addition to RBV and RDT, Medcof (2001) also uses the Vroom-Yetton model of leadership as a third theoretical perspective (Vroom/Yetton 1973).
[205] As discussed in Subsections 3.3.2.3 and Section 3.3.3.2 at more length, Liouka applies both RBV and RDT when investigating the antecedents and the outcomes of entrepreneurial opportunity identification in foreign subsidiaries. While RBV represents the overarching theoretical perspective, RDT is specifically used when discussing aspects of intraorganizational relationships of subsidiaries and their impact on subsidiary entrepreneurship (see e.g. Liouka 2007, pp. 48-49).
[206] The strength of this argument, however, is somewhat diluted when one considers the recent developments of the RBV towards more strongly integrating external contingencies as outlined earlier. In addition, it needs to be remembered that RDT also considers both interorganizational (external) as well as intraorganizational (internal) relationships of organizations.

tioning of the firm (Hagan 1996, p. 149, Barney/Arikan 2001, p. 125, Freiling 2008, p. 36).[207]

Nevertheless, these differences need not be viewed as entirely contradictory. Instead, researchers may actually make use of the complementary potential of the two theoretical approaches. In instances where neither theory is able to fully explain a particular phenomenon, using both RBV and RDT – without necessarily fully integrating both theories – may thus allow an overall resource-oriented perspective to be maintained while extending the reach of both theoretical approaches (zu Knyphausen-Aufseß 1997, p. 479, Freiling 2008, p. 34). For instance, RDT may help to explain how and why organizations acquire control of important and unique resources (from external sources), while RBV could then help to explain how and why these resources may (internally) lead to competitive advantage (Hillman et al. 2009, p. 1417). Moreover, RDT could likely supplement the RBV in investigations of the internal and external shifts in resource-based power resulting from newly acquired or developed resources, as has been done by some of the cited literature (i.e. Medcof 2001, Luo 2003, Liouka 2007).

Corresponding to this reasoning, the present thesis will also take advantage of the complementary potential of both resource-oriented approaches. RBV comes into play to help explain how the initiative-related resource management process may unfold in the foreign subsidiaries and potentially lead to firm-level advantages for the wider MNC. RDT will then be utilized, under the larger umbrella of the RBV, to explain the potential role that resource-based power may play in headquarters-subsidiary interactions and relationships throughout the process of subsidiary initiative-taking.

3.3.5.2 Relationship Between Contingency Theory and RBV

Since the RBV as originally proposed is largely context-insensitive and mostly neglects the environmental and organizational setting of firms, scholars have repeatedly argued in favor of linking the RBV with contingency theory (e.g. Priem/Butler 2001, p. 32;, Ambrosini/Bowman 2009, p. 46). It has been held that such a combined theoretical view provides a more complete picture on the rent creation process, and consequently it could better explain how and under what circumstances resources and resource management activities lead to sustained competitive advantage in firms (Makadok 2001, p. 391, Fahy/Hooley 2002, p. 251).[208] Accordingly, numerous publications have linked contingency approaches with the RBV, for instance in the management literature in

---

[207] This argument can be further underlined when looking at the theoretical roots of these two perspectives. While RDT is to a large extent theoretically grounded in sociology (e.g. Emerson 1962, Blau 1964), RBV is more closely associated with Ricardian and Penrosian economics (e.g. Penrose 1959; see Ulrich/Barney 1984, p. 472, Barney/Arikan 2001, p. 125).

[208] Besides these more recent calls for including a contingency perspective, proponents of the RBV have – although more generally – acknowledged the importance of the contextual perspective for the generation of sustained competitive advantage from earlier on (e.g. Barney 1986a, Amit/Schoemaker 1993, Teece et al. 1997).

general (e.g. Collis 1994, Miller/Shamsie 1996, Brush/Artz 1999, Makadok 2001, Fahy/ Hooley 2002, Aragón-Correa/Sharma 2003, Sirmon et al. 2007, Sirmon/Hitt 2009) and in (corporate) entrepreneurship literature in particular (e.g. Chandler/Hanks 1994, Godfrey/Gregersen 1999, Teng 2007, Hitt et al. 2011).[209]

Certain scholars associate linking the more dynamic and processes-oriented strands of the RBV, in particular, with contingency approaches with various advantages. For instance, it has been stated that such linking should better reflect the understanding that both resources and the internal and external contextual setting play a critical role when it comes to firm performance and success (Mahoney/Pandian 1992, p. 375, Spanos/ Lioukas 2001, p. 912, Makadok 2001, p. 391, Fahy/Hooley 2002, p. 251, Kutschker/ Schmid 2011, p. 844). Such a combined view may also help overcome the criticism of contingency theory as an overly deterministic and static theory since it may help better explain how resources can be managed in different contextual settings to create value for the firm (e.g. Aragón/Sharma 2003, p. 83, Sirmon et al. 2008, p. 923).

In line with these arguments and in view of the complementary nature of the two theories[210] (see also Pertusa-Ortega et al. 2010, p. 1294), the present research takes a contingency perspective on the initiative-related resource management process. While the dynamic and process-oriented strands of the RBV will provide guidance on the resource management activities related to entrepreneurial initiatives, contingency theory will help explain how these activities are influenced by different subsidiary role contexts.

3.3.5.3 Relationship Between Contingency Theory and RDT

It has been claimed that contingency theory and RDT are closely related and share many fundamental assumptions (Hillman et al. 2009, p. 1418). While some scholars consider RDT to be "an important correction to structural contingency theory" (Foss 1997, p. 16), others take a more inclusive view and think of it as "a branch of structural contingency theory ... concerned with the power aspects of organizational structure" (Donaldson 2001, p. 153).[211] Analogous to contingency theory, RDT highlights the importance of (mostly external) contingencies for organizational structure and behavior. As a result, it has been stated that the distribution of power and control and organiza-

---

[209] See also Subsection 3.3.2.2 herein which outlines contingency approaches to the RBV in more detail.
[210] It has been suggested that linking these two theories is possible given their "fundamental compatibility". For instance, it has been proposed that both theories attempt to explain heterogeneity in firms' performance – yet with different emphasis: one with an inside-out view (RBV) and the other one with an outside-in perspective (contingency theory). Hence, drawing from both, one could obtain a more balanced view on how competitive advantage is created. Furthermore, both theories attempt to explain the same phenomenon of interest, that is, sustained competitive advantage. Last, both theoretical approaches use the same unit of analysis, that is, the firm (see Spanos/Lioukas 2001, p. 912).
[211] These arguments can be further substantiated when looking at the theoretical antecedents of RDT. For instance, in their book publication, Pfeffer and Salancik draw from contingency theory works, such as Thompson (1967) or Hickson et al. (1971; see e.g. Pfeffer/Salancik 2003, pp. 230-231), emphasizing the importance of organizational context for organizational structure and activities.

tional structure is "context specific" and hence dependent on contingencies internal or external to organizations (Astley/Sachdeva 1984, p. 104, Pfeffer/Salancik 2003, p. 231).[212] Given the similarities and complementarities, scholars have encouraged the integrative use of the two theoretical approaches (e.g. Ghoshal/Nohria 1989, p. 324, Ambos/Schlegelmilch 2007, p. 474, Hillman et al. 2009, p. 1418). For instance, Ghoshal and Nohria state that a synthesis of contingency theory and resource dependence theory "may readily by extended to multi-unit organizations, such as MNCs, in which different components, such as the various national subsidiaries, face vastly different environmental and resource contingencies" (Nohria/Ghoshal 1989, p. 324). Consequently, the authors use both contingency and resource dependence arguments in order to explain internal differentiation within MNCs. Ambos and Schlegelmilch similarly claim that "both perspectives show a great potential to unify many ... contingencies into one framework" (Ambos/Schlegelmilch 2007, p. 474).

Despite the common fundamental assumptions, contingency theory and RDT also differ in certain regards. *First*, traditional contingency theory takes a rather functional and bureaucratic perspective. It argues that organizational structure and behavior are mechanistically determined by the contextual setting, leading to differences in organizational performance. In contrast, RDT, taking a stronger sociological view, focuses less on efficiency aspects and more on structural change based on power imbalances resulting from resource exchanges in view of organizational functioning and survival (Astley/Van De Ven 1983, pp. 248-249, Foss 1997, pp. 16-18). *Second*, while contingency theory is supposedly deficient in describing the mechanisms through which changes in context impact organizations and assumes "inevitable contextual determinism," RDT provides a more detailed model of how changes in context are linked to organizational actions and structures through the distribution of power and control in an organization (e.g. Pfeffer/Salancik 2003, pp. 226-228). *Third*, partially linked to the previous point, RDT takes a less deterministic view than contingency theory and argues that organizations are not limited to "mere adaptive (re)actions" but can make strategic choices within contextual constraints. Hence, from a resource dependence perspective, the contextual setting acts less as an "intractable constraint," giving organizations and their managers some discretion over how to structure their organization (Astley/Van De Ven 1983, p. 249, Greening/Gray 1994, p. 471, Donaldson 2001, p. 155). *Fourth*, in comparison to contingency theory, RDT also incorporates aspects related to organizational politics, such as conflict, power or bargaining. It has been stated that "since contingencies determine power and there are benefits to having control within the

---

[212] Yet, while contingency theory refers to a broad range of contingencies, RDT more narrowly focuses on one contingency, that is, the "critical challenge" facing the organization (Pfeffer/Salancik 2003, p. 230, Donaldson 2001, p. 154). As argued by Pfeffer and Salancik, such critical challenge or contingency may stem from both within and from outside the organization. Nevertheless, more emphasis is placed on critical contingencies arising from the external environment (see, for instance, Pfeffer/Salancik 2003, pp. 228-231).

organization, one can be certain that enactments are not apolitical interpretations of events" (Pfeffer/Salancik 2003, p. 234). Unlike contingency theory, RDT does not view organizational structure and actions as being shaped by impersonal mechanisms but rather as resulting from political processes within organizations (Astley/Van De Ven 1983, p. 249, Pfeffer/Salancik 2003, p. 229). *Fifth*, while traditional contingency theory holds that situational factors, as independent variables, cannot be influenced by the organization, RDT argues that organizations not only adapt to the context, but they "may take actions to modify the environment to which the organization then responds ... altering the system of constraints and dependencies confronting the organization" (Pfeffer/Salancik 2003, pp. 266-267). Therefore, in RDT organizations and their managers can, at least in part, influence contingencies to regain fit, thereby reducing the need to adapt their structure to the context (Foss 1997, p. 16, Donaldson 2001, p. 133).[213]

Given the close relationship between contingency theory and RDT, this work will take a combined view which assumes that subsidiary context influences (but does not determine) power distribution in general and headquarters-subsidiary alignment as part of initiative-taking in particular. Instead of following traditional contingency thinking, which would imply that role context directly shapes headquarters-subsidiary alignment, this work takes a less deterministic view. Here it is assumed that subsidiary management has some leeway or strategic choice to influence the sub-process of alignment and interaction with headquarters within contextual constraints.

3.3.5.4 Application of Theoretical Lenses

As outlined in Subsection 3.3.1.2, this thesis takes an overall contingency and resource-oriented view. Both the resource-based view and resource dependence theory provide the theoretical foundations for the two central aspects of the subsidiary initiative-taking behavior under investigation. The resource-based view is used to describe and explain the entrepreneurial resource management activities necessary to realize initiative opportunities. Resource dependence theory provides theoretical guidance with regard to the alignment and interactions between headquarters and the subsidiary. As both aspects of subsidiary initiative-taking behavior and the outcomes are expected to be contingent on the subsidiary's role setting, a contingency perspective is applied as an overarching theoretical lens to link these different elements within one comprehensive framework. Figure 3.16 once again provides an overview of the basic research framework and specifies how the three theoretical lenses are applied.

---

[213] It needs to be noted that this difference mostly applies to the traditional contingency theories. Certain strands of contingency theory, such as the "strategic choice" view advocated by Child, reflect a less deterministic perspective and acknowledge that organizations have some degree of choice regarding their structure and actions (see e.g. Child 1972).

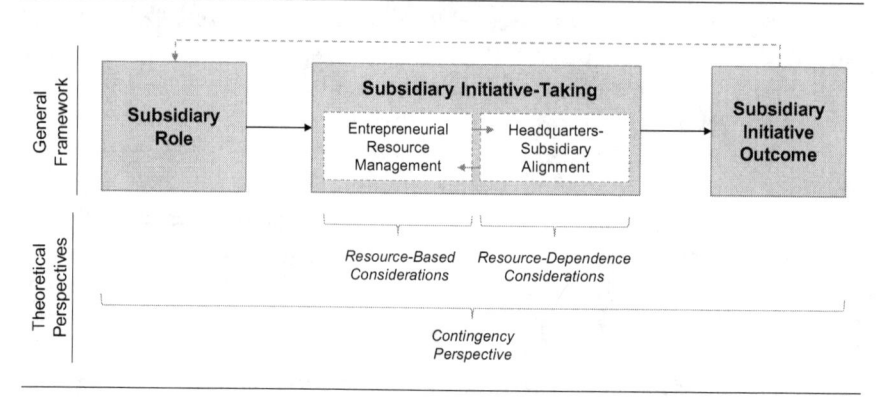

Figure 3.16: Theoretical perspectives and their application in the research framework

3.4 Contingent and Dynamic Resource-Based Framework

3.4.1 Introduction and Basic Assumptions

Building on the previously outlined resource-oriented and contingency considerations, this thesis views subsidiary initiative-taking as a context-dependent entrepreneurial process in foreign subsidiaries that is primarily concerned with identifying, acquiring, developing and bundling of resources and capabilities in order to exploit perceived entrepreneurial opportunities. Moreover, such a view of subsidiary initiatives entails (1) the assumption that unique resources and capabilities can be held at the subsidiary level, (2) a dynamic resource-based perspective acknowledging that unique resources and capabilities can be acquired and developed over time at the subsidiary level, (3) a process perspective on subsidiary initiative-taking that involves activities related to opportunity identification, resource utilization and (4) headquarters-subsidiary alignment. Finally, it is acknowledged that (5) the initiative process activities are contingent upon environmental and organizational factors.

(1) First, in line with the RBV (e.g. Wernerfelt 1984, Barney 1991), the MNC is viewed as a bundle of heterogeneous resources and capabilities that represents a potential source of sustained competitive advantage for the firm. Furthermore, extending the RBV to the MNC and its subsidiaries entails acknowledging that unique resources and capabilities are not held by a monolithic entity but are instead dispersed throughout the MNC network and may therefore also reside in foreign subsidiary units (e.g. Ghoshal/ Bartlett 1990, pp. 610-611, Roth 1995, p. 201, Birkinshaw 2000, pp. 103-104).[214] Within the differentiated MNC network, subsidiaries are conceptualized as semi-autonomous entities that have some discretion over their actions and that are, at least in part, capable of shaping their own strategic direction and of developing their own unique resource profiles. Given their strategic leeway, these foreign units are able to somewhat independently undertake entrepreneurial initiatives involving the development and deployment of specialized resources, even without explicit permission from headquarters (Birkinshaw 1997, p. 210, 2000, p. 103, Ambos et al. 2010, p. 1101). Subsidiary units are therefore not only regarded as important means for the development of specialized resources and capabilities for the wider MNC but also as potential sources of competitive advantage for the entire firm (Bartlett/Ghoshal 1986, p. 94, Birkinshaw et al. 1998, p. 225, Birkinshaw et al. 2005, p. 228).[215]

---

[214] As was shown in Subsections 3.3.1.2 and 3.3.2.3 herein, the RBV can be and has been usefully applied at the subsidiary level of MNCs.
[215] Following the resource-based logic, it is presumed that competitive advantage is still developed at the firm level rather than at the subsidiary level. Consequently, in order for these dispersed subsidiary resources and capabilities to contribute to firm-level advantages, they must be usefully leveraged in the wider MNC and therefore fulfill the requirements of being (a) specialized and (b) not fully location-bound (Birkinshaw et al. 1998, Birkinshaw 2000, Rugman/Verbeke 2001; see also section 3.3.2.3.2 herein).

(2) Second, taking a more dynamic resource-based perspective (e.g. Dierickx/Cool 1989, Teece et al. 1997, Makadok 2001, Helfat/Peteraf 2003), resources and capabilities in the MNC and their potential to generate competitive advantage are not viewed in a static manner. Instead, it is recognized that the dispersed resources and capabilities need to change and evolve over time. As the result of, for instance, variations in environmental conditions, customer demand, or imitative efforts by competitors, existing resource-based advantages can be more or less quickly eroded, thus requiring MNCs and their subsidiaries to frequently create, adapt and reconfigure their resource bases (Ambrosini/Bowman 2009, p. S13, Hitt et al. 2011, p. 69, Sirmon et al. 2011, pp. 1398-1399).[216] Such a dynamic resource-based perspective also entails that equilibrium conditions might only hold true for a certain (shorter or longer) period of time and that competitive advantage must be sustained through continuous efforts to adapt and (re)deploy the MNC's and the subsidiaries' resource bases in order to achieve a sequence of temporary competitive advantages (Ambrosini/Bowman 2009, p. 43, Sirmon et al. 2010, p. 1387). Corresponding to this more dynamic view, the possession or control of unique resources is not *per se* the only factor that provides the potential for sustainable competitive advantage; it also derives from effective actions related to the management of resources in response to the specificities of the contextual settings of the MNC and its subsidiaries (Eisenhardt/Martin 2000, p. 1118, Ahokangas et al. 2010, p. 127).[217]

(3) Third, recognizing the importance of resource management activities for sustained competitive advantage, this contribution also adopts a resource-based process perspective on subsidiary initiative-taking (e.g. Lichtenstein/Brush 2001, Bowman/Collier 2006, Helfat et al. 2007, Sirmon et al. 2007).[218] In order to bring more transparency to the entrepreneurial initiative-taking activities and their possible outcomes, the process is further unbundled into the distinct stages of initiative opportunity identification, initiative realization (consisting of resource structuring and resource bundling) and initiative implementation through resource leveraging activities (e.g. Alvarez/Busenitz 2001, Lichtenstein/Brush 2001, Sirmon et al. 2007).

(4) Fourth, it is recognized that subsidiary initiative-taking is not a straight-forward resource development and deployment process. Instead, it also depends on the alignment and interactions between headquarters and subsidiaries that are typically required to push subsidiary initiatives through the socio-political system of the MNC.

---

[216] Aside from such "resource risks," changes in the external or internal firm context may also offer new resource development and/or deployment opportunities for MNCs and their subsidiaries (Helfat/Peteraf 2003, p. 1007).

[217] As shown in Subsection 3.3.2.2, dynamic approaches to the RBV are considered well-suited for studying entrepreneurial phenomena as they can more appropriately address such dynamic issues.

[218] By taking a process perspective and outlining the specific process activities to alter and deploy the MNC's resource base, the tautology concern of the RBV is addressed (Eisenhardt/Martin 2000, p. 1108; see also Subsection 3.3.2.1 herein, which outlines the central criticisms of the RBV).

These more political aspects of the initiative process are expected to be, at least in part, shaped by resource dependencies and the resulting power distribution within the MNC (Astley/Sachdeva 1984, Pfeffer/Salancik 2003). To the extent that subsidiaries possess and/or are able to develop specialized resources on which headquarters or other MNC units depend, they can presumably exert and utilize their resource-based power to, for example, become more autonomous or to promote their interests and influence decisions in the MNC with regard to their initiatives (Birkinshaw/Ridderstråle 1999, p. 152, Ambos et al. 2010, p. 1101).

(5) Fifth, the two central elements of the initiative process, and consequently the resulting initiative outcomes, are expected to be influenced by the contextual setting of the subsidiary. Therefore, a contingency perspective is taken both on sub-processes of entrepreneurial resource management (see e.g. Covin/Slevin 1991, Bowman/Collier 2006, Helfat et al. 2007, Sirmon et al. 2007) and on headquarters-subsidiary alignment and interactions throughout the initiative process (see e.g. Ghoshal/Nohria 1989, Ambos/Schlegelmilch 2007). Accordingly, the previously specified subsidiary roles are incorporated as the independent variables, while the two central elements of subsidiary initiative-taking behavior and the initiative outcomes are included as dependent variables in the framework.

Following the overview of the basic assumptions of the contingent and resource-oriented framework, further details are presented on the entrepreneurial resource management sub-process (Subsection 3.4.2), the headquarters-subsidiary alignment sub-process (Subsection 3.4.3), the initiative outcomes (3.4.4) as well as subsidiary roles contexts as contingency factors (Subsection 3.4.5). This part of the dissertation then ends with concluding remarks on the research framework presented (Subsection 3.4.6).

3.4.2 Entrepreneurial Resource Management

As previously argued, through a contingent and dynamic resource-based lens, subsidiary initiative-taking can be understood as a context-dependent entrepreneurial process aimed at advancing new ways to use or expand a subsidiary's resources and capabilities in order to respond to opportunities that are perceived in the internal or external market (e.g. Birkinshaw 1997, p. 207, 1999, pp. 9-10, Birkinshaw/Ridderstråle 1999, p. 151). This perspective is in line with various publications stressing that value creation through innovation and entrepreneurship entails the identification, exchange and combination of resources to generate novel deployments of resources in the form of, for example, new or better products, services or processes (Schumpeter 1934, Burgelman 1983a, Moran/Ghoshal 1997, Tsai/Ghoshal 1998, Godfrey/Gregersen 1999,

Shane 2003).[219] Successfully implemented initiatives in the form of, for example, innovative products, services or processes, therefore lead to the accumulation and enhancement of specialized subsidiary resources and capabilities that, if further leveraged in the wider MNC, may even contribute to firm-level advantages (Peng 2001, p. 811, Rugman/Verbeke 2001, p. 245, Birkinshaw/Pedersen 2009, p. 379).[220]

Taking a resource-based perspective, Alvarez and Busenitz argue that entrepreneurship relates to two different aspects. First, it "involves the founder's unique awareness of opportunities" and second "the ability to acquire the resources needed to exploit the opportunity, and the organizational ability to recombine homogenous inputs into heterogeneous outputs" (Alvarez/Busenitz 2001, p. 771). Following their contribution and other resource-based publications on entrepreneurial activities (e.g. Bhave 1994, Moran/Ghoshal 1997, Boccardelli/Magnusson 2006), the present thesis considers two particular parts of the entrepreneurial initiative-taking process in foreign subsidiaries of MNCs: (1) the identification and (2) the "physical" realization of the initiative opportunity involving the structuring and bundling of existing and/or new resources and capabilities.[221] These particular aspects of the entrepreneurial initiative process are further described in the following Subsections 3.4.2.1 and 3.4.2.2.

---

[219] This view of entrepreneurial initiatives essentially builds on resource-oriented approaches to entrepreneurship, which posit that it entails the identification, development and realization of new combinations of resources to exploit marketplace opportunities. See also Subsection 3.3.2.4 herein, which discusses the link between the RBV and entrepreneurship.

[220] Nevertheless, entrepreneurial subsidiary initiatives do not merely represent the use and expansion of a subsidiary's resource base. In contrast to the gradual resource development and deployment that often comes with the regular business activities of the subsidiary, it is a key feature of initiatives to achieve exceptional growth that goes beyond the established mandate of the subsidiary (Birkinshaw/Hood 1997, p. 343, Bouquet/Birkinshaw 2008b, p. 582). In order to achieve such exceptional growth, initiative-taking subsidiaries must be proactive, risk-taking and innovative when pursuing opportunities to use or expand their resources (Miller 1983, p. 780, Covin/Slevin 1991, p. 7, Birkinshaw 1997, p. 208, Zahra et al. 2000, p. 5). Subsidiary initiative-taking is a proactive undertaking as it represents deliberate and conscious efforts by the subsidiary to seek out and develop new opportunities that others have not recognized or not actively pursued (Birkinshaw/Hood 1998b, p. 785, Covin/Miles 1999, p. 54). It represents activities that lie outside the assigned and accepted responsibility of the subsidiary and requires that foreign units be alert and/or sensitive to resource deployment and development opportunities that may emerge in the internal or external market (Birkinshaw/Hood 1997, p. 343). Initiative-taking is also risk-taking as it involves the pursuit of opportunities regardless of the resources currently controlled by the subsidiary (Stevenson/Jarillo 1990, p. 23, Birkinshaw 1997, p. 208, Dimitratos et al. 2009b, p. 181). This implies that subsidiaries are involved in entrepreneurial activities that will stretch their current resource-base "without entirely breaking with [it]" (Teng 2007, p. 122). Initiative-taking is also risk-taking because new initiative opportunities are often uncertain, as new resources need to be obtained and bundled before their outcomes and value can be fully determined (Shane 2003, p. 161). Finally, initiative-taking represents innovative activities as it typically involves creating and introducing new products, production processes or organizational systems through novel combinations of resources and capabilities (Tseng et al. 2004, p. 94, Bouquet/Birkinshaw 2008b, p. 582).

[221] Similarly, Bouquet and Birkinshaw (2008, p. 490) describe subsidiary initiative-taking as a process that in general involves (1) the identification and pursuit of new opportunities, (2) the reorganization and creative deployment of resources and (3) the acquisition and use of power. While the first two parts of this process view are addressed in Subsections 3.4.2.1 and 3.4.2.2, the headquarters-subsidiary alignment activities that involve the acquisition and use of power are described in Subsection 3.5.3.

3.4.2.1 Initiative-Related Opportunity Identification

Subsidiary initiatives typically begin with the identification of a new business opportunity or business improvement opportunity within the foreign units of an MNC. Through a resource-based lens, an initiative opportunity, such as an innovative product or service, can be viewed as a possibility to create new resources and/or combine existing ones in novel ways to generate superior value for the firm (e.g. Schumpeter 1934, Birkinshaw 1997, Ireland et al. 2001, Alvarez/Barney 2002). The identification of subsidiary initiative opportunities frequently occurs through subsidiary managers and can be seen as a deliberate and conscious effort to discover or create new resource development and deployment opportunities.[222] These can take various forms and range from, for instance, smaller internal business improvement opportunities to more extensive new product development opportunities. The identification of initiative opportunities can take place either (a) *externally* through interactions with local suppliers, customers and other market players (external market initiatives) or (b) *internally* through interactions with actors from within the corporate system, such as headquarters or other subsidiary units (internal market initiatives; Stevenson/Jarillo 1990, p. 23, Birkinshaw/Hood 1998b, pp. 785-786).

After a resource creation and deployment opportunity in the form of a subsidiary initiative is identified, the broader idea is usually further developed and framed by project or initiative champions in the subsidiary, leading to a more concrete proposal (e.g. a preliminary business concept) that may also come into play when approaching subsidiary and/or headquarters management for approval, resources or support (Birkinshaw 1995, p. 35, Birkinshaw/Fry 1998, p. 54 Ardichvili et al. 2003, p. 109). It can be expected that such a proposal specifies the resource and capability configurations required to exploit the given initiative opportunity and to gain a competitive advantage in the internal or external market (Sirmon et al. 2007, p. 284). Comparing the resources needed to realize the opportunity with the resources currently available to the subsidiary may then lead to the determination of a resource gap or "investment need," including the type (e.g. physical, human and financial resources), quantity or timing of the resources required. After the resource need is specified, potential resource suppliers and provid-

---

[222] The entrepreneurship literature often further differentiates between opportunity discovery (e.g. Kirzner 1973) and opportunity creation (e.g. Schumpeter 1934). Opportunity discovery refers to the recognition of new and better utilization possibilities of given resources (i.e. discovering a fit between market needs and specific resources), whereas opportunity creation involves the more extensive redirection and recombination of resources (i.e. creating a fit between market needs and resources; see Shane 2000, pp. 449-450, Ardichvili et al. 2003, pp. 109-111). Hence, it can be assumed that both possibilities also apply to subsidiary initiatives (see Liouka 2007, pp. 54-55).

ers must be identified, or the possibility of internal development has to be assessed (Grant 1991, p. 115, Brush et al. 2001, pp. 74-75).[223]

3.4.2.2 Initiative-Related Resource Structuring

Obtaining the resources needed for "physical" realization has been described as an essential part of entrepreneurial initiative (Kuratko et al. 2005, p. 706). After specifying their resource need, subsidiaries can undertake different resource structuring activities to attain the resources required to realize the identified initiative opportunity. The resource-based literature presents two basic mechanisms through which organizations can obtain new resources and capabilities, which should also apply to foreign subsidiary units of MNCs: resource acquisition in strategic factor markets (Barney 1986) and internal resource accumulation or development (Dierickx/Cool 1989, see also Maritan/Peteraf 2011, p. 1374). Furthermore, in the particular case of foreign subsidiaries in MNCs, previous literature highlights two distinct sources from which needed resources and capabilities for subsidiary initiatives can be obtained: external sources outside the MNC network (e.g. in local host country networks) and internal sources within the MNC network (e.g. through intra-firm relationships; see e.g. Andersson et al. 2001a, Foss/Pedersen 2002, Schmid/Schurig 2003). Bringing together these two dimensions, the "mechanism of resource structuring" and "source for resource structuring," results in the two-by-two matrix illustrated in Figure 3.17, which briefly portrays the four principal approaches that foreign subsidiaries may take to resource structuring. Accordingly, subsidiaries may (1) *externally acquire* resources from outside the MNC network, (2) *internally acquire* resources from within the MNC network, (3) *exclusively accumulate resources internally* within the subsidiary itself or through interactions with internal MNC network partners, and (4) *accumulate resources internally* but also involving external market actors from outside the MNC network (see Subsections 3.3.2.6 and 3.3.2.7).[224]

---

[223] It should be noted that the identification of the "exact" resource need is a challenging task, as subsidiary initiatives may evolve in their scope, content and focus as they progress and develop (Kuratko et al. 2005, p. 706). Therefore, the resource need may have to be repeatedly adjusted or refined over time.
[224] Subsidiaries may also divest resources. However, this will not be further discussed at this point, as the focus is on the development of resources rather than the optimization of the entire resource portfolio.

	Source for Resource Structuring	
	Internal (intra MNC)	External
Resource Acquisition	② Internal resource acquisition	① External resource acquisition
Resource Accumulation	③ Internal resource accumulation	④ Internal-external resource accumulation

(Mechanism of Resource Structuring — row labels on left)

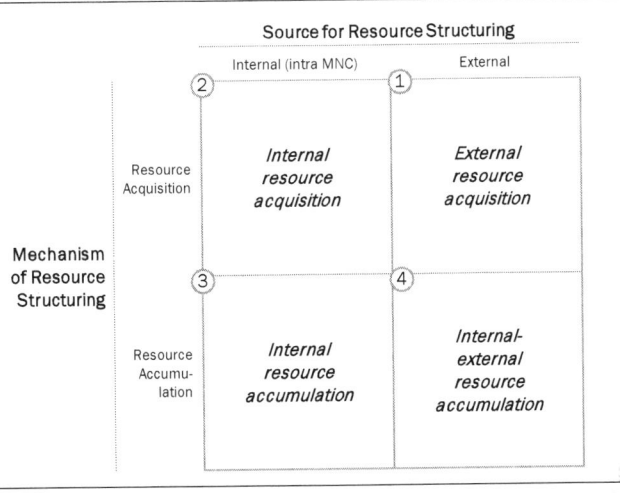

Fig. 3.17: Mechanisms and sources for subsidiary initiative-related resource structuring

(1) First, subsidiaries can *externally acquire* resources from strategic factor markets. The external acquisition can range from commodity-like resources (e.g. equipment or machinery) and more intangible resources (e.g. intellectual property) to complex bundles of tangible and intangible resources. Subsidiaries may either purchase particular resources in a relevant factor market (e.g. research and development skills obtained in the research scientist labor market) or acquire larger and more complex sets of resources and capabilities via, for instance, mergers and acquisitions (Barney 1986, p. 1232, Sirmon et al. 2007, p. 278, Wiklund/Shepherd 2009, pp. 195-198, Maritan/Peteraf 2011, pp. 1375-1376). Furthermore, subsidiaries can obtain access to specific resources through their local host country networks and their relationships and interactions with local actors, such as customers, suppliers or even governments (e.g. McEvily/Zaheer 1999, p. 1135, Frost 2001, p. 101, Andersson et al. 2002b, p. 979, Almeida/Phene 2004, p. 848).[225]

---

[225] However, the external acquisition of critical resources is likely influenced by different factors such as acquisition costs, resource availability or resource accessibility in these markets. Based on the strategic factor market logic (e.g. Barney 1986), the costs for obtaining a resource determine the extent to which a firm can earn above-normal returns from the acquired resources. If a subsidiary is able to purchase resources externally at costs below their true economic value, it can be expected that it will gain a resource-based advantage. In order to identify such "undervalued" resources, a subsidiary's abilities for environmental scanning and internally analyzing its resource situation could prove particularly relevant. This enhances its chances to develop more accurate foresights about the potential value of external resources and thus allow it to acquire them below their true market value (Barney 1986, p. 1234, Sirmon et al. 2007, p. 278). Moreover, it is to be assumed that not all resources are freely or easily available in the local (or possibly even global) factor markets. First, some critical resources may not be available because they are simply not tradable at all. In particular, the idiosyncratic nature of many firm-specific resources or capabilities largely limits their tradability (Dierickx/Cool 1989, pp. 1505-1506). Second, other resources may in general be tradable, but simply not exist in particular factor markets. Market munificence, reflecting "the scarcity or abundance of critical resources needed by (one or more) firms operating within an environment" (Castrogiovanni 1991, p. 542), therefore also determines whether a subsidiary can actually acquire the needed

(2) In addition to the external acquisition, foreign subsidiary units may also *internally acquire* resources that exist within the intra-organizational network of the MNC in order to realize identified subsidiary initiative opportunities. It is suggested that the subsidiary's embeddedness in the intra-organizational network (e.g. Hedlund 1986, Bartlett/ Ghoshal 1989) plays an important role when accessing the collective resource base of the MNC (Schmid/Schurig 2003, p. 761). Specifically, close and frequent relationships between the subsidiary and other MNC units may enhance internal resource acquisition (e.g. Tsai/Ghoshal 1998, p. 465, Tsai 2001, Tseng et al. 2004, p. 99). Previous research highlights the various internal sources that subsidiaries can approach when needing to acquire resources and capabilities internally, such as corporate headquarters, internal suppliers, internal R&D units or internal customers (e.g. Schmid/Schurig 2003, p. 776, Lyles/Salk 2007, p. 5, Phene/Almeida 2008). The option of internal resource acquisition may be specifically relevant if critical resources are not externally available or if they can be obtained more effectively or efficiently internally.[226] However, approaching other actors within the MNC for the acquisition of resources also implies that headquarters or other units will probably become aware of the initiative-taking intentions of the subsidiary. It is to be expected that the request for internal MNC resources might "stimulate" the corporate immune system, thereby initiating activities related to initiative selling, evaluation and approval. Internal subsidiary initiatives in particular seem to rely strongly on internally acquired resources and hence more likely need to follow the vertical line of authority (Birkinshaw/Fry 1998, p. 167).

(3) Rather than purchasing available resources and capabilities "off-the-shelf" in the external or internal market, subsidiaries can also grow and accumulate resources and capabilities internally in what is referred to as *internal resource accumulation*. Accumulation is understood as the organic process of developing resources within the subsidiary unit and involves prior investment decisions to build new resources and capabilities (e.g. constructing a new manufacturing site) or to augment existing ones (e.g. expanding an existing manufacturing site). Although subsidiary resources and capabilities can be accumulated through different mechanisms, research and development activities and subsidiary learning more generally should be the most important ones (Dierickx/Cool 1989, p. 1505, Makadok 2001, p. 391, Zollo/Winter 2002, p. 339, Sirmon/ Hitt 2003, p. 350, Sirmon et al. 2007, p. 279). Consequently, resource accumulation often involves learning through repetition and experimentation. The internal devel-

---

critical resources externally. Third, direct resource access might be limited as, for instance, some resources are intertwined with others or may be more deeply embedded in other organizations (Das/Teng 2000, p. 36). Therefore, closer collaboration or partnerships with local market actors (e.g. in the form of joint ventures or strategic alliances) may enhance the possibility of acquiring such critical resources and capabilities (e.g. Hart 1995, Eisenhardt/Schoonhoven 1996, Inkpen 1998, Chetty/Wilson 2003).

[226] For instance, research indicates that resource transfer within MNCs is easier than with outside organizations, thus providing an important advantage to the MNC (e.g. Andersson 2003, p. 426).

opment of resources is considered necessary, as it cannot be expected that all initiative-related resources are to be found in the external or internal factor markets. Especially under conditions of limited resource availability and/or accessibility, the subsidiary has to rely more strongly on internal development. Subsidiaries may reactively develop resources (after identifying an existing initiative opportunity) or proactively accumulate resources in anticipation of future opportunities (Dierickx/Cool 1989, p. 1506, Sirmon et al. 2007, p. 279, Maritan/Peteraf 2011, p. 1378). However, in comparison to resource acquisition, internal resource development is often considered more risky and time-consuming, making it particularly difficult in highly dynamic and competitive markets (Brush et al. 2001, Teng 2007, p. 123). Internal resource development may be based on the sole activities and efforts of the subsidiary (e.g. inexperienced subsidiary employees learning new skills from more experienced subsidiary employees), but it may also involve interactions with other units of the MNC (e.g. internal transfer of best practices; see Özsomer/Gençtürk 2003, p. 7).

(4) In addition to "pure" internal accumulation, subsidiaries can also develop resources through interactions with external network partners through *internal-external development* (Sirmon et al. 2007, p. 279, Maritan/Peteraf 2011, p. 1376). Close collaboration or partnership with local or even global market actors (e.g. in the form of joint ventures or strategic alliances) allows subsidiaries to better learn from their partners and improve their chances to develop critical resources and capabilities internally but through interactions with external actors (e.g. Hart 1995, Eisenhardt/Schoonhoven 1996, Lane/Lubatkin 1998, Chetty/Wilson 2003, Knott et al. 2003). For instance, subsidiaries can learn through strategic alliances by imitating resources from their partners that are valuable but not directly transferable, or they can enhance their capabilities by transferring best practices (Tsang 1998, p. 214). However, obtaining valuable new resources or resource bundles through internal-external resource development requires, first, the identification and selection of appropriate partners that offer complementary resources and, second, effective relationship management enhancing the resource-sharing between the business partners (Sirmon et al. 2011).[227]

These four resource structuring approaches should not, however, be viewed as separate and mutually exclusive ways for subsidiaries to obtain the required resources and capabilities necessary to realize identified initiative opportunities. It is argued that often a single resource structuring approach (such as the external acquisition) may not be sufficient to obtain the necessary specialized resources. Instead, subsidiaries may have to rely on, for example, a mixture of utilizing existing resources and acquiring and

---

[227] See also, for example, the publications by Inkpen and colleagues on knowledge resource accumulation through collaborative activities such as alliances or joint ventures (Inkpen 1996, 1998, 2005).

developing new ones if they wish to create more sustainable advantages (Maritan/ Peteraf 2011, p. 1379).

3.4.2.3 Initiative-Related Resource Bundling

As resources and capabilities are often of little use in isolation, subsidiaries will in most cases need to take further bundling steps in order to realize an initiative opportunity and thereby add potential value for the subsidiary or even the wider MNC (Kogut/Zander 1992, p. 391, Tsai/Ghoshal 1998, p. 468, Sirmon et al. 2011, p. 1397).[228] Bundling refers to the sub-process in which existing and/or newly obtained resources from the subsidiary's resource portfolio are further integrated and combined in order to generate new and unique resource bundles or capabilities in pursuit of subsidiary initiative opportunities such as innovative products, services or new market entries (Ireland et al. 2003, p. 979, Morrow et al. 2007, p. 272, Sirmon et al. 2007, p. 281, Wiklund/Shepherd 2009, p. 196).[229] For example, the development and introduction of a new product to the market may require the combination of knowledge resources newly developed through R&D activities in the subsidiary (e.g. new technology), existing resources and capabilities related to manufacturing (ranging from raw material to specific production expertise) as well as the skills and competencies necessary to promote and market the product (e.g. access to sales and distribution channels or marketing expertise).

Bundling and integrating can involve resources that were obtained externally (e.g. market research data on customer requirements, patented technology acquired from external partners) or internally (e.g. internally developed new product designs, experience of sales force; see Godfrey/Gregersen 1999, p. 40, Bowman/Ambrosini 2003, p. 295). These internal and external input resources may also differ in their degree of uniqueness. While some resources may represent rather "common inputs" that are standard in an industry (e.g. standard manufacturing process), others may be much more specialized and unique (patented technology or strong brand image; see Bowman/ Collier 2006, pp. 199-200).[230] Furthermore, the sub-process of resource (re)combination can, depending on the scope of bundling activities involved, range from minor resource combination efforts for incremental initiatives to more extensive combination activities for initiatives entailing more radical changes. Accordingly, bundling activities have been further broken down into those that are (1) incremental (or stabilizing), (2) intermediate

---

[228] The view that entrepreneurial activities involve the (re)combination of resources (e.g. when developing new products/services or processes, entering new markets or introducing organizational changes) can be traced back to Schumpeter, who argues that entrepreneurship involves a special process of "carrying out of new combinations" (see Schumpeter 1934, pp. 65-66 and 74-81).

[229] Resource bundling has also been referred to by other scholars as, for instance, "combinative capacities" (Kogut/Zander 1992), "realized absorptive capacity" (Zahra/George 2002) and "subsidiary combinative capabilities" (Phene/Almeida 2008).

[230] Although the bundling may involve different types of resources, they should ideally be complementary, related or co-specialized if they are to create further value for the subsidiary or the wider MNC (Lockett et al. 2009, p. 14).

(or enriching) and (3) radical (or pioneering) (see e.g. Sirmon et al. 2007, pp. 281-282, Sirmon et al. 2011, p. 1392).

(1) Incremental bundling refers to the recombination of resources in order to maintain or incrementally enhance existing capabilities. This more subtle type of resource combination represented, for example, by continuous organizational learning or continuous improvement programs may help to prevent the erosion of specialized subsidiary resources and capabilities in the face of slowly changing environmental conditions. Incremental bundling activities may help to maintain or slightly enhance current subsidiary-level advantages by improving existing operations and enhancing operational and organizational efficiency. (2) Intermediate or enriching bundling relates to the extension and elaboration of current subsidiary capabilities. It frequently entails the combination of newly obtained resources with existing resource bundles from the subsidiary's portfolio. Enriching bundling can, for example, manifest as product line extensions or new market entries in which existing resources and capabilities are used to solve similar or related problems. Existing resource bundles (e.g. an existing product line) may thus be enriched through newly acquired or developed resources (e.g. access to and information about a certain market niche). Although this intermediate form of resource combination may produce somewhat unique and specialized resource bundles for the subsidiary, greater enrichment or even radical bundling may be necessary to realize capabilities that can be used in uncertain and dynamic environments. (3) Finally, radical bundling frequently involves the extensive combination of mostly new resources to create entirely new bundles. This form of resource bundling is typically based on Schumpeterian logic and may likely generate new avenues for value generation for the subsidiary or even the wider MNC. Radical resource combinations may come into play when a subsidiary attempts to realize a highly novel product or service offering (Ireland et al. 2003, p. 979, Sirmon et al. 2007, pp. 281-282, Worthington 2007, pp. 21-32, Hitt et al. 2011, p. 65, Sirmon et al. 2011, p. 1392).[231]

These different bundling activities can also be linked to different types of subsidiary initiatives. For example, internal subsidiary initiatives that often deal with efficiency improvement or organizational restructuring efforts and that typically remain within the parameters of existing subsidiary activities may only require incremental and continuous resource combination efforts that allow the organization to maintain or enhance its level of efficiency (e.g. initiating a continuous improvement program to enhance the manufacturing process at the subsidiary). In contrast, a highly complex and highly innovative subsidiary initiative that challenges the existing fabric of the wider MNC (e.g. a global

---

[231] In order to "physically" realize an initiative opportunity, subsidiaries may not necessarily have to stick to one specific bundling form but instead use a mixture of these types. However, given the contingent nature of the initiative process, including the bundling sub-process, it is expected that, given different situations, certain bundling forms will be pursued more vigorously than others (see also Worthington 2007, pp. 32-33).

market initiative involving the development and introduction of a completely new product or service for global application) may necessitate an extensive and novel synthesis of many highly specialized resources and capabilities that are newly obtained from different internal and external sources. However, both cases are likely to bring value-adding potential to the local subsidiary or the wider MNC (Birkinshaw 2000, pp. 72-73, Dimitratos et al. 2009a, p. 411).[232]

3.4.3 Headquarters-Subsidiary Alignment

In addition to the process activities concerning the identification and "physical" realization of initiative opportunities through structuring and bundling activities, the initiative process also depends critically on the successful alignment and interaction in the MNC between headquarters and the initiative-taking subsidiaries. Although subsidiaries are frequently viewed as semi-autonomous entities in the MNC that, at least to some degree, follow their own interests and, for example, pursue entrepreneurial opportunities in the local market or establish relationships with local actors more or less independently, they typically remain dependent on strategic decisions of headquarters when it comes to decisions such as the approval or allocation of resources for subsidiary initiatives (e.g. Birkinshaw/Ridderstråle 1999, p. 151, Andersson et al. 2001b, p. 6).

As stated earlier, subsidiary initiative-taking represents proactive, risk-taking and innovative behavior aiming to achieve exceptional growth that goes beyond the established mandate of the subsidiary (Birkinshaw/Hood 1997, p. 343, Bouquet/Birkinshaw 2008b, p. 582). However, as the mind-sets of managers at headquarters are typically focused on maintaining the current business model, creation-oriented activities such as subsidiary initiatives are often viewed with suspicion as they bear potential risks, imply changes to organizational routines and behaviors and threaten existing power-relations in the MNC (Amit/Schoemaker 1993, p. 42, Birkinshaw 2000, p. 39). It is to be further assumed that headquarters often lacks familiarity with the novel resource combinations that are advocated by entrepreneurial subsidiaries and the initiative details are relatively difficult to understand and evaluate for headquarters management (Burgelman 1983a, p. 1360). So, in order for subsidiaries to gather support and help initiatives gain momentum in the MNC, they must select and pursue appropriate alignment strategies and tactics in order to push initiatives through the socio-political system of the MNC and towards implementation (Birkinshaw 2000, p. 39, Mahnke et al. 2007, p. 1283, Ambos et al. 2010, p. 1104).

---

[232] It has also been argued that some external (i.e. local and global market) initiatives can be viewed as a Schumpeterian form of entrepreneurship because they challenge the technological foundations or business logic of the MNC (Birkinshaw 2000). Similarly, radical (pioneering) bundling is also said to be usually based on Schumpeterian logic (Sirmon et al. 2007, p. 282).

3 – Research Framework

It has been argued that innovative activities often involve power and politics in order to overcome resistance in organizations (Pfeffer 1992, p. 71, Freiling 2008, p. 41).[233] Similarly, subsidiary initiatives are said to require the acquisition and use of power and influence to gather support or to overcome the resistance that headquarters or other MNC units may exert to hinder or suppress the advancement of such entrepreneurial activities in the MNC (Birkinshaw et al. 2005, p. 246). Consequently, the sub-process is assumed to be largely dependent upon the relative power of the subsidiary and the influence it has vis-à-vis headquarters (Birkinshaw/Ridderstråle 1999, p. 152). Subsidiary power in general has been described as "the subsidiary's ability to influence their parent companies in their strategic and operational decision-making activities" (Dörrenbächer/Gammelgaard 2011, p. 32). Previous work has outlined two important sources of subsidiary power that play a critical role for headquarters-subsidiary alignment and hence initiative progress and survival: resource-based power[234] and structural power[235] (Birkinshaw/Ridderstråle 1999, p. 152, Delany 2000, p. 238, Forsgren et al. 2005, p. 143).[236]

---

[233] Likewise, Amit and Shoemaker, adopting a resource-based perspective, state that the development and deployment of strategic assets (SA) often leads to intra-organizational conflict as "any change in the existing bundle in SA may benefit some employees and hurt others." Furthermore, the scholars also refer to the problem of nestedness, since, for example, strategic business unit level choice "impact divisional as well as corporate capabilities and vice versa" (Amit/Shoemaker 1993, pp. 41-42).

[234] Subsidiaries may accrue resource-based power from resource-dependence situations in which the foreign MNC units have control over critical and scarce resources on which others in the organization depend (Astley/ Sachdeva 1984, p. 106, Astley/Zajac 1991, pp. 401-402, Pfeffer/Salancik 2003, p. 230). In particular, when viewing MNCs as less hierarchical and more loosely-coupled federations in which strategic resources are dispersed throughout the organization, it is to be expected that internal resource exchanges between different MNC units and the resulting internal resource dependencies to a great extent determine the distribution of intra-organizational power (Andersson et al. 2007, p. 805, Dörrenbächer/Gammelgaard 2011, p. 33). Power stemming from the control of critical resources can be assumed to be multidirectional, with power flowing upwards, downwards or horizontally, that is, for instance, from subsidiaries to headquarters (or other MNC units) or vice versa (Andersson/Forsgren 1996, p. 490, Lioukas 2007, p. 31).

[235] Structural power or systemic power stems from the subsidiary's position or location within the MNC network and its role with regard to performing tasks in the intra-firm division of labor (Ghoshal/Bartlett 1990, p. 616, Birkinshaw/Ridderstråle 1999, p. 152, Forsgren et al. 2005, p. 146). It is assumed that subsidiaries, as subunits within the MNC, may acquire structural power to the extent that they take on central responsibilities for specific functions that are critical for the proper functioning of the wider firm (Astley/Zajac 1991, p. 404, Dörrenbächer/ Gammelgaard 2011, p. 477). Put differently, subsidiaries that are centrally engaged in the MNC's system of inter-dependent activities and that occupy pivotal roles in the intra-organizational network are essential to organizational functioning and therefore become powerful (Hickson et al. 1971, p. 221). However, in contrast to resource-based power, which typically involves asymmetric resource dependencies in dyadic relationships, structural power arises in a system of mutually dependent resource flows and thus leads to a system of non-directional interdependencies between a focal subsidiary and other MNC units (Forsgren et al. 2005, pp. 146-147).

[236] Similarly, other publications have differentiated sources of power in this manner. For instance, Astley and Zajac (Astley/Zajac 1991, pp. 401, 403) distinguish between "resource power" and "systemic power" in their contribution on the intra-organizational power of subunits. Moreover, Bartlett and Ghoshal (Ghoshal/Bartlett 1990, p. 615) refer to the two concepts of hierarchical power and resource-based (linkage-based) power when discussing centrality and power in the MNC network. Other contributions that apply a similar differentiation are, for instance, those of Ambos and Schlegelmilch (2007, pp. 476-477) or Dörrenbächer and Gammelgaard (2011, p. 33). It is also recognized that there is some overlap between the two types of subsidiary power, making a clear distinction somewhat difficult. For example, the enhanced ability of a central and thus structurally integrated subsidiary unit to access multiple resources could also positively affect its ability to generate power based on resource dependencies. While some authors argue that this overlap should not eliminate the need to analytically differentiate between the two sources of power (e.g. Astley/Sachdeva 1984, p. 106, Astley/Zajac 1991, p. 404) others take a more inclusive approach and view them as variants of a broader resource dependence perspective (see e.g. Pfeffer 1981, p. 101, Ambos/Schlegelmilch 2007, p. 477).

From the two sources of subsidiary power that are of potential importance for subsidiary initiative-taking, structural power is not viewed as being particularly relevant.[237] In comparison, power based on resource-dependencies in the MNC should play a much more important role in the initiative sub-process concerned with headquarters-subsidiary alignment. First, it is expected that resource-based power, better than structural or systemic subsidiary power, provides a foundation upon which to understand and explain the relationships between initiative-taking (and therefore competence-creating) subsidiaries and headquarters in less hierarchically-structured MNCs. Here, resource dependence theory better incorporates the multiple and asymmetric dependence relationships that often exist in such organizations. Moreover, a resource dependence perspective also allows for a more political view of intra-organizational relationships as they manifest during the initiative process, including the "power games" that may result from the sometimes diverging agendas and objectives of the different units (Mudambi/Pedersen 2007, pp. 10-11, Ambos et al. 2010, p. 1100). Third, previous research indicates that a subsidiary's resource-based power stemming from resource dependence situations is generally stronger and more sustainable than other forms of subsidiary power (Becker-Ritterspach/Dörrenbächer 2009, p. 208, Dörrenbächer/Gammelgaard 2011, p. 34). Often, certain subsidiary resources (e.g. local market knowledge or local market access) are important or even critical to the performance of the entire MNC. Furthermore, such resources can frequently only be effectively accessed and leveraged by the foreign MNC unit since they are bound to the host country location or to the local business network of the subsidiary. Hence, these critical resources may provide a strong and unidirectional source of power that can be used by subsidiaries to influence the decision-making processes and behavior in MNCs (e.g. concerning initiative-related resource allocation or strategic investments decisions in the MNC; Forsgren et al. 2005, pp. 147-148).

Following resource dependence logic, it is hence expected that subsidiaries that have control over current or potential important resources and capabilities for which no alternative resources exists and on which others in the MNC depend may develop resource-based power. More specifically, resources and capabilities that allow the subsidiary to cope with the MNC's critical internal and external problems will help the

---

[237] A subsidiary's structural power is not considered to be very strong. As this type of power arises in a system of mutual dependence in which the MNC cannot function without the focal subsidiary and vice versa, it makes it difficult for the subsidiary to utilize it to influence the behavior and decision-making process of other units in the MNC. Thus, it represents a greater problem for a subsidiary to exploit this type of power than power resulting from resource dependencies when, for instance, engaging in the selling and bargaining activities that often occur in the initiative process (Forsgren et al. 2005, p. 148, Yamin/Sinkovics 2010, p. 957). Furthermore, it is assumed that the structural power of a subsidiary is also not very sustainable. It has been suggested that subsidiaries using this type of power might provoke changes in the organizational structure and/or the value chain configuration in the long run, which then leads to a decline in power, e.g. a change in the official mandate of a subsidiary by headquarters would also eradicate the power associated with it (see also Astley/Zajac 1991, p. 404;, Dörrenbächer/Gammelgaard 2011, p. 33).

unit acquire power within the organization (Pfeffer/Salancik 2003, pp. 45, 230, Bouquet/ Birkinshaw 2008a, p. 482).[238] However, subsidiary resource-based power is assumed to be of a "relative nature." Although foreign MNC units may increase their power by creating resource dependencies with other units in the firm, their power may decrease to the extent that the other units develop countervailing power through reciprocal resource contributions to the subsidiary in question (Astley/Zajac 1991, p. 402, Pfeffer/ Salancik 2003, p. 53, Forsgren et al. 2005, p. 144). Moreover, subsidiary resource-based power is presumably context-specific (Astley/Sachdeva 1984, p. 104, Birkinshaw/Ridderstråle 1999, p. 152, Pfeffer/Salancik 2003, p. 230). It is assumed that the environmental and organizational setting of the subsidiary to at least some extent determines the resource-based power of the foreign MNC unit.[239]

In addition to critical resources in their broadest sense, existing research has provided more concrete examples of important subsidiary resources that may represent potential sources of power and should also be relevant for headquarters-subsidiary alignment. For example, the subsidiary's proximity and access to favorable host markets and to lucrative new market opportunities in the local environment may form an important basis of subsidiary power (Dörrenbächer/Gammelgaard 2006, p. 267, Yamin/Sinkovics 2010, p. 957, Dörrenbächer/Gammelgaard 2011, p. 33). Similarly, it has been posited that a subsidiary's external network relationships with local business partners embodies a resource from which power can be derived if the linkages can only be accessed through the subsidiary (Andersson/Forsgren 1996, p. 490, Birkinshaw/Ridderstråle 1999, p. 152). In addition, it has been argued that the subsidiary's capacity to develop unique bundles of resources and capabilities – such as innovative products, services or processes – that are well-adapted to environmental contingencies and thereby help the MNC better cope with environmental challenges and opportunities, represents an important source of power and influence in the MNC (Andersson/Pahlberg 1997, p. 323, Bouquet/Birkinshaw 2008a, p. 484).

With regard to the initiative sub-process of headquarters-subsidiary alignment and interaction, subsidiaries should be able to use their resource-based power in two different ways. First, they may use it to become more autonomous and hence reduce headquarters' involvement in the initiative process or, second, they can apply it to promote

---

[238] In line with Pfeffer and Salancik's arguments, it is assumed that the importance of subsidiary resources and capabilities is determined by both the magnitude of resource flows from the subsidiary to other MNC units and the criticality of the subsidiary resource for the functioning of the wider organization (Pfeffer/Salancik 2003, p. 46).

[239] For various reasons, the relationships between organizational context and the internal power distribution may not always be straight-forward and perfectly determined. For example, it is suggested that power is socially constructed or enacted and as such is subject to the perceptions and interpretations of individuals and groups within the MNC. Second, internal power often becomes institutionalized, represented, for example, through relatively permanent structures and policies that help to preserve the existing power distributions for some time (see e.g. Birkinshaw/Ridderstråle 1999, p. 152, Pfeffer/Salancik 2003, pp. 234-235).

their interests by influencing initiative-related decisions by headquarters or other units of the MNC (Andersson/Pahlberg 1997, p. 321, Ambos et al. 2010, p. 1102). Although the ways in which this sub-process plays out may vary widely, initiative-related alignment and interactions between subsidiaries and headquarters can perhaps best be characterized by (a) the extent that headquarters is involved in the initiative-taking process, (b) the level of resistance an initiative encounters in the MNC and (c) the intensity of subsidiary managers' selling activities at headquarters or other units. These three aspects of the sub-process and the potential impact of subsidiary power are further outlined in the following subsections.

3.4.3.1 Headquarters Involvement

As has been shown, foreign subsidiary units can be viewed as semi-autonomous entities that may to some extent set their own strategic agenda and pursue innovative and entrepreneurial opportunities somewhat independently. This view implies that headquarters-subsidiary relationships become mixed-motive dyads in which the interests of the two parties are not always aligned (Ghoshal/Nohria 1989, pp. 324-325). For example, in cases where the subsidiary may desire autonomy to pursue local entrepreneurial opportunities that yield benefits for the local unit, headquarters may want to exert control to ensure that the unit does not engage in mere empire-building behavior to improve its position and standing at the expense of MNC (Birkinshaw 1998a, pp. 361-362). Thus, in order to monitor and control subsidiary entrepreneurial activities, headquarters is typically interested in becoming (more or less directly) involved in the initiative process, thereby attempting to shape or influence the entrepreneurial activities of the subsidiary so that they are aligned with the overall corporate strategy (Ambos et al. 2010, p. 1102).[240]

Headquarters involvement, as one specific facet of the headquarters-subsidiary relationship, relates to the direct participation and engagement of the corporate center in the initiative process. Although it may manifest itself in many different ways, previous research often emphasizes two particular aspects to describe the degree of headquarters involvement in subsidiary entrepreneurial and innovative activities: (1) subsidiary autonomy and (2) headquarters-subsidiary communication and interaction (see e.g. Birkinshaw et al. 1998, pp. 227-228, Birkinshaw 1999, p. 16). (1) Subsidiary autonomy generally refers to the strategic and operational decision-making authority of the foreign unit. It represents a key structural attribute of MNCs and "allows subsidiary managers to

---

[240] Similarly, various publications have also dealt with headquarters involvement in subsidiary innovative activities, arguing that corporate headquarters may act as orchestrators in the MNC that direct and steer innovation development at the subsidiary level (e.g. Ambos/Schlegelmilch 2007, Ciabuschi/Martín Martín 2010, Yamin et al. 2011, Ciabuschi et al. 2012).

exercise greater discretion in dealing with the demands of the local market and task environment" (O'Donnell 2000, p. 528). With regard to initiative-taking, subsidiary autonomy may thus be understood as the subsidiary's ability to take initiative-related decisions and actions autonomously and independently on its own behalf without having to obtain permission or approval from headquarters (Birkinshaw 2000, p. 24, Young/ Tavares 2004, p. 228). (2) In addition to the (granted or acquired) autonomy of a subsidiary, headquarters involvement is also often described in terms of headquarters-subsidiary communication and interaction. However, the related activities may come in many forms and take place either throughout or only in part of the entire initiative process. For example, headquarters may be closely involved from the beginning when assisting the subsidiary in refining and further developing newly identified opportunities. Likewise, the corporate center may also be engaged in assessing and evaluating initiative proposals or in specifying requests at different points in time in order to select the most promising subsidiary initiatives and support their continuation. Finally, headquarters may also be involved in providing final approval for an initiative and providing the subsidiary with resources necessary to launch or further progress with the initiative (Birkinshaw 1997, p. 221, Birkinshaw/Ridderstråle 1999, p. 153, Rugman/Verbeke 2001, p. 242, Keupp 2008, p. 33)

In general, headquarters involvement in the initiative process has been shown to vary widely. While in some cases subsidiaries may enjoy large degrees of freedom and have little or even no contact with headquarters when pursuing entrepreneurial initiatives, in other cases they may be faced with low levels of autonomy and a high level of headquarters-subsidiary communication. For instance, internally-oriented subsidiary initiatives are typically characterized by close alignment and interactions with headquarters from the beginning. These types of initiatives usually aim at internal improvements or obtaining investments from headquarters and as such they depend more heavily on earning formal approval and resources from headquarters. In situations of more centralized resource allocation decisions, and when subsidiaries have a higher need for central resources, headquarters involvement in subsidiary initiatives is also usually higher. In such cases, an explicit approval process frequently takes place that involves repeated rounds of credibility building with headquarters and initiative proposal refinement. Alternatively, in the event of externally-oriented initiatives and when resource allocation decisions are less centralized, headquarters involvement remains limited throughout the entire process (in the case of global initiatives) or takes place only in later stages once the viability of an initiative can be better proven (e.g. in the form of external market approval) (Birkinshaw 1997, p. 221, Birkinshaw/Ridderstråle 1999, pp. 166-167, Birkinshaw 2000, pp. 25-30).

Following the proposed resource-dependence logic, it is expected that the characteristics of headquarters involvement in the initiative sub-process is at least in part influenced by the relative power of the subsidiary vis-à-vis headquarters. Presumably, subsidiary units that possess extensive power based on the control of critical resources may enjoy larger degrees of freedom and face less involvement from headquarters, whereas units low in power may be confronted with stronger involvement from the corporate center throughout their initiative-taking activities (Ghoshal/Nohria 1989, p. 326, Ambos/Schlegelmilch 2007, p. 478).

3.4.3.2 Corporate Resistance

Aside from attempts by the corporate center to monitor and control a subsidiary's entrepreneurial activities, subsidiary initiatives also frequently encounter corporate resistance (i.e. the corporate immune system) from other organizational actors in the MNC that attempt to hinder their progression. Corporate resistance, as a complex and multifaceted phenomenon, is understood as "the set of organizational forces that suppress the advancement of creation-oriented activities such as initiatives" and may come from different MNC actors and/or units that represent existing power bases within the organization (Birkinshaw/Ridderstråle 1999, p. 153). As described earlier, subsidiary initiatives are often seen with suspicion because they involve potential risks, imply changes to organizational routines and behaviors and threaten existing power-relations in the MNC (Amit/Schoemaker 1993, p. 42, Birkinshaw 2000, p. 39). Furthermore, headquarters regularly lacks familiarity with the novel resource combinations that are advocated by entrepreneurial subsidiaries, and initiative details are relatively difficult to understand and evaluate for headquarters management both *ex ante* and from the geographical distance (Burgelman 1983a, p. 1360). Initiatives may also be perceived by corporate managers as being undertaken for opportunistic and empire-building motives, such as to improve the standing and position of the subsidiary at the expense of the wider MNC (Birkinshaw 1998a, pp. 361-362, Birkinshaw/Fry 1998, p. 59). Thus, given the potential risks associated with subsidiary initiatives, corporate hesitation or even resistance may be deemed appropriate in certain cases.

Corporate resistance typically manifests itself as (1) requests for greater justification by headquarters, delay and rejection, (2) lobbying and rival initiatives by competing MNC units, and (3) a lack of recognition of the initiative in other parts of the organization. [241]

---

[241] As briefly discussed in Subsection 2.2.3.3 herein, the corporate immune system involves, aside from the visible manifestations described here, less visible predispositions of individuals that exhibit resistance to initiatives. Birkinshaw and colleagues identify three groupings of predispositions in their works: (1) ethnocentrism of the corporate managers: the preoccupation of the individuals with their own nationality and their conviction of its superiority over others, (2) suspicion of the unknown as a reluctance to listen to/engage with subsidiary managers that headquarters is not familiar with and (3) resistance to change resulting from parochial self-interest and/or misunderstanding and lack of trust on the part of corporate management (see e.g. Birkinshaw 2000, pp. 40-42).

(1) As corporate managers are often uncertain about proposed initiatives (e.g. concerning the potential return on investment, the fit with the strategic priorities of the MNC or the subsidiary's ability to implement the initiative), they may make requests for greater justification and ask subsidiaries to provide further evidence for the viability of an initiative. In addition to this "soft" form of resistance, headquarters can also delay an initiative. This frequently indicates complete disinterest in the topic by corporate management, which might, for example, not respond at all to an initiative proposal made by the subsidiary or respond only after a very long time. Finally, as a stronger form of resistance, headquarters may also simply reject initiatives. (2) Moreover, the corporate immune system may manifest itself in the form of lobbying and rival initiatives by competing units of the MNC. This form of resistance is often experienced in firms that use internal market principles, such as having different units internally compete for the right to develop and market a new product. Since this implies that certain parts of the business could be shifted or taken away from a particular unit, competing units may actively lobby against each other or engage in competitive rivalry, including working independently on a similar or even identical topic (e.g. a new product or service). (3) Finally, corporate resistance can come in the form of lacking legitimacy, which refers to the insufficient or missing consistency of an initiative with the prevailing norms of the MNC. The absence of legitimacy may, for example, materialize as lengthy and tedious alignments or as a lack of buy-in to the initiative by other units in the company, sometimes even after the initiative has been started (Birkinshaw/Ridderstråle 1999, pp. 162-166, Birkinshaw 2000, pp. 42-44).

The level of corporate resistance that subsidiary initiatives face has been shown to differ notably and seems to be influenced by various factors. For example, the characteristics and attitudes of headquarters managers (e.g. ethnocentrism or self-interest) or the particular attributes of the initiative (e.g. perceived risks, benefits or feasibility) may impact the resistance it encounters in the MNC. However, in order to overcome this resistance, the level of subsidiary power appears to play a crucial role. This view has been supported by claims that innovation "often, if not inevitably involves obtaining the power and influence necessary to overcome resistance" (Pfeffer 1992, p. 71). Thus, in keeping with the resource-dependence considerations outlined earlier, it is expected that subsidiary resource-based power is closely associated with overcoming resistance and with winning political fights in the MNC (Birkinshaw 2000, p. 39, Andersson et al. 2007, p. 805).[242] For this purpose, subsidiaries can leverage a wide array of different resources, such as their relationships with internal and external partners, proven

---

However, as this research is primarily is interested in the observable manifestations and activities related to corporate resistance, these underlying predispositions are not further considered at this point.

[242] The findings of Birkinshaw and colleagues suggest that the level of influence the subsidiary has is often more important to the success of an initiative than its technical or financial implications (see e.g. Birkinshaw/Hood 1997, p. 218, Birkinshaw/Ridderstråle 1999, p. 154, Birkinshaw 2000, p. 40).

subsidiary resources, and the subsidiary's reputation and track record. Accordingly, it been posited that, when facing corporate resistance, an important condition for initiative success is the subsidiary's ability to demonstrate to headquarters that is has the necessary resources and capabilities to pursue the envisioned initiative. Similarly, the reputation and track record of a subsidiary has been viewed as a critical resource through which resource-based power can be obtained in order to overcome resistance and push the initiative through the organizational system of the MNC (Birkinshaw 1997, pp. 218-219, 1999, p. 17, Birkinshaw/Ridderstråle 1999).

3.4.3.3 Subsidiary Initiative Selling

Viewing foreign subsidiaries within the MNC as semi-autonomous entities implies that, although they may possess a certain level of strategic choice, they are still somewhat bound to decisions made at the corporate center (Birkinshaw 1997, pp. 209-210). Since subsidiary entrepreneurial initiatives frequently depend on central approval and resources, subsidiaries engage in (more or less extensive) selling or championing activities in order to promote their initiatives in the MNC and help them move through the organizational system towards implementation (Burgelman 1983b, p. 232, Birkinshaw/Hood 1997, p. 343). As with issue selling, initiative selling activities refer to subsidiary managers' behaviors that are directed toward bringing the opportunity to the attention of headquarters and making them understand the issue so it can eventually be approved and implemented (Dutton/Ashford 1993, p. 398, Ambos/Birkinshaw 2010, p. 457). As such, it typically involves communication and bargaining efforts to gather central support, for instance, in the form of financial, technical or managerial resources or even moral support (Medcof 2007, p. 455, De Clercq et al. 2011, p. 1270). Initiative champions appear to play an important role in this sub-process, as "individuals that are willing to take risks by enthusiastically promoting the development and/or implementation of an innovation inside a corporation ... without regard of the resources currently controlled" (Jenssen/Jørgensen 2004, p. 65). Throughout the initiative process, champions play a critical part in fostering and advocating the identified opportunity and thus may be involved in activities such as further developing an initiative, making proposals, and using personal contacts when promoting or presenting the initiative at headquarters or other MNC units (Birkinshaw/Fry 1998, pp. 54-56). Apparently, champions may use a wider variety of influence and sales tactics in order to bring an initiative to the attention of headquarters and to obtain approval and resources to continue with their entrepreneurial efforts. For example, in some cases individuals from the subsidiary may decide to follow the official lines of authority and make formal proposals at headquarters in the form of thoroughly prepared presentation of the opportunity, including the documentation of benefits and financial implications. However, in other cases champions may choose to bypass bureaucracy and employ more informal tactics such as personal appeals or behind-the-scene negotiations.[243] Despite the manifold selling and bargaining possibilities that may be pursued by foreign subsidiaries, three central aspects of issue-selling activities seem to prevail: (1) attracting headquarters attention, (2) making headquarters understand an issue and (3) lobbying at the parent company (Gammelgaard 2009, pp. 217-218).

(1) One important part of issue-selling strategies is concerned with attracting the attention of headquarters for a subsidiary and its initiative opportunity. It can be assumed that headquarters managers' allocation of attention to an initiative "is a necessary precursor" to decision-making activity that may involve the approval and/or allocation of resources to a proposed initiative opportunity (Dutton/Ashford 1993, p. 404). However, given the large size of most MNCs and the differentiated activities that are often dispersed across foreign subsidiaries, headquarters attention can generally be viewed as a scarce and critical resource. Organizational attention is limited and selective in its focus, so corporate management must carefully select the issues and topics on which to focus (Bouquet/Birkinshaw 2008b, p. 577, Ambos/Birkinshaw 2010, p. 450). Thus, for the purpose of directing attention towards the entrepreneurial opportunities in foreign subsidiary units, different tactics can be employed. First, subsidiaries can strategically frame an initiative so that it better fits the preferences of headquarters or corporate management better comprehends its relevance for the performance of the wider MNC. This may be done, for example, by highlighting certain attributes (e.g. potential benefits or urgency of the initiative) or downplaying negative ones (e.g. potential risks). Second, subsidiaries can draw attention to themselves and their entrepreneurial activities by emphasizing the strategic significance of the foreign unit and its activities for the overall MNC. In this context, highlighting the strategic significance of the local market environment and the strength of the subsidiary within the MNC network may prove useful when attempting to gain headquarters attention (Bouquet/Birkinshaw 2008b, p. 582, Gammelgaard 2009, p. 218).[244] (2) A second important aspect of subsidiary selling efforts relates to making headquarters understand an initiative opportunity. Subsidiary managers must decide how to reveal information and how to communicate initiative details to reduce the perceived uncertainty at headquarters. For this purpose, foreign units can use different "issue packaging" tactics that define "how an issue is linguistically framed, the way an issue is presented, and how an issue's boundaries are established" (Dutton/Ashford 1993, p. 410). This may include activities such as the communication of detailed project descriptions or face-to-face meetings in order to substantiate the subsidiary's requests for approval and the commitment of resources. It

---

[243] For overviews on different selling and influence strategies that can be employed by champions, see e.g. Dutton and Ashford (1993, pp. 417-420), Birkinshaw and Ridderstråle (1999, p. 175), Jenssen and Jørgensen (2004, pp. 71-75) and Ling et al. (2005, pp. 640-641).
[244] These attention-generating activities should be of relevance not only for attracting attention to certain subsidiary initiatives but also more generally for the subsidiary as a whole.

is expected that by offering information that can help reduce the perceived uncertainty and complexity of an initiative and by providing details that give headquarters management a greater sense of control, subsidiaries can enhance their chances to obtain approval and funding (Dutton/Ashford 1993, p. 412, Gammelgaard 2009, p. 218). (3) Finally, foreign subsidiary units may engage in lobbying efforts that involve activities such as "personal appeals, behind-the-scenes negotiations, or discussions..." in order to influence corporate management's attitude towards the initiative. In addition to these rather informal tactics, subsidiaries can also apply more formal and rational means to convince headquarters, for example, by presenting a solid business idea or by making a scheduled formal presentation to corporate management. Here, through conversations, meetings or active coordination, subsidiary units can gather support at the corporate center or at other relevant units of the MNC and motivate them to remove social and structural barriers or to provide active support for an initiative (Dutton/Ashford 1993, pp. 419-420, Jenssen/Jørgensen 2004, pp. 71-73).

Despite the distinction made here between these central aspects of initiative-selling, in reality subsidiaries will most likely use multiple tactics at different levels of the organization to increase awareness, showcase the potential advantages and benefits and gather support for the identified initiative opportunities (Ling et al. 2005, p. 641, Bouquet/Birkinshaw 2008b, p. 490). In addition to the different tactics, the level of selling activities has been shown to vary widely. For example, active selling by subsidiary managers appears to be particularly relevant when sponsorship or additional resources from a corporate division are required and when headquarters is more strongly involved in an initiative (Birkinshaw/Ridderstråle 1999, p. 172). Likewise, the level of subsidiary selling seems to differ by initiative type. While external initiatives that are often undertaken without headquarters awareness and do not require central resources involve little to moderate active selling efforts by subsidiary management, internal initiatives are often characterized by high levels of active selling in order to build broad support among different subsidiary and headquarters actors (see e.g. Birkinshaw 1997, Birkinshaw/Ridderstråle 1999, Birkinshaw 2000).

In line with the theoretical expectations concerning the other two sub-process of headquarters-subsidiary alignment (i.e. headquarters involvement and corporate resistance), initiative selling activities are expected to depend, at least in part, on the relative power of the subsidiary. Previous research indicates that advocating and selling efforts by subunits to obtain central approval and resources are positively influenced by the power they possess (Pfeffer/Salancik 2003, p. 234). Similarly, it is expected that the subsidiary's ability to gain support for an initiative and to influence central resource allocation decisions in the MNC varies directly with the power base of the championing subsidiary unit and its managers (Ghoshal/Bartlett 1990, p. 615, Birkinshaw 2000, p.

39). In this context, subsidiaries may, for instance, employ their resource-based power to counteract the hierarchical power of headquarters and thereby enhance their bargaining position to influence initiative-related decisions at headquarters (Andersson/Pahlberg 1997, p. 321, Forsgren/Pedersen 2000, p. 69, Ambos et al. 2010, p. 1102).

3.4.3.4 Summary of Subsidiary Initiative-Taking Behavior

For the purpose of this study, two particular aspects of subsidiary initiative-taking have been emphasized since they crystallized as important elements in previous works: (1) entrepreneurial resource management activities related to the identification and "physical" realization of initiative opportunities and (2) the alignment and interactions between headquarters and the subsidiary in order to gather support for initiatives and help them move through the socio-political system of the MNC.[245]

(1) Based on the contingent and dynamic resource-based considerations presented herein, the first element of initiative-taking is viewed as a context-dependent entrepreneurial process at the subsidiary level aimed at advancing new ways to use or expand subsidiary resources and capabilities when responding to newly identified opportunities. More specifically, the entrepreneurial process involves (a) identifying new opportunities and "physically" realizing them by (b) obtaining (i.e. structuring) the necessary resources and capabilities and (c) bundling them in the end. (a) As depicted, the identification can take place in either the *external market* through interactions with, for instance, local or global customers, suppliers and other market players, or in the *internal marketplace* with actors from within the corporate system. (b) Furthermore, in order to obtain the resources and capabilities that are necessary to realize an identified initiative opportunity, subsidiaries may rely on *acquisition* in the *external* or *internal market* system or on resource *development* either solely *within the MNC* (internal resource accumulation) or together with *external* partners outside the MNC (internal-external resource accumulation). (c) As resources and capabilities are often of little use in isolation, subsidiaries in most cases need to combine and bundle them in order to realize an opportunity (such as an innovative product or service) and thereby create potential value for the subsidiary or the MNC as a whole. As shown above, resource bundling can, depending on the scope of combinative activities, entail *incremental* (stabilizing bundling), *intermediate* (enriching bundling) or *radical* efforts (pioneering bundling). Figure 3.18 summarizes the key elements of the subsidiary initiative-taking process that represent the focus of the present research.

---

[245] Although these two components of subsidiary initiative-taking are – for the sake of clarity – viewed somewhat separately in this contribution, they are nevertheless to be seen as strongly intertwined and most likely impacting each other. For example, the way the entrepreneurial resource management takes place (e.g. identification of a radical initiative opportunity in an only little developed subsidiary) should also affect the headquarters-subsidiary alignment activities (e.g. headquarters involvement or corporate resistance). Vice versa, the way headquarters-subsidiary interactions take place may also impact the entrepreneurial resource management process.

(2) In addition to the identification and "physical" realization of opportunities, subsidiary initiatives are also critically dependent on the appropriate alignment and interactions between headquarters and the subsidiary. Resource-dependence considerations lead to the expectation that this sub-process is largely driven by the relative resource-based power of the subsidiary vis-à-vis headquarters. Subsidiaries that have control over resources and capabilities on which others in the MNC depend and for which no alternatives exist accrue relative power that they can use to become more autonomous and/or to influence initiative-related decisions in the MNC (concerning, e.g., initiative approval or resource allocation). Although the ways in which this sub-process proceeds may vary greatly, previous contributions have typically emphasized the following aspects when investigating and describing headquarters-subsidiary alignment and interactions: (d) headquarters involvement in the initiative-taking process, (e) corporate resistance against subsidiary initiatives and (f) subsidiary initiative selling. (d) As described earlier, headquarters involvement relates to the direct participation and engagement of the corporate center in the initiative process and is usually described in terms of subsidiary autonomy along with headquarters-subsidiary communication and interaction. The extent of headquarters involvement may vary widely[246] and is expected to be influenced to some extent by the power position of the subsidiary vis-à-vis the corporate center. (e) Moreover, subsidiary initiatives frequently encounter resistance from other units within the MNC that attempt to hinder their advancement and progression. Corporate resistance may differ greatly (e.g. ranging from none or little to intense resistance) and typically manifests itself in the form of requests for greater justification by headquarters, lobbying and rival initiatives by other units and a lack of recognition of the initiative in other parts of the MNC. The subsidiary's ability to overcome this resistance is also expected to be linked to the resource-based power it has available. (f) Finally, since subsidiaries in many cases depend on central approval and/or resources to continue with their entrepreneurial efforts, they engage in various degrees of selling or championing activities to promote their initiatives in the broader MNC. Initiative-selling, similar to issue-selling, encompasses activities related to attracting headquarters attention for an initiative, making the corporate center understand the issue and engaging in lobbying to influence parent management's attitude towards the initiative. Similar to the other headquarters-subsidiary alignment sub-processes, subsidiary initiative-selling efforts are believed to be, at least to a certain extent, influenced by the relative power of the subsidiary.[247]

---

[246] A low level of headquarters involvement implies a high degree of subsidiary autonomy and a low degree of headquarters-subsidiary communication/interaction. In contrast, a high level of headquarters involvement is expressed through a low degree of subsidiary autonomy and a high degree of headquarters-subsidiary communication/interaction through initiative-taking.

[247] These process elements and activities may convey the impression that initiative-taking can be modeled in a somewhat "standardized" manner. However, this clearly is not the case. As posited in the literature review chapter above, it is important to note the initiative process may take a variety of forms and will likely vary from case to

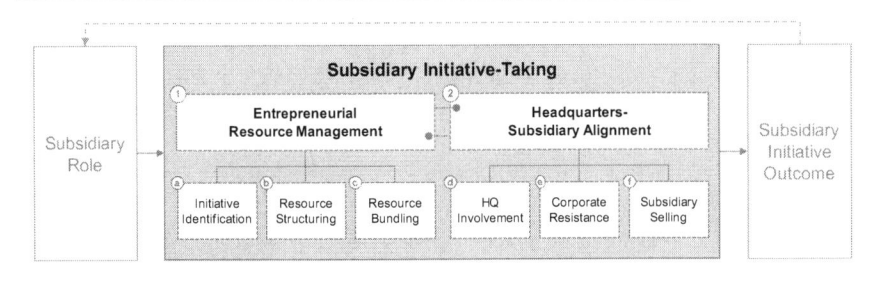

Fig. 3.18: Key elements of subsidiary initiative-taking behavior

3.4.4 Subsidiary Initiative-Taking Outcomes

Researchers in strategic management and international management are often concerned with key variables – such as characteristics of the business environment, organizational structure and processes – and their impact on performance outcomes. Similarly, the contingent and resource-based logic that underlies the research framework suggests that not only initiative-taking behavior but also the outcomes should vary with the contextual setting of the subsidiary. Existing studies have shown a wide array of possible consequences at the environmental and organizational levels that have been linked to subsidiary entrepreneurial initiatives. For example, at the environmental level, subsidiary initiatives may contribute to economic development in the host country (e.g. Dimitratos et al. 2009b) or lead to changes in the industry offerings and structure (e.g. Jindra et al. 2009). Similarly, at the organizational level, these activities can result in improved subsidiary performance (e.g. Liouka 2007), enhanced worldwide learning in the MNC (Birkinshaw 1997), increased efficiency of the corporate system (e.g. Birkinshaw/Fry 1998), or an improved subsidiary mandate (e.g. Birkinshaw/Hood 1997, Delany 2000).[248] However, as not all possible outcomes can and should be incorporated into the present framework, only the most appropriate ones must be selected. For this purpose, two particular aspects are considered of particular importance: the proximity of the outcome(s) to entrepreneurial subsidiary behavior and compatibility with the underlying theoretical foundations.

---

case. The outlined phases and underlying activities do not necessarily have to take place in sequence; they may overlap and some may not even materialize in every initiative. Furthermore, the initiative process is inherently dynamic, thus allowing for its continuous adaption to changing contextual settings; it may even entail feedback loops between the different process phases and activities. Nevertheless, the elements described are still considered to be of value for this study. They were carefully derived from previous research in the subsidiary initiative field and further substantiated through theoretical considerations. They represent important cornerstones of subsidiary initiative-taking that can help shed more light specifically on how entrepreneurial opportunities are "physically" realized and politically sanctioned in the MNC in different contextual settings. Moreover, the process elements outlined should make it possible to better structure the complex and manifold activities throughout the subsidiary initiative development and permit a more systematic investigation of this phenomenon.

[248] See Subsection 2.2.5 herein for further details on outcomes and consequences of subsidiary initiatives as explained in previous work.

First, many of the previously outlined consequences seem to represent secondary or "downstream" outcomes of successfully approved and/or implemented subsidiary initiatives. For example, subsidiary autonomy, subsidiary influence in the MNC, intrafirm competition and headquarters attention have been shown to subsequently result from past subsidiary initiatives (Bouquet/Birkinshaw 2008a, Becker-Ritterspach/Dörrenbächer 2009, Ambos et al. 2010). However, as the present study focuses particularly on initiative-taking behavior as it unfolds within the subsidiary (and to some extent in the wider MNC), outcome measures are deemed suitable if they best capture the immediate results of these entrepreneurial undertakings rather than secondary or "downstream" outcomes. Second, the proposed framework follows contingency and resource-based considerations. Accordingly, the outcomes emphasized should be consistent with those of the underlying theoretical foundations. While contingency theory represents an open and flexible framework that allows for the inclusion of various performance measures (e.g. revenue, profitability or innovation rate), resource-based approaches at the subsidiary level typically aim at explaining heterogeneity of outcomes in terms of specialized resources that, if further leveraged in the MNC, may contribute to firm-level advantage and thereby help ensure the survival of the organization in the longer term. In view of these requirements, two outcomes were selected to represent the dependent variables of the framework, which will be further explained in the following subsections: (1) the level of realized subsidiary initiatives and (2) the level of specialized resources and capabilities that can be further leveraged in the wider MNC.

3.4.4.1 Realized Subsidiary Initiatives

Entrepreneurship literature generally asserts that there exists a positive relationship between entrepreneurship and organizational performance (e.g. Covin/Slevin 1991, Zahra 1993, Zahra/Covin 1995, Lumpkin/Dess 1996, Covin/Miles 1999, McDougall/Oviatt 2000). For example, Zahra and Covin argue that "a theoretical link between corporate entrepreneurship and company financial performance can be readily inferred from the literature" (Zahra/Covin 1995, p. 46). Likewise, as Covin and Miles state, research in corporate entrepreneurship recognizes that "[it] can be used to improve competitive positioning and transform corporations, their markets, and industries as opportunities for value-creating innovation are developed and exploited" (Covin/Miles 1999, p. 47). Similarly, subsidiary entrepreneurial initiatives have been shown to lead to subsidiary-level benefits (e.g. increased sales or profitability) or even firm-level advantages (e.g. enhanced worldwide learning or increased efficiency of the corporate system; see e.g. Birkinshaw 1997, Birkinshaw/Fry 1998, Birkinshaw et al. 1998).[249]

---

[249] Certainly, not all subsidiary initiatives necessarily lead to subsidiary-level or firm-level advantages and some may even fail to deliver the expected outcomes. Furthermore, some initiatives may only help to preserve the status quo rather than helping to improve revenues or profitability of the subsidiary (or the wider MNC) while perhaps in

However, subsidiary initiative-taking has been described as a complex phenomenon that extends over various levels of the MNC organization and unfolds over different stages. In order for subsidiary initiatives to make it "all the way" to implementation, they not only need to be identified by the subsidiary in the first place, but they also have to be created, and then, in most cases, evaluated and approved by different actors in the MNC. It is plausible to assume that, along this path, initiatives may fail at any given point for various reasons, perhaps due to a lack of resources and capabilities that are beyond the subsidiary's control or perhaps as a result of insufficient corporate support and approval (see e.g. Birkinshaw/Ridderstråle 1999, Keupp 2008). Therefore, many "pieces of the puzzle" must fall into place for initiative-taking to occur and be successful in the end.

In order to examine the immediate outcomes of successful subsidiary initiative-taking, the present study incorporates the "level of realized subsidiary initiatives," which refers to all entrepreneurial initiatives by foreign subsidiaries in MNCs that have been approved and/or implemented in the end. This approach is in line with previous works that examined the effects of different environmental and organizational characteristics on the level of subsidiary initiatives (e.g. Birkinshaw 1997, 1999, Tseng et al. 2004, Borini et al. 2009a, Borini et al. 2009b, Williams/Lee 2011) or, relatedly, the level of subsidiary innovation (e.g. Ghoshal/Bartlett 1988, Nohria/Gulati 1996, Phene/Almeida 2008). Nevertheless, previous research has revealed that different forms of subsidiary initiatives may take place. Accordingly, the present study examines the level of realized initiatives with regard to the commonly defined types: global market initiatives, local market initiatives, internal market initiatives, and global-internal hybrid initiatives.[250]

3.4.4.2 Resource-Based Outcomes

As shown previously, entrepreneurship involves the creation of new resources or the combination of existing resources in new ways to, for example, develop and commercialize new products and services or to move into new markets. Consequently, these activities are said to lead to the development of new resource bundles or capabilities that have the potential to generate advantages for the firm (e.g. Godfrey/Gregersen 1999, Hitt et al. 2001). Likewise, successfully implemented subsidiary initiatives such as innovative products, services or processes can, through a resource-based lens, be viewed as newly generated bundles of resources and capabilities that may subse-

---

other cases the expected outcomes or the "pay-off" can only be realized at a later point in time. However, although there may be certain instances in which entrepreneurial initiatives by subsidiaries do not (directly) lead to advantages for the subsidiary and/or MNC, a positive relationship is to be assumed in general (for similar arguments on entrepreneurship in general see, e.g., Zahra 1993, Zahra/Covin 1995).

[250] By explicitly considering different types of subsidiary initiatives, this work also addresses a shortcoming of previous writings, which were mostly interested in subsidiary initiatives as a group rather than the different types that exist. See also Subsection 2.2.3.1, which deals with the different types of subsidiary initiatives as identified in earlier work.

quently lead to the accumulation and enhancement of specialized resources and capabilities at the subsidiary level.[251] Furthermore, the resulting resource outcomes may not only be of benefit for the subsidiary itself, but they can provide foundations for firm-level advantages (Birkinshaw et al. 1998, p. 225, Bouquet/Birkinshaw 2008b, p. 581). However, in order to do so, two particular resource characteristics are considered critical: the degree of specialization and the applicability for the wider MNC (see, e.g., Rugman/Verbeke 2001, p. 245, Birkinshaw/Pedersen 2009, p. 379).[252]

(1) Specialized subsidiary resources have been defined as superior to those that exist elsewhere in the MNC, or, put differently, those that represent a capability gap within the MNC (Birkinshaw et al. 1998, Rugman/Verbeke 2001). It can be assumed that the resource bundles newly developed through subsidiary initiatives possess some degree of specialization since initiatives are produced through unique and idiosyncratic processes. The initiative processes are unique and idiosyncratic, because the particular environmental and organizational conditions in which subsidiaries operate also lead to distinct initiative processes that will be heterogeneous across the subsidiary units of an MNC. For instance, different subsidiaries possess unique resource profiles as a result of their particular geographical settings or as a consequence of their historical development (Birkinshaw/Hood 1998b, p. 781). Different subsidiaries should also possess unique and idiosyncratic patterns of external and internal network relationships that expose them in different ways to new resources, knowledge, ideas and opportunities (McEvily/Zaheer 1999, p. 1135). In addition, it is to be expected that the entrepreneurial initiative processes of identifying opportunities and transforming them into unique resource bundles is not trivial and involves distinct entrepreneurial know-how, experience and insight by subsidiary managers (Helfat et al. 2007, p. 63, Ambrosini/Bowman 2009, p. 41). Consequently, the particular environmental and organizational conditions and imprinting of subsidiaries should result in distinct initiative processes able to deliver specialized and unique resource bundles and capabilities that also differ across subsidiary units of an MNC.[253]

(2) Additionally, subsidiary initiatives should generally have the potential to produce resource bundles or capabilities that are partially location-bound or non-location-bound

---

[251] Even failed entrepreneurial initiatives can produce useful resources (e.g. in the form of new knowledge/expertise) and thereby help the subsidiary or the wider MNC effectively compete in its market. However, as this study is primarily concerned with "successful" initiatives as outcomes, resource and capability enhancement through failed initiatives are not further considered.

[252] In a similar vein, Schmid and Schurig (2003, p. 759) speak of superior subsidiary capabilities "if the subsidiary performs these activities better than other organizations or other units within the same MNC ... and if these capabilities are not only relevant for the focal subsidiary, but also for other MNC units." For further detail on the link between subsidiary resources/capabilities and firm-level advantage see also subsection 3.3.2.3.2 herein.

[253] The degree of specialization may certainly vary and should likely be a function of both the uniqueness of input resources and the uniqueness of the initiative process itself (Bowman/Collier 2006, p. 198).

and thus can be applied by the wider MNC.[254] Supporting this argument, it has been claimed that subsidiary initiatives in most cases should represent activities that have implications for the wider MNC rather than being projects of limited scope that are only of interest for the local unit (Birkinshaw/Ridderstråle 1999, p. 155). This should come as no surprise, as such initiatives are typically pursued with the objective of changing the subsidiary's mandate or enhancing its international responsibilities by strengthening its contributory role within the MNC. In order to achieve this, subsidiaries must develop specialized resources and capabilities through initiatives that then lead to the transfer of proprietary capabilities within the corporate network and hence can benefit the entire organization (Birkinshaw 1997, pp. 223-224, Ambos/Birkinshaw 2010, p. 456).[255]

In sum, it can be stated that subsidiary initiatives should deliver new resource bundles that are, to varying degrees, both specialized and directly applicable in other parts of the MNC. By meeting these criteria they may not only lead to advantages at the subsidiary level but they can also provide the grounds for firm-level advantages. The two emphasized resource characteristics, and thus the potential to generate firm-level advantages, can also be linked to different types of initiatives. First, *global market initiatives* typically aim at creating new solutions around existing businesses and business relationships for non-local actors that are situated outside the subsidiary's local market. They represent "larger-scale" entrepreneurial activities that, in some cases, even follow a Schumpeterian logic and thus can challenge "the technological foundation or business logic of the MNC" (Birkinshaw 2000, p. 77).[256] In the end, they should deliver highly specialized capabilities (in a specific business area) that can also be transferred to other units or directly applied internationally (e.g. in the form of globally marketed products), therefore offering the greatest potential for firm-level advantages (Birkinshaw 1997, p. 223, 2000, p. 25, Rugman/Verbeke 2001, p. 241).[257] Second, *local market initiatives* involve new products, markets or processes that are first identified and developed locally but that

---

[254] Non-location-bound resources and capabilities refer to those that can be easily transferred within the MNC without substantial adaptation and thus can be exploited globally to generate "benefits of scale, scope or exploitation of national differences." In contrast, location-bound resources and capabilities cannot be easily transferred and require significant adaptation before they can be used in other locations of the MNC. Thus, they typically benefit the MNC only in one or few particular locations and help to enhance local responsiveness, for instance (e.g. Rugman/Verbeke 1992, p. 763, 2001, p. 241).

[255] However, the extent to which the newly generated resource bundles (or single resources therein) can be directly exploited globally seems to differ. Some appear to represent non-location-bound resources that can be immediately transferred and used effectively in different parts of the MNC (e.g. in the form of internationally marketed products) while others first require the "transformation" into non-location-bound resources by the subsidiary (e.g. products first developed for the local market and then adapted to the needs of other markets; Rugman/Verbeke 2001, pp. 241-242).

[256] In this case, their realization should involve the extensive combination of mostly new resources to create entirely new bundles (i.e. radical bundling) that could likely generate new avenues for value generation for the subsidiary, the wider MNC, or even beyond. See also Subsection 3.3.2.2 for details on bundling activities required for a Schumpeterian type of entrepreneurship.

[257] Not surprisingly, these types of initiatives are expected to result from subsidiary units that are considered "centers of excellence" or from more advanced types such as Strategic Leaders (Birkinshaw 2000, p. 25, Rugman/Verbeke 2001, p. 242). See also Subsections 3.5.1.3 and 3.5.2.3, which discuss the link between distinct subsidiary roles and initiative types.

are subsequently exploited on a global scale. Similar to global initiatives, it can be expected that they will deliver specialized capabilities as they often involve subsidiary-specific resources (e.g. existing local network linkages or product-related knowledge) and newly obtained resources (e.g. newly identified customer requirements or newly developed technology) that are further bundled when "physically" realized. In comparison with global initiatives, however, they initially lead to partially location-bound capabilities that need to be transformed by the subsidiary into non-location-bound ones before they can be used by others in the MNC (Birkinshaw 2000, pp. 22-23, Rugman/ Verbeke 2001, p. 242). Third, *internal market initiatives* arise through opportunities that are identified within the internal market of the MNC. They represent smaller-scale entrepreneurial projects that aim at improving the efficiency of the corporate system through reconfiguring and rationalizing efforts (e.g. optimization of subsidiary operations). In the end, these should also deliver new capabilities, but possibly somewhat less specialized than externally oriented initiatives. This is assumed to be the case because their development is more strongly linked to corporate center guidelines and decisions and hence should remain somewhat closer to the "dominant logic" and current capabilities of the MNC (Prahalad/Bettis 1986, Bettis/Prahalad 1995).[258] Also, given the close alignment between headquarters and the subsidiary throughout the initiative process, the newly generated resource bundles can be easily diffused to other parts of the MNC or incorporated into internationally marketed products or services (Birkinshaw 2000, pp. 27-28, Rugman/Verbeke 2001, p. 242). Fourth, *global-internal hybrid initiatives* represent larger-scale projects that lead to the reallocation of value-adding functions to the subsidiary location (e.g. bidding for investments to relocate production facilities to the subsidiary location). These contain elements of both global and internal market initiatives as they involve opportunities that are identified outside a subsidiary's local market but require the internal process of convincing headquarters to relocate activities and provide funding for implementation. With regard to the outcomes, global-internal hybrid initiatives should produce resource bundles that are somewhat similar to those of internal market initiatives since they are also geared towards optimizing the efficiency of the broader corporate system.[259] Rather than creating new and highly specialized resource bundles (as in some external initiatives), this type more strongly emphasizes the reconfiguration and the incremental enhancement of existing resources and capabilities in close alignment with the corporate center. Consequently, these entrepreneurial activities also result in (incrementally improved) capabilities that are

---

[258] It has also been suggested that entrepreneurial efforts aimed at enhancing operational and organizational efficiency typically only require incremental forms of bundling that lead to smaller enhancements of existing capabilities (e.g. Birkinshaw 2000, p. 28, Sirmon et al. 2007, p. 281).
[259] In comparison to internal market initiatives that aim to enhance "local" efficiency, global-internal hybrid ones are usually large-scale projects that may have more far-reaching effects for the MNC as a whole (Birkinshaw 2000, p. 30).

non-location-bound and thus have a direct impact for the wider MNC (Birkinshaw 1997, p. 224, 2000, pp. 28-30, Rugman/Verbeke 2001, p. 242).

In addition to these four types of subsidiary initiatives that are viewed as having implications for the wider MNC (as proposed by Birkinshaw and colleagues), literature suggests that subsidiary entrepreneurship may also encompass subtle and incremental forms that are more "operational" in nature (e.g. restructuring of local departments or development of innovative local work practices; see e.g. Birkinshaw 1997, p. 211, Liouka 2007, p. 1). Hence, it seems plausible to assume that such *"trivial initiatives"* would deliver resource bundles with relatively little specialization and that are primarily of use for the local subsidiary. Thus, they may only indirectly benefit the wider MNC by strengthening the performance of the subsidiary rather than directly benefiting the MNC as a whole (Dimitratos et al. 2009a, p. 411, Dimitratos et al. 2009b, p. 184).[260] Figure 3.19 below presents these different initiatives types alongside the two specified dimensions, "degree of specialization" and "degree of direct applicability for wider MNC," as outlined in this section.

It has been previously argued that the particular advantage of the multinational firm may lie in its ability to combine and bundle the diverse resources and capabilities scattered throughout its network to, for instance, generate product or process innovations for firm-wide application. Although the individual resources and capabilities that are geographically dispersed in the MNC may already create value for the firm by themselves, the firm-level ability to bundle and combine them effectively may lead to even greater advantages (e.g. Kogut/Zander 1993, p. 636, Andersson et al. 2001a, p. 1018, Rugman/ Verbeke 2001, p. 245, Andersson 2003, p. 426, Dellestrand 2011, p. 230). In this context, subsidiary initiatives may play a critical role for the development of competitive advantage of the entire firm. In particular, initiative-related resources and capabilities may provide the greatest potential for firm-level advantages when they possess a high degree of specialization (i.e. better than those elsewhere in the MNC) and can be effectively transferred and combined (i.e. applied) with other resources and capabilities of the firm (see e.g. Birkinshaw et al. 1998, p. 225, Birkinshaw 2000, p. 106, Rugman/ Verbeke 2001, p. 224). Accordingly, global market initiatives could offer the highest potential for MNC-level advantages while, in contrast, trivial initiatives should only be able generate benefits for the local subsidiary (e.g. in the form of reduced costs). Local market initiatives that produce specialized but (initially) location-bound resource bundles, as well as internally-oriented initiatives that produce less specialized bundles

---

[260] The term "trivial" in this context is not meant to imply that such entrepreneurial initiatives of limited scope are not important or even of no use for the MNC. Instead, this word is used to differentiate between initiatives that affect the wider MNC and the more incremental or operational entrepreneurial activities whose impacts do not go beyond the focal subsidiary (see also Birkinshaw 1997, p. 211).

of resources, may occupy an intermediate position regarding their potential for firm-level advantages, as indicated in Figure 3.19 below.

```
                                  Degree of Specialization
                                  (of Resources/Capabilities)
High  ┌─────────────────────────────────────────────────────┐
      │   Local Market              Global Market           │
      │   Initiatives               Initiatives             │
      │                                                     │
      │   Medium potential for      High potential for firm-│
      │   firm-level advantage      level advantage         │
      │                                                     │
      │   "Trivial Initiatives"     Internal Market and     │
      │                             Global-Internal         │
      │                             Hybrid Initiatives      │
      │                                                     │
      │   Low potential for firm-   Medium potential for    │
      │   level advantage           firm-level advantage    │
Low   └─────────────────────────────────────────────────────┘  High
           Degree of Direct Applicability for Wider MNC
                    (of Resources/Capabilities)
```

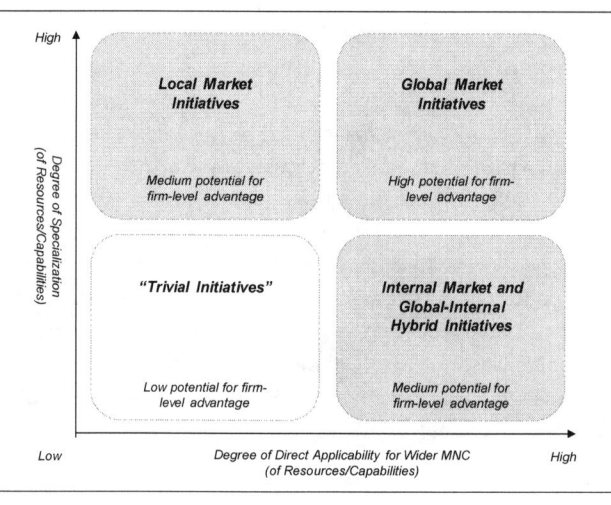

Fig. 3.19: Subsidiary initiative types and the associated resource and capability characteristics

3.4.4.3 Subsidiary Evolution

Although not explicitly incorporated in the present model as an outcome, it is nevertheless useful to briefly address the possible impact of subsidiary entrepreneurial initiatives on subsidiary role development, sometimes also termed subsidiary evolution.[261] Existing research suggests not only that initiative-taking is influenced by the role a subsidiary currently holds in the MNC, but also that the entrepreneurial efforts should impact subsidiary role development in the longer term (see e.g. Gupta/Govindarajan 1994, Birkinshaw 1996, 1998b, Birkinshaw/Hood 1998b, 1998a, Delany 1998, 2000, Dörrenbächer/Gammelgaard 2006, Johnston/Menguc 2007, Bouquet/Birkinshaw 2008b, Cavanagh/Freeman 2012).[262] In view of this, it has been stated that "subsidiary-driven development is a bottom-up, entrepreneurial process. It is characterized by the creation of new business opportunities within the subsidiary that are nurtured and gradually built up by subsidiary managers ..." in order to "demonstrate their expertise and willingness to take on additional responsibilities to head office managers" (Birkinshaw/Hood 1998a,

---

[261] Subsidiary role development or subsidiary evolution has not explicitly been incorporated as an outcome measure in the present model because it is viewed as a somewhat indirect or downstream result of initiative-taking. However, it is included here to underline the expected reciprocal relationship between subsidiary initiatives and subsidiary role change.

[262] This indicates that the relationship between subsidiary roles and subsidiary initiatives is likely reciprocal in nature, with the role determining initiative behavior (and outcomes) which in turn seems to impact the role of the subsidiary in the long run.

pp. 273-274, Birkinshaw et al. 1998, p. 225). More specifically, it is proposed that the initiative-related accumulation of specialized capabilities[263] that can be further leveraged in other parts of the MNC can lead the subsidiary's role to change over time.[264]

Despite the apparent importance of specialized capability development, one must be careful not to view alterations in a subsidiary's capability profile as synonymous with role change for the following reasons. First, the mere enhancement of the subsidiary's specialized capability base through initiatives alone may not be sufficient. Research suggests that specialized capabilities also need to be recognized as such by headquarters. Only if subsidiaries are able to convince headquarters managers (e.g. through selling and championing efforts) that they possess the specialized capabilities or the necessary expertise to fulfill a new role it can be "officially" granted (Birkinshaw et al. 1998, p. 227, Dörrenbächer/Gammelgaard 2006, p. 271). Second, requiring the recognition by headquarters also implies that role change may lead or lag behind capability change. For instance, a sudden change in the subsidiary's capability base may lead to a mismatch between the actual capability profile and its "official" role because the corporate center may not immediately become aware of it (Birkinshaw/Hood 1998b, p. 782, Delany 2000, p. 239).[265] Third, it is to be assumed that within many MNCs there exists an internal competition for new roles or charters. At any given time, different units of the MNC may engage in efforts to defend or enhance their roles and positions in the firm. As it is unlikely that the MNC can and will allow all subsidiary units to change their given role, changes in a subsidiary's capability profile should be considered in the larger realm of the MNC and in relation to efforts of other (competing) units (Galunic/Eisenhardt 1996, p. 257, Birkinshaw/Hood 1998b, p. 782). Fourth and finally, as the numerous role typologies in IB literature show, subsidiary roles cannot be defined only by the capability profile of a foreign unit. Instead, they have been characterized along many other dimensions such as market scope, product scope, value added scope (White/Poynter 1984), decision-making autonomy and market involvement (D'Cruz 1986).[266] Therefore, focusing merely on variations in subsidiary capabilities as an indicator of role change

---

[263] According to Delany (2000, p. 239), examples of specialized resources and capabilities that can support subsidiary evolution include special relationships with important external and internal market players, business-specific competencies, growth-enabling skills and privileged assets.
[264] Essentially, the roots of this particular perspective on resource-based or capability-based subsidiary growth can be traced back to the work of Penrose (1959), who views firms as a collection of resources and thus links firm growth to resource growth. Accordingly, it has been maintained in different publications that the resource-based view can offer useful guidance on the phenomenon of subsidiary role development since it can help to explain how subsidiaries develop their contributory role and thereby further support the development of competitive advantages in the MNC (see e.g. Birkinshaw/Hood 1997, p. 343, 1998b, p. 781, Dörrenbächer/Gammelgaard 2006, p. 270, Cavanagh/Freeman 2012, p. 605).
[265] This likely represents one possible cause for perception gaps between headquarters and subsidiaries concerning the subsidiary role. For further details on perceptions gaps see, e.g., Daniel (2010) or Schmid and Daniel (2010).
[266] Nevertheless, a larger number of role typologies in fact explicitly or implicitly recognize subsidiary resources and capabilities as a critical determinant (e.g. Bartlett/Ghoshal 1986, Gupta/Govindarajan 1991, Hoffman 1994, Randøy/Li 1998, Benito et al. 2003). See also Subsection 3.2.1.1 herein, which outlines different subsidiary role typologies and their respective dimensions.

may be too narrow, and developments in other dimensions should be considered as well. Figure 3.20 provides an overview of the outcomes relating to different forms of subsidiary initiatives and types of resources.

```
                                    ┌─────────────────────────────────────────────────────┐
                                    │          Subsidiary Initiative Outcome              │
                                    │  ┌──────────────────────────┬──────────────────────┐│
                                    │  │ Realized Subsidiary       │  Resource Outcomes   ││
                                    │  │ Initiatives               │                      ││
┌───────────┐   ┌───────────┐       │  │  Global Market Initiatives│  Degree of           ││
│Subsidiary │──▶│Subsidiary │──▶    │  │                           │  Specialization      ││
│Role       │   │Initiative-│       │  │  Local Market Initiatives │  Degree of MNC       ││
│           │   │Taking     │       │  │                           │  Applicability       ││
└───────────┘   └───────────┘       │  │  Internal Market          │                      ││
                                    │  │  Initiatives              │                      ││
                                    │  │  Global-Internal Hybrid   │                      ││
                                    │  │  Initiatives              │                      ││
                                    │  └──────────────────────────┴──────────────────────┘│
                                    └─────────────────────────────────────────────────────┘
```

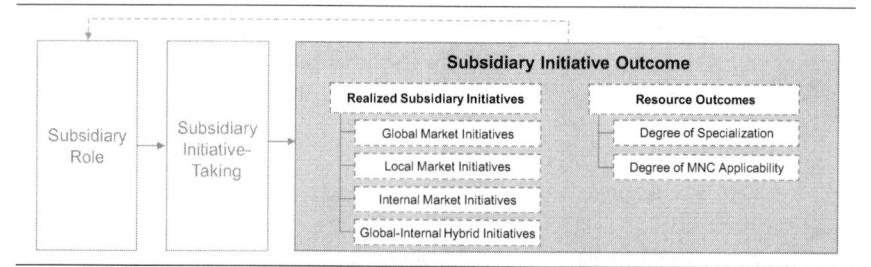

Fig. 3.20: Outcomes of subsidiary initiatives in the research framework

3.4.5 Subsidiary Roles as Contingency Factors

As argued above, it is expected that the way in which the subsidiary initiative process unfolds and produces distinct outcomes in the end is contingent upon the environmental and organizational context of the subsidiary.[267] In general, the literature has already provided broad theoretical and empirical support for the contingent nature of entrepreneurship, suggesting that entrepreneurial behavior and processes vary systematically with differences in firms' contextual settings (e.g. Miller 1983, Covin/Slevin 1989, 1991, Zahra/Covin 1995, Lumpkin/Dess 1996, Dess et al. 1997, Teng 2007, Hitt et al. 2011). Similarly, research in the subsidiary initiative field shows that different variables from the environmental, organizational, and individual-level contexts influence entrepreneurial behavior in foreign units of MNCs.[268] As addressed earlier in this publication, among the numerous influencing factors that have been identified in association with subsidiary initiatives in previous research, several ones represent or are closely related to dimensions of different subsidiary role typologies from the IB domain. This provides support for the assumption that the role a subsidiary holds may critically influence its initiative-taking behavior.[269] This view is also expressed in other works suggesting that foreign units with more advanced roles should be more entrepreneurial and show more initiative on their part (e.g. Gupta/Govindarajan 1994, pp. 448, 455, Birkinshaw/Fry 1998, p. 58, Boojihawon et al. 2007, p. 553, Verbeke et al. 2007, p. 586).

---

[267] Most likely it is also contingent upon individual-level factors. However, due to the emphasis on subsidiary roles as influencing factors, additional variables from the individual level are not incorporated in the proposed model.
[268] See also Subsection 3.3.4.3 herein on the relationship between different contingent variables and subsidiary initiatives.
[269] See also Section 3.1 and Subsection 3.2.1.3, which discuss the possible relationship between subsidiary roles and subsidiary entrepreneurial initiatives.

Through a contingent and dynamic resource-based lens, subsidiary roles, representing multivariate combinations of contextual dimensions,[270] are expected to influence the two central elements of initiative-taking behavior in the present framework as follows. First, a subsidiary's role should affect its position to identify and realize entrepreneurial opportunities that deliver specialized capabilities, which can subsequently provide the grounds for firm-level advantages (i.e. the entrepreneurial resource management sub-process). Second, it should also influence the sub-process of headquarters-subsidiary alignment as it impacts the resource-based power of a subsidiary, which it can employ during its entrepreneurial undertakings. From the numerous role typologies presented in IB literature throughout the past two and a half decades, two in particular were chosen as contingency factors for this study based on the outlined selection criteria, namely those of Bartlett and Ghoshal (1986, 1989) and Jarillo and Martinez (1990).[271] These two typologies consist altogether of four role dimensions relating to (a) environmental factors (i.e. strategic importance of the subsidiary environment) and (b) organizational factors (i.e. subsidiary resources and capabilities, degree of localization/local responsiveness and degree of integration). These four role dimensions and their potential impact on subsidiary entrepreneurial behavior are briefly addressed below and discussed in more detail in Section 3.5.

(a) The external environment has been viewed in several studies as a key determinant for entrepreneurial behavior, and different environmental variables have been recognized as important influencing factors. Among these are market dynamism, competitive pressure, environmental hostility, complexity, and technological sophistication (e.g. Miller 1983, Covin/Slevin 1991, Zahra/Covin 1995, Lumpkin/Dess 1996). Similarly, environmental dynamism, competitive pressure, hostility and complexity in the subsidiary's local market have also been identified as factors affecting the entrepreneurial initiatives of foreign subsidiary units in MNCs (e.g. Zahra et al. 2000, Borini et al. 2009b). In view of these findings, it is also expected that the externally oriented subsidiary role dimension from Bartlett and Ghoshal's (1986, 1989) role typology, referred to as "**strategic importance of the subsidiary's environment**," impacts the entrepreneurial behavior of foreign subsidiary units.[272] As discussed in detail in the following section, it is expected that foreign subsidiary units operating in strategically important markets should, in general, be more entrepreneurial than those located in less important areas since the complex and dynamic environmental conditions encourage or even necessitate more proactive, risk-taking and innovative behavior. Furthermore, it is assumed that

---
[270] It has been claimed that multivariate configurations (rather than bivariate configurations), which include two or more contingency elements, can offer more useful or complete explanations of complex organizations and should also have more predictive power (see Dess et al. 1997 p. 682).
[271] See subsection 3.2.1.4 herein for more on the process of selecting the role typologies for this study.
[272] As is further explained in section 4.3.1.1, a market is considered of high strategic importance for the MNC if the market is large and if it is characterized by high levels of competitive intensity, technological dynamism, and sophisticated customer demands.

the strategic importance of the local environment also positively impacts the resource-based power that the foreign units can employ when aligning and interacting with headquarters throughout their initiative-taking activities.

(b) In addition to environmental contingencies, various organizational context factors have also been shown to play an important role as determinants of entrepreneurial behavior, such as an organization's resources and competencies, its strategy, structure or culture (see e.g. Covin/Slevin 1991, Lumpkin/Dess 1996, Hitt et al. 2011). Thus it is expected that the three selected role dimensions linked to the organizational context will influence entrepreneurial initiatives of foreign subsidiaries as well. With regard to the second dimension of Bartlett and Ghoshal's typology, concerned with **subsidiary resources and capabilities**, previous theoretical and empirical works have highlighted their positive influence on the entrepreneurial activities of foreign subsidiary units in MNCs (e.g. Birkinshaw 1997, Birkinshaw et al. 1998, Birkinshaw 1999, Tseng et al. 2004). As they represent the necessary resource inputs, skills and expertise (e.g. technical or market-based knowledge resources) on which entrepreneurial initiatives are built, it is presumed that the foreign unit's ability to engage in such activities depends in part on the level of resources and capabilities it has.[273] A high level of subsidiary resources and capabilities can also, under certain conditions, positively impact the resource-based power that the subsidiary can employ throughout the entrepreneurial process when aligning and interacting with the corporate center.

The first dimension of Jarillo and Martinez' (1990) typology termed the **degree of localization**, or relatedly the dimension referred to by Taggart (1997) as the degree of local responsiveness, is a context factor expected to strengthen subsidiary initiatives. This assumption is theoretically and empirically supported by a number of publications in the subsidiary initiative field positing a positive effect of localization, local responsiveness, or local market orientation on innovative and entrepreneurial activities of foreign units of MNCs (e.g. Luo 2001, Tseng et al. 2004, Birkinshaw et al. 2005, Liouka 2007, Scott et al. 2010). Moreover, subsidiary units characterized by high degrees of local responsiveness and localization should also hold more resource-based power. Based on the belief that they possess a broader and more diverse set of resources and that they are well-positioned to access critical resources in their local markets, such foreign units should hold stronger resource-based power positions, which likely impacts their alignment and interaction with headquarters throughout the process.

Finally, with regard to the **degree of integration,** representing the second role dimension in the typologies of both Jarillo/Martinez and Taggart, previous research generally

---

[273] As argued previously, it is expected that the relationship between resources/capabilities and initiatives is reciprocal in nature in that resources/capabilities impact entrepreneurial behavior, which in turn impacts the resource and capability base of the subsidiary.

asserts that a high level of integration should facilitate subsidiary initiatives (e.g. Birkinshaw 1997, Birkinshaw/Fry 1998, Tseng et al. 2004).[274] It is presumed that a high level of integration may enhance the subsidiary's ability identify new opportunities from inside the MNC network and improve its access to resources of other internal MNC units for the realization of initiatives. However, a high degree of subsidiary integration with the rest of the MNC is likely associated with higher levels of resource exchange between the subsidiary and other MNC units, thereby creating a situation of mutual resource dependency rather than of one-sided dependency to the "power benefit" of the subsidiary. Although this may endow the subsidiary with some (weaker) structural power based on its critical position in the MNC network, it does not truly provide it with stronger resource-based power that it can utilize throughout the initiative process.

Summarizing the above arguments, it is posited that the subsidiary roles in the typologies of Bartlett and Ghoshal (1986, 1989) and of Jarillo and Martinez (1990) represent distinct contextual settings that are viewed as more or less conducive for different forms of entrepreneurial subsidiary behavior and that should consequently result in distinct initiative outcomes for the subsidiary or even the wider MNC in the end. More precisely, the different role types are predicted to impact the two central sub-processes of initiative-taking as outlined in the framework, that is, the entrepreneurial resource management sub-process related to identification and the "physical" realization of an initiative, as well as the sub-process concerned with the alignment and interactions between the subsidiary and headquarters. Figure 3.20 shows an overview of the final research framework regarding role-specific subsidiary initiative-taking.

---

[274] As discussed in more detail in Subsection 3.5.2.2, high levels of subsidiary integration are particularly linked to internally oriented subsidiary initiatives (i.e. internal markets and global-internal hybrids).

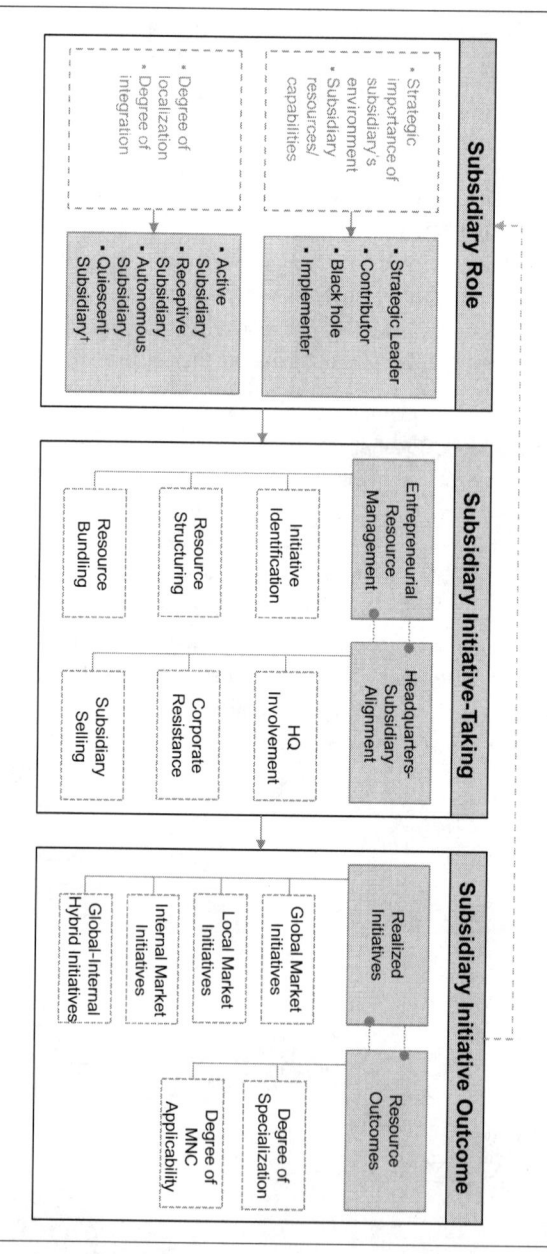

Fig. 3.21: Overview of final research framework on role-specific subsidiary initiative-taking

Although traditional contingency theory (e.g. Burns/Stalker 1961, Lawrence/Lorsch 1967, Thompson 1967) would suggest that the subsidiary situation mechanistically and unidirectionally regulates subsidiary initiative-taking and its outcomes, this thesis takes a somewhat less deterministic view and acknowledges some degree of "strategic choice" on the side of subsidiary units and their managers. Rather than viewing the role context as "dictating" subsidiary entrepreneurial behavior, it is presumed that the units abroad have a certain "freedom of manoeuvre" and as such some choice as how best to deal with their contextual setting (Child 1972, p. 14).[275] This view underlines the critical role of subsidiary managers in converting resources into something of value and implies that a direct linkage between context and entrepreneurial behavior may be somewhat problematic for the following reasons. First, the current subsidiary role context may be viewed not only as an "objective reality," but it is also subject to the perceptions and interpretations of the subsidiary decision-makers (Child 1972, p. 17).[276] Second, subsidiary managers play an important part in defining entrepreneurial strategies and in taking related actions to deal appropriately with the various situations they face. For example, subsidiary managers must identify, develop, bundle and deploy resources in a way that delivers some form of advantage for the subsidiary or the wider firm in view of their specific settings. This requires that they accurately frame opportunities and challenges, anticipate possible futures or overcome corporate resistance to change in the organization. However, as prior values, experience, training and other aspects are likely to influence their decisions and activities, this should lead to variations in how managers in similar or even identical situations deal with their contextual setting (see e.g. Amit/Schoemaker 1993, pp. 40-43, Aragón-Correa/Sharma 2003, p. 73, Ambrosini/Bowman 2009, pp. 41-42). Third, while traditional contingency theory assumes that situational factors are fully independent variables, the recognition of strategic choice also entails that subsidiary managers are at least to some extent in a position to change their context as well. The proposed framework infers a reciprocal relationship between subsidiary initiative-taking behavior (and its outcomes) and the role context of the subsidiary (Child 1972, p. 16).[277] Consequently, by acknowledging some degree of

---

[275] Child (1972, 1997) introduces the notion of strategic choice in contingency theory in order to address some of the shortcomings and critiques that this theoretical perspective has faced (e.g. its overly deterministic nature and its neglect of organizational politics; see also Subsection 3.3.4.1, which outlines the central critiques of contingency theory). For instance, strategic choice introduces managerial decisions as well as the notion of perceptions, beliefs, politics and power in a theory that otherwise focuses on the link between impersonal variables such as context, structure and performance. For a more detailed discussion of the adaptations made in the strategic choice concept see, for instance, Donaldson (2001, pp. 131-137) and Kieser (2006, pp. 239-240).

[276] A similar argument has been put forward in RDT by Pfeffer and Salancik who claim that "... the environment does not come knocking on the organization's door announcing its critical contingencies. Rather, organizational participants must enact and interpret their environment and its effects on the organization" (Pfeffer/Salancik 2003, p. 234). Similarly, the RBV acknowledges the important role of managers in converting resources into positions of sustainable competitive advantage.

[277] Closely related to this argument, subsidiary initiative literature has presented the notion of "subsidiary choice," which reflects the strategic decisions and activities of subsidiaries to define their role context in the MNC for themselves (e.g. Birkinshaw/Hood 1998b, p. 775, Birkinshaw et al. 1998, p. 223, Ambos/Birkinshaw 2010, p.

strategic choice, the subsidiary role context is not viewed as an immutable "determinant" of subsidiary entrepreneurial behavior and its outcomes. Rather, the subsidiary role setting is understood as a context that induces or constrains certain patterns of subsidiary initiative-taking behavior, which in the longer term can in turn impact the subsidiary role context.

3.4.6 Conclusion

The previous subsections of this thesis have developed a contingent and dynamic resource-oriented framework for role-specific initiative-taking by foreign subsidiaries. This framework represents an attempt to more comprehensively model the complex relationships between potentially important contextual variables in the form of well-established subsidiary roles, central elements of subsidiary initiative-taking behavior and selected outcomes. In addition to building on insights from the current literature in the subsidiary initiative field, three specific theoretical perspectives were utilized to further guide and substantiate this effort: RBV, RDT and contingency theory.

This framework addresses various gaps that were identified in existing work and aims to bring a novel theoretical approach to research in the subsidiary initiative field. First, the research framework may aid in explaining why and how different subsidiary role types engage in different forms of subsidiary initiatives and ultimately produce different outcomes. As described in Sections 2.3 and 3.1, previous work has only generally stated that foreign units of MNCs with more advanced roles should be more entrepreneurial, but in-depth research appears to be lacking. Second, it represents a more holistic approach since it links potentially important contextual variables and key elements of subsidiary initiative-taking behavior to resource- and performance-related subsidiary initiative outcomes. Third, the framework explicitly incorporates core subsidiary initiative process activities related to entrepreneurial resource management and headquarters-subsidiary alignment and thereby attempts to shed light on the "process black box" and better understand how subsidiaries obtain and utilize resources to create subsidiary-level or firm-level advantages through entrepreneurial efforts. Fourth, previous work has applied 19 different theoretical lenses, often at a rather high level.[278] From among these, the present framework draws from three specific theories, which are discussed thoroughly and presented extensively in Section 3.3. For example, it draws from the newer dynamic and process-oriented strands of the RBV that also recognize the contingent nature of the resource management process (e.g. Helfat et al. 2007, Sirmon et al. 2007, Hitt et al. 2011, Sirmon et al. 2011) and that are more suitable for studying

---

451). See also Subsection 3.2.1.2 herein regarding different perspectives on subsidiary role determination and development, including the subsidiary choice perspective.

[278] See Subsection 2.2.6 for a summary of previously employed theories in the subsidiary initiative field.

entrepreneurial subsidiary behavior from a processual viewpoint. In addition, it links the resource-oriented RBV and RDT with contingency theory to better connect the subsidiary context to the inner workings of the foreign unit. In the end, it is expected that this novel approach will help better explain how subsidiary initiatives can lead to subsidiary and firm-level advantages in different contextual settings.[279]

Nevertheless, the research framework also has a number of limitations that are important to mention. First, only certain initiative antecedents, in the form of four subsidiary role dimensions, are incorporated as contextual variables. This means that many of the previously studied antecedents are not part of the investigation and it might therefore be possible that other important ones are left out. Second, although the most important core initiative sub-processes and activities are believed to have been included in the framework, the approach is unable to fully account for all possible variations and dynamics of the subsidiary initiative process. Furthermore, not all possible process activities are included in the framework. For instance, initiative-related alignment and interaction within the foreign units themselves and the actual implementation of subsidiary initiatives are not made part of the framework. Therefore, the included sub-processes and activities should be viewed as a "snapshot" of the critical process elements, rather than as a comprehensive or all-inclusive picture. Third, while the proposed framework acknowledges the critical role of subsidiary managers in the initiative process – for example, to help identify opportunities or realize initiatives – it does not aim to explain individual managers' ambitions, motivations or decisions. A complete model of subsidiary initiatives would benefit from the inclusion of these elements to better illuminate how and why the whole process is set in motion (see e.g. Birkinshaw 1997, p. 227). Fourth and finally, the focus of the framework is on initiative-taking behavior and outcomes predominantly at the subsidiary level. Why and how resulting resource bundles are further transferred in the MNC and hence may lead to firm-level advantages is not modeled or investigated.

---

[279] For similar arguments on the benefits of linking context, process and outcomes in RBV see e.g. Helfat et al. 2007, p. 43, Crook et al. 2008, p. 1153, or Sirmon/Hitt 2009, p. 1392.

3.5 Predictions for Role-Specific Initiative-Taking

This section develops predictions with regard to the potential effects of the specified subsidiary role types on subsidiary initiative-taking behavior and outcomes. These predictions are intended to guide the empirical study and to help the research "move into the right direction" and to "look for relevant evidence" (Yin 2009, p. 28). However, in comparison to the comprehensively elaborated hypotheses that are often used in quantitative research designs, the predictions derived in this study are of a more tentative and preliminary nature (Wrona 2005, pp. 19-23, Lee/Lings 2008, pp. 127-131). Whenever possible, predictions are based on existing works and empirical findings from relevant contributions in the field. For this purpose, predictions are presented first for the subsidiary role typologies of Bartlett and Ghoshal in Subsection 3.5.1 and of Jarillo and Martinez in Subsection 3.5.2. For each of these role typologies, there will be, first, a separate discussion on the possible effects of the individual role dimensions and, second, a joint consideration of the specified role types.

3.5.1 Role Typology by Bartlett and Ghoshal

3.5.1.1 Strategic Importance of the Subsidiary Environment

In general terms, the strategic importance of the subsidiary environment is said to reflect the importance of the respective subsidiary market for the for the overall MNC (Schmid et al. 1998, p. 34) or, alternatively, the external resources that a subsidiary can potentially access in a particular location (Rugman et al. 2011, p. 254). When analyzing the underlying elements used for the operationalization of this subsidiary role dimension by Bartlett and Ghoshal, one can see that the importance of the subsidiary's environment is determined by four different characteristics: (1) market size, (2) competitive intensity, (3) technological dynamism, and (4) customer demand intensity.[280] Taken together, these four aspects determine the strategic importance of a subsidiary's environment for the wider MNC. The following paragraphs discuss the potential impact of the strategic importance of the subsidiary market environment on initiative-taking, and more specifically its effect on the overall propensity to engage in subsidiary initiatives (Paragraph 1), the sub-processes concerned with entrepreneurial resource management (Paragraph 2) and headquarters-subsidiary alignment (Paragraph 3).

(1) Subsidiary Initiative-Taking Propensity

The strategic importance of the overall market should positively influence the likelihood that subsidiaries will engage in entrepreneurial initiatives for the following reasons. First, subsidiaries in strategically important environments should have access to larger mar-

---

[280] See Subsection 4.3.1.1 herein for details on the operationalization of this role dimension.

kets where it is expected that they encounter more potential entrepreneurial opportunities *per se*. In such cases, subsidiary managers have the possibility to interact with more external actors, such as customers, suppliers or other entities, which exposes them to more stimuli and potential opportunities for entrepreneurial initiatives. Second, in environments marked by strong dynamism and frequent shifts in technology, new entrepreneurial opportunities should arise more often than in stable environments. Dynamism suggests that innovations are fast-paced, thus pressuring subsidiaries to upgrade and enhance their resources and capabilities more rapidly and more aggressively if they want to remain competitive in their respective markets (e.g. Miller 1983, p. 775, Covin/Slevin 1991, p. 12, Zahra et al. 2000, pp. 12-13). Third, environments characterized by high competitive intensity also require that subsidiaries more strongly engage in proactive, innovative and risk-taking behavior. Given situations with strong competitive forces, existing advantages cannot be sustained for long, so subsidiaries must more frequently develop product or process improvements and ideas to keep up with or stay ahead of competition (e.g. Covin/Slevin 1989, p. 77, Holm et al. 2005, p. 201, Bowman/Collier 2006, p. 204). Fourth and finally, strategically important markets are typically characterized by sophisticated and complex customer demands. This implies that products or services requested from customers involve, for instance, complex technologies and/or means of production with extensive R&D efforts required. Due to the challenges and the high pace of change that often come with (technologically) sophisticated demands, it is expected that these conditions stimulate innovative and entrepreneurial subsidiary behavior and positively impact the foreign unit's ability to develop or improve products, services or processes over time (Covin/Covin 1990, pp. 31-32, Porter 1991, pp. 111-112, Zahra et al. 2000, pp. 14-15). In sum, these considerations suggest that subsidiaries located in strategically important environments should respond to the more demanding and challenging environmental conditions by pursuing more innovative and entrepreneurial activities. In comparison, foreign units in more stable environments should be less pressured to upgrade their resources and capabilities through entrepreneurial initiatives, as in such less challenging situations it may be sufficient to continuously and incrementally adjust and improve the subsidiary's resource base (Ambrosini et al. 2009, p. 14). Summarizing these assumptions it is predicted that:

*The higher the strategic importance of the subsidiary environment, the **more likely** subsidiaries will **pursue subsidiary initiatives**.*

(2) Entrepreneurial Resource Management Activities

Initiative Opportunity Identification: The strategic importance of the local environment can also be expected to influence the identification of new initiative opportunities. First, it can be assumed that entrepreneurial opportunities are generally more prevalent in more complex, dynamic and sophisticated environments (Zahra et al. 2000, pp. 12-15, DeTienne et al. 2008, p. 553, Hitt et al. 2011, p. 60). Frequent changes in, for example, customer needs, technologies or regulatory settings may result in existing solutions (in the form of particular resource and capability bundles) becoming inadequate or even obsolete more quickly, thereby creating "space" for new solutions and thus initiative opportunities. However, not only may strategically important markets provide a richer set of opportunities, but subsidiaries operating in changing and more dynamic environments need to be more proactive and aggressive in identifying and pursuing initiative opportunities (Covin/Covin 1990, p. 38). As technological standards are typically shorter-lived and undergo constant changes, subsidiaries must also be more active and aggressive in their entrepreneurial initiative-taking (Dess et al. 1997, p. 681). Consequently, it is predicted that more challenging environmental conditions in strategically important markets increase both the chances and the pressure for foreign subsidiaries to identify new resource development and deployment opportunities in the form of subsidiary initiatives, leading to the following prediction: [281]

*The higher the strategic importance of the subsidiary environment, the **more likely** subsidiaries will **identify initiative opportunities.***

In addition, it may be presumed that the importance of the local environment also results in the subsidiary focusing its attention more strongly on changes and opportunities in the external environment rather than on opportunities from within the MNC network. In more dynamic and complex environments, subsidiary managers must be aware of external changes, potential threats and opportunities, and thus more frequently need to assess the implications of their responses to local developments (Sohail/Ayadurai 2007, p. 44). A subsidiary that wants to remain competitive in such a challenging environment must therefore analyze and scan the external conditions more extensively for new external initiative opportunities in the form of, for example, new products or services. In contrast, in less dynamic and competitive environments, external scanning

---

[281] Although there might be a higher prevalence of initiative opportunities in strategically important environments, there are also certain arguments suggesting that their identification could, at the same time, become more difficult in such situations. For instance, market dynamism and competitive intensity are said to result in higher market uncertainties which again make it more difficult to assess current and future market conditions and hence to identify new opportunities. Thus, in these more challenging situations, subsidiaries with existing resources in the form of, for example, critical market knowledge or experienced and/or entrepreneurially minded managers may be in a better position to take advantage of opportunities that present themselves in these environments (Sirmon et al. 2007, p. 282, Hitt et al. 2011, p. 61).

and opportunity identification should play a less critical role, allowing the subsidiary to focus on internal initiative opportunities such as process or quality improvement (Barringer/Bluedorn 1999, p. 423). Previous research also indicates that subsidiaries in more dynamic and competitive environments often engage in more external networking activities (Holm et al. 2005, p. 204), thereby again enhancing their chance to identify potential initiative opportunities in the external environment (McEvily/Zaheer 1999, p. 1138, Hitt et al. 2001, p. 481, Ardichvili et al. 2003, p. 115, Holm et al. 2005, p. 204). Accordingly, the following prediction is made:

*The higher the strategic importance of the subsidiary environment, the **more likely** subsidiaries will **identify external initiative opportunities** (rather than internal initiative opportunities).*

Resource Structuring: As outlined earlier, subsidiaries may often need to structure their resource portfolios before they engage in resource bundling activities. Particularly in more demanding and dynamic markets, it is likely that customers will require more sophisticated or even radical solutions that consequently involve more complex bundles of unique resources and capabilities (Holm et al. 2005, p. 204). Moreover, in strategically important markets where conditions and demand can change suddenly, subsidiaries may often need new and improved resources to respond to those sophisticated and/or frequently shifting customer needs (Zahra et al. 2000, p. 12, Sirmon et al. 2007, p. 280). It can therefore be concluded that in such environments, subsidiaries must obtain and maintain richer and more diverse portfolios of (ideally flexible) resources that can be utilized to respond quickly to new opportunities or threats that may arise, thus leading to the following prediction:

*The higher the strategic importance of the subsidiary environment, the **more likely** subsidiaries will engage in **resource structuring** activities.*

Further evidence suggests that subsidiaries operating in highly competitive environments are more likely to leverage external sources rather than internal ones to obtain critical resources and capabilities. Obtaining resources from external partners enables them to share costs and risks and obtain resources that can help further differentiate their offerings, particularly in difficult and challenging market situations (Eisenhardt/ Schoonhoven 1996, pp. 137-139, Hitt et al. 2011, p. 61). The use of cooperative partnerships in dynamic and competitive environments can help subsidiaries better acquire or jointly develop needed resources and protect themselves from possible market risks and uncertainties (Holm et al. 2005, pp. 204, 213). In addition, in markets where customer demand and technology are changing rapidly, innovative and entrepreneurial processes are often informed by developments occurring outside the organization. This necessitates participation in external networks or even beyond (e.g. technological communities) and makes it more likely that subsidiaries will incorporate externally acquired resources (Frost 2001, pp. 104-105). Especially in situations in which the MNC network cannot adequately provide the necessary resources or in which subsidiary management deliberately decides not to involve other MNC units, it seems likely that subsidiaries will obtain resources from external sources (Almeida et al. 2003, pp. 357-358). This leads to the predication that:

*The higher the strategic importance of the subsidiary environment, the **more likely** subsidiaries will rely on **external sources** (rather than internal sources).*

Additionally, dynamic and competitive markets create uncertainty about the future value of specific resources and their potential to generate advantages for the subsidiary and the MNC as a whole. Sudden shifts in customer demand or technology could render existing subsidiary resources and capabilities more or less useless or, alternatively, transform less valuable ones into critical ones (Bowman/Collier 2006, p. 201). Subsidiaries should therefore gain the most benefit from a rich repertoire of resources that can be used flexibly in the event that local market conditions or competitive behaviors change suddenly or unpredictably (Sirmon et al. 2007, p. 278). The (internal) development of resources and capabilities often takes place through subsidiary learning, which involves repetition and experimentation. Resource accumulation can hence be seen as longer-term investment in the gradual and path-dependent development of subsidiary-specific resources and capabilities. However, in dynamic, demanding and competitive markets, subsidiaries may need to act more quickly and more flexibly. In these situations, the acquisition of resources could provide a more viable alternative rather than internal development. In contrast, in more stable and less competitive markets, subsidiaries should have more time to develop and accumulate the necessary resources and capabilities (Bowman/Collier 2006, pp. 202-203). Furthermore, fewer uncertainties should allow for better predictability of future market developments and hence reduce the potential risks associated with longer-term resource investments. Therefore, gradual resource accumulation would represent a more viable option in stable and less demanding markets, leading to the following prediction:

*The higher the strategic importance of the subsidiary environment, the **more likely** subsidiaries will **acquire resources** (rather than internally develop resources).*

Resource Bundling: It has been argued that different bundling processes result in specific types of capabilities. For instance, stabilizing bundling processes will result in smaller incremental improvements of existing capabilities, whereas pioneering bundling processes will result in more substantial or even radical changes. In more demanding and competitive subsidiary markets, it has to be assumed that initiative-taking that leads to the gradual development of resources and capabilities is often not sufficient. Instead, bundling processes are needed that continuously produce more substantial change in the firm's capabilities if subsidiaries wish to maintain or gain an advantage over competitors in their respective markets. Thus, repeated enriching and pioneering bundling that involves more extensive combinations of, for instance, newly acquired resources with existing ones, appears more suitable under these market conditions (Bowman/Collier 2006, pp. 205-206, Sirmon et al. 2007, pp. 281-283). This leads to the following prediction:

*The higher the strategic importance of the subsidiary environment, the **more likely** subsidiaries will use **extensive bundling processes** (i.e. pioneering rather than stabilizing bundling processes).*

(3) Headquarters-Subsidiary Alignment

Headquarters Involvement: It is also expected that the strategic importance of the local environment influences how headquarters and subsidiaries align and interact throughout entrepreneurial initiatives. Following resource-dependence considerations, it is assumed that subsidiary units that operate in strategically important markets possess higher levels of resource-based power, which they can employ to avoid control from headquarters or to influence central decision-making in their favor. The reasons for this are as follows. First, as indicated, strategically important markets are usually large. As MNCs normally gain (better) access to the significant sales opportunities in these markets through their foreign subsidiaries, these units, at least to some degree, control the important resources of local market access, which provides them with resource-based power vis-à-vis headquarters (Bouquet/Birkinshaw 2008b, p. 582, Dörrenbächer/ Gammelgaard 2011, p. 33). Second and more importantly, strategically important markets are characterized by high levels of competitive intensity, technological dynamism and customer demand intensity. Given the subsidiary's position in these critical environments, it is expected that they can provide the MNC with access to the advanced and sophisticated resources and capabilities that exist in their respective markets (Rugman/Verbeke 1992, p. 767, 2003, p. 129, Rugman et al. 201). For example, subsidiaries may have better access to cutting-edge technologies in their environment or to advanced knowledge or specialized information on local developments that have strategic implications for the MNC as a whole (Bouquet/Birkinshaw 2008b, p. 582, 2008a, p. 482). Consequently, subsidiary units in strategically important markets often represent critical contributors to the MNC's firm-specific advantages (Birkinshaw et al. 1998, p. 228, Bouquet/Birkinshaw 2008b, p. 582), thereby putting them into a strong power position vis-à-vis headquarters. Third, subsidiaries in strategically important markets tend to possess stronger linkages with local entities through which they can obtain the critical resources and capabilities in their markets (Holm et al. 2005, pp. 204, 213).

These local linkages by themselves have been argued to constitute a strong source of resource-based power for subsidiaries (Andersson/Pahlberg 1997, p. 329). Summarizing these considerations, it is expected that subsidiaries operating in strategically important markets have higher levels of resource-based power that they can utilize to counter headquarters control and limit its involvement in the entrepreneurial endeavors of the subsidiary. Thus, it is predicted that:

*The higher the strategic importance of the subsidiary environment, the **less likely** subsidiaries will face **headquarters involvement** in the initiative process.*

Corporate Resistance: With regard to the impact of the strategic importance of the local environment on the level of corporate resistance, two alternative lines of reasoning are possible. On the one hand, it could be assumed that the strategic importance of the local environment affects the characteristics of the emerging initiatives, which in turn influence the intensity of the corporate immune system. As stated previously, in strategically important markets, entrepreneurial initiatives should more often involve close collaborations with external network partners such as customers, suppliers or research institutions. Such collaborative efforts often produce initiatives that involve context-specific or even relation-specific knowledge and capabilities that can be difficult for outsiders to understand (Furu 2001, p. 137, Andersson 2003, p. 430). In addition, in dynamic, competitive and technologically advanced markets, subsidiary initiatives should often represent complex and sophisticated solutions that may involve radical and creation-oriented activities. Such initiatives offer less certain and more remote returns, and they are more risky and imply greater changes to existing routines and behaviors (Birkinshaw 2000, p. 39). Therefore, subsidiary initiatives stemming from strategically important markets may involve entrepreneurial knowledge (or resources and capabilities in general) that are co-specialized, tacit and socially complex and hence more difficult to communicate to headquarters (Mahnke et al. 2007, p. 1283, Keupp/Gassmann 2009, p. 199). Besides the communicative uncertainties, more radical and explorative initiatives also imply greater value uncertainties as they often do not fit established processes or existing values in the MNC, making it more difficult for headquarters to assess and evaluate them (Mahnke et al. 2007, p. 1283). In sum, the increased risks and uncertainties associated with more radical and sophisticated initiatives that originate in strategically important markets could also increase their chances of encountering corporate resistance.

On the other hand, and in contrast to the previous assumptions, arguments can be found that support an alternative line of reasoning. It might also be expected that subsidiaries operating in strategically important markets not only receive more headquarters attention, but are also positively recognized as potential contributors to the

MNC's firm-specific advantages (Birkinshaw et al. 1998, p. 228, Bouquet/Birkinshaw 2008b, p. 582). Additionally, subsidiaries in more competitive and dynamic environments tend to possess stronger linkages with local entities through which they may better access critical resources and capabilities in the local market (Holm et al. 2005, pp. 204, 213). The positive attention and recognition of the subsidiary at headquarters, combined with better external linkages, could help to increase the subsidiary's power base vis-à-vis headquarters and other units (Ghoshal/Bartlett 1990, p. 616, Mudambi/ Navarra 2004, p. 392). Such an enhanced power base has been shown to be an important factor in reducing corporate resistance and gaining central support for initiatives (Birkinshaw/Ridderstråle 1999, pp. 152-153, Birkinshaw 2000, p. 39), leading to the following two alternative predictions:[282]

*Alternative 1: The higher the strategic importance of the subsidiary environment, the **more likely** subsidiaries will face **corporate resistance** in the initiative process.*

*Alternative 2: The higher the strategic importance of the subsidiary environment, the **less likely** subsidiaries will face **corporate resistance** in the initiative process.*

Subsidiary Selling: As outlined previously, subsidiary initiatives typically involve more or less extensive selling and championing activities to promote them in the wider MNC and to help them move through the socio-political system of the firm. In line with the previous considerations related to corporate resistance, two opposing predictions concerning the impact of the strategic market importance on subsidiary initiative selling efforts are conceivable.

First, the challenging environmental conditions (i.e. large market size, high level of competitive intensity, technological dynamism and strong customer demand intensity) should require subsidiaries to continuously devise entrepreneurial initiatives that lead to sophisticated, complex or even radical solutions that may involve cutting-edge knowledge to help the units remain competitive in their respective markets (Cui et al. 2005, pp. 37-38, Holm et al. 2005, p. 204, Cui et al. 2006, pp. 102-103). The realization of these more complex and sophisticated solutions should also necessitate a broader and more diverse set of resources obtained from different internal and external sources and integrated through extensive bundling efforts (Sirmon et al. 2007, pp. 278-282). This may therefore lead to initiatives that represent bundles of resources that are more co-

---

[282] Although two alternative arguments are presented here, previous empirical work suggests that the effects of the subsidiary's resource-based power (see Alternative 2) should be stronger than the ones resulting from risks and uncertainties associated with the context-specific and more uncertain initiatives (see e.g. Andersson et al. 2002b, pp. 984-985, 2007, p. 807). Similarly, Birkinshaw and Ridderstråle (1999, p. 154) argue that the level of subsidiary power and influence is more critical to initiative success than initiative characteristics such as technical of financial implications.

specialized, tacit and socially complex in nature, thereby not only making it more difficult to communicate or explain them to others in the MNCs (Mahnke et al. 2007, p. 1283, Keupp/Gassmann 2009, p. 199), but also making it problematic to transfer the inherent resources to other MNC units in the end (Andersson et al. 2001a, pp. 1019-1020, 2002b, pp. 984-985). The increased risks and uncertainties associated with such initiatives should require more extensive initiative-selling activities on the part of the foreign subsidiaries. As argued above, by offering information that can help to reduce the perceived uncertainty and complexity of an initiative and by providing details that give headquarters managers a sense of greater control, subsidiaries can enhance their chances to obtain approval and funding for the initiative (Dutton/Ashford 1993, p. 412, Gammelgaard 2009, p. 218).[283]

Second, in contrast to the previous line of reasoning, it could also be claimed that the enhanced resource-based power of subsidiaries in strategically important markets makes it less necessary that they engage in active initiative-selling. As argued earlier, subsidiaries with high levels of power can use it to either become more autonomous and avoid hierarchical control by headquarters, or they may employ it to influence decision-making at headquarters in their favor. Consequently, it could be maintained that the more powerful units abroad should be less inclined to engage in selling efforts, as they could either bypass headquarters altogether (in view of their enhanced autonomy) or directly influence initiative-related decisions at the corporate center rather than having to employ lobbying or sales efforts. These contrasting considerations lead to these two alternative predictions:

*Alternative 1: The higher the strategic importance of the subsidiary environment, the **more likely** a subsidiary will engage in **initiative-selling** activities.*

*Alternative 2: The higher the strategic importance of the subsidiary environment, the **less likely** a subsidiary will engage in **initiative-selling** activities.*

3.5.1.2 Subsidiary Resources and Capabilities

The role typology presented by Bartlett and Ghoshal employs the "level of local resources and capabilities" as a second dimension to differentiate between subsidiary types (see e.g. Bartlett/Ghoshal 2002, p. 122). The authors further describe this as the "organizational competence of a particular subsidiary ... in technology, production, marketing, or any other area" (Bartlett/Ghoshal 1986, p. 90, 2002, p. 121). Drawing from a wider range of their publications, the level of subsidiary resources and capabilities is more comprehensively understood in this publication as the level of specialized

---

[283] See also Subsection 3.4.3.3 of this publication which discusses the topic of subsidiary initiative selling.

resources and capabilities a subsidiary possesses in the functional areas of research and development, production, marketing and sales, logistics, purchasing, human resource management, general management and finally innovation and entrepreneurship.[284] The next paragraphs develop predictions as to how the level of resources and capabilities might impact the subsidiary's propensity to undertake entrepreneurial initiatives in general (Paragraph 1), the entrepreneurial resource management sub-process (Paragraph 2) and finally the headquarters-subsidiary alignment sub-process (Paragraph 3).

(1) Subsidiary Initiative-Taking Propensity

A multitude of research studies conceptually and empirically support the notion that the level of resources and capabilities that a subsidiary controls or can access will influence its ability to pursue entrepreneurial and innovative activities (e.g. Ghoshal 1986, Ghoshal/Bartlett 1988, Birkinshaw 1997, Birkinshaw et al. 1998, Birkinshaw 1999, 2000, Delany 2000, Tseng et al. 2004, Krishnan 2006, Zucchella et al. 2007). Consistent with the view taken herein, entrepreneurial efforts have been claimed to represent resource-consuming activities (see e.g. Covin/Slevin 1991, Dess/Lumpkin 2005, Hitt et al. 2011). Therefore, the resources and capabilities that a subsidiary controls play a critical role, since they represent the necessary inputs that provide the grounds for future initiatives (Birkinshaw 1999, p. 17). While certain entrepreneurship literature suggests that relevant resources and capabilities in this context should be defined in their broadest sense to include common inputs such as raw material, monetary resources, plant and equipment or personnel (see e.g. Covin/Slevin 1991, pp. 15-16, Hitt et al. 2011, pp. 60-64), publications in the subsidiary initiative field more strongly emphasize distinctive or specialized capabilities as critical drivers of subsidiary entrepreneurial behavior (e.g. Birkinshaw 1997, Birkinshaw et al. 1998, Birkinshaw 1999, 2000, Tseng et al. 2004, Dörrenbächer/Geppert 2010).[285] In addition to their importance as more or less unique "input factors," high levels of (slack) resources have also been said to put the subsidiary in a better position to deal with the high risks and costs of entrepreneurial initiatives and allow it to better engage in trial-and-error approaches (Ghoshal/Bartlett 1988, p. 369, Tseng et al. 2004, p. 98). Furthermore, the accumulation and demonstration of distinctive subsidiary resources has been claimed to enhance the credibility of the foreign unit

---

[284] As will be explained in more detail in Subsection 4.3.1.1 of this publication, Bartlett and Ghoshal do not use a consistent wording or terminology in their different contributions with regard to this role dimensions. Instead they refer to it as resources, abilities, capabilities or competencies. Therefore, the present study also views this dimension in a broader sense involving both resources and capabilities of various kinds in the outlined eight functional areas.

[285] Birkinshaw and colleagues define distinctive or specialized capabilities as superior to those that exist elsewhere in the MNC and suggest that they may involve, for example, entrepreneurial, technical or market-based expertise (see e.g. Birkinshaw et al. 1998, p. 224, Birkinshaw 1999, p. 17). In his empirical study, Birkinshaw recognizes distinctive subsidiary capabilities as the single most important predictor of subsidiary initiatives (Birkinshaw 1999, p. 24).

in the eyes of headquarters management. This in turn should "lubricate" the initiative process and help the subsidiary overcome corporate resistance by demonstrating that it has the necessary skills and expertise to pursue the identified initiative opportunity (Birkinshaw 1997, pp. 218-219, 1999, pp. 16-17). Taken together, these considerations lead to the following proposition:

The higher the level of subsidiary resources and capabilities, the **more likely** *it will pursue* **subsidiary initiatives***.*

(2) Entrepreneurial Resource Management

Initiative Opportunity Identification: The propensity of subsidiaries to identify new initiative opportunities is also expected to be influenced by its level of resources and capabilities. Aside from resources and capabilities in their broadest sense, three distinct types that possibly play a particularly important role in this context are described in more detail below: (1) the entrepreneurial knowledge or capabilities of subsidiary managers, (2) the subsidiary's network linkages and (3) slack resources (see also Zucchella/ Scabini 2007, p. 127).

(1) A given entrepreneurial opportunity is not necessarily equally obvious to all potential entrepreneurs. Instead, an individual's past entrepreneurial experience and idiosyncratically developed knowledge may allow him or her to recognize opportunities that others would not (Ardichvili et al. 2003, p. 114, Baron/Ensley 2006, p. 1332). Entrepreneurial knowledge as a resource can be understood as accumulated practical skills or expertise that allow entrepreneurs to recognize and exploit entrepreneurial opportunities better than others (Alvarez/Busenitz 2001, p. 767). It has been stated that the more often an individual has been exposed to entrepreneurial opportunities, the more knowledge chunks and heuristics will be developed in what one research team called "opportunity pattern recognition templates" (Linsday/Craig 2002, p. 17). These developed recognition patterns or heuristics may help entrepreneurs to identify and assess initiative opportunities better and more quickly, especially in complex and ambiguous situations where information is uncertain or not fully available (Alvarez/Busenitz 2001, p. 758). Thus, the identification of new initiative opportunities can be viewed as a path-dependent process that is reliant on entrepreneurial experience and knowledge accumulated over time (Alvarez/Busenitz 2001, p. 769). Consequently, it might be stated that the more entrepreneurial knowledge resources and capabilities exist within a subsidiary (and its employees), the more likely that it will be able to discover future initiative opportunities (Haynie et al. 2009, p. 341).

(2) Another factor of potential relevance for initiative identification is a subsidiary's network-embeddedness, which has also been identified as a critical resource (e.g. Anders-

son/Pahlberg 1997, Andersson et al. 2002b, Zaefarian et al. 2011, p. 863). Subsidiary units may be embedded both in inter-organizational and intra-organizational networks (Schmid/Schurig 2003, pp. 760-761). The more strongly a subsidiary is engaged in unique internal and external network relationships, the better its chances to detect emerging initiative opportunities that present themselves in the external or internal market (e.g. Tsai/Ghoshal 1998, McEvily/Zaheer 1999, p. 1135, Delany 2000, p. 239, Andersson et al. 2002b, p. 981); it may thus have more privileged access to opportunities (Denrell et al. 2003, p. 988).

(3) Finally, a certain degree of slack resources at the subsidiary level, understood as "the pool of resources in an organization that is in excess of the minimum necessary to produce a given level of organizational output" (Nohria/Gulati 1996, p. 1246), has been shown to have a positive effect on opportunity identification. Slack resources, in the form of excess funding, time or qualified personnel, for example, should enable the subsidiary to better engage in the "search and trial and error activities" required for entrepreneurial and innovative activities (Ghoshal/Bartlett 1988, p. 370). For instance, it has been argued that subsidiary managers who want to identify and pursue initiative opportunities need excess time to engage with customers or extra funding to further develop an idea. Subsidiaries that consume their entire resource base to fulfill a given mandate are hence less able to engage in the quest for new value-adding opportunities such as entrepreneurial initiatives (Birkinshaw/Fry 1998, p. 53, Delany 2000, pp. 239-240). As suggested in previous research (e.g. Shane 2000, Alvarez/Busenitz 2001, Ardichvili et al. 2003, Denrell et al. 2003, Baron/Ensley 2006), it is hence is presumed that a high level of subsidiary resources and capabilities should allow it to better identify new initiative opportunities, which can be expressed in the following prediction:

*The higher the level of subsidiary resources and capabilities, the **more likely** it will **identify initiative opportunities** in general.*

Concerning the location where initiative opportunities are predominantly identified in situations of high subsidiary resources and capabilities (i.e. within the MNC or outside the MNC), no clear prediction can be derived. As the identification of new entrepreneurial opportunities is viewed as a path-dependent process (see e.g. Alvarez/Busenitz 2001, p. 769), it is expected that the identification of new opportunities will more likely take place in areas in which the subsidiary already has distinctive resources and capabilities. For example, if a subsidiary has well-established and unique relationships with important external customers, then it should be more likely that new initiative opportunities arise in this area.

Resource Structuring: With regard to the development and/or acquisition of the resources needed to realize subsidiary initiatives, two alternative predictions may be made. First, it has been suggested that organizations that are well-endowed with resources should be less inclined to develop or acquire new resources for their entrepreneurial undertakings (Hitt et al. 2002, p. 5). Likewise, with regard to subsidiary initiative-taking, it can be expected that the need for resource structuring varies with the availability of relevant resources the subsidiary possesses. More specifically, it is expected that resource structuring activities are especially needed when larger gaps exist between the resources needed to realize the initiative and the resources available to the subsidiary (Brush et al. 2001, p. 74). Hence, foreign entities already possessing a larger share of (relevant) resources and capabilities can more likely rely on their existing resource portfolio. In contrast, in situations in which the subsidiary only possesses a limited amount of resources and capabilities and in which the resource demand is high (e.g. for more sophisticated initiatives in demanding markets), subsidiaries will have to engage more strongly in resource structuring activities.[286]

Second, although it has been argued that there should be less of a need for resource-endowed subsidiaries to engage in resource structuring activities, they could, nevertheless, be better positioned to do so than units with a lower level of resources and capabilities. For example, existing subsidiary resources in the form of network linkages provide them with better access to the strategic resources and capabilities of their network partners (e.g. Andersson et al. 2002b, p. 980, Mu et al. 2007, p. 82, Phene/Almeida 2008, p. 904). In addition, existing resources, such as prior related knowledge, make it easier to obtain and absorb new knowledge resources and apply them to commercial ends (Cohen/Levinthal 1990, p. 128). Accordingly, it has been stated that organizations differ in terms of their entrepreneurial absorptive capacity, suggesting that the more entrepreneurial experience and knowledge a firm has, the better it will be able to recognize and integrate new resources and capabilities (Alvarez/Busenitz 2001, p. 766). Moreover, subsidiaries that possess a high level of distinctive resources and capabilities can more easily gain access to new resources, since a well-endowed resource portfolio makes the subsidiary more attractive to others for the sharing of their resources and capabilities as well (Almeida et al. 2003, p. 363). These arguments yield two alternative predictions:

*Alternative 1: The higher the level of subsidiary resources and capabilities, the **less likely** it will engage in **resource structuring** activities.*

*Alternative 2: The higher the level of subsidiary resources and capabilities, the **more likely** it will engage in **resource structuring** activities.*

---

[286] The argumentation presented here indicates that the need for resource structuring may actually depend on two aspects, that is, (a) the "demand side" in the form of new resources/capabilities needed to realize an initiative and (b) the "supply side" represented by the resources available to the subsidiary. However, as the resource "demand" side is not considered at this point, emphasis is placed on developing predictions concerning the "supply" side, embodied by the level of subsidiary resources and capabilities.

With regard to the mode and sources of resource structuring, no clear conclusions can be drawn based only on the level of existing subsidiary resources and capabilities. Although it could be argued that, in a situation in which a subsidiary possesses extensive resources and capabilities for the initiative in question, there will be less of an incentive to obtain resources from external partners (Eisenhardt/Schoonhoven 1996, p. 137), the same could hold true for other forms of resource structuring as well. However, in view of the path-dependent nature of resource acquisition and development activities, it could be maintained that resources and capabilities are more easily obtained in areas in which the subsidiary already possesses resources and capabilities (see e.g. Dierickx/ Cool 1989, pp. 1507-1508, Barney 1991, pp. 107-108, Kogut/Zander 1992, p. 392). For instance, subsidiaries endowed with resources in the form of strong external network linkages might be more inclined to obtain new resources or capabilities through these sourcing channels.

Resource Bundling: Subsidiaries equipped with a larger portfolio of resources can be expected to be in a better position to (extensively) combine and integrate them to obtain more distinctive resource bundles or capabilities. A larger set of available subsidiary resources can, in general, make resource bundling easier, allowing subsidiaries to select from a broader range of potentially relevant resources (Sirmon et al. 2007, p. 282). Moreover, structuring activities, such as resource acquisition or development, require investments, time and effort by subsidiary employees. If the subsidiary already possesses many or even all of the required resource inputs necessary for a particular initiative, local managers should be better able to channel their time, efforts and investment towards bundling activities, allowing for more extensive forms such as enriching or pioneering. Lastly, existing subsidiary resources in the form of the prior knowledge and experience of subsidiary managers should enable them to combine and integrate different resources more effectively and efficiently into more complex bundles (Alvarez/Busenitz 2001, p. 769). Such knowledge resources can help managers determine how best to make use of the subsidiary's pockets of expertise and how to further combine or extend its current set of resources so that they better fit customer and market demands (Brush et al. 2001, p. 76). Therefore, it is predicted that:

*The higher the level of subsidiary resources and capabilities, the **more likely** it will use **extensive bundling processes** (i.e. pioneering rather than stabilizing bundling processes).*

(3) Headquarters-Subsidiary Alignment

Headquarters Involvement: Lastly, it is suggested that the level of specialized subsidiary resources and capabilities also affects the headquarters-subsidiary alignment subprocess. Consistent with the resource-dependence considerations used in other parts of this thesis, it is expected that the level of specialized resources and capabilities that a subsidiary controls and that are important for other parts of the MNC should allow it to accrue resource-based power (e.g. Astley/Sachdeva 1984, Medcof 2001, Pfeffer/Salancik 2003). As described above, such specialized resources and capabilities may include, among many others, the subsidiary's proximity and access to local markets, its external network relationships with local business partners, its market knowledge and the subsidiary's entrepreneurial and innovative capabilities.[287] With regard to headquarters involvement in the entrepreneurial initiatives, it is anticipated that subsidiaries in control of such specialized resources and capabilities are in a better position to increase their degree of autonomy vis-à-vis headquarters (Ambos et al. 2010, p. 1102, Yamin/Sinkovics 2010, p. 953), thereby potentially reducing the level of headquarters involvement in the process.[288] Furthermore, in situations in which subsidiaries already possess a high level of resources and capabilities, it is less likely that they will need to approach headquarters for additional resource allocation and approval for their initiatives (Birkinshaw/Morrison 1995, p. 737). Accordingly, it is predicted that:

*The higher the level of subsidiary resources and capabilities, the **less likely** it will face **headquarters involvement** in the initiative process.*

Corporate Resistance: Furthermore, it is to be expected that a high level of subsidiary resources and capabilities also reduces the level of corporate resistance that an initiative will encounter. This may occur in various ways. First, subsidiaries that are well-endowed with resources and capabilities should be less inclined to involve head-

---

[287] See Subsection 3.3.3.2 herein which outlines different sources of subsidiary resource-based power.

[288] As outlined in Subsection 3.3.3 of this publication, RDT suggests that maximum resource dependence and thus maximum power of a subsidiary should develop when it has (a) full control of (b) specialized resources that are (c) important to others in the MNC. However, it needs to be noted that this subsidiary role dimension only (implicitly) addresses two of the three criteria, namely those of resource control and of resource specialization. Therefore, solely relying on "the level of specialized subsidiary resources and capabilities" to predict the full extent of potential subsidiary power may fall somewhat short since the issue of resource importance is not directly addressed. Nevertheless, this concern might, at least in part, be possibly mitigated by the following two arguments. First, it would seem unlikely that a subsidiary – as a semiautonomous unit that is under partial control of headquarters – accumulates large amounts of specialized resources and capabilities that are not critical or important for the proper functioning of the MNC. Hence, for the purpose of this study, it will be implicitly assumed that the specialized resources and capabilities a subsidiary possesses or controls – to the most part – are also of some relevance for the proper functioning of the wider MNC. Second, the importance of a resource for the proper functioning of an organization is to a large degree dependent on the characteristics of the external environment (e.g. environmental uncertainty and instability; see Pfeffer/Salancik 2003, p. 47, 231). Therefore, the joint consideration of both subsidiary role dimensions of Bartlett and Ghoshal's typology later on in this publication, including "the strategic importance of the local environment" (which also relates to aspects of environmental uncertainty and dynamism) should have better predictive power. For example, the subsidiary's possession of specialized resources and capabilities should even be more critical for the MNCs functioning in strategically important markets as they should allow it to better cope with the particularly challenging conditions in such a market (see e.g. Nohria/Bartlett 1994, p. 492).

quarters, thus allowing the foreign unit to bypass or circumvent the "corporate immune system" entirely or at least in the early stages of an initiative (Birkinshaw/Ridderstråle 1999, p. 171, Birkinshaw 2000, p. 46). Second, a high level of proven resources and capabilities should help strengthen the subsidiary's credibility at headquarters by demonstrating that it has the necessary expertise or skills to pursue the initiative, thereby possibly reducing the level of corporate resistance (Birkinshaw 1997, pp. 218-219, Birkinshaw/Fry 1998, p. 58, Birkinshaw 1999, p. 17). Third, and in line with the arguments above, a high level of specialized resources and capabilities should enhance the subsidiary's resource-based power, which has been claimed to be critical in gaining corporate support for an initiative (Birkinshaw/Ridderstråle 1999, p. 152, Birkinshaw 2000, p. 39). Subsidiaries possessing a higher level of relevant resources can be expected to have a stronger influence on the headquarters' (strategic) decisions related to the initiatives (Holm/Pedersen 2000a, p. 37). Thus, it is predicted that:

*The higher the level of subsidiary resources and capabilities, the **less likely** it will face **corporate resistance** in the initiative process.*

Subsidiary Selling: In line with the considerations outlined above, it is predicted that foreign units with high levels of resources and capabilities should also have a lower need to engage in lobbying and bargaining efforts aimed at promoting the initiative at headquarters. The reasons for this are as follows. First, the possession of abundant resources should allow the subsidiary to pursue initiatives more autonomously without having to involve headquarters or other units of the MNC. Thus, by bypassing other units or by being able to better "hide" the initiative, the need to sell or promote it should be reduced. Second, the positive effects of proven resources and capabilities on the credibility of the subsidiary and its ability to pursue the opportunity may also lessen the need for lobbying and sales efforts at headquarters. Thus, well-endowed units abroad should also have less of a need obtain further resources from headquarters, thereby limiting the central resource "investment" and hence the perceived risks at the corporate center. Third, the stronger power of resource-rich units could make selling activities less imperative as such subsidiaries are in a stronger position to "force" the initiative through the socio-political system of the MNC rather than having to "convince" other units of the MNC. Consequently, the following prediction is made:

*The higher the level of subsidiary resources and capabilities, the **less likely** it will engage in **initiative selling** activities.*

3.5.1.3 Role-Specific Predictions

Having presented the predictions for the individual role dimensions in the previous subsection, propositions are now given in this subsection for the four subsidiary role types of Bartlett and Ghoshal, specifically the Strategic Leader (Paragraph 1), the Contributor (Paragraph 2), the Black Hole (Paragraph 3), and the Implementer (Paragraph 4). Each of these paragraphs has a similar structure. Initially, the specific role is introduced and described briefly. Then, predictions are outlined with regard to (a) the entrepreneurial resource management sub-process, (b) the headquarters-subsidiary alignment sub-process, and finally (c) the potential outcomes of subsidiary initiative-taking behavior.

(1) Strategic Leader

Strategic Leaders are subsidiary units that operate in strategically important markets for the MNC and possess high levels of resources and capabilities for one specific function or even for all functions. They are seen as important and legitimate partners for headquarters in the development and implementation of firm-wide strategies and they also play a critical role in the scanning and analysis of opportunities and threats in their respective markets (Bartlett/Ghoshal 1986, p. 90, Schmid et al. 1998, p. 36, Bartlett/ Ghoshal 2002, pp. 121-122). Ideally, Strategic Leaders are given greater autonomy and flexibility in decision-making than other role types, allowing them to better deal with the complex and dynamic environments in which they operate (Nohria/Ghoshal 1994, p. 493). As Strategic Leaders are located in important markets, they are presumed to provide the MNC with access to the advanced and sophisticated resources and capabilities that reside in their environments. At the same time, they can also utilize their own extensive set of resources, providing the grounds for the idiosyncratic bundling of internal and external resources that forms the basis for sustained advantages (Rugman/ Verbeke 1992, p. 767, 2003, p. 129, Rugman et al. 2011, p. 254). As a result, it can be expected that Strategic Leaders represent the entrepreneurial and "innovative spark plugs" in MNCs that generate sophisticated resources and capabilities that are not only of use for the focal subsidiary, but often also for the MNC as a whole (Bartlett/Ghoshal 2002, p. 153, Manolopoulos 2008, p. 31).

Entrepreneurial Resource Management: Concerning the entrepreneurial resource management sub-process, it can be expected that Strategic Leaders have, relative to other role types, the *greatest chance to identify initiative opportunities*. First, this subsidiary type operates in complex and dynamic markets in which it can be expected that entrepreneurial opportunities are generally more prevalent. Second, in such environments subsidiaries are also under more pressure to identify initiative opportunities more frequently if they want to stay competitive, as resource-based advantages are more

3 – Research Framework

quickly eroded. Third, although the identification of new opportunities in strategically important markets could be more challenging, Strategic Leaders should possess a richer set of distinctive capabilities (such as existing internal and external network relationships, entrepreneurial capabilities or experienced subsidiary management), as well as slack resources, all of which allows them to better identify existing or future initiative opportunities. Fourth, they are commonly granted greater levels of autonomy and local decision-making, allowing them to pursue new opportunities more freely and more flexibly. Due to the criticality of the environment, however, it can also be assumed that Strategic Leaders will focus more strongly on the *identification of external initiative opportunities* rather than on internal ones, as this is where most of the pressure for change should originate.

With regard to resource structuring activities, previous work suggests that the demanding environment of this subsidiary type will require subsidiaries to obtain and maintain rich and diverse portfolios of flexible resources that can be used to respond quickly to frequently changing market needs. Strategic Leaders should be in a superior position to obtain required resources from various internal and external sources, such as their internal and external network partners. Moreover, given their existing knowledge and experience, they should also possess a high absorptive capacity, making it easier to retrieve and integrate new resources and capabilities. Nevertheless, taking into account the extensive set of resources that this type of subsidiary should already control, it is expected that it will show a *moderate to high level of resource structuring* activities throughout the initiative process. Concerning the mode and source of resource structuring, it is expected that Strategic Leaders would tend to acquire resources needed for initiatives *from external sources* rather than engaging in internal development. Due to the high importance of the external market, it seems plausible to assume that these subsidiaries would focus more strongly on the external environment and more readily participate in external networks, thus making it more likely that they rely on external sources. Furthermore, as subsidiaries that operate in dynamic and challenging environments need to react more quickly and more flexibly to market changes, the *acquisition* of resources, rather than the gradual resource accumulation, should provide a more viable option in those cases.

Finally, Strategic Leader subsidiaries are more likely to engage in more *extensive resource bundling* and combination efforts. Not only does the more dynamic and challenging market environment require more substantial or even radical entrepreneurial activities, but the existing knowledge and experience in more resource-endowed subsidiaries should additionally provide better grounds to extensively combine resources and capabilities into unique bundles.

Headquarters-Subsidiary Alignment: Strategic Leaders should, relative to the other role types of Bartlett and Ghoshal's typology, have the strongest position when it comes to the alignment and interactions with headquarters. Given their high level of distinctive resources and capabilities and their position in strategically important markets, they play a critical role as contributors to the firm-specific advantages of the MNC. Consequently, they are of high relevance for the functioning of the wider MNC and should thus possess a high level of power, which they can employ to increase their autonomy or to influence initiative-related decisions in the MNC. Pertaining to the level of headquarters involvement, it seems reasonable to assume that Strategic Leaders will face few attempts by the corporate center to become involved or to interfere in their entrepreneurial initiatives. In support of this view, existing work suggests that in this role setting, the corporate management's primary task should be to support the innovative and entrepreneurial subsidiary activities with both the resources and the necessary freedom that are needed to carry out these endeavors (see e.g. Ghoshal 1986, p. 423, Ghoshal/ Nohria 1989, p. 327). Also, given their extensive resources and capabilities, they are expected to be in a good position to pursue many initiatives without having to approach or involve headquarters (or other units of the MNC) for additional resources or approval. Therefore, it is predicted that Strategic Leaders should only face *low involvement of headquarters* in the initiative process.

Moreover, the contextual setting in which Strategic Leaders operate should likely influence the level of corporate resistance they encounter when engaging in entrepreneurial activities. Besides being in a better position to bypass or circumvent headquarters when pursuing initiatives (and thereby evading potential confrontation with the corporate immune system), Strategic Leaders are also presumed to have more credibility and legitimacy in the eyes of headquarters to engage in entrepreneurial activities. As they are considered to have the resources and capabilities required for the realization of initiatives and the skills and expertise necessary to bring it to completion, they are less likely to encounter corporate resistance than all other role types (see e.g. Birkinshaw/ Fry 1998, p. 58). In addition, given their strong power position in the MNC, it is believed that these units are better equipped to gain support for their initiatives or to overcome possible resistance, as they can exert stronger influence on decision-making in the organization. Taken together, these considerations indicate that Strategic Leaders should encounter little resistance from within the MNC. However, it also needs to be taken into account that the often complex, sophisticated and somewhat uncertain entrepreneurial initiatives that are required in strategically important markets may also increase their chances of producing resistance within the MNC.[289] In view of these

---

[289] As argued in Paragraph 3 of Subsection 3.5.1.1, it is expected that the "negative" effects resulting from the uncertainties and complexities of the initiatives are weaker than the "positive" effects stemming from the enhanced power and credibility of the subsidiary.

arguments, it is predicted that Strategic Leaders should, relative to the other role types, face a *low to moderate level of corporate resistance*.

Likewise, with regard to initiative-related selling activities, it is assumed that subsidiaries in the role of Strategic Leaders should show a *low (to moderate) level of initiative-selling* or lobbying. On the one hand, the rather complex and sophisticated initiatives arising in this environment require somewhat stronger selling and championing efforts on the part of the foreign subsidiary units. On the other hand, the strong resource positions and the enhanced credibility of Strategic Leaders in the MNC should make them both less dependent on headquarters for resources and/or approval and also put them in a better position to convince or even force the initiative through the socio-political system of the firm. Hence, it is predicted that they exhibit a *low to moderate level of selling activities*.

Subsidiary Initiative Outcome: With regard to subsidiary initiative outcomes, Strategic Leaders should show the *highest level of realized subsidiary initiatives* of all four subsidiary role types as defined by Bartlett and Ghoshal. While their environmental context encourages or even requires them to engage in proactive and autonomous entrepreneurial behavior, their organizational context in the form of a rich resource and capability base reflects their superior ability to identify and realize initiative opportunities. Moreover, owing to their critical role for the wider MNC as contributors to firm-wide advantages, they are not only regarded as legitimate or equal partners for headquarters, but they are also in a strong bargaining position that allows them to push their initiatives towards completion.

Concerning the types of initiatives that are pursued, Strategic Leaders should be well equipped to undertake all forms of external and internal entrepreneurial initiatives. However, in view of the particular challenges that exist in their external market environment, it seems more likely that they would focus on *externally-oriented initiatives*, as this is where most of the pressures should arise. More specifically, taking into account that global environmental change often originates from their markets, and considering the extensive set of resources they possess, it is argued that Strategic Leader subsidiaries of all role types are the ones most likely to pursue global market initiatives (Ghoshal 1986, p. 32).[290] As a consequence, Strategic Leaders should be in the best position to engage in entrepreneurial initiatives that produce both *highly-specialized and non-location-bound resource bundles* for wider application in the MNC (Birkinshaw et al. 1998, p. 225, Rugman/Verbeke 2001, p. 242, Bartlett/Ghoshal 2002, p. 153, Rugman/Verbeke 2003, p. 129) and as such provide the grounds for subsequent advantages for the entire firm (Birkinshaw et al. 1998, p. 225).

---

[290] As further substantiation, Birkinshaw provides examples in his book of global initiatives only in association with subsidiary units that had a worldwide customer base or that possessed a world product mandate (see Birkinshaw 2000, p. 24).

(2) Contributor

Foreign subsidiary units in the role of Contributors are, like Strategic Leaders, characterized by a high level of distinctive resources and capabilities, but they are located in markets of less strategic relevance for the MNC. Typically, Contributors represent older and more established subsidiary units that have accumulated their pool of "sticky" resources through a long process of resource accumulation (Ghoshal/Nohria 1994, p. 328). These units are important for the MNC because of their high level of existing resources and capabilities in specific areas (e.g. particular technological capabilities) and their ability to internally develop new resources and capabilities that can be applied on a local or sometimes even global basis (Bartlett/Ghoshal 1986, pp. 90-91, Schmid et al. 1998, p. 37, Bartlett/Ghoshal 2002, pp. 123-125). However, in contrast to Strategic Leaders, which can access a larger portfolio of internal and external resources, Contributors have to rely mostly on internally available resources and capabilities (Rugman/ Verbeke 1992, p. 767, 2003, p. 129). Subsidiaries belonging to this role type do have "some potential to advance the firm's global innovation processes ... but lack the exposure to stimulating environments" (Bartlett/Ghoshal 2002, p. 154). Furthermore, Contributors may, if not managed appropriately, pose a particular problem for MNCs as they lack external market challenges that guide their resources and capability development efforts. This could result in resource development activities that are not deemed necessary or that could even be harmful for the overall MNC strategy (Bartlett/Ghoshal 2002, p. 125). Hence, with regard to headquarters-subsidiary relationships, it has been suggested that Contributors should be given some degree of autonomy to reduce potential conflict and dissonance between the two parties, yet at the same time they should be managed through high levels of formalization in order to constrain potentially adverse or non-aligned subsidiary behavior (Ghoshal/Nohria 1989, p. 328, Nohria/ Ghoshal 1994, p. 493).

Entrepreneurial Resource Management: In comparison to the other role types of Bartlett and Ghoshal's typology, Contributors are expected to show a *moderate level of initiative opportunity identification* for the following reasons. First, this role type is typically endowed with distinctive resources and capabilities (at least in certain areas), which enhances the foreign unit's ability to identify new opportunities. For example, besides the considerable expertise and skills that have been accumulated over time, slack resources in the form of excess funding, time or qualified personnel could also improve the Contributor's capacity to engage in the search and trial and error activities that are often needed when looking for new entrepreneurial or innovative opportunities. Second, despite the extensive resources such a unit should possess, the rather undemanding and stable environmental market conditions provide little pressure or stimulus to engage in the identification of new entrepreneurial opportunities. Hence, in view of these two opposing effects, it is predicted that Contributors will exhibit a rather moderate level of initiative opportunity identification. Concerning the locus of opportunity identification, it is argued that, due to the low strategic relevance of the external market environment, Contributors should have less of a need to focus on changes, potential threats and opportunities in the external market. Instead, it is expected that these foreign units can act in a more inward-focused way and therefore are more likely to *identify initiative opportunities in the internal market system* of the MNC.

When realizing the identified initiative opportunities, it is presumed that subsidiaries in the role of Contributors would show a *low to moderate level of resource structuring* activities. As previously argued, the environments of low strategic importance in which Contributors operate are characterized by lower degrees of competitive intensity, technological dynamism and sophistication in customer demand. Here, initiatives are not only needed less frequently, but they should also be of less complex and sophisticated nature. Consequently, Contributors, already possessing a rich pool of resources and capabilities, can more strongly rely on their existing resource base and should be less inclined to obtain new sources in these relatively undemanding markets. Nevertheless, given the path-dependent nature of resource structuring activities, well-endowed Contributors should still be in a better position to obtain new resources and capabilities. Together, these two opposing arguments lead to the prediction that Contributors should exhibit a low to moderate level of resource structuring activities. Lastly, in view of their stable and less competitive market environments, Contributors should have more time to internally develop and accumulate the necessary resources and should be less pressured to obtain acquire them externally. Thus, it is predicted that Contributor subsidiaries are more likely to engage in *internal resource development* efforts when realizing identified initiative opportunities.

Additionally, Contributors should exhibit a *moderate level of less extensive bundling* activities. Although such units could be expected to be in a better position to (extensively) combine and integrate resources to obtain more complex and distinct bundles, the relatively undemanding environment necessitates only incremental or intermediate bundling to maintain or incrementally improve existing products, service or processes. Therefore, the bundling of mostly existing subsidiary resources with some newly obtained ones should be sufficient in such a context.

Headquarters-Subsidiary Alignment: Contributors should, relative to the other role types, possess a moderately strong position when it comes to the alignment and interactions with the corporate center with regard to their initiatives. On the one hand, Contributors are, similar to Strategic Leaders, important for the MNC because of their high level of distinctive resources and capabilities, thereby providing them with some resource-based power that they can employ to increase their autonomy or to influence initiative-related decisions in the MNC. However, in comparison to Strategic Leaders, which can derive an even stronger power position due to their location in strategically important markets, Contributors should be somewhat less critical for the MNC, as their environments do not provide them with access to more advanced or sophisticated resources and capabilities. Hence, considering their somewhat moderate level of resource-based power, it may be concluded that headquarters is able to exert more hierarchical power than it would with Strategic Leaders. As a result of the particular power distribution, Contributors should be less able to avoid central control attempts and thus face *moderate levels of headquarters involvement* in the initiative process.

As to effects of the corporate immune system, Contributors are predicted to encounter a *moderate level of corporate resistance* against their entrepreneurial initiatives based on the following considerations. First, the moderately strong resource position of these units should give them some resource-based power that can be used to reduce resistance in the MNC and help gain central support for their initiatives. Second, given their often long history in the MNC and their high level of proven resources and capabilities in specific areas, Contributors should have earned a certain level of credibility and trust in their abilities, which has been shown to reduce corporate resistance in multinational firms and help subsidiaries better overcome it. Third, the less demanding external market environment should more strongly encourage internally-oriented initiatives that are less complex, sophisticated and radical in nature and that should remain closer to the current capabilities of the subsidiary. Consequently, such entrepreneurial activities by Contributors and their implications for the wider MNC should be easier to communicate and perceived as less uncertain and risky by headquarters. Taken together, given their moderately strong power position in the MNC along with their location in strategically unimportant markets requiring less complex, sophisticated and radical initiatives, Contributors should face a moderate level of corporate resistance.

Similarly, Contributors should show a *moderate level of selling activities* aimed at promoting their initiatives in the wider MNC. First, it is expected that the moderately strong resource base of this subsidiary type should decrease its propensity to engage in active selling activities, as it should have less of a need to involve headquarters for further resources, higher credibility in the eyes of the corporate center as well as some resource-based power that it can use to "force" its initiative through the socio-political system of the MNC. Second, given the low strategic importance of their environment, Contributors are expected to take on less complex, sophisticated and radical (rather internal market) initiatives. Since such initiatives pose less risk and uncertainty and are easier to communicate to headquarters, the need for active selling should be reduced. However, contrary to the previous two considerations, the low strategic importance of their environment should also somewhat limit the importance and the resource-based power of Contributors. While Strategic Leaders can also provide the MNC with the advanced and sophisticated resources and capabilities in their markets, Contributors must primarily deliver those that were developed internally. In view of these somewhat opposing effects, it is predicted that these units should exhibit a moderate level of selling activities.

Subsidiary Initiative Outcome: In comparison to the other role types described by Bartlett and Ghoshal, Contributors are expected to exhibit a *moderate level of realized subsidiary initiatives*. While the extensive set of resources and capabilities strengthens this role type's ability to identify and realize entrepreneurial initiatives, the relatively undemanding market should inhibit entrepreneurial subsidiary behavior as it lacks the stimuli and opportunities for entrepreneurial initiatives. Furthermore, owing mostly to their strong resource and capability profile, Contributors are in a moderate or even strong power position to navigate their initiatives through the political system of the MNC. Overall, this should lead to a moderate level of successful initiatives.

With regard to the initiative types, Contributors should be generally able to engage in both internal and certain external initiatives. However, in view of the lacking external pressures or stimuli and given their rather tight integration in the corporate network (see e.g. Birkinshaw/Morrison 1995, Manolopoulos 2008), it is expected that Contributors should show a relatively higher propensity to engage in *internally-oriented entrepreneurial initiatives*. As outlined previously, Contributors are more likely to identify new initiative opportunities from within the corporate system. Moreover, considering the less demanding and challenging environmental conditions they face, more incremental internal initiatives that involve gradual resource and capability development efforts to, for instance, improve existing products or services or enhance operational and organizational efficiency, should often be sufficient in such a context.[291]

In the end, initiatives undertaken by Contributors should produce some new resource bundles of *low to moderate specialization* that are, however, *readily applicable in other units* of the MNC. This conclusion is based on the following considerations. Given the low strategic importance of their external environment and their rather tight integration in the MNC system, it is expected that Contributors will tend to pursue initiatives that are internally rather than externally oriented and that are more incremental than radical in nature. As was argued earlier, internally oriented initiatives should (in comparison with external ones) deliver somewhat less specialized resource bundles, as they are more strongly influenced by corporate center guidelines and decisions and hence should

---

[291] These characteristics are typically associated with internally-oriented initiatives. As described in Subsection 3.4.4 of this publication, internal market initiatives arise through opportunities that are identified within the internal market of the MNC and which are geared towards improving the efficiency of the corporate system through reconfiguring and rationalization efforts.

remain somewhat closer to the dominant logic and the current capabilities of the MNC.[292] Similarly, less complex and sophisticated initiatives should only require the reconfiguration and incremental enhancement of existing resources and capabilities, thereby leading to resource outcomes that may be less specialized. Furthermore, due to the low strategic importance of their environment, Contributors should, in contrast to Strategic Leaders, lack the access to the advanced and sophisticated resources and capabilities that typically exist in more important markets. Consequently, Contributors will have to rely primarily on internal resources, thereby limiting their ability to produce highly specialized resource bundles.[293] In sum, these considerations would suggest that the initiatives by Contributors should commonly deliver resource bundles of low to moderate specialization.[294]

With regard to the applicability of the resource outcomes for the wider MNC, however, Contributors should deliver resource bundles that are mostly non-location-bound and thus can be more or less directly applied in the wider MNC. As their initiatives should largely revolve around existing resources and capabilities and only involve few resources that were acquired externally, the resulting resource bundles should be less idiosyncratic, context-specific and/or tacit, thus making it easier to use them in other parts of the MNC (Andersson et al. 2001a, pp. 1019-1020, 2002b, pp. 984-985). Furthermore, assuming that initiatives undertaken by Contributors are more strongly influenced and guided by headquarters (than those of Strategic Leaders, for example), the resulting resource bundles should remain closer to the current capabilities of the MNC, thus making it easier for other parts of the corporation to absorb and utilize them (Cohen/Levinthal 1990, pp. 135-136, Ambos et al. 2006, p. 299).

(3) Black Hole

Foreign subsidiary units that operate in strategically important markets but only possess limited resources and capabilities are labeled "Black Holes." They often represent young or recently established units or cases in which subsidiaries were unable to build up resources at the speed of rapidly changing environments (Ghoshal/Nohria 1989, p. 328). Although they are situated in important environments that could allow them to benefit from critical resources and capabilities that reside in their respective markets, this subsidiary type usually lacks the capabilities and preconditions to adequately exploit

---

[292] See Subsection 3.4.4.2 of this publication which also deals with the link between different subsidiary initiative types and resource-based outcomes.

[293] In comparison to the other role types, Contributors are expected to take a somewhat intermediate position between Strategic Leaders and Implementers with regards to the specialization of resource outcomes. On the "high" side of the spectrum, Strategic Leaders can utilize both the advanced external resources in their markets and their own extensive set of internal resources for idiosyncratic bundling activities. In contrast, Implementers, at the other side of the spectrum, should be very limited in their bundling activities as they are not able to access many unique resources internally or externally.

[294] Relatedly, it has been suggested that – more generally – resources and capabilities provided by Contributors should remain close or, to a certain extent, even overlap with those of the parent company (Rabbiosi 2011, p. 99).

the learning and resource development potentials that exist in their specific environments (Rugman/Verbeke 1992, p. 767, Furu 2001, p. 135, Bartlett/Ghoshal 2002, p. 154, Manolopoulos 2008, p. 31). Therefore, this role is only deemed acceptable for a limited period of time and should only be tolerated while building up a strong local presence in such markets (Bartlett/Ghoshal 1986, p. 91, Schmid et al. 1998, p. 38, Bartlett/Ghoshal 2002, pp. 126-128). Nevertheless, Black Holes can still serve as observation posts that help monitor the developments and changes in important markets, even if the market potential itself cannot be leveraged immediately (Bartlett/Ghoshal 2002, p. 128, Enright/Subramanian 2007, p. 913).

Entrepreneurial Resource Management: Relative to the other role types of Bartlett and Ghoshal's typology, Black Holes are expected to show a *moderate level of initiative opportunity identification* based on the following considerations. First, this role type is to be found in strategically important markets in which new opportunities for entrepreneurial endeavors are expected to arise more frequently due to such things as quickly changing market conditions and rapid technological advancements. Furthermore, in view of quickly eroding competitive advantages in such challenging environments, subsidiary units are also required to more frequently identify new innovative or entrepreneurial opportunities that help them to keep up with competition. However, in spite of the more frequent opportunities that should surface in such critical markets, the low level of distinctive resources and capabilities of Black Holes should impede their ability to identify new initiative opportunities. For example, limited managerial expertise or market knowledge in these subsidiaries could make the identification of new opportunities more difficult for Black Holes. Similarly, lacking external network linkages (of these often young units) with, for instance, customers, suppliers or other external actors should severely constrain their chances to recognize new opportunities for entrepreneurial initiatives. Together, these assumptions suggest that Black Holes should, relative to the other role types, show a moderate level of initiative opportunity identification. Given their criticality of their external environment, it is furthermore expected that Black Holes would tend to *identify new opportunities in their external market* rather than from within the MNC network.

As concerns obtaining new resources and capabilities to realize initiatives, it is predicted that Black Holes should exhibit a *moderate or even low level of resource structuring*. On the one hand, the challenging market conditions, together with the limited resource base of the subsidiary, should increase the Black hole's need to attain new resources and capabilities to further pursue the rather complex and sophisticated initiative opportunities that are often needed in this context.[295] On the other hand, the low level of

---

[295] As outlined in Subsection 3.4.2.1, such a situation indicates that there exists a large "resource gap" between the resources needed to realize an identified initiative opportunity and the resources available to the subsidiary. It was suggested that this increases the need for subsidiaries to engage in resource structuring activities.

existing resources and capabilities in the subsidiary should also make it somewhat difficult to obtain them from internal or external sources. Thus, despite the high need for new resources and capabilities, Black Holes should be limited in their ability to acquire or develop them. With regard to the mode and source of resource structuring, it is expected that, due to the dynamic, complex and sophisticated environment of Black Holes, these units would be more inclined to *acquire new resources and capabilities from external sources*.

In addition, it is presumed that Black Holes should show a *moderate or even low level of resource bundling* and that is less extensive in nature. Although these units are situated in environments requiring initiatives that imply extensive or even radical change (and therefore require more extensive bundling activities), their own limited resource base and their inability to access most of the advanced and sophisticated resources in their environment should largely impede their capacity for more extensive bundling activities.[296]

Headquarters-Subsidiary Alignment: Relative to the other role types of Bartlett and Ghoshal's typology, Black Holes are expected to have a low to moderately strong power position in their headquarters-subsidiary alignment. Due to their location in strategically important markets, it is expected that Black Holes can, at least to some extent, accrue resource-based power that they can use when aligning and interacting with headquarters. Although they are not well-positioned to directly access the advanced and sophisticated resources and capabilities in their environment, they nevertheless can provide the MNC with specialized information on local developments that have strategic implications for the wider firm (Bartlett/Ghoshal 2002, p. 128, Bouquet/Birkinshaw 2008a, p. 482). However, in comparison with Strategic Leaders, Black Holes are unable to derive a strong power position in the MNC due to their poor resource and capability base. Concerning to the level of headquarters participation and engagement in subsidiary initiative-taking activities, the rather weak bargaining position of this role type should then translate into *moderate to high levels of headquarters involvement*. This can also manifest in, for instance, low to moderate degrees of subsidiary autonomy and more frequent interaction and communication between the two parties.

Furthermore, the role setting of Black Holes in the MNC may also impact the level of corporate resistance they face when undertaking entrepreneurial initiatives. As was argued previously, the challenging conditions in strategically important markets should necessitate or motivate more complex, sophisticated and exploratory entrepreneurial initiatives. As a result, they should not only be more difficult for headquarters to

---

[296] In line with these assumptions, it has been claimed that "in the case of black hole subsidiaries, no such bundling can occur, meaning that the mere location of the subsidiary in a particular geographic space is insufficient for it to access and utilize the valuable external resources present in that space" (Rugman/Verbeke 2011, p. 255).

understand and assess, but they may also be perceived as more risky and uncertain by the parent company, thereby "stimulating" the corporate immune system. Moreover, as subsidiaries in the role of Black Holes do not possess many distinctive resources or capabilities that allow them to autonomously pursue initiatives or could lend them greater credibility in the eyes of headquarters, it is anticipated that this role type should encounter a *moderate to high level of corporate resistance*.

In line with the previous reasoning, it is also expected that Black Holes will show a *moderate to high level of subsidiary initiative selling*. The increased risks and uncertainties associated with initiatives that often originate in their challenging environments should require more extensive selling and lobbying efforts from Black Holes. Likewise, the low level of resources and the limited bargaining power of this role type should necessitate stronger sales activities, as they cannot easily bypass or circumvent the corporate immune system and are less able to influence headquarters initiative-related decision-making in the MNC.

Subsidiary Initiative Outcome: In contrast to the other role types, Black Hole subsidiaries can be expected to exhibit a *moderate to low level of entrepreneurial initiatives*. Although their demanding environment should function as a driver for initiative-taking activities, their limited resource and capability base should considerably constrain such entrepreneurial efforts. Moreover, because of their relatively low power and bargaining position in the MNC, it is also assumed that it will be easier for the corporate immune system to inhibit or reject the entrepreneurial initiatives of Black Holes.

Regarding the types of initiatives undertaken, it is expected that Black Holes will be more likely to focus on *externally oriented initiatives* as most of the pressures for entrepreneurial behavior should stem from the challenging and demanding external environment. However, although global environmental change may frequently originate from their strategically important markets, their lack of resources and capabilities should not allow them to fully engage in global market initiatives. Instead, it would seem more likely for Black Holes to engage in local market initiatives that are identified in their immediate local environment. Given the smaller scale of these entrepreneurial initiatives, even less well-endowed Black Holes could be in some position to pursue and realize them.

In view of the moderate or even low level of (local market) initiatives that are anticipated to stem from subsidiaries in the role of Black Holes, it is predicted that they should only produce a *moderate to low level of specialized resources and capabilities*. Given the limited access to resources in the external environment and in view of their own limited resource base, these units should thus be quite limited in creating unique or specialized resource bundles through their entrepreneurial initiatives. Furthermore, as a consequence of the particular environmental conditions and the complex and sophisticated demand in strategically important markets, it could be assumed that the resource bundles resulting from the (rather local market) initiatives are also not directly applicable for other parts of the MNC. Instead, they should first lead to *partially location-bound resource bundles* that need to be transformed subsequently by the subsidiary into non-location-bound ones before they can be transferred and effectively utilized in other parts of the firm.

(4) Implementer

Finally, subsidiaries in the role of Implementers are located in markets of little strategic relevance for the MNC and at the same time do not possess any distinctive resources or capabilities. It has been suggested that subsidiaries from developing countries or from smaller European countries often fall into this category. Foreign units in such a position often have only the resources and capabilities necessary to sustain their local operations. Because the market is of little relevance for the MNC's sustained competitiveness, they typically only receive limited resources from headquarters for the implementation of the company's strategies (Bartlett/Ghoshal 2002, p. 125, Manolopoulos 2008, p. 31). In such a context, subsidiaries may be only loosely integrated with the rest of the MNC and at the same time not deeply embedded in their local environment (Taggart 1997, p. 301). As a result, Implementers are not expected to deliver significant innovations for wider application within the MNC and thus they do not contribute much to the sustained competitiveness of the MNC (Bartlett/Ghoshal 2002, p. 153).[297] Instead, they are more likely to create some minor innovations to adapt global products or processes to the needs of their local environment (Ghoshal 1986, p. 35). Yet, despite their rather unimportant role for innovations in the MNC, Implementers are still considered crucial for the firm. They generate the cash flows that are important for the survival of the firm and they deliver resources that can support the strategic and innovative efforts of the company. Implementers also provide opportunities for the MNC to achieve economies of scale and scope, as their activities focus on efficient resource exploitation rather than on resource exploration and development (Bartlett/Ghoshal 1986, p. 91, Schmid et al. 1998, p. 38, Furu 2001, p. 135, Bartlett/Ghoshal 2002, pp. 125-126, Rugman/Verbeke 2003, p. 129).

Entrepreneurial Resource Management: In comparison to the other role types, Implementers should exhibit the *lowest level of initiative opportunity identification*. Neither their undemanding environmental context nor their limited resource base should encourage or enable them to engage in the identification or generation of new initiative opportunities. Furthermore, their loose integration in the MNC network should prevent

---

[297] However, they still should be able to make minor modifications to global products or forward local needs to other parts of the MNC (Bartlett/Ghoshal 2002, p. 153).

them from identifying potential opportunities that exist or emerge within the multinational network (Tsai/Ghoshal 1998, p. 467, Tseng et al. 2004, p. 99), while their rather low local embeddedness also limits their chances to detect new opportunities in the external environment (Andersson et al. 2001a, p. 1015, Holm et al. 2005, p. 202).[298] Therefore, Implementers should be mostly restricted to *internal initiative opportunities* that emerge within the confines of the subsidiary unit itself.

As to the efforts to obtain new resources and capabilities to realize the (few) identified initiative opportunities, it is presumed that of all role types, Implementers will show the *lowest level of resource structuring* activities. In their strategically unimportant markets, it is not expected that frequent initiative-taking is required that involves complex bundles of unique resources and capabilities, and as such reduces the need to obtain many new ones. Furthermore, the small resource base of Implementers also limits their ability to subsequently acquire or develop new resources and capabilities. For example, lacking resources in the form of network linkages could keep them from recognizing and accessing the knowledge and capabilities of external and internal network partners. Concerning the mode and source of resource structuring, it is assumed that Implementers tend to *internally develop new resources and capabilities* over time. In view of their stable and less competitive market environments, Implementers not only have more time to internally accumulate them, but, given their lack of internal and external embeddedness, this role type may also not have many other alternatives.

Lastly, Implementers should show the *lowest level of resource bundling* activities and these should be generally incremental in nature. Considering the few minor initiatives that could possibly stem from these units, incremental bundling activities that enhance existing capabilities through, for instance, continuous organizational learning or improvement programs are often likely to be sufficient. Additionally, as a result of the limited access to internal and external sources, Implementers should largely lack the resource inputs needed for more extensive forms of combinative activities.

Headquarters-Subsidiary Alignment: Among all the role types of Bartlett and Ghoshal's typology, Implementers should be in the "weakest" power or bargaining position with regard to initiative-related alignment and interactions with the corporate center. The inability of these units to deliver critical resources to the wider MNC and, at the same time, their strong dependence on resources from headquarters put them in a very weak relative power position. Based on this assumption, it should be quite difficult for Implementers to obtain significant autonomy throughout their initiatives or to influence initiative-related decision-making in the organization in their favor. Therefore,

---

[298] The effects of subsidiary integration and subsidiary local embeddedness on the identification of subsidiary initiative opportunities are more thoroughly discussed in Subsections 3.5.2.1 and 3.5.2.2 of this publication.

the low level of autonomy that is typically associated with Implementers and the high resource need from the parent company should also affect initiative-taking activities by subsidiaries with *headquarters becoming strongly involved* in these entrepreneurial subsidiary endeavors.

Implementers are also presumed to encounter the *highest level of corporate resistance* when taking entrepreneurial initiatives. First, as a consequence of their own weak resource base, it appears more likely that they would need to approach headquarters to obtain the resources and approval necessary to realize their initiatives. Second, given their low level of proven resources and capabilities, they should lack the credibility and legitimacy in the eyes of the corporate center to engage in entrepreneurial initiatives. Third, the limited power of Implementers should make it difficult for them to gain support or overcome possible resistance in the MNC. Taken together, these considerations suggest that, of all role types, Implementers could face the highest level of corporate resistance when taking initiatives.

Similarly, Implementers are expected to exhibit a *high level of initiative selling*. In line with the reasoning presented above, due to the expected low autonomy, the little credibility and the limited resource-based power, selling and lobbying activities to promote their initiatives should be commonly required for Implementer subsidiaries.

Subsidiary Initiative Outcome: With regard to the outcomes of initiative-taking behavior by Implementers, it is expected that they *exhibit the lowest level of successful initiatives*. Both the undemanding environmental context and their very limited resource base should largely restrict entrepreneurial efforts in these units. In addition, due to their weak power and bargaining position in the MNC, it is also assumed that the corporate immune system can operate to its full extent to inhibit or reject entrepreneurial initiatives brought forward by Implementers.

It has been previously claimed that Implementers should not contribute much to the global innovation process in MNCs. Given the non-critical nature of the market environment and the limited access to key resources and capabilities of the MNC, Implementers are mostly unable to support entrepreneurial or innovative efforts in other parts of the multinational organization. Instead, it has been suggested that they are merely able to deliver some local innovations, usually in the form of minor modifications, which are, however, seldom of use outside their national boundaries (Ghoshal 1986, pp. 35, 421-425). Similarly, the contextual setting of Implementers should largely prevent them from pursuing entrepreneurial initiatives of a larger scale and scope. As they lack the external stimulus and pressures from their strategically unimportant markets, it is also presumed that they would tend to focus on smaller opportunities that arise within the organizational network of the MNC and thus would tend to engage in *"trivial" initiatives* or

3 – Research Framework

perhaps, at most, some *internal market initiatives* that could help with improving the efficiency of the wider corporate system. Table 3.5 below summarizes all predictions made for the role typology by Bartlett and Ghoshal.

	Strategic Leader	Contributor	Black Hole	Implementer
Strat. importance of subsidiary environment	High	Low	High	Low
Competence of local organization	High	High	Low	Low
(I) Entrepreneurial Resource Management				
Opportunity identification (level and source)	• **Highest** level of initiative opportunity identification • **Rather external** than internal identification	• **Moderate** level of initiative opportunity identification • **Rather internal** identification	• **Moderate** level of initiative opportunity identification • **Rather external** than internal identification	• **Lowest** level of initiative opportunity identification • **Rather internal** than external identification
Resource structuring (level, source and mode)	• **Moderate to high** level of resource structuring • **Rather resource acquisition** from external sources	• **Low to moderate** level of resource structuring • **Rather internal development**	• **Low to moderate** level of resource structuring • **Rather external acquisition**	• **Lowest** level of resource structuring • Possibly some **internal resource development** activities
Resource bundling (level and mode)	• **High** level of resource bundling • **More extensive** bundling	• **Moderate** level of resource bundling • **Less extensive** bundling	• **Low to moderate** level of resource bundling • **Less extensive** bundling	• **Lowest** level of resource bundling • **Rather incremental** bundling
(II) Headquarters-Subsidiary Alignment				
HQ involvement (level)	• **Low** level of involvement	• **Moderate** level of involvement	• **Moderate to high** level of involvement	• **High** level of involvement
Corp. resistance (level)	• **Low to moderate** level of resistance	• **Moderate** level of resistance	• **Moderate to high** level of resistance	• **High** level of resistance
Sub. initiative selling (level)	• **Low to moderate** level of selling	• **Moderate** level of selling	• **Moderate to high** level of selling	• **High** level of selling
(III) Subsidiary Initiative Outcome				
Subsidiary initiative-taking (level and type)	• **Highest** level of initiatives • Mostly **external** initiatives (global and local market), some internal market	• **Moderate** level of initiatives • Rather **internal** initiatives (internal market and internal-hybrid), some local market	• **Low to moderate** level of initiatives • Rather **external** initiatives (local market)	• **Lowest** level of initiatives • Rather **internal** initiatives (internal market & trivial)
Subsidiary resource development (level and type)	• **Highest** level of specialized resource development • Rather **non-location bound** resources	• **Low to moderate** level of specialized resource development • Mostly **non-location-bound** resources	• **Low to moderate** level of specialized resource development • **Partially location-bound** resources	• **Lowest** level of specialized resource development • Mostly **location-bound** resources

Table 3.5: Summary of predictions for the subsidiary role typology by Bartlett/Ghoshal

In sum, it has been claimed that subsidiary units in the role of Implementers do not engage in extensive resource- and capability-creating activities and thus seldom produce critical resources that can be utilized in other parts of the MNC (Furu 2001, p. 140, Rugman/Verbeke 2003, p. 129, Ambos et al. 2006, p. 298, Enright/Subramanian 2007, p. 912, Rabbiosi 2011, p. 99). Likewise, it has been argued that their primarily adaptive innovations are rarely of use outside their national boundaries (Ghoshal 1986, p. 35). In a similar vein, it is expected that Implementers should engage in initiatives that produce *few new resources and capabilities*, which are mostly of *use for the local* unit.

3.5.2 Role Typology by Jarillo and Martinez

3.5.2.1 Subsidiary's Localization and Local Responsiveness

Jarillo and Martinez, as well as Taggart, use what they term the "degree of localization" (Jarillo/Martinez 1990) or the "degree of local responsiveness" (Taggart 1997) as one dimension for their role typologies. The degree of localization expresses the extent to which various activities are performed at a subsidiary location, such as manufacturing, purchasing, marketing or R&D. It also indicates to what degree products or services are adapted locally due to pressures arising from customers, competitors or technological developments (see also Jarillo/Martinez 1990, pp. 504-505). Similarly, the degree of local responsiveness as applied by Taggart largely focuses on the driving forces or preconditions that necessitate a subsidiary's response to the specific needs of the local environment (e.g. pressures arising from customers and competitors or technological developments; see Taggart 1997, p. 305).[299] The following paragraphs discuss the potential impact of the subsidiary's degree of localization/local responsiveness on subsidiary initiative-taking, and more specifically the effect on the overall propensity to engage in subsidiary initiatives (Paragraph 1) as well as on the sub-processes concerned with entrepreneurial resource management (Paragraph 2) and headquarters-subsidiary alignment (Paragraph 3).

(1) Subsidiary Initiative-Taking Propensity

Previous empirical research investigating the effects of a subsidiary's local responsiveness and local market orientation lends broad support for the assumption that these conditions should have a positive effect on subsidiary initiative-taking (see e.g. Birkinshaw 1998b, Delany 2000, Tseng et al. 2004, Birkinshaw et al. 2005, Liouka 2007, Scott et al. 2010). For instance, Birkinshaw's research on foreign-owned subsidiaries in Sweden revealed that those units with a broader local value-added scope typically showed a greater level of initiative-taking (Birkinshaw 1998b, p. 293). Likewise, Tseng et al. discovered through their empirical work that a subsidiary's local responsiveness is positively linked to subsidiary initiative (Tseng et al. 2004, p. 100). Other publications

---

[299] Although Taggart attempts to evaluate and extend the model by Jarillo and Martinez, he applies somewhat different measures and scales for the operationalization and assessment of this role dimension. Apparently, he follows the approach previously used by Prahalad and Doz (see Taggart 1997, p. 303 and for comparison Prahalad/Doz 1987, p. 32) while Jarillo and Martinez' operationalization relies on a mixture of Porter's configuration/coordination framework and the integration-responsiveness framework by Prahald and Doz (see also Venaik et al. 2002, p. 11). The deviations are further discussed in Subsection 4.3.1.3 of this publication.

also generally acknowledge the positive effects of local responsiveness on the entrepreneurial and innovative behavior of foreign subsidiaries. Dunning, for instance, argues that foreign subsidiaries engaged in more value-adding activities locally should also show a higher propensity to pursue higher-order activities such as innovation and entrepreneurship (Dunning 1998, p. 51). Moreover, Luo suggests that subsidiaries that respond to the specific needs in their host countries and maintain the necessary local responsiveness should be in a better position to take initiatives (Luo 2001, p. 453). Additionally, it seems plausible to assume that a high degree of localization also implies that subsidiaries are more deeply embedded in their local environment (Manolopoulos 2008, p. 36).[300] For instance, handling production, marketing and sales or R&D activities in the host country frequently involves closer interactions and more solid relationships with local stakeholders, such as suppliers, end customers or research institutions (Harzing 2000, p. 109, Tseng et al. 2004, pp. 99-100). The stronger external embeddedness should in turn also positively influence the subsidiary's ability to be entrepreneurial and innovative and to develop new resources and capabilities (see e.g. Andersson et al. 2001a, p. 1018, Andersson 2003, p. 428, Holm et al. 2005, p. 202). When subsidiaries are embedded in dynamic, sophisticated or technologically diverse environments, initiative-taking may be fostered even further (Zahra et al. 2000, pp. 12-15, Almeida/Phene 2004, p. 859). Hence, the following prediction is made:

*The higher a subsidiary's degree of localization/local responsiveness, the **more** **likely** it will pursue **subsidiary initiatives**.*

(2) Entrepreneurial Resource Management Activities

Initiative Opportunity Identification: In line with the previous arguments, it is also assumed that a higher degree of a subsidiary's localization/local responsiveness should increase its propensity to identify new initiative opportunities for the following reasons. First, foreign units that perform a wider range of value-adding activities in the host country can be expected to possess a broader and more diverse set of resource configurations (Taggart 1997, p. 301, Tseng et al. 2004, p. 98). Consequently, a more extensive spectrum of activities and resources should broaden the subsidiary's opportunity space and thus increase its chances to identify new initiative opportunities (Tseng et al. 2004, p. 98, Ambos et al. 2010, p. 1108). Second, a high degree of local responsiveness also implies that products and services are better adapted to local needs. It therefore seems reasonable to assume that subsidiary managers need to be more alert

---

[300] The view that the dimensions of "local responsiveness" and "external embeddedness" are closely related can be further substantiated by looking at the way they are both often operationalized. For instance, Andersson and Forsgren measure the degree of subsidiary (technological) embeddedness by assessing the "extent the subsidiary's product development and production process development are adapted to the requirements of the specific customer/supplier" (Andersson/Forsgren 2000, p. 339).

and/or sensitive to environmental demands and changes such as shifts in customer requirements, technology or competitive setting (Luo 2001, p. 460, Ambrosini/Bowman 2009, p. 41). This should require more extensive scanning and analyzing of the local environment, thereby enhancing the subsidiary's chances of detecting market signals from customers or initiative opportunities in more general (Barringer/Bluedorn 1999, pp. 423-424, Frost 2001, p. 106). Third, as argued previously, a high degree of local responsiveness also involves closer interactions and more solid relationships with local actors. Unique business relationships with local network actors have been shown to positively influence the identification of new opportunities (e.g. Tsai/Ghoshal 1998, McEvily/Zaheer 1999, Delany 2000, Andersson et al. 2002b, Ardichvili et al. 2003). The underlying assumption is that actors that are more closely tied are more willing and able to exchange resources, knowledge and information with each other (Andersson et al. 2007, p. 806). For instance, close relationships provide subsidiaries with an improved understanding of their counterparts' resources and capabilities, thereby enhancing the chances of detecting new resource development or deployment possibilities based on the resources both organizations control (Holm et al. 2005, p. 202). Often, such business relationships are the result of path-dependent processes involving complex and idiosyncratic interactions that cannot be easily replicated (Andersson et al. 2002b, p. 980). Hence, they may reveal opportunities that are relation-specific or tacit in nature and cannot be sensed by actors outside the network, or to which only partners are granted preferential access (Andersson et al. 2001a, p. 1015, Denrell et al. 2003, p. 988). In addition to such strong network ties, even weaker connections can expose the subsidiary to new initiative opportunities. For example, more general interactions or contacts of subsidiary employees with local customers or other local firms can serve as important stimuli for potential initiative opportunities (Birkinshaw 1999, p. 18, Hansen 1999, p. 84). These arguments lead to the following prediction:

*The higher a subsidiary's degree of localization/local responsiveness, the **more likely** it will **identify initiative opportunities**.*

In addition, it is expected that the subsidiary's localization/local responsiveness is positively linked to the identification of new initiative opportunities in the external market environment (rather than in the internal MNC system). In order to appropriately and quickly respond to changes in the external environment, locally responsive subsidiaries must have a better understanding of their local customer needs, their competitors' strategies and other external developments. This requires that they be alert and/or sensitive to demands and developments in their external environment, such as shifts in customer requirements, technologies or competitive settings. Local responsiveness also often implies that subsidiary units maintain solid external relationships with, for instance, customers, suppliers or governmental authorities, thereby exposing them to new external opportunities and stimuli (Luo 2001, p. 453, Tseng et al. 2004, p. 100). In sum, both the strong focus on external market demands and changes and the more developed external business relationships of locally responsive subsidiaries should particularly enhance their chances to recognize new opportunities externally (e.g. McEvily/Zaheer 1999, p. 1138, Holm et al. 2005, p. 204, Mu et al. 2007, p. 83). Thus it is expected that:

*The higher a subsidiary's degree of localization/local responsiveness, the **more likely** it will **identify external initiative opportunities** (rather than internal initiative opportunities).*

Resource Structuring: Concerning resource structuring activities, it is expected that a higher degree of localization/local responsiveness positively influences the subsidiary's propensity to obtain the new resources necessary to realize the identified initiative opportunities. First, it is presumed that locally responsive subsidiaries are typically well-informed about their local environmental context. This puts them into a better position to identify undervalued resource inputs that are available in their factors markets or to recognize value that others do not see in available resources (Bowman/Collier 2006, p. 197). Second, it has been suggested that locally responsive subsidiaries are often more strongly embedded in their local networks. This could provide them with better (possibly even privileged) access to the resources and capabilities of their network partners, including capital, knowledge or physical assets (e.g. Andersson et al. 2002b, p. 980, Mu et al. 2007, p. 82, Phene/Almeida 2008, p. 904). Finally, it has also been claimed that the need for subsidiary units to be locally responsive arises, among other factors, from heterogeneous customer demands, rapid technological developments, environmental complexities and competitive intensity (see e.g. Taggart 1997, p. 305, Luo 2001, p. 455). As outlined earlier, these circumstances should also require subsidiaries to obtain new and improved resources more frequently in order to respond to the particular needs and the more dynamic developments in such environments.[301] As a result, it is presumed that:

*The higher a subsidiary's degree of localization/local responsiveness, the **more likely** it will engage in **resource structuring** activities.*

With regard to the sources from which new resources and capabilities are obtained to realize entrepreneurial endeavors, it appears likely that foreign units of MNCs that are strongly localized/locally responsive would tend to obtain them externally (rather than from within the MNC system). Given their external orientation and their frequent engagement in external networks, such units should be better able to identify and obtain resources and capabilities from their local environment and the local actors therein,

---

[301] See also Subsection 3.5.1.1 herein which discusses the impact of certain environmental contingencies on resource structuring activities.

making them less dependent on resources from within the MNC network at the same time (Andersson et al. 2002b, p. 983, Tseng et al. 2004, p. 100, Andersson et al. 2007, p. 806). Furthermore, in view of the path-dependent nature of resource acquisition and development activities, it appears likely that units abroad would tend to obtain new resources and capabilities in areas where they already are well endowed (see e.g. Dierickx/Cool 1989, pp. 1507-1508;, Barney 1991, pp. 107-108, Kogut/Zander 1992, p. 392). Hence, strongly localized/locally responsive units should be more inclined to obtain resources and capabilities through external sourcing channels. Finally, strongly localized/locally responsive subsidiary units that have to react to the particular needs and demands of their local environment may need to access the more diverse set of resources and capabilities that is available externally rather than internally. As resources and capabilities within the MNC are frequently related or even duplicative in nature (Yamin/Andersson 2011, p. 154), the internal MNC network may not offer those needed to respond to particular local demands. Instead, localized/locally responsive subsidiaries may be more inclined to draw from the wider array of resources and capabilities that are available locally. These considerations suggest that:

> The higher a subsidiary's degree of localization/local responsiveness, the **more likely** it will rely on **external sources** (rather than internal sources).

As outlined previously, subsidiaries may obtain resources externally via acquisition or via external-internal developments in the form of, for instance, strategic alliances or joint research efforts with local market actors. No clear prediction can be derived as to which of these two modes is more likely to occur merely based on the degree of subsidiary localization/local responsiveness. However, following the line of reasoning that the need for local responsiveness, at least in part, results from subsidiaries operating in more demanding and uncertain environments (Taggart 1997, p. 305, Luo 2001, p. 455), it could possibly be argued that external resource acquisition, rather than resource development with external partners, represents the better option in such circumstances (Bowmann/Collier 2006, pp. 201-203).[302]

Resource Bundling: Certain conclusions can also be drawn with regard to the effect of subsidiary localization and local responsiveness on resource bundling activities. First, it may be tentatively assumed that the broader set of resources of a locally responsive subsidiary, resulting from its wider range of value-adding activities and better access to the external resources of its network partners, could enhance a subsidiary's overall ability to integrate and combine different resources (Sirmon et al. 2007, p. 282). Second, the need for local responsiveness is frequently driven by more demanding and

---

[302] See also Subsection 3.5.1.1 of this publication which discusses the potential effects of certain environmental contingencies on resource structuring activities.

uncertain environments. Given the particular local requirements, more distinct bundling processes may be needed to produce the specific products and services that are applicable in such markets rather than relying on more standardized solutions that involve less complex resource bundles. In addition, the more uncertain environmental conditions should require frequent and more extensive bundling activities in the form of enriching or pioneering to keep up with more rapid technological developments or with unpredicted competitor moves (Bowman/Collier 2006, pp. 205-206, Sirmon et al. 2007, pp. 281-283). Lastly, the potentially better access to a broader set of resources (of both the subsidiary and of external partners) may allow the subsidiary to focus more time, efforts and investments on bundling activities instead of attempting to obtain resources from new and more distant sources. Based on these assumptions, it is predicted that:

*The higher a subsidiary's degree of localization/local responsiveness, the **more likely** it will use **extensive bundling** processes (i.e. pioneering rather than stabilizing bundling processes).*

(3) Headquarters-Subsidiary Alignment

Headquarters Involvement: The degree of subsidiary localization/local responsiveness is likely to affect the headquarters-subsidiary alignment sub-process as well. Following the proposed resource-dependence considerations outlined earlier (e.g. Astley/Sachdeva 1984, Medcof 2001, Pfeffer/Salancik 2003), this role dimension is expected to be positively associated with resource-based power in the MNC, which potentially impacts the headquarters involvement in subsidiary initiatives as follows. First, foreign units that perform a wider range of value-adding activities in the host country can be expected to possess a broader and more diverse set of resource configurations (Taggart 1997, p. 301, Tseng et al. 2004, p. 98). Consequently, the more extensive spectrum of activities and (distinctive) resources and capabilities should strengthen the subsidiary's position and hence its recognition as a potential contributor to the MNC's firm-specific advantages (Birkinshaw et al. 1998, p. 228, Bouquet/Birkinshaw 2008b, p. 582). Second, as stated above, localized/locally responsive units typically need to be better informed about changes and developments in their environment. This provides them with unique knowledge of local market and competitive developments with potential implications for the wider firm, and thus may represent an important source of subsidiary power (Bouquet/Birkinshaw 2008a, p. 482). Third, stronger subsidiary linkages with local network partners may allow the MNC as a whole better access to critical resources and capabilities that exist in the local market, thereby strengthening the power base of the foreign unit (Andersson 2003, p. 428, Andersson et al. 2007, p. 807). Fourth, more demanding and dynamic market conditions that typically necessitate a higher level of local responsiveness (Taggart 1997, p. 305, Luo 2001, p. 455) could also be perceived by headquarters as a signal for the availability of critical location-specific resources and capabilities at the subsidiary location (Bouquet/Birkinshaw 2008b, p. 582). Taken together, these considerations suggest that such units may likely be recognized by headquarters as important providers of critical resources and capabilities and hence as potential contributors to firm specific advantages. This has been shown to enhance the resource-based power that can be applied to increase the subsidiary's degree of autonomy vis-à-vis headquarters when engaging in entrepreneurial initiatives (Ambos et al. 2010, p. 1102, Yamin/Sinkovics 2010, p. 953).[303] Thus, it is predicted that:

*The higher a subsidiary's degree of localization/local responsiveness, the **less likely** it will face **headquarters involvement** in the initiative process.*

With regard to the impact of subsidiary localization/local responsiveness on the extent of corporate resistance that subsidiary initiatives may face within the MNC, two alternative predictions appear plausible. On the one hand, subsidiaries that are more locally responsive should come up with initiatives that are more strongly tailored to the requirements of the local environment. It may also be expected that they typically result from closer interactions and more solid relationships with local stakeholders. The complex and idiosyncratic interaction processes with local business partners may produce initiatives that involve entrepreneurial knowledge, resources and capabilities that are more co-specialized, tacit and socially complex, and as such they might not only be more difficult to communicate to headquarters (Mahnke et al. 2007, p. 1283;, Keupp/ Gassmann 2009, p. 199) but may also be more difficult to apply in other MNC units' business contexts (Andersson et al. 2001a, pp. 1019-1020, 2002b, p. 985). It could therefore be concluded that the complexity, context-specificity and tacitness of initiatives from such a context should result in a higher level of corporate resistance.

However, arguments can be found to support a contrasting line of reasoning. As argued before, subsidiaries that are more locally responsive should possess higher levels of resource-based power (Mudambi/Navarra 2004, p. 392, Andersson et al. 2007, p. 807), which is critical to reduce corporate resistance and gain central support for initiatives (Birkinshaw 1999, p. 17, Birkinshaw/Ridderstråle 1999, p. 152, Birkinshaw 2000, p. 39). Hence, an alternative prediction is that more locally responsive subsidiaries should face lower levels of corporate resistance.[304]

---

[303] In line with this argumentation, it has been stated that locally-oriented and locally-embedded subsidiaries typically face lower levels of central control (Andersson/Forsgren 1996, p. 493) and are endowed with greater levels of autonomy (Young/Tavares 2004, p. 221).

[304] As outlined earlier in this publication, previous empirical work suggests that the effects of the subsidiary's resource-based power (see Alternative 2) should be stronger than the ones resulting from risks and uncertainties associated with the context-specific and more uncertain initiatives (see e.g. Andersson et al. 2002b, pp. 984-985, 2007, p. 807).

*Alternative 1: The higher a subsidiary's degree of localization/local responsiveness, the **more likely** it will face **corporate resistance** in the initiative process.*

*Alternative 2: The higher a subsidiary's degree of localization/local responsiveness, the **less likely** it will face **corporate resistance** in the initiative process.*

Following the two alternative arguments above, two contrasting predictions can also be developed concerning the level of active subsidiary selling in the initiative process. Assuming that initiatives from more locally responsive subsidiaries involve more co-specialized, tacit and socially complex knowledge, resources and capabilities that are more difficult to employ in other MNC units' business contexts, it might be predicted that subsidiaries need to sell such initiatives more actively if they are to be further pursued in the MNC. Alternatively, higher levels of resource-based power could reduce the subsidiaries' need to actively sell initiatives to headquarters, as they have enough bargaining power to "push" them through the corporate immune system. Therefore, the following two predictions are derived:

*Alternative 1: The higher a subsidiary's degree of localization/local responsiveness, the **more likely** it will engage in **initiative selling** activities.*

*Alternative 2: The higher a subsidiary's degree of localization/local responsiveness, the **less likely** it will engage in **initiative selling** activities.*

3.5.2.2 Subsidiary Integration

Jarillo and Martinez (1990) and Taggart (1997) use the "degree of integration" as the second dimension for their role typologies. This dimension expresses the extent to which the value-adding activities performed by the subsidiary are integrated and coordinated with the same activities in other parts of the MNC. This can range from "very autonomous" to "highly integrated" and hence, at least implicitly, incorporates the aspect of subsidiary autonomy (Jarillo/Martinez 1990, p. 503). Higher levels of subsidiary integration have been linked to increased interchanges of products, knowledge, or resources more generally, between the subsidiary and other MNC units (Gammelgaard/Pedersen 2003, p. 7), higher degrees of central control and coordination (Roth/Nigh 1992, p. 280, Andersson/Forsgren 1996, p. 495, Yamin 2005, p. 98) and more centralized decision-making and lower degrees of subsidiary autonomy (Young/ Tavares 2004, p. 221). The following paragraphs address the possible impact of a subsidiary's degree of integration on subsidiary initiative-taking, and in particular the effect on the subsidiary's overall propensity to engage in initiatives (Paragraph 1), as well as on the sub-processes concerned with entrepreneurial resource management (Paragraph 2) and headquarters-subsidiary alignment (Paragraph 3).

(1) Subsidiary Initiative-Taking Propensity

Existing research on the influence of subsidiary integration on the intensity of subsidiary initiative-taking remains somewhat ambiguous. While some empirical research indicates that a tight subsidiary integration into the corporate system could facilitate initiative-taking (Birkinshaw 1997, Birkinshaw/Fry 1998, Borini et al. 2009a), other studies provide contradictory findings that suggest an inverse relationship between integration and initiative-taking (Krishnan 2006, Borini et al. 2009b).[305] However, when these findings are analyzed more closely, it becomes clearer that integration can be seen as a "double-edged sword" that both positively and negatively affects subsidiary initiative-taking in the MNC. On the one hand, high subsidiary integration can positively impact initiative-taking efforts, as it should facilitate the subsidiary's access to resources and capabilities of the MNC network. Moreover, it could enhance the flow of information between headquarters and subsidiaries, thereby strengthening credibility and trust and reducing communicative, behavioral and value uncertainties, which is important when subsidiaries attempt to obtain central support for their initiatives (e.g. Birkinshaw 1999, p. 16, Mahnke et al. 2007, pp. 1282-1286, Borini et al. 2009b, p. 262, Yamin/Andersson 2011, p. 153). On the other hand, a high degree of integration could adversely affect initiative-taking, as it reduces the level of subsidiary autonomy. Subsidiary autonomy has been found to be an important factor that promotes initiative-taking (e.g. Birkinshaw 1997, Birkinshaw et al. 1998, Birkinshaw 1999, Sargent/Matthews 2006, Liouka 2007). More specifically, high degrees of autonomy are critical for external initiatives identified in the external market, while internal initiatives require only low degrees of autonomy (Birkinshaw 1997, p. 224, Birkinshaw/Fry 1998, pp. 53-55, Birkinshaw 2000, pp. 22-30). Based on this more differentiated view it is predicted that subsidiary integration will impact internally and externally oriented initiatives in different ways.

First, it is argued that subsidiaries that are more deeply integrated in the MNC are more likely to pursue internally oriented initiatives, for the following reasons. Internal initiatives represent entrepreneurial undertakings that are recognized within the boundaries of the corporation and which emerge through interactions of subsidiary managers with other actors from within the MNC network (Birkinshaw 1998a, p. 359, 2000, p. 73). Furthermore, they are facilitated by low degrees of subsidiary autonomy and by close headquarters-subsidiary interaction and communication (Birkinshaw 1997, p. 227). As subsidiaries that are more deeply integrated are characterized by higher levels of cooperation and information exchange between headquarters and subsidiaries (Andersson/Forsgren 1994, p. 5) and by lower degrees of autonomy (Young/Tavares 2004, p. 221), they should provide conditions conducive for internally oriented initiatives (rather than

---

[305] More precisely, the publications by Birkinshaw and his colleagues observe that a tight integration into the corporate system specifically facilitates internal initiatives.

external ones). It is also to be expected that integrated subsidiaries are more likely to pursue initiatives that are closer to the "dominant logic" of the MNC (Prahalad/Bettis 1986, Bettis/Prahalad 1995). Hence, their entrepreneurial activities should be more in line with the developments and directions of headquarters (Yamin 2005, p. 97). Moreover, as the value-adding activities of integrated subsidiaries are closely tied to those of headquarters or other MNC units, their entrepreneurial activities should remain close to the current capabilities of the MNC and the technological trajectory of the group (Pearce 1999, p. 127, Yamin/Andersson 2011, p. 153). New initiative development should therefore be more closely aligned with headquarters' needs, revolve around existing resources and capabilities and be adaptive and exploitative rather than disruptive and explorative in nature (Frost 2001, p. 105). Accordingly, it has been suggested that integrated and internally embedded subsidiaries should more strongly engage in innovative and entrepreneurial activities that focus internally on improving the efficiency of existing operations and activities (i.e. internal subsidiary initiatives) rather than on developing new products and services for the external market (see Yamin 2005, p. 101, Yamin/Andersson 2011, p. 154). In contrast, external initiatives that focus on the development of new products and services are identified in the external market. They require high levels of subsidiary autonomy and low levels of headquarters-subsidiary interaction and communication (see e.g. Birkinshaw 1997, 1998a, pp. 356-357, 2000). Thus, it is conversely argued that subsidiaries that are more integrated and more closely tied to the MNC will show a lower propensity to pursue external initiatives. These considerations lead to the following predictions:

*The higher a subsidiary's degree of integration, the **more likely** it will undertake **internally-oriented subsidiary initiatives**.*

*The higher a subsidiary's degree of integration, the **less likely** it will undertake **externally-oriented subsidiary initiatives**.*

(2) Entrepreneurial Resource Management

Initiative Opportunity Identification: In line with the predictions made previously, it is expected that a high degree of subsidiary integration will positively affect the internal recognition of initiative opportunities but negatively influence external recognition. Subsidiaries that are more deeply integrated within other units of the MNC and hence have closer and more frequent interactions with them should be more strongly exposed to the vast information resources and entrepreneurial opportunities that exist or emerge from within the MNC network (Tsai/Ghoshal 1998, p. 467, Delany 2000, p. 239, Tseng et al. 2004, p. 99). Moreover, close relationships within the corporation provide the subsidiary with an improved understanding of the resources and capabilities controlled by the other units, thus enhancing the chances to detect new resource development and deployment opportunities based on the complementary resources the units hold within in the MNC (Holm et al. 2005, p. 202). It is therefore expected that a tight subsidiary integration with the MNC should enhance its chances to identify new initiatives from the internal MNC market. In contrast, it is assumed to be more difficult for highly integrated subsidiaries to identify initiative opportunities in the external market. As they typically face higher levels of central control, coordination and decision-making, tightly integrated subsidiaries should have less autonomy and flexibility to pursue external opportunities, especially when they go in new directions and are more explorative in nature (Almeida/Phene 2004, p. 850). Furthermore, identifying new business opportunities entails, among other subsidiary resources, effort, time and entrepreneurial capabilities. As subsidiaries can be expected to be limited in such resources, attempts at internal identification of initiative opportunities should undermine or "crowd out" externally-oriented activities (Yamin/Andersson 2011, p. 155). Based on these arguments the following two predictions are formulated:

*The higher a subsidiary's degree of integration, the **more likely** it will **identify internally-oriented initiative opportunities**.*

*The higher a subsidiary's degree of integration, the **less likely** it will **identify externally-oriented initiative opportunities**.*

Resource Structuring: It has been argued that more integrated and internally focused subsidiaries will pursue initiatives that are closely aligned with headquarters' needs, rely more on existing resources and capabilities and be comparatively adaptive and exploitative in nature (Frost 2001, p. 105, Yamin/Andersson 2011, p. 154). Here, it can be expected that the overall need to obtain new resources and capabilities remains limited, so the intensity of resource structuring activities should also remain fairly low. In addition to the reduced pressure to engage in structuring activities, the subsidiary's ability should also be limited by its tight integration in the MNC system. While it can be expected that such a subsidiary will, relative to less integrated units, have better access to the resources and capabilities in the internal network of the MNC, those from within the corporation should often be closely related or possibly even identical to those of the subsidiary, as they developed in a similar business context (Yamin 2005, p. 100, Yamin/Andersson 2011, p. 154). Additionally, integrated subsidiaries that focus on the internal MNC network to obtain the resources and capabilities needed for the progression of initiatives access "only part of the system" and miss out on the many resources that might exist in their external network (Birkinshaw et al. 2005, p. 234). Based on these arguments it is predicted that:

*The higher a subsidiary's degree of integration, the **less likely** it will engage in **resource structuring** activities.*

Given the strong relationships and resource ties between an integrated subsidiary and other MNC units, it is assumed that such subsidiaries should be more willing and better able to attain resources from within the corporation rather than from sources outside the MNC network (Andersson et al. 2007, p. 806). Units that are more integrated typically have a better understanding of each other's resources and capabilities, and hence they should be better able to identify and access resources inside the MNC than less integrated units (Tsai/Ghoshal 1998, p. 467). Moreover, tight integration of foreign MNC units has been shown to improve the flow of information between headquarters and subsidiaries, strengthen credibility and trust and thus reduce communicative, behavioral and value uncertainties (e.g. Ghoshal/Bartlett 1988, p. 372, Birkinshaw 1999, p. 16, Mahnke et al. 2007, pp. 1282-1286, Borini et al. 2009b, p. 262, Yamin/Andersson 2011, p. 153). Furthermore, it appears likely that highly integrated subsidiaries possess a higher degree of internal relationship resources, thereby increasing their absorptive capacity for resources from within the MNC network (Cohen/Levinthal 1990, p. 128). Taken together, these conditions should make it more likely that integrated subsidiaries would obtain resources from headquarters or other units from within the MNC rather than from external sources. Especially in situations in which the external environment does not offer the needed resources or in which a subsidiary is unable to access them (e.g. due to weak or non-existent external network relationships), internal MNC resources become even more critical. Accordingly, it is predicted that:

*The higher a subsidiary's degree of integration, the **more likely** it will rely on **internal sources** (rather than external sources).*

Concerning the mode of resource structuring, there are certain indications that more integrated subsidiaries might tend to develop resources internally rather than to acquire them. As outlined, integrated and internally focused subsidiaries are more likely to pursue initiatives that are closely aligned with headquarters' needs, focus on the refinement and extension of existing resources and capabilities and be adaptive and exploitative in nature (Frost 2001, p. 105, Yamin/Andersson 2011, p. 154). Under such circumstances, in which initiatives are largely based on the existing resource portfolio and there is little need to quickly react to unexpected (external) shifts, it seems more likely that subsidiaries would engage in the steady development of required resources. Thus, resource accumulation as a longer-term investment in the gradual accumulation of subsidiary resources and capabilities should be a more useful option in such a situation. Consequently, it is predicted that:

*The higher a subsidiary's degree of integration, the **more likely** it will develop **resources** (rather than acquire them).*

Resource Bundling: Overall, it can be expected that highly integrated subsidiaries will be less inclined to engage in resource bundling activities, particularly more extensive ones. As argued above, integrated subsidiaries should have access only to a narrower set of resources from within the MNC network, and these should also be somewhat related to the ones the subsidiary already possesses. Consequently, such a portfolio of less diverse resources should generally make the combination and integration of different resources more difficult. Moreover, the incremental and internally-oriented initiatives that are said to occur more frequently in integrated subsidiaries only require bundling activities that result in less substantial change, such as stabilizing bundling processes. In contrast, more extensive bundling (i.e. pioneering) requires exploratory learning and typically involves the integration of completely new resources that were acquired from external factor markets (Sirmon et al. 2007, pp. 281-282). Therefore, more integrated subsidiaries should show a lower degree of bundling activity overall, and extensive bundling in particular. Accordingly, it is predicted that:

> The higher a subsidiary's degree of integration, the **less likely** it will engage in **bundling activities**.

> The higher a subsidiary's degree of integration, the **more likely** it will use **incremental bundling** processes (i.e. stabilizing rather than pioneering bundling processes).

(3) Headquarters-Subsidiary Alignment

Headquarters Involvement: In addition, it is assumed that the degree of subsidiary integration also impacts the initiative sub-process concerned with the alignment and interactions between headquarters and the focal subsidiary throughout the initiative process; these effects are described below. First, it was previously argued that a higher degree of subsidiary integration should also imply a higher level of headquarters-subsidiary communication, interchanges of products and knowledge (or resources in more general), higher degrees of central control and coordination as well as more centralized decision-making. Therefore, not only is headquarters more likely to become aware of subsidiary initiative-taking attempts, but it should be more strongly involved in the entrepreneurial process itself (Dellestrand 2011, p. 233). Moreover, subsidiaries that are more closely linked to the internal MNC network rather than the external network should have less resource-based power (Andersson et al. 2007, pp. 806-807) that they can use to increase their degree of autonomy and limit headquarters involvement in the initiative process (Ambos et al. 2010, p. 1102, Yamin/Sinkovics 2010, p. 953).[306] Hence,

---

[306] Instead, highly integrated subsidiaries could perhaps possess some structural power (rather than resource-based power). However, as outlined in Subsection 3.4.3, structural power is not considered to be very strong and not

the following prediction is derived as to the potential relation between subsidiary integration and headquarters involvement in the initiative-taking process:

*The higher a subsidiary's degree of integration, the **more likely** it will face **headquarters involvement** in the initiative process.*

Corporate Resistance: As to the effect of subsidiary integration on the level of corporate resistance that a subsidiary initiative might encounter, two opposing predictions appear possible. First, it could be argued that more deeply integrated subsidiaries should face lower levels of corporate resistance. It can be expected that, due to stronger ties and closer interactions between headquarters and subsidiaries in general, there should be a greater level of trust and credibility and hence a lower level of uncertainty associated with initiatives that are presented to headquarters (Tsai/Ghoshal 1998, pp. 465-466, Mahnke et al. 2007, p. 1284, Borini et al. 2009a, p. 262). These aspects have been shown to be important drivers for headquarters' acceptance of initiatives (Birkinshaw 2000, p. 40). Second, as integrated subsidiaries typically act in close alignment with the corporate center, their entrepreneurial initiatives should be more in tune with the needs of the wider MNC and remain close to the technological trajectory of the parent firm. Therefore, initiatives stemming from highly integrated subsidiaries should be mainly "adaptive" in nature and contain elements that are known and familiar to headquarters, thereby limiting the chance that they will encounter corporate resistance (Yamin 2005, pp. 100-101, Dellestrand 2011, p. 233).

On the other hand, certain factors might also yield a contrasting line of reasoning. As highly integrated subsidiaries typically face higher degrees of central control, coordination and decision-making, it will also be more difficult for them to "hide" their initiatives from headquarters until they are *fait accomplis,* hence making it more likely that headquarters will become aware and counteract them (Birkinshaw/Ridderstråle 1999, p. 171, Yamin/Andersson 2011, p. 153). Furthermore, as particularly integrated subsidiaries are expected to function and behave in line with the "dominant logic" of the MNC, proactive and autonomous entrepreneurial behavior on the part of the subsidiary is likely to instigate corporate resistance. Finally, more integrated subsidiaries should also possess less resource-based power that they can use to reduce corporate resistance and obtain central support for their initiatives (Birkinshaw/Ridderstråle 1999, pp. 152-153, Birkinshaw 2000, p. 39). The above arguments lead to the following two alternative predictions:

*Alternative 1: The higher a subsidiary's degree of integration, the **less likely** it will face **headquarters resistance** in the initiative process.*

---

very sustainable, making it difficult for subsidiary units to employ it to become more autonomous or to influence decision-making in the MNC.

*Alternative 2: The higher a subsidiary's degree of integration, the **more likely** it will face **headquarters resistance** in the initiative process.*

Based on the discussion above, two contrasting predictions are also derived with regard to the level of active subsidiary selling in the initiative process. Presuming that subsidiary initiatives from more integrated units are more closely aligned with headquarters needs, focus on refinement and extension of existing resources and capabilities and are adaptive and exploitative in nature (Frost 2001, p. 105, Yamin/Andersson 2011, p. 154), it can be expected that they will require less active selling efforts. Alternatively, lower levels of power and influence and the difficulty of "hiding" initiatives throughout the process could require higher selling efforts by subsidiaries to convince headquarters and to gain central support. Accordingly, it is predicted that:

*Alternative 1: The higher a subsidiary's degree of integration, the **less likely** it will engage in **initiative selling** activities.*

*Alternative 2: The higher a subsidiary's degree of integration, the **more likely** it will engage in **initiative selling** activities.*

3.5.2.3 Role-Specific Predictions

Following the expectations presented for the single role dimensions in the previous subsection, predictions are now developed for each of the subsidiary role types presented by Jarillo and Martinez and by Taggart. Hence, the potential initiative-taking behavior and outcomes are discussed for the Active Subsidiary (Paragraph 1), the Receptive Subsidiary (Paragraph 2), the Autonomous Subsidiary (Paragraph 3), and finally the Quiescent Subsidiary type (Paragraph 4). Each of these paragraphs first briefly introduces and describes the role type under consideration. Second, predictions are developed with regard to (a) the entrepreneurial resource management sub-process, (b) the headquarters-subsidiary alignment sub-process and finally (c) the potential outcomes of the subsidiary initiative-taking behavior.

(1) Active Subsidiary[307]

Active Subsidiaries are foreign units characterized by a high degree of localization and integration. Here, many (or even all) value-adding activities are located in the host country, including manufacturing, purchasing, marketing or R&D, all of which are, at the same time, strongly integrated with the same activities in the rest of the MNC. This

---

[307] In comparison to Jarillo and Martinez (1990) who termed this role type "Active Subsidiary", Taggart (1997) decided to rename it into "Constrained Independent". As the typology by Jarillo and Martinez represents the "original" one, it was decided to rely on their denomination. For further details, see Subsection 3.2.1.5 of this publication in which the different role typologies are presented in more detail.

subsidiary type often directs a large part of its local output to other units of the MNC, while also receiving many products or components from them, hence representing an "active node" in the MNC network (Jarillo/Martinez 1990, p. 503, Martinez/Jarillo 1991, p. 433, Taggart 1997, p. 307, Schmid et al. 1998, p. 54, Maitland/Sammartino 2009, p. 68). Although most value-adding activities are performed in close relation with other MNC units, requiring heavier use of coordination mechanisms, Active Subsidiaries nevertheless experience a high degree of decision-making autonomy (Martinez/Jarillo 1991, p. 441, Tsai et al. 2006, p. 8). This, together with their strong localization and responsiveness, allows them to better engage in innovative and entrepreneurial activities that are more extensive (e.g. going beyond mere product adaptations) and that are also applicable for other geographical areas in which the MNC is active (Manolopoulos 2008, p. 37). Although Active Subsidiaries are primarily (or even exclusively) found in transnational companies, not all subsidiaries in such firms will possess an active role and represent an active node in the MNC network. Instead, most subsidiaries in transnational MNCs are likely to have low(er) degrees of local responsiveness and therefore more often take the role of Receptive Subsidiaries (Jarillo/Martinez 1990, p. 503, Schmid et al. 1998, p. 54).

Entrepreneurial Resource Management: Concerning the sub-process of entrepreneurial resource management, it is assumed that Active Subsidiaries have, in comparison to the other role types, the *highest chance to identify initiative opportunities*; this situation comes about for the following reasons. First, their broad range of value-adding activities and resources should broaden their opportunity space and thus their chances to identify new initiative opportunities. Second, their high degree of local orientation and close interaction with external actors should enhance their chances to identify new entrepreneurial opportunities in the external environment. Third, their high degree of integration with other parts of the MNC should simultaneously expose them to the diverse opportunities that may exist in the internal network of the multinational firm. Hence, given both their high level of localization/local responsiveness and their tight integration, this subsidiary role type should also be equally equipped to frequently identify new initiative opportunities *both externally and internally*.

Furthermore, Active Subsidiaries should exhibit a *moderate to high level of resource structuring* activities. Based on the assumption that this subsidiary role type is typically well informed about its internal and external context and also strongly embedded internally and externally, subsidiary units of this type should be in a superior position to identify and access the resource inputs available in both the internal and external MNC network. In addition, Active Subsidiaries are often required to respond to particular local needs due to their operation in challenging and demanding market environments (e.g. in the form of rapid technological developments, competitive intensity, and environmental complexity). In such a context it would seem likely that more sophisticated solutions are needed that involve relatively complex bundles of unique resources and capabilities (Zahra et al. 2000, p. 12, Holm et al. 2005, p. 204). While these considerations would suggest that this role type exhibits a high level of resource structuring activities, the possibly high level of resources and capabilities that may already be present in Active Subsidiaries may somewhat alleviate the need to obtain new resources and capabilities for the realization of entrepreneurial opportunities. With regard to the source of resource structuring, it is expected that this role type is equally well-equipped to obtain them *from either external or internal sources* given both its strong local orientation and its integration in the MNC. Concerning the mode of resource structuring, no clear prediction can be derived, as arguments were found to support the assumption that both resource acquisition and more gradual resource development are likely to occur.

Finally, Active Subsidiaries are expected to *frequently* engage in more *extensive resource bundling efforts* in relation to their entrepreneurial initiatives. In view of their large existing resource base and their easy access both to new internal and external resources and capabilities, these subsidiary units should be well-positioned to develop new (extensive) resource bundles. Furthermore, based on the premise that Active Subsidiaries often operate in dynamic and challenging environments that frequently require more sophisticated innovative solutions, extensive combinative activities should be expected in this context (i.e. enriching or pioneering bundling).

Headquarters-Subsidiary Alignment: In comparison to the other role types, Active Subsidiaries should be in a moderate to strong power position when it comes to alignment and interaction with headquarters in the subsidiary initiative process. Given the extensive spectrum of value-adding activities that are performed locally, as well as their presumably broad resource base, these units should be recognized as important contributors to firm-specific advantages in the MNC (Birkinshaw et al. 1998, p. 228, Bouquet/Birkinshaw 2008b, p. 582). Moreover, the subsidiaries' knowledge about the local market and competitive developments and their often strong linkages with local network partners should provide them with further resource-based power. Although these circumstances should give them the possibility to accrue a rather high degree of power, their tight integration in the corporate system and the high interdependencies with other MNC units should partially weaken these effects (Holm/Pedersen 2000b, p. 7, Young/Tavares 2004, p. 221). Overall, this should lead to a moderate to strong level of subsidiary power that such units can employ to increase their autonomy or to influence initiative-related decisions in the MNC.[308]

---

[308] Moreover, the subsidiary power of Active Subsidiaries could be limited since it should, at least to some extent, represent structural or systemic power. As described above, Active Subsidiaries represent "active nodes" in a system of mutual dependencies in which the foreign MNC units function as both senders and receivers of

As to the level of headquarters involvement in the initiative process, it is assumed that Active Subsidiaries will commonly face a *low to moderate level of active engagement of the corporate center*. On the one hand, their relatively strong resource base should provide them with the resource-based power and the autonomy to independently pursue initiatives without having to approach or involve headquarters for additional resources and/or approval. On the other hand, their tight integration in the corporate system could allow headquarters to exert at least some control over the entrepreneurial activities of Active Subsidiaries, resulting in an overall low to moderate level of headquarters involvement (Dellestrand 2011, p. 233, Yamin/Andersson 2011, p. 153).

In addition, the contextual role setting of Active Subsidiaries is expected to influence the level of corporate resistance these units encounter when pursuing entrepreneurial initiatives. As described above, Active Subsidiaries hold a dual-focused position in the MNC that is characterized by a high degree of localization/local responsiveness as well as a high degree of integration at the same time. Consequently, subsidiary initiatives that originate in these units should typically be both strongly tailored to local market requirements, and at the same time also aligned with the needs of the wider MNC, thus resulting in a *low to moderate level of corporate resistance*. More specifically, their strong localization/local responsiveness should induce initiatives that involve resources and capabilities that are co-specialized, tacit and socially complex, and thus the initiatives will not only be more difficult to communicate to headquarters but should also pose a challenge in use at other locations of the MNC. However, some countervailing effects can be expected from the tight integration in the MNC system, since this ensures that the initiatives are usually closely aligned with the corporate center as well. Furthermore, the high degree of integration often leads to stronger ties and closer interactions between headquarters and the focal subsidiary, thereby strengthening trust and credibility between the two units and possibly leading to lower levels of corporate resistance against entrepreneurial initiatives (e.g. Birkinshaw 1999, pp. 16-17, 2000, p. 40). In addition to the expected characteristics of initiatives that should typically stem from Active Subsidiaries, their level of resource-based power is also assumed to impact corporate resistance to their initiatives. As was argued earlier, these units should possess a moderate to strong degree of subsidiary power that they can use to influence initiative-related decisions in the company or to overcome resistance from other MNC

---

resources and capabilities. This gives them some structural power rather than resource-based power which is said to arise through asymmetric resource dependence situations (rather than through mutual dependencies). As was argued in Subsection 3.4.3 herein, structural power is not considered particularly strong and not very sustainable in comparison with power based on resource dependency.

units. Overall, these considerations suggest that Active Subsidiaries should encounter a moderate level of corporate resistance.[309]

Similarly, this subsidiary role type is expected to exhibit a *low to moderate level of initiative selling* and lobbying activities. On the one hand, the high degree of localization/local responsiveness of Active Subsidiaries should lead to initiatives that are, in part, location-specific and hence difficult to communicate to headquarters and also more difficult to use at other MNC locations. Consequently, this should require stronger selling and championing activities on the part of the subsidiaries to promote their initiatives and push them towards implementation. On the other hand, due to their strong integration in the MNC, Active Subsidiaries may at the same time benefit from enhanced communication, trust and credibility vis-à-vis headquarters, which should reduce the need to sell and promote their initiatives. Finally, given their moderate or even strong resource and power position, they should be well positioned to influence others in the MNC, reducing their need to actively sell and promote their entrepreneurial initiatives.

Subsidiary Initiative Outcome: With regard to subsidiary initiative outcomes, it is suggested that Active Subsidiaries should show the *highest level of subsidiary initiatives* among all role types. Previous work suggests that the high degree of autonomy these units enjoy, as well as their strong localization and responsiveness, should enable them to better engage in innovative and entrepreneurial activities that are more extensive (beyond mere product adaptations) and also applicable for other locations within the MNC (Manolopoulos 2008, p. 37). Likewise, the arguments developed earlier in this thesis provide further support for this view. First, Active Subsidiaries should be in a superior position to identify new initiative opportunities both externally in the local environment and internally from within the MNC network. Second, these foreign units should, in general, already be well-equipped with resources and capabilities. Furthermore, their strong external and internal linkages should enable them to more easily obtain new resources and capabilities that may be required to realize identified opportunities from various sources. Third, their comparatively tight integration in the multinational firm ensures that initiatives are closely aligned with the needs of the wider MNC. Additionally, the close interaction and alignment with headquarters may help to reduce the likelihood for empire-building behavior on the part of the foreign subsidiaries aimed at improving their position at the expense of MNC. Thus, corporate resistance against subsidiary initiatives should remain fairly low, allowing them to progress towards implementation. Fourth and finally, even if the entrepreneurial activities of Active Subsidiaries trigger the corporate immune system, their strong resource and power position

---

[309] It needs to be noted, however, that the impact of the different (and partially opposing) effects is difficult to predict precisely. Therefore, the consolidated prediction on the influence of the subsidiary role setting on corporate resistance and on active subsidiary selling activities is to be viewed as somewhat speculative in nature.

should give them the possibility to bypass it or help push their initiatives through the socio-political system toward implementation.

Concerning the types of initiatives pursued, Active Subsidiaries should be well-positioned to undertake all forms of entrepreneurial initiatives. As maintained earlier, their high degree of localization/local responsiveness and the integration of their activities with those at other locations in the MNC facilitate the identification of *both internally and externally-oriented initiatives*. More specifically, it seems likely that foreign units in the role of Active Subsidiaries are capable of pursuing initiatives of a larger scale and scope, such as global market initiatives or global-internal hybrid initiatives that usually have direct implications for the multinational firm. Given their wide range of value-adding activities and their extensive set of resources and capabilities, these units are well-prepared to engage in such broader entrepreneurial activities. Furthermore, their high degree of integration simultaneously ensures that their entrepreneurial initiatives are in line with the needs and requirements of the wider company and thus can be more or less directly applied subsequently at other locations of the MNC (e.g. Yamin 2005, pp. 100-101, Yamin/Andersson 2011, pp. 153-154).

As to the resource-based outcomes of their initiative-taking efforts, Active Subsidiaries can greatly benefit from their "dual-focused" position, which allows them to access and bundle the various resources that exist both within the MNC and in their local environment (Andersson et al. 2002a, p. 993, Birkinshaw et al. 2005, p. 246). These units should be able to deliver new resource bundles that are *highly specialized*,[310] yet at the same time also *directly transferable to other MNC units* (e.g. through global market initiatives),[311] thereby providing the greatest potential among all role types for firm-level advantages (see also Birkinshaw et al. 1998, p. 225). Nevertheless, these MNC units may also develop new resource bundles that are less specialized (e.g. through internally-oriented initiatives) or that must be adapted before use at other locations (e.g. through local market initiatives).

---

[310] The resulting resources and capabilities should potentially be highly specialized as they involve somewhat unique input resources that are further combined and bundled in distinct entrepreneurial processes. For example, the resources which are obtained through the unique internal or external network relationships of Active Subsidiaries should also be relatively inimitable and non-substitutable (see e.g. McEvily/Zaheer 1999, p. 1135, Andersson et al. 2002b, p. 980). Furthermore, the rather extensive bundling processes that are expected to typically take place in these units as part of the initiative-taking activities could further enhance the uniqueness or specialization of the resulting resource bundles or capabilities (see e.g. Bowman/Collier 2006, p. 198, Sirmon et al. 2007, p. 281).

[311] Various publications provide support for the assumption that a subsidiary's integration and embeddedness in the corporate network can facilitate the transfer of capabilities that are developed by foreign units through external network relationships (see e.g. Forsgren et al. 2000, p. 57, Andersson et al. 2002b, p. 992, Gammelgaard/ Pedersen 2003, p. 7, Meyer et al. 2011, p. 242).

(2) Receptive Subsidiary

Foreign subsidiary units that perform few value-adding activities locally (i.e. a low degree of localization) but that are highly integrated in the MNC are labeled Receptive Subsidiaries. They frequently focus on the local execution of particular activities such as marketing and sales or manufacturing. Receptive subsidiaries often exist in firms that are active in global industries (Jarillo/Martinez 1990, p. 503, Taggart 1997, p. 307, Schmid et al. 1998, p. 53). It has also been stated that subsidiaries of this type are often older and established ones that supply a wider geographical market with their exports. Receptive Subsidiaries usually have lower levels of decision-making, central coordination is high, and critical resources and capabilities tend to be located at headquarters rather than at the subsidiary level. These subsidiary characteristics, together with their strong internal focus, may constrain their entrepreneurial and innovative behavior towards more internal efforts such as the adaptation of manufacturing technologies or efficiency-seeking (Jindra 2005, p. 55, Qu 2007, p. 1184, Manolopoulos 2008, p. 37).

Entrepreneurial Resource Management: In comparison to the other role types, Receptive Subsidiaries should exhibit a *moderate level of initiative opportunity identification* based on the following assumptions. In view of their tight integration in the firm and thus their closer and more frequent interactions with actors from inside the MNC, it can be expected that these subsidiary units should be well-positioned to identify new initiative opportunities that exist or emerge particularly from within the multinational network. However, their low degree of localization/local responsiveness should impede their chances to recognize new opportunities that exist in the external market environment. As argued previously, these units usually lack the focus on external market developments and have only limited linkages and relationships with external market actors, thereby reducing their odds of identifying new business opportunities in the external market. Furthermore, they are also expected to be located in less challenging and demanding market environments, in which new opportunities may be less prevalent or in which there is less pressure or stimulus to engage in the identification of new entrepreneurial opportunities *per se*. Finally, their narrow scope of value-adding activities and their presumably limited resource base may also lessen their chances for new opportunity recognition. Concerning the location where new opportunities are identified, Receptive Subsidiaries should predominantly detect them in the *internal market system* of the MNC rather than in the external environment. Not only should their tight integration in the MNC direct their focus towards internal initiative opportunities but the higher levels of central control they face should also limit their freedom and flexibility to pursue opportunities in the external market.

In order to "physically realize" new initiative opportunities, this role type might be expected to exhibit a rather *low to moderate level of resource structuring* activities based on the following considerations. Due to their high degree of integration in the multinational firm, Receptive Subsidiaries have better access to the resources and capabilities of the MNC.[312] However, their low degree of localization/local responsiveness should limit their ability to obtain new resources and capabilities from the external environment. Furthermore, their presumably stronger focus on internally oriented initiatives that are adaptive and exploitative in nature should only require limited resource structuring activities, as they typically involve only the refinement and extension of existing subsidiary resources and capabilities (see e.g. Frost 2001, p. 105, Yamin 2005, p. 100, Dellestrand 2011, p. 233, Yamin/Andersson 2011, p. 153). Finally, because of the path-dependent nature of resource acquisition and development activities, their limited resource base should also restrict their ability to obtain new resources and capabilities (see e.g. Dierickx/Cool 1989, pp. 1507-1508, Barney 1991, pp. 107-108, Kogut/Zander 1992, p. 392). In sum, these arguments suggest that such units will only show a low to moderate level of resource acquisition or development effort when taking initiatives. Concerning the source of resource structuring activities, Receptive Subsidiary units should primarily rely on sources from within the MNC. As these units are characterized by a low degree of localization/local responsiveness and a high degree of integration, it is expected that these units would rely on their strong internal network linkages rather than attempting to obtain new resources and capabilities from their external environment (see also Maitland/Sammartino 2009, p. 69). With regard to the mode of resource structuring it is presumed that Receptive Subsidiaries will rely more strongly on the *internal development of new resources and capabilities* needed for the realization of entrepreneurial opportunities. As their initiatives should often focus on the refinement and extension of existing resources and capabilities and be adaptive and exploitative, gradual (internal) development should often be sufficient in such circumstances.

Lastly, as to bundling activities, Receptive Subsidiaries can be expected to display a *low to moderate level of less extensive bundling* activities. Their potentially narrower set of existing resources and capabilities and their restricted access to new resources and capabilities largely from within the MNC network should make it difficult for these units to engage in more extensive bundling activities. In addition, the more internally-oriented adaptive initiatives that are expected to occur more frequently in Receptive Subsidiaries should only require incremental and continuous resource combination efforts to maintain or enhance the units' efficiency.[313]

---

[312] As was outlined above, many of them could be closely related or even identical to those that exist in the subsidiary unit which could limit their applicability for entrepreneurial initiatives and particular those that go into new directions (e.g. radical global or local market initiatives; Yamin 2005, p. 100, Yamin/Andersson 2011, p. 154).

[313] See also Subsection 3.4.2.3 herein which addresses the link between different forms of resource bundling and different types of subsidiary initiatives.

Headquarters-Subsidiary Alignment: Based on the predictions made above for each of the separate role dimensions, it is assumed that units in the role of Receptive Subsidiaries face *high levels of headquarters involvement* in their initiative-taking activities. First, these highly integrated units should generally face more central control and decision-making, as well as higher levels of communication with headquarters.[314] Furthermore, given their low degree of localization/local responsiveness, these subsidiaries should only possess limited resource-based power to employ in increasing their autonomy and limiting the involvement of the corporate center in their entrepreneurial endeavors (see also Qu 2007, p. 1184).

Furthermore, the role setting of Receptive Subsidiary units might impact the extent of corporate resistance they encounter.[315] On the one hand, the close integration of these subsidiary units should ensure that their initiatives are more in tune with the needs of the wider MNC, remain close to the technological trajectory of the MNC and contain elements that are familiar to the corporate center. Furthermore, the closer interactions between headquarters and Receptive Subsidiaries should result in greater levels of trust and credibility, which may in turn reduce the resistance against subsidiary initiatives. On the other hand, their high degree of integration and limited resource base should make it more difficult for these units to autonomously pursue initiatives and bypass the corporate immune system until the initiative is a *fait accompli*. This should make it more likely that headquarters will become aware of initiative attempts early on and impede or stop them. Finally, the low level of resource-based power that Receptive Subsidiary units hold should make it more difficult for them to gain central support and overcome possible opposition from within the MNC. Therefore, it is assumed that these units should encounter a *moderate to high level of corporate resistance* when engaging in entrepreneurial initiatives.[316]

Similarly, it is presumed that Receptive Subsidiary units exhibit a *moderate to high level of initiative selling* and lobbying activities. As argued above, the high level of integration should lead to internally oriented, adaptive and exploitative initiatives that are also closely aligned with headquarters needs. These considerations suggest that less active selling by the foreign MNC units is necessary. However, the limited resource base of Receptive Subsidiaries and their stronger dependence on resources and capabilities

---

[314] See also Subsection 3.5.2.2 herein which develops predictions for the relationships between subsidiary integration and subsidiary initiative-taking.

[315] It needs to be noted, however, that the impact of the different (and partially opposing) effects is difficult to predict precisely. Therefore, the consolidated prediction on the influence of the subsidiary role setting on corporate resistance and on active subsidiary selling activities is to be viewed as quite speculative in nature.

[316] As outlined earlier in this publication, previous empirical work suggests that the effects of the subsidiary's resource-based power should be stronger than the ones resulting from risks and uncertainties associated with the context-specific and more uncertain initiatives (see e.g. Andersson et al. 2002b, pp. 984-985, 2007, p. 807). Consequently, the resource-based power effects are assumed to be potentially stronger than those associated with initiative characteristics. The same holds true for the subsequent predictions relating to subsidiary initiative selling activities.

from other MNC units put them in a rather weak position and make it more difficult for them to autonomously pursue entrepreneurial efforts. Overall, these contrasting considerations are expected to lead to a moderate to high level of initiative selling efforts by these units.

Subsidiary Initiative Outcomes: In contrast to the other role types, Receptive Subsidiaries should exhibit a *moderate level of entrepreneurial initiatives*. On the one hand, their close and frequent interactions with headquarters (or other MNC units) should allow them to better recognize the entrepreneurial opportunities and access the necessary resources that exist within the multinational firm. Furthermore, enhanced information flows between the parties should strengthen trust and credibility and help reduce (perceived) uncertainties on the part of headquarters, which has been shown to be important when subsidiaries are attempting to obtain central approval or support for their entrepreneurial endeavors. Taken together, these aspects should strengthen the ability of Receptive Subsidiaries to identify and realize new initiatives. On the other hand, their narrow scope of value-adding activities, their limited resource base and their lack of local responsiveness should prevent them from recognizing and realizing entrepreneurial initiatives, thus potentially leading overall to a rather moderate level of successfully realized initiatives in the end. More specifically, with regard to the type of initiatives that should be pursued by Receptive Subsidiaries, it is presumed that these highly integrated units more frequently engage in *internally oriented initiatives* that aim at improving the efficiency of the corporate system rather than externally oriented ones that deliver, for instance, new products or services for local or even global application (e.g. Birkinshaw 1997, p. 220, Yamin 2005, pp. 101-102).[317] As a result, the entrepreneurial initiatives by Receptive Subsidiaries should produce resource bundles that are characterized by a *moderate or even low level of specialization*,[318] but which are mostly non-location-bound and as such *easily transferable* to other units of the MNC.[319]

(3) Autonomous Subsidiary

If a subsidiary performs most of its value-adding activities locally and at the same time is largely independent of the parent organization or other MNC units, it is considered an Autonomous Subsidiary (Jarillo/Martinez 1990, p. 503, Schmid et al. 1998, p. 53).

---

[317] See also Paragraphs 1 and 2 of Subsection 3.5.2.2 which discuss the potential influence of subsidiary integration on the overall propensity to engage in entrepreneurial initiatives.

[318] The resulting resource bundles or capabilities that represent the e.g. new or improved products, processes or technologies, are thought to be only of moderate specialization as they, first, involve less specialized input resources mostly from within the MNC that are, second, combined in less extensive and complex bundling processes. See also Subsection 3.4.4.2 of this publication which discusses the possible resource-based outcomes of internally-oriented subsidiary initiatives.

[319] As already presented in Paragraph 1 of this subsection, numerous publications indicate that a subsidiary's integration and embeddedness in the corporate network should improve the transfer of capabilities that are developed by the foreign units (see e.g. Forsgren et al. 2000, p. 57, Andersson et al. 2002b, p. 992, Gammelgaard/Pedersen 2003, p. 7, Meyer et al. 2011, p. 242).

Subsidiaries belonging to this group typically have a narrow market scope (i.e. only the host country), as they are often established solely to serve the local market. As implied by the term "autonomous," they possess few network linkages with other MNC units, they enjoy high levels of local decision-making (or autonomy), while central control and coordination remain low. It has also been shown that, within Autonomous Subsidiaries, local executives often have different backgrounds and typically do not closely identify with the overall MNC and its corporate culture. In addition, Autonomous Subsidiaries must be more locally responsive, as external market conditions such as customer needs and competitor strategies are more difficult to identify and to assess, technology is still changing and product lines are relatively new. The high local responsiveness coupled with higher degrees of autonomy and frequently well-developed R&D activities within the subsidiary could provide conditions that are conducive for locally-oriented entrepreneurial and innovative activities, in some instances even for other geographical locations of the MNC (Martinez/Jarillo 1991, p. 441, Taggart 1997, p. 307, Young/Tavares 2004, p. 221, Manolopoulos 2008, p. 38).

Entrepreneurial Resource Management: With regard to the identification of new entrepreneurial opportunities, it is assumed that Autonomous Subsidiaries should show a *moderate to high level of initiative opportunity identification*. First, the wide range of value-adding activities and the diverse set of local resources may broaden the opportunity space and hence improve the foreign units' chances of identifying new entrepreneurial initiatives. Moreover, their high degree of local market orientation and their often strong linkages with external network partners should be helpful in identifying new opportunities, particularly in the external environment. Their potentially more demanding and uncertain environments, which are often thought to drive their strong local responsiveness, should also be conducive for the identification of new entrepreneurial opportunities in the external environment. However, while these factors are expected to support the external recognition of potential opportunities, the low degree of subsidiary integration could make the identification of new opportunities from within the MNC more difficult. For example, less interaction and communication with internal MNC actors could diminish the chances to detect new initiative opportunities from within the MNC network. As a result, Autonomous Subsidiaries are assumed to exhibit an overall moderate to high level of opportunity identification activities specifically *from the external* rather than from the internal *MNC network*.

In addition, foreign units in the role of Autonomous Subsidiaries are likely to exhibit a *moderate to high level of resource structuring activities* to obtain the necessary resources and capabilities for their entrepreneurial endeavors. Given their high degree of localization/local responsiveness, these units should be well-positioned to access the resources and capabilities present in their respective environments. Furthermore, the generally more demanding and uncertain environments of Autonomous Subsidiaries should necessitate externally oriented initiatives in the form of, for example, more specialized or sophisticated solutions that therefore involve more complex bundles of novel resources and capabilities. Taken together, these characteristics suggest that this role type should engage in resource structuring activities to a larger extent. However, two further considerations could indicate less of a need and/or ability for resource structuring. First, Autonomous Subsidiary units may already possess a somewhat stronger resource base. This should allow them to rely more strongly on their existing resources and capabilities rather than having to obtain new ones from other sources. Second, given their low level of integration in the corporate system, these foreign units may be restricted in accessing resources and capabilities from within the MNC. Taken together, these considerations lead to the assumption that Autonomous Subsidiaries will typically exhibit a moderate to high level of resource structuring activities when pursuing entrepreneurial initiatives. Concerning the origin of new resources and capabilities, Autonomous Subsidiaries are expected to obtain them from external rather than internal MNC sources (see also Jindra 2005, p. 62, Maitland/Sammartino 2009, p. 69). In view of their strong external orientation and their frequent engagement in external networks, these units should be better equipped to identify and obtain resources from their local environment. Moreover, Autonomous Subsidiaries must react to the particular needs and demands of their local environment. As resources and capabilities from within the MNC are often closely related or even identical, this role type may be more inclined to access the potentially more diverse set of resources and capabilities in their external environment. Lastly, as the autonomous units are also characterized by a low degree of integration, it might be claimed that they are less willing and/or able to obtain resources from within the MNC. Next, with regard to the mode of resource structuring, the previously presented arguments suggest that Autonomous Subsidiaries may tend to rely more strongly on *external resource acquisition*. As argued above, this subsidiary role type should operate in comparatively demanding and uncertain environments in which sudden shifts in, for instance, customer demand or technology are more likely. Thus, in order to react quickly and flexibly to these changes, (external) resource acquisition, rather than gradual resource development, should provide a more useful option under these circumstances.

Finally, it is anticipated that Autonomous Subsidiaries exhibit a *moderate to high level of more extensive resource bundling activities* (e.g. intermediate or radical bundling). Due to their extensive scope of value-adding activities, their broader set of existing resources and capabilities and their often strong linkages to external network partners, they should be better able to access and bundle a relatively diverse set of resources and capabilities. Furthermore, given the demanding and uncertain environment and the specific demands in their markets, Autonomous Subsidiaries may need to engage in more distinct bundling processes that deliver differentiated and potentially more complex products, services or technologies. However, their limited access to the resources and capabilities of the MNC network may partially impede their ability to produce highly unique bundles based on both internal and external resources.

Headquarters-Subsidiary Alignment: Considering the predictions made earlier for each separate role dimension, it can be concluded that Autonomous Subsidiaries should possess a moderate to strong resource-based power position in their alignment and interaction with headquarters (see also Qu 2007, p. 1185). Aside from their existing set of diverse resources and capabilities, these units can accrue further power from their specific knowledge of local market and competitive developments as well as their strong linkages with external network partners. This power may then be employed to increase their autonomy or to influence initiative-related decision-making in the MNC when engaging in entrepreneurial activities.[320]

Hence, with regard to the engagement of the corporate center in the initiative process, it is presumed that Autonomous units – at least in part due to their resource-based power and their relevance for the development of new resources and capabilities in the MNC – will face only *low to moderate levels of headquarters involvement*. Furthermore, their diverse resource base makes them less dependent on other MNC units and therefore enables these autonomous units to bypass or circumvent headquarters, at least in the early development phases of initiatives. In line with this view, several publications suggest that a subsidiary's external orientation and local embeddedness will generally reduce headquarters control and enhance subsidiary autonomy (e.g. Mudambi/ Navarra 2004, p. 392, Young/Tavares 2004, p. 226, Andersson et al. 2007, p. 807).

This particular role stetting is also expected to impact the level of corporate resistance a subsidiary should face when pursuing entrepreneurial initiatives. On the one hand, Autonomous Subsidiaries are more likely to be engaged in entrepreneurial activities that are adapted to the requirements of the local environment and have developed through close interactions with local actors. Consequently, these initiatives should involve new (local) resources and capabilities that are context-specific, tacit and socially-complex, and as such difficult to communicate to outsiders and difficult to use in other MNC units'

---

[320] However, following the resource-dependence logic as outlined earlier in this publication, it could be maintained that the resources and capabilities controlled by Autonomous Subsidiaries only provide them with a moderate level of power. As discussed in Subsections 3.3.3 and 3.4.3, subsidiaries may develop resource-based power to the extent that they (a) control resources that are (b) important to others in the MNC and (c) for which no alternatives exist. While it seems likely that Autonomous Subsidiary units can gain control over resources for which no alternatives exist (e.g. obtaining location-specific resources in their environment that only they can access through their local network relationships), the aspect of resource importance for the wider MNC is to be questioned. Since the resources these units control may be largely location-bound and thus cannot be employed to solve problems at other locations of the MNC, these subsidiary resources may only help to address localized problems. Consequently, they may only provide it with some weaker power in comparison to those resources that are applicable or helpful for the wider MNC.

business contexts (e.g. Forsgren et al. 2000, pp. 60-61, Andersson 2003, p. 430). It may therefore be presumed that these initiative aspects increase the level of corporate resistance. On the other hand, the moderate to strong resource and power position and high degree of autonomy of this role type could allow it to better bypass the corporate immune system or use this power to overcome possible resistance in the MNC. Together, this would suggest that Autonomous Subsidiaries encounter a *low to moderate level of corporate resistance* when engaging in entrepreneurial initiatives.[321]

Likewise, this subsidiary role type should exhibit a *low to moderate level of active initiative selling*. First, it can be expected that the context-specific and complex initiatives require higher selling efforts on the part of the subsidiary to provide information that can help headquarters better understand them and their potential implications for the wider MNC. Yet, contrastingly, their relatively strong resource and power position should allow this role type to circumvent the corporate center or better influence central decision-making in its favor and thus help initiatives move through the MNC system. Furthermore, previous research suggests that externally-oriented initiatives are often undertaken without headquarters' awareness and without central resources, and as such involve fewer initiative-selling activities.[322]

Subsidiary Initiative Outcomes: Compared to the other role types, Autonomous Subsidiaries are assumed to show a *moderate to high level of entrepreneurial initiatives*. Earlier contributions indicate that these units' high level of local responsiveness, coupled with higher degrees of autonomy and fairly well-developed R&D capabilities, provide conditions that encourage entrepreneurial and innovative activities, in particular those for local application (Martinez/Jarillo 1991, p. 441, Taggart 1997, p. 307, Young/ Tavares 2004, p. 221, Manolopoulos 2008, p. 38). The predictions developed herein similarly suggest that the broad value-added scope, the relative strong resource base, the strong external orientation and the close relationships with local actors should help Autonomous Subsidiaries engage in entrepreneurial activities, particularly in local market initiatives.[323] However, in contrast to Active Subsidiaries, which can also benefit

---

[321] As discussed previously in this publication, empirical work suggests that the effects of the subsidiary's resource-based power should be stronger than the ones resulting from risks and uncertainties associated with the context-specific and more uncertain initiatives (see e.g. Andersson et al. 2002b, pp. 984-985, 2007, p. 807). Consequently, the resource-based power effects are assumed to be potentially stronger than those associated with initiative characteristics. The same holds true for the subsequent predictions relating to subsidiary initiative selling activities.

[322] See also Subsection 3.4.3.3 of this publication which also addresses the link between subsidiary initiative selling activities and different types of subsidiary initiatives.

[323] Other publications can be found which provide further support for the assumption that the contextual setting of Autonomous Subsidiaries should specifically facilitate local entrepreneurship and innovation. For example, Ghoshal and Bartlett argue that local innovations are, among other aspects, driven by decentralized resources in the MNC and high degrees of subsidiary autonomy (see e.g. Ghoshal 1986, pp. 215-216, Ghoshal/Bartlett 1988, pp. 370-371). Relatedly, Birkinshaw shows that local market initiatives are positively influenced by a moderate level of subsidiary resources, a high level of subsidiary autonomy as well as by low headquarters-subsidiary interactions and communication (Birkinshaw 1997, p. 224). Lastly, Mu et al. argue that local market embeddedness should facilitate specifically localized subsidiary innovation (Mu et al. 2007, p. 83).

from their strong integration in the MNC network for the identification and realization of (internally-oriented) initiatives, foreign units in the role of Autonomous Subsidiaries should be somewhat limited in this regard. In particular it is presumed that these units are more likely to pursue local market initiatives embodied in, for instance, new products, processes or technologies that are first identified and realized in the local market, but which can subsequently be exploited at other locations of the MNC as well.

Concerning the resource-based outcomes, the entrepreneurial initiatives of Autonomous Subsidiaries should produce *resource bundles of moderate or even high specialization* (e.g. in the form of an innovative product that is strongly tailored to the needs of local customers)[324] but that are often *partially location-bound* and thus are not immediately applicable at other MNC locations.[325]

(4) Quiescent Subsidiary[326]

Finally, Quiescent Subsidiaries are characterized by a low degree of both integration and local responsiveness. Their low degree of integration indicates that they possess only weak linkages to the rest of the MNC network, and local decisions concerning, for instance, manufacturing, products or quality are not made with the objective of supplying customers in other geographical areas of the MNC. Furthermore, headquarters has only very limited control or none at all over local quality, production or stocks of the subsidiary. The development of technology is largely centralized, with only a limited amount of technology, product or knowledge transfer taking place between headquarters and the subsidiary. With regard to local responsiveness, Quiescent Subsidiaries perform very few value chain activities and they do not perform these activities on a global scale. Furthermore, they do not typically adapt either operations or products to local needs, as there is little environmental pressure for subsidiaries in this

---

[324] The resulting resources bundles should potentially be moderately or even highly specialized as they involve unique input resources that are further combined in distinct entrepreneurial processes. For example, the resources which are obtained through the unique external network relationships of Autonomous Subsidiaries should also be relatively inimitable and non-substitutable (see e.g. McEvily/Zaheer 1999, p. 1135, Andersson et al. 2002b, p. 980). Furthermore, their rather extensive bundling processes could further enhance the uniqueness or specialization of the resulting resource bundles or capabilities (see e.g. Bowman/Collier 2006, p. 198, Sirmon et al. 2007, p. 281). However, in comparison to Active Subsidiary units that can access and bundle various resources from their external environment as well as from within the MNC, Autonomous Subsidiaries could be more restricted in their bundling, as it should be more difficult for them to access the resources at other MNC locations.

[325] Various publications provide support for the assumption that a subsidiary's high degree of localization/local responsiveness may lead to resource outcomes that are potentially context-specific, tacit and socially-complex and as such more difficult to transfer to other locations of the MNC (e.g. Kogut/Zander 1992, p. 637, Forsgren et al. 2000, pp. 60-61, Andersson et al. 2001a, pp. 1019-1020, Andersson 2003, p. 430, Mahnke et al. 2007, p. 1283). Likewise, it can be inferred from other works that a subsidiary's lacking integration may impede the transfer of resources and capabilities from the foreign unit to other parts of the MNC (e.g. Forsgren et al. 2000, p. 57, Andersson et al. 2002b, p. 992, Gammelgaard/Pedersen 2003, p. 7, Meyer et al. 2011, p. 242). As Autonomous Subsidiaries are characterized by both a high degree of localization/local responsiveness as well as by a low degree of integration, it can be assumed that the resource bundles from their often locally-oriented initiatives should be partially or even fully-location bound.

[326] As mentioned above, this type of subsidiary was originally not included in Jarillo and Martinez typology and was only subsequently introduced by Taggart (1997).

context to be more locally responsive. Overall, they tend to operate in relatively stable markets in which customers, customer needs, competitors and their strategies are easily identified. In addition, technology and technological development are stable, products are often rather mature, and manufacturing processes are at the higher end of the learning curve. It has also been proposed that the low responsiveness could be associated with lower subsidiary resources and capabilities. In sum, it can be expected that subsidiaries in such a context show very little entrepreneurial and innovative activities and thus resource and capability development for both local and global application remains very limited (Taggart 1997, p. 307, Schmid et al. 1998, p. 59, Manolopoulos 2008, p. 38, De Beule 2011, p. 206).

Entrepreneurial Resource Management: Concerning initiative opportunity identification, it is predicted that Quiescent Subsidiaries exhibit the lowest level of all role types proposed by Jarillo and Martinez and by Taggart based on the following considerations. First, their limited range of value-adding activities and their small resource base should weaken the foreign units' overall chances to identify new entrepreneurial initiatives. More specifically, their low degree of external market orientation and their lack of linkages to actors in the external environment should make it difficult for them to identify new externally oriented initiative opportunities. Likewise, their potentially less demanding and more stable environments should provide few chances or stimuli for new entrepreneurial undertakings. Second, their low degree of integration, leading to weaker ties and looser interactions with other MNC units, should decrease the likelihood that they will recognize opportunities within the MNC network. Taken together, these factors suggest that Quiescent Subsidiaries exhibit the *lowest level of initiative opportunity identification, both internally and externally oriented* ones.

Pertaining to resource acquisition and development activities, it is anticipated that Quiescent Subsidiaries should show a *low level of resource structuring* as well. Due to their low degree of localization and weak linkages with external actors, these units should be quite restricted in accessing the resources and capabilities present in their external environment. Furthermore, their less demanding and less uncertain environments should not only require innovative solutions less frequently, but any such solutions should also of less complexity and sophistication. Consequently, the need for Quiescent Subsidiaries to obtain new resources and capabilities should be very limited. Furthermore, taking into consideration the path-dependent nature of resource acquisition and development activities, their limited resource base should also restrict their ability to obtain new resources and capabilities (see e.g. Dierickx/Cool 1989, pp. 1507-1508, Barney 1991, pp. 107-108, Kogut/Zander 1992, p. 392). Finally, the low degree of integration with other MNC units may impede the foreign units' ability to access the different resources and capabilities within the multinational firm (see also Qu 2007, p.

1185). In sum, this should lead to the lowest level of resource structuring activities among all subsidiary role types. With regard to the sources from which new resources and capabilities are obtained, no clear prediction can be made. However, given the limited access to external and internal MNC sources and their frequently less demanding and more predictable market environments, it may be tentatively assumed that Quiescent Subsidiaries must rely more on the *internal and more gradual development* of resources and capabilities within the foreign unit itself, or in some cases turn to the parent company for additional resources (Jindra 2005, p. 62, De Beule 2011, p. 206).

Moreover, it can be predicted that this particular role type shows *the lowest level of resource bundling activities*. In view of the few minor entrepreneurial initiatives that should originate from these units, few resource bundling activities are expected to take place. Also, their own restricted resource base and their limited access to further internal and external resources and capabilities should make bundling activities more difficult for them. Finally, their operation in rather undemanding and more predictable environments, where only less complex and sophisticated initiatives are needed, suggests that *less extensive bundling activities* (e.g. incremental bundling) should be sufficient in these circumstances.

Headquarters-Subsidiary Alignment: In comparison to the other role types, Quiescent Subsidiaries are likely to possess a relatively weak resource and power position in the MNC, which should subsequently also impact the interactions and alignment with the corporate center throughout the initiative process. More specifically, attributable to their own small resource base and their limited capacity to obtain resources from their local environment, Quiescent Subsidiaries are expected to gain little resource-based power in the multinational firm (see also Qu 2007, p. 1185). Specifically with regard to headquarters engagement in subsidiary initiative-taking, it is assumed that Quiescent Subsidiaries should face a *moderate to high level of involvement* from the corporate center for the following reasons. First, their limited resource and power base and their limited links to the external environment do not allow them to pursue initiatives autonomously or to easily bypass the corporate immune system. Instead, it appears more likely that these units would have to approach the parent company for further resources and/or approval when attempting to realize identified initiative opportunities, in particular those of large scale or scope (see also De Beule 2011, p. 206). Additionally, given their rather undemanding and stable environments, Quiescent Subsidiaries may not be perceived by headquarters as potential providers of critical location-specific resources and capabilities, which could weaken their power position in the multinational firm even further. Consequently, this should imply a low degree of subsidiary autonomy, and inversely a somewhat higher level of central control, leading to potentially higher levels of headquarters involvement in the initiative-taking activities. Nevertheless, as Quiescent Subsidiaries are also characterized by a low degree of integration in the MNC, this should give them at least some local decision-making autonomy in relation to their local markets. As outlined above, low degrees of integration imply low degrees of central control and lower levels of cooperation and communication. Therefore, Quiescent Subsidiary units should face an overall moderate to high level of headquarters involvement when engaging in entrepreneurial initiatives.

In addition, this role type should encounter a *moderate or possibly even high level of corporate resistance* when pursuing initiatives. On the one hand, the (few) adaptive entrepreneurial activities of possibly smaller scale and/or scope that may originate from Quiescent Subsidiaries should, given their limited local responsiveness, involve mostly resources and capabilities that are not very context-specific, tacit or socially complex. Hence, the initiatives should be relatively easy to communicate and easier to use at other locations of the MNC, resulting in a comparatively low level of corporate resistance. On the other hand, however, their low degree of integration should result in looser ties and less frequent interactions between headquarters and the foreign units. This again may impede the development of trust and credibility and therefore increase perceived uncertainties associated with subsidiary initiatives presented to the parent company for central support and/or approval. Furthermore, the relatively weak resource and power position of Quiescent Subsidiaries should make it less likely that these units can either bypass the corporate immune system or overcome corporate resistance by, for example, demonstrating that they have the necessary skills or expertise for the envisioned initiatives. On the whole, this suggests that these units may encounter a moderate or possibly even high level of resistance from other parts of the MNC.

Consistent with the previous arguments, Quiescent Subsidiaries are expected to show a *moderate or even strong level of initiative selling*. As their initiatives should mostly involve resources and capabilities that are not context-specific, tacit or socially complex and that can be relatively easily transferred to other MNC locations, this should reduce the need for them to sell or promote their entrepreneurial endeavors in the MNC. However, in contrast to these assumptions, it could be maintained that their low degree of integration at the same time reduces the chance that their initiatives will be closely aligned with the needs of the wider MNC or will remain close to the existing resources and capabilities of the firm. Moreover, these less integrated units could suffer from lower levels of trust and credibility, thus requiring stronger efforts to explain and promote their initiatives in the multinational firm. Hence, based on these considerations, along with their rather weak resource and power position, Quiescent Subsidiaries should need to engage in active initiative-selling to a moderate or even high degree.

Subsidiary Initiative Outcome: In comparison to the other role types, Quiescent Subsidiaries might be expected to show the *lowest level of successful initiatives*. First, given their low degree of local responsiveness and their low degree of integration, it should be difficult for these units to identify new initiative opportunities both internally and externally. Furthermore, their role context (e.g. their weak resource base and their limited access to new internal and external resources and capabilities) should largely prohibit them from realizing any entrepreneurial opportunity of larger scale and/or scope. In addition, considering their rather weak power position in the MNC it would appear likely for them to encounter corporate resistance, which should also be difficult for them to overcome.

With regard to the types of initiatives that can be expected to originate from this role type, Quiescent Subsidiaries should commonly engage in what was earlier termed *"trivial initiatives,"* which aim at improving processes or products for primarily local purposes and typically not for subsequent use in the wider MNC. Corresponding to this assumption, previous research indicates that Quiescent units should show only limited creative activities that go beyond adapting the existing products or technologies of the MNC. For example, these foreign entities are expected to modify existing products or services in minor ways or to alter production processes so that they better fit local conditions (Manolopoulos 2008, p. 38, De Beule 2011, p. 206). As a result, the entrepreneurial initiatives undertaken by Quiescent Subsidiaries should typically be of *little specialization*[327] and in many cases also *not directly applicable at other locations* of the MNC.[328] As a result, the initiatives that are typically undertaken by this subsidiary role type should only contribute little to the firm-level advantages of the MNC, underlining their weak contributory role. Table 3.6 summarizes the predictions for all four role types presented by Jarillo and Martinez.

---

[327] The resulting resource bundles or capabilities should only be of little specialization as they, first, involve less specialized input resources that are, second, combined in less extensive and complex bundling processes. For example, the input resources employed in their initiatives should largely stem from either the subsidiary unit itself or possibly from the parent company. As was argued previously, these units are thought to lack the access to more unique resources and capabilities that could exist in their environment given their low degree of local responsiveness. In addition, the different resources should only be combined through incremental bundling efforts and thus only deliver bundles of little specialization in the end (e.g. in the form of slightly modified products that are already well-established in the MNC; see e.g. De Beule 2011, p. 206).

[328] As was outlined earlier in this publication, it can be inferred from other works that a subsidiary's lacking integration may impede the transfer of resources and capabilities from the foreign unit to other parts of the MNC (e.g. Forsgren et al. 2000, p. 57, Andersson et al. 2002b, p. 992, Gammelgaard/Pedersen 2003, p. 7, Meyer et al. 2011, p. 242). Hence, the new resource bundles associated with the Quiescent Subsidiaries' initiatives could be somewhat difficult to transfer.

3 – Research Framework

	Active Subsidiary	Receptive Subsidiary	Autonomous Subsidiary	Quiescent Subsidiary
Degree of localization	High	Low	High	Low
Degree of integration	High	High	Low	Low
(I) Entrepreneurial Resource Management				
Opportunity identification (level and source)	• **Highest** level of initiative opportunity identification • Both **external** and **internal**	• **Moderate** level of initiative opportunity identification • Rather **internal** identification	• **Moderate to high** level of initiative opportunity identification • Rather **external** identification	• **Lowest** level of initiative opportunity identification • Both **external** and **internal**
Resource structuring (level, source and mode)	• **Moderate to high** level of resource structuring • **All sources and modes** equally possible	• **Low to moderate** level of resource structuring • Rather **internal** development	• **Moderate to high** level of resource structuring • Rather **external** acquisition	• **Low** level of resource structuring • Possibly some **internal** resource development activities
Resource bundling (level and mode)	• **High** level of resource bundling • **More extensive** bundling	• **Moderate** level of resource bundling • **Less extensive** bundling	• **Moderate to high** level of resource bundling • **More extensive** bundling	• **Low** level of resource bundling • **Very limited** bundling
(II) Headquarters-Subsidiary Alignment				
HQ involvement (level)	• **Low to moderate** level of HQ involvement	• **High** level of HQ involvement	• **Low to moderate** level of HQ involvement	• **Moderate to high** level of HQ involvement
Corp. resistance (level)	• **Low to moderate** level of resistance	• **Moderate to high** level of resistance	• **Low to moderate** level of resistance	• **Moderate to high** level of resistance
Subsidiary initiative selling (level)	• **Low to moderate** level of selling	• **Moderate to high** level of selling	• **Low to moderate** level of selling	• **Moderate to high** level of selling
(III) Subsidiary Initiative Outcome				
Subsidiary initiative-taking (level and type)	• **Highest** level of initiatives • Both **external** and **internal** initiatives	• **Moderate** level of initiatives • Rather **internal** initiatives (internal market and internal-hybrid)	• **Moderate to high** level of initiatives • Rather **external** initiatives (local market)	• **Lowest** level of initiatives • Rather trivial initiatives
Subsidiary resource development (level and type)	• **Highest** level of specialized resource development • Rather **non-location bound** resources	• **Moderate to low** level of specialized resource development • Mostly **non-location-bound** resources	• **Moderate to high** level of specialized resource development • Partially **location-bound** resources	• **Lowest** level of specialized resource development • Partially **location-bound** resources and possibly **some non-location-bound**

Table 3.6: Summary of predictions for the subsidiary role typology by Jarillo/Martinez

4 Empirical Study

Having presented the theoretical framework and the preliminary predictions in Chapter 3, this part now focuses on presenting the research philosophy employed (Section 4.1), the selected design of the empirical study (Section 4.2), the collection of the data (Section 4.3), the techniques for analyzing the data (Section 4.4), and finally the scientific quality criteria (Section 4.5).

4.1 Research Philosophy

Since the research philosophy adopted for any study has important implications for the research methodology employed, it is useful to briefly address the philosophical stance of this research prior to presenting the research design in the following subsections. More specifically, outlining the key assumptions concerning the particular "philosophy of science" of a study may, first, help the researcher clarify the research design, refine what is considered appropriate evidence, and determine how it is to be best collected and interpreted. Transparency regarding the philosophical stance may thus help when evaluating and selecting research methodologies and prevent the use of inappropriate empirical approaches. Moreover, positioning the research relative to certain philosophical paradigms is also important, since this helps others better understand the worldview that guides the researcher and his or her work, what he or she perceives as acceptable knowledge or "quality" and which evaluation criteria should apply to ensure meaningful outcomes (Bøllingtoft 2007, p. 407, Easterby-Smith et al. 2012, p. 17).

At the core, the research philosophy usually involves assumptions regarding ontology, epistemology and the methodology of the research. When aligned, ontological, epistemological and methodological considerations form a coherent philosophical paradigm or perspective. While ontological assumptions relate to the researcher's view of reality, epistemological assumptions touch upon his or her understanding on what constitutes acceptable knowledge and, finally, methodological assumptions deal with the combination of techniques that a researcher uses for his or her investigation (see e.g. Guba 1990, p. 18, Guba/Lincoln 1994, p. 108, Saunders et al. 2012, p. 129). Different positions with regard to ontology, epistemology and methodology have produced diverse philosophical stances, such as positivism, realism and constructivism. In line with other writings, this study assumes that the philosophical paradigms can be organized as a continuum with positivism at one end and constructivism at the other. In between the two extreme positions, other philosophical perspectives can be found, for example, realism or critical theory (see e.g. Morgan/Smircich 1980, Collis/Hussey

2009).[329] The two extreme (and often considered incommensurable) orientations and the somewhat intermediate paradigm of realism are portrayed in an attempt to position the philosophy of the present research thereafter (for a summary see Table 4.1).[330]

A *positivistic* stance maintains that an objective and apprehensible reality exists which is shaped by immutable natural laws and mechanisms. It is the main objective of scientific research to uncover the causal relationships between the different elements that constitute reality so that natural phenomena can eventually be better predicted and controlled. In the search for regularities that may allow the development of time- and context-free generalizations, researchers can obtain new knowledge from "positive" or objective information. As the investigator and the object under study are expected to be independent of each other, it is deemed possible that the researcher studies the object without influencing it, allowing the retrieval of "objective" and credible data. As to the methodology, questions and hypotheses are typically formulated on the basis of theories, which are then tested in empirical studies (i.e. theory-testing based on deduction). Here, emphasis is usually placed on collecting quantifiable data that is more apt for statistical analysis. Thus, principal data collection techniques under this paradigm include larger-scale surveys or quantitative experiments (see e.g. Guba 1990, pp. 19-20, Guba/Lincoln 1994, pp. 109-110, Collis/Hussey 2009, p. 56, Saunders et al. 2012, pp. 134-135).

On the other side of the continuum lies the paradigm frequently referred to as *constructivism*.[331] Here, it is maintained that there is no singular and objective reality. Instead, various subjective realities exist that are shaped by individual perceptions and are constructed in people's minds. Epistemologically, the constructivist researcher is expected to take a subjectivist position and to adopt an empathetic stance in order to investigate and understand the world from the research object's point of view, since new scientific findings are actually created through the interaction of the investigator and the investigated object. Thus, while the positivist stance advocates that the investigator remains objective and independent, the constructivist perspective conversely acknowledges that the researcher is a necessary part of what is being observed. Methodologically, the subjective nature of reality and the specificities of social construction necessitate that the researcher interacts with the social actors to produce rich, subjective and qualitative

---

[329] However, not all research philosophies can necessarily be positioned between the two extremes. For example, the philosophical approach of pragmatism may lie somewhat outside this continuum. Rather than adhering to a fixed and coherent profile regarding ontological, epistemological and methodological assumptions, pragmatists may adopt different views and perspectives from different philosophical positions as they see fit for their specific research (see e.g. Saunders et al. 2012, p. 130).

[330] As it is outside the scope of this publication to provide an extensive overview and discussion of the various philosophical positions developed over time, only the central aspects of the three specified paradigms are outlined.

[331] It should be noted that the literature is not always consistent in the wording with regard to the different philosophical paradigms. For example, constructivism is sometimes also referred to as social constructivism (e.g. Easterby-Smith et al. 2012) or interpretivism (e.g. Collis/Hussey 2009 and Saunders et al. 2012).

data from which new ideas and/or theories can be induced. Hence, data collection ideally involves the detailed investigation of small samples through a broader array of methods, such as action research, ethnographic approaches or in-depth interviews (e.g. Guba 1990, pp. 25-27, Guba/Lincoln 1994, pp. 110, Collis/Hussey 2009, pp. 56-68, Saunders et al. 2012, p. 137).

Finally, a somewhat intermediate position is represented by the *realist* position (sometimes also referred to as post-positivism), which contains elements of both positivism and constructivism (see e.g. Järvensivu/Törnroos 2010, p. 101, Bechara/Van De Ven 2011, p. 348, Easterby-Smith et al. 2012, p. 29). As to ontological assumptions, this philosophical approach takes a critical realist position, believing that reality exists which is, however, only imperfectly and probabilistically apprehensible given the "flawed human intellectual mechanisms and the fundamentally intractable nature of phenomena." Furthermore, the dualism between the investigator and the investigated object is largely abandoned. Nonetheless, although it is recognized that true objectivity cannot be achieved completely, it remains a "regulatory ideal" (Guba/Lincoln 1994, p. 110). For this purpose, mechanisms to "safeguard" objectivity are deemed to play a critical role, such as critical traditions or critical communities that are present to examine new findings. Consequently, replicated findings are expected to be probably true, yet they remain subject to subsequent falsification. In order to best capture the multiple perceptions of a single reality, realism emphasizes the importance of multiplism or triangulation with regard to methodology. Accordingly, both qualitative and quantitative methodologies are considered appropriate, and methods such as case studies and in-depth interviews are just as acceptable as statistical analyses or structural equation modeling (Healy/Perry 2000, pp. 119-122, Bøllingtoft 2007, p. 413, Easton 2010, pp. 119-120, Järvensivu/Törnroos 2010, p. 101).

	Positivism	Realism	Constructivism
Ontology	Naïve realism: Reality is "real" and apprehensible	Critical realism: Reality is "real" but only imperfectly apprehensible	Relativism: Reality is "subjective" and constructed
Epistemology	Objectivist: Investigator and investigated object are independent entities; observations provide true and credible data	Modified objectivist: Dualism between investigator and investigated object abandoned; objectivity as regulatory ideal; findings are open to misinterpretation	Subjectivist: New findings are created only through interactions of investigator and investigated object
Methodology	Quantitative: Verification of hypotheses through mainly quantitative methods	Quantitative and qualitative: Triangulation and interpretation of issues through quantitative and qualitative methods	Qualitative: Development of patterns and/or theory through in-depth investigations using mainly qualitative methods

Table 4.1: Comparison of different research philosophies
Sources: Compiled from the works of Guba and Lincoln (1994, p. 109), Healy and Perry (2000, p. 119, 122), Jill et al. (2009, p. 58), and Saunders et al. (2012, p. 140)

Another useful framework in this context has been offered by Burrell and Morgan, who derive four paradigms for the analysis of social theory and thereby provide what has been termed "the major belief systems of management and business researchers" (Saunders et al. 2012, p. 141). Central to the authors' work is the view that "all theories of organization are based upon a philosophy of science and a theory of society" (Burrell/Morgan 1979, p. 1). Accordingly, the scholars differentiate their four paradigms based on two dimensions relating to (1) a philosophy of science and (2) a theory of society. As to the first dimension, it is assumed that researchers base their work on different viewpoints regarding ontology, epistemology, human nature, and methodology. Here, two extreme positions are considered possible, with objectivist approaches at one end and subjectivist approaches at the other. *Objectivist* approaches are characterized by a realist standpoint on ontology, a positivist epistemology, a deterministic view on human nature, and a nomothetic methodology.[332] In contrast, *subjectivist* approaches represent a nominalist view on ontology, an anti-positivist epistemology, a voluntaristic

---

[332] Although certain scholars suggest that ontological, epistemological and methodological assumptions form the core of a research philosophy (e.g. Guba 1990, Guba/Lincoln 1994, Healy/Perry 2000 and Bechara/Van De Ven 2011), other researchers use a wider array of characteristics to describe different research philosophies. For example, in addition to the three core aspects, Morgan and Smircich also refer to assumptions about human nature and favored metaphors (Morgan/Smircich 1980, p. 492), while Saunders et al. add axiology (view of values; see Saunders et al. 2012, p. 140) and Collis and Hussey include rhetorical aspects (language of research) and axiological considerations (see Collis/Hussey 2009, p. 58).

view on human nature and an ideographic methodology (see Table 4.2).[333] However, corresponding with the previous arguments, these two positions do not form a strict dichotomy. Instead, they represent two extreme positions along a continuum with several other research philosophies lying in between.[334]

	Objectivist Approach		Subjectivist Approach
Ontology	**Realism:** Reality as a concrete structure	↔	**Nominalism:** Reality as a projection of human imagination
Epistemology	**Positivism:** Construct a positivist science	↔	**Anti-Positivism:** Obtain phenomenological insights
Human Nature	**Determinism:** Man as a responder	↔	**Voluntarism:** Man as a creator
Methodology	**Nomothetic:** Utilization of systematic techniques to test hypotheses through mostly quantitative methods (deductive testing)	↔	**Ideographic:** Analysis of subjective accounts through mostly qualitative methods (inductive development)

Table 4.2: Comparison of objectivist and subjectivist approach
Sources: Adapted from Burrell and Morgan (1979, p. 3) and Morgan and Smircich (1980, p. 492)

In addition to making assumptions concerning the "philosophy of science" Burrell and Morgan argue that researchers may also hold different views about the "nature of society," as reflected in their second dimension, which essentially differentiates between the extremes of regulation and radical change. Researchers following the "regulation" perspective typically attempt to explain society in ways that emphasize its underlying unity and cohesiveness. Thus, they are concerned with what Burrell and Morgan describe as "status quo, social order, consensus, social integration, solidarity, need satisfaction as well as actuality." In comparison, the "radical change" perspective takes a more dynamic standpoint that focuses on process and change, reflected in aspects such as "radical change, structural conflict, modes of domination, contradiction, emancipation, deprivation, and potentiality" (Burrell/Morgan 1979, p. 18). Assumptions that researchers make with regard to these two independent dimensions lead to delineation of four distinct paradigms referred to as "functionalist," "interpretative," "radical humanist" and "radical structuralist" (see Figure 4.1).[335]

---

[333] A deterministic view on nature assumes that human beings are essentially conditioned by their external circumstances, while a voluntaristic perspective assumes a much more creative role of human beings, with social actors controlling or creating their environment (see e.g. Burrell/Morgan 1979, p. 2).
[334] For example, Morgan and Smircich place four additional philosophical standpoints in between the two extremes (see Morgan/Smircich 1980, p. 492).
[335] In order to keep the discussion about the adopted philosophical stance at a manageable length, the relative positioning of this study will only be discussed for the dimension relating to the "philosophy of science", that is, alongside the continuum between objective and subjective approaches.

	The Sociology of Radical Change		
	Radical Humanist	Radical Structuralist	
Subjective			Objective
	Interpretative	Functionalist	
	The Sociology of Regulation		

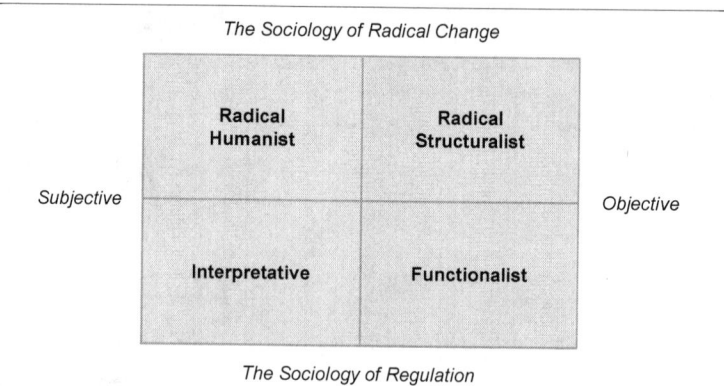

Figure 4.1: Four paradigms for the analysis of organizations
Source: Burrell and Morgan (1979, p. 22)

In line with the majority of both management and entrepreneurship research, the present work remains located largely within the bounds of the Functionalist paradigm (see e.g. Jennings et al. 2005, p. 146, Scherer 2006, p. 35, Kutschker/Schmid 2011, p. 474). However, instead of adhering to an extreme objectivist position, this study takes a somewhat intermediate or moderate position that also incorporates certain assumptions that are more subjectivist in nature. In order to better position the present research on the continuum of objective versus subjective approaches, the ontological, epistemological and methodological positions this work adopts are now briefly described.

Ontologically, this study takes a critical realist perspective, acknowledging that while a true reality exists, it is only imperfectly and probabilistically apprehensible. Moreover, in contrast to strictly objective approaches that view the social world as a "hard, concrete structure," it is assumed that it is more dynamic and changing, providing opportunities for those (e.g. entrepreneurs) who have the will and ability to act (Morgan/Smircich 1980, p. 495). Concerning human nature, it is expected that social actors (or other entities such as firms or their subunits) have both causal powers and liabilities that also allow them to cause events to occur or to change. In comparison with strictly objective approaches that view entities merely responding to situational forces in a mechanistic and predictable way, a more relaxed position is taken that recognizes that they are neither fully determined by their context nor are they fully autonomous. Instead, it is presumed that actors are both enabled and constrained by situational factors, indicating a contingent rather than a purely deterministic relationship (Whittington 1988, p. 528, Easton 2002, p. 120, Sousa 2010, p. 475).

Epistemologically, the need to understand processes and investigate how phenomena change over time in relation to their specific contextual settings is highlighted (Morgan/ Smircich 1980, p. 493, Healy/Perry 2000, p. 123, Easton 2002, p. 120). Recognizing that the knowledge of reality is interpreted through social conditioning, it is also acknowledged that it cannot be accessed directly, but needs to be derived in association with the social actors involved in the knowledge generation process (Easterby-Smith et al. 2012, p. 19, Saunders et al. 2012, p. 136). Based on the belief that complex reality is only imperfectly and probabilistically apprehensible and true objectivity cannot be achieved completely, this study will attempt to collect data from various sources and multiple levels in order to paint a more comprehensive picture and obtain a more differentiated view of reality (Guba/Lincoln 1994, p. 110, Easton 2002, p. 123).

With regard to the research aim and research process, the present thesis takes a somewhat intermediate position as well. As described before, while strict objectivist approaches tend to begin with a theoretical argument (e.g. hypothesized regularities) and then test it empirically (i.e. a deductive approach), subjectivist approaches lean towards inductively building theory on the basis of "lived experiences" (Collis/Hussey 2009, p. 58, Järvensivu/Törnroos 2010, p. 102). As is explicated in more detail in the next Section (4.2), this work incorporate aspects of both theory-testing and theory-building research. Given the still emerging state of research in subsidiary entrepreneurship and the rather weak theoretical foundations in the field, research methodologies are warranted that allow not only for testing existing theories but also for modifying and further developing them. Consequently, obtaining various types of data (quantitative and qualitative) and using different data collection methods is considered appropriate, as this better allows for the triangulation of data to obtain a rich picture of reality that is "as objective as possible." In particular, case study design that can incorporate different types of data and various forms of data collection methods is frequently considered a useful research approach in the realist paradigm (e.g. Perry 1998, Healy/Perry 2000, Easton 2010, see also Figure 4.2).

```
                        Methodology                    Philosophical Paradigm

                                                              ↑
         Grounded theory                              Constructivism

         In-depth interviewing and
              focus groups
  ─ ─ ─ ─ ─ ─ ─ ─ ─ ─ ─ ─ ─ ─ ─ ─ ─ ─ ─ ─ ─ ─ ─ ─ ─ ─ ─ ─ ─ ─
         Instrumental case research                  Realism

              Survey and structural
               equation modelling
  ─ ─ ─ ─ ─ ─ ─ ─ ─ ─ ─ ─ ─ ─ ─ ─ ─ ─ ─ ─ ─ ─ ─ ─ ─ ─ ─ ─ ─ ─
                   Survey and other
                multivariate techniques              Positivism
                                                              ↓
              Theory-testing research:
              emphasis on measurement
```
(Left axis: *Theory-building research: emphasis on meaning*)

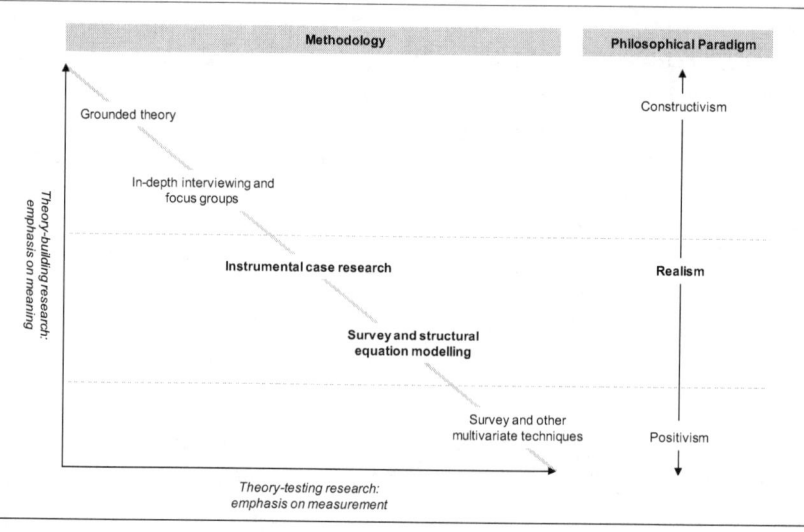

Figure 4.2: Research methodologies and related philosophical paradigms
Source: Adapted from Healy and Perry (2000, p. 121)

This research is certainly not alone in taking such a realist position towards subsidiary entrepreneurship. Various other scholars have previously argued in favor of adopting a (critical) realist perspective for this topic and have provided different arguments for doing so (see e.g. Blundel 2007, Bøllingtoft 2007, Alvarez/Barney 2010, Chiles et al. 2010, Mole/Mole 2010). First, realism is said to have "long intellectual roots in entrepreneurship research" (Blundel 2007, p. 58). For example, the works of Schumpeter (1943), Penrose (1959) and Kirzner (1973) have been linked to a realist perspective (see e.g. Alvarez/Barney 2010, Chiles et al. 2010). Second, as outlined before, critical realism stresses the importance of investigating reality as a process and specifically incorporates the effects of context. Thus, this philosophical approach is considered useful to frame the phenomenon of subsidiary entrepreneurship, which is viewed as a "context-dependent entrepreneurial process" in this dissertation.[336] More specifically, its intermediate position between the extremes of "determinism" and "voluntarism" may permit a more fine-grained understanding of the contextual conditions under which managers in foreign units exercise strategic choice when engaging in entrepreneurial activities (Whittington 1988, p. 528, Blundel 2007, p. 60). Third, a critical realist position recognizes the importance of multi-level research (e.g. at the level of the individual, the subunit and the organization; see e.g. Easton 2010, p. 121, Saunders et

---

[336] See also Subsection 3.4.2 herein for more detail on the entrepreneurial management process of subsidiary initiative-taking.

al. 2012, p. 137). As entrepreneurship in general (e.g. Low/MacMillan 1988, Davidsson/ Wiklund 2007, Hoskisson et al. 2011) and subsidiary entrepreneurship in particular are viewed as complex and multi-level phenomena, a methodology inspired by a critical realist position may be well-suited for studying these phenomena across the different levels of analysis (Blundel 2007, p. 61). Fourth, a critical realist approach lends itself well to both quantitative and qualitative methods. In particular, case study research that can accommodate different types of data (e.g. quantitative and qualitative) and various data collection procedures (e.g. interviews, archival data analysis, surveys or observations) is considered well-applicable under this paradigm (Perry 1998, p. 787, Easton 2010, p. 123). Likewise, case study designs are viewed as highly suitable for investigating the phenomenon of entrepreneurship in general and subsidiary entrepreneurial initiative in particular, as is described in more detail in the next Section on the research design and the underlying rationale.

4.2 Research Design

The research design provides a plan or structure to link the conceptual research problem and research questions to the empirical research (Ghauri/Grønhaug 2005, p. 56). It helps the researcher focus the research efforts and provides guidance throughout the process of data collection, data analysis ,and data interpretation (Yin 2009, p. 26). Important elements of a research design are, aside from the research questions and propositions, specification of the unit of analysis, the selection of sources and types of data, the methodological procedures, and the criteria for analyzing and interpreting the findings (Lee 1999, p. 58, Flick 2004, pp. 146-147, Wilson 2010, p. 105). The determination of an appropriate research design and the underlying research methodologies should, in general, be determined by the research objective and research questions, the nature of the research problem, and the theoretical framework that informs the study. Further aspects that can influence the choice of research design include the availability of data, and the presence of temporal, material or resource constraints in general (Marschan-Piekkari/Welch 2004b, p. 9, Zalan/Lewis 2004, p. 512, Wilson 2010, pp. 114, 130). Furthermore, the detailed description of the selected research design is important as it provides transparency and traceability as to why a specific research design was chosen and how the data for the study was obtained and analyzed. Making the logical chain of evidence explicit can enhance validation and reinterpretation by other researchers, in particular with qualitative research (Zalan/Lewis 2004, p. 509, Sinkovics et al. 2008, p. 709). Accordingly, the following two subsections provide insights as to why a case study design was chosen (Subsection 4.2.1) and describe in more detail the multiple case study design that is applied for the present research (Subsection 4.2.2).

4.2.1 Rationale for Case Study Design

Researchers can choose from a wide array of research designs, such as experimental, survey, case study, longitudinal or archival analysis (e.g. Yin 2009, p. 8, Wilson 2010, p. 106). Among them, case study design, which has been selected as a research method for the present thesis, is becoming increasingly prominent in the management domain in general (Eisenhardt/Graebner 2007, p. 30) and within the field of IB in particular (Welch et al. 2011, p. 740). A case study can be understood as "an empirical enquiry that investigates a contemporary phenomenon in depth and within its real-life context, especially when the boundaries between phenomenon and context are not clearly evident" (Yin 2009, p. 18). Although case study design is often associated with qualitative approaches, it does not represent a specific methodological approach, but rather reflects the selection of a particular object that is to be studied. The present study will rely primarily on qualitative data obtained through semi-structured interviews, but will also use data acquired through a survey and through archival data analysis, thereby making use of the possibility to include quantitative and qualitative data from multiple sources in the case study design (Eisenhardt 1989, p. 534, Ghauri 2004, p. 109, Wilson 2010, p. 129).

The literature review has already underlined the importance of case study design for the investigation of the subsidiary initiative phenomenon. Of the 39 publications that involved empirical work, 18 employed a case study design, often incorporating different types of data obtained through interviews, surveys and the analysis of archival or secondary data. Despite the prevalence of case study approaches in the subsidiary initiative field, the specificities of this particular research study must be taken into account when selecting an appropriate design. Overall, the use of a case study design is suggested by arguments concerning (1) the research objectives and research questions, (2) the nature of the research problem and (3) the theoretical framework.

(1) Nature of the Research Problem: Case study design is particularly useful when the area of research is relatively unknown, when the phenomenon under investigation is broad and complex and when it is a contemporary, real-life object that is difficult to study outside its natural setting (Bonoma 1985, p. 207, Lee 1999, p. 60, Ghauri 2004, pp. 109-112, Yin 2009, pp. 11-12). Moreover, case studies often represent the appropriate design when studying dynamic phenomena such as organizational processes in general or innovation and entrepreneurship processes in particular (Gummesson 2000, p. 83, Perren/Ram 2004, p. 84). As argued previously in this thesis, the subject of subsidiary initiatives remains an underexplored topic. In particular, the question of how the initiative process unfolds in different subsidiary settings has not yet been the subject of detailed empirical investigation. In particular, the qualitative data collection methods that often form the core of case study designs allow opening the "process black box" and permit in-depth investigation of context-specific initiative processes in different contextual settings (Lee 1999, p. 54, Birkinshaw et al. 2005, p. 236, Doz 2011, p. 583).

Subsidiary initiative-taking has also been identified as a complex and multi-level phenomenon that unfolds over several process phases and involves numerous actors from different levels of the organization. Thus, case study design appears well suited, as it permits research of dynamic phenomena covering a certain period of time, incorporating a variety of viewpoints, and involving numerous levels of analysis. Additional complexity arises through the cross-cultural context of the research, as the initiative process will be investigated in different foreign subsidiaries of MNCs. Here, a case study method is helpful as it gives researchers the chance to collect data and ask questions until sufficient insights and interpretations are obtained. In-depth interviews are considered an especially valuable data collection approach in case study design to understand and compare the behavior and actions of decision-makers in different cultural settings (Eisenhardt 1989, p. 534, Ghauri 2004, p. 112).

Lastly, subsidiary initiative-taking as a contemporary phenomenon must be studied in its real-life context in order to shed light on the decisions and actions of the involved actors in different subsidiary contexts. Here, the particular strength of case study research in allowing the detailed observation and investigation of the numerous process facets, of how they relate to each other and of how the process unfolds in its "total environment," best enable the researcher to study the dynamic phenomenon in its natural setting (Gummesson 2000, p. 86). Furthermore, it is not necessary for the researcher to exert control or manipulate the behavior of the actors. Therefore, the particular characteristics of the present research problem concerning subsidiary initiatives make case study design the preferred approach (see also Yin 2009, p. 11).

(2) Research Questions and Research Objectives: The use of case studies is also the recommended design when "how" or "why" questions are to be answered, when the research objective is exploratory or explanatory and when the phenomenon is to be studied in a holistic and integrative manner (Ghauri 2004, p. 112, Gerring 2007, p. 49, Yin 2009, p. 9). The present study is both explanatory and exploratory in nature. It is interested in understanding "how" the initiative process takes place in different subsidiary role settings, or more precisely "how" and "why" a particular subsidiary role influences the different phases and activities of the initiative process, and "how" and "why" this could lead to different subsidiary initiative outcomes. In addition to "how" and "why" questions, this research also intends to answer exploratory "what" questions, such as "what" are the crucial factors, other than the subsidiary role dimensions, that impact the initiative process and its outcomes. Case study design is also relevant for this study, as it allows integrating a temporal dimension into the research. As case design often involves, in addition to interviews, the review of archival and secondary material, it bears some similarities with historical review and thus permits better study of the initiative process as it unfolds over time (Ghauri 2004, p. 111). Moreover, it has been presented as one of the objectives of this particular research to approach role-specific initiative-taking in an integrative and holistic manner (see Section 1.3). While many earlier writings in this field focus only on particular aspects of the phenomenon, this study intends to include and link different aspects, such as certain antecedents, process aspects and performance outcomes. Therefore, the strength of case study research to "study an object with many dimensions and then draw the various elements together in a cohesive interpretation" is an ideal fit for the research objective (Ghauri 2004, p. 110; see also Yin 2009, p. 9). The rich possibilities for data gathering in case study design should also facilitate the development of deep knowledge about the entrepreneurial initiative process and the effects of environmental and organizational context thereon. Hence, given the particular research questions and research objectives, a case study approach seems suitable for this study.

(3) Theoretical Framework: In general, a case study approach is advised when existing theory appears inadequate and when researchers are engaged in theory-building or theory-extending types of research (Eisenhardt 1989, p. 536, Ghauri 2004, p. 109).[337] As shown in Subsection 2.2.6, the theoretical foundation of the subsidiary initiative phenomenon remains somewhat weak. Previous research has been largely inductive and has been able to make only minor theoretical progress, leaving ample room for further theory-building and theory-testing (Johnson/Medcof 2002, p. 187). Among other theoretical elements, the present study predominantly applies dynamic and process-oriented resource-based considerations for the subject of subsidiary initiatives. No previous empirical study could be found that applies and empirically tests this particular theoretical approach in the subsidiary initiative field. Several scholars specifically recommend qualitative (case study) methods when using the RBV as a theoretical perspective since resources and capabilities, the underlying development process and the relationship between resources and performance is difficult to measure quantitatively (e.g. Barney et al. 2001, pp. 636-637, Peng 2001, p. 821, Ambrosini/ Bowman 2009, p. 46, Lockett et al. 2009, p. 25). For example, Easterby-Smith et al. (2009, p. S6) argue that qualitative studies can "provide detailed descriptions of what processes are involved, the role of management, the reconfiguration of the dynamic capabilities, and the interaction with the environment." Similarly, Ambrosini and Bowman suggest that fine-grained case studies and "qualitative, smaller sample studies are ... more appropriate for understanding the subtlety of resource creation and

---

[337] Moreover, methodological issues concerning the RBV in particular, which is applied as one central theoretical pillar, suggest the use of a qualitative (case study) approach (e.g. Barney et al. 2001, pp. 636-637, Easterby-Smith et al. 2009, p. S6, Lockett et al. 2009, p. 25).

regeneration processes" (Ambrosini/Bowman 2009, pp. 37, 46). All in all, it can be concluded that both the rather weak theoretical foundation in the subsidiary initiative field and the need for further theoretical development in the RBV domain provide arguments for the application of case study design.[338]

Despite its suitability for this particular research problem, case study design also has certain limitations that should be taken into account. First, case study research is often confronted with the concern that it lacks scientific rigor. It is presumed that the limited number of publications providing guidance, as well as the less strict and less systematic procedures for how to conduct case study research, might have given rise to such concerns (Gibbert et al. 2008, p. 1465, Yin 2009, p. 14). Nevertheless, a number of publications have emerged over time that attempt to give more precise guidance on the case study approach in general (e.g. Stake 1995, Ghauri/Grønhaug 2005, Gerring 2007, Yin 2009) or in IB in particular (e.g. Marschan-Piekkari/Welch 2004a). Furthermore, different criteria for judging the quality of case study designs (i.e. validity and reliability measures) have been presented in order to better evaluate the rigor or assess the trustworthiness of case study research (see e.g. Gibbert et al. 2008, Yin 2009). Second, case study approaches are also criticized for providing little grounds for scientific generalization (Stake 1995, p. 7, Siggelkow 2007, p. 20, Yin 2009, p. 15, Welch et al. 2011, p. 742). While "statistical generalization" is typically difficult to achieve with a case study approach, it nevertheless allows for "analytical generalization," in which theoretically-based propositions are generalized rather than findings about a population (Yin 2009, pp. 15, 38). Third, case study approaches are considered time-consuming, involving a large amount of empirical evidence and leading to massive and rich data that can be overly complex and difficult to analyze. However, as the case study approach allows for the inclusion of different types of data collected by various methods, this critique does not necessarily have to apply for case study design in general (Eisenhardt 1989, p. 547, Yin 2009, p. 15). Having outlined both the reasons for using a case study design and also the potential shortcomings of this approach, the following subsection explains in more detail the multiple case study design that has been chosen for this research.

---

[338] The need for additional theoretical development in the RBV domain has been expressed by Crook et al., who state that "theory building about and empirical inquiry into the process through which strategic resources lead to high performance, how value is appropriated, and how resources interact with the environment and strategy is essential" (Crook et al. 2008, p. 1153).

4.2.2 Description of the Multiple Case Study Design

4.2.2.1 Selection of the Case Study Design

The general case study approach portrayed above can be further differentiated into more specific case study designs. Yin (2009, pp. 46-60) defines four different designs based on two distinguishing attributes: single versus multiple case study designs and holistic versus embedded case study designs. A single case study design can be viewed as single experiment and is the preferred approach when, for example, testing a well-formulated theory, when investigating extreme, unique, typical, or revelatory cases or when pursuing longitudinal investigations (Ghauri/Grønhaug 2005, p. 120, Yin 2009, pp. 47-49, Wilson 2010, p. 108). Conversely, multiple case designs are to be viewed as multiple experiments that can be used, for instance, to replicate earlier findings (i.e. literal replication) or to obtain contrasting results (theoretical replication). In multiple case study designs, the same set of questions is typically posed in different organizations or organizational units and the findings are subsequently compared to each other. As each case serves a specific purpose, a solid theoretical framework is a critical element of multiple case study designs, as it guides the selection of the cases and provides the grounds for generalizing to new cases. Evidence stemming from multiple case designs is often viewed as more convincing and more robust, yet it also may require more extensive use of resources and time (Ghauri 2004, p. 114, Ghauri/ Grønhaug 2005, p. 120, Yin 2009, pp. 53-55).

Both single and multiple case studies can involve one or more units of analysis, of which the former is referred to as holistic and the latter as an embedded case study design. In a holistic design, only one single unit, such as the global nature of an organization, is analyzed. This approach is usually applied when no logical sub-units can be derived or when the underlying theory is of a holistic nature. In contrast, embedded designs contain more than one sub-unit of analysis within one case, requiring several steps of selection from the main case(s) to the different subunits (Neergaard 2004, pp. 267-269). The present study applies an embedded and multiple case study design in order to investigate how the subsidiary initiative process takes place in distinct subsidiary role settings. The use of multiple cases allows for the analysis and comparison of the findings both within and across cases and helps improve the robustness of the results. Moreover, multiple cases provide better grounds for a broader exploration of the research questions, a more thorough comparison with the predictions and further theoretical elaboration on the subsidiary initiative phenomenon (Eisenhardt/Graebner 2007, p. 27, Piekkari et al. 2009, p. 571).

4.2.2.2 Determination of Units of Analysis and Units of Observation

A critical aspect of the case study design is the determination, specification and justification of the appropriate *units of analysis*, which broadly represents the "who" or "what" is to be studied (Zalan/Lewis 2004, p. 513, Yin 2009, p. 29). While some scholars may create the impression that it is a rather clear-cut and straightforward matter (e.g. Yin 2009), others assert that it is often an ambiguous tasks for IB researcher given the typically complex and interlinked concepts to be investigated (Fletcher/Plakoyiannaki 2011, p. 174). However, in order to help them identify and select the appropriate unit of analysis, researchers may, for example, turn to their main research questions and propositions (Yin 2009, p. 29, Fletcher/Plakoyiannaki 2011, p. 173). In view of the main research questions posed in this thesis, and in line with previous research in the field (e.g. Birkinshaw 1997, Birkinshaw/Ridderstråle 1999), this research project defines the subsidiary and its initiative-taking process as the main unit of analysis. As outlined, the central interest of this project is to investigate how initiative-taking and its outcomes are impacted by the different roles that foreign subsidiary units hold. More specifically, the focus is on how the two sub-processes concerned with (a) entrepreneurial resource management and with (b) headquarters-subsidiary alignment unfold in different subsidiary role settings. As to the *units of observation* – representing the entities from which the researcher collects data – this thesis will obtain information from both managers at foreign subsidiary units and from executives located at their respective headquarters. As described above, the phenomenon of subsidiary initiative-taking relates not only to the entrepreneurial activities of managers in the units abroad, but typically also involves the actions and decisions of managers at the corporate center. Thus, in order to investigate subsidiary initiative-taking more comprehensively as it unfolds in the wider MNC, relevant managers from organizational levels are included in the study.[339]

4.2.2.3 Case Selection

Another critical aspect in case study research concerns the selection of appropriate cases for the investigation. Of the "total population," or all the entities that can potentially be accessed (such as firms, individuals, groups or elements), the ones represented in the study must be selected (Ghauri 2004, p. 112). The proper selection of cases is important as it helps to, for example, control for irrelevant variation and to define the limits for the generalization of the findings (Eisenhardt 1989, p. 536). The selection process and criteria should be consistent with the research problem and may, for instance, be guided by the main research questions, the theoretical framework, and

---

[339] Previous literature has emphasized the difficulty of accurately determining the role of foreign subsidiaries as both headquarters and managers abroad may have different perceptions of this aspect (see e.g. Birkinshaw et al. 2000, Daniel 2010, Schmid/Daniel 2010). Hence it is considered important to assess the relevant subsidiary role dimensions (e.g. level of subsidiary resources and capabilities) from both perspectives.

the variables under study. In addition, further aspects should also be taken into consideration, such as time restrictions, financial resources, or other practical issues (Ghauri 2004, p. 113, Ghauri/Grønhaug 2005, p. 118). Concerning the number of cases in comparative case study design, no clear lower or upper limit can be defined. While in certain research settings one case can be sufficient (e.g. in-depth analysis of one specific phenomenon within one MNC), in other instances multiple cases might be more appropriate, for example, to replicate or contrast different findings (Ghauri 2004, p. 114).

As specified earlier, the present thesis intends to investigate entrepreneurial initiatives within distinct contextual settings of foreign subsidiary units of MNCs. More specifically, the proposed framework of this study suggests that key elements of entrepreneurial initiative-taking (i.e. the entrepreneurial resource management and headquarters-subsidiary alignment) and the resulting outcomes will be contingent upon particular role settings of the foreign subsidiaries. Given the already well-defined nature of the research setting, a purposeful multi-level sampling strategy involving predefined criteria (rather than a random sampling strategy) is deemed appropriate (see e.g. Fletcher/ Playkoyiannaki 2001, p. 181, Patton 2002, p. 230). More precisely, criteria were set for the selection of suitable (1) industries, (2) multinational firms and (3) foreign subsidiary units.

(1) It is evident that not all industries are equally suitable for this particular research. Since the differentiation of subsidiary roles is primarily expected to occur in network MNCs, transnational industries are of specific interest for this research (Kutschker/ Schmid 2011, p. 298). MNCs operating in transnational environments are typically faced with strong forces of both global integration and localization. As a result of these contingencies, multinational companies must attain global efficiency, local adaptation and worldwide learning more or less simultaneously. In order to achieve this, transnational firms are expected to adopt an integrated network configuration, differentiate subsidiary roles and responsibilities and simultaneously manage the multiple innovation processes that take place across the geographically dispersed units (Bartlett/Ghoshal 2002, p. 74).[340] Typical transnational industries that display the need for both globalization and localization and which are deemed more suitable for the present research are, for instance, drugs and pharmaceuticals, IT and telecommunications, photographic equipment, automotive industry, and postal services (see Figure 4.3).

---

[340] It should be noted, however, that in reality the ideal type of a network MNC is not likely to be found (Schmid et al. 2002, pp. 65-68, Kutschker/Schmid 2011, p. 546).

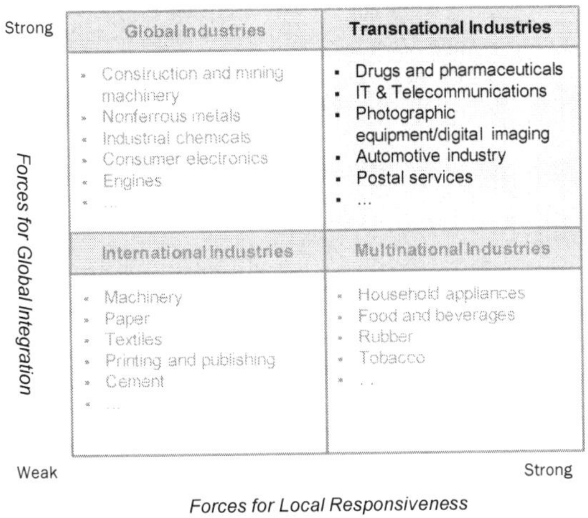

	Global Industries	Transnational Industries
Strong ↑ Forces for Global Integration	• Construction and mining machinery • Nonferrous metals • Industrial chemicals • Consumer electronics • Engines • ...	• Drugs and pharmaceuticals • IT & Telecommunications • Photographic equipment/digital imaging • Automotive industry • Postal services • ...
	International Industries	Multinational Industries
Weak	• Machinery • Paper • Textiles • Printing and publishing • Cement • ...	• Household appliances • Food and beverages • Rubber • Tobacco • ...

Weak ←―――― Forces for Local Responsiveness ――――→ Strong

Figure 4.3: The environment of MNCs
Sources: Adapted from Ghoshal and Nohria (1993, p. 27) and Kutschker and Schmid (2011, p. 301)

(2) Moreover, not all MNCs operating in transnational industries are equally appropriate. Preference is given to (a) internationally operating firms of medium to large size that (b) conduct "significant" business outside their home market, ideally in many different countries.[341] Here, it is expected that these companies could provide a wider range of subsidiary units (with potentially many different roles) for investigation. Based on preliminary guidance from previous works investigating subsidiary initiatives (e.g. Ambos et al. 2010, Ambos/Birkinshaw 2010), only MNCs with total annual revenues of more than 2 billion Euros were considered. With regard to "significant business" outside the home market, it was determined that the share of foreign sales out of total sales should be equal to or greater than thirty percent. (c) Moreover, given the objective of this research, to study subsidiary initiative-taking in different contextual settings (i.e. different subsidiary roles), it was further determined that a suitable MNC had to possess eight or more foreign subsidiary units. This is to allow for sufficient variety and role differentiation within the MNC. (d) Finally, in order to facilitate personal contact and access to the corporate center, only companies with global headquarters located in

---

[341] Various quantitative and qualitative measures can come into play to differentiate between an international and national corporation. For example, the number of foreign offices or subsidiaries, as well as revenues or costs abroad, can be applied to measure the internationalization of firms (for a more extensive overview see also Kutschker/Schmid 2011, pp. 259-339). In order to limit the effort expended on analysis and selection for the present thesis, it was decided to focus primarily on the following two quantitative measures which are often relatively easy to obtain: (1) foreign sales out of total sales and (2) number of foreign sites.

Germany, Austria, Switzerland, France and the Benelux countries were considered for this research.

Suitable MNCs from the automotive, IT & telecommunications and postal and logistics industry were contacted via postal mail and/or electronic mail. This correspondence included a cover letter and a brief study overview, which were sent to relevant headquarters managers at the selected companies.[342] Five firms signaled their initial interest. With those organizations, telephone calls were arranged to introduce the researcher, present the research project, and to determine further interest in participating in the empirical study. In the end, two companies decided to take part in the study, one from the automotive industry (referred to as Company A) and one from the IT & telecommunications industry (referred to as Company B). Personal meetings with these two firms at group headquarters were set up to explain the research project and details as to the involvement and effort firm required from the firm. Given the large size of both companies and the diverse fields of their activity, it was decided in the personal meetings to focus on only one particular division or strategic business unit in each of the MNCs. The selected division of Company A will be referred to as "Autocomp," while the division of Company B will be referred to as "Telecomp." A preliminary overview of both divisions is given in Table 4.3.[343] In the following, personal meetings with divisional managers were held at divisional headquarters[344] to discuss the overall research approach and to jointly select potential subsidiary units for the present research.[345] Moreover, the divisional managers functioned as "sponsors" who not only endorsed the research within their firms, but also facilitated access to subsidiary managers and ensured cooperation in the wider MNCs.

	Autocomp	Telecomp
Industry	Automotive	IT & telecommunications
Annual revenue	> 5 billion EUR	> 10 billion EUR
Share of foreign sales	> 70%	> 90%
Employees	> 25,000	> 30,000
Foreign subsidiaries	> 20 countries	> 15 countries

Table 4.3: Overview of Autocomp and Telecomp cases

---

[342] Appropriate contact persons were identified in advance through, for example, the investigation of company reports and websites, telephone inquiries at the MNCs and online social and business networks such as such as xing.de or linkedin.com. Typical addressees were, for instance, CEOs, divisional managers, global innovation managers or global heads of research and development. In total, more than 50 invitation letters were sent out between May and September 2012.

[343] The information provided refers to 2013. Further information on Companies A and B and their different divisions is provided in Sections 5.1 and 5.2 herein.

[344] Hereafter, these two divisional headquarters, rather than the group headquarters, will be defined as "headquarters level" for the study, since they directly manage and interact with the single subsidiaries of their division.

[345] When choosing an appropriate division, the same selection criteria that were used for the selection of MNCs came into play (e.g. significant business outside the home market, number of foreign subsidiaries).

(3) In order to select appropriate subsidiary units, further selection criteria came into play. (a) First, a unit had to be a national or foreign subsidiary fully owned by the parent companies. A foreign subsidiary was understood as "any operational unit controlled by the MNC and situated outside the home country" (Birkinshaw 1997, p. 207). More specifically, fully owned subsidiary units were defined as local affiliates whose parent companies held more than 50% of their ownership (Bouquet/Birkinshaw 2008, p. 585). This was to ensure that further complexities due to shared ownership were avoided. (b) Second, the present research intends to investigate initiative-taking over a period of five years. Consequently, only subsidiary units were considered that were at least five years old, so that the periods of investigation among the foreign units were comparable and the unfolding initiative processes could be studied in their entirety.[346] (c) Third, foreign subsidiaries had to perform both manufacturing/service delivery and R&D/engineering activities locally. This criterion was set in order to exclude, for example, foreign units with a very narrow set of value functions, such as sales-only subsidiaries or mere R&D centers. As previous research has shown, subsidiaries with a limited range of value chain activities might not have the necessary size or latitude necessary for initiatives (see e.g. Birkinshaw 1999, p. 19). (d) Fourth, it had to be ensured that, ideally, all relevant role types that were previously determined in Subsection 3.2.1.4 were covered in this research. (e) Moreover, the subsidiary role assessments by both headquarters and subsidiary managers had to largely match, and cases with significant deviations between headquarters and subsidiary perspectives were excluded.[347] (f) Lastly, it was required that subsidiaries had engaged in some initiative-taking activities during the past five years. As this research is interested in investigating how the initiative process unfolds in distinct contextual subsidiary settings, it was deemed necessary that foreign units at least showed some attempts at entrepreneurial initiatives regardless of their success. Other aspects such as subsidiary size[348] or mode of subsidiary formation were not considered to be relevant selection criteria but were included as control measures.[349] Figure 4.4 provides an overview of the previously outlined selection criteria that were applied for this study.

---

[346] Typically, subsidiary initiatives will develop and unfold over a certain amount of time rather than emerging "out of thin air." Consequently, previous research usually analyzes subsidiary initiatives over a period between three and ten years. For this reason, the present work uses a five-year time span for the investigation, as is further described in Subsection 4.3.3.1 herein.
[347] The notion "largely match" did not imply that both assessments on role positions in the subsidiary role grids had to be entirely identical. Instead, it was only required that the role types matched, that is, subsidiary and headquarters managers chose the same role type for one particular unit (e.g. both chose "Strategic Leader") but not necessarily selected the exact same position in the respective role quadrant.
[348] Previous research on subsidiary initiatives has taken place in subsidiaries of various sizes in terms of the subsidiary revenue or the number of subsidiary employees. For example, research by Birkinshaw and colleagues used samples of subsidiaries with annual revenues between $65 million and $1.5 billion (Birkinshaw/Hood 1997) or between $2 million and $6.0 billion (Bouquet/Birkinshaw 2008).
[349] It would also have been preferred to select only subsidiary units from similar cultural backgrounds to eliminate a further potential source of variation (see e.g. Bouquet/Birkinshaw 2008). However, given the vast geographical

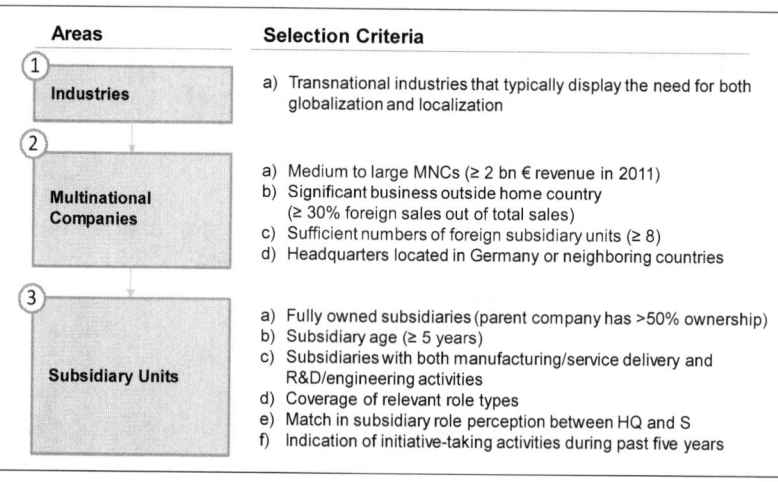

Areas	Selection Criteria
① Industries	a) Transnational industries that typically display the need for both globalization and localization
② Multinational Companies	a) Medium to large MNCs (≥ 2 bn € revenue in 2011) b) Significant business outside home country (≥ 30% foreign sales out of total sales) c) Sufficient numbers of foreign subsidiary units (≥ 8) d) Headquarters located in Germany or neighboring countries
③ Subsidiary Units	a) Fully owned subsidiaries (parent company has >50% ownership) b) Subsidiary age (≥ 5 years) c) Subsidiaries with both manufacturing/service delivery and R&D/engineering activities d) Coverage of relevant role types e) Match in subsidiary role perception between HQ and S f) Indication of initiative-taking activities during past five years

Figure 4.4: Overview of applied selection criteria

Based on the first four selection criteria for subsidiary units, 14 sites from Autocomp and 12 affiliates from Telecomp were initially identified as potential subsidiaries for the present research. The identification took place together with the two headquarters managers during the personal visits at the beginning of the empirical research. During these two meetings, the managers were also asked to determine the subsidiary role positions based on their perceptions for both applicable role typologies using a short questionnaire. Similarly, the perceptions of subsidiary managers were collected afterwards through a questionnaire. For this purpose, all 26 subsidiary units were invited to participate in surveys, mostly online but sometimes paper-based, investigating, among other aspects, the role position and previous initiative-taking activities of these units.[350] The headquarters and subsidiary evaluations of subsidiary role positions were then compared and units with large deviations in role perception and/or no evidence of initiative-taking activities during the past five years were excluded.[351] In the end, seven subsidiaries from Autocomp and seven units from Telecomp were finally included in the analysis. These are further described in Table 4.4 below.

---

distribution within the two firms and the overall limited number of subsidiaries available in each firm, it was decided not to apply this criterion.
[350] Detailed information on the approach and content of this survey is provided in Subsection 4.4.1 herein.
[351] Of the 26 foreign units that were invited to participate in the study, five did not respond. The subsequent comparison of headquarters and subsidiary role assessments of the remaining 21 units revealed significant deviations for two Autocomp and five Telecomp subsidiaries. This led to the elimination of another seven foreign units in both cases, resulting in 14 foreign sites for final investigation.

№	Unit	Role Types[352]	Host Country	Date and Mode of Formation	Employees	Questionnaires	Interviews
Autocomp Subsidiaries							
1	Alpha	SL/AcS	Germany	1960s; Greenfield	2,500	1	1
2	Beta	SL/AcS	Mexico	2000s; Acquisition	3,000	1	1
3	Gamma	C/RS	South Korea	2000s; Acquisition	2,300	1	1
4	Delta	C/RS	Australia	1950s; Greenfield	350	2	1
5	Epsilon	BH/AuS	China	2000s; Acquisition	3,000	1	1
6	Zeta	I/QS	Romania	2000s; Greenfield	2,600	2	1
7	Eta	I/QS	India	2000s; Acquisition	1,700	1	1
Telecomp Subsidiaries							
8	Theta	SL/AcS	Hungary	1990s; Acquisition	10,000	1	1
9	Iota	SL/AcS	Poland	2000s; Acquisition	5,000	1	1
10	Kappa	SL/AcS	Croatia	2000s; Acquisition	5,000	1	1
11	Lambda	C/RS	Slovak Republic	1990s; Acquisition	4,000	1	1
12	Mu	BH/AuS	Greece	2000s; Acquisition	10,000	2	1
13	Sigma	I/QS	Romania	1990s, Acquisition	8,000	1	1
14	Omega	I/QS	Montenegro	1990s; Acquisition	1,000	1	1

Table 4.4: Sample of subsidiaries included in research

4.2.2.4 Types of Data

Among the strengths of case study research is the possibility to incorporate different types of data and use diverse data collection procedures (Creswell 2003, p. 15, Eisenhardt/Graebner 2007, p. 28, Piekkari et al. 2009, p. 572). For example, Birkinshaw presents different case study designs for research in international business that incorporate both qualitative and quantitative data obtained through interviews, questionnaires, and the analysis of archival data (Birkinshaw 2004, pp. 572-579). Yin also advises case study researchers to use multiple sources of evidence, as this allows for the triangulation of data and thus can lead to findings that are "more convincing and accurate" in the end (Yin 2009, p. 116). Thus, following these suggestions and in line with other case study designs repeatedly applied in the subsidiary initiative field (e.g. Birkinshaw 1997, Birkinshaw/Hood 1997, Birkinshaw 1999, Birkinshaw/Ridderstråle 1999), the data collection procedure in the present research consists of three methods: (1) administration of a questionnaire, (2) use of semi-structured interviews and (3) gathering of additional archival and secondary data. While these data collection approaches and their interplay will be explained in more detail in Section 4.4, the following Section 4.3 first addresses the operationalization of the theoretical framework.

---

[352] SL = Strategic Leader, C= Contributor, BH = Black Hole, I = Implementer; AcS = Active Subsidiary, RS = Receptive Subsidiary, AuS = Autonomous Subsidiary, QS = Quiescent Subsidiary

4.3 Operationalization of the Research Framework

In order to empirically test and further explore the proposed research framework, the various elements must be operationalized. Eisenhardt argues that in case study design the "a priori specification of constructs ... is valuable because it permits researchers to measure constructs more accurately," thereby giving them "firmer empirical grounding for the emergent theory" (Eisenhardt 1989, p. 536). As previously outlined in detail, the research framework consists of three major elements as shown again in Figure 4.5: (1) the subsidiary role context, (2) the subsidiary initiative-taking process and (3) the subsidiary initiative outcome.

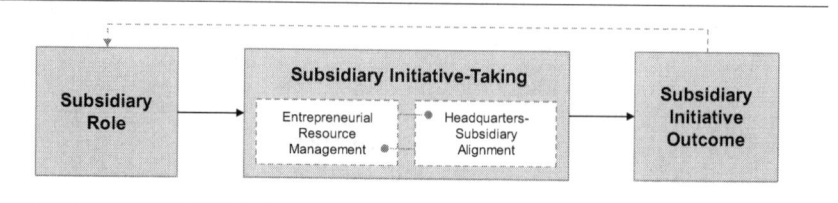

Figure 4.5: Proposed research framework

The following subsections address the operationalization and measurement of these three elements. Subsection 4.3.1 outlines the operationalization of the subsidiary role context. More specifically, the four role dimensions of the two selected role typologies are addressed. Subsection 4.3.2 then focuses on the operationalization of the initiative process and the sub-processes related to entrepreneurial resource management and to headquarters-subsidiary alignment. Finally, in Subsection 4.3.3 the relevant aspects of subsidiary initiative outcome are operationalized. For all subsequent constructs, the study attempts to draw from existing operationalization approaches and measurement scales when possible. In the end, the operationalization will be used both for data collection and for data analysis. For instance, it will be employed for the development of the questionnaire and also serve as a basis for structuring and formulating interview questions. Moreover, it will aid in the development of an initial categorization scheme that comes into play for the analysis of data.

4.3.1 Subsidiary Role Dimensions

4.3.1.1 Strategic Importance of the Subsidiary Environment

In order to operationalize the subsidiary role dimension "strategic importance of the subsidiary environment," one can turn to Bartlett and Ghoshal's relevant contributions, which present and characterize the different subsidiary types of their role typology (e.g. Bartlett/Ghoshal 1986, 2002). In these publications, the authors argue that the strategic importance of a specific subsidiary environment is strongly influenced by its significance for the MNC's global strategy. Accordingly, they state that "a large market is obviously important, and so is a competitor's home market or a market that is particularly sophisticated or technologically advanced" (Bartlett/Ghoshal 1986, p. 90, 2002, p. 121). As the role typology is conceptually rather than empirically determined (Schmid et al. 1998, p. 33), a more precise operationalization cannot be identified in these publications. Nevertheless, it becomes apparent that the strategic importance of the subsidiary environment is generally based on four different indicators: subsidiary market size, competitive intensity, sophistication of customer demand and technological dynamism. In addition to these two publications, one can also draw further conclusions from empirical studies by Ghoshal and Nohria that present a more precise description of operationalization and measurement. The authors use two equally-weighted variables, the level of local competition and technological dynamism, in order to assess the subsidiary role dimension, which is termed slightly different as "environmental complexity" (see Ghoshal/Nohria 1986, 1989, Nohria/Ghoshal 1994). In the studies, respondents at headquarters and at subsidiaries are asked to rate the intensity of competition and the rate of product and process innovations in the subsidiary's market on a five-point scale. Furthermore, Bouquet and Birkinshaw also measure the strategic significance of a local market through two indicators: the size of the local subsidiary market and the presence of MNCs in the local market. However, instead of asking respondents to evaluate these aspects, both indicators are computed based on data from different databases (Bouquet/Birkinshaw 2008, p. 587).[353]

Drawing from these publications, the strategic importance of the subsidiary's market environment is measured in the present study through the four following, equally-weighted indicators: (1) subsidiary market size, (2) competitive intensity in the subsidiary market, (3) technological dynamism, and (4) customer demand intensity. These indicators are assessed by both headquarters and subsidiary managers on a five-point scale ranging from "very small" to "very high."[354] Moreover, as subsidiaries can take on responsibilities that go beyond their national borders, the market characteristics are assessed not only for the local country market but for the entire market environment for

---

[353] The first indicator, "size of the local subsidiary market," is calculated as the proportion of worldwide industry sales realized in a given subsidiary's host country, based on data from the "Compustat Global Vantage" database. The second indicator, "presence of MNCs in the local market," is computed as the ratio of foreign direct investment (FDI) inflows to FDI outflows over ten years based on data from the United Nations 2005 World Investment Report.

[354] The present study will use five-point scales for a number of reasons. First, they are said to be the "preferred scales" and they are among the most widely used in field research. Second, five-point scales can be expected to produce similar or even the same results as seven-point scales without "burdening" the respondents with overly differentiated scales. Third, as the same operationalization and measurement will be used for both the survey and the semi-structured interviews, a five-point scale is deemed more practical, as it should require less extensive judging efforts by respondents (Bortz/Döring 2006, pp. 180-181, Dawes 2008, p. 75).

which the units are responsible. The final operationalization of the role dimension "strategic importance of the subsidiary's market environment" is shown in Table 4.5.[355]

Indicator	Operationalization	Scale	Supporting Literature[356]
Strategic importance of subsidiary environment	Assessment of the following subsidiary market characteristics: • Market size • Competitive intensity • Technological dynamism • Customer demand intensity	Five-point Likert scale	C: Bartlett/Ghoshal 1986, 2002 E: Ghoshal/Nohria 1986, 1989, Nohria/Ghoshal 1994

Table 4.5: Measurement of the strategic importance of the subsidiary's market environment

4.3.1.2 Subsidiary Resources and Capabilities

Bartlett and Ghoshal use "competence of the local organization" as the second dimension to distinguish between different subsidiary role types. They define this as an "organizational competence of a particular subsidiary ... in technology, production, marketing, or any other area" (Bartlett/Ghoshal 1986, p. 90) and thus further differentiate subsidiary competencies by functional areas (see also Amit/Schoemaker 1993, p. 35). Although the authors do not specify how they operationalize the level of competence of the local organization in this particular publication, other contributions by Ghoshal and Nohria (Ghoshal/Nohria 1986, Nohria/Ghoshal 1994) provide insights into the measurement of this dimension. In line with Bartlett and Ghoshal's definition, a number of other empirical studies also assess the level of subsidiary competence for different functional areas (e.g. Roth/Morrison 1992, Holm/Pedersen 2000, Moore 2001, Benito et al. 2003, Tseng et al. 2004). The number of functional areas (or items) that are included in the operationalization of this dimension varies from four (Schmid/Schurig 2003) to eight (Roth/Morrison 1992). With regard to the scale, the studies predominantly apply a seven-point Likert-type scale, measuring subsidiary resources and capabilities from, for example, "far below average" to "far above average" (Roth/Morrison 1992, p. 725, Birkinshaw 1999, p. 34), "weak" to "very strong" (Benito et al. 2003, p. 450) or simply from "low" to "high" (Nohria/Ghoshal 1994, p. 500).

It is to be noted that the studies do not use a consistent wording or terminology when it comes to subsidiary resources and capabilities, but rather refer to the dimension as subsidiary "resources", "abilities", "capabilities" or "competencies". Bartlett and Ghoshal themselves apply different terms in their various publications, referring to them as, for

---
[355] As a subsidiary's situation may change over time, the operationalization can be used to assess not only the current situation of the subsidiary but also situations in the past or the future. For instance, Jarillo and Martinez ask respondents to assess the subsidiary situation both five years ago and the predicted situation three years in the future (see Jarillo/Martinez 1990, p. 504).

[356] "C" refers to supporting literature that is purely conceptual, while "E" represents literature that is of empirical nature.

example, subsidiary capabilities (Bartlett/Ghoshal 2002, p. 72), subsidiary competencies (e.g. Bartlett/Ghoshal 1986, p. 90, 2002, p. 121) or subsidiary resources (e.g. Ghoshal/ Bartlett 1988, p. 381, Nohria/Ghoshal 1994, p. 500, Bartlett/Ghoshal 2002, p. 152). The alternative use of the different terminology is not uncommon in business literature and is, at least in part, the result of the numerous definitions that have been brought forward for resources, capabilities and competencies (Schmid/Schurig 2003, p. 757). Despite the different terms used by Bartlett and Ghoshal, their operationalization of the role dimension shows that the authors primarily focus on subsidiary capabilities and include subsidiary resources only to a lesser degree (see e.g. Ghoshal/Nohria 1986, Nohria/ Ghoshal 1994). Therefore, the present study will view the dimension as a broader concept that encompasses both subsidiary resources and capabilities, but will focus primarily on capabilities.

Following the operationalization approaches of the outlined studies (in particular those of Birkinshaw 1999, Holm/Pedersen 2000 and Moore 2001), this study assesses this subsidiary role dimension by determining the level of subsidiary resources and capabilities relative to those of other subsidiary units for the following eight different functional areas: (1) research and/or development, (2) production of goods and/or services, (3) marketing and/or sales, (4) logistics and/or distribution, (5) purchasing, (6) HR management, (7) general management and (8) innovation and/or entrepreneurship. For reasons of consistency with regard to the measurement of the other elements in the research framework, this study uses a five-point scale from "not capable" to "highly capable." The overall level of resources and capabilities that a subsidiary possesses is represented by the mean average value of all eight functional resource and capability level assessments. The final operationalization of the role dimension "subsidiary resources and capabilities" is shown in Table 4.6.

Indicator	Operationalization	Scale	Supporting Literature
Subsidiary resources and capabilities	Level of subsidiary resources and capabilities for the following functions: • Research and/or development • Production of goods/services • Marketing and/or sales • Logistics and/or distribution • Purchasing • HR management • General management • Innovation and/or entrepreneurship	Five-point Likert scale	E: Ghoshal/Nohria 1986, 1989, Nohria/Ghoshal 1994, Birkinshaw 1999, Holm/Pedersen 2000, Schmid/Schurig 2003

Table 4.6: Measurement of subsidiary resources and capabilities

4.3.1.3 Subsidiary's Localization and Local Responsiveness

Jarillo and Martinez, as well as Taggart, use the "degree of localization" (Jarillo/Martinez 1990) and the "degree of local responsiveness" respectively (Taggart 1997) as one differentiating dimension of their role typologies. According to Jarillo and Martinez, the degree of localization expresses to what extent different value chain activities, such as manufacturing, purchasing, marketing or R&D, are performed at a subsidiary location. Following a principal-component factor analysis, the role dimension is operationalized through three variables: (1) percentage of input that comes from the group, (2) percentage of locally produced goods as part of total sales and (3) local content in locally produced goods (Jarillo/Martinez 1990, p. 504).

Although Taggart attempts to "carry out an evaluation and extension of the derived model of Jarillo and Martinez" (Taggart 1997, p. 296), the author nevertheless uses different measures and scales for the operationalization and assessment of this role dimension (see also Schmid et al. 1998, pp. 56-57). Instead of three, the author uses five variables and applies a seven-point rather than five-point scale for evaluation. Taking a closer look at the five variables, it can also be seen that Taggart takes a different perspective. Whereas Jarillo and Martinez variables can be primarily understood as a reflection of the extent of locally performed value chain activities (e.g. local input and local content in locally sold products and services), Taggart's operationalization focuses on the "driving forces" or preconditions (i.e. pressures arising from customers, competitors or technological developments) that necessitate a subsidiary's response to the particular local needs. Similar to the view and operationalization of Taggart, a number of other scholars also use variables that reflect the subsidiary's response to specific local needs and/or that assess the underlying driving forces (e.g. Harzing 2000, Luo 2001, Tseng et al. 2004). Accordingly, these authors view local responsiveness as the extent to which subsidiaries respond to different customer preferences, distribution constraints, business cultures, or governmental regulations, which is driven by the complexity and dynamism of market conditions and by the sociopolitical and macroeconomic environments (Harzing 2000, p. 108, Luo 2001, p. 453). Furthermore, Tseng et al. underline the important linkage between local responsiveness and the subsidiary's local embeddedness and thus incorporate two additional variables reflecting the subsidiary's interaction with local actors (Tseng et al. 2004, p. 103).[357]

Based on these conceptualizations of localization and local responsiveness, the present study uses three different indicators for the operationalization of the role dimension termed "subsidiary's localization and local responsiveness," as shown in Table 4.7: (1) the extent of value-adding activities performed locally, (2) the pressure for local adapta-

---

[357] In line with Tseng et al.'s view, Manolopoulos argues that the degree of localization or local responsiveness comprises a proxy for a subsidiary's embeddedness in the local environment (Manolopoulos 2008, p. 36).

tion of goods and services and (3) local engagement. The first indicator related to the local value-adding activities is directly adopted from Jarillo and Martinez (1990) and consists of three variables reflecting the extent to which value chain activities are performed at the subsidiary location. The second indicator is primarily concerned with the local adaptation of goods and services and is based on the five variables applied by Taggart (1997).[358] For the third indicator, one additional variable is drawn from the operationalization of Tseng et al. (2004) in order to incorporate the aspect of local subsidiary engagement and interaction with local actors.[359] The resulting nine variables are measured on a five-point scale ranging from "very low" to "very high." The overall degree of the subsidiary's localization and local responsiveness is represented by the mean average value of all nine variables.[360]

Indicator	Operationalization[361]	Scale	Supporting Literature
Extent of value adding activities performed locally	• Extent of inputs the subsidiary receives from other units of the company (i) • Share of sales (from total sales) that come from goods or services created at the subsidiary location • Extent of local content in locally produced goods or services	Five-point Likert scale	E: Jarillo/Martinez 1990, Martinez/ Jarillo 1991
Local adaptation of goods and services	• Extent to which subsidiary's customers and their needs differ from those of other units of the company • Extent to which competitors and their strategies are easily identified (i) • Stability of technology and level of manufacturing/service delivery sophistication (i) • Maturity of life cycle stage of product/service line(s) and manufacturing processes (i) • Heterogeneity of subsidiary executive group	Five-point Likert scale	E: Taggart 1997
Extent of local engagement	• Extent to which subsidiary interacts with local actors	Five-point Likert scale	E: Tseng et al. 2004

Table 4.7: Measurement of the subsidiary's localization and local responsiveness

---

[358] In comparison to the wording presented by Taggart (1997, p. 303-305), some slight adaptations have been made to the questions to ease understanding for respondents.
[359] The two variables "extent to which subsidiary interacts with local firms" and "extent to which subsidiary interacts with host governments, research and other institutions" were joined into a single variable.
[360] As the operationalization includes all variables applied by both Jarillo and Martinez (1990) and Taggart (1997), the findings from the present study can be attributed to both role typologies accordingly.
[361] Unfortunately, not all variables are formulated by the original authors in a unidirectional manner (i.e. a "very low" evaluation represents a "very low" degree of localization/local responsiveness). Consequently, the value of the scales is reversed for the following four variables indicated by "(i)" in Table 4.7: (1) extent of inputs the subsidiary receives from other units of the company, (2) extent to which your competitors and their strategies are easily identified, (3) stability of technology and level of manufacturing/service delivery sophistication and (4) maturity of life cycle stage of product/service line(s) and manufacturing processes. In these four cases, a "very low" evaluation would indicate a "very high" degree of localization/local responsiveness. This is also substantiated in the contributions of the authors. For example, concerning the identification of competitors and their strategies, Taggart states that "pressures for responsiveness will be low when competitors are few in number and easily identified" (see Jarillo/Martinez 1990, pp. 504-505 and Taggart 1997, p. 303 for all variables).This is also taken into account for the development and the analysis of the survey.

4.3.1.4 Subsidiary Integration and Subsidiary Autonomy

The degree of "subsidiary integration" used by Jarillo and Martinez (1990) and Taggart (1997) as a second dimension of their role typologies broadly expresses the extent to which the value-adding activities performed by the subsidiary are integrated and coordinated with the same activities in other parts of the MNC. Jarillo and Martinez originally operationalize and measure the degree of subsidiary integration through six variables on a seven-point scale. These variables mostly assess the integration of different value chain functions (i.e. purchasing, manufacturing, R&D and marketing), but they also evaluate the adaptation of products to the local market and the proportion of local R&D out of the total R&D incorporated in the goods sold by the subsidiary (Jarillo/Martinez 1990, pp. 503-504).[362] Although intending to test and extend Jarillo and Martinez's typology, Taggart again uses different measures and scales for the operationalization and assessment of the second role dimension. In contrast to Jarillo and Martinez, who are mostly concerned with the integration of value-adding activities, he uses six variables that refer to different facets, such as the (de)centralization of different decisions and activities, the geographical servicing area of the subsidiary and the subsidiary dependence on other MNC units (Taggart 1997, p. 305).[363]

Following primarily the existing conceptualizations by Jarillo and Martinez and Taggart, the present study uses a total of 12 different variables for the operationalization of the role dimension "subsidiary integration." These 12 variables can be further grouped into four indicators: (1) subsidiary's integration and dependence, (2) local R&D and adaptation of products and/or services, (3) centralization of decisions and (4) subsidiary's scope of operations. The 12 variables are measured on a five-point scale ranging from "very low" to "very high."[364] The overall degree of the subsidiary's integration is represented by the mean average value of all 12 variables. The final operationalization of the role dimension as used in the questionnaire is shown in Table 4.8.[365]

---

[362] As indicated previously, the six variables are the results of a principal-components factor analysis (see Jarillo/Martinez 1990, p. 504).
[363] Additional insight into the operationalization of this subsidiary role dimension can be obtained from subsequent publications on the topic of subsidiary initiatives (e.g. Tseng et al. 2004, Borini et al. 2009b). For instance, Tseng et al. (2004, p. 103) use five variables for operationalization that are closely related to those proposed by Jarillo and Martinez and are concerned with the level of integration and coordination of different value chain activities.
[364] Similar to the previous role dimension, not all variables are formulated by the original authors in a unidirectional manner (i.e. a "very low" evaluation representing a "very low" degree of subsidiary integration). Consequently, the values of the scales for the following two variables are reversed: (1) adaptation of products to the local market and (2) proportion of local R&D as part of total R&D (see also Taggart 1997, p. 303).
[365] As the operationalization includes all variables applied by both Jarillo and Martinez (1990) and Taggart (1997), the findings from the present study can be subsequently attributed to both role typologies accordingly.

Indicator	Operationalization	Scale	Supporting Literature

Subsidiary's integration and dependence	• Extent to which the following activities are integrated with the rest of the group:
	  - Purchasing
	  - Manufacturing/service delivery
	  - Research and/or development
	  - Marketing
	• Dependence of subsidiary on linkages within the internal network
		Five-point Likert scale	E: Jarillo/Martinez 1990, Martinez/Jarillo 1991, Taggart 1997

Local R&D and adaptation	• Adaptation of products/services to the local market (i) • Proportion of local R&D out of total R&D (i) • Product and quality specifications developed by HQ (versus development by subsidiary)	Five-point Likert scale	E: Jarillo/Martinez 1990, Martinez/Jarillo 1991, Taggart 1997
Centralization of decisions	• Centralization of production planning, inventory and quality control • Centralization and sharing of technology development within the internal network	Five-point Likert scale	E: Taggart 1997
Subsidiary's scope of operations	• Extent to which subsidiary serves its MNC customers worldwide • Manufacturing/service delivery decisions linked to world-wide market areas (versus local market areas)	Five-point Likert scale	E: Taggart 1997

Table 4.8: Measurement of subsidiary integration

The operationalization of subsidiary integration presented above contains certain elements relating to the centralization of decision-making in the MNC or conversely to the decision-making autonomy of subsidiary units.[366] This is not surprising, as subsidiary autonomy has often been explicitly or implicitly linked to different subsidiary roles (Paterson/Brock 2002, p. 144). As shown in previous writings, higher levels of subsidiary autonomy are usually associated with subsidiaries that hold more advanced roles in the MNC, such as "Strategic Leaders," "Active Subsidiaries" or "World Product Mandates" (see e.g. Nohria/Ghoshal 1994, p. 493, Birkinshaw/Morrison 1995, p. 742, Young/Tavares 2004, p. 221, Manolopoulos 2008, p. 37). Similarly, a number of earlier studies provide empirical support for the positive link between a subsidiary's autonomy and its ability to engage in innovative and entrepreneurial activities (e.g. Ghoshal/Bartlett 1988, Birkinshaw et al. 1998, Birkinshaw 1999). Given the high relevance of subsidiary autonomy for the research topic of entrepreneurial initiatives and the close link to subsidiary roles, it was decided to include the construct.

In general, subsidiary autonomy refers to the extent to which a foreign subsidiary and its managers have strategic and operational decision-making authority and can render

---

[366] Centralization of decision-making and autonomy are typically seen as two extremes on a continuum (see e.g. Young/Tavares 2004). Consequently, centralization is typically operationalized as the opposite of autonomy (see e.g. Nohria/Ghoshal 1994, p. 501, Nobel/Birkinshaw 1998, p. 495).

decisions without headquarters involvement (O'Donnell 2000, p. 528, Ambos et al. 2010, p. 1108). Accordingly, a multitude of empirical work investigating subsidiary autonomy asks respondents to indicate the level of the organization (e.g. subsidiary or headquarters) at which various types of decisions are made (e.g. Ghoshal/Bartlett 1988, Birkinshaw/Morrison 1995, Nobel/Birkinshaw 1998, Birkinshaw 1999, Foss/Pedersen 2002, Ambos et al. 2010). For the purpose of this study, the operationalization is largely based on the work of Ghoshal and Bartlett (1988), which similarly investigates the link between local subsidiary autonomy and the creation, adoption and diffusion of subsidiary innovation. In line with additional research by Birkinshaw and colleagues (Birkinshaw/Morrison 1995, Nobel/Birkinshaw 1998), the present study further differentiates between strategic and operational decision-making. As a result, the following two indicators were used, as displayed in Table 4.9: (1) strategic decision-making autonomy, consisting of four variables, and (2) operational decision-making autonomy, comprising three variables.[367] The total of seven variables were measured by asking respondents, on a five-point scale, to indicate the extent to which it was "decided centrally by headquarters" or "decided independently by the subsidiary." The average scores in each of the two categories represented the estimates for strategic and operational autonomy of the subsidiary, while the overall average of the seven items is used to calculate the overall degree of subsidiary decision-making autonomy.

Indicator	Operationalization	Scale	Supporting Literature
Subsidiary strategic decision-making autonomy	• Development of a major new product and/or service offering • Major modification of a production and/or service delivery process • Restructuring of the subsidiary organization involving the creation or abolition of departments • Formulating and approving subsidiary's annual budgets	Five-point Likert scale	E: Ghoshal/Bartlett 1988, Birkinshaw 1999, Bouquet/ Birkinshaw 2008
Subsidiary operational decision-making autonomy	• Minor but significant modification of an existing product • Recruitment and promotion to positions just below that of the subsidiary's general manager • Career development plans for departmental managers	Five-point Likert scale	E: Ghoshal/Bartlett 1988

Table 4.9: Measurement of subsidiary decision-making autonomy

---

[367] The first three variables of strategic decision-making autonomy were directly adopted from Bartlett and Ghoshal's approach (1988) and only slightly reworded, while the fourth relating to the subsidiary's budget was added from the works of Birkinshaw and colleagues (Birkinshaw 1999, Bouquet/Birkinshaw 2008). The three items of operational decision-making autonomy were directly adopted from Bartlett and Ghoshal (1998, pp. 375, 387).

4.3.2 Subsidiary Initiative-Taking

Generally speaking, empirical work on the initiative-taking process remains scarce, with many of the studies being of exploratory nature. Therefore, these studies can only provide limited support regarding how to best operationalize and measure the different sub-processes and activities. In addition, the dynamic resource-oriented literature that largely represents the theoretical foundation for the research framework is still considered "nascent" and offers largely conceptual insights with very little empirical work to be found (Sirmon et al. 2011, pp. 1391-1392). Consequently, there exists only a small body of empirical work that can offer guidance in this matter. The following subsections explain how the sub-processes of initiative-taking behavior are measured, including subsidiary initiative opportunity identification (Subsection 4.3.2.1), resource structuring and bundling (Subsections 4.3.2.2 and 4.3.2.3), and headquarters-subsidiary alignment (Subsection 4.3.2.4).

4.3.2.1 Subsidiary Initiative Opportunity Identification

As previously described in Subsections 2.2.3.3 and 3.4.2.1, initiative-taking usually begins with the identification of a new business opportunity or business improvement opportunity by the foreign subsidiary. Based on the literature review and analysis, it was derived that the initiative opportunity identification can take place (a) externally through interactions with, for instance, local suppliers, customers and government entities, or (b) internally through interactions with actors from within the MNC, such as headquarters or other subsidiary units (see e.g. Birkinshaw 1997, 1998a, Birkinshaw/Fry 1998, Birkinshaw/Hood 1998b, Delany 2000). With regard to the operationalization of this process activity, only one contribution could be identified that offers relevant insights into the empirical measurement of this item (i.e. Liouka 2007).[368] Based on the findings of earlier exploratory case studies, Liouka subsequently operationalizes "subsidiary opportunity identification" through 11 items to measure the extent to which subsidiaries identified opportunities from different internal and external sources. In line with previous writings in the field, the study explicitly considers four internal and seven external sources of subsidiary opportunities and applies a five-point scale to assess the extent (Liouka 2007, p. 216).[369]

---

[368] In addition to the literature on subsidiary initiatives, empirical work on entrepreneurial opportunity identification and recognition was examined with the intention to identify potentially useful approaches to operationalizing and measuring this construct. The basis for further investigation was the work of Hansen et al. (2011). Of the 56 publications on entrepreneurial opportunity and opportunity-related processes that the authors analyze, only 26 offer insights into the operationalization of opportunity-related processes. Of these, 10 merely assess the opportunity identification as a count of the number of ideas or opportunities recognized. The remaining 16 articles were further analyzed, but no applicable constructs for the particular aspect of subsidiary initiative opportunity identification could be identified (for an overview see Hansen et al. 2011, p. 289).

[369] The four internal sources are subsidiary employees, subsidiary management, corporate headquarters and other subsidiary units in the MNC. The seven external sources are the subsidiary's customers, suppliers, distributors,

Consistent with what is stated in the subsidiary initiative literature and the operationalization used by Liouka, the present study also measures the extent to which a subsidiary identified opportunities from different internal and external sources during the past five years. However, as the focus of this research is not on the identification of particular sources of opportunities, but instead on the more general locus or origin (i.e. internal, local or global; see Birkinshaw 1997, pp. 211-214, 2000, pp. 71-77), broader categorizations for (1) internal and (2) external sources are applied. Overall, the following three variables are used to assess the extent of opportunities identified from three internal sources: opportunities stemming solely from within the subsidiary, opportunities originating from any type of interaction with corporate headquarters and opportunities from any type of interaction with sister subsidiaries or other MNC units. Furthermore, two variables are employed to measure the level of opportunities identified from external sources: opportunities identified through any type of interaction with local actors from within the subsidiary's local (domestic) market environment, and those identified through any type of interaction with global actors from the subsidiary's global (international) market environment.[370] Consequently, these five variables measure the extent to which internal, local and global opportunities had been identified in a particular subsidiary over the past five years, using a five-point scale ranging from "never" to "plentifully." The overall level of internal opportunity identification is represented by the averages scores of the first three internally-oriented variables, and the total level of external opportunity identification by the average score for the last two externally-oriented variables. Table 4.10 shows the indicators and items used to measure the sub-process activity concerning "subsidiary opportunity identification."

---

external consultants, government organizations, academic and research institutions and professional and trade associations.

[370] The operationalization proposed by Liouka does not further differentiate between local and global market opportunities. However, existing work clearly indicates that initiative opportunities can stem not only from the local market environment but also from the global market environment (see e.g. Birkinshaw 1997, p. 213, 2000, pp. 23-24). Hence, a second variable is introduced to account for opportunities originating in the global market.

Indicator	Operationalization	Scale	Supporting Literature
Internal initiative opportunity identification	Extent to which new entrepreneurial opportunities emerged through the following internal sources: • Solely from within the subsidiary • Through any type of interaction with sister subsidiaries or other units of your company • Through any type of interaction with corporate headquarters	Five-point Likert scale	E: Liouka 2007
External initiative opportunity identification	Extent to which new entrepreneurial opportunities emerged through the following external sources: • Through any type of interaction with local actors outside the subsidiary • Through any type of interaction with global actors outside the company	Five-point Likert scale	E: Liouka 2007

Table 4.10: Measurement of subsidiary initiative opportunity identification

As shown in Subsection 2.2.3.1, subsidiary initiative opportunities can be characterized not only by their amount and source of origin, but also by the extent or scale of changes they can cause. Accordingly, it has been stated that subsidiary (initiative) opportunities may comprise not only radical change but also more incremental and continuous improvement (Andersson/Pahlberg 1997, p. 323, Birkinshaw 2000, pp. 76-77, Liouka 2007, p. 2, Dimitratos et al. 2009, p. 411). Although the importance of considering not only the number but also the innovativeness of identified opportunities is generally acknowledged (Shepherd/DeTienne 2005, p. 98), only one empirical study could be identified that actually assesses the level of innovativeness of subsidiary initiative opportunities (i.e. Liouka 2007). However, Liouka aims only at identifying radical opportunities and therefore uses three variables to measure the innovativeness of subsidiary opportunities based on how many opportunities were identified that (1) are far from current business practices of the subsidiary, (2) are far from existing subsidiary organizational goals and that (3) led to significant changes in products, processes, and/or technologies (Liouka 2007, p. 217). Nevertheless, further insights concerning the possible operationalization of this construct could be obtained from previous empirical work on entrepreneurial and innovative opportunity recognition in general (e.g. DeTienne/Chandler 2004, Shepherd/DeTienne 2005, DeTienne/Chandler 2007, Hartmann 2011). For instance, DeTienne and Chandler assess the innovativeness of opportunities using a six-item scale with categories ranging from the "incremental" (1) replication of existing products/services used in similar applications to "radical" (6) product/service that is new to the world (DeTienne/Chandler 2007, p. 378). Since the approach by DeTienne and Chandler represents a more comprehensive operationalization and allows for better measurement of the full range of innovativeness, it is applied for the present thesis. Therefore, the innovativeness of subsidiary initiative opportunities is measured by having respondents assess the six variables on a five-point scale ranging from "never" to "plentifully." The final operationalization of subsidiary initiative opportunity innovativeness as used in the questionnaire is shown in Table 4.11.

Indicator	Operationalization	Scale	Supporting Literature
Innovativeness of initiative opportunity	• Replication of existing products/services or processes used in similar applications • New application for existing products/services or processes with little or no modification • Minor changes in existing product/services or processes • Significant changes in existing products/ services or processes • Combination of two or more existing products/ services into one unique product/service • Product/service that is "new to the world"	Five-point Likert scale	E: DeTienne/ Chandler 2004, 2007

Table 4.11: Measurement of the innovativeness of subsidiary initiative opportunities

4.3.2.2 Resource Structuring

As stated above, scholarly work dealing with the process of resource management is considered nascent and provides primarily conceptual insights with little empirical work to be found. As a result, the present thesis draws from conceptual and, where possible, empirical work to develop appropriate means for the operationalization and the measurement of this initiative sub-processes. Next, the development of constructs related to the following sub-processes is described: (1) external resource acquisition, (2) internal resource acquisition, (3) internal resource accumulation and (4) intern-external resource accumulation.

(1) External Resource Acquisition: Unfortunately, none of the few empirical studies rooted in the dynamic resource-based view that deal with resource acquisition from strategic factor markets are able to offer applicable insights for the operationalization of this process activity, so a new measure had to be developed.[371] Development of such a measure was guided by (a) conceptual work on the dynamic resource-based view and (b) empirical studies on competence and knowledge acquisition by foreign subsidiaries.[372] The conceptual publications dealing with the dynamic RBV provide insights into different modes of resource acquisition in general, while the empirical contributions in

---

[371] Maritan and Peteraf (2011, p. 1378) outline different empirical studies concerned with resource acquisition in strategic factor markets (i.e. Poppo/Weigelt 2000, Coff 2002, Knott 2003, Capron/Shen 2007). However, examination of these publications yielded no applicable measurement approaches of use for the present study.

[372] Since no works could be identified in the subsidiary literature field that deal with the broader notion of resource acquisition, it was necessary to resort to those addressing the specific resource of knowledge. Knowledge not only represents a specific type of resource but it is also considered one of the most critical ones. For instance, Conner and Prahalad refer to it as "... the essence of the resource-based perspective" and "... a basic source of competitive advantage" (Conner/Prahalad 1996, p. 477, see for similar arguments Inkpen 1998, p. 70, Eisenhardt/Martin 2000, p. 1107, Giroud/Scott-Kennel 2009, p. 560).

the subsidiary field outline potential sources or sellers of resources. (a) Following the strategic factor market logic as proposed by Barney, external resource acquisition by foreign subsidiary units refers to buying or purchasing those tradable resources from sellers in factor markets that are necessary to realize an identified initiative opportunity. Subsidiaries may either purchase particular resources in a relevant factor market directly or acquire larger and more complex sets of resources and capabilities indirectly via, for instance, mergers and acquisitions (Barney 1986, p. 1232, Sirmon et al. 2007, p. 278, Maritan/Peteraf 2011, pp. 1375-1376).[373] (b) As outlined in Section 3.3.2.3, resource-based work on subsidiary resource and capability development highlights, along with the subsidiary units itself, two important sources a subsidiary can turn to when needing to acquire new resources: externally from actors in their business network and internally from actors within the MNC (e.g. Frost 2001, Andersson et al. 2002b, Foss/Pedersen 2002, Schmid/Schurig 2003, Almeida/Phene 2004, Phene/ Almeida 2008). Accordingly, empirical work on external knowledge acquisition by subsidiaries frequently involves the assessment of knowledge obtained from different external actors. For instance, Foss and Pedersen measure the knowledge that subsidiaries acquire in their external networks through four variables relating to different external organizations. In their study, the authors ask respondents to assess the impact of external market customers, external market suppliers, specific distributors and specific external R&D units on the development of the subsidiary competencies on a seven-point scale, ranging from "no impact at all" to "very decisive impact" (Foss/ Pedersen 2002, p. 61). Similarly, Schmid and Schurig have respondents assess the influence of six different external network partners (customers, suppliers, distributors, competitors, R&D units and governmental institutions) on the subsidiary's capability development on a seven-point scale (Schmid/Schurig 2003, p. 768).[374] Other empirical studies in the subsidiary field measure the extent of knowledge acquisition from external sources more broadly and only incorporate external customers and/or competitors (e.g. Yli-Renko et al. 2001, Cui et al. 2005, Holm et al. 2005).

Based on these conceptual and empirical contributions, the external acquisition of resources is operationalized through two variables, each reflecting a particular acquisition mode. (1) First, respondents are asked to indicate the extent to which their subsidiary externally acquired resources and capabilities that were needed to realize their initiative(s) *directly* from external actors such as suppliers, competitors, governmental or research institutions over the past five years. (2) Second, they are asked to assess the

---

[373] In addition to the conceptual contributions on the dynamic RBV, literature on subsidiary initiatives also describes M&A activities as a viable option to externally acquire new resources and capabilities (see Birkinshaw/Hood 1997, p. 341).
[374] It should be noted, however, that the contributions by Foss and Pedersen (2002) and Schmid and Schurig (2003) do not further differentiate between "acquiring" resources (i.e. purchasing them from external actors) and "developing" resources (i.e. accumulating them through learning from external actors, for example). Instead, both publications use the terms "acquisition" and "development" more or less interchangeably.

extent to which their subsidiaries externally acquired needed resources and capabilities *indirectly*, e.g. through merging with or acquiring another entity in the local or global marketplace over the past five years. As can be seen, in contrast to the two described empirical studies,[375] respondents are not asked to indicate the influence or importance of different external actors on subsidiary capability development. Instead, they are required to assess to what extent they actually acquired resources and capabilities either directly or indirectly in the external business network. It is presumed that the "direct" measure is more appropriate, as the core interest here is on the actual mode and source of acquisition rather than the subsequent effects on subsidiary capability development. Both variables are measured on a five-point scale ranging from "never" to "plentifully" as shown in Table 4.12. The final measure, "external resource acquisition," is represented by the average of the two individual scores.

(2) Internal Resource Acquisition: In addition to buying resources from external actors, subsidiaries can also acquire them from different sources or actors within the MNC.[376] For instance, literature on subsidiary initiatives suggests that foreign subsidiaries can acquire different forms of resources from headquarters when pursuing initiatives, such as new plant facilities, proprietary technology or financial investments (Birkinshaw/Hood 1997, p. 341). In addition to headquarters, empirical work dealing with subsidiary capability development more generally highlights many other internal MNC sources, such as sister subsidiaries, internal suppliers or internal R&D units that subsidiaries can potentially turn to when needing to acquire resources and capabilities (e.g. Schmid/Schurig 2003, Lyles/Salk 2007, Phene/Almeida 2008, Williams 2009). Although these contributions acknowledge different internal sources for resource acquisition, they nevertheless take different approaches towards operationalization and measurement. For example, while Phene and Almeida assess the extent of knowledge acquired from two internal sources (headquarters and other subsidiaries of the MNC) through a patent portfolio analysis (2008, p. 908),[377] Schmid and Schurig have respondents use a seven-point scale to evaluate the degree to which network relationships with four internal partners (headquarters, internal customers, internal suppliers and internal R&D units) had influenced subsidiary capability development (2003, p. 776).

In order to operationalize and measure the construct of "internal resource acquisition," the present study applies three variables that reflect three important internal sources: (1) corporate headquarters, (2) sister subsidiaries in the MNC and (3) other internal MNC units besides headquarters and sister subsidiaries. As the present study aims at identifying and assessing the extent to which subsidiaries have applied a specific

---

[375] Here, the studies by Schmid and Schurig (2003) and Foss and Pedersen (2002) are specifically referred to.
[376] See Subsections 3.3.2.3 and 3.4.2.2 for further detail on internal resource acquisition.
[377] The authors argue that patents are used to identify the technical antecedents of (subsidiary) innovation as they reflect the knowledge acquired to create an innovation (Phene/Almeida 2008, p. 908).

structuring mode (i.e. external/internal acquisition or internal/internal-external accumulation), it was not deemed necessary to further differentiate the particular internal MNC actors from which resources and capabilities were obtained. Respondents are therefore asked to indicate to what extent their subsidiary acquired resources and capabilities from these three sourcing possibilities over the past five years when pursuing entrepreneurial initiatives, using a five-point scale ranging from "never" to "plentifully." The average score of these three variables represents the overall measure for the construct of "internal resource acquisition."

(3) Internal Resource Accumulation: As a third approach, resources and capabilities can be internally accumulated by a subsidiary, which is understood as their gradual development over time (Dierickx/Cool 1989, p. 1506). Rather than purchasing available resources and capabilities in the external or internal market "off the shelf," resources or capabilities may be built-up internally. Similar to the process activity of resource acquisition, there exists only "a relatively small body of work that focuses on the details and properties of the asset accumulation process itself" (Maritan/Peteraf 2011, p. 1376).[378] As a consequence, the dynamic resource-based perspective literature can provide mostly conceptual guidance on the operationalization and measurement of this construct. However, further insights can be obtained from empirical studies concerned with internal subsidiary knowledge and competence development (e.g. Foss/Pedersen 2002, Williams 2009).

The conceptual work on the dynamic RBV highlights different modes through which new resources and capabilities can be accumulated. It appears that research and development activities, and (subsidiary) learning more generally, represent the most important cornerstones of internal (subsidiary) resource accumulation (Dierickx/Cool 1989, p. 1505, Makadok 2001, p. 391, Zollo/Winter 2002, p. 339, Sirmon/Hitt 2003, p. 350, Sirmon et al. 2007, p. 279).[379] Similarly, empirical studies focusing on subsidiary innovation and competence development also acknowledge the importance of internal resource and capability development through investment in R&D, or through subsidiary learning more generally (e.g. Foss/Pedersen 2002, p. 55, Phene/Almeida 2003, p. 354).[380] Nonetheless, despite the focus on R&D investments and learning, it can be

---

[378] Maritan and Peteraf mention four particular contributions that have previously investigated the resource accumulation process in more detail (i.e. Thomke/Kuemmerle 2002, Knott et al. 2003, Pacheco-de-Almeida/Zemsky 2007, Pacheco-de-Almeida et al. 2008). However, the examination of these four journal articles yielded no applicable information on the operationalization and measurement of this particular construct.

[379] More specific examples of resource accumulation refer to the development of new managerial knowledge and skills of employees (e.g. by moving employees between headquarters and subsidiaries or by on-the job training activities), the enhancement of technical or operational capabilities, the improvement of a firm's reputation or the development of intellectual capital (e.g. Sirmon et al. 2007, p. 279, Pacheco-de-Almeida et al. 2008, p. 518, Sirmon et al. 2011, p. 1396).

[380] A number of other empirical studies have used R&D investment to measure the level of resource accumulation (e.g. Helfat 1997, Knott et al. 2003, Pacheco-de-Almeida et al. 2008). However, these studies did not rely on managers to assess the level of R&D investments but instead used data available from various databases.

expected that internal resource development is a much broader phenomenon that can take place in different functional areas and in connection with different value chain activities.

Therefore, the present study slightly adapts the operationalization proposed by Foss and Pedersen (2002, pp. 60-61), who measure internal (knowledge) resource accumulation for six different subsidiary activities. The construct of "internal resource accumulation" is measured by asking respondents to assess the level of investments that the subsidiary has made over the past five years in the following seven functional areas in order to realize/implement the identified opportunities:[381] (1) research and/or development, (2) production, (3) marketing and/or sales, (4) logistics and/or distribution, (5) purchasing, (6) HR management and (7) general management.[382] In line with the previously described constructs, a five-point scale is applied, ranging from "very limited" to "substantial." The total score for "internal resource accumulation" is calculated as the average of the seven individual scores.

(4) Internal-External Resource Accumulation: A fourth possibility for subsidiaries to obtain the resources and capabilities needed for initiatives is to do so through internal accumulation not solely from within the MNC but also involving interactions with external business partners. In contrast to external resource acquisition that entails purchasing "off-the-shelf" resources and capabilities that are directly accessible from external actors, internal-external resource accumulation refers to the more gradual process of resource building through collaboration with external business partners. Literature taking a resource-based view highlights strategic alliances and joint ventures as important forms of resource accumulation in partnerships, although other forms of inter-organizational resource accumulation, such as strategic technology partnering, are also possible (e.g. Eisenhardt/Schoonhoven 1996, Inkpen 1998, Tsang 1998, Sirmon et al. 2007, Sirmon et al. 2011). Internal-external resource accumulation essentially represents subsidiary learning in which the inter-organizational transfer of knowledge resources plays a dominant role (Eisenhardt/Schoonhoven 1996, p. 139, Mowery et al. 1996, p. 77, Inkpen 1998, p. 70, Giroud/Scott-Kennel 2009, p. 560). Consequently, empirical studies dealing with collaborative resource development efforts with external partners frequently focus on assessing different aspects of knowledge transfer, but take different approaches with regard to operationalization and measurement.

---

[381] Measuring the level of investment in different subsidiary activities should be understood only as a proxy for internal resource accumulation. As a certain level of investment does not necessarily have to lead to an equivalent increase in resources or capabilities, it can only serve as an indirect measure (Mowery et al. 1996, p. 82).

[382] The two functional areas "HR management" and "general management" were added for consistency, as these seven functional areas are used for other constructs in this thesis.

For instance, Mowery and colleagues measure inter-firm knowledge transfer in strategic alliances by capturing the number of "cross-citations" in the patents held by the two companies (Mowery et al. 1996, p. 83, 2002, p. 300). The studies thereby assess the actual outcomes of knowledge transfer rather than evaluating the development of the knowledge resources themselves. Mothe and Quelin also evaluate the outcomes of cooperative R&D efforts. Instead of using patent data, the authors ask respondents to assess the effect of cooperative R&D on the creation of new tangible and intangible resources. This is then operationalized through ten and four variables respectively (Mothe/Quelin 2001, p. 125). Other empirical contributions concentrate more directly on the development of new knowledge resources. For example, Lane and Lubatkin measure inter-organizational learning in alliances by having respondents asses to what extent the collaborative efforts have helped with regard to learning new skills and capabilities, technology and research developments, using a five-point scale ranging from "very poorly" to "very well" (Lane/Lubatkin 1998, p. 468). Similarly, Simonin measures knowledge transfer in international strategic alliances by asking respondents to what extent they agree with three different statements concerning the knowledge transfer itself and the subsequent effects on the company, applying a seven-point scale from "strongly disagree" to "strongly agree" (Simonin 2004, p. 426).

Although focusing on *intra*-organizational rather than *inter*-organizational knowledge transfer, empirical work on knowledge flows and knowledge transfer in MNC subsidiaries also provides valuable insights for the possible operationalization and measurement of this particular construct (e.g. Gupta/Govindarajan 1991, 1994, Chung et al. 2000, Gupta/Govindarajan 2000, Harzing/Noorderhaven 2006). Gupta and Govindarajan use a nine-item instrument relating to different types of knowledge and skills to measure the exchange of mostly procedural knowledge between internal MNC units.[383] Respondents are asked to indicate the extent of knowledge transfer on a seven-point Likert scale ranging from "not at all" to "a very great deal" (Gupta/Govindarajan 1991, p. 23, 1994, p. 450).[384]

In order to measure and operationalize this particular process activity, the present study assesses the resources and capabilities developed through collaborative efforts with external partners for the following seven value chain activities:[385] (1) research and/or

---

[383] These are: (1) market data on customers, (2) market data on competitors, (3) products designs, (4) process designs, (5) marketing know-how, (6) distribution know-how, (7) packaging design/technology, (8) purchasing know-how and (9) management systems and practices.

[384] In the most recent of these three contributions, Gupta and Govindarajan combine knowledge resources relating to market data on customers, market data on competitors and marketing know-how into one single item, "marketing know-how," thereby reducing it to seven knowledge types (Gupta/Govindarajan 2000, p. 483).

[385] Frequently, inter-organizational knowledge transfer is measured by changes in knowledge resources, level of innovativeness, or performance of the recipient firm (Easterby-Smith et al. 2008, p. 681). However, based on the theoretical framework of this work, the present work only focuses on the level of knowledge-resources that were accumulated through collaborative efforts.

development, (2) production, (3) marketing and/or sales, (4) logistics and/or distribution, (5) purchasing, (6) HR management and (7) general management as shown in Table 4.12.

Indicator	Operationalization	Scale	Supporting Literature
External acquisition of resources and capabilities	Extent to which subsidiary acquired needed resources and capabilities externally that were: • Directly available from external actors in the local or global marketplace • Indirectly available through merging with or acquiring another organization in the local or global marketplace	Five-point Likert scale	C: Barney 1986, Sirmon et al. 2007 E: Foss/Pedersen 2002, Schmid/ Schurig 2003, Holm et al. 2005
Internal acquisition of resources and capabilities	Extent to which subsidiary acquired needed resources and capabilities internally from: • Corporate headquarters • Sister subsidiaries • Other MNC units besides headquarters and sister subsidiaries	Five-point Likert scale	C: Barney 1986, Sirmon et al. 2007 E: Foss/Pedersen 2002, Schmid/ Schurig 2003
Internal accumulation of resources and capabilities	Extent to which subsidiary made deliberate investments to develop needed resources and capabilities internally in the following functional areas: • Research and/or development • Production • Marketing and/or sales • Logistics and/or distribution • Purchasing • HR management • General management	Five-point Likert scale	C: Dierickx/Cool 1989, Sirmon et al. 2007, 2011 E: Foss/Pedersen 2002
External-internal accumulation of resources and capabilities	Extent to which subsidiary developed needed resources and capabilities through collaborative efforts with external network partners in the following functional areas: • Research and/or development • Production • Marketing and/or sales • Logistics and/or distribution • Purchasing • HR management • General management	Five-point Likert scale	C: Sirmon et al. 2007 E: Gupta/Govindarajan 1991, 1994, 2000, Lane/Lubatkin 1998

Table 4.12: Measurement of initiative-related resource structuring

Although this operationalization is largely based on the one proposed by Gupta and Govindarajan (1991, 1994, 2000), some deliberate modifications were made. First, instead of referring to the more specific resource of knowledge, the broader notion of resources and capabilities is used. Second, while Gupta and Govindarajan refer to different areas of knowledge, resource and capabilities, accumulation is evaluated here in relation to different value chain activities.[386] Third, for reasons stated before and to

---
[386] Measuring knowledge transfer relating to value chain functions is not uncommon and in accordance with previous operationalization of, for example Chung et al. (2000) or Harzing and Norderhaven (2006).

ensure consistency for the empirical study, a five-point scale is used, ranging from "very limited" to "substantial."

4.3.2.3 Resource Bundling

Resource bundling refers to the process stage in which the different resources of the subsidiary's resource portfolio are combined and integrated to achieve, for instance, new product or service offerings, or to realize new business improvements efforts. Overall, there is very little empirical that is concerned with the resource bundling process and that can provide information on existing items to measure the process activity (Worthington 2007, p. 49, Wiklund/Shepherd 2009, p. 196). Hence, in order to develop appropriate measures for the empirical assessment, insights from both conceptual literature and the limited number of existing empirical studies were considered.[387]

Empirical studies dealing with resource integration and resource combination take different approaches to operationalizing and measuring this process activity. While some studies more strongly emphasize resource structuring activities and thereby infer that it also implies (re)combination efforts, other contributions more closely consider the actual integration and bundling efforts. Among the first type of empirical measurement is, for example, the study by Tsai and Ghoshal in which they assess resource exchange and resource combination, arguing that the "resource combination process often takes place in conjunction with resource exchange." The authors develop four sets of questions for their survey to address the intra-firm exchange of information, products or services, personnel and support between different business units. Respondents are asked to indicate which of these resource types are exchanged (and hence combined) with other business units of their company (Tsai/Ghoshal 1998, p. 470).[388] Similarly, in order to measure resource combination activities in alliances, Wiklund and Shephard apply a six-item construct that emphasizes different aspects of resource structuring (i.e. resource accumulation and development) rather than addressing the actual bundling and combination efforts (Wiklund/Shepherd 2009, p. 208). Among the studies that more strongly stress concrete resource bundling attempts, are, for example, those by Cui et

---

[387] Conceptual literature suggests that bundling can range from minor resource combination efforts for incremental initiatives to extensive combination activities for initiatives entailing more substantial changes. Incremental forms of bundling aim at maintaining or stabilizing existing capabilities and should therefore involve some limited combination of existing resources. Intermediate modes of resource combination with the objective of extending or enhancing capabilities refer to the integration of newly acquired resources with existing ones, while extensive bundling activities demand far-reaching combinations of newly obtained resources (Sirmon et al. 2007, pp. 281-282, Sirmon et al. 2011, p. 1392). See Subsections 3.3.2.2 and 3.4.2.3 for theoretical considerations on resource bundling.

[388] In order to create a single-item measure that takes into account exchanges between the different business units, the authors combined the four resource types into a matrix, allowing them to subsequently compute a single in-degree centrality measure (see Tsai/Ghoshal 1998, p. 470).

al. (2005), Tiwana (2008) and Phene and Almeida (2008).[389] Overall, however, there appears to be little consistency with regard to the measurement of resource bundling activities. Moreover, the extent or intensity of resource bundling activities is seldom considered in these studies.

The search for appropriate measures for the process stage of resource bundling yielded one empirical study conducted by Worthington (2007) that explicitly tested the three theoretically derived bundling processes proposed by Sirmon and colleagues (i.e. stabilizing, enriching and pioneering bundling; see Sirmon et al. 2007, Sirmon et al. 2011).[390] The author developed a four-item construct to measure the incremental (stabilizing) bundling process, consisting of the following indicators: (1) converting repetitive actions into codified procedures to increase efficiency, (2) discovering new ways of using existing capabilities to create new opportunities, (3) combining existing capabilities from two departments to add new products and (4) exchanging personnel from different departments to transfer ideas internally. In line with the conceptual work by Sirmon et al., incremental or stabilizing bundling is hence operationalized to reflect the minor (re)combination of existing resources to maintain or refine existing capabilities. Intermediate (enriching) bundling is also assessed through four indicators mainly representing the (re)combination of newly obtained resources with existing ones: (5) reconfiguring capabilities from within the firm to create new business opportunities, (6) discovering new ways of using existing capabilities to create new opportunities, (7) combining existing capabilities from two departments to add new products and (8) exchanging personnel from different departments to transfer ideas internally. Finally, radical (pioneering) bundling activities that involve the extensive bundling of newly-obtained resources are determined through the following four items: (9) acquiring a new capability from outside the firm to implement a new strategy, (10) acquiring another firm to add a new product to the existing portfolio, (11) adding a manufacturing capability to an existing R&D capability (or vice versa) and (12) partnering with another firm to offer a blended product. These twelve items are measured on a five-point scale extending from "little" to "much" (Worthington 2007, pp. 50-51).

---

[389] Cui et al. apply a three-item scale asking respondents in foreign subsidiaries of MNCs to what extent they agree or disagree that their company has (1) ways of converting knowledge into the design of new products or services, (2) processes for organizing knowledge, and (3) processes for converting competitive intelligence into plans of action (Cui et al. 2005, p. 42). Tiwana measures the extent to which members of innovation-seeking project alliance teams had synthesized their knowledge and skills through a three-item construct, having respondents evaluate the extent to which members of a team (1) had competently blended new knowledge with existing knowledge, (2) span several areas of expertise and (3) synthesize and integrate their individual expertise (Tiwana 2008, p. 272). A different method is applied by Phene and Almeida, who investigate innovation in MNC subsidiaries through internal and external knowledge assimilation and integration. The scholars use patent and patent citation analysis to assess "subsidiary combinative capability," reflecting the extent of knowledge integration from different sources (Phene/Almeida 2008, pp. 908-909).

[390] It appears that the dissertation by Worthington (2007) is the first attempt to empirically test the conceptual framework previously proposed in the publication by Sirmon, Hitt and Ireland (2007). Two of the three authors (i.e. Hitt and Ireland) were also members of Worthington's thesis committee.

Primarily based on the conceptual works by Sirmon et al. and the operationalization proposed by Worthington, a refined measure for resource bundling was developed for this thesis. Instead of using four different items for each bundling type (i.e. incremental/ stabilizing, intermediate/enriching and radical/pioneering) as in the study by Worthington, it was decided to only use only item for three reasons. First, Worthington largely assesses bundling activities indirectly by having respondents evaluate the extent of structuring activities related to different sources. As the detailed measurement of resource acquisition activities is already included in this study (see previous subsection), a duplication is unlikely to yield any additional insights. Instead, stronger emphasis can be placed exclusively on bundling activities.[391] Second, the conceptual literature provides a detailed description of the different resource bundling types, allowing for the precise specification of adequate questions. Third, in order not to overburden respondents with too many (and even partially duplicated) questions, it was deliberately chosen to use a total of three questions to measure resource bundling activities. As a result, (1) the degree to which incremental bundling was used to realize entrepreneurial initiatives is measured by asking respondents to indicate the extent to which the new business opportunities or business improvement opportunities required "some minor combinations of already existing resources and capabilities" over the past five years. (2) In order to determine the extent of intermediate bundling activities respondents are asked to evaluate the extent to which "combinations of newly obtained resources and capabilities with already existing ones in the subsidiary" were necessary. Finally, (3) radical bundling is assessed through one question concerning the use of "extensive combinations of completely new resources and capabilities that were obtained specifically for new initiative opportunities." In line with the measurement of the other constructs in the present study, a five-point rating scale is used for all three indicators ranging from "never" to "plentifully." The operationalization and measurement for all three resource bundling activities is shown in in Table 4.13.

---

[391] It could also be argued that resource bundling should, as in previous studies, only be indirectly measured through the extent to which resource structuring from different sources occurs. However, the use of different sources does not necessarily have to lead to an equivalent amount of bundling (e.g. if some acquired resources or resource bundles are directly applied without having to combine them with other subsidiary resources). Therefore, it was decided to use a more direct measure to assess the extent of the three different resource bundling activities.

Indicator	Operationalization	Scale	Supporting Literature
Incremental resource bundling (stabilizing)	▪ Requiring some minor combination of already existing resources and capabilities of the subsidiary	Five-point Likert scale	C: Sirmon/Hitt 2003, Sirmon et al. 2007 E: Worthington 2007
Intermediate resource bundling (enriching)	▪ Requiring the combination of newly obtained resources and capabilities with already existing ones in the subsidiary	Five-point Likert scale	C: Sirmon/Hitt 2003, Sirmon et al. 2007 E: Worthington 2007
Radical resource bundling (pioneering)	▪ Requiring the extensive combination of completely new resources and capabilities that were obtained specifically for a new initiative opportunity	Five-point Likert scale	C: Sirmon/Hitt 2003, Sirmon et al. 2007 E: Worthington 2007

Table 4.13: Measurement of initiative-related resource bundling

4.3.2.4 Headquarters-Subsidiary Alignment

Besides the resource management activities described previously, the subsidiary initiative-taking process is said to critically depend also on the successful alignment and interaction in the MNC between headquarters and entrepreneurially active foreign subsidiaries. As outlined in Subsections 3.2.2.2 and 3.4.3, existing works emphasize three central aspects of initiative-related alignment and interaction. Their operationalization will be presented in this subsection: (1) headquarters involvement in subsidiary initiatives, (2) corporate resistance in the MNC, and (3) subsidiary initiative selling.

(1) Headquarters Involvement: Throughout the initiative development process, headquarters can be more or less strongly involved. As discussed in Subsection 3.4.3.1, headquarters involvement in the initiative process relates to aspects of both (a) the centralization of initiative-related decision-making and (b) the extent of headquarters-subsidiary communication and interaction. Accordingly, Birkinshaw and colleagues frequently consider these two aspects when describing and empirically assessing headquarters involvement as one particular aspect of the headquarters-subsidiary relationship (e.g. Birkinshaw 1997, p. 224, Birkinshaw et al. 1998, p. 231, Birkinshaw 1999, p. 34, 2000, pp. 22-30). In addition to the work related to subsidiary initiatives, a number of other empirical studies dealing with subsidiary innovation capture, in a somewhat similar manner, the extent of headquarters involvement through aspects of subsidiary autonomy (or decision-making centralization) and headquarters-subsidiary communication (e.g. Ciabuschi et al. 2010, Ciabuschi et al. 2011, Dellestrand 2011, Yamin et al. 2011, Ciabuschi et al. 2012). While most of these studies focus on headquarters involvement specifically in knowledge and innovation transfer, only one study addresses and measures headquarters involvement in the development of subsidiary innovations (i.e. Ciabuschi et al. 2012). The authors use four items measured on a seven-point Likert scale relating to frequent interaction with headquarters, close participation and support from headquarters in the development of innovations and development of the innovation within the facilities of the headquarters organization. In order to measure the extent of headquarters involvement in subsidiary initiatives, the present study largely relies on the conceptual and empirical work of Birkinshaw and colleagues (Birkinshaw 1997, 1998b, Birkinshaw et al. 1998, Birkinshaw 1999, 2000) and on the study by Ciabuschi et al. (2012). The newly developed construct contains four items, with two of them relating to (a) initiative-related headquarters-subsidiary communication, interaction and participation, and two items to (b) headquarters involvement regarding initiative evaluation and approval.[392] This is illustrated in Table 4.14. The construct is measured using a five-point rating scale ranging from "never" to "plentifully."

(2) Corporate Resistance: As described in Subsection 3.4.3.2, subsidiaries may also be confronted with corporate resistance when engaging in entrepreneurial initiatives from what is sometimes termed "the corporate immune system." Empirical findings suggest that this typically manifests itself as (a) rejection of initiatives by headquarters, (b) delay and/or request for greater justification by headquarters, (c) lobbying and rival initiatives by competing divisions and (d) lack of recognition of an initiative by other divisions of the MNC (Birkinshaw/Ridderstråle 1999, p. 158). As no other empirical studies were found that provide relevant insights into the potential measurement of corporate resistance to entrepreneurial initiatives, these manifestations were applied directly as the four items for this construct. In line with the other constructs in this study, a five-point rating scale from "never" to "plentifully" was applied.

(3) Subsidiary Initiative Selling: An additional element of headquarters-subsidiary alignment is concerned with initiative selling. Foreign units may engage in more or less extensive selling or championing activities in order to promote their entrepreneurial initiatives in the MNC and push them through the organizational system towards implementation. Qualitative research has identified a variety of selling strategies and tactics that can be applied in initiative selling. For example, foreign affiliates can engage in selling and championing activities at headquarters, they can pursue internal lobbying with various corporate bodies or they can use personal contacts within the MNC to establish credibility for an initiative (e.g. Birkinshaw/Ridderstråle 1999, pp. 169-170, 173-174). However, as outlined in Subsection 3.4.3.3, from the many possibilities that may be pursued by the foreign sites, three central aspects of issue-selling appear to prevail: (a) attracting headquarters attention, (b) making headquarters understand an issue and (c) lobbying at the parent company (Gammelgaard 2009). Consequently,

---

[392] The construct applied by Birkinshaw and colleagues to decision-making centralization measures subsidiary autonomy in general and not specifically with regard to subsidiary initiative-taking activities. Since the measure of subsidiary autonomy has already been introduced in this study, decision-making centralization was included only with the specific focus on initiative evaluation and approval.

these three items, which are largely based on the empirical work by Gammelgaard on subsidiary issue selling, were used to operationalize the construct of initiative selling. However, initiative-related corporate resistance may be encountered not only vertically from headquarters but also from various other directions, such as sister divisions or even other units of the MNC. Similarly, subsidiary initiative selling also takes place vertically as well as horizontally in the MNC (Birkinshaw 2000, p. 27). Consequently, an additional item concerning the extent to which the subsidiary engaged in "horizontal lobbying at sister subsidiaries or other MNC units" was included. The total of four items were measured on a five-point rating scale from "never" to "plentifully" as shown in Table 4.14.

Indicator	Operationalization	Scale	Supporting Literature
Headquarters involvement	<ul><li>Extent to which subsidiary managers communicated and/or interacted with counterparts in headquarters w/ regard to opportunities</li><li>Extent to which headquarters participated closely in the refinement and development of opportunities</li><li>Extent to which presentations of opportunity proposals at headquarters were necessary</li><li>Extent to which headquarters' approval was required for continuation or implementation of opportunity</li></ul>	Five-point Likert scale	C: Birkinshaw 1997, 2000 E: Birkinshaw 1998b, Birkinshaw et al. 1998, Birkinshaw 1999, Ciabuschi et al. 2012
Resistance from headquarters and other units	<ul><li>Rejection of initiative by headquarters</li><li>Delay of initiative and/or requests for greater justification by headquarters' managers</li><li>Lobbying and rival initiatives by competing divisions</li><li>Lack of recognition of initiative by other MNC units</li></ul>	Five-point Likert scale	E: Birkinshaw/ Ridderstråle 1999
Subsidiary initiative selling	Extent of subsidiary efforts aimed at:<ul><li>Attracting HQ attention to the new opportunity</li><li>Making HQ understand the new opportunity</li><li>Lobbying at HQ to gain support for new opportunity</li><li>Lobbying at sister subsidiaries or other MNC units to gain support for new opportunity</li></ul>	Five-point Likert scale	C: Birkinshaw 1997, Birkinshaw/ Ridderstråle 1999 E:Gammelgaard 2009, De Clercq et al. 2011

Table 4.14: Measurement of headquarters-subsidiary alignment

4.3.3 Subsidiary Initiative-Taking Outcome

It has been suggested that studies investigating the relationships between context, behavior and performance should not only rely on a single performance measure but instead use multiple ones, id possible (Prescott 1986, p. 340). Following this recommendation, the present work addresses a number of different outcomes of subsidiary initiatives. As has been outlined in Subsection 3.2.3, the "immediate" performance of a subsidiary initiative is measured through two different constructs. First, the extent of subsidiary initiatives (i.e. those that are approved and/or implemented) is assessed. However, in contrast to most previous studies, the extent will not only be determined for subsidiary initiatives in general, but for the four different initiative types as described in Subsection 4.3.3.1. Second, the extent of new and specialized resources and capabilities that result from the initiatives and that are also applicable for the wider MNC will be evaluated. The respective constructs and measurement methods are described in Subsection 4.3.3.2. Third, although not part of the proposed research framework, more "intermediate" performance measures were also included and are further explained in Subsection 4.3.3.3.

4.3.3.1 Extent and Types of Subsidiary Initiatives

A number of different empirical studies apply the "level" or the "extent" of subsidiary initiative-taking as an outcome measure (e.g. Birkinshaw/Hood 1998a, Birkinshaw et al. 1998, Birkinshaw 1999, Tseng et al. 2004, Borini et al. 2009a, Borini et al. 2009b, Ambos et al. 2010). In these studies, subsidiary managers are asked to indicate the level of different entrepreneurial activities pursued by their subsidiary over a certain period of time. However, operationalization and measurement vary among the studies. Scales range from three (e.g. Ambos et al. 2010) to nine items (e.g. Borini et al. 2009b), and periods under investigate typically stretch from five years (e.g. Ambos et al. 2010, Ambos/Birkinshaw 2010, Scott et al. 2010) to ten (e.g. Birkinshaw et al. 1998, Birkinshaw 1999). Nevertheless, most of these studies base their measurements on the empirical study conducted by Birkinshaw (1997) that identifies and describes the four different types of initiatives also employed for this research. In line with the research framework applied there, the present study also measures the extent of all four different types of subsidiary initiatives that occurred over a period of five years. The operationalization is based both on the early research findings of Birkinshaw (1997) and on the subsequent measurement approaches that employed a six-item scale (Birkinshaw 1998b), as seen below and illustrated in Table 4.15.

(1) Global market initiatives refer to new products or markets that are developed for non-local actors situated outside the subsidiary's local market. Although they may arise through interaction with all kinds of customers or suppliers throughout the world, they typically occur as extensions of existing mandates (e.g. existing international product responsibilities) and relationships with global actors outside the MNC (Birkinshaw 1997, pp. 213-214, 2000, pp. 23-25). Consequently, the following two items were used to measure the extent of global initiatives: (a) significant extensions to existing international responsibilities and (b) enhancements to product/services lines which are already sold internationally. (2) Local market initiatives represent new products, markets or

processes that are first identified and developed locally but are subsequently exploited on a global scale (Birkinshaw 1997, p. 218, 2000, p. 22). Hence, this initiative type is measured through two items: (a) new international business activities that were first started locally and (b) new products/services developed locally and sold internationally. (3) Internal market initiatives arise through opportunities identified within the internal market of the MNC. They represent smaller-scale entrepreneurial efforts that aim at improving the efficiency of the corporate system through reconfiguring and rationalization efforts. In the end, they are said to "promote the redistribution of existing corporate assets or resources such that they are more efficiently deployed" (Birkinshaw 1997, p. 218). Thus, two corresponding items are used: (a) proposals to transfer manufacturing/service delivery to subsidiary locations from elsewhere in the corporation and (b) reconfiguring of local subsidiary operations from domestic to international orientation.

Indicator	Operationalization[393]	Scale	Supporting Literature
Global market initiatives	• Significant extensions to existing international responsibilities • Enhancement to product/service lines already sold internationally	Five-point Likert scale	C: Birkinshaw 1997 E: Birkinshaw 1998b, Birkinshaw et al. 1998, Birkinshaw 1999
Local market initiatives	• New international business activities that were first started locally • New products or services developed locally and sold internationally	Five-point Likert scale	C: Birkinshaw 1997 E: Birkinshaw 1998b, Birkinshaw et al. 1998, Birkinshaw 1999
Internal market initiatives	• Proposals to transfer manufacturing/service delivery to subsidiary location from elsewhere in the corporation • Reconfiguring of local subsidiary operations from domestic to international orientation	Five-point Likert scale	C: Birkinshaw 1997 E: Birkinshaw 1998b, Birkinshaw et al. 1998, Birkinshaw 1999
Global-internal hybrid initiatives	• Successful bids for corporate investment in subsidiary location • New corporate investment in R&D or manufacturing/service delivery attracted by local subsidiary management	Five-point Likert scale	C: Birkinshaw 1997 E: Birkinshaw 1998b, Birkinshaw et al. 1998, Birkinshaw 1999

Table 4.15: Measurement of subsidiary initiative-taking by initiative type[394]

(4) Finally, global-internal hybrid initiatives involve the reallocation of value-adding functions to the subsidiary unit. Typically, subsidiary management identifies opportunities outside the subsidiary's local market. It then seeks to attract global investments in the subsidiary location and engages in the internal process of convincing headquarters to

---

[393] As the measurement by Birkinshaw and colleagues referred to manufacturing subsidiaries, some items were slightly adapted to allow for their use with non-manufacturing units as well, for example in the service industry.

[394] It should be noted, however, that Birkinshaw and colleagues have previously attempted to measure different initiative types as separate sub-constructs. However, their provisional PLS analysis indicated that the discriminant validity between these sub-constructs was poor, so it was subsequently decided to view subsidiary initiatives as a single construct (see Birkinshaw et al. 1998, p. 231).

relocate activities from other parts of the MNC. Accordingly, the following two items were used: (a) successful bids for corporate investment in subsidiary location and (b) new corporate investment in R&D or manufacturing/service delivery attracted by local subsidiary management. Hence, in order to measure the successful pursuit of all four types of initiatives, respondents were asked to indicate to what extent successfully approved and/or implemented entrepreneurial opportunities at their location related to the eight items displayed in Table 4.15. The items were measured on a five-point scale ranging from "never" to "plentifully," and the overall average of all eight items is used to calculate the overall level of subsidiary initiative during the past five years.

4.3.3.2 Specialized Subsidiary Resources and Capabilities for MNC Application

In addition to assessing the extent of the different initiative types, this research project also attempts to evaluate the level of specialized or distinctive resources and capabilities resulting from the entrepreneurial behavior of subsidiaries that can subsequently provide the grounds for competitive advantage at firm level. When applying the RBV as a firm-level theory, the dependent performance variable is typically represented by what is termed "competitive advantage," "sustained competitive advantage" or "economic rents" (Barney/Clark 2007, p. 24). However, as explained in Subsection 3.4.4.2, when applying the RBV at the subsidiary level, one must first focus on the precursors to firm-level advantage at the subsidiary level, which are (1) specialized or distinctive subsidiary resources that can (2) be further applied throughout the MNC, as competitive advantage will be achieved at firm level rather than subsidiary level (Birkinshaw et al. 1998, Rugman/Verbeke 2001).

(1) As previously argued, unique or distinctive subsidiary resources and capabilities are those that are assessed as "superior to those in sister units around the world" and that may, if also applicable at other locations of the MNC, "have the potential to enhance the competitiveness of the entire MNC" (Birkinshaw 1999, p. 17, Rugman/Verbeke 2001, p. 244, Schmid/Schurig 2003, p. 767). In line with this understanding, existing empirical studies often assess the level of distinctive resources and capabilities for different functional areas. For example, in studies by Birkinshaw and colleagues, respondents are asked to indicate the subsidiary's capability or distinctive expertise relative to other subsidiaries in the MNC in five areas (product or process R&D, manufacturing, marketing, managing international activities and innovation/entrepreneurship) using a seven-point scale from "far below average" to "far above average" (Birkinshaw et al. 1998, Birkinshaw 1999). Similarly, Schmid and Schurig (2003) analyze the development of critical subsidiary capabilities in four functional areas (development, production, marketing and logistics) using a seven-point scale from "weak competence" to "very high competence." Comparable to these studies, the present thesis measures the extent of

new and distinctive resource development in the eight value chain areas used previously. These are used to ensure consistency and allow for comparison with the role dimensions relating to the level of subsidiary resources and capabilities as presented in Subsection 4.3.1.2. Respondents are asked to indicate to what extent their subsidiary developed new and specialized capabilities or competencies in the eight areas as a result of their entrepreneurial activities during the past five years.[395] All eight items were measured on a five-point scale from "no capability development at all" to "extensive capability development," as shown in Table 4.16.[396] The mean average of all eight items is used to calculate the overall level of specialized resource development by the foreign subsidiary unit through initiative-taking during the past five years.

Indicator	Operationalization	Scale	Supporting Literature
Enhancement of specialized subsidiary resources and capabilities	• Research and/or development • Production of goods and/or services • Marketing and/or sales • Logistics and/or distribution • Purchasing • Human resource management • General management • Innovation and/or entrepreneurship	Five-point Likert scale	E: Birkinshaw et al. 1998, Birkinshaw 1999

Table 4.16: Measurement of the enhancement of distinctive subsidiary resources and capabilities through subsidiary initiatives

(2) A number of empirical studies have investigated the extent to which subsidiaries' resources and capabilities can be transferred and used in other parts of the multinational firm or to which they impact the overall competence development in the MNC (e.g. Birkinshaw et al. 1998, Andersson et al. 2001a, Andersson et al. 2002a, Andersson et al. 2002b, Schmid/Schurig 2003, Holm et al. 2005). For example, the work by Holm and Pedersen assesses to what degree the subsidiary has contributed to competence development of the MNC in six areas: research, development, production, marketing and sales, logistics and distribution as well as purchasing. Andersson et al. (2001a, 2002a, 2002b) evaluate the extent of a subsidiary's competence transfer to the other MNC units in two areas (product development and production development), while Schmid and Schurig (2003) measure the use of critical subsidiary capabilities by other corporate units in the four areas presented above. For the purpose of this study, the operationalization of this construct is primarily based on those developed by Holm and

---

[395] It should be noted that in Schmid and Schurig's study (2003), only those subsidiaries were said to have "critical" capabilities that achieved scores of 6 or 7 on two different scales (i.e. level of competence and level of use of these capabilities to other corporate units). In contrast, the present research evaluates only the extent to which "specialized" resources or capabilities are developed. Therefore, no further distinction of "resource criticalness" based on the respondent assessment is needed.

[396] It is acknowledged that directly measuring resources is a difficult endeavor for researchers since critical resources are often intangible and unobservable (Barney et al. 2001, p. 636, Barney et al. 2011, p. 1311). Therefore, different data collection methods are used in the present research to allow for a comprehensive analysis of the phenomenon from multiple angles (see also Subsection 4.2.1 on the rationale for selecting a case study design).

Pedersen and Schmid and Schurig. Accordingly, respondents are asked to indicate the extent to which the new and specialized subsidiary resources and capabilities are also of use for other MNC units. For consistency and comparability with the previous construct (i.e. development of distinctive subsidiary resources and capabilities), the assessment uses the eight items presented in Table 4.17 on a five-point scale ranging from "no use at all" to "very useful." The mean average of all eight items is used to determine the overall subsidiary impact on MNC capability development through initiative-taking during the past five years.

Indicator	Operationalization	Scale	Supporting Literature
Subsidiary initiative impact on MNC capability development	• Research and/or development • Production of goods and/or services • Marketing and/or sales • Logistics and/or distribution • Purchasing • Human resource management • General management • Innovation and/or entrepreneurship	Five-point Likert scale	E: Holm/Pedersen 2000, Schmid/ Schurig 2003

Table 4.17: Measurement of the subsidiary initiative impact on MNC capability development

4.3.4 Additional Measures

4.3.4.1 Subsidiary Role and Position in the MNC

(1) Subsidiary Role Development: Although not explicitly incorporated in the research framework as a separate outcome, it is nevertheless deemed important to also consider the potential impact of subsidiary initiative-taking on subsidiary role development and the subsidiary position in the MNC. Although subsidiary role development has yet to be clearly defined in the literature (Dörrenbächer/Gammelgaard 2006, p. 268), it is typically associated with positive or negative changes in the subsidiary role dimensions. For example, White and Poynter categorize subsidiaries based on the three role dimensions: product scope, market scope and valued-added scope. They further argue that "changes along one or more of these dimensions represent a fundamental shift in the strategy of a subsidiary" (White/Poynter 1984, p. 59). In line with this view, various empirical studies assess subsidiary role change based on these facets (e.g. Birkinshaw 1996, Benito et al. 2003, Dörrenbächer/Gammelgaard 2006). In accordance with these studies, the construct of subsidiary role change consists of three items related to changes in the subsidiary's geographical scope, product scope and value-added scope, as indicated in Table 4.16. Respondents are asked to assess the extent to which the entrepreneurial subsidiary initiatives resulted in changes along these three dimensions over the past five years.

(2) Subsidiary Influence: Following resource dependence logic, it has been argued that subsidiaries can create valuable resources for the MNC through entrepreneurial initiatives and hence potentially increase their influence and power in the firm over time (Ambos et al. 2010, p. 1103).[397] Subsidiary influence is understood as the "actual influence subsidiaries have on the strategic behavior of the MNC as a whole" (Andersson et al. 2007, p. 804). Various works have dealt empirically with subsidiary influence and power in general (e.g. Andersson/Pahlberg 1997, Forsgren/Pedersen 2000, Andersson et al. 2007) or specifically with regard to subsidiary initiatives (Bouquet/Birkinshaw 2008, Ambos et al. 2010). While the first three publications focus on the extent to which foreign subsidiaries can influence different strategic decisions in the MNC, the latter two assess the relative strength or influence of a subsidiary based on the influence it has on the outcomes of other subsidiaries.[398] Since this thesis also intends to measure the change in subsidiary influence specifically as the result of entrepreneurial subsidiary initiatives, the approach by Bouquet and Birkinshaw is used and adapted here. More precisely, only the item relating to subsidiary influence is applied, as this research is primarily interested in assessing changes in subsidiary influence rather than its relative influence vis-à-vis other foreign units. Thus, respondents are asked to assess, on a five-point scale, to what extent the subsidiary influence on the outcomes/performance of other subsidiaries in the MNC has changed within the past five years as a result of its entrepreneurial initiatives (see Table 4.18).

(3) Subsidiary Credibility: Research also provides support for the assumption that subsidiary initiatives impact subsidiary credibility (e.g. Birkinshaw/Fry 1998, p. 58, Birkinshaw 1999, p. 29, Delany 2000, p. 222, Dimitratos et al. 2009, p. 416). However, only one empirical study was identified that provided insight into the operationalization and measurement of this construct (Birkinshaw 1999). From this approach, the four items are directly adopted for the purpose of this study, as presented in Table 4.18. In line with the two previous indicators, a five point scale is applied from (1) major decline, (3) no change to (5) major improvement.

---

[397] See also Subsection 3.3.3.3 for further detail on the link between RDT and subsidiary initiatives.
[398] More specifically, relative subsidiary influence is calculated by measuring (a) the extent to which a focal subsidiary can influence the outcomes of other subsidiaries in the MNC and dividing it by (b) the average assessment of three items that measure the extent to which other subsidiary units influence or impact the focal unit.

Indicator	Operationalization	Scale	Supporting Literature
Change in subsidiary role	Change along the following role dimensions: • Geographical market scope • Product scope • Value-added scope	Five-point Likert scale	C: White/Poynter 1984 E: Birkinshaw 1996, Benito et al. 2003, Dörrenbächer/ Gammelgaard 2006
Change in subsidiary influence	• Change in subsidiary influence on the outcomes/performance of other subsidiaries	Five-point Likert scale	E: Bouquet/Birkinshaw 2008, Ambos et al. 2010
Change in subsidiary credibility	• Subsidiary history of delivering what it promised to the parent company • Significant value-added contribution to the corporation • Global competitiveness in subsidiary area of operation • Regarded by the parent as strategically important subsidiary	Five-point Likert scale	E: Birkinshaw 1999

Table 4.18: Measurement of changes in subsidiary role, influence and credibility

4.3.4.2 Subsidiary Performance

Following the resource-based logic outlined earlier in this publication, entrepreneurial initiatives, as newly developed resource bundles, may result in subsidiary or even firm-level advantages. Correspondingly, a number of empirical studies suggest that subsidiary initiatives will also lead to improved subsidiary performance (Birkinshaw 1997, Birkinshaw/Fry 1998, Liouka 2007, Ambos/Birkinshaw 2010). For example, externally-oriented subsidiary initiatives have been shown to result in enhanced sales, revenues and profits. Likewise, internally-oriented initiatives are said to lead to cost reductions and enhanced efficiency of the corporate system (Birkinshaw 1997, pp. 222-224, Birkinshaw/Fry 1998, pp. 54-56). In general, financial measures related to sales or profit are widely used to measure subsidiary performance (Andersson et al. 2001b, p. 5, Luo 2003, p. 299). Similarly, studies in the field of subsidiary entrepreneurship and innovation often focus on financial performance measures (e.g. Birkinshaw et al. 2005, Ambos et al. 2010, Ambos/Birkinshaw 2010). In order to assess changes in subsidiary performance resulting from entrepreneurial initiatives this study follows the same approach. Consequently, six items related to enhancements in sales/revenues, market share, costs, productivity, return on investment and profit are applied, as shown in Table 4.19.[399] Moreover, a five-point scale was used to measure the extent of performance enhancements for the six items ranging from "very limited" to "substantial".

---

[399] Moreover, it is expected that these six items should well capture the outcomes of both internally-oriented (e.g. improved costs or efficiency/productivity) and externally-oriented initiatives (e.g. enhanced sales or profits).

Indicator	Operationalization	Scale	Supporting Literature
Change in subsidiary performance	• Enhanced sales or revenues • Reduced costs • Improved market share • Improved profit • Improved return on investment • Improved productivity	Five-point Likert scale	E: Birkinshaw et al. 2005, Ambos et al. 2010, Ambos/Birkinshaw 2010

Table 4.19: Measurement of change in subsidiary performance

4.3.4.3 Control Measures

In addition to the main dependent and independent constructs of the framework, three (control) variables concerning further characteristics of the subsidiary are included in the study since they are also expected to influence subsidiary initiative-taking behavior and outcomes. In line with other empirical studies investigating the phenomenon of entrepreneurial initiatives (e.g. Jindra et al. 2009, Ambos et al. 2010, Ambos/Birkinshaw 2010), this research adds the following controls: (a) subsidiary size, (b) subsidiary age, (c) value scope, and (d) subsidiary mode of establishment. The considerations for their inclusion are as follows. First, subsidiary size can be seen as an indication of the level of subsidiary resources, which has been linked to the occurrence of subsidiary initiatives (e.g. Nohria/Gulati 1996, p. 1255, Yamin/Andersson 2011, p. 158). Hence, this variable, represented as the number of full time employees in the subsidiary unit, is incorporated in this research. Second, subsidiary age, i.e. years since subsidiary formation, is also positively linked to the occurrence of subsidiary initiatives. It is assumed that foreign units with many years of experience in their businesses and their local markets are better equipped to pursue entrepreneurial initiatives (Ambos et al. 2010, p. 1109). Third, a broader value-added scope has been linked to higher levels of initiatives in foreign affiliates, as it potentially broadens the opportunity space for entrepreneurial activities (Birkinshaw/Hood 1998b, p. 293). Fourth and finally, the subsidiary mode of formation is considered potentially relevant. It may be the case that subsidiary units established through acquisition rather than greenfield investment might engage more frequently in entrepreneurial initiatives (Birkinshaw/Hood 1998b, p. 293).

4.4 Collection of Data

Gaining access to the MNC and its multiple units is considered a particular challenge for researchers in IB. Scholars typically not only have to obtain permission for access to the organization itself but often need to approach various units in different geographical locations as well (Marschan-Piekkari et al. 2004, p. 252). In the light of these constraints, it has been found helpful to employ a "top-down" approach in which personal relationships with top executives are first established, and these individuals then facilitate access to other units of the MNC (Welch et al. 2002, p. 614). It was decided in this study to follow such a "cascading" procedure. Consequently, in each of the company cases, a central point of contact was identified who not only served as entry point into the MNCs but also then facilitated access to the subsidiary units abroad.

As illustrated in Figure 4.6, data was obtained (a) through different collection methods and (b) from different levels of the organization.[400] Taking advantage of the case study design, the present research collected quantitative and qualitative data from various sources, more specifically through (1) questionnaires, (2) interviews and (3) secondary and archival data. In case study research in the subsidiary initiative field, these particular three sources are common and are frequently employed in combination (e.g. Birkinshaw 1997, Birkinshaw/Hood 1997, Birkinshaw 1999, Lee/Chen 2003, Boojihawon et al. 2007). More specifically, the use of the three data collection methods served two purposes. First, their application was intended as convergent means aimed at obtaining a cumulative validation of research results through different sources. This is assumed to be beneficial since the same aspects of role-specific initiative-taking are investigated from different perspectives and through different data collection methods. Second, these approaches also served as "complementary means," allowing for "an enlargement of perspectives that permits a fuller treatment, description and explanation" of the phenomenon under investigation (Kelle/Erzberger 2004, pp. 174-175).[401] In addition to the use of these three sources, data was also obtained both from headquarters and the subsidiary level, which made it possible to study the phenomenon of subsidiary initiatives from different angles and incorporate the different perceptions that might exist at home and abroad (Marschan-Piekkari et al. 2004, pp. 254-255). In the end, the multiple sources of evidence should allow for the development of "convergent lines of inquiry" and for triangulation, thereby enhancing the validity and reliability of the study (Eisenhardt 1989, p. 538, Yin 2009, pp. 115-116). In the following Subsections, 4.4.1 to

---

[400] This multifaceted approach is believed to not only provide the possibility for subsequent "data triangulation" (i.e. data drawn from different data sources; see e.g. Kelle 2004, p. 179) but also to offer the opportunity for "unit triangulation" (i.e. compare or contrast responses from HQ and subsidiaries, see Marschan-Piekkari et al. 2004, p. 254).
[401] For example, through the post-survey interviews, the researcher intended to gain various insights into the phenomenon of role-specific initiative-taking for each subsidiary unit in its distinct contextual setting and hence "help to explain the meaning of data at a deeper level than otherwise" possible (Peterson 2004, p. 38).

4.4.3, these three different data collection methods are explained in more detail, along with their objectives and the approaches chosen.

(a) Data Collection Methods

	(1) Questionnaires	(2) Interviews	(3) Secondary Data
HQ-Level	• Assess **current subsidiary roles** from HQ perspective	• Obtain **additional information on foreign subsidiary units** from HQ perspective (e.g. entrepreneurial activities and outcomes)	• Obtain **additional information on foreign subsidiary units** (e.g. entrepreneurial activities and outcomes)
Sub.-Level	• Assess **current subsidiary roles/contexts** from subsidiary perspective • Acquire data on defined facets of **subsidiary initiative-taking** and selected **outcomes**	• Validate **current subsidiary roles** and investigate **role development** over time • Explore subsidiary **initiative-taking and outcomes in more detail**	• Obtain **additional information on foreign subsidiary units** and their entrepreneurial activities

(b) Organizational Level — Possibility for data triangulation — Possibility for unit triangulation

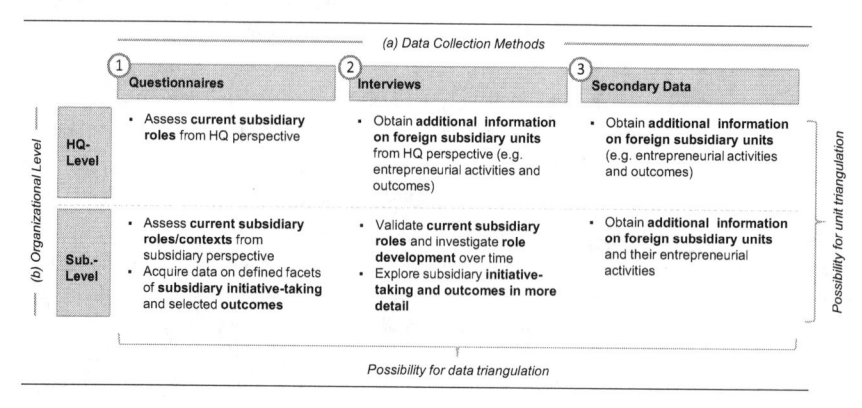

Figure 4.6: Overview of data collection approaches used in this study

4.4.1 Questionnaire

4.4.1.1 Objectives

The first step in the data collection process was the application of a questionnaire at both headquarters and the subsidiary level. At the corporate center, the aim was to assess the headquarters managers' perceptions of their foreign subsidiaries roles using the four role dimensions of the two role typologies. Given previous empirical studies on subsidiary role typologies, the use of a questionnaire was considered appropriate in order to systematically and efficiently assess role types from the perspective of headquarters.[402] At the foreign subsidiary units, a longer questionnaire was administered in order to collect data not only on subsidiary managers' perception of their units' roles, but also to acquire initial data on specific facets of subsidiary initiative-taking behavior and on subsidiary initiative outcomes. As stated earlier herein, there already exists a good understanding of the basic aspects of subsidiary initiatives. Therefore, it was deemed most efficient to first assess key initiative aspects through a standardized subsidiary and then employ interviews thereafter to further elaborate on the main findings, as is explained in more detail in Subsection 4.4.2.

---

[402] The questionnaire employed for headquarters was considerably shorter than the one used for the subsidiary units. It included questions to assess only the four role dimensions that are part of underlying the research framework. The questionnaires (one for each potential subsidiary to be included in the research) were handed out during the personal visits at the two divisional headquarters and completed by the main points of contact there.

4.4.1.2 Approach

(1) Application at Headquarters Level: In both cases (i.e. Autocomp and Telecomp), initial personal visits to the two headquarters locations in Germany were undertaken.[403] During these meetings, potentially relevant subsidiary units were selected jointly with headquarters managers based on the predefined criteria outlined above.[404] Managers at the corporate centers were then asked to complete a short questionnaire that intended to collect their perceptions of the current subsidiary roles of the 26 foreign units that were identified as suitable and potentially relevant in both companies. The role assessment questionnaire was based on the operationalization and measurement approaches outlined in Subsection 4.3.1. A sample questionnaire section for the evaluation of the "strategic importance of the subsidiary environment" is presented in Figure 4.7.[405]

1. Strategic Importance of the Subsidiary Environment					
The following questions will assess your opinion about different characteristics of the **current market environment** of the subsidiary unit located *in country xy*. Please indicate, for each characteristic listed below, to what extent it applies to the market environment for which the subsidiary is responsible at the moment.					
	Very small 1	2	3	4	Very high 5
Market size (e.g. sales value/volume, number of customers)...........................	☐	☐	☐	☐	☐
Competitive intensity (e.g. number of major customers, quality and sophistication of competitive products/services)................................	☐	☐	☐	☐	☐
Technological dynamism (e.g. number of innovations and patents developed in the market each year)..	☐	☐	☐	☐	☐
Customer demand intensity (e.g. sophistication and complexity of products/services demanded by customers).......................................	☐	☐	☐	☐	☐

Figure 4.7: Section of headquarters questionnaire on subsidiary roles

(2) Application at Subsidiary Level: Following the selection of all relevant subsidiary units at the two headquarters locations, one or two members of each subsidiary's top

---

[403] Following the first contact via telephone, personal meetings were scheduled at the headquarters of both companies in Germany. These initial personal meetings were used, to present the research project in more detail to headquarters managers, to select potential subsidiary units for the study, to assess – through the paper-based questionnaire – headquarters managers' perception of the current subsidiaries' roles, and to conduct preliminary interviews.

[404] See Subsection 4.2.2.3 for more detail on the subsidiary selection criteria.

[405] The application of a standardized questionnaire to assess subsidiary roles in conjunction with case study research is not uncommon in IB literature (see e.g. Birkinshaw et al. 2000, Daniel 2010). Among the advantages of such an approach is the possibility for direct comparison by the respondents between the different foreign units along particular dimensions, and the opportunity of the researcher to provide further explanations or to ask additional questions to enhance understanding and confidence in responses (see also Birkinshaw et al. 2000, p. 334).

management team were identified as potential respondents for the subsequent survey. Afterwards, the two headquarters managers also functioned as corporate-level sponsors for the research project. Previous work suggests that, given the particular complexities of international firms, the use of internal sponsors is "of utmost importance in view of the geographically dispersed activities of the firm" (Welch et al. 2002, p. 620). The same holds true for the present study. For example, the two sponsors not only enabled access to the foreign units' management but also informed the respective respondents via telephone and/or email of the research and the upcoming survey. This helped to raise awareness of the study and increase the foreign managers' motivation to participate in both the surveys and the interviews.

Following the initial information provided by the two sponsors, an email invitation was sent out shortly afterwards to the managers at the 26 subsidiaries. In addition to a brief overview of the research project and details on the survey,[406] the email included a link to the online questionnaire.[407] Two reminder emails were sent to managers who had not yet completed the survey, the first two weeks after the initial email, and the second four weeks after.[408] In total, respondents in both firms were given six weeks to complete the survey. After this period, the online survey was closed and no further entries were accepted. The choice to use an email invitation and an online survey (rather than postal survey) was based on several advantages that are associated with such a data collection approach. First, it allowed for direct contact with the geographically dispersed managers at a high speed and low cost. Second, the online survey provided the respondents with the convenience of answering the questions at a time and location suitable for them. Moreover, the completed questions were directly transmitted and no effort was required from the respondents to send back the completed questionnaire (as with postal questionnaires, for example). Third, all data received was automatically stored in a secure database. This facilitated data entry and subsequent analysis for the researcher. Moreover, respondents that did not finish the entire questionnaire could be quickly contacted by the researcher and were kindly asked to complete only the remaining questions. This significantly eased the follow-up process and increased the final response rate. Fourth and finally, the online survey allowed for the designation of "required questions" that had to be answered by the managers before advancing to the next question. For the key questions of the survey, this eliminated item non-response and the necessity of discarding answers that were not finished properly.[409]

---

[406] For example, the email contained information on the main question areas of the survey, the approximate time needed for completion and the confidentiality of the responses.
[407] The online questionnaire was hosted by www.unipark.de.
[408] As respondents had to provide their names and email addresses in the survey as contacts for the subsequent interviews, reminder emails could be specifically targeted at those who had yet to complete the survey.
[409] Disadvantages that are typically linked to online questionnaires are dismissal as junk mail, skewed attributes of internet population, or concerns as to the selection and representativeness of samples (see e.g. Evans/Mathur

In total, the subsidiary questionnaire consisted of 19 core questions that aimed at collecting subsidiary managers' perceptions of (a) current subsidiary role and context, (b) subsidiary initiative-taking and (c) outcomes as shown in Table 4.20.[410] The four subsidiary role dimensions and subsidiary autonomy were operationalized as presented in Subsection 4.3.1 and measured using five-point scales. Questions on subsidiary initiative-taking related to the identification of initiatives, resource structuring and bundling and to headquarters-subsidiary alignment activities. The respective nine questions were operationalized using the constructs outlined in Subsection 4.3.2 and assessed on five-point scales.

Subsidiary Role	Subsidiary Initiative-Taking	Subsidiary Initiative Outcome
Typology by Bartlett/Ghoshal (1) Strategic importance of the subsidiary environment (2) Subsidiary resources and capabilities **Typology by Jarillo/Martinez** (3) Subsidiary localization/local responsiveness (4) Subsidiary integration **Other Context Factors** (5) Subsidiary decision-making autonomy	**Identification** (6) Identification of subsidiary initiative opportunities (7) Innovativeness of identified opportunities **Resource Structuring and Bundling** (8) Acquisition of resources and capabilities (9) Internal resource/capability development (10) Internal-external resource/capability development (11) Bundling of resources and capabilities **HQ-Subsidiary Alignment** (12) HQ involvement (13) Resistance from HQ and other MNC units (14) Subsidiary initiative selling	**Direct Initiative Outcomes** (15) Extent of subsidiary initiatives (16) Development of specialized subsidiary resources/capabilities (17) Impact on MNC capability development **Additional Measures** (18) Performance outcomes (19) Changes to subsidiary role and position

Table 4.20: Elements of subsidiary-level questionnaire

With regard to initiative outcomes, one question block was designed to assess the extent of various types of initiatives that were successfully pursued during the past five years, based on the operationalization described in Subsection 4.3.3. Two further questions were included to evaluate the extent of newly developed and specialized resources/capabilities of use for other MNC units as well. In line with previous works, these questions were measured on five-point scales. Finally, two questions on additional measures were incorporated. For this purpose, the operationalization described in Subsection 4.3.4, regarding changes to subsidiary role and position and performance outcomes, was employed and measured on a five-point scale.

At Autocomp, managers from 14 country units were invited to participate at the beginning of June 2012. The online survey was then conducted between mid-June 2012 and

---

2005, pp. 201-202). Given the criteria-led selection of subsidiary units and respondents as well as the direct approach through corporate sponsors, these weaknesses were not considered relevant.

[410] Admittedly, given the inclusion of several subsidiary role typologies, the different sub-processes and multiple outcomes, the questionnaire ended up longer than desired. Hence, the average time for respondents to complete the online questionnaire was approximately 25 minutes, with extremes between 18 minutes on the lower end and 45 minutes on the upper end.

the end of July 2012. By the end, 11 managers from nine countries had fully completed the questionnaire. In the case of Telecomp, the survey took place exactly one year later, between mid-June 2013 and the end of July 2013. Here, managers from a total of 12 subsidiaries were invited at the beginning of June. After six weeks of survey time, 13 managers from all 12 country units had responded and completed the online questionnaire.

As is explained in detail in Subsection 4.5.1, the survey results were subsequently analyzed by the researcher and the subsidiary roles were determined based on the foreign managers' evaluation of their own units. Next, the resulting relative subsidiary positions were graphically presented in the form of 2 two-by-two matrices (one matrix for each subsidiary role typology). The illustrations were shared with all survey respondents by email, and they were asked to verify or, if necessary, alter the relative role position of their own unit or any other units that they have relevant knowledge of.[411] Interestingly, there was wide agreement as to the overall role positions among the subsidiary managers. All units remained within the quadrant of their role types and only minor adjustments were made.[412] As a final step, the role matrices as assessed by subsidiary managers were also shared with the two corporate sponsors. There were larger deviations between subsidiary and headquarters role perceptions of two foreign units of Autocomp (Brazil and Malaysia) and five subsidiaries of Telecomp (Albania, Czech Republic, Germany, Macedonia and Netherlands). These seven units were excluded, resulting in a total of 14 foreign subsidiaries (seven each in Autocomp and Telecomp) in which further interviews were conducted. The interviews are described in the following subsection.

4.4.2 Interviews

4.4.2.1 Objectives

The second step in the data collection for this research consisted of interviews, that is, "purposeful discussions between two or more people" (Saunders et al. 2012, p. 245). Interviewing requires direct interaction between the researcher and the respondent and allows for gathering rich data that can then be analyzed qualitatively and quantitatively. Interviews can range from highly formalized and structured to informal and unstruc-

---

[411] The two-by-two matrices were shared as Microsoft PowerPoint files. This allowed for the easy repositioning of the units via "drag and drop" by each respondent. Files were then saved and sent back to the researcher along with further explanations and comments for alterations. In some instances, the subsidiary managers were also contacted via telephone to discuss changes in role positions.

[412] Subsequent telephone conversations with a number of subsidiary respondents revealed that some of them lacked deeper insights into the role dimensions of other units (i.e. specific market environments, subsidiary resources/ capabilities or localization and integration). Hence, they were only able to provide limited feedback or none at all on other units.

tured.[413] Between those extreme positions are semi-structured interviews, which were employed in the present research. Here, the researcher applies a list of questions that are to be covered in the interview (e.g. in the form of an interview guideline), but these may vary from case to case. Semi-structured interviews are considered particularly useful not only for understanding the "what" and "how" of a research topic, but also for exploring the "why." Furthermore, semi-structured interviews are considered appropriate not only for exploratory purposes, but also when trying to understand the relationship between variables, for explanatory purposes, or to validate and extend findings from questionnaires (Ghauri/Grønhaug 2005, pp. 132-133, Saunders et al. 2012, p. 248).

Accordingly, the semi-structured interviews applied in this study served two major purposes. First, the interviews were intended to provide additional validation of the findings derived from the structured subsidiary-level questionnaire. For example, the interview questions relating to subsidiary role dimensions aimed at substantiating and enriching the preliminary results from the survey and at helping understand the basis on which the assessments were made. Moreover, the interviews were intended to aid in further explaining the themes and patterns that emerged from the questionnaire and in better understanding the relationships between the different elements of the framework. Here, interview questions such as "how" (e.g. the initiative process took place) and "why" (e.g. certain activities were undertaken) came into play. Second, aside from these more explanatory objectives, the interviews were used to further explore and investigate aspects that were not covered in the questionnaire. For example, the interviews allowed for a deeper exploration of "how" or "why" subsidiary roles changed over time and "how" or "why" this affected entrepreneurial initiatives. Between May 2012 and January 2014, a total of 16 interviews both at headquarters and at the foreign subsidiary level were completed in the two multinational firms. Among these, the two interviews at headquarters level lasted between 2 and 2.5 hours each, while the 14 interviews with subsidiary-level respondents ranged from 40 to 70 minutes. The interview modes, procedures and content are described in more detail below for both headquarters and the subsidiary level.

4.4.2.2 Approach

(1) Application at Headquarters Level: At the two corporate centers, semi-structured interviews were conducted during the initial personal meetings. Interviews were performed with suitable headquarters representatives who were centrally responsible for innovative and/or entrepreneurial activities across the MNC and who possessed far-reaching knowledge and expertise of the various national and international subsidiaries

---

[413] In addition to formalization and structure, interviews can be categorized based on "standardization," "type of respondents," "number of interviewees" or "interview mode" (see e.g. Bortz/Döring 2006, p. 315, Saunders et al. 2012, pp. 246-247).

within their organizations. At Autocomp, the interview partner and main sponsor for the present research was the global innovation manager. A central element of this role is the responsibility for managing and coordinating centralized and decentralized innovative and entrepreneurial activities across the regions of the MNC. The interview partner and sponsor at Telecomp was the global head of product marketing and product development, responsible for, among other things, managing the portfolio of existing products and for globally steering innovative and entrepreneurial activities across the division.

In both cases, the initial interviews at headquarters were conducted face-to-face during personal site visits by the researcher, which lasted between 2 and 2.5 hours. In-person interviews were considered particularly appropriate for the following reasons. First, given the importance of the central sponsors at headquarters for the subsequent research in the each MNC, visits to establish first contact and to start building a personal relationship were considered critical. Second, given the very small number of headquarters respondents, the researcher needed both to cover a breadth of topics and to collect deep and rich data from these informants. This was not deemed feasible with other interview forms such as telephone or mail interviews. Third, personal interactions enabled the researcher to develop a deeper rapport with interviewees and hence to obtain more open and honest responses, particularly on sensitive and complex issues such as headquarters-subsidiary interaction or subsidiary development over time. Fourth, the in-depth interviews (in longer in-person interview sessions) made it possible to obtain a clearer and more accurate picture of the respondents' position and views. The interviewer was able to ask for further elaboration of answers and attitudes, which was helpful at the beginning of research in each MNC at a time when many topics and aspects were not yet sufficiently detailed. Fifth and finally, pragmatic and cost-oriented aspects were taken into consideration. Since both headquarters are located in Germany, travel time and travel costs were less of an issue (see e.g. Shuy 2001, p. 539, Marschan-Piekkari et al. 2004, pp. 186-187, Ghauri/Grønhaug 2005, pp. 132-133).

Each interview used a short guide, representing "essentially a checklist for the researcher to follow to help ensure that all topic areas are covered during the interview" (Daniels/Cannice 2004, p. 192). The interview guide focused on the following key aspects: basic information on the MNC and the role of the headquarters manager, overview and information on foreign subsidiary units, the headquarters manager's interaction with foreign subsidiary units, selection of subsidiary units for the present research and the subsidiary role assessment.[414] In contrast to the subsidiary-level interviews, these were not recorded, as it was expected that particularly during the first personal meeting with the researcher, headquarters managers would be "more guarded when tape-recorded" and might answer less openly and freely (Daniels/Cannice 2004, p.

---

[414] See also the Appendix for the complete interview guide used at the headquarters level.

198). Instead, detailed notes were taken during the interviews. Moreover, additional points and recollections were added directly after the interviews and were documented in the same order as the interview guide. In the end, notes were also shared with the headquarters representatives to ensure that all information was documented correctly and comprehensively.[415]

(2) Application at Subsidiary Level: As at the corporate level, semi-structured interviews were conducted with the foreign units. However, interviews with subsidiary managers were performed only after the subsidiary-level questionnaires were returned and analyzed.[416] In total, 14 subsidiary-level interviews with 14 subsidiary managers were conducted between August 2012 and January 2014.[417] Suitable respondents were jointly determined in advance with the corporate sponsors in each company. As is common in subsidiary initiative research, the interview partners were senior managers or managing directors of the foreign units (see e.g. Birkinshaw 1997, Birkinshaw/Hood 1997, 1998a, Boojihawon et al. 2007, Dörrenbächer/Geppert 2009). This was to ensure that the interviewees had a comprehensive view of the innovative and entrepreneurial activities undertaken in the foreign unit. Accordingly, the respondents held positions such as managing director, head of research and development, and head of product management. In all cases, the interviews with subsidiary managers were conducted via telephone due to the dispersed locations of the foreign units across various countries and due to the budget and time constraints of this study. Most interviews were conducted in English and only a smaller number in German when the interviewer and interviewee shared the same native language. All interviews were recorded and transcribed, as detailed in Subsection 4.5.2.

As with the headquarters interviews, an interview guide was applied at the subsidiary level (see Figure 4.8). The guide was developed based on the concepts and theories presented in Chapter 3 of this publication. Because the intention was to substantiate and enhance the information gathered through the questionnaire, the interview followed a similar structure.

---

[415] Both headquarters managers largely agreed with all notes and documentations and only minor adaptations were suggested.
[416] This was necessary because certain interview questions were adapted based on the results of the survey. Moreover, it helped the researcher obtain a preliminary view on subsidiary initiative-taking activities in the past five years and to better prepare for the interview sessions.
[417] The subsidiary interview phases took place at Autocomp from August 2012 to February 2013 and at Telecomp from October 2013 to January 2014. The interview phase at Autocomp was somewhat longer as some interviews had to be rescheduled multiple times due to the unavailability of some subsidiary managers.

Introduction
1. Basic Subsidiary Characteristics
2. Changes in Subsidiary Characteristics
3. General Information on Entrepreneurial Activities
4. Subsidiary Initiative Process – Entrepreneurial Resource Management 4.1 Initiative Opportunity Identification 4.2 Resource Structuring 4.3 Resource Bundling
5. Subsidiary Initiative Process – HQ-S Alignment 5.1 Headquarters Involvement 5.2 Corporate Resistance 5.3 Subsidiary Initiative Selling
6. Subsidiary Initiative Outcomes
Closing

Figure 4.8: General structure of the subsidiary interview guide

First, it focused on the respondent's perception of selected subsidiary characteristics related to its role in the MNC.[418] Second, respondents were asked to provide information on how the role of the foreign unit has changed over the past five years. Third, interviewees were invited to share some general insights into entrepreneurial activities pursued in the local unit, such as the frequency of initiatives or the motivation and objectives for doing so. In cases where subsidiaries pursued multiple initiatives during the past five years, respondents were asked to make reference to the three most important during this time frame, as was done in similar cases previously (e.g. Delany 1998, p. 223). Fourth and fifth, the initiative process was examined in more detail, particularly in relation to entrepreneurial resource management and headquarters-subsidiary alignment. The objective here was to better understand how and why certain sub-processes took place as communicated by the subsidiary manager in the questionnaire. Finally, the outcomes of subsidiary initiatives for both the subsidiary and the wider MNC were addressed.

---

[418] As the role perceptions for both role typologies are already addressed in the questionnaire, the focus here is on additional role aspects that were not covered in the survey, such as product scope, market scope or value-adding scope.

4.4.3 Archival and Secondary data

4.4.3.1 Objectives

As is often done in case study research in the subsidiary initiative field, secondary and archival data were collected. Examples of secondary data that are commonly applied in international business are financial reports, budget and operating statements, public company reports, internal company documents and press releases (Daniels/Cannice 2004, p. 201, Ghauri 2004, p. 110). Likewise, in the subsidiary initiative field secondary data may consist of annual reports, internal company documents, press clippings or handbooks, for example (see e.g. Birkinshaw 1997, p. 216, 1999, p. 21, Dörrenbächer/ Geppert 2010, p. 609). Typically, secondary and archival data can be used to obtain comparative or contextual information, to contrast or compare with findings from other sources, or even to make unforeseen or unexpected new discoveries (Saunders et al. 2012, p. 201). In the present study, the primary objective was to provide confirmation and substantiation of interview and survey data relating to aspects such as current subsidiary context, subsidiary role development and entrepreneurial activities pursued by the local affiliates during the past five years.

4.4.3.2 Approach

Secondary data was obtained from sources within and outside the two companies. For example, the sponsors at headquarters were encouraged during the face-to-face meetings to provide further documents on the overall company as well as on the subsidiary units to be included in the study. Similarly, subsidiary-level respondents were asked at the end of each interview whether additional documentation on the local unit and on subsidiary initiatives was available and could be shared with the researcher. Various internal company presentations and documents were acquired in this way. In addition, annual company reports from Autocomp and Telecomp, press reports and company presentations were obtained from other sources such as websites and the public relations departments of both companies.

4.5 Data Analysis

4.5.1 Questionnaire

As was described above in Subsection 4.2.2.4, case study research can incorporate both qualitative and quantitative data. Among the different data sources employed in this study, the questionnaire provided quantitative data. However, given the small sample size, a sophisticated statistical analysis was not deemed appropriate. Instead, the quantitative data obtained through the questionnaire was used primarily for descriptive purposes. Commonly, descriptive statistics involve basic summaries of survey results.

These are often supplemented by simple graphic representations such as pie charts or bar graphs. By displaying, for example, frequencies, frequency distribution (e.g. numbers or percentages), measures of central tendencies (e.g. mean, median or mode) or variations (e.g. range or standard deviation), an overview and simple comparison of samples can be attained (Ghauri/Grønhaug 2005, pp. 160-168, Bortz/Döring 2006, pp. 371-372, Fink 2009, pp. 78-81).

Accordingly, this research presents the survey results in the form of basic summaries and bar charts for each of the 19 question categories. When more than one survey was completed by a subsidiary unit, the mean average for each question was displayed for the subsidiary unit.[419] A sample graph showing the subsidiary managers' assessment of select role dimensions is shown in Figure 4.9. This chart provides the following information: (1) Which question category is concerned? (2) What scale is applied? (3) How many responses were received? (4) What individual questions within the category are concerned? (5) What is the average rating by subsidiary respondents at one location for each question? (6) What is the mean average value per question category for one specific subsidiary location?[420] (7) What is the mean average value per question category across all subsidiary units in one company case?

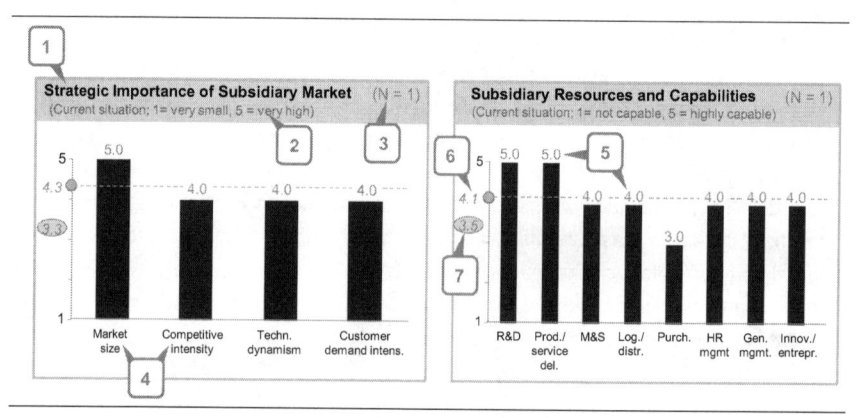

Figure 4.9: Sample graph chart on subsidiary role dimensions

---

[419] Typically, average ratings of multiple respondents are considered more reliable and more valid than individual ratings. However, given the limited number of suitable and available respondents at the subsidiary locations, in many cases this study had to rely on single responses (Bortz/Döring 2006, p. 185).
[420] Admittedly, this is a simplification that is not without possible problems. One possible critique is that each question carries the same weight or that not all potentially relevant questions are covered in each category. However, when reviewing previous empirical work and when operationalizing the different constructs (see section 4.3), no arguments for weighted differentiation or additional questions were identified.

4.5.2 Interviews and Secondary Data

Before performing the subsidiary-level interviews, short reports containing the survey results for each location were shared by email with respective local managers. This was to give them the opportunity to review the findings and help better prepare for the upcoming interviews. The vast majority of interviews were tape-recorded to ensure that all content was captured as comprehensively as possible. In addition, some notes were taken to ensure that the researcher listened attentively and recorded all potentially relevant information, and to provide him with an intermediate overview of which questions had already been addressed during each interview (Ghauri/Grønhaug 2005, p. 135, Saunders et al. 2012, pp. 263-264). The recorded interviews were transcribed shortly afterwards and rechecked by the researcher by listening to the entire audio-tape and comparing it to the transcripts (Miles/Huberman 1994, p. 50). Moreover, a preliminary analysis of the collected material was performed to allow for an intertwined process of data collection and analysis and to permit adjustments to the data collection process if necessary (Eisenhardt 1989, p. 539).

Data analysis started after all interview data was obtained and transcribed. Following Miles and Huberman, the qualitative data analysis consisted of three main activities: data reduction, data display and drawing/verification of conclusions (Miles/Huberman 1994, pp. 10-12). (1) Data reduction refers to "selecting, focusing, simplifying, abstracting and transforming" data from notes or transcriptions in order to "create meaning from the mass of words" (Ghauri/Grønhaug 2005, p. 206). It involves the creation of categories and the identification of themes and patterns through activities such as writing summaries, coding or clustering to reduce and sharpen content. (2) Data display then deals with the organization and assembly of information so that conclusions can be drawn and action can be taken. This can occur as extended text or, to make comprehensive and complex information more accessible, as graphs, charts or matrices. (3) The drawing and verification of conclusions relates to activities such as seeking to identify regularities, patterns or explanations and to derive possible configurations and propositions. Verification typically takes place as the researcher proceeds and conclusions are continuously tested for plausibility and conformability (Miles et al. 2007, pp. 12-14).

For the purpose of reducing the data in this study, coding of interview transcripts and additional material (e.g. research notes and secondary data) was performed. In general, coding refers to the process of identifying a unit or chunk of data (e.g. a passage of text) and assigning it to some more general phenomenon or category. A code therefore represents a label assigned to a certain text passage that consists of, for example, a few words, sentences or paragraphs (Ghauri/Grønhaug 2005, pp. 207-208, Kuckartz 2010, pp. 57-60). In general, codes can be developed inductively or deductively. Inductive coding can be viewed as more of an exploratory approach in which new codes and coding schemes gradually evolve over the course of analyzing different texts. Here, certain phrases are selected and assigned to preliminary codes or categories, which are then further developed, summarized or differentiated. Conversely, deductive coding implies that a coding scheme is first designed, based on, for example, existing literature, research, or prior theoretical knowledge. Instead of developing new codes, text passages are assigned to one or more existing codes if they are identified as indicators of certain phenomena. However, qualitative research often utilizes hybrid modes in which initiative coding schemes are first developed and new codes are then added during further analysis (Gibbs 2007, pp. 44-46, Kuckartz 2010, pp. 60-61).

In addition to these two general coding approaches, specific coding forms have been described in the literature, such as open or theoretical coding (Glaser/Strauss 1967, Glaser 1978), thematic coding (Kuckartz 2010, Flick 2014), or qualitative content analysis (Mayring 2002, 2010).[421] The present study uses thematic coding, as this has been recognized as a structured approach that is particularly apt for analyzing and comparing different groups or cases. It is typically based on prior theoretical knowledge and assists in validating or further advancing theories rather than generating new ones (Flick 2009, p. 318, Kuckartz 2010, p. 85, Flick 2014, p. 378). The coding of interview and secondary data was conducted as follows.

(1) First, an initial coding scheme was developed based on the structure and operationalization of the proposed research framework.[422] Using an existing theoretical framework for coding is considered advantageous and more reliable than developing new codes merely through analyzing data. This method helps tie the research question and conceptual interests directly to the data (Miles/Huberman 1994, pp. 58, 65). The initial coding scheme used for this study consisted of all the central elements of the research framework as shown in Figure 4.10. In total, 29 codes were initially used, of which 5 relate to the subsidiary role context, 16 to subsidiary imitative-taking activities, and 8 to outcomes.

(2) The coding scheme was then employed to codify data obtained from subsidiary and headquarters management through the interviews and secondary data, for example. This was performed using a two-step coding approach. First, printouts of all texts were made and read several times by the researcher. Relevant text passages were color marked,[423] research notes were added and one or more codes were written next to the text elements. Subsequently, QDA software was applied to enter all assigned codes into

---

[421] For a more comprehensive overview of different coding methods see, for example, Flick 2014, pp. 378-379.
[422] When developing the coding scheme, the interview guide also served as an important foundation, which again follows the structure of the research framework. See Sections 3.4 and 4.3 for further detail on the research framework and the operationalization of the different elements.
[423] As not every part of the notes is of relevance and needs to be coded, emphasis was placed on coding elements related to the research framework and research questions (see Miles/Huberman 1994, p. 65).

the computer.[424] Finally, all codes were monitored and adjusted as necessary (Miles/ Huberman 1994, p. 65, Kuckartz 2010, pp. 82-83). In the course of the coding process, several new codes emerged throughout the data analyses and were then added to the initial coding scheme.

(3) After completion of the coding process, each subsidiary unit was analyzed in detail. The purpose of the individual analysis was to achieve a deeper understanding of the particular context of a subsidiary and examine its specific initiative-taking behavior and the related outcomes. To this end, detailed write-ups were generated for each subsidiary unit based on the elements of the research framework. The primary objective of this step was to "describe, understand and explain what has happened in a single bounded context" of a foreign unit (Miles et al. 2007, p. 100). A further purpose was to allow the researcher to become "intimately familiar" with each subsidiary unit and its entrepreneurial undertakings before attempts were made to generalize findings across subsidiary units and cases (Eisenhardt 1989, p. 540).[425]

(4) Following the unit-by-unit analysis and presentation, pattern matching was conducted. In general, this implies the comparison of empirically based patterns with *a priori* predictions and is commonly applied in causal case studies. If systematic patterns emerge, predictions or assumptions can be accepted (Ghauri 2004, p. 121, Ghauri/ Grønhaug 2005, p. 215, Yin 2009, p. 136, Saunders et al. 2012, p. 390). As to the present research, subsidiary initiative-related patterns that emerged from empirical findings were compared with the predictions for each role type as posited in Section 3.5. The goal of this was to determine consistencies or differences between different subsidiary role types in each case and to enhance understanding and provide explanations. Following the within-case examinations (see Sections 5.1 and 5.2), an analysis across subsidiaries of Autocomp and Telecomp was performed to determine whether role-specific predictions were also met across cases (see Section 5.3). Although statistical generalization was neither intended nor deemed possible with the approach chosen, it can be assumed that if role-specific predictions can be replicated both within and across cases, compelling support for the initial predictions is obtained (Yin 2009, pp. 54-56).

---

[424] In the present thesis, the software program MAXQDA was used. The application of QDA software is greatly beneficial for qualitative data analysis as it helps, for example, to generate overviews of all codes, identify overlaps and show the proximity of different codes to each other (see e.g. Kuckartz 2010, p. 83).
[425] Detailed descriptions of the unit-by-unit analysis are presented in Chapter 5.

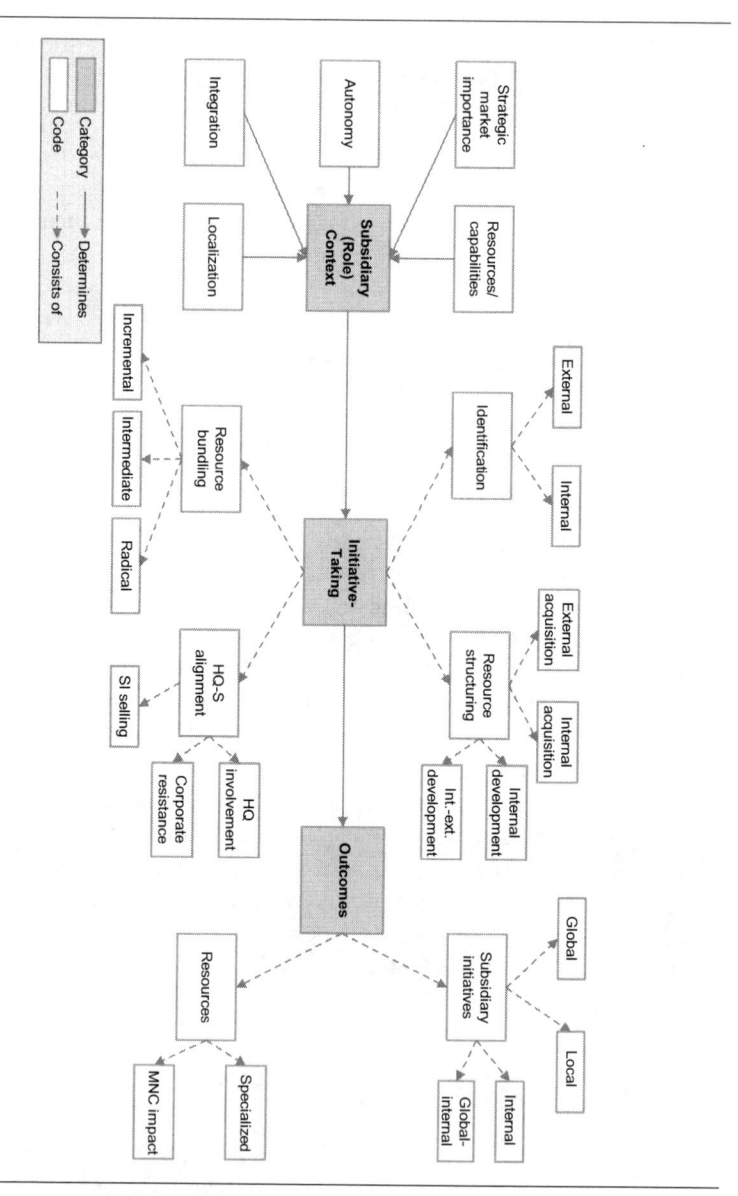

Figure 4.10: Initial coding scheme used for the analysis

4.6 Scientific Quality Criteria

As with quantitative studies, qualitative research can also be assessed through various criteria. Although it is often argued that qualitative criteria are less rigorous and less well-established than their quantitative counterparts, the following four criteria are commonly applied to judge the quality of case study design and are also applied for the present thesis: (1) construct validity, (2) internal validity, (3) external validity and (4) reliability (see e.g. Gibbert et al. 2008, pp. 1466-1468, Sinkovics et al. 2008, p. 695, Göbel 2009, pp. 371-374, Yin 2009, pp. 40-45).

(1) Construct validity refers to the quality of the operational constructs that are used to measure the concept being studied. Case study research is often criticized for failing to develop an appropriately operational set of measures and instead relying on subjective judgments when collecting data. In order to mitigate such concerns, the following measures can be taken: (a) develop constructs *a priori* based on existing literature and previous studies, (b) use multiple sources of evidence, (c) establish a chain of evidence and (d) have informants review the draft case study reports (Gibbert et al. 2008, pp. 371-372, Yin 2009, pp. 41-42). Accordingly, these measures were incorporated in the present research as follows. First, in order to appropriately measure the different elements of the research framework, this study relied largely on existing operationalizations derived from previous empirical studies. Second, data was obtained from multiple sources at headquarters and at the subsidiary level. Moreover, data was collected from questionnaires, interviews and archival and secondary data. These multiple sources of evidence not only allow for the investigation of the subsidiary initiative phenomenon from various perspectives, but it can also be expected that convergent findings indicate that the phenomenon was accurately measured. Third, a clear chain of evidence was maintained to allow external observers to reconstruct how new evidence is derived from the initial research questions to the final case study conclusions. For this purpose, a detailed description of how data was collected, analyzed and interpreted in this research is provided. Moreover, the case study reports describe the findings *en detail* and also link to the relevant sources of evidence. Fourth, summary findings were shared with key informants at headquarters and the subsidiary level.[426] Results were discussed and feedback was requested to ensure that all data was recorded and interpreted appropriately by the researcher.

(2) The test for internal validity is particularly relevant for explanatory case studies and ensures that the research provides a plausible and logical reasoning for the proposed causal relationships. Here an assessment is made as to whether the resulting conclu-

---

[426] For example, subsidiary role assessments were shared and discussed with both headquarters and subsidiary representatives to determine commonalities or differences in role perception. Moreover, subsidiary-specific findings obtained through questionnaires were sent to subsidiary managers prior to interviews.

sions are correct and whether possible rival or conflicting explanations are sufficiently addressed. In order to strengthen internal validity, researchers can (a) formulate a clear research framework that outlines causal relationships and/or (b) engage in pattern matching (Gibbert et al. 2008, p. 1466, Göbel 2009, pp. 372-373, Yin 2009, pp. 42-43). To meet these requirements, the present thesis first develops and describes a clear research framework and predictions on potential causal relationships in Chapter 3. Second, pattern matching was conducted as described in Subsection 4.5.2. Thus the thesis tests the extent to which the *a priori* predictions and the empirically derived patterns matched.

(3) External validity relates to the "generalizability" of findings beyond the immediate case study. While large quantitative survey research can commonly rely on statistical generalization, this is neither intended nor possible with case studies. Instead, case studies can follow the logic of analytical generalization from empirical observations to theory rather than generalize based on a population. In order to strengthen external validity, the following generally available measures are utilized for this research: (a) replicate findings within and across cases, (b) provide a clear rationale for case study design and (c) give generous details on the case study context so the reader can follow the researcher's sampling choices (Gibbert et al. 2008, p. 1468, Göbel 2009, p. 373, Yin 2009, pp. 43-44). Consequently, attempts were made to, first, replicate findings for specific role types not only within each embedded case but across the two nested cases as well. It can be presumed that if the findings can be replicated in a second or third setting, this provides increasingly strong support for generalization (see Yin 2009, p. 44).[427] Second, this study provided a clear rationale for why a case design was adopted (Subsection 4.2.1) and how the case study research was designed (Subsection 4.2.2). Third, details on the case study context were provided both in Section 4.2 and at the beginning of each section presenting the empirical findings (Sections 5.1 and 5.2). Taken together, these detailed descriptions are intended to provide the reader with a high degree of transparency on the particular case study design and context and hence help better assess to what extent the findings can be generalized beyond the immediate case study.

(4) Reliability is concerned with the absence of random error and biases, implying that subsequent investigators would come to the same results and conclusions if they were to follow the same procedures as the original research. Therefore, transparency regarding the methodological approach and the possibility of replicating the same case

---

[427] As outlined in Subsection 4.2.2.1, this research utilizes an embedded and multiple case study design (see also Yin 2009, pp. 46-50). Accordingly, each subsidiary unit can be viewed as an embedded unit of analysis within a case. In sum, both cases contain 14 embedded units of analysis that can be used for replication purposes and as such should provide a good basis for analytical replication (see also Gibbert et al. 2008, p. 1468).

4 – Empirical Study

study are emphasized in order to enhance the reliability of case studies. Accordingly, measures a researcher can take include (a) using a case study protocol to report how the research was conducted and (b) developing a case study database, which should include all relevant documents such as interview transcripts, study notes and secondary data (Gibbert et al. 2008, p. 1468, Göbel 2009, p. 373, Yin 2009, p. 45). In view of these requirements, the following actions were taken in this study. First, Chapter 4 outlines in detail how the present research is conducted, including, for example, the selected case study design, the operationalization of the different elements of the research framework and the data collection methods and procedures. Second, findings on all cases and embedded units are thoroughly documented in Chapter 5. In addition, a case study database was established that contains all materials used, such as codified transcripts of all interviews, questionnaire data and secondary data.[428] Finally, to strengthen reliability further, select interviews were transcribed twice and the results subsequently compared to ensure consistency.[429] Furthermore, approximately a quarter of the interview transcripts were recoded by the researcher a few days later in order to assess the stability and consistency of the content analysis.[430] Taken together, these activities aimed at ensuring a high level of reliability in this study.

---

[428] This case study database and all respective documents were also shared with the supervisor of the dissertation.
[429] Overall, four interviews were transcribed twice by the researcher and one other person. Transcriptions were nearly identical, thereby implying a high degree of reliability.
[430] High intra-coder reliability of more than 85% was achieved, which is considered a good value (see Miles/Huberman 1994). Reliability is calculated by the number of correct code assignments divided by the total number of all code assignments.

5 Empirical Findings

5.1 Company A: Strategic Business Unit Autocomp

Company A is a German-based firm that offers products and solutions for the automotive industry. In 2013, the company had more than 100,000 employees at hundreds of locations in numerous countries around the world. In the same year the company achieved a turnover of more than 20 billion Euros, of which approximately 75% was realized outside the home country. Company A consists of different divisions with each focusing on delivering products and solutions for distinct areas of the automotive industry, such as rubber and plastic materials, driving and safety assistance, engine components, or information management systems (A1).[431]

The division included in the present study develops and produces various components and systems related to information management and information presentation in vehicles, and it is here referred to as "Autocomp." Based on annual revenue, it represents the third largest division of the MNC with more than 5 billion € of turnover in 2013.[432] Moreover, this particular division has more than 25,000 employees in more than 20 countries worldwide with its headquarters located in Germany. Most of the foreign subsidiaries represent manufacturing locations, of which many also have engineering and administrative functions (A1, A3, A4). Of the foreign units, seven subsidiaries participated both in the survey and the interview phase of this study: Germany, Mexico, South Korea, Australia, China, Romania and India (see Figure 5.1).

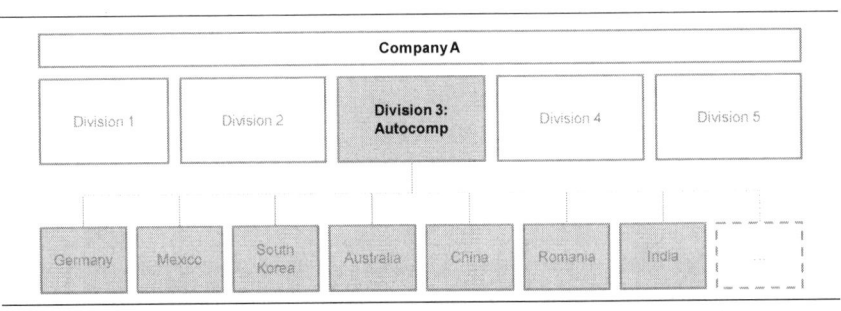

Figure 5.1: Organizational structure of Company A and its Autocomp division

With regard to the subsidiary **role typology by Bartlett and Ghoshal** (1986, 1989), the assessment by headquarters and subsidiary managers suggests that two units can be classified as "Strategic Leaders" (Germany and Mexico), two as "Contributors" (South Korea and Australia), one as "Black Hole" (China) and two as "Implementers" (Romania

---

[431] The letters and numbers in brackets refer to the source(s) of information. "A" refers to archival and secondary data, "I" to interview data and "S" to survey data. See the Appendix for further details.
[432] Thereof, 70% of total sales were achieved outside of the home country in 2012. (A2, A3).

and India). Concerning the **role typology by Jarillo and Martinez** (1990), responses indicate that two units can be characterized as "Active Subsidiaries" (Germany and Mexico), two as "Receptive Subsidiaries" (South Korea and Australia), one as an "Autonomous Subsidiary" (China) and two as "Quiescent Subsidiaries" (Romania and India), as shown in Figure 5.2 below. In the following subsections, empirical findings on each subsidiary unit, its initiative-taking activities in the past five years and the outcomes are described in detail.

Role Typology by Bartlett/Ghoshal	Role Typology by Jarillo/Martinez
High — Competence of local organization (3) South Korea / (1) Germany (4) Australia (2) Mexico Contributor / Strategic Leader Implementer / Black Hole (6) Romania (7) India (5) China Low — Strategic importance of the subsidiary environment — High	High — Degree of integration (3) South Korea / (1) Germany (2) Mexico (4) Australia Receptive / Active Quiescent / Autonomous (7) India (6) Romania (5) China Low — Degree of localization — High

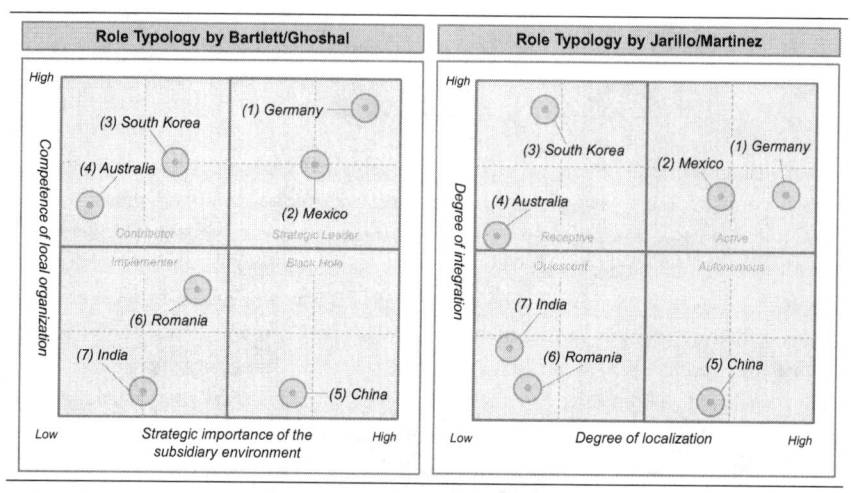

Figure 5.2: Survey Results: Subsidiary roles at Autocomp

5.1.1 German Subsidiary

The German subsidiary[433] was originally founded in the early 1960s through Greenfield investment and represents the oldest of all Autocomp subsidiary units in this research. In 2012 it had approximately 2,500 employees, of which about one half were engaged in production and the other half in other areas such as R&D, marketing and sales, human resource management, or other administrative functions. Accordingly, all major value chain functions are performed at this German site (I2, S2). The German unit also represents one of three major R&D hubs of Autocomp where research and development activities are somewhat centralized. However, in comparison to the two other R&D hubs, which focus on designing and developing solutions mostly for local markets and local customers, the German subsidiary represents the "global hub" responsible for the core development of products and applications, which are then often transferred to other locations for further adaption and refinement, for example (I1, I2).

---

[433] The German subsidiary of the Autocomp division is separate from both divisional and MNC headquarters and is situated in a distinct location as well.

5 – Empirical Findings

5.1.1.1 Subsidiary Roles

(1) Strategic Market Importance and Subsidiary Competence: Strategic Leader

According to the assessments by headquarters and subsidiary management, the German unit represents a "Strategic Leader" subsidiary within Autocomp. The strategic importance of the subsidiary market (4.3)[434] and the level of subsidiary resources and capabilities (4.1) are both evaluated as higher than all other Autocomp units included in this research. With regard to the **strategic importance of the subsidiary market**, the market size is viewed as very high (5.0) as shown in Figure 5.3 (S2). The German unit designs, manufactures and sells its products to all major Original Equipment Manufacturers (OEMs) located in Europe. Moreover, relationships with European and many non-European customers are centrally managed from this location (I1, I2). Consequently, it competes with numerous other internationally active automotive suppliers in these markets, resulting in a high degree of competitive intensity and increasing pressure on prices. Moreover, the technological dynamism and customer demand intensity of these OEMs are considered high (I2, S2).

Strategic Importance of Subsidiary Market (N = 1)
(Current situation; 1= very small, 5 = very high)

	Market size	Competitive intensity	Techn. dynamism	Customer demand intens.
	5.0	4.0	4.0	4.0

4.3 ⌀ (3.3)

Subsidiary Resources and Capabilities (N = 1)
(Current situation; 1= not capable, 5 = highly capable)

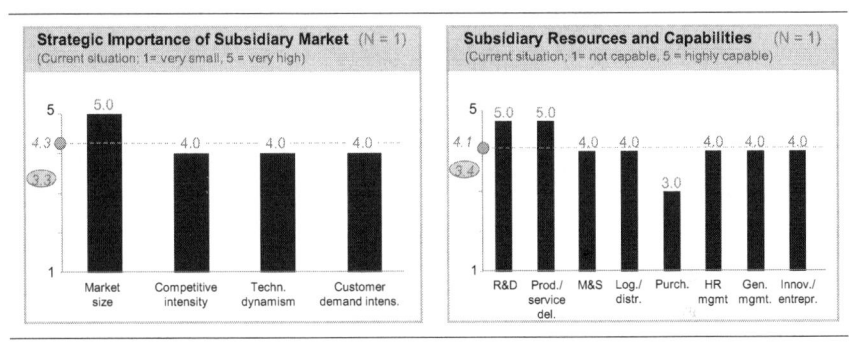

R&D	Prod./service del.	M&S	Log./distr.	Purch.	HR mgmt	Gen. mgmt	Innov./entrepr.
5.0	5.0	4.0	4.0	3.0	4.0	4.0	4.0

4.1 ⌀ (3.4)

Figure 5.3: Survey Results: Germany – Strategic importance and subsidiary resources/capabilities

Concerning the extent of **subsidiary resources and capabilities,** the German unit has been assessed as having the highest level among all Autocomp units included in this research (S2). Particularly in R&D and production of goods, the unit is seen as highly capable. Moreover, resources and capabilities are evaluated as high in most areas with the exception of purchasing, in which it is viewed as moderately capable. As to the high

---

[434] The figures in brackets represent the mean average value for the preceding topic. For example, in this case it represents average value for strategic importance of the subsidiary market of the German Autocomp unit. The following nomenclature is applied hereafter. Values are termed "medium" or "moderate" if they deviate up to ±5%from the average value of all subsidiary units in the respective MNC. Values are labeled "moderate to high" if they are between >5% and ≤10% larger, or inversely, regarded as "low to moderate" if they are between >5% and ≤10% smaller than the average value of all subsidiary units. Values that differ more are called "high" (>10% higher than average) or "low" (>10% lower than average).

level of R&D resources and capabilities, the German subsidiary not only holds the responsibility for core product development and the design of global platform solutions, but also hosts a pre-development center. Therefore, the location employs the largest number of R&D personnel among all Autocomp subsidiaries worldwide (I1, I7).

> "Ja gut, wir haben fast 800 Entwickler am Standort. ... Da ist einiges an Manpower da und da ist einiges an Finanzmitteln da. Deswegen, das ist eben der Vorteil, wenn sie an der Zentrale sitzen. Wir haben in den Hubs, in [Singapur] und in [Mexico] selbstverständlich auch Leute sitzen. Aber noch nicht in dem Maße und in der Anzahl und der Ausprägung ..." (I2)

The general evaluation that the German unit possesses a high level of knowledge and experience in various areas is also shared by other subsidiary managers of Autocomp such as those in Mexico or Romania. For example, the Mexican manager asserted that "*in terms of knowledge of the technology ... [Germany] is superior. They have much more experience.*" (I3). Similarly, the Romanian manager stated: "*considering also the vast experience that is available in [Germany] ... a lot more projects, much more ideas of improvement come from there than from our location. So this comes with responsibility on a wider range [of products] and with that experience. ... but we are not at that level of knowledge and experience and product responsibility.*" (I7).[435]

(2) Subsidiary Localization and Integration: Active Subsidiary

Based on the survey results, the German unit can also be characterized as an "Active Subsidiary" within Autocomp. Both the degree of localization/local responsiveness (4.3) and the degree of integration (3.8) were evaluated as high, as shown in Figure 5.4 (S2). Regarding the **degree of localization/local responsiveness**, particularly the extent of local content in locally produced goods, the share of sales that comes from locally produced goods and the extent of local interaction were assessed as very high (each 5.0). The German unit designs and manufactures most of the products for its European customers. Consequently, local content in locally produced goods, as well as the share of local inputs, is very high. Furthermore, the unit interacts closely with its customers, which are typically actively involved in product development activities. In addition to interaction with local customers, the subsidiary also cooperated with universities, government-funded development groups and competitors (I2). The remaining aspects related to this role dimension were all assessed as high with values of 4.0.

---

[435] As is outlined in more detail below, many foreign subsidiaries also approach the German location in order to obtain or acquire particular technology or expertise needed to realize their entrepreneurial initiatives.

5 – Empirical Findings

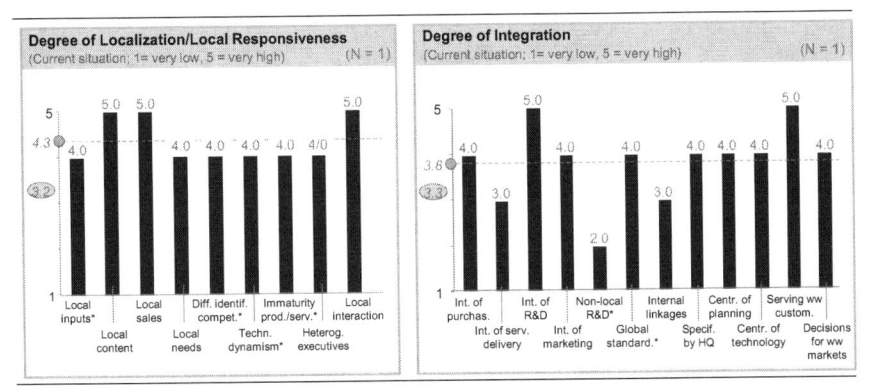

Figure 5.4: Survey Results: Germany – Subsidiary localization/local responsiveness and subsidiary integration

Similarly, the **degree of subsidiary integration** was evaluated as high (S2). The integration of different functions varies, with R&D being the most integrated and manufacturing the least (5.0 and 3.0 respectively). R&D activities are highly integrated since the German unit interacts closely with the two other R&D hubs and with other units of the multinational firm (I1). Since most R&D activities are performed locally, the share of non-local R&D remains low. Moreover, the subsidiary designs and manufactures many products and product platforms for a larger geographical area. Consequently, these product platforms are often highly standardized (4.0), leaving other foreign sites with limited possibilities for changes and adaptations to local needs. The dependence of the German subsidiary on linkages within the MNC network is seen as moderate (3.0). Additionally, product specifications are typically still developed by headquarters and the centralization of both production planning and technology is high (all 4.0). Finally, the German entity to a very large extent serves customers worldwide and thus manufacturing decisions are often linked to worldwide markets (5.0 and 4.0).

(3) Subsidiary Decision-Making Autonomy

With a mean average of 3.9, the German subsidiary enjoys a high degree of decision-making autonomy (see Figure 5.5; S2). In contrast to most other units of Autocomp it has a large degree of freedom for both operational and strategic decisions (4.0 and 3.8). With regard to strategic decisions, major new product developments, major product modifications or the restructuring of the unit can be decided on largely independently by the German entity. One area with less leeway concerns the formulation and approval of the unit's annual budget. Relatedly, the annual budget for entrepreneurial and innovative activities is determined by an innovation steering board that consists of, for example, people from the division, different customer segment teams, the core development group, and the central innovation management team. However, once the annual budget is determined by this board, the German subsidiary is largely free to set the focus or to reprioritize topics and projects where needed, as the subsidiary manager explains:

> „ ... da können wir relativ frei agieren. Und auch unterjährlich, wenn wir feststellen jetzt das Thema wird wichtiger als ein anderes Thema ... dann haben wir auch die Möglichkeit letztendlich die Priorisierung dieser Projekte ... zu verändern." (I2)

Similarly, for operational decisions the unit can either decide on its own regarding minor but significant modifications of existing products, or with some central involvement for recruitment and promotions and for career development plans for departmental managers (S2). In addition to the high degree of subsidiary autonomy, the German unit also holds some decision-making power over other units, for example concerning new product development activities or changes to existing global platform solutions, as is explained in more detail below (I2).

Subsidiary Autonomy (Current situation, 1 = decided centrally by HQ; 5 = decided independently by subsidiary) (N = 1)

	Strategic Decisions: 3.8			Operational Decisions: 4.0		
Major new product developm.	Major modification of process	Orga restructuring	Annual budget	Minor modification	Recruitment/ promotions	Career developm.
5.0	4.0	4.0	2.0	5.0	4.0	3.0

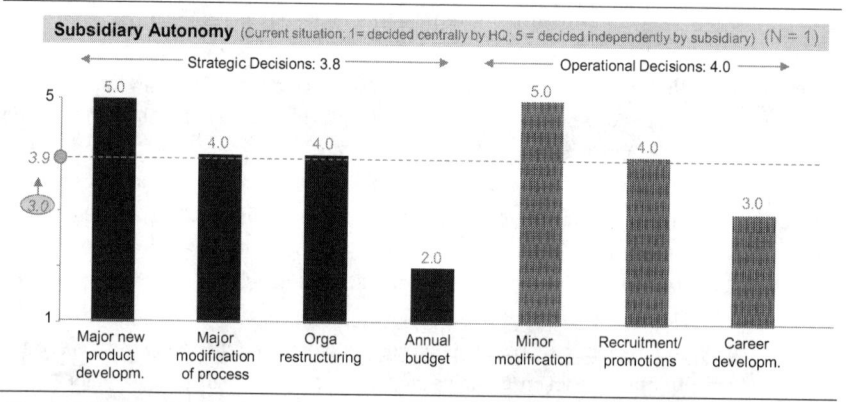

(3.9 overall; 3.0 other)

Figure 5.5: Survey Results: Germany – Subsidiary decision-making autonomy

5.1.1.2 Subsidiary Initiative-Taking

(1) Entrepreneurial Resource Management

The German unit exhibited a high level of **initiative identification** during the past five years (3.2; S2). The discovery of new initiative opportunities took place to a similar extent internally and externally, as illustrated in Figure 5.6. Internally, the identification occurred most frequently within the subsidiary itself through, for example, subsidiary employees or subsidiary management (4.0). As the subsidiary manager described:

> "Wichtige Quelle für neue Ideen sind natürlich auch immer unsere Mitarbeiter, die wir haben. Da kommen viele kleine Lösungen, die auf der einen Seite natürlich im Bereich der Software liegen, der Algorithmus der Anzeige, aber wie auch im Bereich von einfachen Produktentwicklungen." (I2)

Additionally, other units at headquarters or other units of the MNC were recognized as frequent sources of internal initiative opportunity identification (both 3.0). Externally, new ideas and opportunities were often detected through interactions with global actors, or less often with local actors from outside the company (4.0 and 2.0, S2). According to subsidiary management, global OEMs play an important role for the identification as they are typically deeply involved in new product development activities and many requirements are defined by them (I1, I2). Moreover, the participation of and interaction with external network partners such as competitors, universities and research institutions were mentioned as critical external sources:

> *"Als Quelle kann auch mitbenutzt werden ... die Diskussionen in Gremien, also wenn man jetzt in Gremienarbeiten unterwegs ist, ... aber auch die Interaktion ... mit dem Markt, mit anderen Marktteilnehmern."* (I2)

As to their **innovativeness**, most initiative opportunities were assessed as incrementally innovative, as shown in Figure 5.6 (S2). They typically involved the replication of existing products or processes for use in similar applications, or they represented new applications for existing products or processes with little or no modification. The German unit also repeatedly identified moderately innovative initiative opportunities during the past five years, including minor or even significant changes in existing products or processes. Lastly, of all Autocomp subsidiaries, the German unit most frequently detected radically innovative initiative opportunities, representing, for example, combinations of two or more products into one unique new one, or even products or processes that were "new to the world."

Identification of Subsidiary Initiative Opportunities (Extent during past five years; 1 = never, 5 = plentifully) (N = 1)					Innovativeness of Subsidiary Initiative Opportunities (Extent during past five years; 1 = never, 5 = plentifully) (N = 1)		
Only from within subsidiary	From HQ	From other units within the MNC	From local actors (external)	From global actors (external)	Incrementally innovative	Moderately innovative	Radically innovative
3.2 / 2.6	4.0	3.0	3.0	2.0	4.0	5.0	4.0	3.0

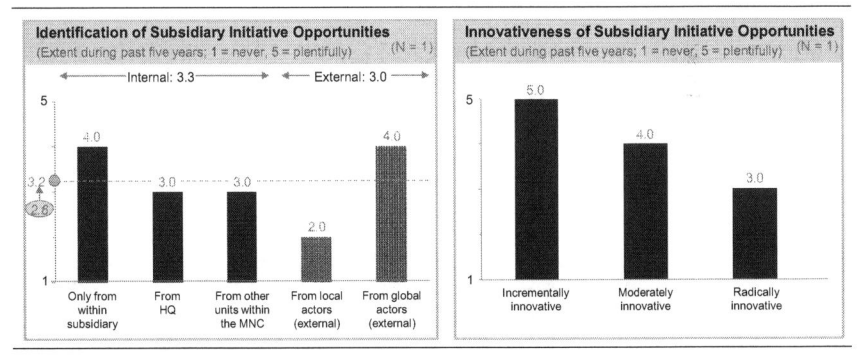

Internal: 3.3   External: 3.0

Figure 5.6: Survey Results: Germany – Identification and innovativeness of initiative opportunities

For the realization of subsidiary initiatives, the German organization engaged in a high level of **resource structuring** activities (2.8). Here, the unit made use of many possibilities to obtain resources from various internal and external sources, as shown in Figure

5.7. Internally, resources were frequently acquired from other parts of the MNC, such as headquarters, the central development department of Company A, or other R&D hubs (S2, I2:81). In comparison, sister subsidiaries played a less important role for resource structuring activities. Moreover, the German subsidiary regularly engaged in resource development activities within the unit itself and, somewhat less often, in collaboration with external partners such as global OEMs, competitors or research institutions (S2, I2). In addition to such collaborative resource development, resources were often acquired directly from external partners. The various resource structuring mechanisms are further described by the subsidiary manager as follows:

> „Also die meisten Ressourcen kommen aus der eigenen Unit heraus. Finanziell aber auch von der Manpower her. Wir bedienen uns aber auch zentraler Einheiten. [Company A] hat ja auch eine zentrale Entwicklung. Und da werden Projekte mit anderen Business Units, Divisionen zusammengebracht, die werden dann teilweise auch zentral finanziert. ... Natürlich auch in Gemeinschaftsprojekten mit Wettbewerbern. ... da haben wir mit Wettbewerbern und mit OEMs zusammen in einem Forschungsprojekt unter einem EU-Schirm gearbeitet. Das kommt genauso in Frage." (I2)

The various resources and capabilities were further **bundled** together in order to realize new initiatives. Here, the German unit most often applied incremental bundling and intermediate bundling (both 4.0, S2). However, radical bundling, involving the extensive combination of completely new resources and capabilities, was also used repeatedly by the subsidiary in pursuit of entrepreneurial activities (3.0).

Resource Structuring Activities (Extent during past five years; 1 = never, 5 = plentifully) (N = 1)

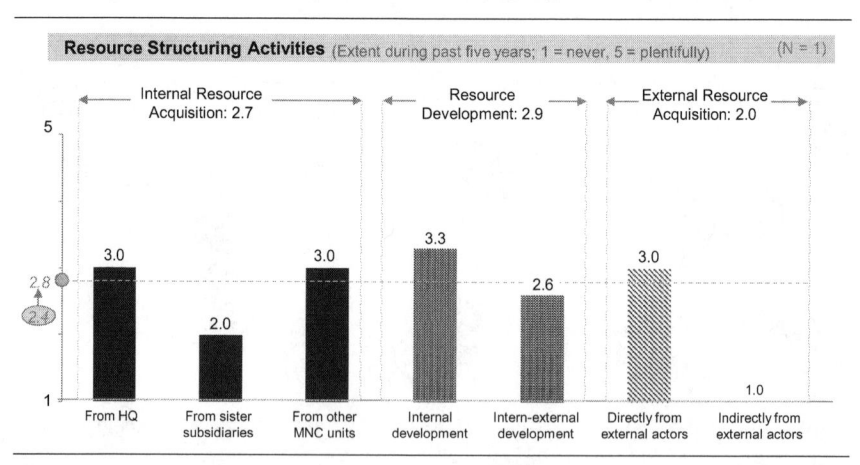

Internal Resource Acquisition: 2.7			Resource Development: 2.9		External Resource Acquisition: 2.0	
From HQ	From sister subsidiaries	From other MNC units	Internal development	Intern-external development	Directly from external actors	Indirectly from external actors
3.0	2.0	3.0	3.3	2.6	3.0	1.0

Figure 5.7: Survey Results: Germany – Initiative-related resource structuring activities

(2) Headquarters-Subsidiary Alignment

On the whole, the German unit experienced a low level of **headquarters involvement** in subsidiary initiatives during the past five years (2.5). While the extent of communications with other units at headquarters was assessed as high, presentations of new initiative opportunities, direct participation in the refinement and development of initiatives and the need for headquarters approval were viewed as moderate or even low. Similarly, the extent of **corporate resistance** was evaluated as low by subsidiary management (2.0). Although the unit experienced some delaying of entrepreneurial initiatives, few lobbying and rival activities by competing units or divisions and lack of recognition and acceptance by other units of the MNC occurred. Direct rejection by the corporate center was not experienced at all during the past five years. Although to a low extent, the German affiliate nevertheless engaged in some **initiative-selling** activities (2.5). Actions such as attracting the attention of headquarters or making them understand a new initiative opportunity were taken repeatedly. Lobbying and selling at headquarters and at other units was assessed as less extensive during the past five years, as can be seen in Figure 5.8.

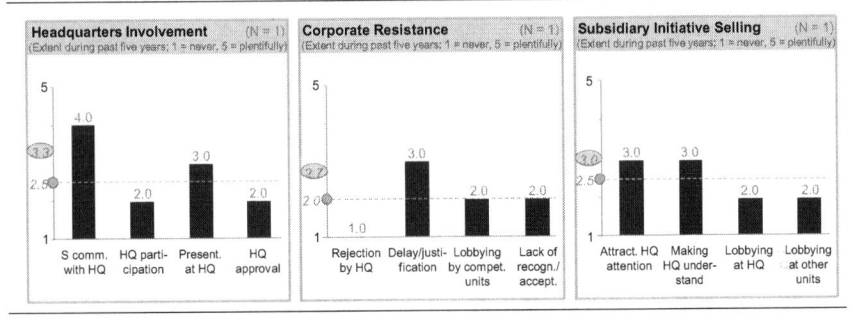

Figure 5.8: Survey Results: Germany – HQ-S alignment and interaction

The survey outcomes are further substantiated by the interview results. According to headquarters and subsidiary management, the German unit enjoys extensive latitude with regard to innovative and entrepreneurial activities. Once per year, a central innovation board determines the annual budget and core projects to be pursued. From that point on, the German site can relatively freely reprioritize projects or even engage in newly defined entrepreneurial initiatives. Nevertheless, alignment and interaction with the central innovation management board is necessary from time to time, as it is involved in the selection of entrepreneurial ideas and opportunities (I1, I2).

5.1.1.3 Subsidiary Initiative-Taking Outcome

(1) Extent of Subsidiary Initiative-Taking

With an overall mean average of 3.6 in the survey, the German unit exhibited the highest level of subsidiary initiatives among the Autocomp units included in this research (S2). During the past five years, the unit engaged to a large extent in both internally oriented and externally oriented entrepreneurial initiatives. In the external market the subsidiary most frequently pursued global market initiatives that involved, for example, significant extensions to existing international responsibilities and enhancements to product lines already sold internationally (see Figure 5.9). Given the international scope of subsidiary operations as described in Subsection 5.1.1.1, many entrepreneurial initiatives that arose through interactions with global OEMs represented global market initiatives. In addition to such initiative types, the local unit also successfully pursued local market initiatives that represented new international business activities first started locally, as well as new products developed locally and then sold internationally. Furthermore, internal market initiatives and global-internal hybrid initiatives were repeatedly pursued by the German subsidiary throughout the past five years (both 3.5).

Subsidiary Initiative-Taking	(Extent of subsidiary entrepreneurial initiatives within past five years: 1= never, 5 = plentifully)	(N = 1)
External initiatives: 3.8		Internal initiatives: 3.5
Global market initiatives: 4.0	Local market initiatives: 3.5	Internal market initiatives: 3.5	Global-internal hybrid initiatives: 3.5

Overall mean: 3.6; reference: 2.6

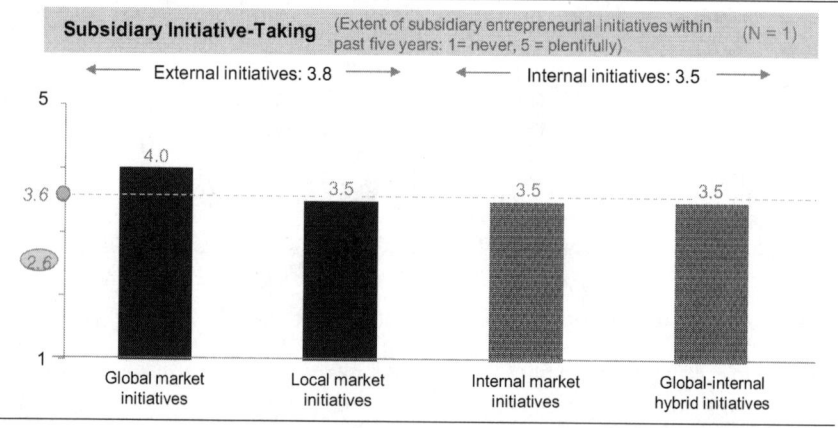

Figure 5.9: Survey Results: Germany – Types and extent of subsidiary initiatives

(2) Resource-Related Outcomes

As a consequence of its entrepreneurial initiatives, the German affiliate developed more **new resources and capabilities** than all other Autocomp subsidiaries in this research (3.8, S2). Extensive capability development was seen particularly in research and development, production and innovation/entrepreneurship (both 5.0). Moderate to high resource development was also experienced in many other areas, such as marketing and sales, logistics and distribution, purchasing or general management. In addition, many of the newly obtained resources were seen as **useful for other MNC locations** (3.4). Especially those in R&D, production and marketing and sales were assessed as highly applicable for other sites (all 4.0). Resources in the remaining areas were viewed as moderately useful for other units of the MNC as can be seen in Figure 5.10.

New Subsidiary Resources and Capabilities (N = 1) (Extent during past five years; 1= no capability development at all, 5 = extensive capability development)		Impact on MNC Capability Development (N = 1) (Extent during past five years; 1= no use at all, 5 = very useful)	
Research and development	5.0	Research and development	4.0
Prod. of goods/ services	5.0	Prod. of goods/ services	4.0
Marketing and/ or sales	4.0	Marketing and/ or sales	4.0
Logistics and/ or distribution	3.0	Logistics and/ or distribution	3.0
Purchasing	3.0	Purchasing	3.0
HR management	2.0	HR management	3.0
General management	3.0	General management	3.0
Innovation/ entrepreneur.	5.0	Innovation/ entrepreneur.	3.0
(1) min. Ø 3.8 max. (5)		(1) min. Ø 3.4 max. (5)	

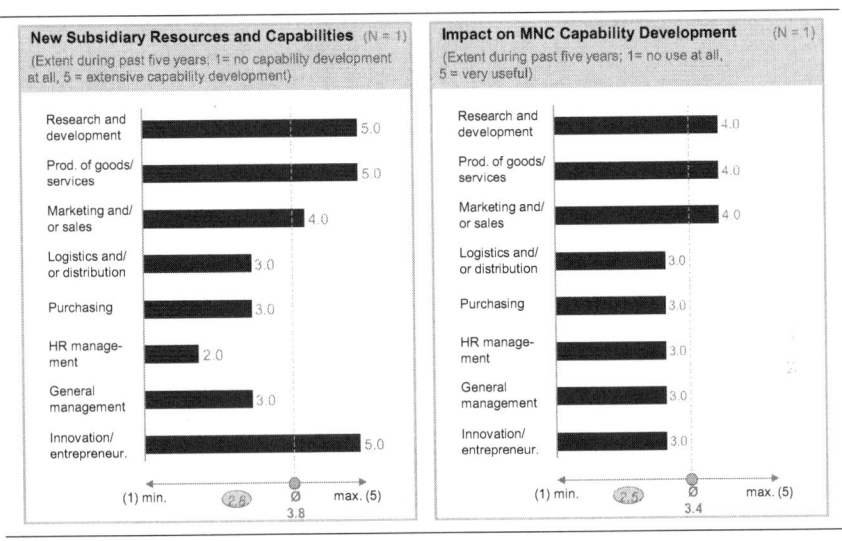

Figure 5.10: Survey Results: Germany – New subsidiary resources and impact on MNC capabilities

(3) Further Outcomes

As to **performance outcomes**, the German unit was able to improve various aspects, such as sales, profit, market share and productivity, through initiative-taking activities (all 4.0). Concerning **changes to its role and position** in the MNC, the German subsidiary enhanced various aspects of its credibility in the MNC such as its recognition by headquarters as a strategically important unit or its value-added contribution within the corporation. Likewise, certain facets of its role improved, including its geographic, product and value-added scope over the past five years. This was expressed by the local manager as follows:

„*Kernbenefit, sagen wir mal so ist die Erweiterung des Produktspektrums. Also wir belegen heute deutlich mehr, deutlich breiteres Produktspektrum als vor 5-10 Jahren.*" (I2)

Performance Outcomes (N = 1)
(Extent during past five years; 1 = very limited, 5 = substantial)

- Enhanced sales/revenues: 4.0
- Reduced costs: 3.0
- Improved market share: 4.0
- Improved profit: 4.0
- Improved ROI: 3.0
- Improved productivity: 4.0
- Ø: 3.7

Subsidiary Role and Position in MNC (N = 1)
(Extent during past five years; 1 = major decline, 3 = no change, 5 = major improvement)

Subsidiary role development:
- Geographical market scope: 4.0
- Product scope: 4.0
- Value-added scope: 4.0

Subsidiary influence:
- Subsidiary influence: 3.0

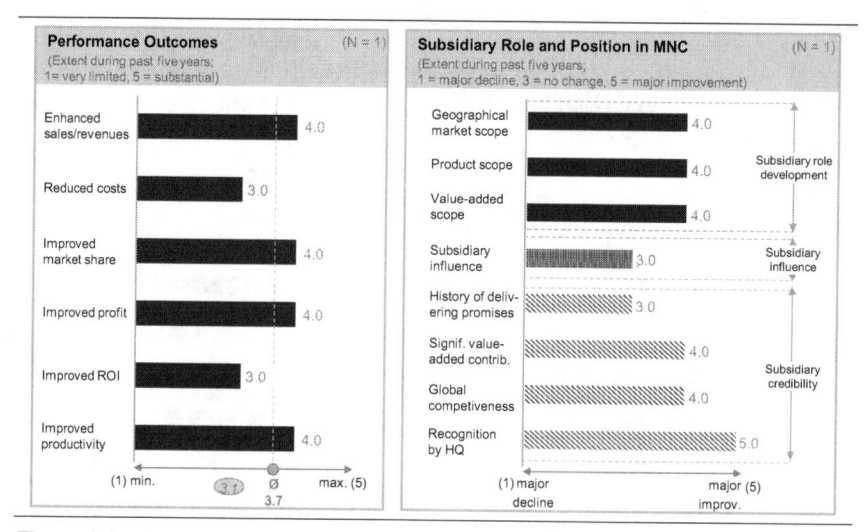

Subsidiary credibility:
- History of delivering promises: 3.0
- Signif. value-added contrib.: 4.0
- Global competiveness: 4.0
- Recognition by HQ: 5.0

Figure 5.11: Survey Results: Germany – Performance outcomes and subsidiary role and position

5.1.2 Mexican Subsidiary

The Mexican subsidiary was originally founded in the 1950s and later acquired by Company A in the early 2000s. In 2012, approximately 3,000 people were employed locally, thus making it one of the largest foreign subsidiaries of Autocomp. All main value chain functions are currently carried out at the location, including production, R&D, marketing and sales, purchasing and HR management (S3). Aside from Autocomp, two other divisions are also present at the location. In addition to production facilities, the location also hosts a research and development center that represents one of three main R&D hubs of Company A worldwide (A2, I1).

5.1.2.1 Subsidiary Roles

(1) Strategic Importance and Subsidiary Competence: Strategic Leader

Based on the survey results, the Mexican unit can be classified as a "Strategic Leader" subsidiary within Autocomp. The strategic importance of the subsidiary's market environment is comparatively high, with an average value of 3.8. Likewise, the overall level of subsidiary resources and capabilities is viewed as high with an average value of 3.8, as outlined in Figure 5.12 (S3).

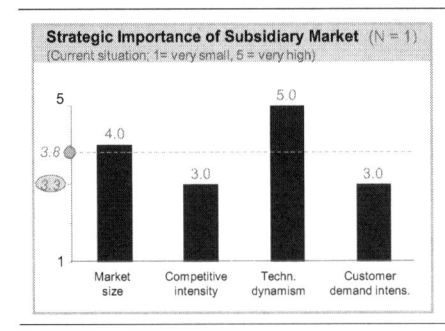

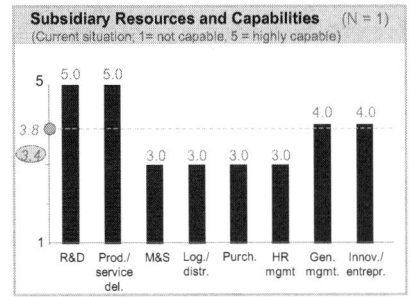

Figure 5.12: Survey Results: Mexico – Strategic importance and subsidiary resources/ capabilities

With regard to the **strategic importance of the subsidiary's market**, the technological dynamism is, in particular, considered very high (5.0). Being part of an emerging and dynamic market clearly plays an important role, as this induces subsidiary innovative behavior that can be of potential benefit for the company as a whole (I1, I3). In terms of size, the Mexican automotive market is considered relatively large, with most major global automotive manufacturers being present in the market (I3, S3). However, the responsibility of the Mexican unit goes beyond the mere local market. For example, most of the products that are manufactured locally are also exported to other parts of the world, particularly to the US and Canada. Even more so, given its role as one of three R&D hubs worldwide, research and development activities are undertaken not only for the Mexican market, but for many other country markets, including the entire NAFTA region (I3, A5). Lastly, the customer demand intensity of the relevant automotive manufacturers and the competitive intensity in the subsidiary market are both seen as moderate.

Concerning the **subsidiary resources and capabilities**, their level is viewed as particularly high in the areas of R&D and production (both 5.0; S3) and also somewhat high in general management and innovation/entrepreneurship (both 4.0). As for the area of R&D, approximately 200 engineers are employed at the subsidiary. In addition to the large amount of personnel resources, their particular expertise is also viewed as high:

"That's what's interesting with that quantity of people; we have a lot of possibility, a lot of engineering power, I'd say. ... The majority of our innovation is really coming based on the experience of the individuals in the market that they are part of." (I3).

(2) Subsidiary Localization and Subsidiary Integration: Active Subsidiary

Regarding the degree of subsidiary localization and subsidiary integration, the Mexican unit constitutes an "Active Subsidiary" unit based on the survey results. With an average value of 3.9, the degree of **localization/local responsiveness** is comparatively high (S3). For example, the extent to which customers and their needs differ from other country units or the degree of local content in locally produced products were assessed as high, as shown in Figure 5.13. The differences in local needs are also addressed by the local manager as follows:

> "...we have needs and situations here in Mexico which the people in Germany don't even -- they've never even thought of. For example, we have an issue here ... in stolen car parts. ... So we may have innovative ideas about how to protect your mirrors. ... And of course we go and talk [in Germany] about this idea and they're like, "Why would you ever want to do that? Who cares?" Because they don't have the same experience or needs." (I3)

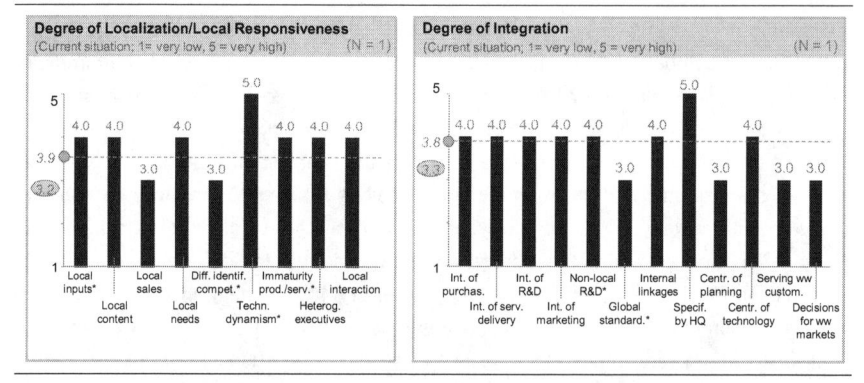

Figure 5.13: Survey Results: Mexico – Subsidiary localization/local responsiveness and subsidiary integration

Likewise, the degree of **subsidiary integration** in the MNC was also evaluated as high, with a mean average of 3.8 (S3). Various value-adding functions are highly integrated with the rest of the group. Moreover, product and quality specifications are typically centrally developed by headquarters and sharing of technology development within the internal network is also centralized. However, the high degree of integration is not only seen as beneficial by local management. For instance, the limited ability in other parts of the firm to fully understand the local setting and to fairly assess the market potential of new ideas developed by the Mexican subsidiary is seen as a disadvantage, as further explained by subsidiary management:

> "From a technology point of view the relationship with the other locations and subsidiaries is a benefit, of course. From a general support [standpoint] it's a

benefit. But ... from [the standpoint of] being able to evaluate our ideas and impact in the whole global market – sometimes it can be not an advantage." (I3)

(3) Subsidiary Decision-Making Autonomy

Based on the assessment by subsidiary management, the Mexican unit possesses a comparatively high degree of autonomy, with an average value of 3.3 (S2). This is also expressed in the interview with the Mexican manager, who stated that:

"... in day-to-day interaction with upper management of [headquarters] we're removed a little bit. So I have the freedom and I've used that freedom in order to do what I want done here ..." (I3)

However, the degree of autonomy is not equally high in all areas. The Mexican entity has less leeway for strategic decisions than it has for operational ones (3.0 vs. 3.7, S3). Similarly, in the area of new product development, the foreign subsidiary possesses more freedom to modify existing products (either minor or major modifications) than to develop major new product offerings, especially when they require central funding or approval (I3, S3). Likewise, its autonomy is limited when it comes to restructuring the local organization or to formulating and approving its annual budget, as shown in Figure 5.14.

Subsidiary Autonomy (Current situation; 1= decided centrally by HQ; 5 = decided independently by subsidiary) (N = 1)

Strategic Decisions: 3.0   Operational Decisions: 3.7

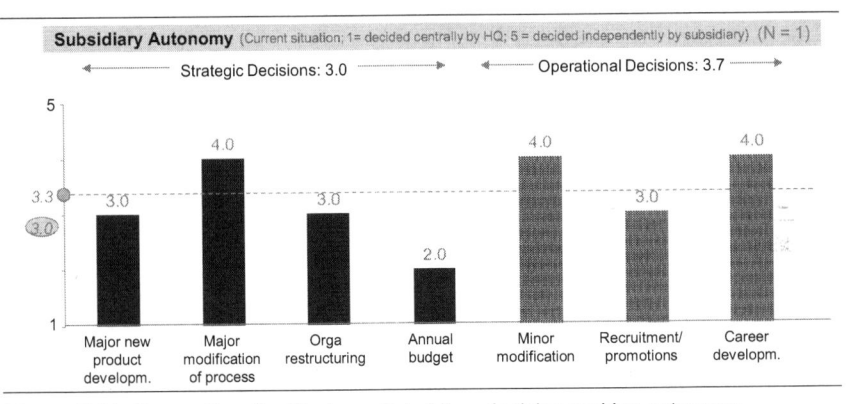

Major new product developm.	Major modification of process	Orga restructuring	Annual budget	Minor modification	Recruitment/ promotions	Career developm.
3.0	4.0	3.0	2.0	4.0	3.0	4.0

(3.3 and 3.0 shown on y-axis as overall averages)

Figure 5.14: Survey Results: Mexico – Subsidiary decision-making autonomy

5.1.2.2 Subsidiary Initiative-Taking

(1) Entrepreneurial Resource Management

As concerns the **identification of new initiative opportunities**, the Mexican subsidiary frequently discovered them both from external and internal sources in the past five years, as shown in Figure 5.15. Internally, initiative identification frequently occurred within the subsidiary alone and, somewhat less often, through interactions with headquarters (5.0 and 4.0, S3). An important source within the Mexican affiliate was a group of engineers formed by the local subsidiary manager two years earlier. While the group initially consisted of few engineers, it continued to grow and now involves almost all R&D personnel at the location.

> "... about two years ago we formed a group of engineers, seven or eight engineers mixed from all the different disciplines, not managers, not necessarily leaders but just a group of engineers who are interested in innovation. So basically what this group was responsible to do is to create and promote a culture of innovation, here at the location. ... This work, of course, generated a lot of attention, a lot of talk, a lot of participation. We rolled out these concepts within this location to the whole organization, all of these 200 engineers. So we start really having people thinking, this cultural idea of being innovative and thinking of ideas and so forth. ... We collect a lot of ideas and we go through a process of evaluating those and picking the ones we think have the most promise." (I3).

Externally, the discovery repeatedly took place through interactions with global or local actors from outside the MNC. Certain global customers played a particularly important role since their requests often triggered innovative behavior at Autocomp (I3). Additionally, a new collaboration model with local universities, initiated by the foreign unit a few years earlier, represented another critical source for the discovery of new opportunities:

> "So we ... started a cooperation with local universities where we have sessions where we collect innovative ideas, we evaluate the ideas and then we select a set of ideas and then students evaluate our selection of ideas and they decide which ones, if any, they would like to be part of ... We have a location inside the university campus, we actually own square footage inside." (I3)

With regard to their **innovativeness**, newly identified opportunities were often moderately innovative, representing minor to significant changes in existing products or services. Radically innovative initiatives seem not to have been needed frequently, given the comparatively less demanding market environment. This is reflected in the following description by the subsidiary manager:

> "This is not something that we've never heard of before; this is not really radically new technology. But what we're really trying to do is, again, we're in more of an emerging market, we're trying to focus on a solution with 80 percent of the functionality and 20 percent of the cost." (I3)

5 – Empirical Findings

Identification of Subsidiary Initiative Opportunities
(Extent during past five years; 1 = never, 5 = plentifully) (N = 1)

Internal: 3.3 External: 3.5

- Only from within subsidiary: 5.0
- From HQ: 4.0
- From other units within the MNC: 3.0
- From local actors (external): 4.0
- From global actors (external): 4.0

Innovativeness of Subsidiary Initiative Opportunities
(Extent during past five years; 1 = never, 5 = plentifully) (N = 1)

- Incrementally innovative: 4.0
- Moderately innovative: 2.0
- Radically innovative: 2.5

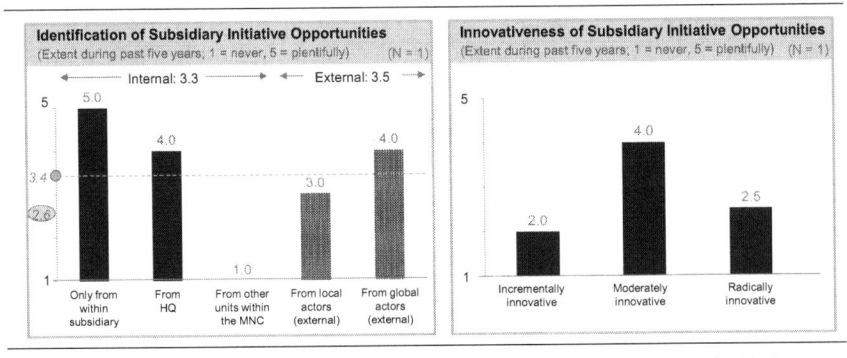

Figure 5.15: Survey Results: Mexico – Identification and innovativeness of initiative opportunities

Concerning the **resource structuring** activities, the Mexican subsidiary obtained resources and capabilities from various sources in order to realize entrepreneurial initiatives (S3). Internally, important sources consisted of other MNC units, particularly an internal engineering service provider within Autocomp. This unit develops technical or engineering solutions for other internal units upon request, including for entrepreneurial initiatives (I3). Additionally, resource development activities within the subsidiary itself were often used when implementing new initiatives (especially in the area of R&D and production). In R&D, the large resource base of engineering personnel played an important role:

"... Now I needed to find resources in my organization; of course that's the first place I look in my organization in order to do the engineering work to build this thing." (I3)

Externally, resources or capabilities were frequently obtained directly from external actors. In such cases, long-term relationships with external partners, such as with one manufacturer of semiconductors, were used to obtain necessary resource inputs either through collaboration or direct acquisition (I3). Indirect acquisition of resources by merging with or acquiring another organization in the local market did not take place in the past five years, as shown in Figure 5.16. Existing and newly developed or acquired resources were then **bundled** together in order to realize subsidiary initiatives. Based on the survey results, bundling took place mostly in the form of incremental or intermediate resource bundling (both 4.0, S3), whereas radical bundling involving the extensive combination of completely new resources and capabilities only occurs from time to time (2.0).

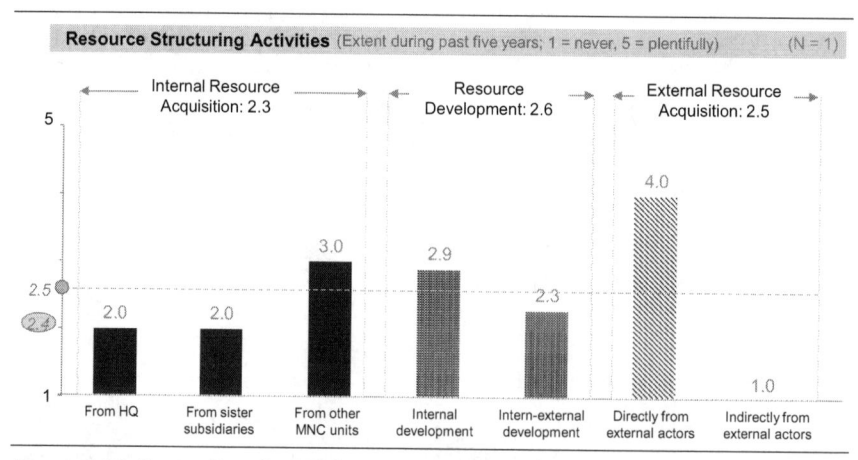

Figure 5.16: Survey Results: Mexico – Initiative-related resource structuring activities

(2) Headquarters-Subsidiary Alignment

Headquarters was comparatively seldom **involved** in the subsidiary initiative process during the past five years (2.3, S3). From time to time, initiative-related communications with headquarters took place, and only in few instances was it necessary to present opportunity proposals at the corporate center. Likewise, headquarters approval was required only a few times. Moreover, direct participation in the refinement or development of entrepreneurial opportunities at the Mexican unit occurred rarely over the past five years. **Corporate resistance was also evaluated as low** (1.8, S3) and the Mexican unit only seldom encountered, for instance, delays of initiatives by headquarters managers, lobbying and rival initiatives by competing divisions or a lack of recognition of their initiatives by other MNC units. No initiatives were rejected during the last five years. Lastly, **initiative selling** was assessed as relatively low, with an average value of 2.3 (S3). Attracting headquarters attention, making headquarters understand new opportunities and lobbying at sister or other units took place infrequently. However, lobbying at headquarters was needed somewhat more often in order to gain support for a new initiative, as shown in Figure 5.17.

Although there exists a standardized approval process within Autocomp for aligning with headquarters on newly identified opportunities and ideas, the Mexican subsidiary was able to circumvent this process repeatedly. Given its geographical distance, its relatively large degree of autonomy and its strong resource base, the foreign unit was often able to pursue initiatives without directly involving the corporate center. This is also expressed in the following statements by the subsidiary manager:

5 – Empirical Findings

"I can also say that we're geographically quite separated and also in day-to-day interaction with upper management [at headquarters] we're removed a little bit. So I have the freedom and I've used that freedom in order to do what I want done here without necessarily advertising or asking for permission." (I3)

"In [the local unit] we do some work, sort of under the table. I mean with 200 engineers I can skim a little bit." (I3)

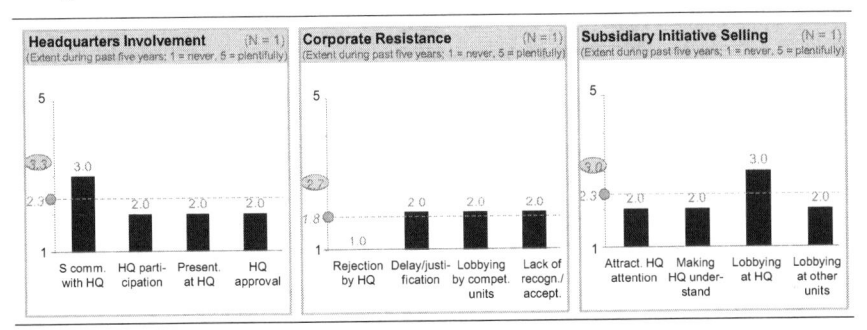

Headquarters Involvement (N = 1)	Corporate Resistance (N = 1)	Subsidiary Initiative Selling (N = 1)
(Extent during past five years; 1 = never, 5 = plentifully)	(Extent during past five years; 1 = never, 5 = plentifully)	(Extent during past five years; 1 = never, 5 = plentifully)
S comm. with HQ: 2.3; HQ participation: 3.0; Present. at HQ: 2.0; HQ approval: 2.0	Rejection by HQ: 1.8; Delay/justification: 1.0; Lobbying by compet. units: 2.0; Lack of recogn./accept.: 2.0	Attract. HQ attention: 2.3; Making HQ understand: 2.0; Lobbying at HQ: 3.0; Lobbying at other units: 2.0

Figure 5.17: Survey Results: Mexico – HQ-S alignment and interaction

Furthermore, there were occasions when the subsidiary manager deliberately decided not to involve headquarters in the early development phase of initiatives in order to gain some speed and to evade corporate bureaucracy.

"... if I go in and I ask for permission it's going to turn into this long process of convincing ... I'd be lucky to have a response by the end of the week. ... And the more you open up to the bureaucracy of the company, of course, the more complicated it's going to get." (I3)

Nevertheless, once a subsidiary initiative reached a certain level of maturity and when it was decided locally that it should be pursued further, headquarters was typically involved in order to obtain central support. In those cases, these more mature initiative opportunities were presented as proposals to the corporate center in the form of, for example, short one- or two-page presentations or as in-person demonstrations (I3). When attempting to convince headquarters managers, three aspects were mentioned by the subsidiary manager as important, as indicated in the interview statements below: the business potential of an idea, the past achievements of the subsidiary unit and the knowledge of how to appropriately package and sell the ideas.

"The idea, of course, is the most important. But if we built a reputation already of being able to execute ideas within the constraints successfully, then of course this is going to help." (I3)

"I think when [the headquarters manager] came here to Guadalajara, he probably saw much, much more than what he expected. And I think at that moment then our collaboration became much closer. And so I think like I said, he's helped us a lot in terms of how to package our ideas in order to get approval, to get budget. ... I think the personal relationship we developed ... and the level of work we've already achieved – I think it was quite impressive for him. And that created a stronger connection than we would have had otherwise." (I3)

5.1.2.3 Subsidiary Initiative-Taking Outcome

(1) Extent of Subsidiary Initiative-Taking

Overall, the Mexican subsidiary showed a relatively high level of subsidiary initiative-taking, with an overall average value of 2.9 (S3). In particular, **local market initiatives** involving products first developed locally and then sold internationally occurred most frequently in the past five years (see Figure 5.18). For example, a low cost product that was initially developed for the Mexican and North American market was later transferred and adapted in other countries as well (I3).

Subsidiary Initiative-Taking	(Extent of subsidiary entrepreneurial initiatives within past five years: 1= never, 5 = plentifully)	(N = 1)
← External initiatives: 3.3 →	← Internal initiatives: 2.5 →	

Global market initiatives	Local market initiatives	Internal market initiatives	Global-internal hybrid initiatives
3.0	3.5	2.0	3.0

Overall average: 2.9 (2.6)

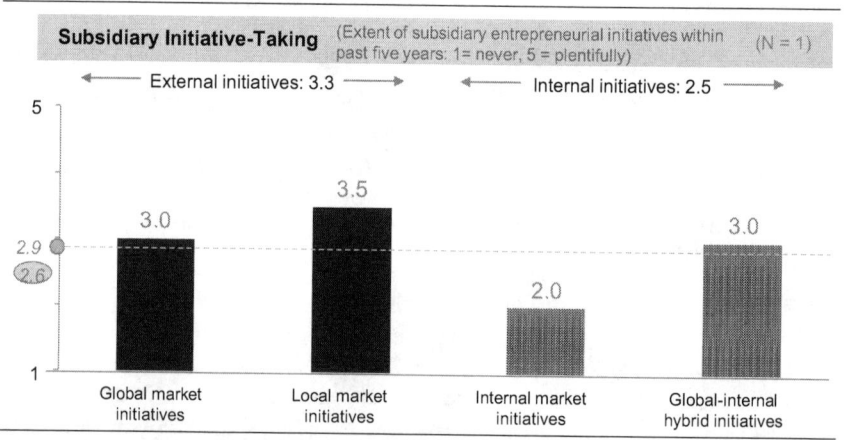

Figure 5.18: Survey Results: Mexico – Types and extent of subsidiary initiatives

Somewhat less often in the last five years, the subsidiary undertook **global market initiatives** and **global-internal hybrid initiatives** (both 3.0). Regarding the latter, the Mexican unit was able to attract a multimillion Euro investment for a new R&D center that focuses on the North American market (A5, I1). With regard to purely internal initiatives such as proposals to transfer manufacturing to the subsidiary location or reconfiguration of local operations, only limited activities took place in the five-year period under study. One example was the development of the collaboration model with local universities to identify innovative ideas, an approach that was later rolled out in two additional countries outside of Mexico (I1, I3).

(2) Resource-Related Outcomes

As a result of its entrepreneurial initiatives in the past five years, the Mexican subsidiary developed **new resources and capabilities** in different areas. With an average value of 3.3 (S3), the extent of newly developed resources was comparatively high. Particularly in the areas of R&D, innovation and entrepreneurship and production, new specialized capabilities were built through initiative-taking that were also seen as quite useful for other MNC locations (see Figure 5.19). The high **applicability** of newly developed resource bundles **at other MNC locations** is also reflected in two examples that were given in the interview with the local manager:

> "So this product that we developed, a low-cost [product] ... the first sample we built we shipped to [headquarters] and they promptly shipped it to Russia. So right now that product is touring Russia somewhere. Clearly you have an example where there is usefulness outside of North America, outside of Mexico." (I3)

> "It's a tool, and ... the idea for this tool ... it started here, then [one person from headquarters] took it and made it global [in Autocomp]. And then [a different division] took it to the next level in the organization ... And now it's being rolled out across [Company A] global." (I3)

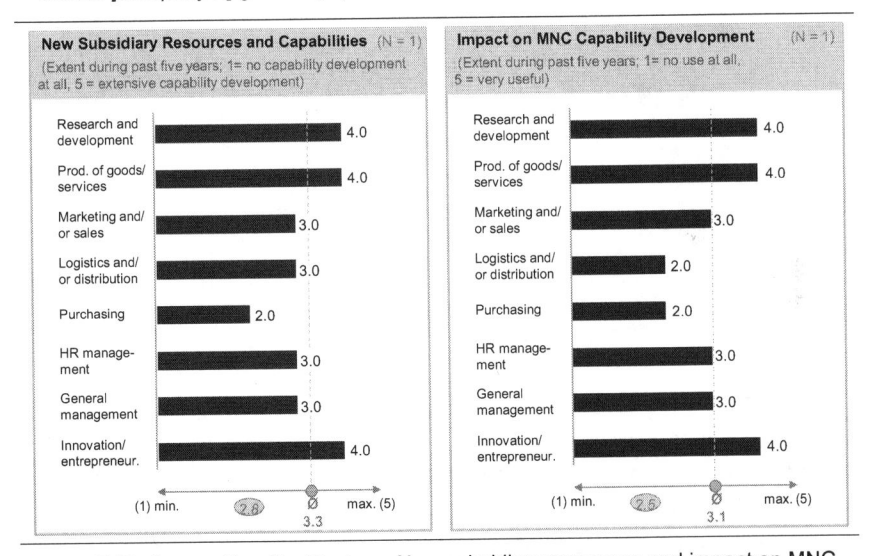

New Subsidiary Resources and Capabilities (N = 1) (Extent during past five years; 1= no capability development at all, 5 = extensive capability development)		Impact on MNC Capability Development (N = 1) (Extent during past five years; 1= no use at all, 5 = very useful)	
Research and development	4.0	Research and development	4.0
Prod. of goods/ services	4.0	Prod. of goods/ services	4.0
Marketing and/ or sales	3.0	Marketing and/ or sales	3.0
Logistics and/ or distribution	3.0	Logistics and/ or distribution	2.0
Purchasing	2.0	Purchasing	2.0
HR management	3.0	HR management	3.0
General management	3.0	General management	3.0
Innovation/ entrepreneur.	4.0	Innovation/ entrepreneur.	4.0
(1) min. — Ø 3.3 — max. (5)		(1) min. — Ø 3.1 — max. (5)	

Figure 5.19: Survey Results: Mexico – New subsidiary resources and impact on MNC capabilities

(3) Further Outcomes

Regarding **performance outcomes**, subsidiary initiative-taking in the past five years resulted in substantial cost reductions. Improvements in other areas, such as market share, profit and productivity seem to have been moderately affected, as can be seen in Figure 5.20. As for **subsidiary role development**, the Mexican unit experienced some improvement, as it was able to enhance its geographical market scope, its product scope and its value-added scope (all 4.0, S3). Moreover, certain aspects related to subsidiary credibility showed some improvement (significant value-added contributions the subsidiary makes to the company) or even major improvement (recognition by headquarters).

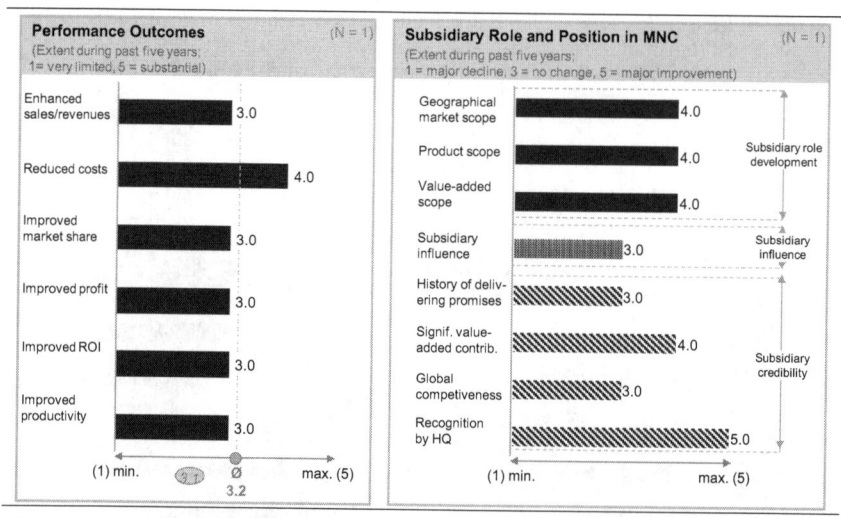

Performance Outcomes (N = 1) (Extent during past five years; 1= very limited, 5 = substantial)		Subsidiary Role and Position in MNC (N = 1) (Extent during past five years; 1 = major decline, 3 = no change, 5 = major improvement)	
Enhanced sales/revenues	3.0	Geographical market scope	4.0
Reduced costs	4.0	Product scope	4.0
Improved market share	3.0	Value-added scope	4.0
Improved profit	3.0	Subsidiary influence	3.0
Improved ROI	3.0	History of delivering promises	3.0
Improved productivity	3.0	Signif. value-added contrib.	4.0
		Global competitiveness	3.0
		Recognition by HQ	5.0
Ø 3.2			

Figure 5.20: Survey Results: Mexico – Performance outcomes and subsidiary role and position

In addition to the survey results, additional outcomes of initiative-taking activities were pointed out by the local subsidiary manager in the interview. Among them are, for example, improved **subsidiary employee motivation, satisfaction, and pride**, as seen in the following two statements:

> "But there are much ... deeper benefits. This is the motivation and the satisfaction of the employees. It's more a soft benefit. We don't see it in the bottom line directly but it is contributing because we attract better engineers, we keep them happy, we keep them creative, we keep them pushing. I think this is probably the biggest benefit." (I3)

"And then I took the sample to [headquarters] ... I showed it to everyone. I mean people – they got some recognition for it. In that case, for example, is not going to give us big business. But the impact it had on this team and the motivation and the sense of pride to be part of [Company A] is probably more valuable than if it would have immediately turned into a product." (I3)

While in the short term, the entrepreneurial activities by the Mexican subsidiary caused conflicts from time to time both at the subsidiary location and with the corporate center, in the longer term it has led to a **stronger connection to headquarters** managers (I3). Finally, as a **risk of initiative-taking,** it was mentioned that some of the entrepreneurial opportunities pursued locally did not fit the overall company needs:

"The downside is that we take off on some idea ... and then we find out, 'Ah, these guys [at headquarters] are working ... on a very similar topic with a slightly different technology.' So maybe we would have been better off to do something different; I don't know. That's the drawback on it; you get some speed but you may pursue something that in the end doesn't really mesh with what the rest of the company is looking for." (I3)

5.1.3 South Korean Subsidiary

The subsidiary in South Korea was first founded in the late 1970s and later acquired by Company A in the late 2000s. Between the founding and the acquisition, the South Korean unit underwent mergers or joint ventures with three other companies. In 2012, more than 2,300 employees worked at this Autocomp country location. All main value chain functions are presently carried out in South Korea, including production, R&D, marketing and sales, purchasing and HR management. In addition to Autocomp, two other divisions are also present at the location. Although it does not represent one of the three global R&D hubs, the foreign unit is considered a competence center in Asia for three particular product areas (I4, S4).

5.1.3.1 Subsidiary Roles

(1) Strategic Importance and Subsidiary Competence: Contributor

Based on the role assessment results obtained through the survey, the South Korean unit is categorized as a "Contributor" subsidiary within Autocomp. The strategic importance of its market environment was deemed low to moderate, with an average value of 3.0 (S4). In contrast, the overall level of resources and capabilities is assessed as high at an average value of 3.8. Concerning the **strategic importance of the subsidiary's market**, the market size and the customer demand intensity yielded particularly high results in the survey, both with a value of 4.0 (see Figure 5.21). Here, the international growth and increasing sales of South Korean OEMs worldwide in recent years have also lead to an expansion of the relevant market size for the foreign subsidiary and resulted in stronger sales contributions from the unit within Autocomp (I4). Furthermore, the South Korean customers request increasingly advanced technological solutions in order to gain a competitive edge over other automotive manufacturers.

> "Korean OEMs, they are very aggressively pushing [Company A] to bring new, or like global world technology, which has not even been introduced to the European OEMs. They are very pushy in this way, very aggressive ..." (I4)

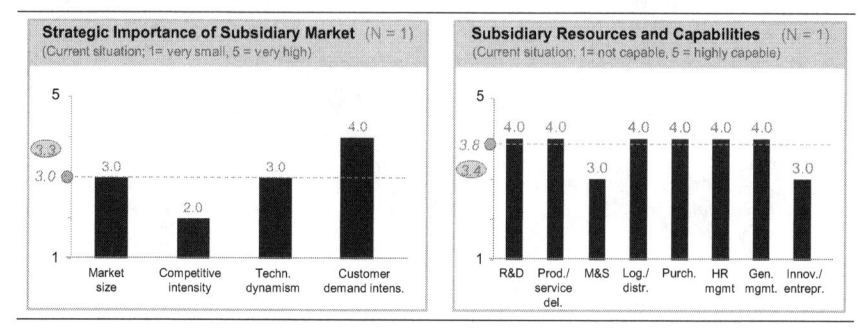

Strategic Importance of Subsidiary Market (N = 1) (Current situation; 1= very small, 5 = very high)					Subsidiary Resources and Capabilities (N = 1) (Current situation; 1= not capable, 5 = highly capable)								
Market size	Competitive intensity	Techn. dynamism	Customer demand intens.		R&D	Prod./ service del.	M&S	Log./ distr.	Purch.	HR mgmt	Gen. mgmt	Innov./ entrepr.	
3.0	3.0	2.0	4.0		4.0	4.0	3.0	4.0	4.0	4.0	4.0	3.0	

(Mean: 3.0) (Mean: 3.8)

Figure 5.21: Survey Results: SK – Strategic importance and subsidiary resources/ capabilities

As to **subsidiary resources and capabilities**, the South Korean unit of Autocomp is at a relatively high level (3.8, S4). All value-chain areas were given a value of 4.0 with the exception of the competencies in marketing and sales and in innovation/entrepreneurship, which achieved scores of 3.0. Specifically, the local R&D competencies for the three product areas in which the unit is considered an Autocomp competence center were highlighted in the interview with the subsidiary manager and mentioned as areas of special subsidiary expertise (I1, I4). In addition, the very good understanding of the local market and the customer culture vis-à-vis other units of the MNC were mentioned by subsidiary management as areas of particular expertise (I4).

(2) Subsidiary Localization and Integration: Receptive Subsidiary

Based on the survey results, this foreign unit also constitutes a "Receptive" subsidiary. The South Korean Autocomp entity shows a comparatively low **degree of localization/ local responsiveness** with an overall mean average of 2.7 (S4), as shown in Figure 5.22. The foreign unit receives extensive input from other units of the company, such as R&D and product expertise from the regional R&D hub in Singapore or from headquarters in Germany (I4), and therefore local input is viewed as rather low (2.0). Furthermore, local content in locally produced goods is limited, competitors and their strategies are easily identified, and the subsidiary interacts little with local actors.

5 – Empirical Findings

However, some aspects received higher scores: the share of sales from locally manufactured goods and the dynamism of technology were both rated at 4.0.

Degree of Localization/Local Responsiveness
(Current situation; 1= very low, 5 = very high)   (N = 1)

Local inputs* / Local content	2.0
Local sales / Local needs	2.0
Diff. identif. compet.* / Techn. dynamism*	4.0
Immaturity prod./serv.* / Heterog. executives	4.0
Local interaction	2.0
(mean)	2.7 (circled); 2.2 (circled)

Values shown: 2.0, 2.0, 4.0, 3.0, 4.0, 3.0, 2.0, 2.0

Degree of Integration
(Current situation; 1= very low, 5 = very high)   (N = 1)

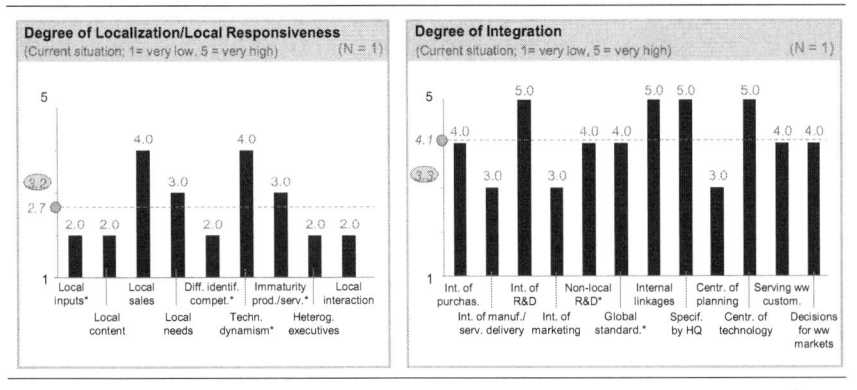

Values shown: 4.0, 3.0, 4.0, 3.0, 4.0, 5.0, 5.0, 5.0, 3.0, 5.0, 4.0, 4.0 — mean 4.1 (circled); 3.3 (circled)

Categories: Int. of purchas. / Int. of manuf./serv. delivery | Int. of R&D / Int. of marketing | Non-local R&D* / Global standard.* | Internal linkages | Centr. of planning / Specif. by HQ | Centr. of technology | Serving ww custom. / Decisions for ww markets

Figure 5.22: Survey Results: SK – Subsidiary localization/local responsiveness and subsidiary integration

Moreover, subsidiary managers evaluated the **degree of subsidiary integration** as high, with a mean average of 4.1 (S4). The degree of integration varies among the functions to some extent, with R&D being the most integrated (5.0) and manufacturing and marketing the least (both 3.0). With regard to product adaptation, globally standardized products are widely applied and only limited local adaptation is implemented at the South Korean unit. Additionally, product and quality specifications are mostly developed at headquarters, thus indicating a higher degree of integration in relation to product specification and adaptation. Moreover, the proportion of non-local R&D is rather high, with many of the advanced and core technologies being centrally developed at the headquarters location (I4, S4). Finally, manufacturing and service delivery decisions are frequently linked to worldwide markets and MNC customers of the subsidiary are typically served worldwide (both 4.0).

(3) Subsidiary Decision-Making Autonomy

On the basis of the assessment by subsidiary management, the South Korean subsidiary has only a moderate degree of autonomy, with a mean average of 3.1 as shown in Figure 5.23. Decision-making autonomy for strategic topics is considerably lower than for operational decisions (2.3 vs. 4.3, S4). Specifically, the capability to influence strategic decisions related to major new product developments and to formulating or approving the subsidiary's annual budget are quite limited. In contrast, minor but significant modifications to existing products can be decided on independently by the South

Korean unit. The limited autonomy related to (major) product development and budget decisions was also addressed by the subsidiary manager in the interview:

> "We are following the rules and guidelines from headquarters; actually we follow standard process for our development projects." (I4)

> "The budget in terms of the human resources and the financial budget ... they are very controlled from headquarters. We have not any freedom regarding that ... not at all." (I4)

Subsidiary Autonomy (Current situation; 1= decided centrally by HQ; 5 = decided independently by subsidiary) (N = 1)

Category	Strategic Decisions: 2.3				Operational Decisions: 4.3		
Major new product developm.	Major modification of process	Orga restructuring	Annual budget	Minor modification	Recruitment/ promotions	Career developm.
1.0	3.0	3.0	2.0	5.0	4.0	4.0

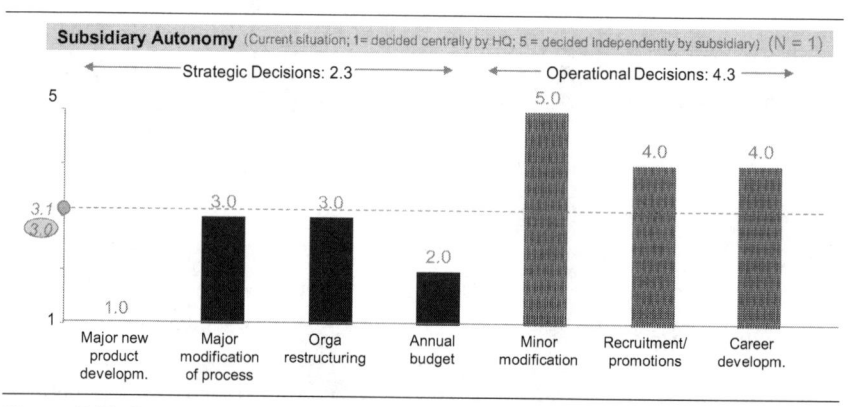

(Ø 3.1 / 3.0)

Figure 5.23: Survey Results: SK – Subsidiary decision-making autonomy

5.1.3.2 Subsidiary Initiative-Taking

(1) Entrepreneurial Resource Management

Within the past five years, certain new **opportunities** for subsidiary initiatives were **identified** by the South Korean unit from both internal and external sources. However, identification occurred internally more often than externally (3.0 vs. 2.0, S4). Internally, opportunities were most frequently recognized through interactions with corporate headquarters (see Figure 5.24). Here, the close alignment and frequent communication with the corporate center to obtain insights on new technologies or new market trends, for instance, played an important role. The relevance of these internal and external sources is also captured in the following statement by the subsidiary manager:

> "Of course we very closely communicate with headquarter[s] to get ... new trends in European market, in long-term market. But also locally, we investigate, where our customers ... are heading." (I4)

As to **innovativeness**, newly identified initiative opportunities during the past five years were only incrementally or moderately innovative (S4). Most frequently, new opportunities represented replications of existing products or processes to be used in similar applications. No radically innovative opportunities for entrepreneurial initiatives were identified at all during the past five years, as shown on the right side of Figure 5.24.

Identification of Subsidiary Initiative Opportunities
(Extent during past five years; 1 = never, 5 = plentifully)   (N = 1)
Internal: 3.0   External: 2.0

Only from within subsidiary	From HQ	From other units within the MNC	From local actors (external)	From global actors (external)
2.6	4.0	2.0	2.0	2.0
3.0				

Innovativeness of Subsidiary Initiative Opportunities
(Extent during past five years; 1 = never, 5 = plentifully)   (N = 1)

Incrementally innovative	Moderately innovative	Radically innovative
3.0	3.0	1.0

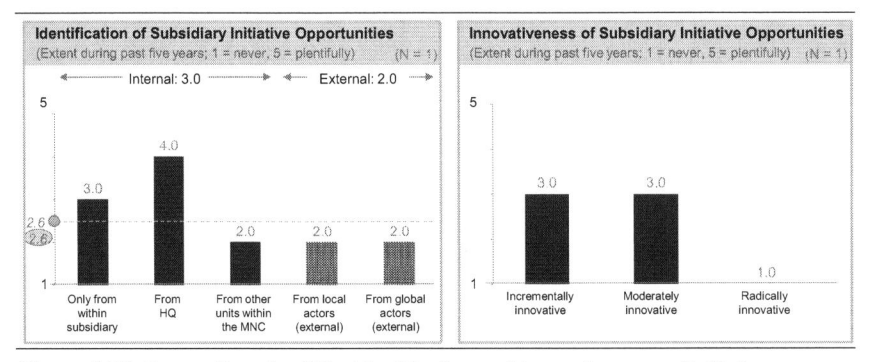

Figure 5.24: Survey Results: SK – Identification and innovativeness of initiative opportunities

With regard to **resource structuring** activities, the foreign subsidiary seldom obtained new resources and capabilities (2.1, S4), and did so only from internal MNC sources in order to realize entrepreneurial initiatives. No resource acquisition from external actors or joint resource development through collaboration with external partners took place over the past five years (see Figure 5.25). Limited subsidiary knowledge and experience in interacting with customers seems to pose a challenge for the South Korean unit.

> *... Headquarter[s] or engineering hub, they only can deliver or provide engineering service. They do not have like, how can I say, a certain manufacturing know-how; they don't have. How to like a working experience with customer OEM directly, they do not deliver those kind of ... solutions. Only they are providing, on a technical side, just this. .... We need both kinds of knowledge and experience, not only engineering knowledge."* (I4)

Internally, an important source where critical resources and capabilities were frequently acquired is headquarters (4.0, S4). As previously described, many of the advanced and core technologies are centrally developed at headquarters in Germany or at the regional R&D hub in Singapore and then afterwards acquired by the South Korean unit. Nevertheless, obtaining resources from the corporate center is not considered easy, as it is often quite restrictive and gives higher priority to other foreign sites, as seen in the following statement:

> *"The idea is mainly they are advanced automotive technology from headquarters in Germany, all the base technology we use came from there."* (I4)

> *"But we have certain limitation or certain, how can I say – resource issues. Currently we're having problems. We get a lot of requests from [customers] but we don't have enough resources to react on that."* (I4)

"We are quite experienced asking ... headquarters. But somehow ... certain technical, certain engineering resources, they are relatively limited. That is why it is very difficult to utilize certain engineering force for these Asian customers as they give ... higher priority to the European OEM projects." (I4)

Resource Structuring Activities (Extent during past five years; 1 = never, 5 = plentifully) (N = 1)

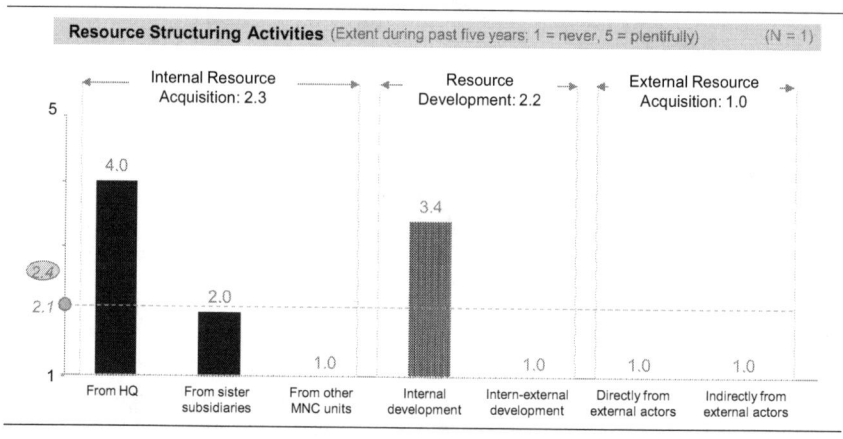

Internal Resource Acquisition: 2.3			Resource Development: 2.2		External Resource Acquisition: 1.0	
From HQ	From sister subsidiaries	From other MNC units	Internal development	Intern-external development	Directly from external actors	Indirectly from external actors
4.0	2.0	1.0	3.4	1.0	1.0	1.0

Overall: 2.1 (2.4)

Figure 5.25: Survey Results: SK – Initiative-related resource structuring activities

Moreover, the necessary resources for subsidiary initiatives were also frequently developed within the subsidiary itself (3.4, S4). Given their extensive product development expertise in particular areas and their strong R&D force, certain products and product adaptations could be developed fully independently by the South Korean unit (I4). In addition to resource structuring activities, the existing and newly acquired and developed resources and capabilities were then **bundled** to realize new initiatives. This most often took the form of incremental bundling with minor combination of already existing resources and capabilities (4.0), as well as some intermediate bundling requiring the mixture of newly obtained resources and capabilities with existing ones (2.0). The subsidiary did not engage in radical resource bundling that necessitated the extensive combination of completely new resources and capabilities during the past five years.

(2) Headquarters-Subsidiary Alignment

Throughout subsidiary initiative-taking, **headquarters involvement** was high, with a mean average of 3.8 (S4; see Figure 5.26). Headquarters-subsidiary communication with regard to new initiative opportunities were particularly frequent (5.0). The content of these communications involved, for example, new and emerging market trends that provided possibilities for new initiatives, presentations and explanations of new initiatives by the foreign unit to headquarters, as well as subsidiary requests for additional resources to further drive initiatives by the local unit (I4). Moreover, linked to the limited subsidiary autonomy and the strict rules and guidelines in the MNC, headquarters approval was often required for the continuation and implementation of new initiatives. With regard to **corporate resistance**, the South Korean unit encountered an overall low to moderate level of opposition from within the corporate system (2.5, S4). Resistance occurred from time to time in the form of initiative rejection by headquarters, delay and requests for greater justification (both 3.0) and, less frequently, as lobbying and rival activities by other units of the MNC or as lack of recognition and acceptance by headquarters (both 2.0). Finally, **initiative selling** activities by the subsidiary were assessed as low to moderate with an average value of 2.8. While attracting headquarters' attention for new initiatives, making headquarters understand new opportunities and lobbying and selling efforts directed at headquarters took place regularly (each 3.0), lobbying and selling efforts at sister subsidiaries or other units occurred less often. Initiative selling was typically undertaken by preparing and communicating initiative proposals to headquarters.

> "We of course are preparing those presentations or certain explanations to the headquarters ... and what the market and what the customer demands and what kind of technology they want. And how we should react on that and how to make a success with the Korean OEM." (I4)

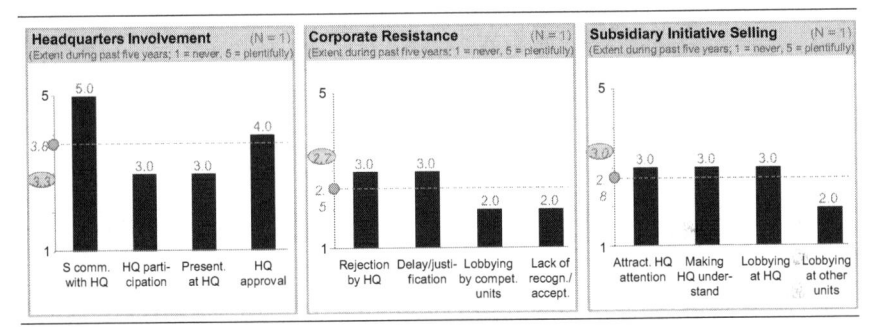

Figure 5.26: Survey Results: SK – Headquarters-subsidiary alignment and interaction

However, convincing the corporate center to accept new initiative opportunities has proved somewhat difficult for the South Korean unit due to limited resources and restrictive investment decisions within Autocomp. Furthermore, higher investment priority was often given to other geographical locations with large markets and more demanding customers, such as European OEMs, or to more advanced foreign units such as the regional R&D hubs (I4).

5.1.3.3 Subsidiary Initiative-Taking Outcome

(1) Extent of Subsidiary Initiative-Taking

Overall, the South Korean unit exhibited a low to moderate level of subsidiary initiatives with a mean average of 2.4 over the past five years (S4). Internally oriented entrepreneurial initiatives occurred slightly more often than externally oriented ones during this time period (2.5 vs. 2.3). Externally oriented entrepreneurial activities occasionally took the form of global and local market initiatives (2.0 and 2.5). Inward-focused initiatives in the form of internal market initiatives, which typically represent smaller-scale efforts aimed at improving the efficiency of the corporate system through reconfiguration or rationalization efforts, were rarely undertaken. In contrast, global-internal hybrid initiatives, which usually involve the relocation of certain value-adding functions to the subsidiary location (e.g. attraction of corporate R&D investment), occurred most frequently of all initiative types, as can be seen in Figure 5.27.

Subsidiary Initiative-Taking (Extent of subsidiary entrepreneurial initiatives within past five years: 1= never, 5 = plentifully) (N = 1)

← External initiatives: 2.3 →   ← Internal initiatives: 2.5 →

- Global market initiatives: 2.0
- Local market initiatives: 2.5
- Internal market initiatives: 2.0
- Global-internal hybrid initiatives: 3.0

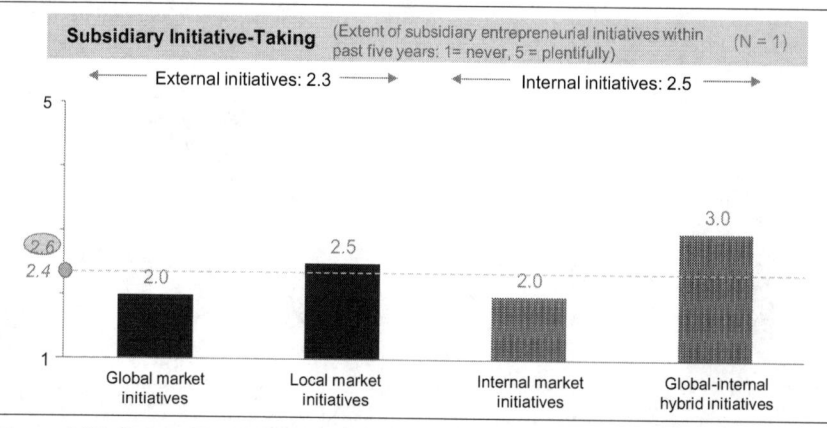

(2.6 / 2.4)

Figure 5.27: Survey Results: SK – Types and extent of subsidiary initiatives

(2) Resource-Related Outcomes

With a mean average of 2.9, the South Korean unit developed a moderate amount of new resources and capabilities as a result of entrepreneurial initiatives in the past five years (2.9, S4). In R&D the unit developed new specialized capabilities to a greater extent than in all other areas (4.0). Here the development of new and advanced technologies within the area of subsidiary competencies was highlighted in the interview with the subsidiary manager (I4). Additionally, newly generated capabilities in R&D, production of goods/services and in the field of innovation and entrepreneurship were considered of moderate use for other MNC locations as well (each 3.0). This indicates that the newly developed capabilities in R&D at the South Korean location also provide some potential for firm-level advantages, given both the extent and the impact on capability development for the wider MNC.

New Subsidiary Resources and Capabilities (N = 1) (Extent during past five years; 1= no capability development at all, 5 = extensive capability development)		Impact on MNC Capability Development (N = 1) (Extent during past five years; 1= no use at all, 5 = very useful)	
Research and development	4.0	Research and development	3.0
Prod. of goods/ services	3.0	Prod. of goods/ services	3.0
Marketing and/ or sales	3.0	Marketing and/ or sales	1.0
Logistics and/ or distribution	3.0	Logistics and/ or distribution	2.0
Purchasing	2.0	Purchasing	2.0
HR management	2.0	HR management	2.0
General management	3.0	General management	2.0
Innovation/ entrepreneur.	3.0	Innovation/ entrepreneur.	3.0
(1) min. Ø 2.9 max. (5)		(1) min. Ø 2.3 max. (5)	

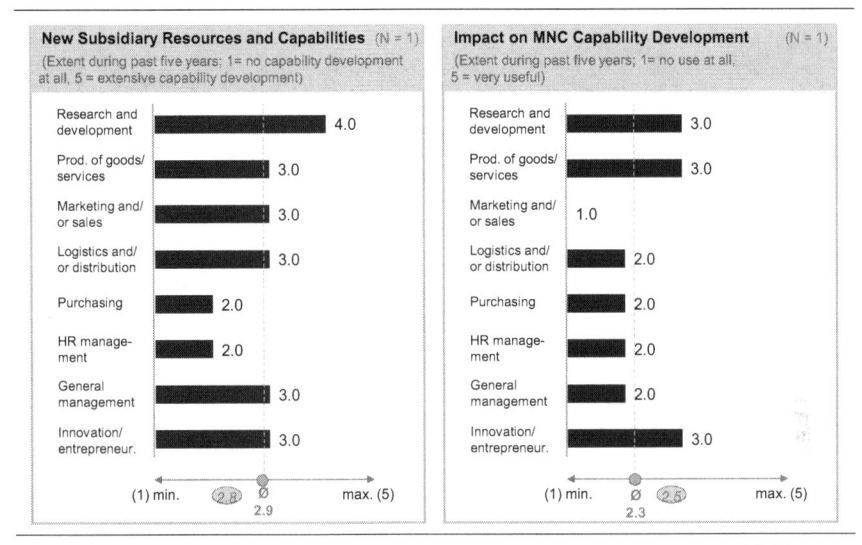

Figure 5.28: Survey Results: SK – New subsidiary resources and impact on MNC capabilities

However, the previously described resource constraints at the subsidiary location were also perceived as impeding more advanced resource building through innovative and entrepreneurial activities that would also be of potential use for other MNC locations. This is expressed in the following statement by the subsidiary manager:

> "If we would have that kind of experience and knowledge or know-how for such kind of advanced engineering product, then we could deliver certain know-how and experience for these other locations, too. ... First we need to invest certain condition resource to the location where this kind of advanced technology will be running. And then we can share a certain kind of experience and knowledge with the other locations or other sites." (I4)

(3) Further Outcomes

As to the **performance outcomes** of subsidiary initiative-taking, the South Korean unit experienced a particularly sharp increase in sales (4.0, S4), as shown in Figure 5.29. Positive developments related to costs, profit and productivity remained moderate (each 3.0), while advancement of market share was assessed as limited in the survey (2.0). The increase in sales was also expressed in the interview with the subsidiary manager:

"We've been making [a] very successful story. We are making more products for customers and we make sustainable increase of sales. That's why ... we can participate ... we have more products, more projects from customers and also we will extend our product range." (I4)

Performance Outcomes (N = 1) (Extent during past five years; 1 = very limited, 5 = substantial)		Subsidiary Role and Position in MNC (N = 1) (Extent during past five years; 1 = major decline, 3 = no change, 5 = major improvement)	
Enhanced sales/revenues	4.0	Geographical market scope	3.0
Reduced costs	3.0	Product scope	4.0
Improved market share	2.0	Value-added scope	3.0
Improved profit	3.0	Subsidiary influence	4.0
Improved ROI	3.0	History of delivering promises	3.0
Improved productivity	3.0	Signif. value-added contrib.	3.0
		Global competiveness	3.0
		Recognition by HQ	3.0

Right-side bracket annotations: Subsidiary role development; Subsidiary influence; Subsidiary credibility.

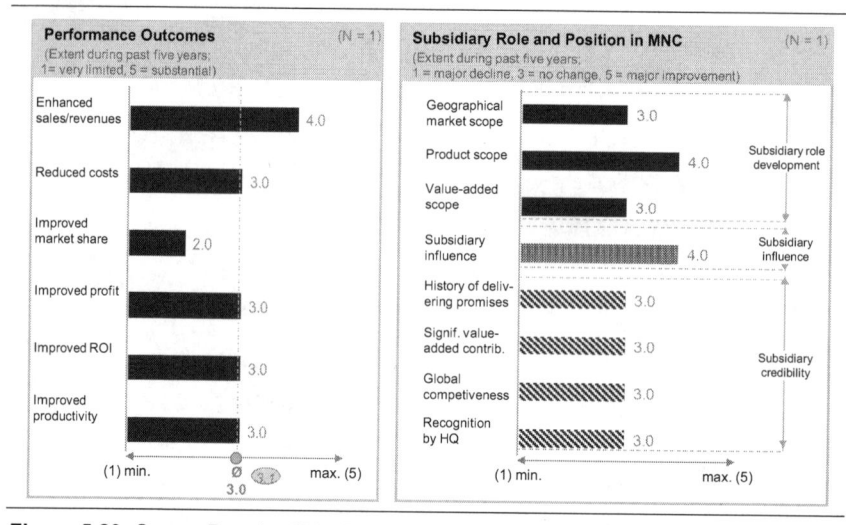

Figure 5.29: Survey Results: SK – Performance outcomes and changes to subsidiary role and position

With regard to the **subsidiary role development** and changes to its position in the MNC, the South Korean unit experienced improvements not only in product scope but also in subsidiary influence within the MNC (both 4.0, S4). According to the subsidiary manager, the growing sales contribution of the foreign unit also positively influenced its position in the corporate network:

"I can say our influence to headquarters has increased. Since [one customer's] market position is getting stronger and they sell their cars more worldwide: NAFTA, Europe and India, all over China, they are getting more like a strong position in the market. ... That's why somehow our ... our sale contribution to the business unit has increased. That's why our influence has ... increased." (I4)

5.1.4 Australian Subsidiary

The Australian Autocomp subsidiary was originally founded in the late 1950s and started initially as a pure manufacturing location providing products for one major customer in the Australian market. Over time, research and development activities were added and further sites were opened. In 2012, approximately 350 people were employed at the two Autocomp locations in Australia. Of these, approximately 200 were involved in production, 100 in administrative functions and 50 in the area of research and development (I5). Although all major value chain functions are carried out locally (S5), the focus of the foreign affiliate is on manufacturing products for the major OEMs present in the Australian market and on certain design and development activities. Besides serving these local customers, selected products are also exported to other geographical markets, including Europe. Furthermore, the foreign affiliate supports some R&D activities for OEMs in Asia. In addition to Autocomp, three other divisions are present in Australia, some of which share locations with Autocomp (I5).

5.1.4.1 Subsidiary Roles

(1) Strategic Market Importance and Subsidiary Resources: Contributor

The assessment of both headquarters and subsidiary management suggest that the Australian unit is a "Contributor" subsidiary. The strategic importance of the subsidiary's market environment achieved a score of only 2.3, which represents the lowest value of all units from Autocomp in the present research. In comparison, the level of subsidiary resources and capabilities was rated at 3.7 and thus is above average among the investigated Autocomp affiliates abroad, as shown in Figure 5.30 (S5). As to the low **strategic importance of the subsidiary market**, the competitive intensity and the customer demand intensity are assessed as relatively moderate (3.5 and 3.0), while the technical dynamism and the market size are viewed as low or very low (1.5 and 1.0). According to the subsidiary manager, local customers have less autonomy to develop their own designs and are instead pushed towards adopting the global platforms that exist in their companies. Consequently, the technical dynamism in the market is not considered very high. Furthermore, the market size is not only viewed as very limited, but has also significantly declined in the past years.

> "So the market has declined quite a lot. An example of that is the [company x] business, volumes were 120,000 I think, something like that, and now you have about 45,000 per annum. So the local car manufacturing has reduced substantially ... due to the pressure from the high Australian dollar, high tariffs and whatnot. So from that regard ... the viability of the business is I guess under some strain at the moment." (I5)[436]

---

[436] Besides "company x," other car manufacturers have also reduced their production volumes considerably or even ceased production in Australia altogether. For example, Mitsubishi discontinued manufacturing activities in the Australian market in 2008. Moreover, Ford Motor Company intends to end production in Australia by the end of 2016 and General Motors by the end of 2017, therefore possibly affecting the future market size of the subsidiary even further (see e.g. Business Monitor 2013).

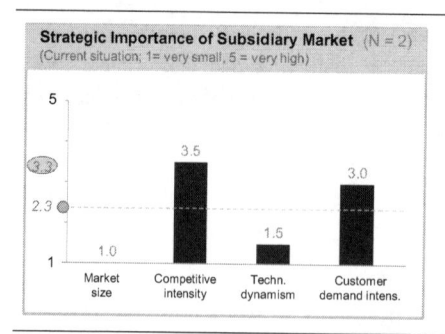

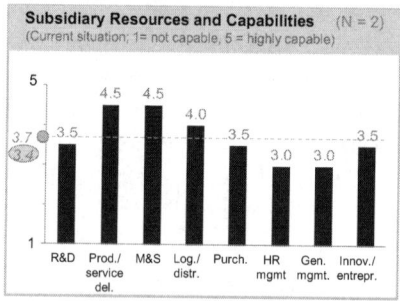

Figure 5.30: Survey Results: AUS – Strategic importance and subsidiary resources/capabilities

Regarding the second role dimension, the current level of **subsidiary resources and capabilities**, the Australian unit was said to possess a moderate to high level of capabilities (3.7, S5), particularly in production, marketing and sales, and logistics and distribution. Given its main focus on manufacturing and on serving customers in Australia, the unit has been able accumulate specific expertise in these areas during more than 50 years of operation. Competencies in the remaining areas are regarded as moderate, with values ranging from 3.0 to 3.5. For example, regarding R&D it is stated that, although experienced personnel exists, their expertise is not highly specialized but rather general in nature:

> "We've got a lot of experienced people. So roughly half of the engineers have long experience in the automotive industry, but they tend to be, because we are such a long way away from other locations ... and also because we have a small terrain, we tend to have more of a spread of capabilities. So every engineer is more of an all-rounder rather than specialized in a particular area ... as opposed to [headquarters], the mother world, where they have very specialized roles." (I5)

(2) Subsidiary Localization and Integration: Receptive Subsidiary

The Australian affiliate of Autocomp can be characterized as a "Receptive" subsidiary. Based on the survey results, the unit has a comparatively low degree of **localization/local responsiveness** with a mean average of 2.4 (S5), as presented in Figure 5.31. Given the unit's strong focus on manufacturing purely for the local market, the share of sales that come from locally produced goods is, of all variables relating to this role dimension, rated highest at 4.0. All other aspects of this dimension are assessed lower, with values ranging from 2.0 to 2.5. For example, the subsidiary receives extensive input from other locations, and local content in locally produced goods is assessed as fairly low. This is in part the result of local products being largely based on global platform solutions that are designed by other units of the company and that are then adapted for the use in Australia. Similarly, given the increasing use of global platforms by their customers (I5), local needs do not differ significantly from other locations.

Degree of Localization/Local Responsiveness
(Current situation; 1= very low, 5 = very high) (N = 2)

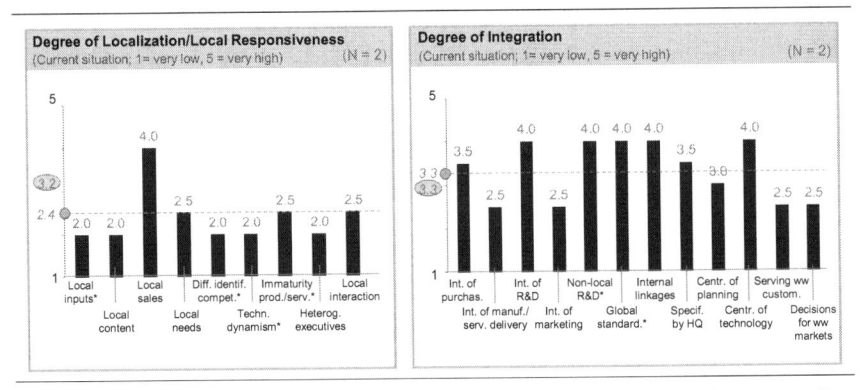

Local inputs*	2.4
Local content	2.0
Local sales	2.0
Local needs	4.0
Diff. identif. compet.*	2.5
Techn. dynamism*	2.0
Immaturity prod./serv.*	2.5
Heterog. executives	2.0
Local interaction	2.5

Degree of Integration
(Current situation; 1= very low, 5 = very high) (N = 2)

Int. of purchas.	3.3
Int. of manuf./ serv. delivery	2.5
Int. of marketing	2.5
Non-local R&D	4.0
Internal R&D*	4.0
Global linkages	4.0
Specif. standard.*	4.0
Centr. of planning	3.5
Centr. of technology	3.0
Serving ww custom.	4.0
Decisions for ww markets	2.5

Figure 5.31: Survey Results: AUS – Subsidiary localization/local responsiveness and subsidiary integration

The degree of **subsidiary integration** in the MNC is moderate, with a mean average of 3.3 (S5), as is further substantiated by the interview statements of the subsidiary manager (I5). With regard to the different functions, purchasing and R&D show a higher extent of integration than manufacturing processes and marketing activities, which are more geared towards local needs. Also, given the existence of global platforms, the use of standardized products and the degree of non-local R&D incorporated in products sold by the Australian unit are viewed as high, thereby indicating higher degrees of integration. Additionally, the subsidiary depends greatly on linkages within the internal network and centralization of technology development is evaluated as high.

(3) Subsidiary Decision-Making Autonomy

Overall, the Australian subsidiary exercises a moderate to high degree of decision-making autonomy with a mean average score of 3.2 (S5). Autonomy for operational decisions is rated much higher than for strategic decisions (4.0 vs. 2.6). With regard to new product development and process improvement efforts, the unit has high levels of autonomy when it comes to minor modifications of existing products, but much less latitude for major modifications of production processes or major developments of new products, as illustrated in Figure 5.32. In part, the limited autonomy for product development is the result of global platform solutions that are often applied within Autocomp, as explained by the subsidiary manager:

"When I say we have little autonomy it also, I guess, is in some ways it is driven by the platform-type solutions we have. Also in a lot of cases we focus on a cost perspective and not so much on a development effort perspective. So this is why I think we only have a certain amount of autonomy." (I5)

Subsidiary Autonomy (Current situation; 1= decided centrally by HQ; 5 = decided independently by subsidiary) (N = 2)

◄──── Strategic Decisions: 2.6 ────► ◄──── Operational Decisions: 4.0 ────►

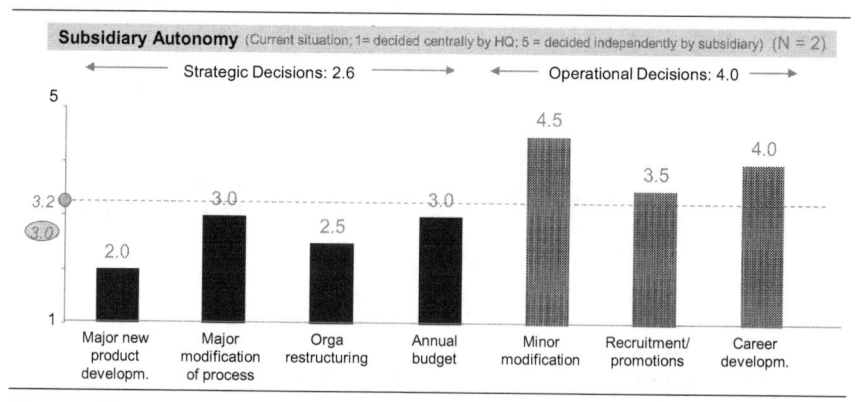

Major new product developm.	Major modification of process	Orga restructuring	Annual budget	Minor modification	Recruitment/ promotions	Career developm.
2.0	3.0	2.5	3.0	4.5	3.5	4.0

Figure 5.32: Survey Results: AUS – Subsidiary decision-making autonomy

5.1.4.2 Subsidiary Initiative-Taking

(1) Entrepreneurial Resource Management

Overall, the level of subsidiary **initiative identification** was rated as moderate with an average value of 2.6 (S5), as indicated in Figure 5.33. While new opportunities for entrepreneurial activities were identified both internally and externally, internal sources played a more important role during the past five years than external ones (3.2 vs. 1.8). Opportunity identification at the Australian location did not follow a structured approach, but instead came in diverse ways, as explained by the subsidiary manager:

"Locally we don't have anything structured in terms of innovative ideas. So any need would be generated out of project teams and project work." (I5)

Internally, most new initiative opportunities were identified within the Australian subsidiary itself. For example, opportunities for product enhancements or for the use of new materials were identified through internal meetings of the local engineering or management teams (I5). Moreover, some opportunities arose through interactions with the innovation teams located at headquarters (3.0) or with other units (2.5) such as the R&D hub located in Singapore.

"What we've done [is] some work with the innovation team in [Germany]. I guess there are some options, some opportunities to participate. But yeah, our resource base is dedicated to local development as opposed to such things." (I5)

5 – Empirical Findings

Identification of Subsidiary Initiative Opportunities
(Extent during past five years; 1 = never, 5 = plentifully) (N = 2)
Internal: 3.2 — External: 1.8

- Only from within subsidiary: 4.0
- From HQ: 3.0
- From other units within the MNC: 2.5
- From local actors (external): 2.0
- From global actors (external): 1.5
- (2.6 / 2.0 markers shown)

Innovativeness of Subsidiary Initiative Opportunities
(Extent during past five years; 1 = never, 5 = plentifully) (N = 2)

- Incrementally innovative: 3.8
- Moderately innovative: 2.8
- Radically innovative: 1.5

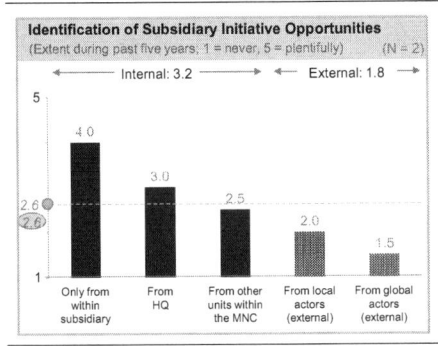

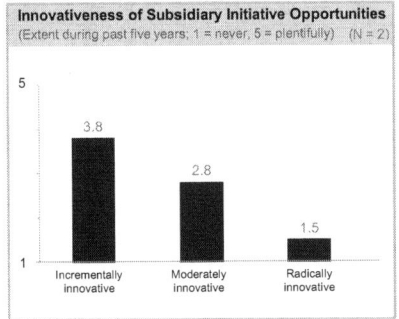

Figure 5.33: Survey Results: AUS – Identification and innovativeness of initiative opportunities

Externally, new initiatives were occasionally identified through interactions with local partners or, rarely, through connections with global actors outside the MNC (2.0 and 1.5, S5). As to **innovativeness**, most of the newly identified opportunities were assessed as incrementally innovative, involving replications of existing products for use in similar applications or new applications for existing products with little or no modification. Moderately innovative opportunities were detected less frequently, and very rarely did radically innovative opportunities emerge during the past five years.

When pursuing initiative opportunities, the Australian affiliate often **obtained new resources** (2.9, S5), and did so primarily from sources within the MNC rather than from external ones. Internally, resources were often acquired from various units of the MNC, or they were developed within the subsidiary itself (both 2.8; see Figure 5.34). As concerns internal resource acquisition, headquarters represents the most important source, followed by other units and sister subsidiaries. Resources obtained from headquarters include, for example, particular knowledge and expertise from the core development group on related or similar projects, special engineering equipment such as optical measurement systems or funding for local development activities (I5). According to the subsidiary manager, internal sources are used more frequently due to corporate policies and superior applicability of internally acquired knowledge:

> "... [at headquarters], there's a number of core development groups and ... they have experts and also we have some alignment with them and the different customer segments. So yes, through that type of network and also Singapore, which is also the R&D hub for the region ... we would get resources." (I5)

> "There is a policy. In fact it is the expectation that we should be using internal services or internal resources if they're available, rather than external. But probably a bigger and more important reason is the specific knowledge of the products is aligned and if you went external that might be lacking." (I5)

Resource Structuring Activities (Extent during past five years; 1 = never, 5 = plentifully)   (N = 2)

- Internal Resource Acquisition: 2.8
- Resource Development: 2.8
- External Resource Acquisition: 1.8

From HQ	From sister subsidiaries	From other MNC units	Internal development	Intern-external development	Directly from external actors	Indirectly from external actors
3.5	2.0	3.0	3.5	2.1	2.5	1.0

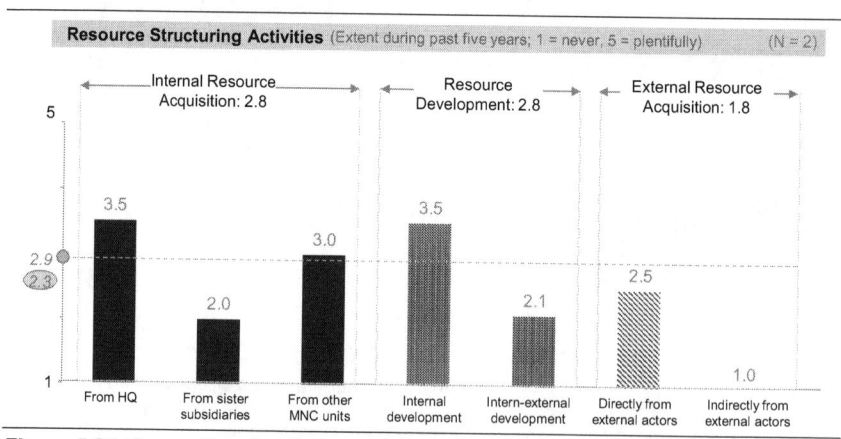

Figure 5.34: Survey Results: AUS – Initiative-related resource structuring activities

The Australian unit also frequently relied on internal resource development when pursuing entrepreneurial activities (3.5). Examples include newly developed software systems, training tools, measurement systems and software applications to be used in conjunction with automotive hardware (I5). In addition to such internal sourcing, new resources were also acquired directly from external actors or sometimes were developed jointly with external partners (2.5 and 2.1). Although opportunities for external collaboration with, for instance, governmental or research institutions did surface during the past five years, they were only seldom pursued (I5). Existing and newly obtained resources and capabilities were then **bundled** when realizing subsidiary initiatives. This occurred primarily in the form of incremental bundling (3.5, S5), with minor combinations of already existing resources, and less frequently as intermediate bundling (2.5) in which existing and newly obtained resources were combined. Radical bundling of completely new resources and capabilities did not occur during the past five years.

(2) Headquarters-Subsidiary Alignment

When engaging in entrepreneurial initiatives, the Australian subsidiary experienced a moderate level of **headquarters involvement** (3.3; S5), as shown in Figure 5.35. Communications with headquarters, presentations of new opportunities and headquarters approval occurred regularly (all 3.5), while headquarters participation in the refinement and development of initiatives took place less frequently (2.5). As a result of the strong centralization of technology development at headquarters and the use of platform-based solutions, new developments or changes to products by the Australian unit often necessitated communication and alignment with the corporate center (I5). **Corporate resistance** only arose from time to time (2.5, S5) and mostly as a lack of recognition and acceptance by other units of Autocomp. Resistance from headquarters often occurred in response to requests for additional resources by the unit abroad. Due to the small size and low importance of the unit for the MNC, this often proved difficult to overcome (I5). Finally, subsidiary **initiative selling** was evaluated as moderate (3.0, S5). The foreign affiliate repeatedly engaged in some lobbying and selling activities at headquarters to obtain support for its initiatives. Aside from selling activities aimed at the corporate center, other opportunities were used for initiative selling to others in the MNC, including at the annual Autocomp global R&D conference:

"We have the engineering conferences at the discipline level as well. Which means all the managers of various functional areas are in the same place and have the opportunity to share information and show around good ideas too, to sell them to their colleagues." (I5)

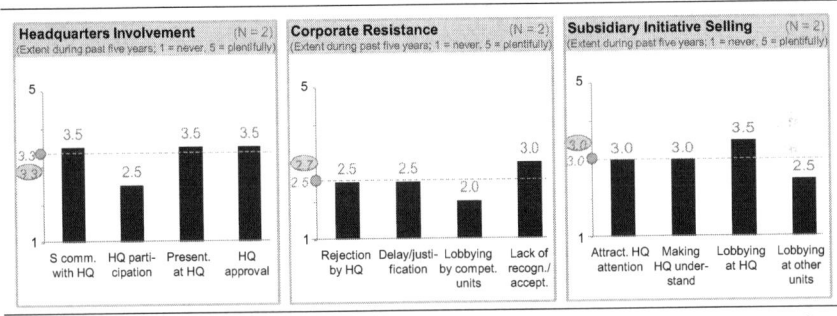

Figure 5.35: Survey Results: AUS – Headquarters-subsidiary alignment and interaction

5.1.4.3 Subsidiary Initiative-Taking Outcome

(1) Extent of Subsidiary Initiative-Taking

During the past five years, the Australian unit showed a moderate level of entrepreneurial initiatives (2.5, S5), as presented in Figure 5.36. With regard to initiative types, internally oriented initiatives originating from opportunities within the MNC were slightly more frequent than external ones (2.6 and 2.4). Of the internally oriented ones, global-internal hybrid initiatives involving the attraction of corporate investment in the subsidiary location took place more often than internal market initiatives, which typically revolve around internal efficiency improvement activities (3.3 and 2.0). Furthermore, the Australian affiliate repeatedly engaged in local market initiatives (3.0) and occasionally even in global ones (1.8). According to the subsidiary manager, many initiatives were on a comparatively small scale and focused on improving existing products or processes:[437]

---

[437] Examples of such smaller entrepreneurial activities given by the local manager include (1) enhancements or adaptations of existing products, (2) the investigation and use of new materials, (3) projects to improve the costs

"At a project level there are some entrepreneurial type activities, but actual fully-funded projects, I would say we don't have any examples of such a thing, where we've had an idea of doing something completely different which was driven by a product need and where we have gone in and investigated it." (I5)

Subsidiary Initiative-Taking (Extent of subsidiary entrepreneurial initiatives within past five years: 1= never, 5 = plentifully) (N = 2)

External initiatives: 2.4 ⇔ Internal initiatives: 2.6

Global market initiatives	1.8
Local market initiatives	3.0
Internal market initiatives	2.0
Global-internal hybrid initiatives	3.3

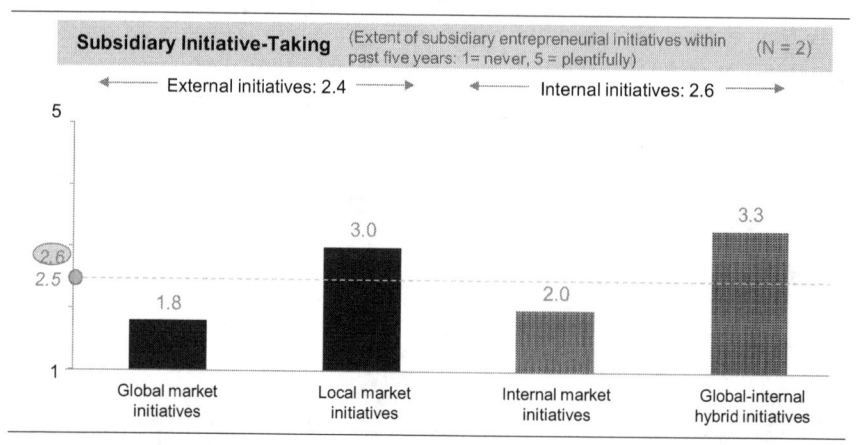

Overall: 2.6

Figure 5.36: Survey Results: AUS – Types and extent of subsidiary initiatives

(2) Resource-Related Outcomes

Subsidiary initiative-taking resulted in a low to moderate increase of resources and capabilities (2.6, S5), as illustrated in Figure 5.37. New resources were obtained with particular frequency in production, research and development and innovation/entrepreneurship. As outlined previously, many initiatives revolved around the enhancement or adaptation of platform-based solutions provided by headquarters or aimed at improving the cost or efficiency of local operations. Consequently, initiative-related resource outcomes in general are not considered highly specialized, as reflected in the following statement:

"So in terms of the complexity of the products and the technical levels I would say now we're probably in the middle. In the past it was probably more at the higher end but now ... we're probably just in the middle here." (I5)

Overall, the contribution of the new resources to the competencies of the MNC was rated as moderate (2.5, S5). According to local management, few *"truly entrepreneurial activities"* took place that could be *"fed back into the larger organization"* (I5). New resources in the area of production appear to be something of an exception, as they were evaluated as highly useful for other MNC units. Resources related to enhance-

---

of products, (4) initiatives for enhancing the profitability of manufacturing and (5) activities to reduce effort spent on development (I5).

ments of platform solutions or achieved cost savings through efficiency improvements were also believed to be easily transferable in MNC:

> "Generally we have the same products around the world so most cost saving ideas can be transferred in some way." (I5)

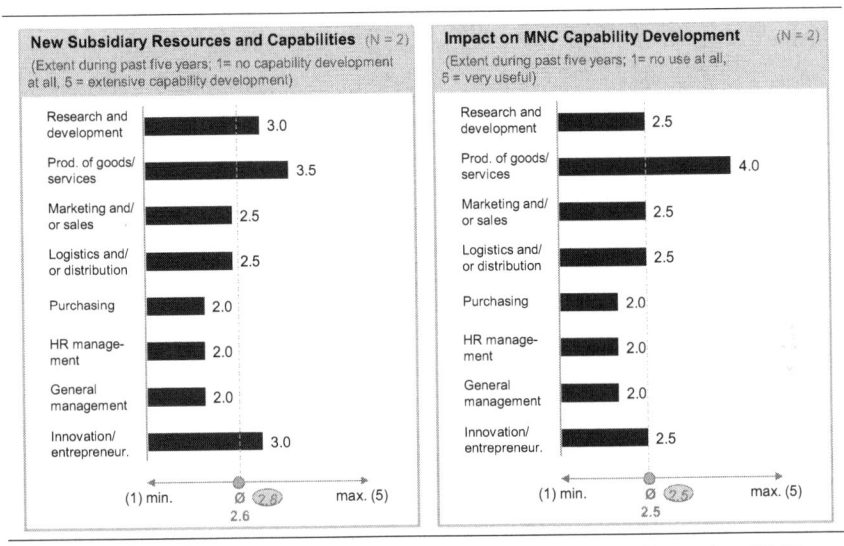

New Subsidiary Resources and Capabilities (N = 2) (Extent during past five years; 1= no capability development at all, 5 = extensive capability development)		Impact on MNC Capability Development (N = 2) (Extent during past five years; 1= no use at all, 5 = very useful)	
Research and development	3.0	Research and development	2.5
Prod. of goods/services	3.5	Prod. of goods/services	4.0
Marketing and/or sales	2.5	Marketing and/or sales	2.5
Logistics and/or distribution	2.5	Logistics and/or distribution	2.5
Purchasing	2.0	Purchasing	2.0
HR management	2.0	HR management	2.0
General management	2.0	General management	2.0
Innovation/entrepreneur.	3.0	Innovation/entrepreneur.	2.5
(1) min. Ø 2.6 max. (5)		(1) min. Ø 2.5 max. (5)	

Figure 5.37: Survey Results: AUS – New subsidiary resources and impact on MNC capabilities

(3) Further Outcomes

In addition to generating new resources and capabilities, subsidiary initiatives also resulted in further **performance outcomes**. Based on the assessment by the subsidiary managers, entrepreneurial activities in the past five years resulted in reduced costs and improved productivity in particular (each 3.5, S5), but also in some advances regarding profit and ROI (each 3.0). Enhancements in sales and market share were evaluated as less substantial than in the other areas. Furthermore, the subsidiary's role slightly declined during the past five years in terms of its geographical market scope and its product scope (both 2.5). Similarly, subsidiary credibility within the MNC deteriorated somewhat in terms of the global competitiveness of the unit in its market environment and the recognition of the subsidiary by headquarters as a strategically important unit (both 2.0). However, slight improvements were observed with regard to the subsidiary's value-added contribution to the company (3.5).

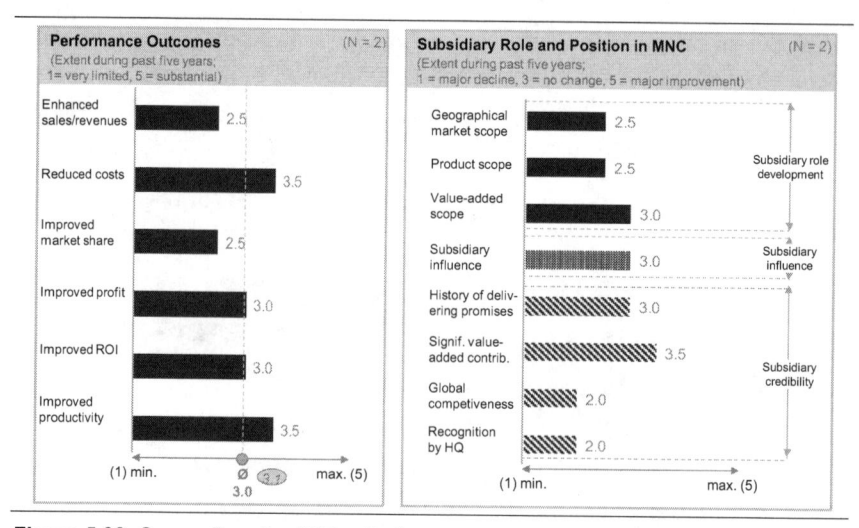

Figure 5.38: Survey Results: AUS – Performance outcomes and changes to subsidiary role and position

5.1.5 Chinese Subsidiary

The Chinese subsidiary unit was originally established in the mid-1990s as a joint venture between a Chinese investor and Company A with a primary focus on becoming a low-cost manufacturing location. Since the mid-2000s, Autocomp has held the majority of shares. In 2013, Autocomp had a presence at multiple locations in China and employed more than 3,000 workers. All major functions, from production, R&D, marketing and sales, to purchasing and HR management were performed by the unit abroad (S6). However, while manufacturing was started with the subsidiary's founding, R&D activities were initiated only in the early 2000s (I6). The foreign unit has a relatively narrow market scope and serves only local customers in China and some international customers present there. While the subsidiary has its own responsibility to develop and manage local Chinese customers, all activities for international customers in the domestic market are driven and decided on by the German headquarters (I6).

5.1.5.1 Subsidiary Roles

(1) Strategic Market Importance and Subsidiary Capabilities: Black Hole

Based on the empirical results, the Chinese subsidiary can be categorized as a "Black Hole" unit within Autocomp. While the strategic importance of the subsidiary market is assessed as moderate to high, the level of subsidiary resources and capabilities is rated the lowest among all units (3.5 and 3.0, S6). As to the **strategic importance of the** subsidiary's market, the market size and competitive intensity are viewed as very high, customer demand intensity is moderate and technical dynamism is seen as very low. **Subsidiary resources and capabilities**, particularly in production, in marketing and sales and in R&D are evaluated as high or very high. All others were seen as moderate or low, as shown in Figure 5.39.

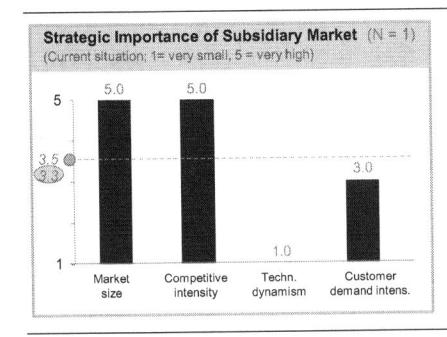

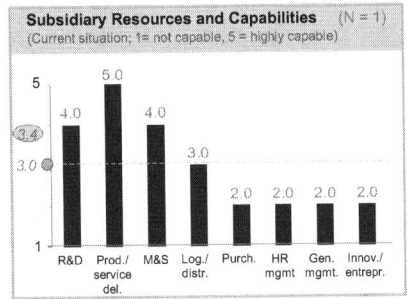

Strategic Importance of Subsidiary Market (N = 1) (Current situation; 1= very small, 5 = very high)	Subsidiary Resources and Capabilities (N = 1) (Current situation; 1= not capable, 5 = highly capable)
Market size: 5.0; Competitive intensity: 5.0; Techn. dynamism: 3.5/2.3; Customer demand intens.: 3.0/1.0	R&D: 4.0/3.4; Prod./service: 5.0; M&S: 4.0; Log./distr. del.: 3.0; Purch.: 2.0; HR mgmt: 2.0; Gen. mgmt: 2.0; Innov./entrepr.: 2.0/3.0

Figure 5.39: Survey Results: China – Strategic importance and subsidiary resources/ capabilities

(2) Subsidiary Localization and Integration: Autonomous Subsidiary

In Jarillo and Martinez's role typology, the Chinese unit represents an "Autonomous Subsidiary" with a high degree of localization/local responsiveness and a low degree of integration (3.7 and 2.5, S6), as presented in Figure 5.40. As to the **degree of localization/local responsiveness**, local input and content as well as the share of sales of locally manufactured goods are assessed as high (4.0). The need for localization is also expressed by the interviewee:

> *"Um dann auf dem hiesigen Markt konkurrenzfähig zu sein, müssen wir eigene Idee haben, um die Kosten zu reduzieren. ... Dann müssen wir natürlich einige Abstriche machen, teilweise bei der Qualität, teilweise im Aussehen des Produktes, manchmal vielleicht ebenso im Hinblick auf die Zuverlässigkeit."* (I6)

> *„Zum anderen müssen wir gleichfalls für unsere lokalen Kunden in China auf dem Markt sein. Denn aus anderen Ländern heraus können die lokalen chinesischen Kunden kaum bedient werden."* (I6)

The Chinese unit also exhibits an overall low **degree of integration** (2.5, S6). Except for the unit's high dependence on linkages within the internal network and the product/ quality specifications often developed by headquarters, all remaining variables were assessed as moderate, low or even very low, as in the case of integration of marketing with the rest of the group.

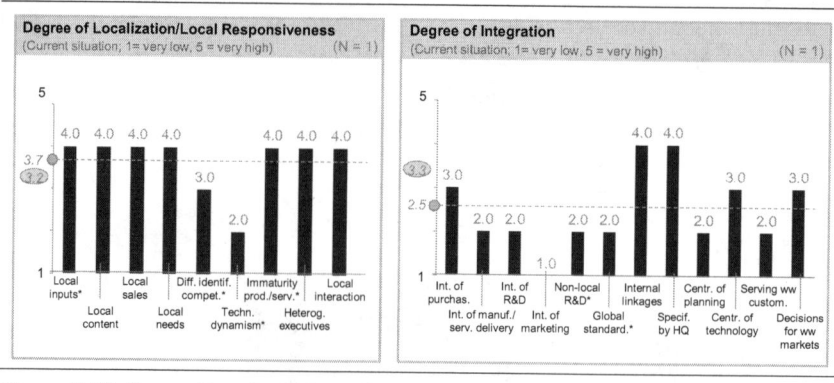

Figure 5.40: Survey Results: China – Subsidiary localization/local responsiveness and subsidiary integration

(3) Subsidiary Decision-Making Autonomy

In comparison to other subsidiaries at Autocomp, the Chinese entity has the lowest level of decision-making autonomy (2.1, S6). As to strategic decisions, the foreign affiliate has some leeway regarding the modification of processes or organizational restructuring. However, the formulation and approval of the unit's annual budget and major new product development activities are decided centrally by headquarters. For example, the Chinese manager needs to align annually with the German headquarters as to planned research and development projects and the related budget requirements:

> „Ich meine, unsere Geschäftsverantwortung liegt ja im Headquarter. Und natürlich müssen wir mit dem Headquarter sprechen, das Budget muss vom Headquarter freigegeben werden. Und ebenso die Headcount-Freigabe, wenn wir Leute einstellen, erfolgt durch das Headquarter." (I6)

> "... für ... internationale OEM ... liegt die Verantwortung bei unserem Headquarter, und wir führen ... nur das aus, was im Headquarter entschieden wird." (I6)

Operational aspects such as minor but significant modifications to existing products are jointly decided on, but recruitment and promotions and career development plans for subsidiary management are primarily the responsibility of headquarters, as seen in Figure 5.41.

5 – Empirical Findings

Subsidiary Autonomy (Current situation; 1= decided centrally by HQ; 5 = decided independently by subsidiary) (N = 1)

◄──── Strategic Decisions: 2.3 ────►   ◄──── Operational Decisions: 2.0 ────►

Major new product developm.	Major modification of process	Orga restructuring	Annual budget	Minor modification	Recruitment/ promotions	Career developm.
1.0	3.0	3.0	1.0	3.0	2.0	2.0

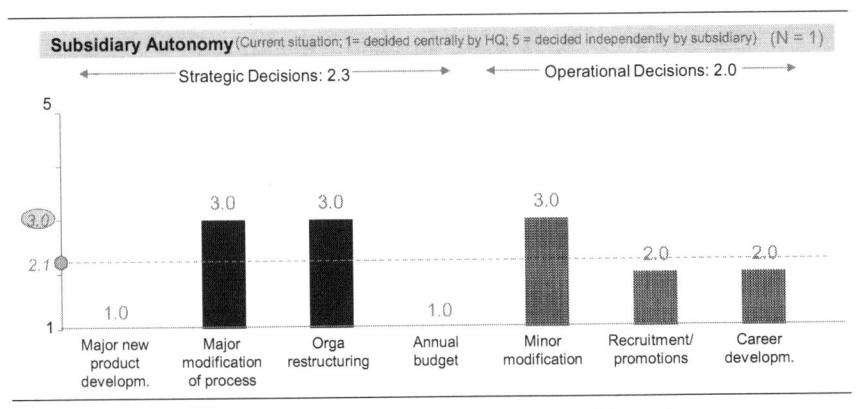

(Overall: 2.1)

Figure 5.41: Survey Results: China – Subsidiary decision-making autonomy

5.1.5.2 Subsidiary Initiative-Taking

(1) Entrepreneurial Resource Management

The Chinese subsidiary displayed a low level of **initiative identification** throughout the past five years (1.8, S6). According to subsidiary management, the most prominent source consisted of local actors in the external market. Global external actors were not relevant for new opportunity identification as the unit abroad is only responsible for the management of local customers, while global customers are managed by headquarters. Internally, headquarters or other units are occasionally used as a source for detecting new opportunities, as shown in Figure 5.42. The relevance of external customers for the identification and evaluation of new opportunities was also noted in the interview. For example, regular meetings and discussions of sales and R&D staff with customers represent an important source:

"Die Sales-Leute gehen ja regelmäßig zu Kunden. Und ich als R&D-Leiter gehe ich ebenfalls jährlich einmal zu unserem großen Kunden, um bei einer Technical Roadshow unsere Produkte vom Headquarter zu zeigen. Und dann diskutiert man mit den Kunden, ob das auch für deren K-Modell in Zukunft infrage kommt. Wenn wir dann alle diese Informationen konsolidieren, erkennen wir ebenso den Markttrend, was der Markt wirklich verlangt." (I6)

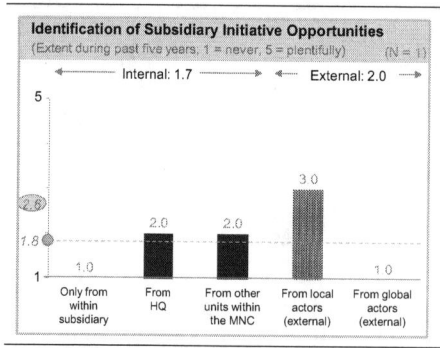

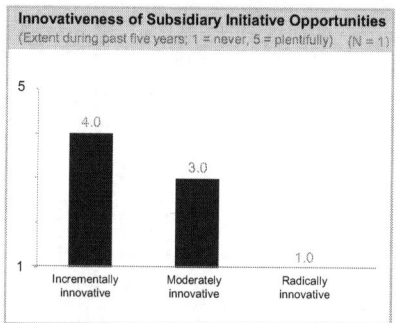

Figure 5.42: Survey Results: China – Identification and innovativeness of initiative opportunities

New initiative opportunities during the past five years were mostly incremental in nature and sometimes moderately innovative. No radically innovative opportunities were identified (S6). According to subsidiary management, new initiative opportunities frequently involved low-cost solutions for the Chinese market as the high-quality and high-priced solutions from Europe typically did not fit the local market needs.

> „Da geht es meistens um sogenannte Lowcost-Lösungen. Ich meine, unser gesamtes Produkt-Portfolio kommt aus Europa. Da gibt es sehr unterschiedliche Standards. Mit unserem europäischen Standard sind wir zwar von der Qualität her die Besten – best in class – aber dann sind wir natürlich auch sehr, sehr teuer gegenüber der lokalen Konkurrenz. Um dann auf dem hiesigen Markt konkurrenzfähig zu sein, müssen wir eigene Idee haben, um die Kosten zu reduzieren. ... Dann müssen wir natürlich einige Abstriche machen, teilweise bei der Qualität, teilweise im Aussehen des Produktes, manchmal vielleicht ebenso im Hinblick auf die Zuverlässigkeit." (I6)

When attempting to realize new initiative opportunities, the Chinese unit engaged in a moderate level of **resource structuring** activities (2.3, S6), as Figure 5.43 illustrates. Internal resource acquisition frequently took place from both headquarters and other MNC units. However, despite the reliance on resources from other internal MNC sources, the latest knowledge, such as specific technologies or know-how, was transferred only reluctantly by headquarters due to the fear of knowledge drain to competitors or product piracy by local actors (I1).

> „Das eine ist die Bereitschaft, Knowhow in einen Emerging Market zu transferieren. Die ist nicht immer gegeben." (I6)

> „Wir haben zum Beispiel 2010 in China bereits eigenständig angefangen, ein [neues Produkt] zu entwickeln. Das ist eine neue Technologie für uns. ... Das ist von der Technologie her viel komplizierter. Und da hat man sehr, sehr lange gezögert, das nach China zu geben." (I6)

Resources were also frequently acquired from external actors to obtain those needed to realize subsidiary initiatives (5.0, S6). In contrast, resource development within the subsidiary or in collaboration with external network partners played less important roles. Some internal development took place, for example, in the form of local training of newly hired employees, but this was with the help and support of headquarters through expatriate transfers to China, for example (I6). Finally, **bundling** of resources only occurred as incremental or intermediate bundling (both 2.0, S6), with existing and new resources being combined in the pursuit of entrepreneurial initiatives.

Resource Structuring Activities (Extent during past five years; 1 = never, 5 = plentifully)   (N = 1)

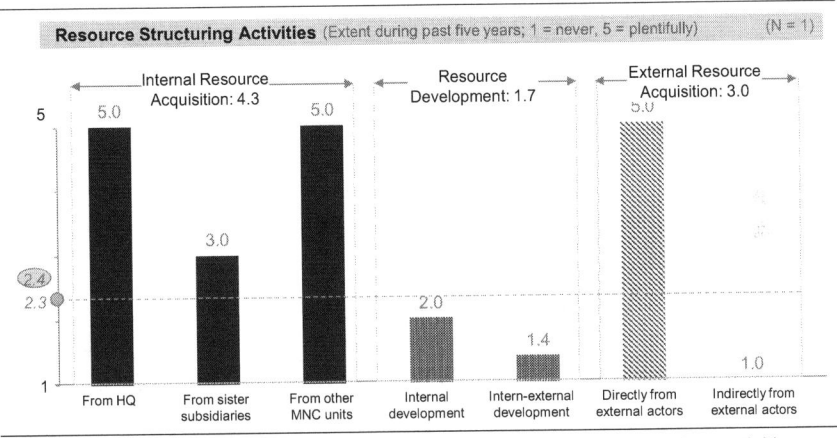

Internal Resource Acquisition	4.3
From HQ	5.0
From sister subsidiaries	2.3 (2.4)
From other MNC units	5.0
Resource Development	1.7
Internal development	3.0
Intern-external development	2.0
External Resource Acquisition	3.0
Directly from external actors	5.0
Indirectly from external actors	1.4 / 1.0

Figure 5.43: Survey Results: China – Initiative-related resource structuring activities

(2) Headquarters-Subsidiary Alignment

In its initiative-taking activities the Chinese subsidiary experienced a very high degree of **headquarters involvement** (5.0, S6). According to subsidiary management, headquarters was typically closely involved throughout the various stages of subsidiary initiatives, as shown in Figure 5.44. For example, the corporate center was informed about new opportunities identified locally and was engaged to obtain budget allocations and approval for entrepreneurial initiatives:

> „... unser erster Ansprechpartner ist da immer das Headquarter. Wir berichten ans Headquarter, dass wir hier Potenzial sehen, welche Produkte wir hier im Markt brauchen, und dann machen wir eine Analyse, ob wir das mit der lokalen Mannschaft können. Und wenn nicht, gucken wir, ob das am Headquarter oder den anderen Standorte schon einmal gemacht wurde, bzw. vergleichen wir das mit unserem globalen Portfolio." (I6)

> „... Und natürlich müssen wir mit dem Headquarter sprechen, das Budget muss vom Headquarter freigegeben werden. Und ebenso die Headcount-Freigabe, wenn wir Leute einstellen, erfolgt durch das Headquarter." (I6)

Moreover, the foreign entity experienced a high degree of **corporate resistance** when engaging in entrepreneurial activities (3.5, S6). This frequently took the form of rejection by headquarters or requests for further justification. The subsidiary manager further explained that the local market requires specific (i.e. lower-cost, lower-quality) solutions and adaptations that are often deemed inappropriate or even risky by headquarters:

> „Um dann auf dem hiesigen Markt konkurrenzfähig zu sein ... müssen wir natürlich einige Abstriche machen, teilweise bei der Qualität, teilweise im Aussehen des Produktes, manchmal vielleicht ebenso im Hinblick auf die Zuverlässigkeit. Aber das Headquarter ist natürlich sehr skeptisch, wenn wir da zu große Kompromisse eingehen, weil das zu Qualitätsproblemen führen könnte, was natürlich längerfristig der Marke ... schaden könnte. ... Das Problem ist allerdings, dass aus europäischer Sicht viele Lösungsvorschläge aufgrund des hohen Standards, den man in Europa gewohnt ist, absurd erscheinen. Und da macht dann natürlich nicht jeder mit. Dieser Konflikt besteht auf jeden Fall." (I6)

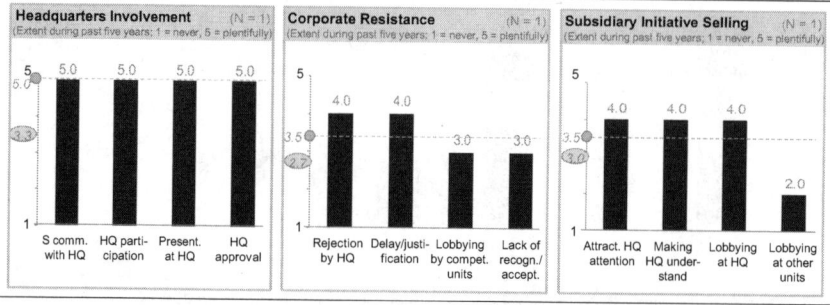

Figure 5.44: Survey Results: China – Headquarters-subsidiary alignment and interaction

Entrepreneurial initiatives during the past five years also typically required high **selling efforts by the subsidiary** within the MNC (3.5, S6). This often took the form of attracting the center's attention, making headquarters understand an initiative and lobbying at the parent company. Along with the more standardized alignment processes, in which new initiative opportunities, customer requirements and budget needs are presented within the MNC, subsidiary management also employed annual R&D meetings at various levels to present new ideas and concepts. Subsidiary management also acknowledged that, in addition to technical data and business case information, good relationships and networking within the MNC are helpful in reaching out to and convincing relevant decision-makers in the firm:

> „... da gibt es verschiedene Wege. Zum einen gibt es immer jährliche Engineering Meetings auf zwei Ebenen. Auf meiner Ebene gibt es jährlich einmal ein Engineering Meeting, und es gibt in jeder Disziplin ebenfalls ein Engineering Meeting. ... Und da hat man die Gelegenheit, etwas zu präsentieren. Auf der

anderen Seite gibt es ebenso zu jedem Projekt einen Genehmigungsprozess, bei dem man ... das Konzept und die Kundenanforderungen präsentiert." (I6)

"... wenn man hier so ein gutes Netzwerk hat, ist es natürlich viel leichter, zu den wichtigen Leuten zu kommen und diese zu überzeugen." (I6)

5.1.5.3 Subsidiary Initiative-Taking Outcome

(1) Extent of Subsidiary Initiative-Taking

With a mean average of 2.5, the Black Hole unit showed a moderate level of entrepreneurial initiatives over the past five years (2.5, S6). Of all external types, local market initiatives occurred most frequently, yet some global market initiatives were also undertaken in this time period. Internally, both internal market initiatives and global-internal hybrid initiatives took place from time to time, as illustrated in Figure 5.45. One example of a local market initiative given by the interviewee involved the proactive adaptation of a high-quality and high-cost product technology originally developed in Germany to the needs of local Chinese customers. It took several rounds of subsidiary selling before a concrete project was approved and finally implemented (I6).

Subsidiary Initiative-Taking	(Extent of subsidiary entrepreneurial initiatives within past five years: 1= never, 5 = plentifully)	(N = 1)

◄──── External initiatives: 2.5 ────►   ◄──── Internal initiatives: 2.5 ────►

Global market initiatives	Local market initiatives	Internal market initiatives	Global-internal hybrid initiatives
2.0	3.0	2.5	2.5

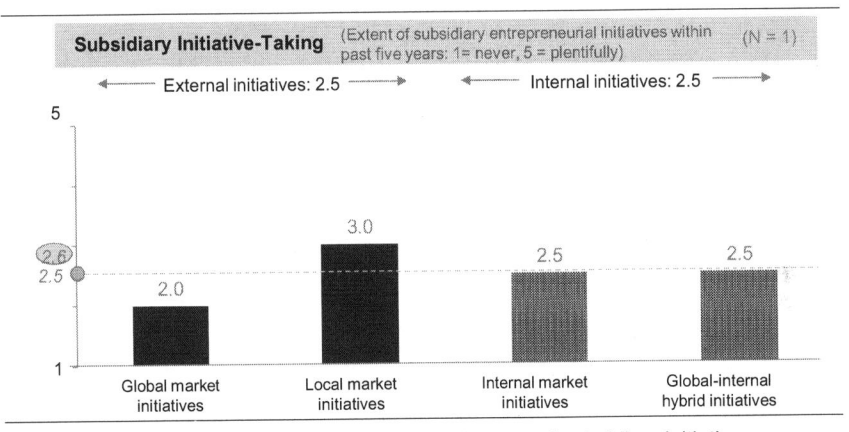

Figure 5.45: Survey Results: China – Types and extent of subsidiary initiatives

(2) Resource-Related Outcomes

Following from the entrepreneurial initiatives, the Chinese unit developed few **specialized capabilities** that were of use in other units of the MNC (see Figure 5.46). Particularly in the area of R&D, the subsidiary was able to grow new resources and capabilities that could be applied elsewhere in the firm. In other areas such as purchasing or logistics/distribution, only moderate capability development occurred. As further described by subsidiary management, resource development was often gradual, through knowledge and technology transfer from headquarters or through continuously expanding the local R&D staff (I6). Moreover, some of the locally developed products, solutions or components are also of **use in other locations** of the MNC, as described by the interviewee:

> „Ich beziehe mich nur auf Engineering. Ja, klar, haben wir unsere Capabilities erweitert. Wie ich vorhin erwähnt habe, sind wir jetzt in der Lage, auch so ein [komplexes Produkt] zu entwickeln. Das wurde ebenfalls in den letzten anderthalb Jahren ausgebaut." (I6)

> „Das Produkt ist ja, sage ich einmal, universell. Man kann es auch in den anderen Standorten einsetzen. Natürlich hat jedes Land eigene Anforderungen. Aber der Kern ist der gleiche." (I6)

New Subsidiary Resources and Capabilities (N=1) (Extent during past five years; 1= no capability development at all, 5 = extensive capability development)		Impact on MNC Capability Development (N=1) (Extent during past five years; 1= no use at all, 5 = very useful)	
Research and development	5.0	Research and development	4.0
Prod. of goods/ services	5.0	Prod. of goods/ services	3.0
Marketing and/ or sales	3.0	Marketing and/ or sales	1.0
Logistics and/ or distribution	2.0	Logistics and/ or distribution	2.0
Purchasing	3.0	Purchasing	3.0
HR management	2.0	HR management	1.0
General management	2.0	General management	2.0
Innovation/ entrepreneur.	1.0	Innovation/ entrepreneur.	1.0
(1) min. Ø 2.9 max. (5)		(1) min. Ø 2.1 max. (5)	

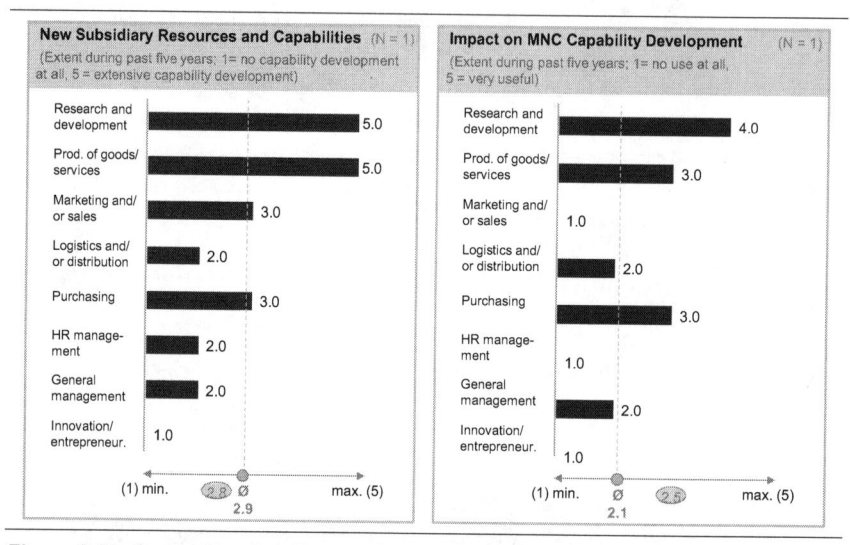

Figure 5.46: Survey Results: China – New subsidiary resources and impact on MNC capabilities

(3) Further Outcomes

Among further **performance outcomes** of subsidiary initiatives, local management stated that enhanced sales and reduced costs were among the most substantial results (both 4.0, S6). As a consequence of local entrepreneurial activities, the Chinese unit was able to win new customer contracts and enhance the profitability of the subsidiary, as described by the interviewee below. Other outcomes were considered less extensive, as illustrated in Figure 5.47. With regard to **subsidiary role and position** in the MNC, the foreign unit positively altered its role in terms of product and value-added scope over time. Particularly in R&D, the subsidiary increased its scope from a manufacturing-focused site towards a unit with stronger research and development for the local market. Finally, as a result of its growing revenue and profit contribution to the wider MNC, the local subsidiary has also been able to increase attention and recognition from headquarters (S6). Changes in the subsidiary's value-added scope and in headquarters recognition were also described by subsidiary management:

> „In den letzten Jahren ist es viel besser geworden. Ich nehme wiederum Engineering als Beispiel. Vor vier Jahren ... hatten wir vierzig Mitarbeiter, und inzwischen sind es 200. Die Zahl hat sich innerhalb von vier Jahren verfünffacht." (I6)

> „Und wir machen sicher ebenso in China viel mehr Umsatz, wir haben mehr EBIT. Und wir gewinnen mehr Fokus vom Headquarter." (I6)

Performance Outcomes (N = 1)
(Extent during past five years; 1 = very limited, 5 = substantial)

Enhanced sales/revenues	4.0
Reduced costs	4.0
Improved market share	2.0
Improved profit	2.0
Improved ROI	2.0
Improved productivity	2.0
Ø	2.7

Subsidiary Role and Position in MNC (N = 1)
(Extent during past five years; 1 = major decline, 3 = no change, 5 = major improvement)

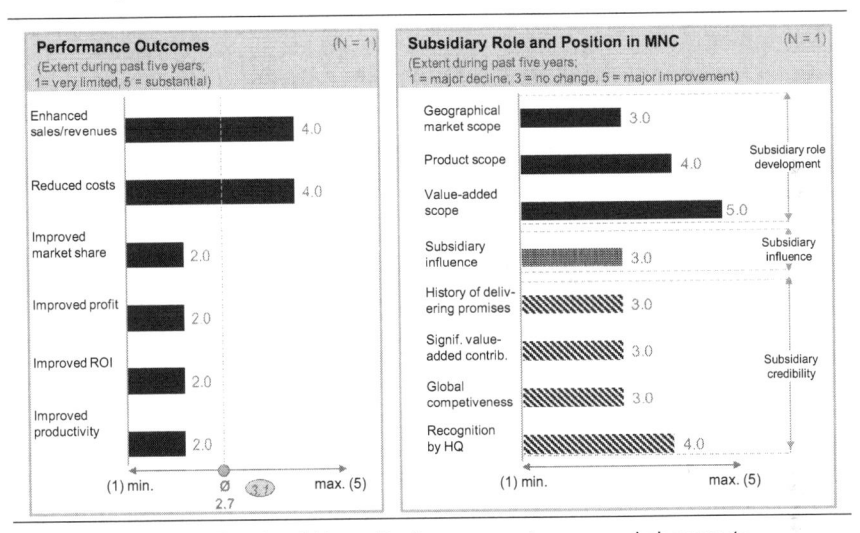

Measure	Value	Category
Geographical market scope	3.0	Subsidiary role development
Product scope	4.0	Subsidiary role development
Value-added scope	5.0	Subsidiary role development
Subsidiary influence	3.0	Subsidiary influence
History of delivering promises	3.0	Subsidiary credibility
Signif. value-added contrib.	3.0	Subsidiary credibility
Global competiveness	3.0	Subsidiary credibility
Recognition by HQ	4.0	Subsidiary credibility

Figure 5.47: Survey Results: China – Performance outcomes and changes to subsidiary role and position

5.1.6 Romanian Subsidiary

The foreign unit in Romania was founded by Company A in the early 2000s. In 2012 close to 2,600 employees were working at this location, of which approximately 600 were employed in production. The remaining 2,000 employees were engaged in non-manufacturing areas such as R&D and other support functions (A6). All major functions are present at the location, including production, R&D, marketing and sales, purchasing, and HR management. In addition to Autocomp, four other divisions of Company A are also active in Romania. However, while most support functions, such as HR management, purchasing, and general management are executed at the Romanian location for all five divisions, manufacturing is only carried out for Autocomp and one other division (I7, S7).

5.1.6.1 Subsidiary Roles

(1) Strategic Market Importance and Subsidiary Capabilities: Implementer

Within Autocomp, the Romanian unit can be classified as an "Implementer" subsidiary. The local managers assessed the strategic importance of the subsidiary's market at a low to moderate value of 3.1, as indicated in Figure 5.48. The overall level of subsidiary resources and capabilities was rated at 3.2 and hence below the average of all subsidiary units of Autocomp in this study (S7).

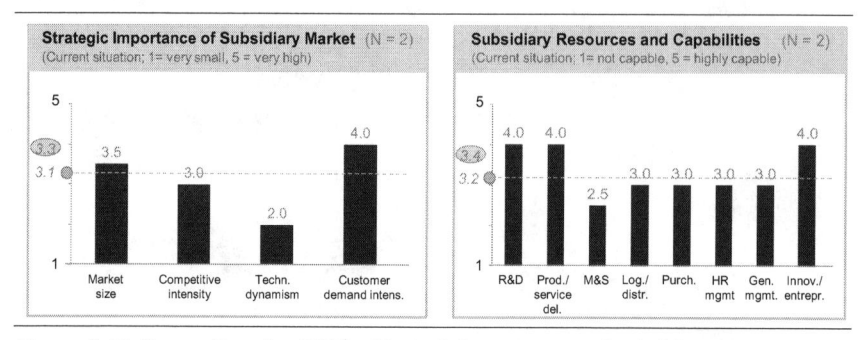

Figure 5.48: Survey Results: ROM – Strategic importance and subsidiary resources/ capabilities

Regarding the **strategic importance of the subsidiary market**, the respective market size and the customer demand intensity are viewed as comparatively high, with values of 3.5 and 4.0 in the survey (S7). Given the unit's status as a "best cost location," locally manufactured products are delivered to a broader customer base in various countries, thus leading to a larger subsidiary market. However, while manufacturing is performed for a wider geographical area, R&D activities are primarily undertaken for customers in Italy. Furthermore, the evaluation of the relatively high customer demand intensity results from the very high expectations of selected customers in terms of the quality of products and solutions (I7).

Concerning the second role dimension, **subsidiary resources and capabilities**, the Romanian unit was assessed as having a low to moderate degree with a mean average of 3.2 (S7). Based on the survey results, the foreign unit possesses a higher level of capabilities in R&D, manufacturing and innovation/entrepreneurship (4.0) than in the other areas (values of 2.5 to 3.0). In R&D and manufacturing, the unit experienced significant investment and growth within the past years, as reflected in the following two statements by the subsidiary manager:

> "This is exactly linked to the fact that over the past years we can run complete R&D projects from here, and this proves a high competence level and this is the experience that was gained in the last ten years." (I7)

> "The growth is really, really visible. From the research and development point of view and also the manufacturing location in the past years, the development was quite big. It's really visible from one year to the other." (I7)

(2) Subsidiary Localization and Integration: Quiescent Subsidiary

According to the evaluation by its managers, the Romanian subsidiary also constitutes a "Quiescent" subsidiary. As shown in Figure 5.49, the foreign unit exhibits a low **degree of localization/local responsiveness**, with an overall mean average of 2.7 (S7). Given its status as a "best cost location," the Romanian subsidiary has been specifically set up to manufacture products for lower-cost markets such as Serbia and Russia. Consequently, the share of sales from locally produced goods is rather high with a value of 4.0 (I7, S7). The extent of inputs from other MNC units and the amount of local content in locally manufactured products are assessed as moderate. Likewise, differences in the subsidiary's customers and their needs as well as the stability of technology are viewed as moderate (all 3.0). The remaining variables, such as difficulties in identifying competitors' strategies and the extent of interaction with local actors, are rated low with a value of 2.0 in the survey.

The degree of **subsidiary integration** in the MNC is also evaluated as rather low, with a mean average of 2.6 (S7; see Figure 5.49). While most variables were assessed as low or moderate (2.0 and 3.0), the integration of R&D and the extent to which quality specifications were developed by headquarters achieved higher scores (4.0). The higher integration of R&D was also further explained in the interview with the subsidiary manager:

> "So from R&D point of view ... the processes are worldwide valid. So everything that is a template here is also a template in Mexico or in China or in Germany or wherever. And from this point of view the level of integration is really high. And also what is used exactly the same is the tools; they are used in the main location but they are used also in all the other locations. So they are not specific processes or tools adapted to the location but they are generally managed. And this is, I believe, a high level of integration here." (I7)

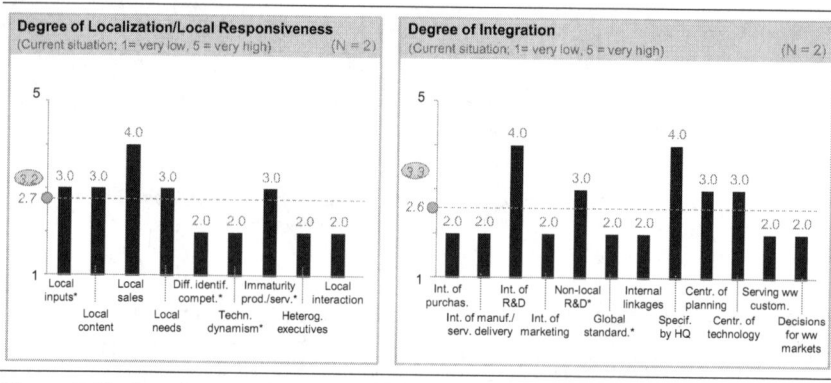

Figure 5.49: Survey Results: ROM – Subsidiary localization/local responsiveness and subsidiary integration

(3) Subsidiary Decision-Making Autonomy

In comparison to the other foreign Autocomp units in this study, the Romanian subsidiary enjoys only a low to moderate degree of decision-making autonomy, with an overall mean average of 2.7 (S7; see Figure 5.50). More specifically, for strategic decisions, it has a much lower degree of decision-making autonomy than for operational decisions (2.0 vs. 3.7). For instance, while major new product development is always centrally decided by headquarters, smaller product modifications or product improvements can, to some extent, be decided on by the foreign subsidiary. As articulated in the interview with the subsidiary manager:

> "The decisions for developing a new product – what we are doing is we are mostly not making products on our own but just if they are awarded from the customer. And this is done always with the management decision from the customer center and this ... is always in the central location. So from a ... location side we can propose improvements on the product for sure and we implement them and different changes in the product. But to discuss over a new product then for sure this is done with customer center ..." (I7)

Subsidiary Autonomy (Current situation; 1= decided centrally by HQ; 5 = decided independently by subsidiary) (N = 2)

← Strategic Decisions: 2.0 → ← Operational Decisions: 3.7 →

Major new product developm.	Major modification of process	Orga restructuring	Annual budget	Minor modification	Recruitment/ promotions	Career developm.
1.0	2.0	3.0	2.0	3.0	4.0	4.0

(Strategic avg: 3.0; Operational avg: 2.7)

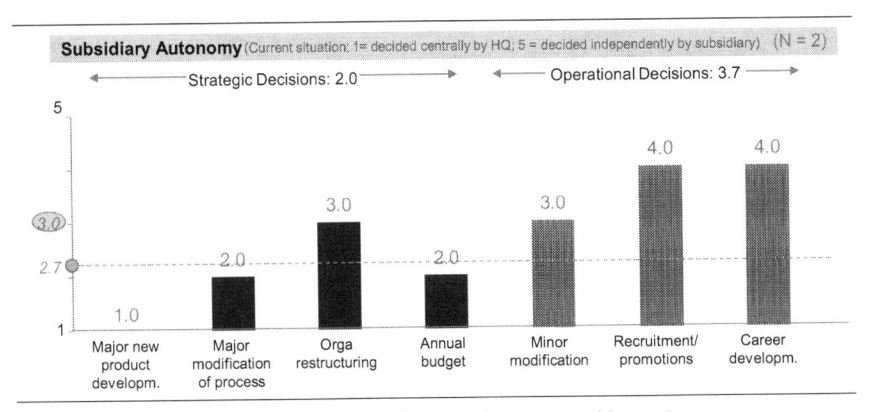

Figure 5.50: Survey Results: ROM – Subsidiary decision-making autonomy

5.1.6.2 Subsidiary Initiative-Taking

(1) Entrepreneurial Resource Management

New opportunities for subsidiary initiatives were **identified** by the Romanian unit through internal rather than through external sources (3.0 vs. 1.5, S7). Internally, opportunities were frequently recognized within the foreign unit itself and somewhat less frequently through interactions with headquarters or other units within the MNC. Opportunities within the subsidiary unit itself were detected, for example, through regular workshops on opportunities to improve production costs or to enhance production stability, for example (I7). Furthermore, a central idea management tool is said to play an important role in the creation and identification of new opportunities. Using this tool, all Autocomp employees can share and discuss their concepts via an online platform. Refined and mature ideas and concepts can then be submitted to senior executives at headquarters for further evaluation and prioritization. Consequently, the identification of new opportunities is said to depend critically on the contribution by individuals from within the subsidiary (I7). In contrast to internal identification, the external detection of opportunities occurred only occasionally through interactions with local actors outside the subsidiary unit, as shown in Figure 5.51.

Newly identified opportunities were mostly incrementally or, somewhat less often, moderately **innovative** in nature (3.5 and 3.0; S7). They typically represented replications of existing products or processes for use in similar applications, as well as minor changes to existing products or processes. Radically innovative opportunities were identified rarely, and only as combinations of two or more existing products into one unique product. Opportunities for products considered "new to the world" were not identified by the Romanian unit at any point during the past five years (see Figure 5.51).

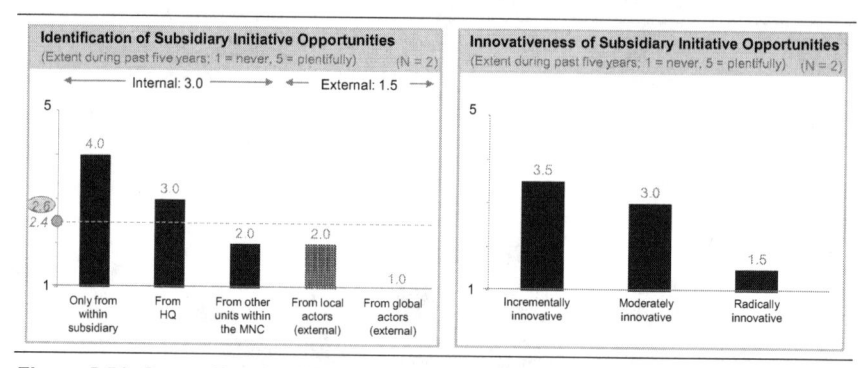

Figure 5.51: Survey Results: ROM – Identification and innovativeness of initiative opportunities

As to the few **resource structuring** activities (1.8, S7), the Romanian subsidiary obtained resources and capabilities needed for the realization of entrepreneurial initiatives mainly from sources within the MNC (see Figure 5.52). Internally, the two central methods of resource structuring were the acquisition of resources from headquarters and development of internal resources within the subsidiary itself (2.5 and 2.4; S7).

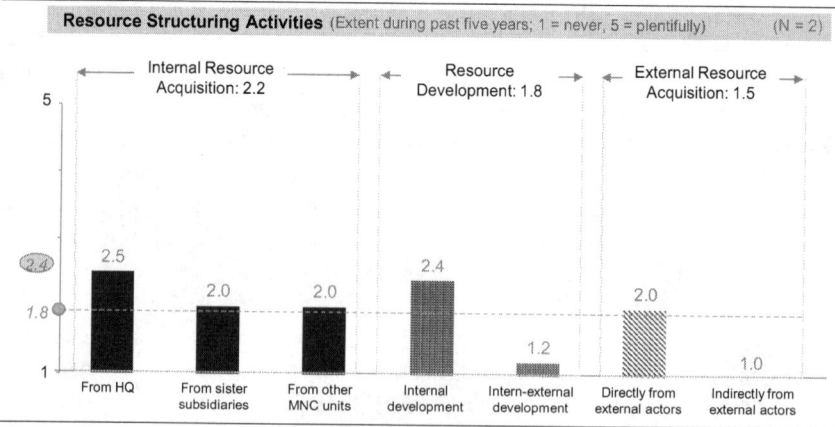

Figure 5.52: Survey Results: ROM – Initiative-related resource structuring activities

Externally, resources and capabilities were occasionally acquired directly from local or global actors, and in very few instances through collaboration with external actors in the area of research and development (2.0 and 1.2). In pursuit of subsidiary initiatives, internal and external resources and capabilities were further **bundled** by the Romanian unit. Incremental (3.5) and intermediate bundling (2.5) were the most frequently used approaches, while there was no radical bundling of completely new resources and capabilities (1.0) in the past five years (S7).

(2) Headquarters-Subsidiary Alignment

In subsidiary initiative-taking in Romania, **headquarters** was **involved** to a moderate extent (3.3; S7), as shown in Figure 5.53. Headquarters approval was often required for the continuation or implementation of initiative opportunities. Initiatives that potentially impacted the wider product landscape of the MNC or that required substantial changes in products particularly necessitated alignment and approval of headquarters. In comparison, smaller changes or enhancements of products required no approval, as described by the subsidiary manager:

"... if there are ideas which are affecting the products then this must be also agreed from the customer center management and this is at the headquarters. If there are ideas which can be implemented locally then they are approved on a local [basis]." (I7)

"... we can propose improvements on the product for sure and we implement them and yeah, different changes on the product. But to discuss over a new product, then for sure this is done with the customer center ..." (I7)

Additionally, the Romanian unit faced a high level of **corporate resistance** (3.1; S7). Within the past five years, the unit experienced this most frequently as delays of entrepreneurial initiatives, requests by headquarters for greater justification, and a lack of recognition and acceptance by other units in the company (both 3.5). Due to the limited budget for entrepreneurial and innovative activities within the MNC, resistance from headquarters was typically experienced with regard to the allocation of central financial resources for initiatives to the Romanian subsidiary (I6). Lastly, **subsidiary initiative selling** by the Romanian unit was evaluated as comparatively high, with a mean average of 3.4 (S7). Specifically, attracting headquarters' attention to new opportunities, making headquarters understand the initiatives, and lobbying and selling efforts at the corporate center were applied most frequently (S7). Selling and lobbying activities took place, for example, as constant reports and clarifications on new opportunities at headquarters or attempts to convince the corporate center to move product responsibility to the Romanian unit (I7). International engineering workshops within Autocomp were also used to present new initiative ideas and to sell them to other units or headquarters (I7).

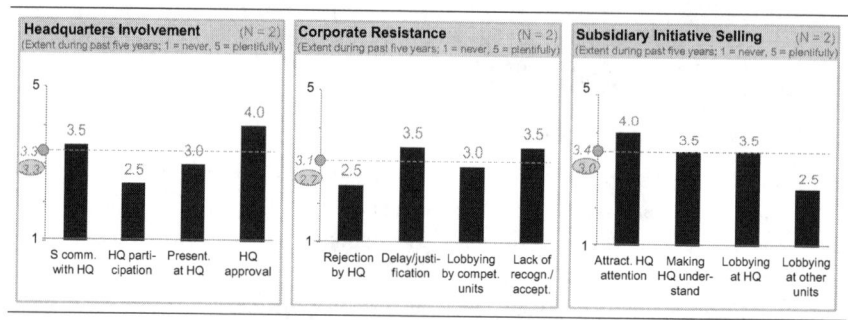

Figure 5.53: Survey Results: ROM – Headquarters-subsidiary alignment and interaction

5.1.6.3 Subsidiary Initiative-Taking Outcome

(1) Extent of Subsidiary Initiative-Taking

In total, the Romanian Autocomp subsidiary exhibited a comparatively low level of entrepreneurial initiatives during the past five years with a mean average of 2.0, as presented in Figure 5.54 (S7). Of the various types, **internal market initiatives** were undertaken most often during this time period, particularly those that involved proposals to transfer manufacturing to the subsidiary location. Additionally, smaller entrepreneurial initiatives aimed at reducing costs or improving efficiency frequently took place at this location, and these were particularly encouraged and supported by Autocomp (I7). Moreover, the unit carried out some **global-internal hybrid initiatives** (2.0) through which, for example, significant corporate investments for R&D activities were attracted by the subsidiary during the past five years.[438] The foreign unit also engaged, albeit to a lesser extent, in externally oriented initiatives. According to the survey, **global market initiatives** (2.0) encompassed some enhancements to product lines already sold internationally by the Romanian subsidiary. Lastly, during the past five years, the foreign affiliate engaged to a very limited extent in **local market initiatives** that were first started locally (1.5).

---

[438] For example, headquarters decided to invest 20 million Euros for a new development center and testing facility in Romania (A7).

Subsidiary Initiative-Taking

(Extent of subsidiary entrepreneurial initiatives within past five years: 1= never, 5 = plentifully) (N = 2)

← External initiatives: 1.8 →   ← Internal initiatives: 2.3 →

- Global market initiatives: 2.0
- Local market initiatives: 1.5
- Internal market initiatives: 2.5
- Global-internal hybrid initiatives: 2.0

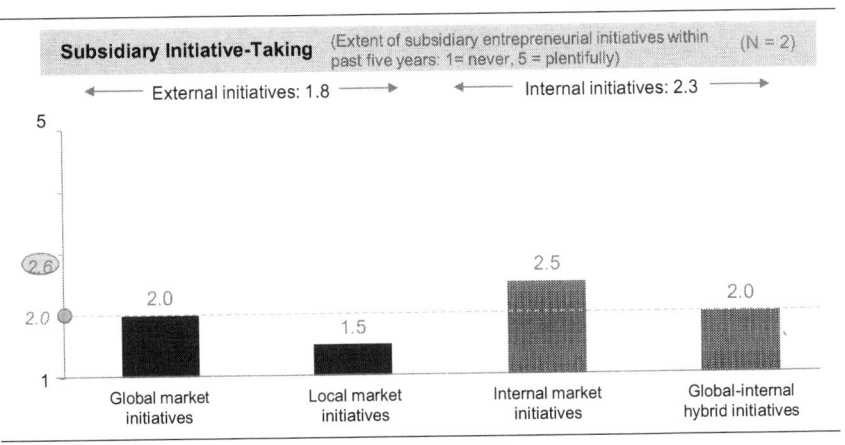

(Overall: 2.0)

Figure 5.54: Survey Results: ROM – Types and extent of subsidiary initiatives

(2) Resource-Related Outcomes

As a consequence of initiative-taking, the Romanian subsidiary generated **new resources and capabilities**. However, given the lower level of initiative-taking activities, the extent of new resources and capabilities remained comparatively low, with a mean average of 2.4 across the value chain functions (S7). More extensive development of specialized resources occurred primarily in R&D and, to a lesser degree, in production and in innovation and entrepreneurship. For instance, the attraction of corporate investment in R&D and manufacturing through global-internal hybrid initiatives subsequently led to the growth of resources, as the manager states:

> "... the growth I was mentioning in the beginning, that what we've managed and what was realized in the past five years is that there is not the specific knowledge on one discipline, for example software, which was the first one started in the department. But now the knowledge is on the complete area of development, management and manufacturing. We are covering the complete area." (I7)

As to the **applicability** of the new resources **for the wider MNC**, the subsidiary assessment indicates that, overall, they are only of little use for the rest of the multinational firm (2.3, see Figure 5.55). However, new resources in the area of R&D and in production (3.5 and 3.0) were considered useful to a larger extent for other company locations. Some of the newly generated knowledge was shared or transferred to other locations through national or international workshops or through presentations to headquarters' management, as described by the subsidiary manager:

> "The knowledge can be used worldwide and transferred to other locations and there are clear cases when this is possible. ... What is done for this type of knowledge transfers – on the one hand ... there are international workshops done to present different ideas or training from each location and what each location is

working on. And then it is done through the reporting part when this type of knowledge is presented to the management and also to the other participants and then this can be shared." (I7)

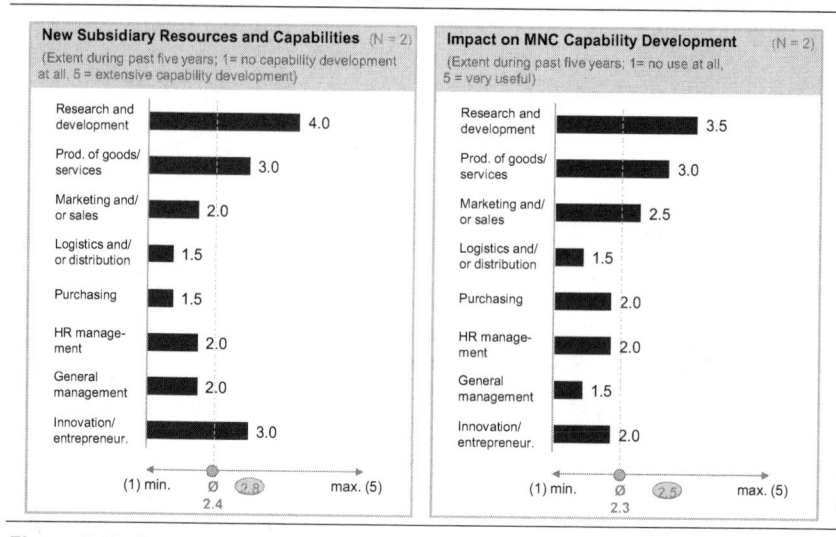

New Subsidiary Resources and Capabilities (N=2)		Impact on MNC Capability Development (N=2)	
(Extent during past five years; 1= no capability development at all, 5 = extensive capability development)		(Extent during past five years; 1= no use at all, 5 = very useful)	
Research and development	4.0	Research and development	3.5
Prod. of goods/ services	3.0	Prod. of goods/ services	3.0
Marketing and/ or sales	2.0	Marketing and/ or sales	2.5
Logistics and/ or distribution	1.5	Logistics and/ or distribution	1.5
Purchasing	1.5	Purchasing	2.0
HR management	2.0	HR management	2.0
General management	2.0	General management	1.5
Innovation/ entrepreneur.	3.0	Innovation/ entrepreneur.	2.0
(1) min. — Ø 2.4 — max. (5)		(1) min. — Ø 2.3 — max. (5)	

Figure 5.55: Survey Results: ROM – New subsidiary resources and impact on MNC capabilities

(3) Further Outcomes

With regard to the **performance outcomes** of subsidiary initiative-taking, the Romanian subsidiary was specifically able to reduce costs and to improve the productivity of its operations, as indicated in Figure 5.56. Encouragement from the corporate center to pursue such activities seems to have led to more significant improvements in these areas. Concerning its **role in the MNC**, the foreign affiliate was able to improve its value-added scope, while its geographical market scope and its product scope remained unchanged (S7). According to the subsidiary manager, the Romanian unit was able to broaden its value-adding activities in manufacturing and in research and development:

> *Also the [R&D] department has grown rapidly. ... We have now just ten years lifetime from the R&D department and the growth is really stable, starting from a small department in the first year with now 360. ... In the past year what we have [taken on] is the complete responsibility for projects, and also the responsibility from all disciplines, meaning all development disciplines and also the sample shop activities are done here at [the location]."* (I7)

Additionally, the foreign unit was able to achieve slight improvement in its **influence** within the multinational firm (3.5) and some aspects of its **credibility** with headquarters, such as its recognition as a strategically important unit within the firm (4.0). Along with the survey results, the subsidiary manager also emphasized one further outcome of entrepreneurial initiatives in the interview, namely the improved satisfaction of employees:

> "For sure, the first thing that comes up in my mind is that the people feel good when they have an idea and when they see that this idea is taken into consideration." (I7)

Performance Outcomes (Extent during past five years; 1 = very limited, 5 = substantial)	(N = 2)
Enhanced sales/revenues	2.5
Reduced costs	3.5
Improved market share	1.5
Improved profit	2.0
Improved ROI	2.0
Improved productivity	3.5

(1) min. — Ø 2.5 — max. (5)

Subsidiary Role and Position in MNC (Extent during past five years; 1 = major decline, 3 = no change, 5 = major improvement)	(N = 2)	
Geographical market scope	3.0	
Product scope	3.0	Subsidiary role development
Value-added scope	4.0	
Subsidiary influence	3.5	Subsidiary influence
History of delivering promises	3.0	
Signif. value-added contrib.	3.5	Subsidiary credibility
Global competiveness	3.0	
Recognition by HQ	3.0	

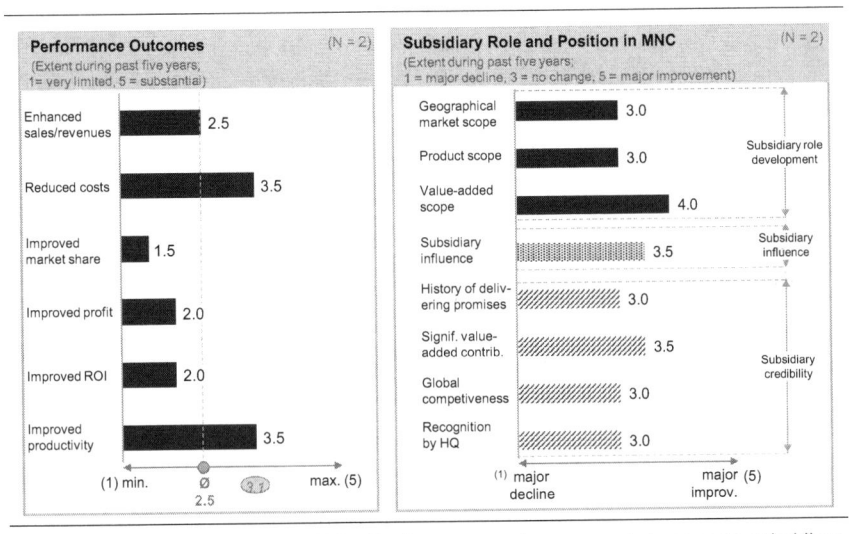

(1) major decline — major (5) improv.

Figure 5.56: Survey Results: ROM – Performance outcomes and changes to subsidiary role and position

5.1.7 Indian Subsidiary

The Indian subsidiary was originally founded in the late 1950s and was acquired by Company A in the late 2000s. The Autocomp division currently operates at four locations in India, where it runs both manufacturing facilities and R&D units. It employs a total of 1,700 people in India, with roughly half of the employees engaged in production and the remainder in either R&D or administrative functions. The focus of the Indian unit is on developing and manufacturing robust systems and components that are customized for the Indian market at affordable costs. In recent years Autocomp has made efforts to further increase the localization of its value chain. Consequently, all major value chain functions, such as R&D, production, marketing and sales and procurement are carried out locally. Along with Autocomp, two other divisions of Company A are present in India, and all four locations in the country also host one or two of the other divisions (A8, I8, S8).

5.1.7.1 Subsidiary Roles

(1) Strategic Market Importance and Subsidiary Competence: Implementer

Based on the assessment of the strategic importance of the subsidiary market environment (2.8) and the level of subsidiary resources and capabilities (3.0), the Indian Autocomp affiliate can be categorized as an "Implementer" subsidiary (S8). With regard to the **strategic importance of the subsidiary market**, the market size is evaluated as relatively small, as shown in Figure 5.57. The foreign unit designs and manufactures products for only two local customers in the Indian market. Furthermore, these customers represent just approximately 30% of the local market share in terms of sales volume (I8):

> "In India, we just have two players, two significant players. And we get to operate only with these two. ... And as you can imagine, these are not necessarily the market leaders in India. They have some decent volumes. They have their own plant. They have their own ways of doing things. But the other factor, and what I wanted to drive home, is that the opportunity that exists in the Indian market, in itself, is very limited." (I8)

With regard to customer demand intensity, these two local customers are not considered to be particularly challenging (2.0; S8) as their primary demand focuses on low-cost products rather than on highly innovative solutions (I8). Likewise, technical dynamism in the market is viewed as moderate. In contrast, competitive intensity in the Indian market is high (I8, S8). According to the subsidiary manager, all major global competitors of Autocomp are also active in the Indian market:

> "In the limited market that we have, we have literally all the companies that you can count in the world, who make [these products]. So it is not a small market sitting somewhere in the corner of the globe, with some limited players that probably do not interest us. It's not the case, obviously. It is an interesting market. No wonder everybody wants a share in it." (I8)

With an average value of 3.0, the evaluation of **subsidiary resources and capabilities** indicates that the foreign affiliate is at a low level in this respect (S8). While the unit holds a higher level of capabilities in R&D and in general management (both 4.0), capability in the other areas is rated moderate or even low. Overall, the level of R&D resources is seen as relatively high given the *"good pool of engineers"* that is *"handy for these innovations"* (I8). Nevertheless, in comparison to the regional R&D hub in Singapore or to central development activities at headquarters, the Indian unit is not seen as having the capabilities for major product development. Instead, the foreign subsidiary engages in smaller-scale development activities such as application development for global platform products or process engineering (I8).

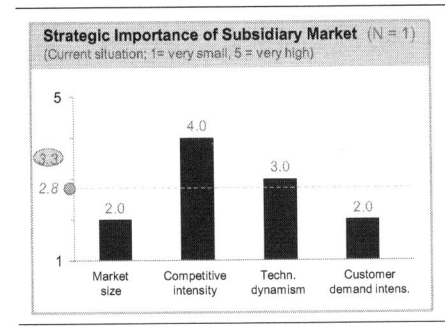

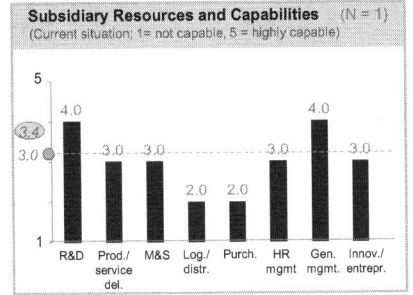

Figure 5.57: Survey Results: India – Strategic importance and subsidiary resources/ capabilities

(2) Subsidiary Localization and Integration: Quiescent Subsidiary

The evaluation by subsidiary management suggests that the Indian unit of Autocomp can be classified as a "Quiescent" subsidiary. The survey returns an average value of 2.6 for subsidiary localization/local responsiveness and 2.8 for subsidiary integration, indicating low levels for both role dimensions (S8). As to the **degree of localization/ local responsiveness**, the share of sales that comes from locally produced goods is seen as high (4.0). As a result of its status as a "best-cost-location," most products are both manufactured and sold in India (I8). All other aspects related to this role dimension were evaluated as moderate or low. For example, the extent of local input and local content in locally produced goods was viewed as limited (both 2.0). Given the use of global platform solutions, many components of automotive products are already designed or predetermined by other units of the company, thereby limiting the input needed from the Indian unit (I8). Likewise, the extent of interaction with local actors is seen as limited, as is the immaturity of the life cycle stage of product lines and manufacturing processes (see Figure 5.58).

As outlined previously, the degree of **subsidiary integration** was stated to be comparatively low. All related aspects were rated between low and moderate with the exception of the proportion of non-local R&D and the extent of technology centralization (both 4.0; S8). Due to global platform design, the majority of R&D inputs come from headquarters in Germany or the regional R&D hub in Singapore. Furthermore, local R&D input is restricted to smaller-scale activities such as software application development (I8). Similarly, technology development within Autocomp is largely centralized at these locations. Moreover, the integration of various functions is viewed as low, with R&D being somewhat more integrated than the others.

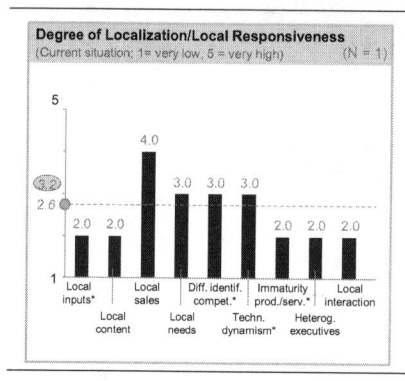

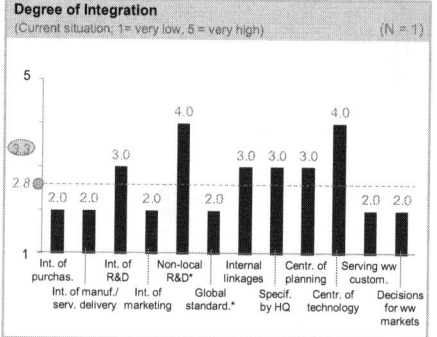

Figure 5.58: Survey Results: India – Subsidiary localization/local responsiveness and subsidiary integration

(3) Subsidiary Decision-Making Autonomy

Overall, the Indian Autocomp subsidiary has only a low degree of decision-making autonomy, with an average value of 2.4 (S8). As outlined in Figure 5.59, it has more leeway for operational decisions than for strategic ones (3.0 vs. 2.0), which are more often centrally decided by headquarters. Overall, decisions on new product development or major/minor product modifications are largely made by the corporate center. While the foreign affiliate has no autonomy to decide on how to interact with global OEMs in the Indian market, it has much more freedom to decide on how to deal with the two local customers for which it holds direct responsibility. This is expressed in the following statements by the subsidiary manager:

> "Whatever the [global] customer wants ... or does not want in the product for a particular car, for which we are being ordered the business – that's decided over there. And it's just populated down into India, and we industrialize this. So often this is the beginning and the end of innovation." (I8)

> "Only where we get to develop products for these two [local] customers will we be allowed to develop on our own. ... For the local car makers, we have an opportunity to discuss innovations, and put a price to it, and push for acceptance, and implement, and so on and so forth." (I8)

With regard to other strategic decisions, the unit has a low degree of autonomy for formulating and approving its own annual budget and a moderate degree of autonomy for restructuring the subsidiary organization (2.0 and 3.0). In comparison, operational decisions linked to the recruitment and promotion to positions below the subsidiary's general manager are made equally by headquarters and the subsidiary (3.0), or largely by the subsidiary alone concerning career development plans for local managers (4.0).

Subsidiary Autonomy (Current situation; 1= decided centrally by HQ; 5 = decided independently by subsidiary) (N = 1)

◄──────Strategic Decisions: 2.0──────► ◄──────Operational Decisions: 3.0──────►

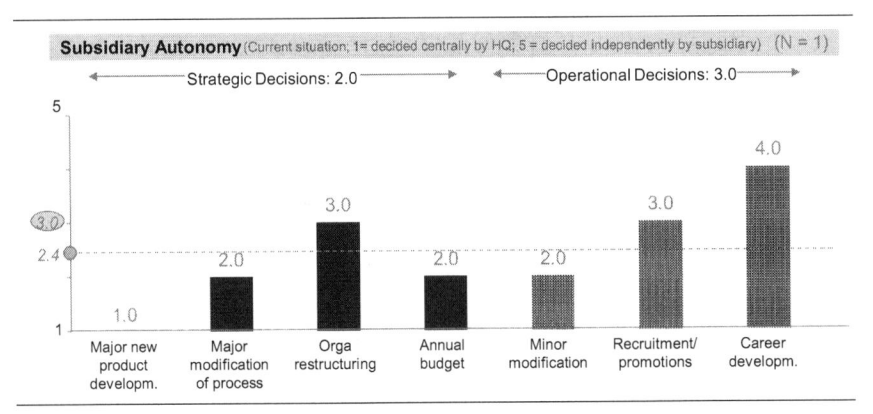

Major new product developm.	Major modification of process	Orga restructuring	Annual budget	Minor modification	Recruitment/ promotions	Career developm.
1.0	2.0	3.0	2.0	2.0	3.0	4.0

Figure 5.59: Survey Results: India – Subsidiary decision-making autonomy

5.1.7.2 Subsidiary Initiative-Taking

(1) Entrepreneurial Resource Management

During the past five years, opportunities for subsidiary initiatives were **identified** by the Indian unit through internal rather than external sources (2.7 vs. 1.5; S8), as illustrated by Figure 5.60. Internally, initiative identification took place most frequently within the subsidiary unit itself or through interactions with headquarters (both 3.0). Other units of the company, such as the regional R&D hub or sister subsidiaries, did not play an important role in this matter. Externally, initiatives were occasionally identified through interactions with local actors. For example, regular discussions and alignments with local customers regarding requirements resulted in the identification of new opportunities (I8).

Concerning their **innovativeness**, the majority of initiative opportunities identified during the last five years could be categorized as incrementally innovative (3.5). Moderately innovative opportunities were identified less frequently (3.0), while no radically innovative opportunities were identified at all during this time period. Many of these opportunities appear to consist of adaptations or minor changes to existing products or improvements to internal processes. The focus on incrementally innovative opportunities was also emphasized by the subsidiary manager:

"None of these things are in the region ... called... something innovative, in terms of research, highly innovative products, highly innovative ideas." (I8)

"Even those aspects or those technologies which can no longer be considered as innovation for the European market or for the North American market – are also not exactly innovations in India. But they're not adopted yet, because of cost reasons." (I8)

Identification of Subsidiary Initiative Opportunities	Innovativeness of Subsidiary Initiative Opportunities
(Extent during past five years; 1 = never, 5 = plentifully) (N = 1)	(Extent during past five years; 1 = never, 5 = plentifully) (N = 1)
Internal: 2.7 External: 1.5	
Only from within subsidiary: 3.0	Incrementally innovative: 3.5
From HQ: 3.0	Moderately innovative: 3.0
From other units within the MNC: 2.0	Radically innovative: 1.5
From local actors (external): 2.0	
From global actors (external): 1.0	
(2.6)	
2.2	

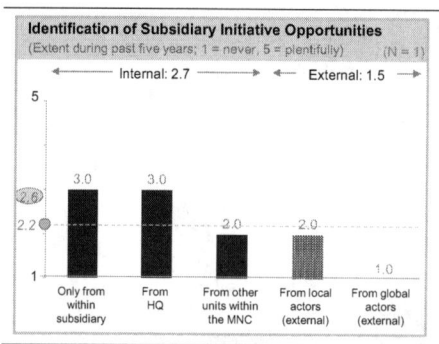

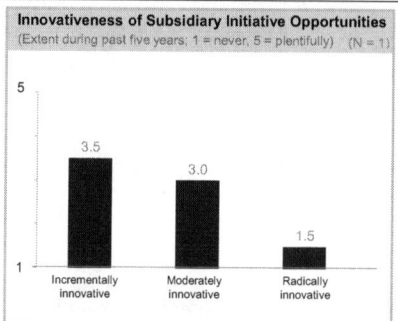

Figure 5.60: Survey Results: India – Identification and innovativeness of initiative opportunities

In order to obtain the necessary resources and capabilities for initiative opportunities, the Indian unit seldom engaged in **resource structuring** activities (2.1; S8). When the subsidiary resource base was not sufficient, the foreign affiliate obtained resources largely from within the MNC network and only to a lesser extent from external sources. Among the different resource structuring possibilities, the Indian subsidiary relied mostly on internal resource acquisition from other parts of the MNC (3.0). Resources were acquired from headquarters, other units of the MNC such as the regional R&D hub, and from sister units (see Figure 5.61). The comments by the subsidiary manager further suggest that the reasons for turning to internal sources include the previous experience and existing knowledge of other units in the multinational firm:

> "If it is a technology that's not been introduced in India, it would inevitably mean that none of our guys would have exposure in it. And we would have to inevitably go back to headquarters or to Singapore, which is one of our engineering hubs worldwide and the engineering hub in Asia." (I8)

> " ... any particular component, any particular software module, for instance, in which we're not that experienced, we go back to one of the locations which has done it before, for them to do it for us. And we have to pay for it." (I8)

5 – Empirical Findings

Resource Structuring Activities (Extent during past five years; 1 = never, 5 = plentifully)   (N = 1)

	Internal Resource Acquisition: 3.0		Resource Development: 2.0		External Resource Acquisition: 1.5	
From HQ	From sister subsidiaries	From other MNC units	Internal development	Intern-external development	Directly from external actors	Indirectly from external actors
2.4	4.0	2.0	3.0	2.3	1.7	2.0	1.0

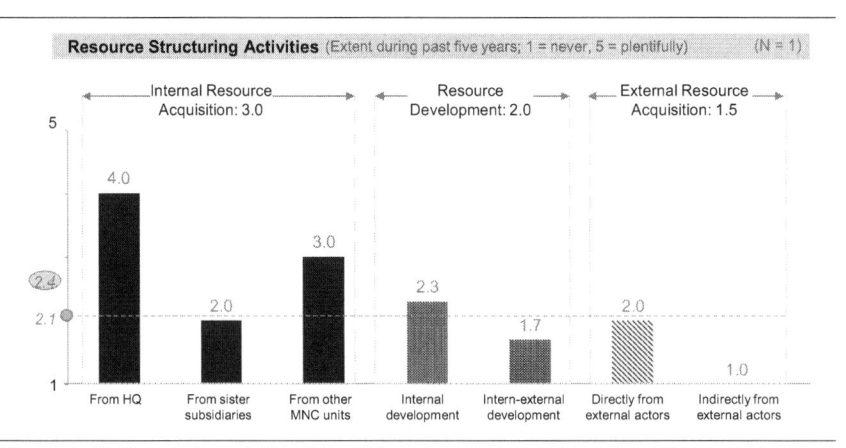

(values: From HQ 2.4; From sister subsidiaries 4.0; From other MNC units 2.0; Internal development 3.0; Intern-external development 2.3; Directly from external actors 1.7; value 2.0; Indirectly from external actors 1.0; baseline 2.1)

Figure 5.61: Survey Results: India – Initiative-related resource structuring activities

Although less often than internal resource acquisition, the Indian subsidiary did rely on resource development, more specifically on internal development within the unit itself, and less often on development in collaboration with external partners (2.3 and 1.7). Finally, direct resource acquisition from external actors occurred from time to time, while indirect acquisition through, for instance, merging with or acquiring another organization did not occur at all. In the end, both internally and externally obtained resources were further **bundled**. Incremental (3.0) and intermediate forms of bundling (2.0) were typically employed, while radical bundling of purely new resources and capabilities did not take place in the past five years (1.0, S8).

(2) Headquarters-Subsidiary Alignment

Throughout the subsidiary initiative-taking endeavors, **headquarters** was **involved** to a moderate extent (3.3; S8). In this context, headquarters-subsidiary communication occurred frequently, for instance, to discuss potential opportunities or request further resources for the realization of initiatives (I8). Moreover, given the use of global platform solutions developed and managed centrally to maintain uniformity, as well as the limited decision-making autonomy for product changes (I8), the subsidiary manager found it necessary to involve headquarters when initiating such changes:

"There is this way and only this way they [headquarters] will operate. Whether it's a small change, a medium, a big change, whatever. It goes right back to the headquarters in Germany. And they say: 'Okay. It does not make sense whatsoever.' We do it this way and only this way." (I8)

Moreover, the extent of **corporate resistance** to subsidiary initiatives was assessed as high with a mean average of 3.5 (S8). According to the survey results, the foreign affiliate frequently experienced rejection by headquarters, delays and requests for greater justification and a lack of recognition and acceptance even by other units of the company (all 4.0), as illustrated in Figure 5.62. According to subsidiary management, resistance was particularly high when the unit attempted to change or adapt global platform solutions that are managed by the corporate center. In comparison, when the subsidiary engaged in initiatives for local customers that were "*implementable*" and made "*a lot of technical and commercial sense,*" resistance was much lower (I8). Likewise, subsidiary **initiative selling** occurred often during the past five years (3.3; S8). In particular, activities to make headquarters understand a new opportunity, as well as lobbying and selling efforts, were frequently employed to inform and persuade the corporate center. The means used for initiative selling were, for example, annual management meetings or regular engineering conferences of Autocomp (I8).

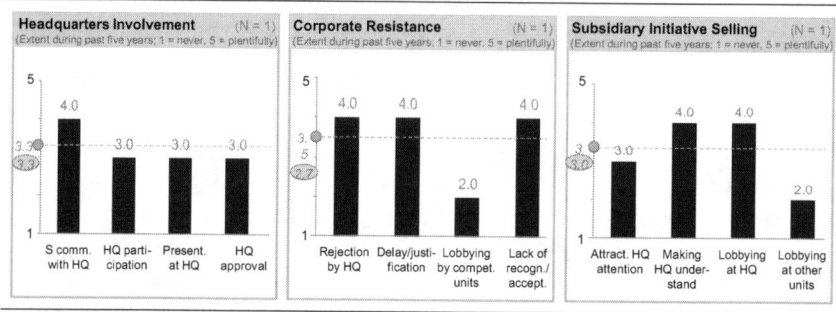

Figure 5.62: Survey Results: India – Headquarters-subsidiary alignment and interaction

5.1.7.3 Subsidiary Initiative-Taking Outcome

(1) Extent of Subsidiary Initiative-Taking

With an average of 2.3, the Indian unit displayed a low level of subsidiary initiatives (S8). This foreign affiliate pursued internally oriented initiatives much more frequently than externally oriented ones (3.3 vs. 1.3) during the past five years, as shown in Figure 5.63. Internally oriented initiatives occurred frequently as **internal market initiatives** and occasionally as **global-internal hybrid initiatives**. Externally oriented initiatives took place very seldom in the form of **global market initiatives** involving significant extensions to existing international responsibilities. According to subsidiary management, entrepreneurial activities did not represent a "*very focused kind of activity*" for the Indian unit and therefore such activities remained very limited (I8). Furthermore, initiatives that occurred were typically incremental rather than radical in nature. External ones often represented enhancements or adaptations of existing products for the Indian market, while internal initiatives involved, for example, improvement of processes or development of new engineering tools.[439]

Subsidiary Initiative-Taking (Extent of subsidiary entrepreneurial initiatives within past five years: 1= never, 5 = plentifully)   (N = 1)

← External initiatives: 1.3 →   ← Internal initiatives: 3.3 →

- Global market initiatives: 1.5
- Local market initiatives: 1.0
- Internal market initiatives: 4.0
- Global-internal hybrid initiatives: 2.5

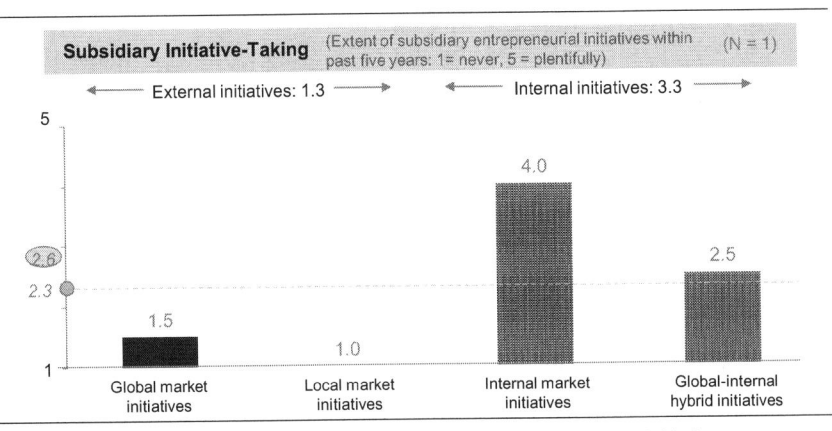

(Reference values: 2.6 and 2.3)

Figure 5.63: Survey Results: India – Types and extent of subsidiary initiatives

(2) Resource-Related Outcomes

As a result of its limited initiative-taking activities, the Indian unit **developed** specialized **resources** only to a small extent (2.1, S8). Based on the survey results, new resources were obtained especially for the production of goods (4.0) and to general management (3.0), while in the remaining areas resource growth remained limited or did not take place at all (see Figure 5.64).

Likewise, the applicability of the newly developed resources for the wider MNC was assessed as low (1.9, S8). With the exception of R&D, new resources were of little or no use for other units of the multinational firm, which was further underlined in the interview with the subsidiary manager as cited below. Although the value of entrepreneurial and innovative activities for the development of subsidiary resources was acknowledged, it was also recognized that they constitute a path-dependent process in which existing resources and capabilities influence future development activities:

> "I can't think of many particular things which happened that way, that we have done an innovative thing locally, and it's been ... adopted globally." (I8)

> "It's a kind of chicken and egg scenario. ... Of course, the objective is for us to be able to do it. But unless we do it once on a project, we won't develop the expertise. And unless we develop the expertise, we won't be doing it. ... So which comes first?" (I8)

---

[439] An exemplary internal market initiative that was mentioned by the subsidiary manager involved the development of a new engineering tool that can be used for the development of instrument clusters. The tool was transferred and subsequently used at various other locations of Autocomp (I8).

New Subsidiary Resources and Capabilities (N = 1)
(Extent during past five years; 1= no capability development at all, 5 = extensive capability development)

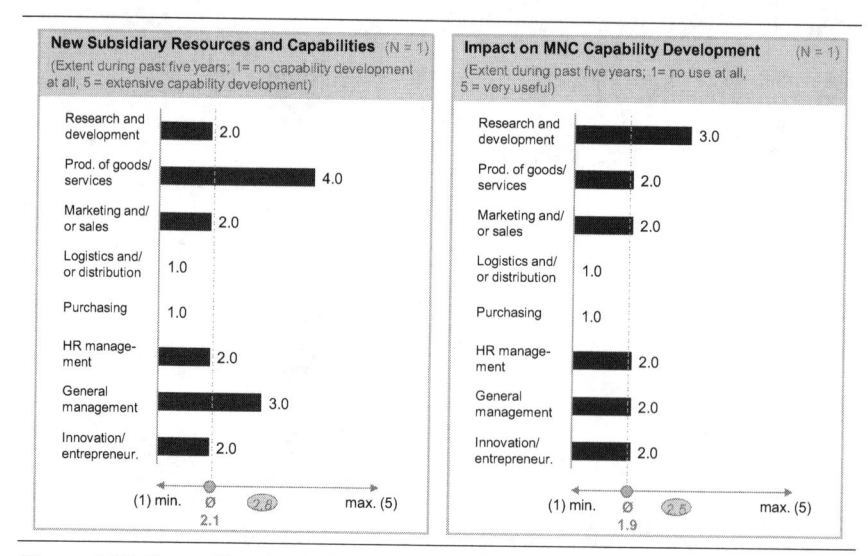

- Research and development: 2.0
- Prod. of goods/services: 4.0
- Marketing and/or sales: 2.0
- Logistics and/or distribution: 1.0
- Purchasing: 1.0
- HR management: 2.0
- General management: 3.0
- Innovation/entrepreneur.: 2.0

(1) min. — Ø 2.1 — max. (5)

Impact on MNC Capability Development (N = 1)
(Extent during past five years; 1= no use at all, 5 = very useful)

- Research and development: 3.0
- Prod. of goods/services: 2.0
- Marketing and/or sales: 2.0
- Logistics and/or distribution: 1.0
- Purchasing: 1.0
- HR management: 2.0
- General management: 2.0
- Innovation/entrepreneur.: 2.0

(1) min. — Ø 1.9 — max. (5)

Figure 5.64: Survey Results: India – New subsidiary resources and impact on MNC capabilities

(3) Further Outcomes

With regard to **performance outcomes**, subsidiary initiative-taking resulted in moderate cost and productivity improvements (both 3.0; S8), as shown in Figure 5.65. Enhancements in other areas, such as growth in sales or market share or increased profit and ROI, remained limited. Similarly, no changes to the subsidiary role or subsidiary influence in the MNC due to entrepreneurial initiatives was noted. According to the assessment by subsidiary management, subsidiary credibility in the MNC even decreased somewhat over the past five years due to weakening global competitiveness of the subsidiary in its market environment and decline in subsidiary recognition by headquarters as a strategically important unit.

5 – Empirical Findings

Performance Outcomes (N = 1) (Extent during past five years; 1= very limited, 5 = substantial)		Subsidiary Role and Position in MNC (N = 1) (Extent during past five years; 1 = major decline, 3 = no change, 5 = major improvement)	
Enhanced sales/revenues	2.0	Geographical market scope	3.0
Reduced costs	3.0	Product scope	3.0
		Value-added scope	3.0
Improved market share	2.0	Subsidiary influence	3.0
Improved profit	2.0	History of delivering promises	3.0
Improved ROI	2.0	Signif. value-added contrib.	3.0
		Global competitiveness	2.0
Improved productivity	3.0	Recognition by HQ	2.0
(1) min. Ø 2.3 max. (5)		(1) min. max. (5)	

Subsidiary role development ↕
Subsidiary influence ↕
Subsidiary credibility ↕

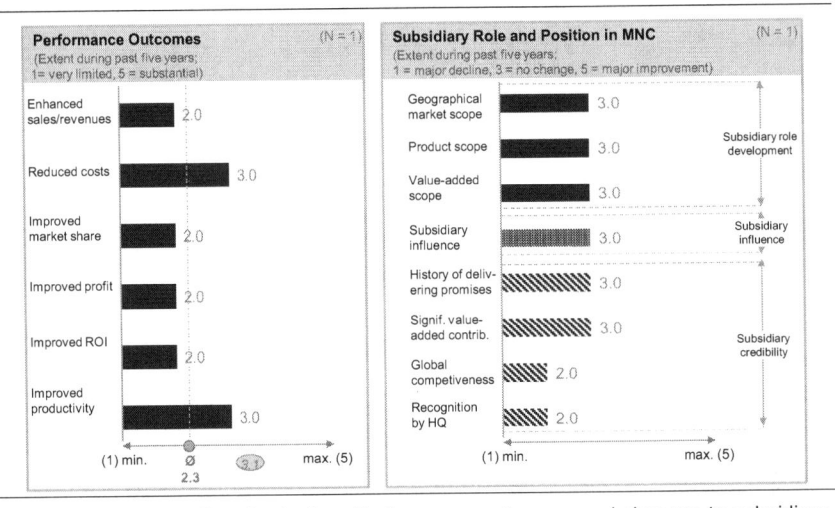

Figure 5.65: Survey Results: India – Performance outcomes and changes to subsidiary role and position

5.2. Company B: Strategic Business Unit Telecomp

Company B is a German-based MNC that provides services related to telecommunications and information technology. In 2013, the company pursued activities in approximately 50 countries and employed more than 100,000 workers at numerous locations worldwide. In total, the firm achieved more than 50 billion Euros in revenues in 2013, of which more than 50% was generated outside the home market in Germany. In addition to the corporate center, the MNC consists of four divisions, with three of them being structured by region and one based on customers and products (A10).

The division included in the present research is referred to as "Telecomp" and provides various telecommunications services for fixed and mobile networks within Europe. Services of this unit include fixed network telephony, internet and television, as well as mobile telephony and data services. In 2013 it generated revenues of more than ten billion Euros and thus represents the third largest division of Company B. Furthermore, this particular division had more than 30,000 employees in more than 15 countries, with its divisional headquarters located in Germany (A10, I9). Of its foreign subsidiaries, the following seven units took part in both the survey and the interview phase of the research: Hungary, Poland, Croatia, Slovakia, Greece, Romania and Montenegro (see Figure 5.66).

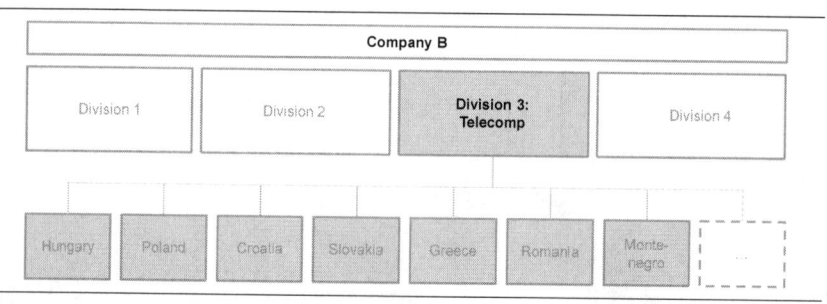

Figure 5.66: Organizational structure of Company B and its Telecomp Division

As to the subsidiary **role typology by Bartlett and Ghoshal** (1986, 1989), the assessments by headquarters and subsidiary managers indicate that three units can be classified as "Strategic Leaders" (Hungary, Poland and Croatia), one as a "Contributor" (Slovakia), one as "Black Hole" (Greece), and two as "Implementers" (Romania and Montenegro), as shown in Figure 5.67. With regard to the role typology developed by **Jarillo and Martinez** (1990), the survey results suggest that three units represent "Active Subsidiaries" (Poland, Hungary and Croatia), one a "Receptive Subsidiary" (Slovakia), one an "Autonomous Subsidiary" (Greece), and two "Quiescent Subsidiaries" (Romania and Montenegro). The following subsections present the empirical findings for each foreign subsidiary unit, its subsidiary initiative-taking activities and the related outcomes in more detail.

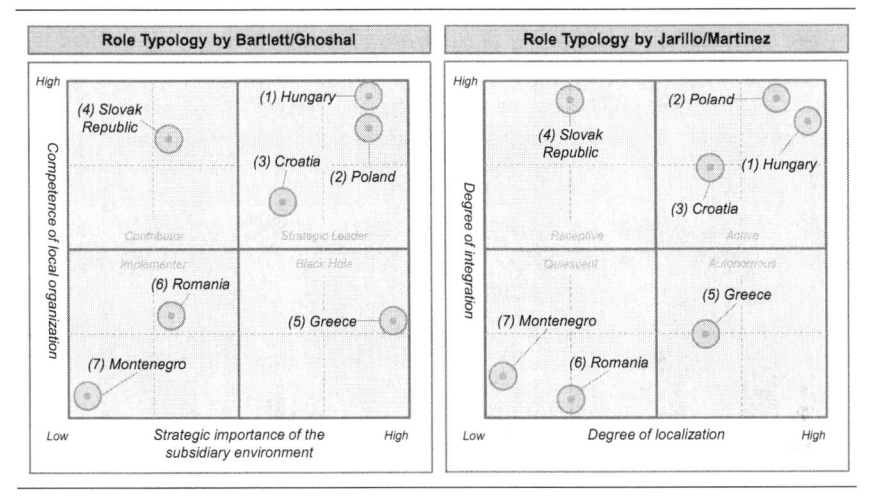

Role Typology by Bartlett/Ghoshal	Role Typology by Jarillo/Martinez
High — Competence of local organization — Low (4) Slovak Republic · (1) Hungary (3) Croatia · (2) Poland Contributor · Strategic Leader Implementer · Black Hole (6) Romania (5) Greece (7) Montenegro Low — Strategic importance of the subsidiary environment — High	High — Degree of integration — Low (2) Poland (4) Slovak Republic · (1) Hungary (3) Croatia Receptive · Active Quiescent · Autonomous (5) Greece (7) Montenegro (6) Romania Low — Degree of localization — High

Figure 5.67: Survey Results – Subsidiary roles at Telecomp

5.2.1 Hungarian Subsidiary

The Hungarian entity was established in the early 1990s via acquisition. In 2013, it employed more than 10,000 people and generated revenues in the amount of two billion Euros, and consequently represents the largest foreign entity of Telecomp in terms of both employees and revenues. Products managed and offered by the unit include fixed-network telephony, broadband internet and IPTV (internet protocol television). Within Telecomp, the unit plays an important role for IPTV and in 2013 became the center of excellence for this specific service area. As such, it has extended new product development responsibilities for the wider company and is also seen as an innovation leader among the foreign units. With regard to value chain functions, most are performed on-location, such as service delivery, marketing, R&D and HR management (A11, S10).

5.2.1.1 Subsidiary Roles

(1) Strategic Market Importance and Subsidiary Competence: Strategic Leader

According to the subsidiary evaluation, the Hungarian entity can be considered a "Strategic Leader" within Telecomp. The strategic importance of the subsidiary market as well as the subsidiary resources and capabilities are assessed as comparatively high (4.0 and 4.1; S10). As concerns the **strategic importance of the subsidiary market**, the competitive intensity in particular is seen as very high, while technological dynamism is assessed as moderate. In addition, the market environment is considered challenging, with declining revenues in the traditional telecom business and ongoing market consolidation through M&A activities. According to subsidiary management, this leads to *"a strong need in the company to innovate ... a strong need for new ideas and new types of services that have to be brought in"* (I10). Likewise, **subsidiary resources and capabilities** are viewed as high in all areas and particularly strong in general management, as Figure 5.68 illustrates.

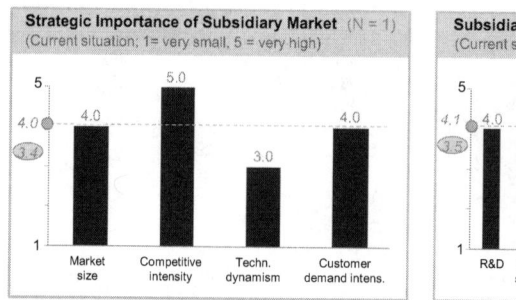

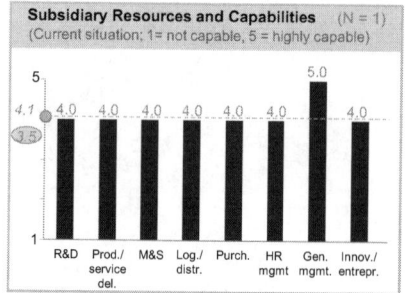

Figure 5.68: Survey Results: HUN – Strategic importance and subsidiary resources/capabilities

(2) Subsidiary Localization and Integration: Active Subsidiary

Based on the survey results, the Hungarian unit also represents an "Active Subsidiary," as both role dimensions are assessed as high by subsidiary management (4.0 and 3.4; S10). Concerning the **degree of localization/local responsiveness**, the extent of local content in locally delivered services and the extent of local interaction were evaluated as particularly high (both 5.0). In comparison, local customer needs are not seen as strongly differing from other MNC locations, and interaction with local actors was considered moderate. As to the **degree of integration** in the MNC, most value-adding functions appear to be closely integrated, such as marketing and R&D. Moreover, the Hungarian unit is highly dependent on linkages within the internal MNC network, as shown in Figure 5.69 (I10, S10).

5 – Empirical Findings

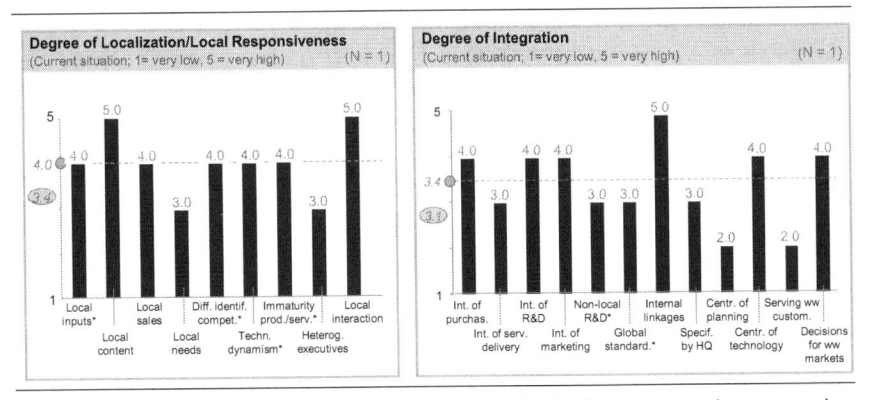

Figure 5.69 Survey Results: HUN – Subsidiary localization/local responsiveness and subsidiary integration

(3) Subsidiary Decision-Making Autonomy

In comparison to other Telecomp subsidiaries, the Hungarian unit enjoys an extensive degree of decision-making autonomy with a mean average of 4.0 (S10; see Figure 5.70). In particular, operational decisions, for example minor modifications of existing services, can be decided locally by the unit itself. In contrast, more strategic aspects such as the formulation and approval of the subsidiary's annual budget are jointly determined by headquarters and the foreign entity.

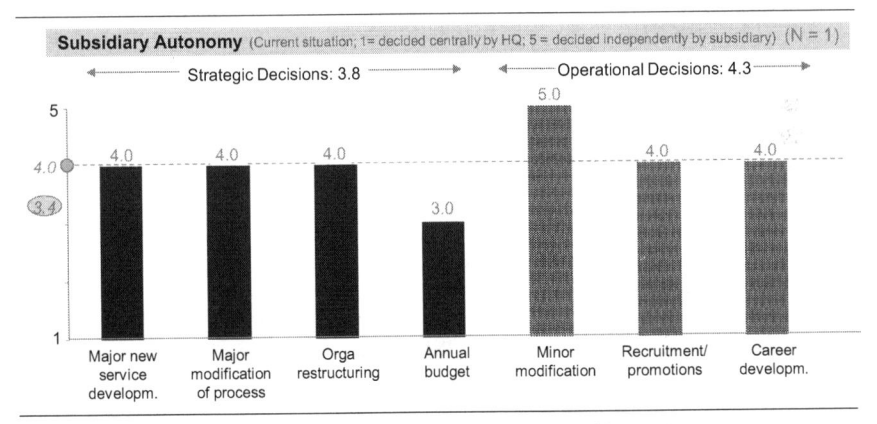

Figure 5.70: Survey Results: HUN – Subsidiary decision-making autonomy

With regard to product development, the unit's autonomy depends on the type of activity. While local product initiatives are largely at the discretion of the Hungarian unit, joint product initiatives with headquarters or initiatives introduced by headquarters into the country are more closely controlled and guided by the corporate center.[440]

> "... for a lot of projects, most of the time we don't have to contact with [headquarters]. There are local product initiatives, which are basically managed in Hungary and directed in Hungary, and they are created in Hungary, built in Hungary, all the resources and BCAs are handled locally." (I10)

5.2.1.2 Subsidiary Initiative-Taking

(1) Entrepreneurial Resource Management

Overall, the Hungarian organization showed a comparatively high level of **initiative identification** over the past five years (3.8; S10). New initiative opportunities were commonly discovered in multiple ways both internally and, somewhat more often, externally. Internally, headquarters and other MNC units often came into play when detecting new opportunities. Other units were, for example, the global R&D unit of Telecomp or sister subsidiaries in other countries (I10). According to subsidiary management, regular conference calls and exchanges with other MNC units regarding more advanced opportunities also played an important role in local initiative detection in Hungary.

> "There is [headquarters] ... organizing a bi-weekly conference call and in this ... all the [subsidiary] representatives, such as high level managers or directors, are participating. And in this session every few weeks there are presentations from the [subsidiaries] on local initiatives and projects from the [headquarters] side or from third party service providers. So this is kind of an idea pool where everybody can push out and share ideas." (I10)

Externally, local actors played a more critical role than global actors for the Hungarian unit (5.0 vs. 3.0). Given strong local relationships, initiative opportunities were frequently identified through interactions with local partners or by companies approaching the subsidiary with new ideas. In both cases, market insights and local relationships are considered important drivers of local initiative detection:

> "So for me, the most important ones are product ideas that came from market insights, local relationships and real user demand because seeing many, many innovations and new products and market ... the most important part of the success of a new service or a service innovation is that it fits a real market demand and has a clear user benefit." (I10)

In terms of their **innovativeness**, most opportunities were considered incrementally or moderately innovative (both 4.0), as presented in Figure 5.71. Radically innovative

---

[440] As explained in the next paragraph, headquarters-driven joint initiatives frequently require the presentation and discussion in bi-weekly conference calls in which both headquarters and representatives from other foreign subsidiaries participate.

5 – Empirical Findings

opportunities were also detected somewhat frequently, but products or services that were "new to the world" arose rarely during the past five years (S10).

Identification of Subsidiary Initiative Opportunities
(Extent during past five years; 1 = never, 5 = plentifully)   (N = 1)

Internal: 3.7   External: 4.0

- Only from within subsidiary: 3.0
- From HQ: 4.0
- From other units within the MNC: 4.0
- From local actors (external): 5.0
- From global actors (external): 3.0

Innovativeness of Subsidiary Initiative Opportunities
(Extent during past five years; 1 = never, 5 = plentifully)   (N = 1)

- Incrementally innovative: 4.0
- Moderately innovative: 4.0
- Radically innovative: 3.5

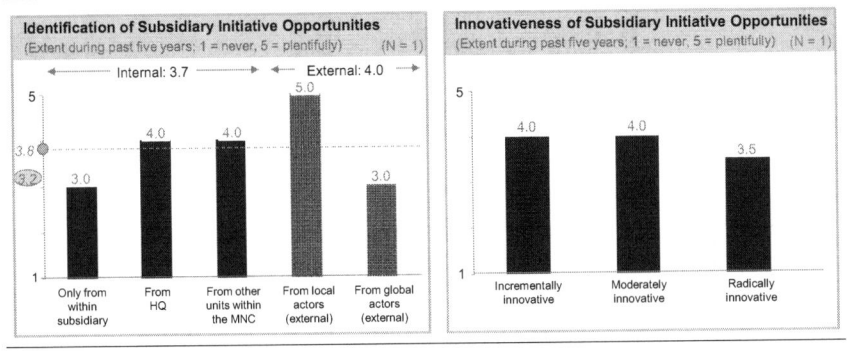

Figure 5.71: Survey Results: HUN – Identification and innovativeness of initiative opportunities

In order to realize initiative opportunities, the Hungarian subsidiary exhibited a comparatively high level of **resource structuring** activities (3.2; S10). Besides leveraging its existing subsidiary resources, the foreign organization acquired needed resources from other places within the MNC and from external sources, or developed new resources and capabilities on its own (see Figure 5.72). However, limited resources within the MNC, a strict resource allocation process and subsidiary competition for scarce resources were seen as a major obstacle to subsidiary initiative (I10).

Resource Structuring Activities (Extent during past five years; 1 = never, 5 = plentifully)   (N = 1)

Internal Resource Acquisition: 3.0   Resource Development: 3.3   External Resource Acquisition: 3.0

- From HQ: 4.0
- From sister subsidiaries: 2.0
- From other MNC units: 3.0
- Internal development: 4.0
- Intern-external development: 2.6
- Directly from external actors: 3.0
- Indirectly from external actors: 3.0

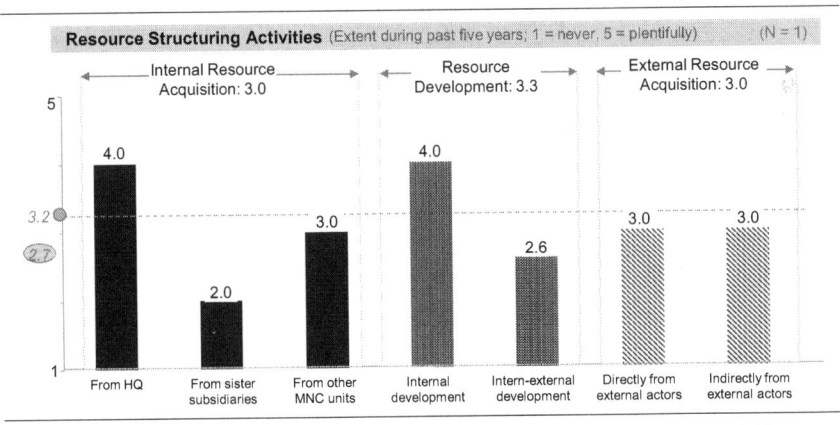

Figure 5.72: Survey Results: HUN – Initiative-related resource structuring activities

As to internal resource acquisition, it made use of central personnel such as product managers from headquarters or obtained financial funding from the corporate center through a defined resource allocation process (I10). In the process of initiative realization, the different resources and capabilities were **bundled**. In this regard, incremental resource bundling was most frequently applied (4.0), but intermediate and even radical bundling were both common as well (both 3.0, S10).

(2) Headquarters-Subsidiary Alignment

Within the past five years, the Hungarian unit experienced low **headquarters involvement** in subsidiary initiative-taking (2.8, S10), as can be seen in Figure 5.73. Communication and presentation of new opportunities to headquarters and its participation in the refinement of new initiatives were all assessed as relatively low. In many cases corporate approval was not even required for continuation. According to local management, for most initiatives the corporate center was not contacted or involved. In particular, locally driven initiatives of smaller scope and scale were managed without headquarters involvement (I10). Likewise, **corporate resistance** occurred only from time to time when engaging in entrepreneurial initiatives (2.3, S10). However, the Hungarian unit faced some lobbying and rival initiatives by competing units and needed to compete with other units for scarce resources, as described below:

> "... it turned out when we were looking around inside the company – that there is a unit [in France] which has already done it in-house. ... And we have now the dilemma that we continue with the in-house development and extend the existing solution with other features ... [this is] a good example for the fact that ideas come from anywhere and sometimes they can also compete with each other. Therefore several versions exist, which have advantages and disadvantages." (I10)

> "There are some big obstacles actually and [these are] mainly about resource allocation, this year this was the biggest obstacle for us. ... A lot of innovation projects are fighting for the resources." (I10)

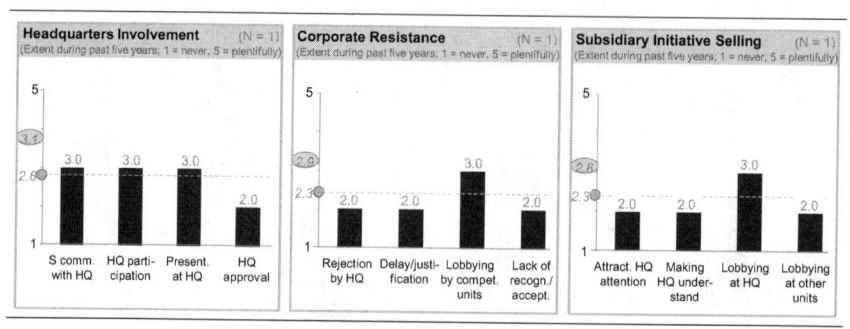

Figure 5.73: Survey Results: HUN – HQ-S alignment and interaction

Finally, the local organization only seldom engaged in **initiative selling** (2.3, S10). While local product initiatives did not require selling to headquarters, advanced ideas and larger scale opportunities were elaborated and evaluated in a more structured manner together with the corporate center as part of a standardized alignment process (I10).

5.2.1.3 Subsidiary Initiative-Taking Outcome

(1) Extent of Subsidiary Initiative-Taking

On the whole, the Hungarian subsidiary engaged in a comparatively high level of subsidiary initiatives in the past five years (3.0, S10). Among these, internally and externally oriented initiatives were undertaken to the same degree, as shown in Figure 5.74. Externally, local market initiatives occurred more frequently than global ones. One illustration of a local market initiative provided by subsidiary management is the design and implementation of a personalized recommendation engine that first started locally and was then further dispersed internationally. Another example of a local market initiative realized in the past five years was the development of a multiscreen application for video-on-demand services. With regard to internally oriented initiatives, the local unit frequently engaged in global-internal hybrid initiatives in the form of bids for corporate investment in the subsidiary location attracted by local subsidiary management.

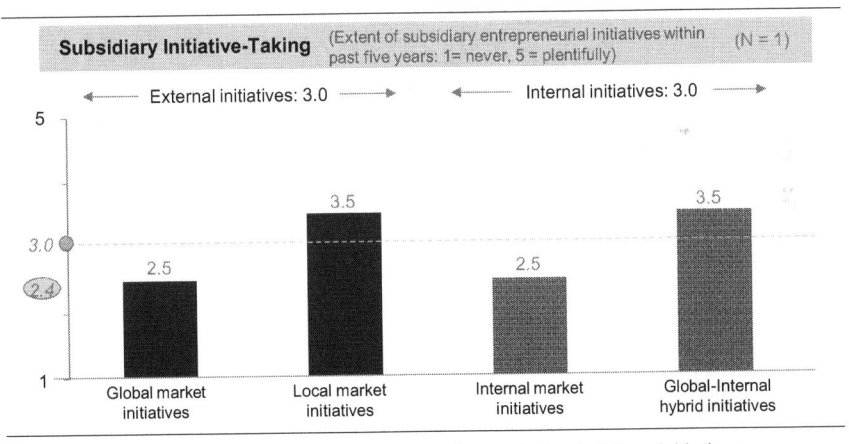

Figure 5.74: Survey Results: HUN – Types and extent of subsidiary initiatives

(2) Resource-Related Outcomes

Resulting from its entrepreneurial initiatives, the Hungarian subsidiary developed an extensive set of **new resources and capabilities** (4.0; S10), particularly in the area of general management. Most new resources and capabilities were also **of use for other MNC units** and hence they also provided the potential for firm-level advantages (see Figure 5.75). For example, the local market initiative concerning the multiscreen application was adapted and later used by the Greek subsidiary as well (I14).

New Subsidiary Resources and Capabilities (N = 2)
(Extent during past five years; 1= no capability development at all, 5 = extensive capability development)

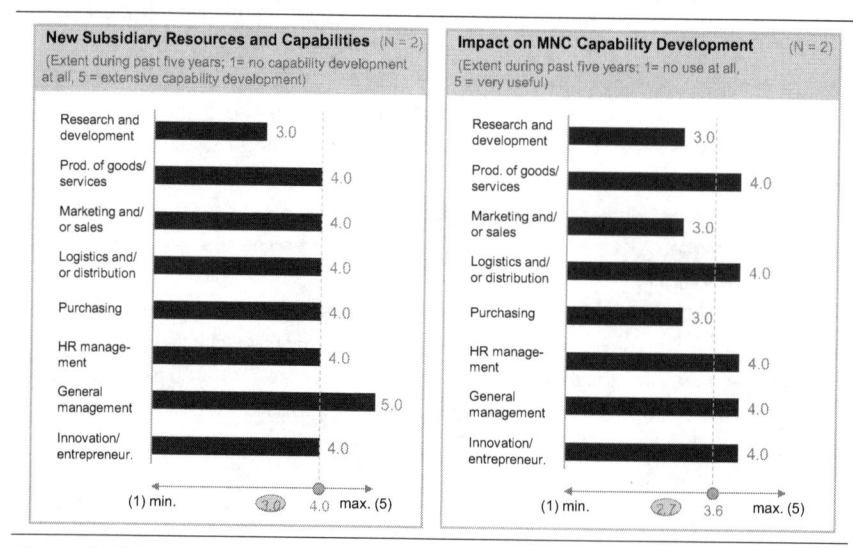

Area	Rating
Research and development	3.0
Prod. of goods/services	4.0
Marketing and/or sales	4.0
Logistics and/or distribution	4.0
Purchasing	4.0
HR management	4.0
General management	5.0
Innovation/entrepreneur.	4.0

Mean: 4.0 (min 1, max 5)

Impact on MNC Capability Development (N = 2)
(Extent during past five years; 1= no use at all, 5 = very useful)

Area	Rating
Research and development	3.0
Prod. of goods/services	4.0
Marketing and/or sales	3.0
Logistics and/or distribution	4.0
Purchasing	3.0
HR management	4.0
General management	4.0
Innovation/entrepreneur.	4.0

Mean: 3.6 (min 1, max 5)

Figure 5.75: Survey Results: HUN – New subsidiary resources and impact on MNC capabilities

(3) Further Outcomes

Concerning the **performance outcomes**, the entrepreneurial subsidiary initiatives in Hungary resulted in the enhancement of market share, revenues, profits and ROI, as well as productivity gains, as shown in Figure 5.76 (S10). As to **role development and position** in the wider MNC, the local unit improved its product and value-added scope (both 5.0) and strengthened its credibility within the multinational organization. Local management also added that the initiatives over the past five years strengthened collaboration with headquarters, improved relations with the corporate center, and helped identify numerous new initiative opportunities:

"I think there clearly is a higher cooperation between the headquarters and [Hungary]. And there is – a lot more projects ... and it is getting much more connected. ... And one of the best signs that I've seen that actually there is a high volume of digital services that are out there in the Group, which are quite good and we know that we can implement them." (I10)

Performance Outcomes (Extent during past five years; 1= very limited, 5 = substantial)	(N = 1)
Enhanced sales/revenues	4.0
Reduced costs	3.0
Improved market share	4.0
Improved profit	4.0
Improved ROI	4.0
Improved productivity	4.0
	(1) min. — 3.8 — max. (5)

Subsidiary Role and Position in MNC (Extent during past five years; 1 = major decline, 3 = no change, 5 = major improvement)	(N = 1)	
Geographical market scope	3.0	
Product scope	5.0	Subsidiary role development
Value-added scope	5.0	
Subsidiary influence	3.0	Subsidiary influence
History of delivering promises	4.0	
Signif. value-added contrib.	5.0	Subsidiary credibility
Global competiveness	4.0	
Recognition by HQ	4.0	
	(1) major decline — major (5) improv.	

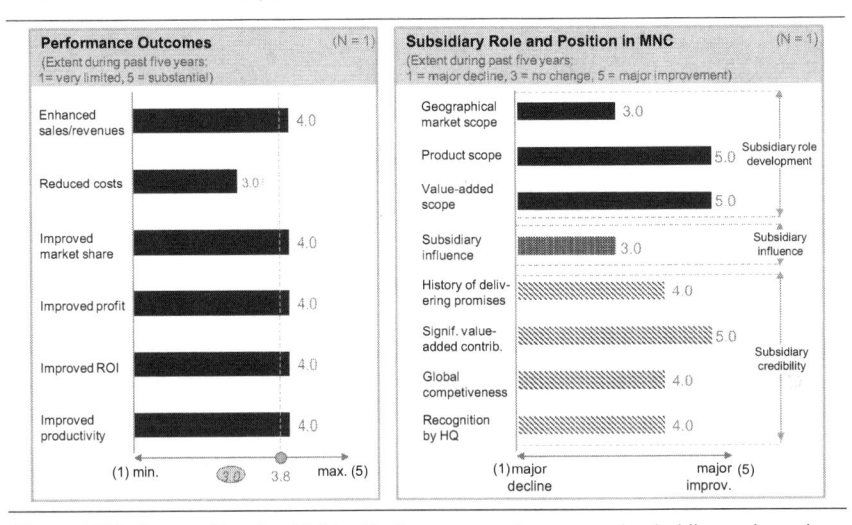

Figure 5.76: Survey Results: HUN – Performance outcomes and subsidiary role and position

5.2.2 Polish Subsidiary

The Polish Telecomp subsidiary was originally established in the mid-1990s. Over time, Company B acquired a large majority of shares and gained full management control over the foreign unit by the early 2000s. In 2013, the Polish organization employed close to 5,000 people and generated more than one billion Euros in annual revenues. Similar to other Telecomp subsidiaries, the Polish unit experienced declining revenues in recent years due to factors such as intense competition and increased regulatory requirements. It provides a wide range of telecommunication services to private and business customers, such as fixed and mobile telephony, broadband internet and IPTV services. The local entity performs all major value-chain functions ranging from service delivery, marketing and sales, customer service to R&D (A10, A13, S11). In addition, the Polish subsidiary has managed the innovation hub for southern and central Europe since 2013. The Polish unit is, along with Croatia and Hungary, considered to be one of the innovative pace setters with a solid track record of delivering innovative services and solutions over the past years (A14, I9, I11, A14).

5.2.2.1 Subsidiary Roles

(1) Strategic Market Importance and Subsidiary Competence: Strategic Leader

Survey results from subsidiary management indicate that the Polish unit represents a "Strategic Leader" unit within Telecomp, with high scores for both the strategic importance of the subsidiary market and subsidiary resources and capabilities (both 4.0, S11), as shown in Figure 5.77 below. As to the first role dimension concerning **strategic importance of the subsidiary market**, all four variables were rated as high. For example, the competitive intensity is seen by local management as very strong and, together with difficult regulatory requirements on price setting, posed challenges for the foreign unit as further explained by subsidiary management below. With regard to **subsidiary resources and capabilities**, the Polish organization has very strong capabilities in service delivery, marketing and sales and distribution, and is strong in R&D and purchasing.

"Und der Preis- und Konkurrenzdruck, der vom Markt ausgeht, der ist enorm. Was natürlich auch an den allgemeinen wirtschaftlichen Bedingungen liegt. Und das ist ganz klar, sobald sich die wirtschaftlichen Bedingungen etwas verschlechtern, wird der Druck ... enorm". (I11)

"Um hier Innovationen zu verkaufen ... muss man ständig ... neue kleine Dinge haben, die einen hohen Funcharakter haben, die einen hohen Anspruch haben im Markt, die also für den Kunden sehr wertvoll sind." (I11)

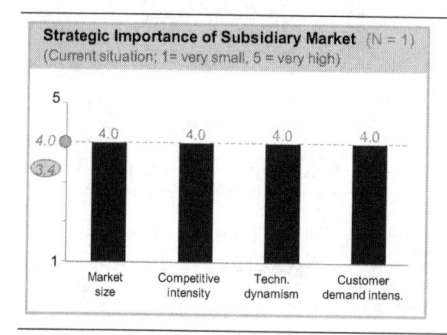

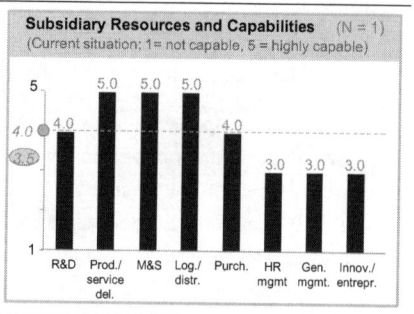

Figure 5.77: Survey Results: PL – Strategic importance and subsidiary resources/capabilities

(2) Subsidiary Localization and Integration: Active Subsidiary

Given the assessment for both role dimensions of localization/local responsiveness and subsidiary integration (3.8 and 3.5, S11), the Polish unit can be described as an "Active Subsidiary." Most of the variables relating to the **degree of localization/localization** received high scores. However, local customer needs differ only partially from other parts of the MNC and competitors and their strategies are somewhat easy to identify (both 3.0). As to the **degree of integration**, the subsidiary's dependence on internal network linkages is seen as particularly high. Moreover, many value-adding functions are highly integrated, such as purchasing, R&D and marketing; technology is largely centralized and shared, and service delivery decisions are strongly linked to worldwide market areas (see Figure 5.78).

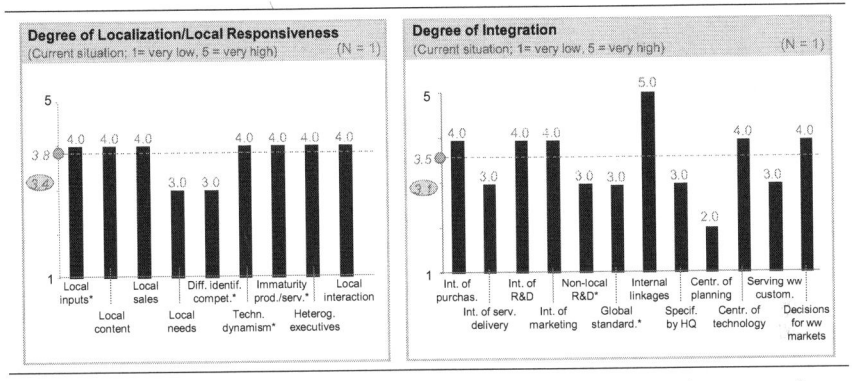

Figure 5.78: Survey Results: PL – Subsidiary localization/local responsiveness and subsidiary integration

(3) Subsidiary Decision-Making Autonomy

In comparison to the other Telecomp subsidiaries, the Polish unit enjoys a relatively high degree of decision-making autonomy (3.9, S11). Both strategic and operational decisions can be made largely by the local unit itself (4.3 and 3.5). More strategic aspects such as the development of major new service offerings, larger changes to service delivery processes, and restructuring of the local organization can be largely decided on by the Polish affiliate alone. One exception is the formulation and approval of the unit's annual budget, which is set centrally by headquarters. In comparison, operational decisions, such as career development plans, minor product modifications and recruitment and promotions are made independently or with only minor headquarters involvement, as illustrated in Figure 5.79.

Subsidiary Autonomy (Current situation; 1= decided centrally by HQ; 5 = decided independently by subsidiary) (N = 1)

◄────── Strategic Decisions: 4.3 ──────► ◄────── Operational Decisions: 3.5 ──────►

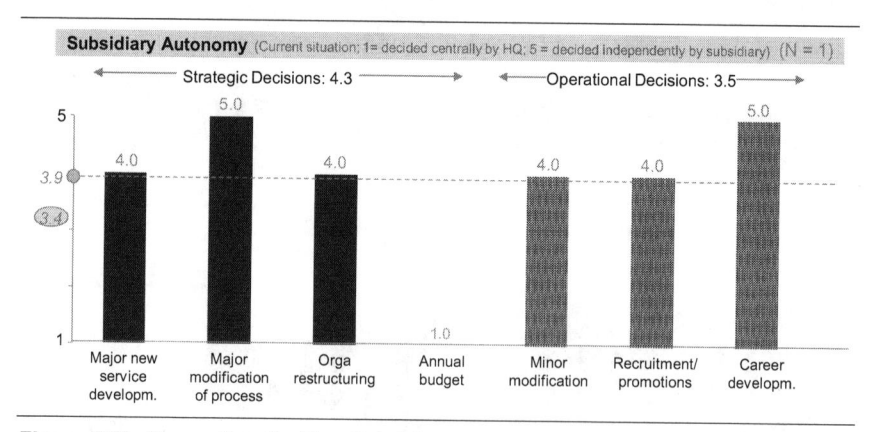

Major new service developm.	Major modification of process	Orga restructuring	Annual budget	Minor modification	Recruitment/ promotions	Career developm.
4.0	5.0	4.0	1.0	4.0	4.0	5.0

(3.9 / 3.4)

Figure 5.79: Survey Results: PL – Subsidiary decision-making autonomy

5.2.2.2 Subsidiary Initiative-Taking

(1) Entrepreneurial Resource Management

Throughout the past five years, the level of new **initiative opportunity identification** by the Polish subsidiary was moderate to high (3.4, S11), with internal discovery occurring somewhat more often than external (3.7 vs. 3.0). Most frequently, new initiative ideas were identified internally within the foreign unit itself, followed by interactions with local actors outside the subsidiary such as local partners or competitors (5.0 and 4.0).

> „Viele Ideen kommen da aus dem Land heraus, also aus Polen. Da werden neue Ideen von uns intern identifiziert und entwickelt, das ist schon so. Und natürlich auch zusammen mit lokalen Partnern oder Wettbewerbern. Dann haben wir haben ja noch in der Zentrale die große P&I Einheit, Product and Innovation. Und man muss auch deutlich sagen, dass da durchaus interessante Produkte rauskommen. Also sowohl Produkte als auch Partnering." (I11)

Other internal sources for new ideas that came into play periodically included regular alignment meetings or calls with headquarters and other MNC units (both 3.0). Identification through interactions with global actors outside the subsidiary was infrequent, as shown in Figure 5.80. Concerning their **innovativeness**, new opportunities were most frequently incrementally or moderately innovative in nature (4.0 and 3.5). However, radically innovative initiative opportunities were also detected more often by the Polish unit than by other foreign units of Telecomp.

5 – Empirical Findings

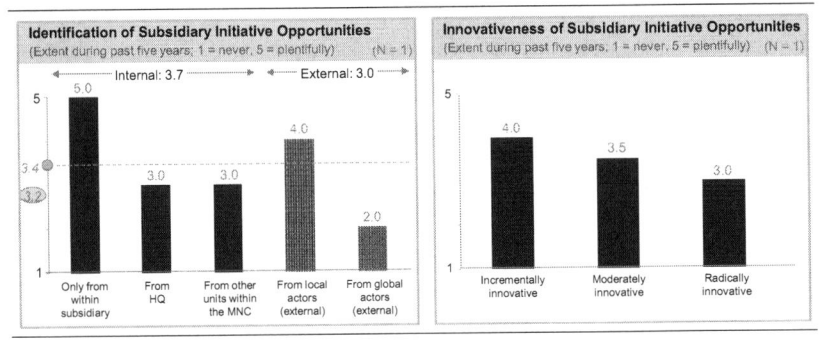

Figure 5.80: Survey Results: PL – Identification and innovativeness of initiative opportunities

Overall, the Polish unit exhibited a high level of **resource structuring** activities (3.0, S11). Resources needed for subsidiary initiatives were obtained more often from internal than from external sources. Externally, direct resource acquisition from external actors in the local or global market was utilized most frequently, while indirect acquisition through mergers or acquisition was rare. Internally, resource development within the Polish unit represented an important means but resource acquisition from headquarters or other MNC units also came into play from time to time, as shown in Figure 5.81. Concerning **bundling activities**, existing and new resources were commonly combined in the form of incremental (4.0) or intermediate bundling (4.0). However, some radical bundling, consisting of the extensive combination of completely new resources and capabilities, was employed as well (2.0, S11).

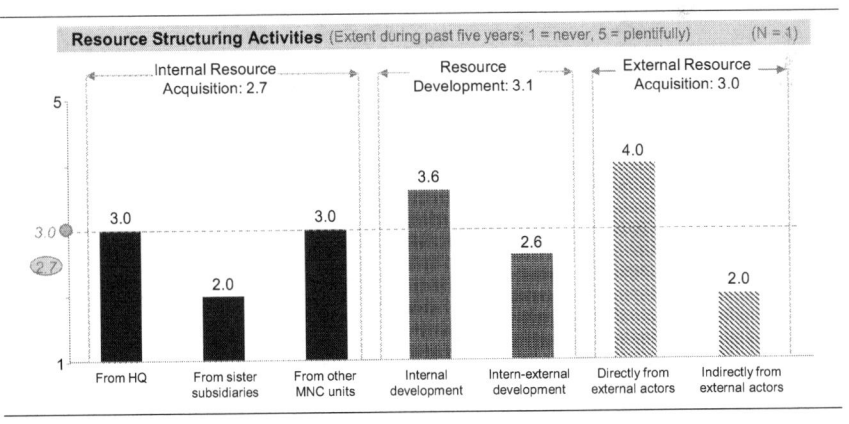

Figure 5.81: Survey Results: PL – Initiative-related resource structuring activities

(2) Headquarters-Subsidiary Alignment

Headquarters was involved in subsidiary initiatives only to a low degree (2.5, S11). While subsidiary management communicated and presented new initiatives to headquarters on occasion, close participation and the need for central approval were rather uncommon. According to local management, subsidiary initiatives could be undertaken largely autonomously, and only more recently were closer alignment and communication processes established by headquarters in Germany. For example, the corporate center implemented quarterly meetings with all foreign subsidiaries and bi-weekly conference calls to better share and discuss new entrepreneurial opportunities (I11). Furthermore, the extent of **corporate resistance** the Polish unit experienced when engaging in initiatives was assessed as low (2.3, S11). Resistance mainly manifested itself as rejection of entrepreneurial activities by headquarters or lobbying and rival activities by other MNC units. As explained in the interview, Company B still frequently ignores or even rejects initiatives and ideas originating from foreign subsidiaries. However, given the importance and size of the Polish market vis-à-vis other countries, headquarters tend to be more open towards entrepreneurial opportunities:

> "Mitunter werden solche Initiativen sogar bekämpft, von Ignoranz bis bekämpft. Bei [Initiative 1] ist versucht worden es [im Heaquarters] totzuschweigen ... Es ist ja nicht so schlicht und einfach, dass da einer kommt und den Stein des Weisen gefunden hat. Sondern da hat jemand eine neue Idee und anstatt zu sagen, so wir setzten uns jetzt wirklich hin mit dieser Idee und überlegen konstruktiv, was können wir aus dieser Idee machen. ... Das findet leider oft nicht statt, sondern wir haben bei der [Company B] immer noch den kulturellen und den strukturellen Clash und Konflikt, dass Deutschland, also das Headquarter, noch immer nicht gerne anerkennt, dass die Tochtergesellschaften im Lead sind. Und sie versuchen, Ideen solange zu ignorieren, bis [Headquarters] sie aufgenommen haben und dann praktisch übernehmen können." (I11)

> "Polen ist als großer und wichtiger Markt besser angesehen. Deshalb ist ... die Möglichkeit Ideen aus Polen zu ignorieren hier geringer als in Tschechien oder Kroatien, wo es nur ein kleiner Markt ist." (I11)

Corresponding to the minimal degree of corporate resistance, the Polish affiliate engaged in a low level of **initiative selling** (2.3, S11), as seen in Figure 5.82. The local entity occasionally attempted to make headquarters understand a new opportunity and tried to attract attention to a new opportunity, or lobby and sell initiatives within the wider MNC. Here, regular quarterly meetings and bi-weekly conference calls with all foreign Telecomp subsidiaries represented a good vehicle for sharing new initiative opportunities and selling them to the wider internal network:

> "Dort gibt es ein Forum, wo neue Ideen und Projekte vorgestellt werden ... Da kann jeder Ideen teilen, Propositions also Vorschläge machen und seine Projekte vorstellen und versuchen sie den anderen [Tochtergesellschaften] schmackhaft zu machen und damit zur Übernahme zu bewegen. ... Aber es gibt ja auch diese

Roadmap-Meetings, die vierteljährlichen Meetings, wo wir ein großes Forum dafür bilden. Wo man auch wirklich ein bisschen ausführlicher präsentieren und diskutieren kann." (I11)

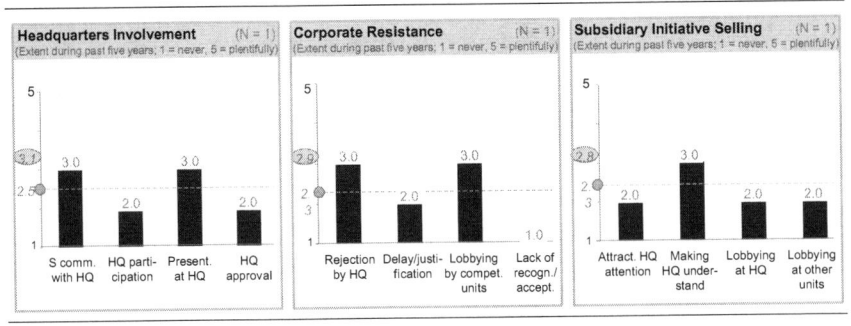

Figure 5.82: Survey Results: PL – HQ-S alignment and interaction

5.2.2.3 Subsidiary Initiative-Taking Outcome

(1) Extent of Subsidiary Initiative-Taking

With an average of 3.3 (S11), the Polish organization displayed the highest level of subsidiary initiatives among all Telecomp units in this study. Based on the survey results, externally oriented entrepreneurial activities were somewhat more prevalent than internally oriented ones (3.5 vs. 3.0). Most frequently pursued were local market initiatives that commonly represented new products, markets or processes first identified and developed locally and then exploited on a global scale. In comparison, global market initiatives, in the form of new global products or markets developed for non-local actors, were only undertaken occasionally. Internal market initiatives and global-internal hybrid initiatives were pursed somewhat more often according to the survey results (see Figure 5.83).

One example of a successful local market initiative undertaken by the Polish unit during the past five years was the development and introduction of an innovative payment system for mobile phones that permits contactless payment of purchases. The idea was first identified in Poland and jointly realized with local partners. Headquarters initially disregarded the local initiative, did not further engage in its development or refinement, and decided not to provide any central support. Nevertheless, the opportunity was driven forward in the country with local resources and finally implemented by the end of 2012. Subsequently, the local solution was partially adapted for other markets and implemented in Germany, Hungary, and the Slovakia in 2014 (A9, I11). A further example of a recent local entrepreneurial activity is the establishment of an online platform where start-up founders, network operators and developers can exchange ideas, obtain funding and jointly initiate new products or services (A15, I9).

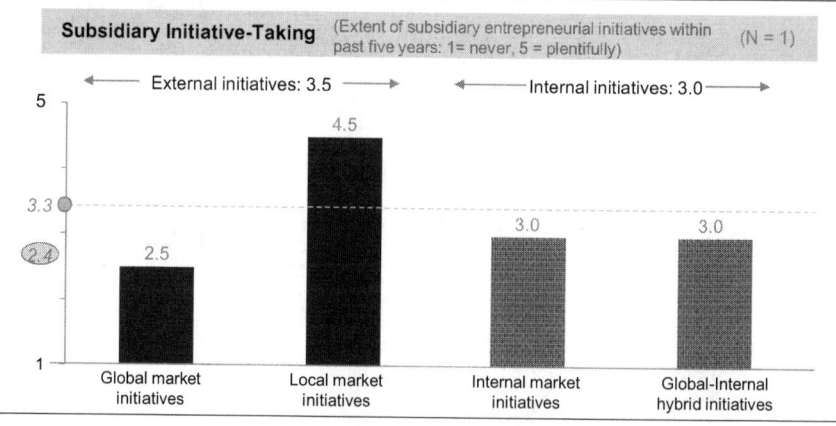

Figure 5.83: Survey Results: PL – Types and extent of subsidiary initiatives

Subsidiary Initiative-Taking (Extent of subsidiary entrepreneurial initiatives within past five years: 1= never, 5 = plentifully) (N = 1)

External initiatives: 3.5 — Internal initiatives: 3.0

Global market initiatives	Local market initiatives	Internal market initiatives	Global-Internal hybrid initiatives
2.5	4.5	3.0	3.0

(Overall mean: 3.3; external mean shown as 2.4)

With regard to internally oriented initiatives, the local management provided two illustrations. First, the Polish unit successfully engaged in a global-internal hybrid initiative. After learning in early 2012 that the corporate center was looking to set up a new innovation center outside its home market in Germany, the Polish unit actively tried to convince headquarters to establish the new innovation hub in Poland. Eventually, the decision was made to start up the innovation unit in the middle of 2013 (A14, I9). Lastly, one example of an internal market initiative that did not succeed was the Polish attempt to realize a cross-country procurement group for mobile devices. Here, the subsidiary's idea was to create a standard portfolio of mobile devices across all countries and thereby leverage the joint buying power of the various units to reduce purchasing costs. However, given the divergent interests of the country units, headquarters ultimately rejected and stopped the initiative (I11).

(2) Resource-Related Outcomes

The entrepreneurial initiatives of the Polish unit resulted in a comparatively high level of new resources and capabilities over the past five years (3.5, S11), as illustrated in Figure 5.84. Many new resources were developed in the areas of R&D, service delivery and innovation/entrepreneurship in particular. Similarly, many of these new resources were also assessed as useful for other MNC locations (3.1), particularly in the areas of R&D, purchasing and innovation/entrepreneurship. For example, some of the elements of the internal market initiative concerning the procurement group were further utilized in the Netherlands as described below:

„Wir haben immer wieder auch Best Pratice Austausch mit anderen Gesellschaften. Wir haben uns zum Beispiel beim Thema Einkaufsgemeinschaft zusammen mit den Niederlanden ausgetauscht. Ja, da es gab sehr viel Austausch, aber das war mehr oder weniger so, dass man dort einige Elemente von uns übernommen hat." (I11)

Similarly, certain resource outcomes from the local market initiative for the mobile payment solution were employed by other foreign subsidiaries as well. However, the solution was not directly transferable but instead required further adaptations to country-specific requirements that differed from those in Poland (I11).

New Subsidiary Resources and Capabilities (N = 1) (Extent during past five years; 1= no capability development at all, 5 = extensive capability development)		Impact on MNC Capability Development (N = 1) (Extent during past five years; 1= no use at all, 5 = very useful)	
Research and development	5.0	Research and development	5.0
Prod. of goods/services	4.0	Prod. of goods/services	3.0
Marketing and/or sales	3.0	Marketing and/or sales	3.0
Logistics and/or distribution	2.0	Logistics and/or distribution	2.0
Purchasing	4.0	Purchasing	4.0
HR management	3.0	HR management	2.0
General management	3.0	General management	2.0
Innovation/entrepreneur.	4.0	Innovation/entrepreneur.	4.0
ø 3.5		ø 3.1	

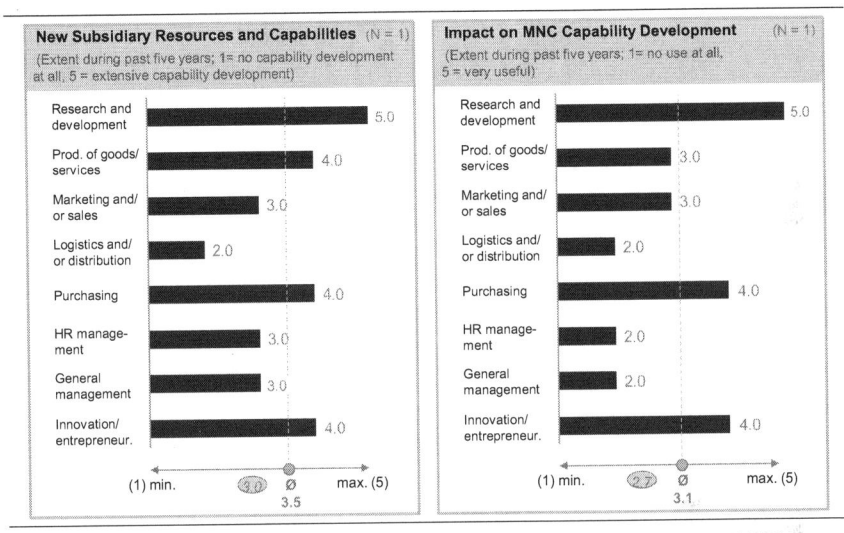

Figure 5.84: Survey Results: PL – New subsidiary resources and impact on MNC capabilities

(3) Further Outcomes

With regard to further performance outcomes, subsidiary initiative-taking activities led to quite substantial improvements in revenues and costs (both 4.0), as shown in Figure 5.85. Moreover, the subsidiary role and position in the wider MNC improved due to the entrepreneurial activities of the local unit. First, the Polish entity was able to strengthen its role within the corporation, particularly its product and value-added scope. Second, its influence on outcomes and performance of other subsidiaries grew over the five-year period. Finally, the Polish unit enhanced various aspects related to its credibility in the wider corporation, such as its recognition as a strategically important unit. In addition, because of its entrepreneurial activities, the local entity received more attention and recognition from headquarters (I11).

Performance Outcomes (N = 1)
(Extent during past five years; 1 = very limited, 5 = substantial)

Enhanced sales/revenues	4.0
Reduced costs	4.0
Improved market share	3.0
Improved profit	2.0
Improved ROI	3.0
Improved productivity	3.0
Ø	3.2

Subsidiary Role and Position in MNC (N = 1)
(Extent during past five years; 1 = major decline, 3 = no change, 5 = major improvement)

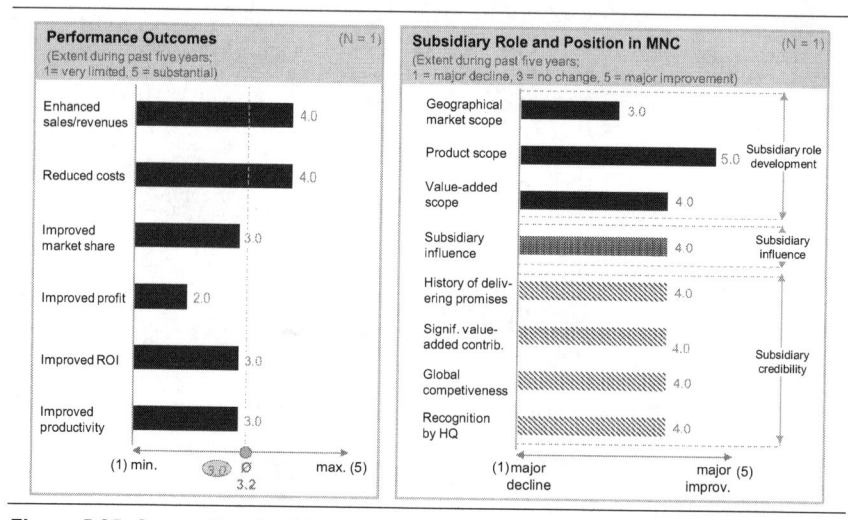

Dimension	Value	Category
Geographical market scope	3.0	Subsidiary role development
Product scope	5.0	Subsidiary role development
Value-added scope	4.0	Subsidiary role development
Subsidiary influence	4.0	Subsidiary influence
History of delivering promises	4.0	Subsidiary credibility
Signif. value-added contrib.	4.0	Subsidiary credibility
Global competetiveness	4.0	Subsidiary credibility
Recognition by HQ	4.0	Subsidiary credibility

Figure 5.85: Survey Results: PL – Performance outcomes and subsidiary role and position

5.2.3 Croatian Subsidiary

The Croatian Telecomp affiliate was first founded in the late 1990s and by the early 2000s Company B had acquired the majority of shares in the local corporation. In 2013, the foreign entity generated revenues of close to one billion Euros and employed more than 5,000 people. Services provided by the local entity include fixed network and mobile network telephony, broadband internet and IPTV. The subsidiary performs all major value-adding functions locally, including R&D, marketing and sales, customer service and HR management. Among the Telecomp subsidiaries, the Croatian unit was one of the first units to launch many innovative services, such as cloud based fleet management, call center services or novel IPTV services, and is viewed as "one of the innovators" within Telecomp (A16, A17, I12, S12).

> "I know that we are one of the maybe two or three ... established leaders or experienced leaders or experienced incumbents ... So we are definitely recognized ... as being innovative and a leader, which of course brings its own expectations from our performance as well." (I12)

5.2.3.1 Subsidiary Roles

(1) Strategic Market Importance and Subsidiary Competence: Strategic Leader

Within Telecomp, the Croatian affiliate can be classified as a "Strategic Leader" subsidiary. Both the strategic importance of the subsidiary market and the level of subsidiary resources and capabilities were evaluated as above average among all Telecomp subsidiaries in this study (3.5 and 3.6, S12), as shown in Figure 5.86 below.

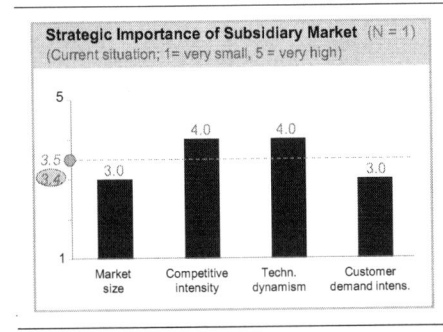

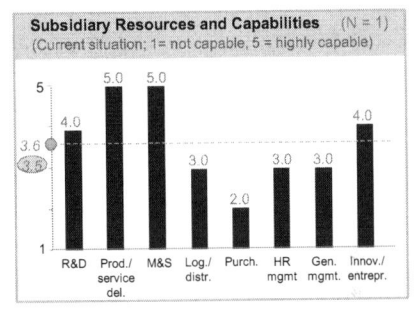

Strategic Importance of Subsidiary Market (N = 1) (Current situation; 1= very small, 5 = very high)	Subsidiary Resources and Capabilities (N = 1) (Current situation; 1= not capable, 5 = highly capable)
Market size: 3.5; Competitive intensity: 4.0; Techn. dynamism: 4.0; Customer demand intens.: 3.0	R&D: 3.6; Prod./service del.: 5.0; M&S: 5.0; Log./distr.: 3.0; Purch.: 2.0; HR mgmt: 3.0; Gen. mgmt.: 3.0; Innov./entrepr.: 4.0

Figure 5.86: Survey Results: CR – Strategic importance and subsidiary resources/ capabilities

Looking at the **strategic importance of the subsidiary market**, the competitive intensity and technical dynamism in particular are evaluated as stronger, while the market size and the customer demand intensity are assessed as moderate. Moreover, the Croatian unit faced several market related challenges over the past five years. For example, the local affiliate had to deal with a contracting telecommunications market, which shrank by more than 5% in value between 2011 and 2013 (A16, S12). Moreover, the subsidiary was confronted with strong regulatory requirements, increasing price competition and growing market saturation in certain areas, as expressed by local management in the interview:

> "The market in general is very competitive. It has in the past four or five years severely changed, so declining prices, so it's a very tough period. ... It's a stagnating market from the global telecom perspective if you look at a telecom business, and that's not helped by the fact that the customer spending power ... is not really where it used to be. So residential customers have less and less disposable income, and business customers are having difficulty with paying their obligations." (I12)

> "What's hindering [our innovations] is really half of the country is still in crisis. Most of EU is on the way out of the crisis, but in Croatia, it's still very much present, and it's making peoples' purchasing decisions very difficult." (I12)

> "So the regulatory environment is really, really tricky, and that's actually, you know, an additional pressure on the innovation part." (I12)

The **subsidiary resources and capabilities** are rated as particularly strong in the areas of marketing and sales as well as in service delivery (both 5.0, S12). Capabilities in R&D and innovation/entrepreneurship are rated as relatively high; as described by local management:

> "We are very good in sales and in implementation. So obviously, as the incumbent, we have the largest budgets for capex, investments, and these kinds of things. And we also have the largest sales force and ... the widest network of distributors and partners and the ... most valuable brand that we can leverage and communicate to the customers ..." (I12)

> "We're also regarded as being one of the innovators and templates for new products and new innovations in the Group. We are willing – or let's say we are never afraid of trying out new things or new models, so this is somehow bringing this aspect to the front." (I12)

(2) Subsidiary Localization and Integration: Active Subsidiary

Survey results further indicate that the Croatian subsidiary constitutes an "Active Subsidiary" within Telecomp, given its above average degrees of localization/local responsiveness and integration (3.6 and 3.3, S12) as shown in Figure 5.87. The above average degree of **localization/local responsiveness** largely results from a high amount of local input and local content in locally delivered services, a strong share of local sales and extensive interactions with local actors (all 4.0) such as suppliers, local entrepreneurs and research institutions (I12). Likewise, the unit's context involves a high degree of technological dynamism and immaturity of life cycle stages of services lines/ processes (both 4.0) as well.

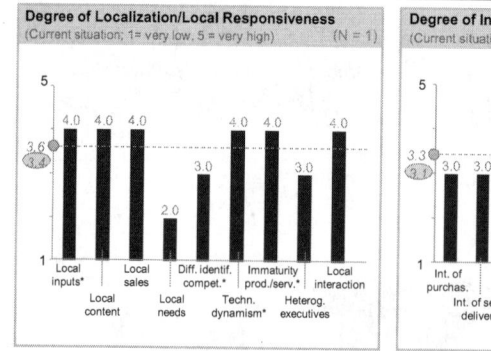

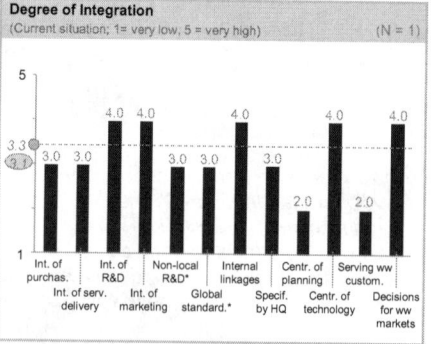

Figure 5.87: Survey Results: CR – Subsidiary localization/local responsiveness and subsidiary integration

The moderate to high degree of **subsidiary integration** in the MNC is mainly driven by the strong integration of select value-chain functions (i.e. R&D, marketing and sales), the high dependence on internal MNC linkages, the centralization of technology sharing and development and the many service delivery decisions that are linked to worldwide markets (all 4.0). Further examples indicating strong collaboration and integration with other units of the MNC include innovation projects driven jointly with headquarters, technology sharing and regular interactions and alignment with all Telecomp units (I12).

(3) Subsidiary Decision-Making Autonomy

Compared to the other Telecomp units, the Croatian subsidiary enjoys a moderate to high degree of decision-making autonomy (3.6, S12) and local management further explained that they are *"actually very autonomous, and ... have a very large freedom to make ... [our] own decisions"* (I12). However, the local organization has more leeway for operational decisions than for strategic ones (4.0 vs. 3.3). With regard to operations, the foreign entity can freely decide on minor but significant modifications to existing services or career development plans for departmental managers. Concerning strategic topics, the Croatian affiliate also benefits from extensive freedom for major process modifications or organizational restructuring (see Figure 5.88).

Subsidiary Autonomy (Current situation; 1= decided centrally by HQ; 5 = decided independently by subsidiary) (N = 1)

◄──── Strategic Decisions: 3.3 ────► ◄──── Operational Decisions: 4.0 ────►

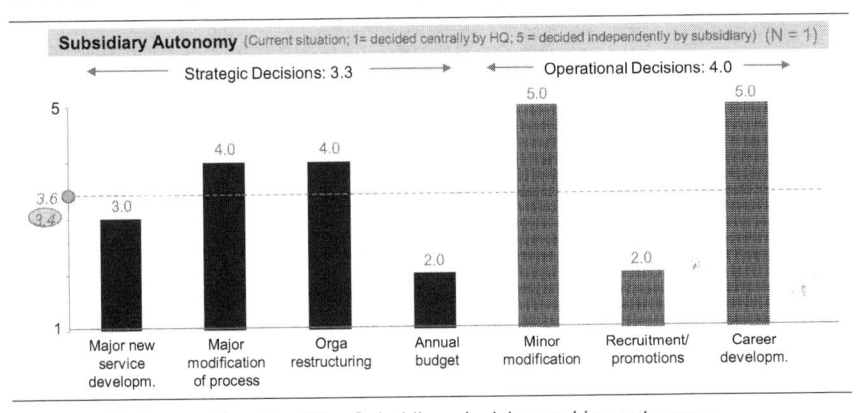

Major new service developm.	3.0
Major modification of process	4.0
Orga restructuring	4.0
Annual budget	2.0
Minor modification	5.0
Recruitment/ promotions	2.0
Career developm.	5.0

3.6
(3.4)

Figure 5.88: Survey Results: CR – Subsidiary decision-making autonomy

5.2.3.2 Subsidiary Initiative-Taking

(1) Entrepreneurial Resource Management

Opportunities for new subsidiary initiatives were frequently **identified** (3.3, S12) from various internal and external sources, as illustrated by Figure 5.89. Ideas were detected internally somewhat more frequently than externally (3.7 vs. 3.0). Important internal sources were other local entities belonging to the Croatian unit that supported the identification and pursuit of local entrepreneurial and innovative efforts and that *"with their own brand are recognized as also being innovative and disruptive in the market ... and* help us with our own activity with regards to innovation ..." (I12). Externally, local actors such as suppliers and vendors, local entrepreneurs and research institutions played a critical role in new initiative opportunity identification, as further explained by local management:

> "So we get ideas from our suppliers, from vendors who come up with new developments on their product platforms. We get them from the local market, from the local entrepreneurs ... We have excellent collaborations with the local technical university. ... There's this faculty of electrical engineering and computer science, with whom we are very much collaborating ... And also from the [headquarters] side ... good connections to third party partners with ... worldwide brand names like Spotify, like Dropbox and these kinds of specific players where Croatia is too small as a country to be noticeable to global entrepreneurs." (I12)

As concerns the level of **innovativeness**, most initiative opportunities were moderately or (somewhat less often) incrementally innovative in nature. Radically innovative opportunities were detected less frequently, as presented in Figure 5.89.

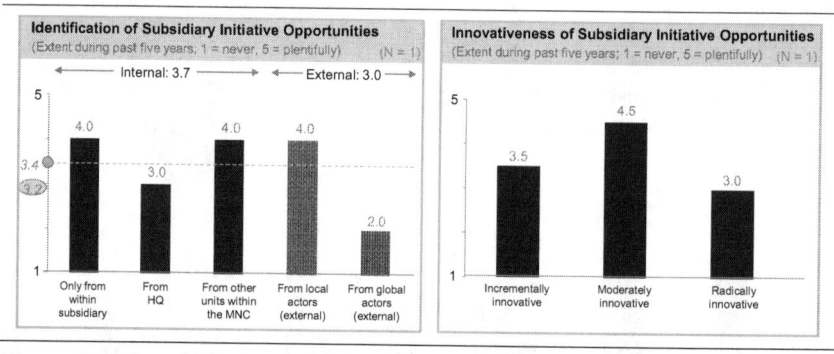

Figure 5.89: Survey Results: CR – Identification and innovativeness of initiative opportunities

When realizing new initiatives, the Croatian organization exhibited a moderate level of **resource structuring** (2.7, S12). In most cases, the subsidiary utilized its own resource base for new entrepreneurial initiatives:

> "It's done mostly locally. There were very few examples where it's done differently. So typically, it is done locally with local resources with local capex, with local opex".(I12)

In cases where new resources were needed, numerous internal and external sources came into play. Externally, resource acquisition from actors outside the MNC, such as local suppliers or vendors, was used most frequently. Resources were acquired from global actors only occasionally, and then often with the support of headquarters helping to establish contact with larger global partners that otherwise would not be directly interested in collaborating on a local level (I12). Finally, joint resource development with local partners such as research institutions took place from time to time (2.9, S12). Internally, resource acquisition from other MNC units or resource development within the subsidiary itself were frequently employed (3.0 and 2.6), as shown in figure 5.90. Resources were **bundled** in order to realize initiatives physically. Bundling was primarily incremental (4.0) and less regularly intermediate (3.0) or radical in nature (2.0).

Resource Structuring Activities (Extent during past five years; 1 = never, 5 = plentifully)							(N = 1)
Internal Resource Acquisition: 2.3			Resource Development: 2.7		External Resource Acquisition: 3.0		
From HQ	From sister subsidiaries	From other MNC units	Internal development	Intern-external development	Directly from external actors	Indirectly from external actors	
2.0	2.0	3.0	2.6	2.9	4.0	2.0	

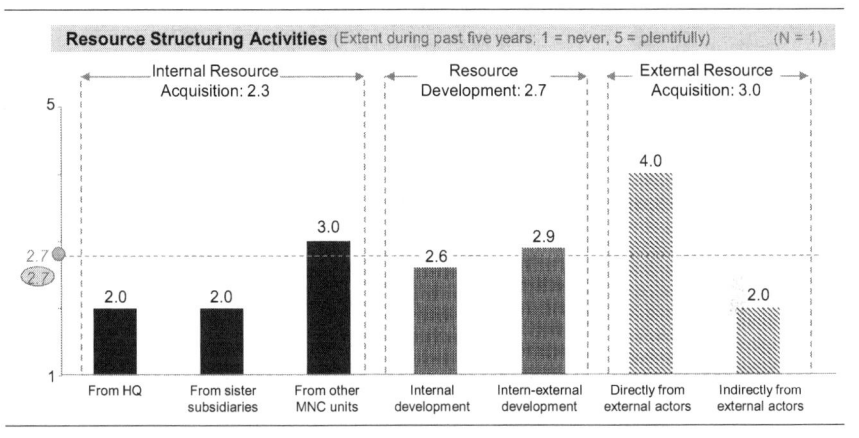

(2.7)

Figure 5.90: Survey Results: CR – Initiative-related resource structuring activities

(2) Headquarters-Subsidiary Alignment

Headquarters involvement in subsidiary initiatives was evaluated as moderate (3.0, S12). More specifically, communication with headquarters on new initiative opportunities was rather frequent, particularly in cases in which they were of potential relevance for other parts of the MNC as well (I12). Close participation in the refinement and development of new initiatives, and presentations to headquarters occurred from time to time, while approval from the corporate center was infrequently required. Moreover, the extent of **corporate resistance** was assessed as comparably low (2.5, S12). While there were occasional delays of entrepreneurial initiatives or lobbying and rival activities by other MNC units, rejections by headquarters or lack of acceptance in other parts of the company were quite rare. Lastly, the foreign affiliate engaged in a moderate level of **initiative-selling** activities (2.8, S12). Only occasionally did the unit attract headquarters attention, try to make it understand a new opportunity, or pursue lobbying or selling efforts at the corporate center. For example, some new initiative opportunities were presented in regular conference calls with other units of Telecomp, or, if they were of relevance for the wider group, they became part of a "common roadmap."[441] Overall, alignment and collaboration with headquarters on new subsidiary initiatives were described positively:

> *"There is a process set up for coming up with a year-long common roadmap of common projects. And this is steered actually by [headquarters]. And there's also product management call, which is happening every two weeks, where new ideas and new concepts are discussed. So based on the ideas that are presented there, we collect feedback and follow up with further interest."* (I12)

> *"We have really good collaboration. We have presented from the Croatian side ... several topics so far that are of interest to other [foreign subsidiaries], and then out of this, based on their interest and relevance, we agreed on doing a common innovation project."* (I12)

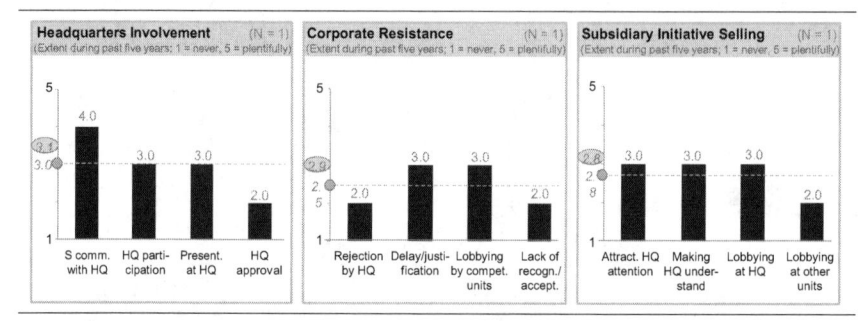

Headquarters Involvement (N=1) (Extent during past five years; 1 = never, 5 = plentifully)				Corporate Resistance (N=1) (Extent during past five years; 1 = never, 5 = plentifully)				Subsidiary Initiative Selling (N=1) (Extent during past five years; 1 = never, 5 = plentifully)			
S comm. with HQ	HQ participation	Present. at HQ	HQ approval	Rejection by HQ	Delay/justification	Lobbying by compet. units	Lack of recogn./ accept.	Attract. HQ attention	Making HQ understand	Lobbying at HQ	Lobbying at other units
4.0	3.0	3.0	2.0	2.0	3.0	3.0	2.0	3.0	3.0	3.0	2.0

Averages (dashed): 3.0 / 2.5 / 2.8

Figure 5.91: Survey Results: CR – HQ-S alignment and interaction

5.2.3.3 Subsidiary Initiative-Taking Outcome

(1) Extent of Subsidiary Initiative-Taking

Overall, the Croatian affiliate exhibited a comparatively high level of initiative-taking activities over the past five years (3.0, S12). Externally oriented initiatives occurred much more frequently than internally oriented ones (3.5 vs. 2.5). Specifically, local market initiatives were pursued regularly. One concrete example of such an initiative was further described in the interview. The Croatian affiliate locally identified and eventually implemented a new recommendation engine for a video-on-demand service. This endeavor was first identified and pursued locally, then realized in collaboration with local vendors and local research institutions. In the end, the solution was also adopted by sister subsidiaries abroad, as described by local management:

---

[441] The "common roadmap" represents a structured documentation and alignment process between headquarters and foreign subsidiaries concerning new innovations and entrepreneurial initiatives that are of relevance for the wider organization. It involves, for example, more detailed documentation of the new opportunity, the required level of capital expenditure or other resources, and the possible timeline. This information is then used for evaluations and discussions on potential ways forward, such as headquarters funding or support (I10, I12, I15).

"We implemented this on our ... commercial TV platform so it's live and running and available to our customers. Now we are currently expanding this ... towards other subsidiaries in the group to have them also use this product. This is a very, very nice example of an innovative research project, started locally and then used elsewhere ... And it's fully done locally, so the discovery, investments, the project management, and the project steering and all that was done locally." (I12)

With regard to internally oriented initiatives, global-internal hybrid initiatives were successfully implemented on occasion, while internal market initiatives targeted at improving the efficiency of the corporate system occurred only seldom (3.0 and 2.0, S12). Two examples of global-internal hybrid initiatives were given in the interviews. First, the Croatian unit learned that headquarters was interested in developing and testing a highly innovative internet network structure in one of the company's European locations. It then persuaded the corporate center to select Croatia as a test and pilot site and also to provide funding and resources for realization. Moreover, it involved the close cooperation of the Croatian organization with headquarters and many sister subsidiaries. According to company information, Croatia was the first country to install this innovative technology (A18, I12). Second, the local entity persuaded the corporate center to provide funding to install and adapt a multi-country platform in Croatia for various southern European countries. The original platform from Germany was adapted to local needs and subsequently serviced other country markets as well (I12).

Subsidiary Initiative-Taking (Extent of subsidiary entrepreneurial initiatives within past five years: 1= never, 5 = plentifully) (N = 1)

External initiatives: 3.5   Internal initiatives: 2.5

Global market initiatives	Local market initiatives	Internal market initiatives	Global-Internal hybrid initiatives
3.0	4.0	2.0	3.0

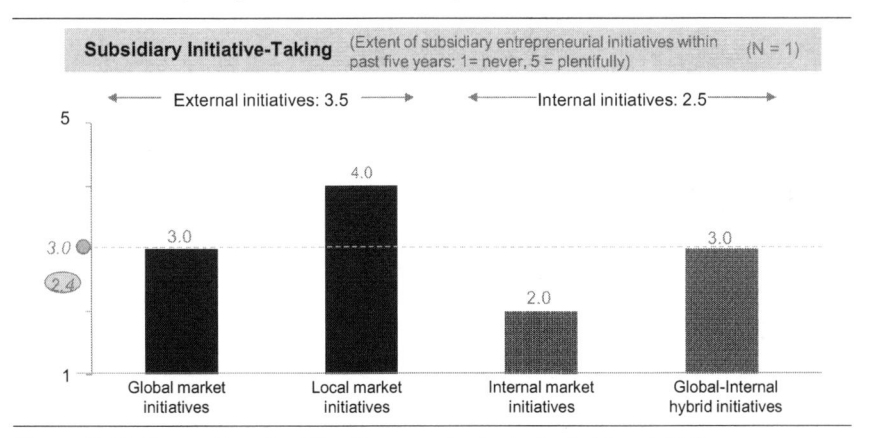

Figure 5.92: Survey Results: CR – Types and extent of subsidiary initiatives

(2) Resource-Related Outcomes

Resulting from the entrepreneurial initiatives, the Croatian unit developed a high level of **new subsidiary resources and capabilities** (3.4, S12), especially in the areas of R&D, service delivery, marketing and sales and innovation/entrepreneurship. With the exception of marketing and sales, resources from these areas also appear to be very useful for other MNC locations as well (see Figure 5.93).

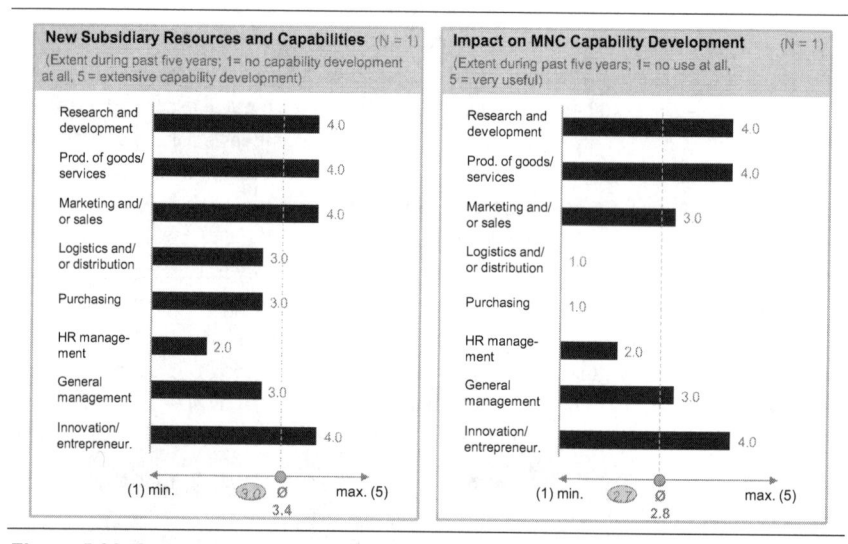

New Subsidiary Resources and Capabilities (N = 1)		Impact on MNC Capability Development (N = 1)	
(Extent during past five years; 1 = no capability development at all, 5 = extensive capability development)		(Extent during past five years; 1 = no use at all, 5 = very useful)	
Research and development	4.0	Research and development	4.0
Prod. of goods/services	4.0	Prod. of goods/services	4.0
Marketing and/or sales	4.0	Marketing and/or sales	3.0
Logistics and/or distribution	3.0	Logistics and/or distribution	1.0
Purchasing	3.0	Purchasing	1.0
HR management	2.0	HR management	2.0
General management	3.0	General management	3.0
Innovation/entrepreneur.	4.0	Innovation/entrepreneur.	4.0
(1) min. ⌀ 3.4 max. (5)		(1) min. ⌀ 2.8 max. (5)	

Figure 5.93: Survey Results: CR – New subsidiary resources and impact on MNC capabilities

(3) Further Outcomes

Concerning further **performance outcomes** of subsidiary initiative-taking, the Croatian affiliate was able to enhance revenues, market share and profits in particular (all 4.0, S12). It also strengthened various aspects of its role in the MNC, namely its geographic, product and value-added scope. Moreover, its recognition by headquarters as a strategically important unit within the multinational firm was strengthened, as seen in Figure 5.94.

Performance Outcomes (N = 1)
(Extent during past five years; 1 = very limited, 5 = substantial)

- Enhanced sales/revenues: 4.0
- Reduced costs: 3.0
- Improved market share: 4.0
- Improved profit: 4.0
- Improved ROI: 3.0
- Improved productivity: 2.0

Ø 3.3

Subsidiary Role and Position in MNC (N = 1)
(Extent during past five years; 1 = major decline, 3 = no change, 5 = major improvement)

- Geographical market scope: 4.0
- Product scope: 4.0
- Value-added scope: 4.0
- Subsidiary influence: 3.0
- History of delivering promises: 3.0
- Signif. value-added contrib.: 3.0
- Global competiveness: 3.0
- Recognition by HQ: 4.0

Subsidiary role development → Subsidiary influence → Subsidiary credibility

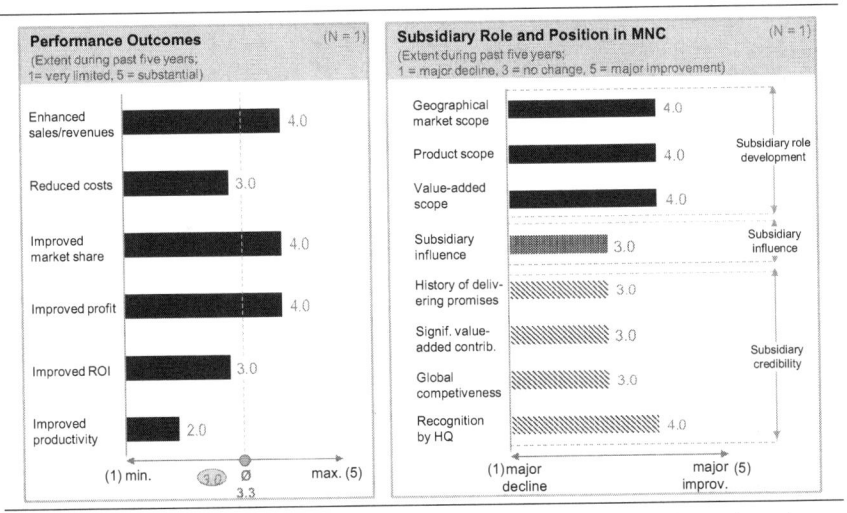

Figure 5.94: Survey Results: CR – Performance outcomes and subsidiary role and position

5.2.4 Slovakian Subsidiary

The Slovakian subsidiary was acquired by Telecomp in the late 1990s. In 2013, it generated revenues of close to one billion Euros and employed approximately 4,000 workers. Based on the number of employees, it is the second smallest foreign Telecomp subsidiary in this study. Some of the services offered by the foreign organization are fixed network and mobile network telephony, broadband internet and IPTV. Value-adding functions performed locally include service delivery, marketing and sales as well as customer service (A19, S13). In the past, the unit was often among the first to implement new technologies and services in select areas, but recently it is seen as having become "somewhat less innovative." The Slovakian subsidiary has also faced declining revenues over the past few years and has seen a reduction in the number of employees (I9).

5.2.4.1 Subsidiary Roles

(1) Strategic Market Importance and Subsidiary Competence: Contributor

The role assessment obtained through the subsidiary survey positions the Slovakian unit as a "Contributor" subsidiary within Telecomp. With an average of 3.0, the strategic importance of the subsidiary market is relatively low, while the level of subsidiary resources and capabilities is assessed as high (3.9, S13). Regarding the low **strategic importance of the subsidiary market**, the Slovakian market size is considered rather small since it is "*limited in population and in purchasing power*" (I13). Technological dynamism and customer demand intensity are regarded as moderate and only the competitive intensity is seen as somewhat higher. **Subsidiary resources and capabilities** are rated as particularly strong in service delivery and general management but only moderate in R&D, purchasing and human resource management, as outlined in Figure 5.95 below. However, despite the relatively high level of resources and capabilities, the local subsidiary manager views its limited financial budget as an obstacle to innovative and entrepreneurial activities:

> "*We don't have enough budget and internal support for making any larger exercises or any bigger entrepreneurial activities. We can only evaluate and maybe create smaller activities successfully here. ... We lost some space to play with new technologies and new ideas because headquarters does not approve enough budget for trials or some trial activities.*" (I13)

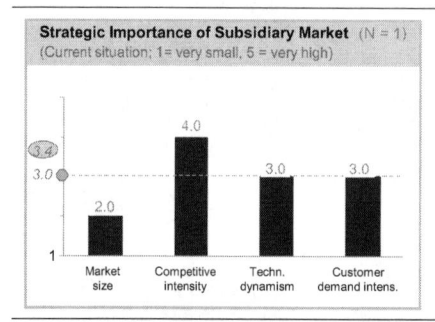

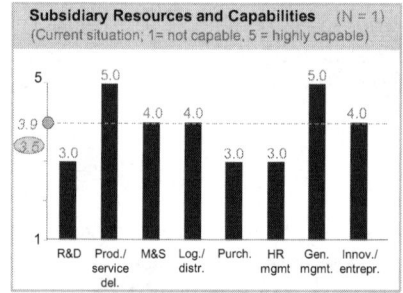

Figure 5.95: Survey Results: SL – Strategic importance and subsidiary resources/capabilities

(2) Subsidiary Localization and Integration: Receptive Subsidiary

Based on both corporate and local assessment, the Slovakian entity constitutes a "Receptive Subsidiary." According to the survey results, the unit is characterized by a relatively low degree of **localization/local responsiveness** (3.1, S13). For example, local customer needs do not significantly differ from other MNC locations, and local inputs and local content in locally provided services are assessed as moderate. Moreover, competitors and their strategies are easily identified and the heterogeneity of the subsidiary executive group is low, indicating a moderate to low degree of localization. In comparison, the **degree of integration** is somewhat higher (3.5, S13). Value-adding functions are integrated to a moderate or high degree, technology development is largely centralized and service delivery decisions are strongly linked to worldwide market areas, as presented in Figure 5.96.

5 – Empirical Findings

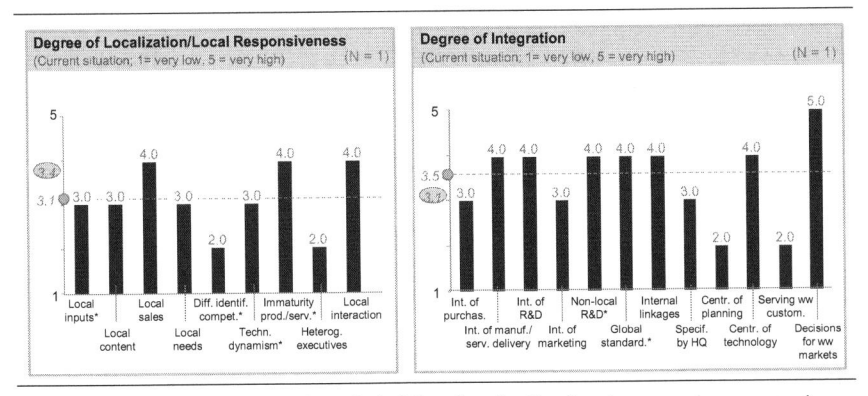

Figure 5.96: Survey Results: SL – Subsidiary localization/local responsiveness and subsidiary integration

(3) Subsidiary Decision-Making Autonomy

On the whole, the Slovakian organization enjoys a moderate level of decision-making autonomy in comparison to the other Telecomp units studied (3.3, S13). Operational decisions are given more leeway than strategic decisions (3.7 vs. 3.0), as shown in Figure 5.97. Concerning strategic decisions, the local unit possesses some freedom to modify service delivery processes without headquarters involvement, develop new service offerings or restructure parts of the local organization, but has only little autonomy regarding decisions on the subsidiary's annual budget. In terms of operational decision-making autonomy, the local organization can independently implement minor but significant modifications to existing services or implement smaller product innovations, as explained by local management:

"When we come with our own ideas here, right, for example we create ... some small products. I mean from a capex point of view, small products, so not expensive ones. We do not discuss these ideas with headquarters." (I13)

"We have limited autonomy but I feel that we have bigger autonomy than our Czech colleagues ... I understand there is a benefit of working with bigger autonomy but we don't have enough budget and internal support for making any larger exercises or any bigger activities. We can only evaluate and maybe create smaller activities successful[ly]" (I13)

Subsidiary Autonomy (Current situation; 1 = decided centrally by HQ; 5 = decided independently by subsidiary) (N = 1)

← Strategic Decisions: 3.0 → ← Operational Decisions: 3.7 →

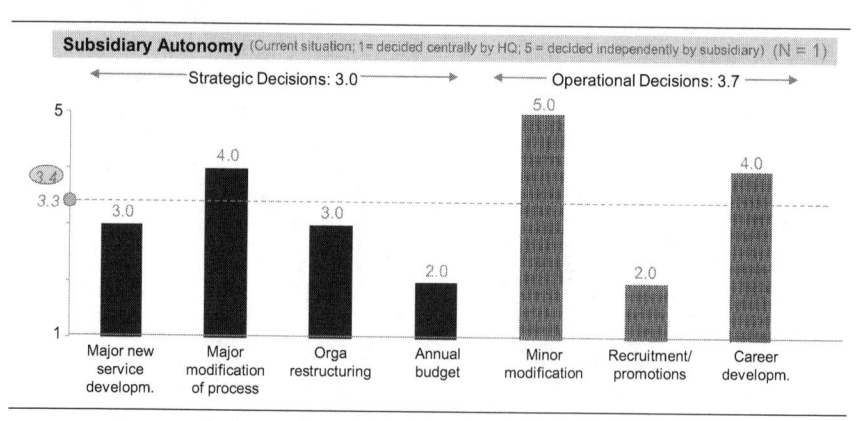

Major new service developm.	Major modification of process	Orga restructuring	Annual budget	Minor modification	Recruitment/ promotions	Career developm.
3.0	4.0	3.0	2.0	5.0	2.0	4.0

(3.4 / 3.3 averages shown)

Figure 5.97: Survey Results: SL – Subsidiary decision-making autonomy

5.2.4.2 Subsidiary Initiative-Taking

(1) Entrepreneurial Resource Management

Within the past five years, the foreign organization showed a moderate level of new subsidiary **opportunity identification** (3.2, S12). Although opportunities were identified from various internal and external sources, internal detection occurred more frequently (3.7 vs. 2.5). Internally, new initiative opportunities were frequently detected within the local subsidiary itself. Market insights and employees' abilities to analyze competitive offerings in the local or foreign markets played an important role, as outlined below. According to subsidiary management, the local market is not considered very innovative or dynamic and few new ideas or products originate in the Slovakian unit:

> "But my view is that local companies are only reselling products from abroad. There are not so many new ideas and products that come from Slovakia. It's not dynamic like that. So for me it is better to cooperate or directly communicate to the owners of the ideas or to the owners or to the managers representing the original idea. ... And they are often abroad in other countries." (I13)

> "So the sources we're considering ... was mostly some benchmarks from abroad ... some from regional market but mostly Japanese market or US market, maybe others ... some Nordic markets like in Norway or Sweden. ... We're considering the competition we have in our region and the products, what they offer and how their products do. So all these aspects we take into the consideration." (I13)

Externally, interactions with local actors, such as customers, technology providers or even competitors, particularly contributed to new initiative opportunity identification for the Slovakian unit (I13, S13). For example, one of the new initiative opportunities was initially identified and discussed in a joint workshop with a local vendor (I13). Interactions or even collaborations with global external actors remained limited. According to subsidiary management, global actors were less motivated to collaborate with the local unit given the small market size and limited purchasing power of the Slovakian population, making it generally less attractive (I13). With regard to the **innovativeness** of new initiative opportunities, most new discoveries were incrementally or moderately innovative. Radically innovative opportunities were only seldom identified within the past five years (see Figure 5.98).

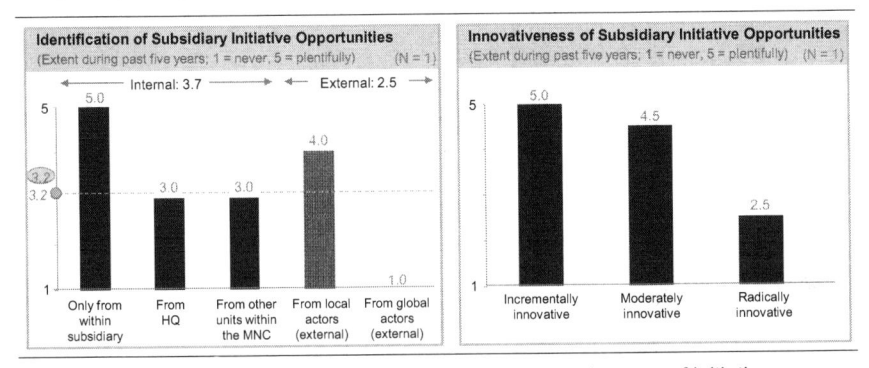

Identification of Subsidiary Initiative Opportunities (Extent during past five years; 1 = never, 5 = plentifully) (N = 1)	Innovativeness of Subsidiary Initiative Opportunities (Extent during past five years; 1 = never, 5 = plentifully) (N = 1)
Internal: 3.7 — External: 2.5	
Only from within subsidiary: 3.2	Incrementally innovative: 5.0
From HQ: 3.0	Moderately innovative: 4.5
From other units within the MNC: 3.0	Radically innovative: 2.5
From local actors (external): 4.0	
From global actors (external): 1.0	

Figure 5.98: Survey Results: SL – Identification and innovativeness of initiative opportunities

When attempting to realize new initiative opportunities, the Slovakian unit exhibited a moderate level of **resource structuring** (2.8, S13) and primarily turned to internal rather than external sources. Furthermore, the local affiliate more frequently developed rather than acquired needed resources. Internally, resources were frequently developed within the subsidiary itself (3.4) or acquired from headquarters or other MNC units (both 3.0). Externally, resources were commonly acquired directly from external actors, as presented in Figure 5.99. Finally, the various resources and capabilities were **bundled** to realize new subsidiary initiatives. In the Slovakian organization, this occurred mostly in the form of incremental and intermediate bundling (both 3.0) and less frequently in the form of radical bundling (2.0).

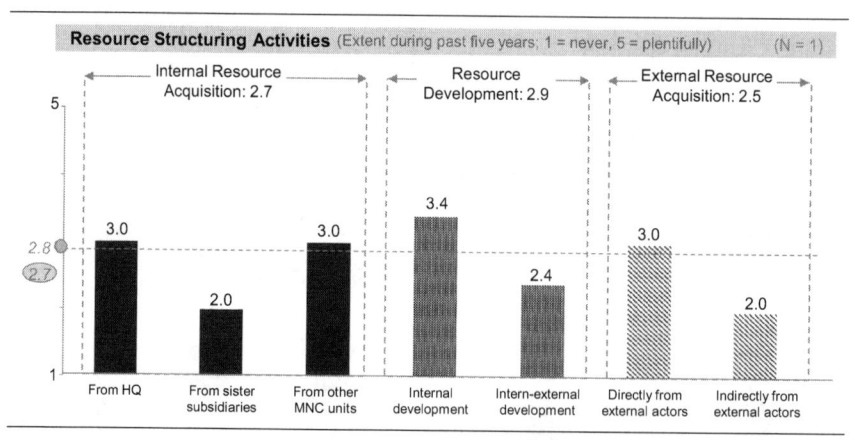

Figure 5.99: Survey Results: SL – Initiative-related resource structuring activities

(2) Headquarters-Subsidiary Alignment

Throughout its initiative-taking activities, the Slovakian affiliate experienced a moderate level of **headquarters involvement** (3.0, S13). While subsidiary managers communicated frequently with stakeholders in the corporate center concerning new opportunities, their central counterparts only seldom engaged in further refining or developing the subsidiary ideas. Moreover, presentations of idea proposals and headquarters approval were needed only from time to time. According to local management, headquarters involvement also differed by the type of new opportunities. While smaller initiatives were commonly not shared or discussed with Germany, larger initiatives were often closely aligned with the corporate center, also in order to monitor financial spending on activities from a central perspective (I13). Likewise, **corporate resistance** was assessed as moderate (3.0, S13). More specifically, lobbying and rival initiatives by competing units and lack of recognition of initiatives by other MNC units were both very infrequent. In contrast, rejection and delay by headquarters were much more common (both 4.0). Finally, the survey results indicate a moderate level of **initiative-selling** activities by the Slovakian affiliate (3.0, S13). While the local unit frequently attempted to attract headquarters attention to new initiative opportunities, efforts to make the corporate center understand the new initiative or to lobby for further support occurred less often, as shown in Figure 5.100. In the interview, the local subsidiary manager further described his selling efforts and headquarters' passive resistance as follows:

> "I had some experiences in the past when I submitted some ideas to the headquarter[s] but in fact there was no answer or a very limited answer." (I13)

"... I submitted some, one, two, three times some ideas. Maybe I submitted to the wrong people, so there was no or limited answer. And then it was about me because once I didn't reach any success then ... I didn't force it. ... And you know, my personal KPIs are not to sell the products to the headquarter[s] or to the other markets." (I13)

"So ... there was ... almost no interaction from the headquarters." (I13)

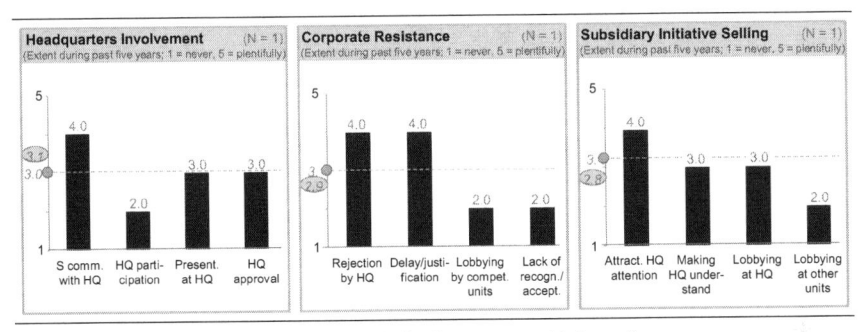

Figure 5.100: Survey Results: SL – HQ-S alignment and interaction

5.2.4.3 Subsidiary Initiative-Taking Outcome

(1) Extent of Subsidiary Initiative-Taking

Over the past five years, the Slovakian unit exhibited a moderate level of entrepreneurial initiatives (2.3, S13). Concerning initiative types, internally oriented and externally oriented initiatives occurred to the same extent (both 2.3). Among internal opportunities, global-internal hybrid initiatives involving the attraction of central investments took place more frequently than internal initiatives concerning internal efficiency improvements (3.0 vs. 1.5). Externally oriented initiatives occurred mostly in the form of local market initiatives and very rarely as global market initiatives (3.0 and 1.5).

One example of a local initiative shared by subsidiary management involved the introduction of an advanced tracking service allowing parents to monitor and track the current location of their children via their mobile phones. The new idea was first identified in a joint workshop with a local technology provider. Subsequently, local and global market research was undertaken to review existing offerings and solutions in the market and to help further refine the concept. Together with the local technology provider, an innovative technical and operational solution was developed that was offered by very few players outside Europe at the time. In the end, it was first implemented in Slovakia using locally available resources and with very limited headquarters involvement. At a later point in time, the initiative idea and content was shared with other foreign subsidiaries of Telecomp and some decided to adopt parts of the solution (I13).

Subsidiary Initiative-Taking (Extent of subsidiary entrepreneurial initiatives within past five years: 1= never, 5 = plentifully) (N = 1)

← External initiatives: 2.3 →   ← Internal initiatives: 2.3 →

- Global market initiatives: 1.5
- Local market initiatives: 3.0
- Internal market initiatives: 1.5
- Global-Internal hybrid initiatives: 3.0

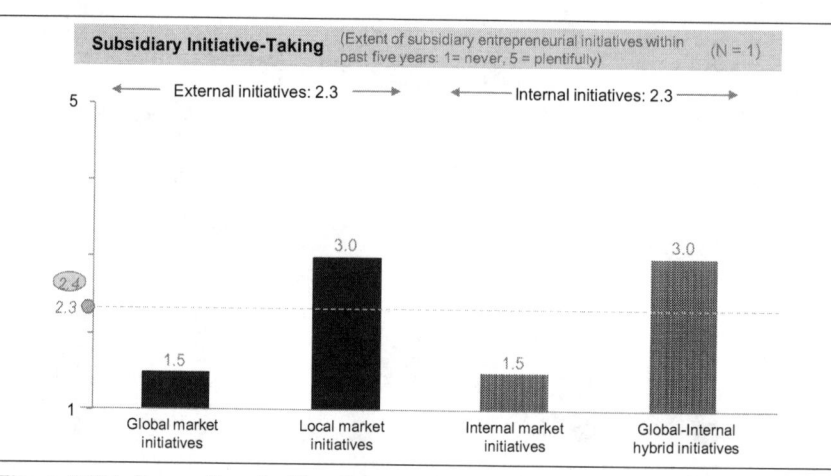

(2.4)
2.3

Figure 5.101: Survey Results: SL – Types and extent of subsidiary initiatives

(2) Resource-Related Outcomes

As a result of the subsidiary initiatives, the Slovakian affiliate was able to moderately increase its level of resources and capabilities over the past five years (3.1, S13), particularly in the areas of R&D, service delivery and innovation/entrepreneurship. As outlined in the previous subsection, the unit successfully implemented some local and global-internal initiatives. For example, the local market initiative regarding the localization service led to the development of new insights on competitive offerings in global and local markets. This also produced new technical solutions in collaboration with the local vendor, and as such somewhat specialized resources and capabilities that had not previously existed in the MNC. The contribution of the newly generated resource bundles to the overall competencies of the MNC was assessed as moderate (2.6, S13). Here, competencies gained in R&D, service delivery, HR and general management as well as innovation/entrepreneurship were believed to be of at least some use for other MNC units, as shown in Figure 5.102.

5 – Empirical Findings

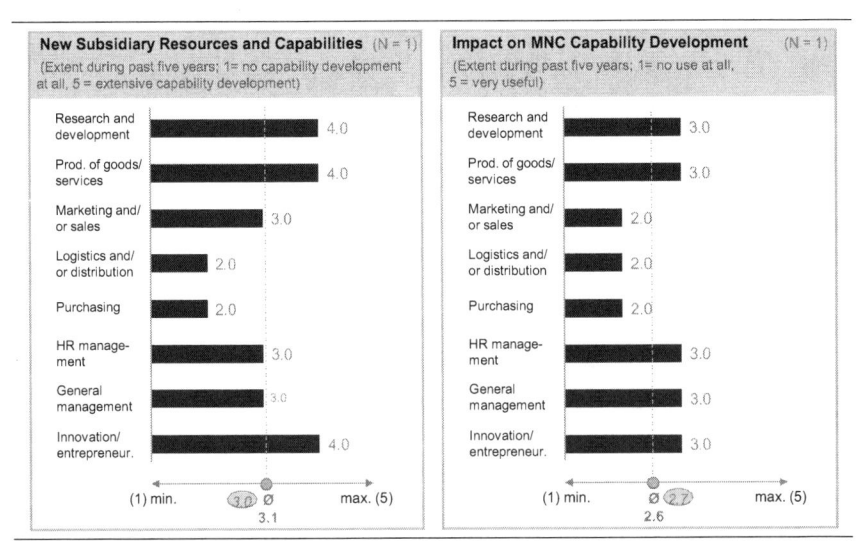

New Subsidiary Resources and Capabilities (N = 1)		Impact on MNC Capability Development (N = 1)	
(Extent during past five years; 1= no capability development at all, 5 = extensive capability development)		(Extent during past five years; 1= no use at all, 5 = very useful)	
Research and development	4.0	Research and development	3.0
Prod. of goods/ services	4.0	Prod. of goods/ services	3.0
Marketing and/ or sales	3.0	Marketing and/ or sales	2.0
Logistics and/ or distribution	2.0	Logistics and/ or distribution	2.0
Purchasing	2.0	Purchasing	2.0
HR management	3.0	HR management	3.0
General management	3.0	General management	3.0
Innovation/ entrepreneur.	4.0	Innovation/ entrepreneur.	3.0
(1) min. Ø 3.1	max. (5)	(1) min. Ø 2.7 2.6	max. (5)

Figure 5.102: Survey Results: SL – New subsidiary resources and impact on MNC capabilities

(3) Further Outcomes

In addition to newly generated resources and capabilities, the entrepreneurial initiatives were seen to positively influence other **performance outcome** measures as well. For example, it helped to partially enhance market share, revenues, profits and ROI (all 4.0, S13). Moreover, the **subsidiary role** in the MNC improved somewhat through enhancements in the product scope (4.0). Likewise, certain aspects relating to the subsidiary's credibility advanced over the past five years as a result of the entrepreneurial initiatives undertaken by the Slovakian unit (see Figure 5.103).

Performance Outcomes (N = 1)
(Extent during past five years; 1 = very limited, 5 = substantial)

Enhanced sales/revenues	4.0
Reduced costs	3.0
Improved market share	4.0
Improved profit	4.0
Improved ROI	4.0
Improved productivity	3.0

(1) min. — Ø 3.7 — max. (5)

Subsidiary Role and Position in MNC (N = 1)
(Extent during past five years; 1 = major decline, 3 = no change, 5 = major improvement)

Geographical market scope	3.0	
Product scope	4.0	Subsidiary role development
Value-added scope	3.0	
Subsidiary influence	3.0	Subsidiary influence
History of delivering promises	4.0	
Signif. value-added contrib.	3.0	
Global competitiveness	4.0	Subsidiary credibility
Recognition by HQ	3.0	

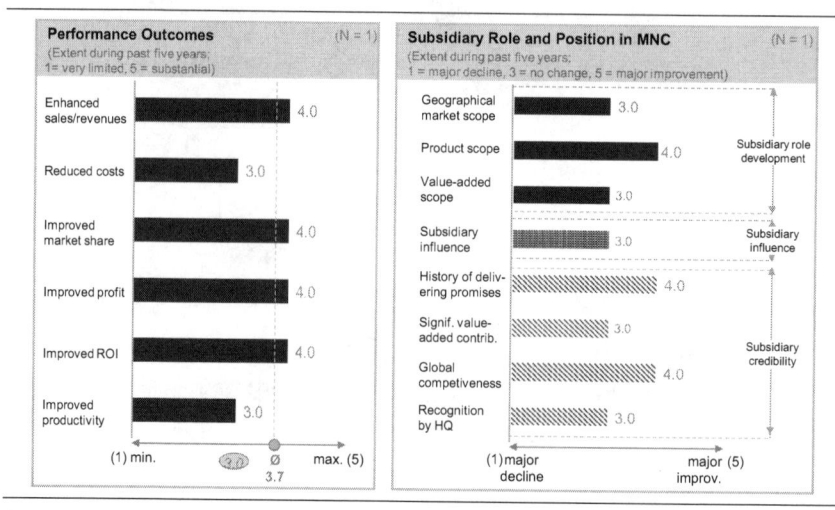

(1) major decline — major (5) improv.

Figure 5.103: Survey Results: SL – Performance outcomes and subsidiary role and position

5.2.5 Greek Subsidiary

The foreign unit located in Greece was originally founded in the late 1940s. Over the last years, Company B gradually increased its number of shares. Now it possesses the majority of the Greek subsidiary's stakes and consequently enjoys management control over the foreign entity. In 2013, close to 10,000 employees were occupied at this location and revenues of more than four billion Euros were generated that year. Except for R&D, all value chain functions are carried out locally. Products and services offered locally include, for example, fixed and mobile telephony and data services, IPTV, online platforms and services as well as a wide range of value-added services (A20, I16, S14).

5.2.5.1 Subsidiary Roles

(1) Strategic Market Importance and Subsidiary Competence: Black Hole

Based on subsidiary managers' assessments, the Greek unit can be classified as a "Black Hole" subsidiary within Telecomp. The **strategic importance of the subsidiary market** is evaluated as high with an average of 4.1 (S14), as shown in Figure 5.104. The competitive intensity, market size and customer demand intensity in particular are considered high or very high, with values ranging from 4.0 to 5.0. Moreover, the Greek unit not only serves the local market but is also engaged in business activities in other countries as well (A20, I14). With regard to competitive intensity and market dynamism, the foreign entity faces strong competition not only in its traditional fixed and mobile telephony market, but also from players in adjacent markets (A10, I14). Given the deterioration and revenue decline in its traditional fixed and mobile business, the local unit is forced to develop new opportunities outside its core business and create offerings in neighboring areas where many other players are already active and well-established (I14, 184).

As to its **resources and capabilities**, the Greek entity was rated at a low level with an average value of 3.1 (S14). Among the various resource areas, the local unit is assessed as particularly capable in the area of marketing and sales. Here, the strong brand, large customer base and customer relationships are mentioned as especially strong assets (I14). In contrast, technical expertise and knowledge in R&D are seen as very limited by subsidiary management, in part due to the lack of a technical department and local R&D activities (I14). The assessment of the remaining subsidiary resources and capabilities are displayed in Figure 5.104 below.

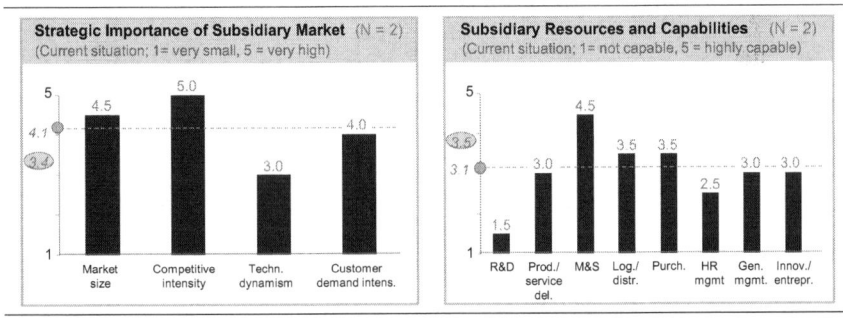

Figure 5.104: Survey Results: Greece – Strategic importance and subsidiary resources/ capabilities

(2) Subsidiary Localization and Integration: Autonomous Subsidiary

According to the survey outcomes, the Greek entity represents an "Autonomous" subsidiary. As to the first role dimension, this local affiliate exhibited a moderate degree of **localization/local responsiveness** (3.6, S14). More specifically, the country unit strongly interacted with external actors in the local market such as technology partners, vendors and competitors (I14, S14). Moreover, local content and technological dynamism are rather high, and the life cycle stage of local services is viewed as relatively immature. In comparison, the degree of **integration** is evaluated as low to moderate (2.9, S14). While many value-adding functions, such as purchasing or service delivery, were not well integrated, this was not the case with R&D or marketing. As the Greek unit does not perform R&D or product development locally, variables related to R&D, marketing and the centralization of technology indicated a somewhat higher degree of integration (all 4.0), as shown in Figure 5.105 below.

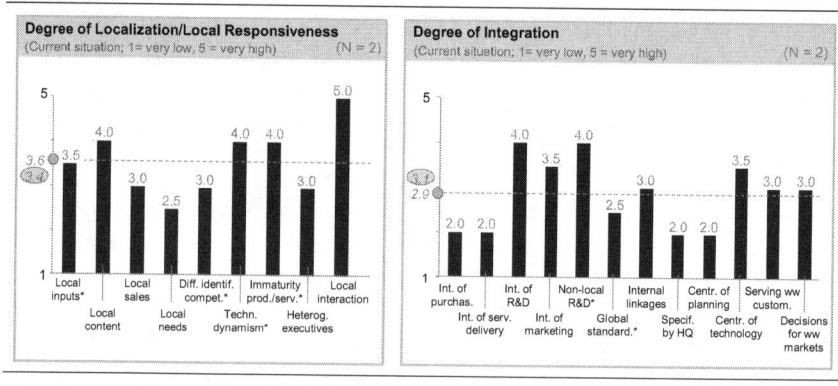

Figure 5.105: Survey Results: Greece – Subsidiary localization/local responsiveness and subsidiary integration

(3) Subsidiary Decision-Making Autonomy

The Greek unit enjoys a low to moderate degree of autonomy in comparison with other Telecomp subsidiaries (3.1, S14), as shown in Figure 5.106. While the local entity has more leeway for operational decisions, it has less autonomy concerning strategic matters such as the formulation and approval of its annual budget (3.8. vs. 2.6). With regard to new product development, the Greek unit also enjoys larger degrees of autonomy when it comes to products purely for the local market. In comparison, autonomy to change or adapt products or services developed and propagated by the corporate center is very limited, as expressed by the local subsidiary manager:

> "For the local products, we have a lot of flexibility because it's a local partner, we can, let's say, change the product. We can add new features – we can ask for new things. So there's big flexibility either from our side or from the partner side in order, let's say, to have a totally different product from ... a group product." (I14)

> "So let's say for ... a corporate project. ... there's no flexibility from their side to change the specification of the product. ... The local needs in Greece ... are different from the local needs in Czech [Republic], Austria or Netherlands. So ... the customization of these products or the extra needs that we'll have from our side in order to customize this product ... is the most difficult thing for us. ... The only thing left we can do is some very minor changes to this product. Minor changes. And this is, let's say, the most difficult thing for us." (I14).

Subsidiary Autonomy (Current situation; 1= decided centrally by HQ; 5 = decided independently by subsidiary) (N = 2)

◄────── Strategic Decisions: 2.6 ──────►   ◄────── Operational Decisions: 3.8 ──────►

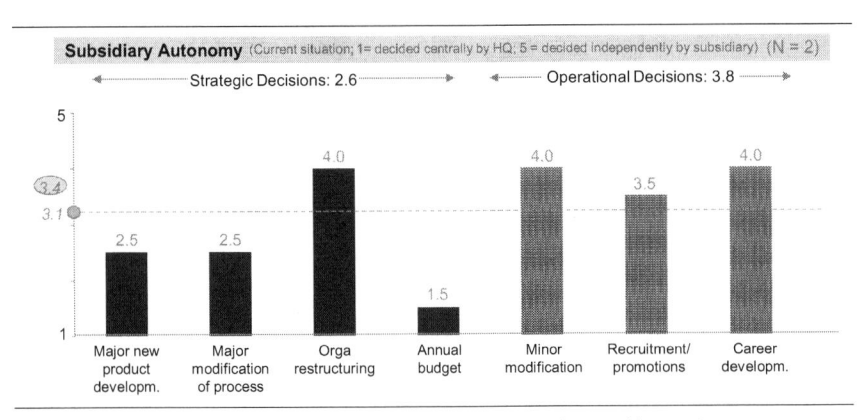

Major new product developm.	Major modification of process	Orga restructuring	Annual budget	Minor modification	Recruitment/ promotions	Career developm.
2.5	2.5	4.0	1.5	4.0	3.5	4.0

(3.4) / 3.1

Figure 5.106: Survey Results: Greece – Subsidiary decision-making autonomy

5.2.5.2 Subsidiary Initiative-Taking

(1) Entrepreneurial Resource Management

New subsidiary **opportunity identification** occurred to a low to moderate extent in the Greek entity (3.0, S14). With regard to the sources, new opportunities were identified externally more frequently than internally, particularly through interactions with local actors such as technology partners or from observation of local competitors (I14, S14). Given the saturation and decreasing revenues in its core market, the local subsidiary frequently aimed at identifying new initiative opportunities in adjacent or even new markets (I14). Internally, new initiative opportunities were often identified in the subsidiary itself (e.g. through local subsidiary experts) or through interactions with the Telecomp global product innovation team (I14, S14).

Concerning the degree of **innovativeness**, most new initiative opportunities identified by the Greek unit were assessed to be of an incremental nature. Moderately or radically innovative ideas were identified less frequently during the past five years (see Figure 5.107). According to subsidiary management, many new initiative ideas are based on existing services of other competitors in adjacent markets and are copied by the Greek entity to gain new revenues in these new markets:

> "To be honest with you, we are trying, let's say, to copy the [other] players' strategy. Okay, for example, we are focusing in music, like Apple. ... They have iTunes, so we also have a proposition from our side. We are focusing on e-books. We have the iBook proposition for example. So mainly we try to copy from our competitors – but for us, these are not the traditional telecom companies .... So we are trying to be there, and of course not to lose revenues to these players." (I14).

Identification of Subsidiary Initiative Opportunities
(Extent during past five years; 1 = never, 5 = plentifully)   (N = 2)

← Internal: 2.8 →   ← External: 3.3 →

- Only from within subsidiary: 3.5
- From HQ: 3.0
- From other units within the MNC: 2.0
- From local actors (external): 4.5
- From global actors (external): 2.0

(3.0 marker)

Innovativeness of Subsidiary Initiative Opportunities
(Extent during past five years; 1 = never, 5 = plentifully)   (N = 2)

- Incrementally innovative: 3.5
- Moderately innovative: 3.0
- Radically innovative: 2.3

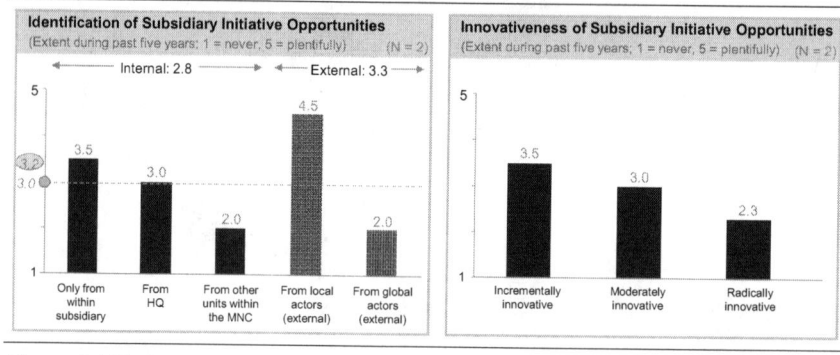

Figure 5.107: Survey Results: Greece – Identification and innovativeness of initiative opportunities

When attempting to realize and create new initiatives, the Greek subsidiary showed a low to moderate level of **resource structuring** (2.5, S14). The foreign unit strongly relied on external sources. In particular, resource acquisition from external sources was most frequent during the past five years, as can be seen in Figure 5.108. According to subsidiary management, this was often needed since the local subsidiary team has only limited knowledge of the new and adjacent markets that it plans to enter. Consequently, capabilities in the form of, for example, consultant expertise or external partner knowledge were acquired externally:

> "If we look at ... the skills of our people, they're, let's say, very – let's say my team, we have very strong skills coming only from telecom services. But we are lacking skills in many of the new areas. So let's say to identify and develop these products, we need a lot of consultants, a lot of external partners." (I14)

> "... there's a lot of local projects, but we are using some experts, some consultants coming from this area. ... We have some people working for us in order, let's say, to prepare the proposition, the product specification, the communication strategy, the go-to-market strategy, and of course the implementation." (I14)

Aside from external acquisition, joint capability development with external partners was also used to some extent (2.4, S14). Given the limited local funding of the Greek unit for new initiative opportunities, they were often developed jointly with new partners to limit financial investment and also to reduce the need to approach headquarters:

> "We don't want the new services or the new products to have an investment. So that's why we have a revenue share model with all of our partners when we try to come up with new products on our own. We don't have a capex, so we are not investing at all. ... We have a specific strategy for this one. ... We share the risk 50 percent each. We cover the costs. We cover the opex from the revenues and we do not have to ask corporate." (I14)

In addition to external acquisition and internal-external development, new resources and capabilities were also acquired and developed internally. Internal acquisition from headquarters or from other units, such as the central product development unit, was particularly relevant for initiatives identified through interactions with the corporate center. Resource acquisition from sister subsidiaries has not yet taken place but is expected to become more likely in the near future (I14:103, 111). Finally, **resource combination** took place most frequently as incremental and intermediate bundling (both 3.0), indicating the use of both existing and new resources and capabilities. Radical bundling, referring to the extensive combination of completely new resources and capabilities, was not used during the past five years (S14).

Resource Structuring Activities (Extent during past five years; 1 = never, 5 = plentifully)   (N = 2)

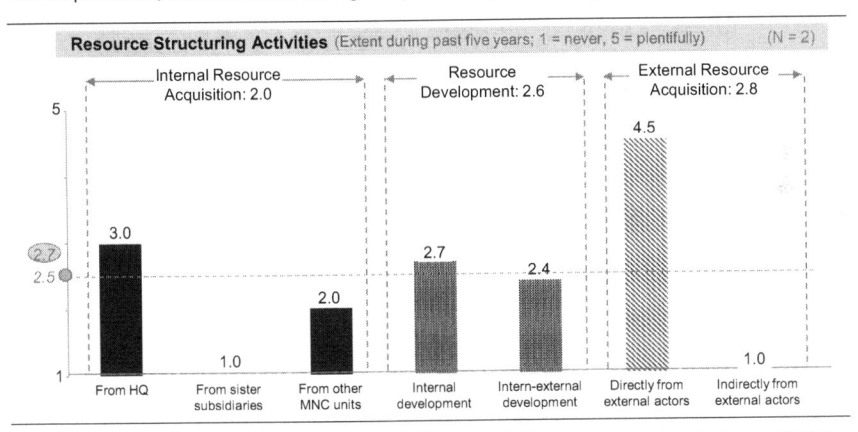

Internal Resource Acquisition: 2.0			Resource Development: 2.6		External Resource Acquisition: 2.8	
From HQ	From sister subsidiaries	From other MNC units	Internal development	Intern-external development	Directly from external actors	Indirectly from external actors
3.0	1.0	2.0	2.7	2.4	4.5	1.0

Figure 5.108: Survey Results: Greece – Initiative-related resource structuring activities

(2) Headquarters-Subsidiary Alignment

In the past five years, the Greek subsidiary experienced a high degree of **headquarters involvement** when engaging in entrepreneurial initiatives (3.8, S14). For example, the unit frequently needed to communicate with the corporate center concerning new initiative opportunities, present them to headquarters and obtain central approval:

> "Every two weeks, we have a conference call to select and see new opportunities. So if we see any opportunities coming from our group locally, we need to do a business case, in order to clarify that this project or this product will bring some extra value to us. ... We need to get the green light from [headquarters]. Then [headquarters] is directly communicating with the product innovation unit, and then we set up a team, a specific team, a local team in Greece. Plus, there is a team coming from [headquarters] and a specific team coming from our product innovation. And only then we have the execution of the product development." (I14)

In addition, the Greek entity faced a relatively high degree of **corporate resistance** when engaging in entrepreneurial activities (3.3, S14). Delay of initiatives and requests for further justification, as well as rejection by headquarters, occurred repeatedly (4.5 and 4.0). In comparison, other units of the MNC exerted less resistance through lobbying and rival initiatives or through lack of recognition of initiatives, for example (see Figure 5.109). Subsidiary management further described some distance and lack of trust by headquarters as it urged them to use existing corporate solutions where possible:

> "Let's say there is a distance and perhaps some lack of trust – and always there's the question 'Guys, we have the same solution already here [at headquarters]. Why not take our solution and you save time to find a local partner? We have already partners in [Company B]. Why not select one of these partners? Why you have to do it locally? Can we see the business case? Is there any, let's say, real opportunity? Can we have a discussion in order to present your solution?' So always there's a question. 'Why don't you take our solution, and you want to have a local solution?' So this is, let's say – it's a lot of discussion – and maybe resistance – in this area." (I14)

In order to promote initiatives in the MNC and push them further through the organizational system, the Greek subsidiary demonstrated a high level of **initiative selling** (3.4, S14). For example, it frequently attempted to lobby and sell new initiative ideas at the corporate center, attract headquarters attention, or make headquarters understand a new initiative. According to subsidiary management, it repeatedly presented new ideas to other units of the MNC:

> "I mean we have done a lot of presentations and a lot of discussions. We have presented our ideas, our propositions, our cases. And to be honest with you ... a lot of [subsidiaries] have shown a lot of interest for these propositions." (I14)

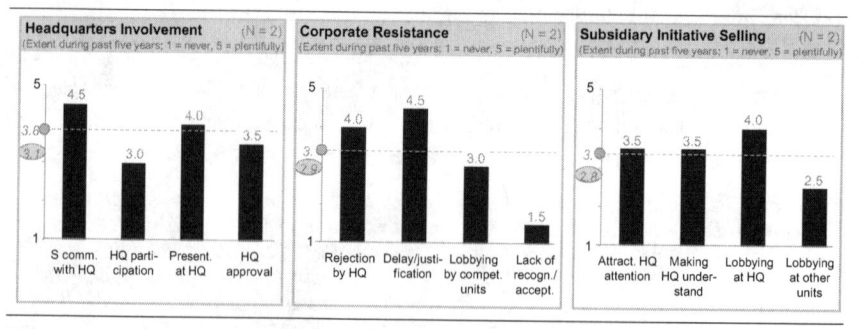

Figure 5.109: Survey Results: Greece – HQ-S alignment and interaction

5.2.5.3 Subsidiary Initiative-Taking Outcome

(1) Extent of Subsidiary Initiative-Taking

The Greek affiliate showed only a low level of subsidiary initiatives over the past five years (1.9, S14). Externally oriented initiatives were undertaken slightly more often than internally oriented ones (2.0 vs. 1.8), as presented in Figure 5.110. Of all types, local market initiatives were pursued most regularly. Examples of local market initiatives include the development of a new cloud storage solution, the introduction of e-book services and entering new market areas with the startup of insurance services (I14). Global-internal hybrid initiatives were pursued from time to time. Illustrations provided by local management included the implementation of a new mobile communication messenger that was identified as an opportunity through interactions with headquarters, the introduction of a new mobile payment system initially developed by another foreign subsidiary and the launch of a new music streaming service supported by the corporate center (I14). Aside from these initiatives types, the Greek entity engaged in a number of "trivial initiatives" that were of a more tactical nature and did not impact the wider MNC. For instance, the local organization developed a new revenue sharing model to make local collaboration with external partners more attractive, it started local initiatives to reduce costs and it developed novel promotional campaigns in one of its service areas (I14).

Subsidiary Initiative-Taking (Extent of subsidiary entrepreneurial initiatives within past five years: 1= never, 5 = plentifully) (N = 2)

◄──── External initiatives: 2.0 ────► ◄──────Internal initiatives: 1.8──────►

- Global market initiatives: 1.0
- Local market initiatives: 3.0
- Internal market initiatives: 1.5
- Global-Internal hybrid initiatives: 2.0

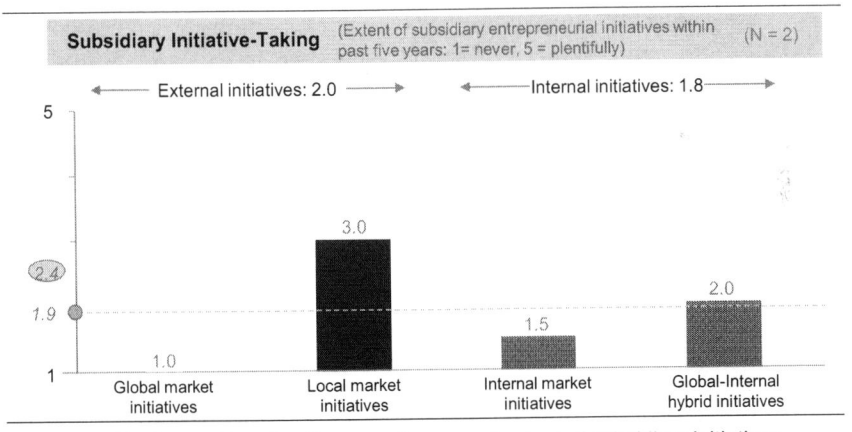

Overall: 2.4 / 1.9

Figure 5.110: Survey Results: Greece – Types and extent of subsidiary initiatives

(2) Resource-Related Outcomes

As a consequence of the small number of entrepreneurial subsidiary initiatives, few new resources and capabilities were developed in the foreign subsidiary (2.4, S14). New resources were obtained particularly in the areas of service delivery and marketing/sales. Only resources from these two areas were also of use for the wider MNC (3.5 and 3.0), as shown in Figure 5.111. For example, the initiative related to e-book services together with an external actor not only strengthened this partnership but also generated new market insights and expertise for the Greek unit. Moreover, the experiences were shared with other foreign subsidiaries that signaled strong interest in joining the partnership and in creating a similar solution in their countries (I14).

New Subsidiary Resources and Capabilities (N = 2)
(Extent during past five years; 1= no capability development at all, 5 = extensive capability development)

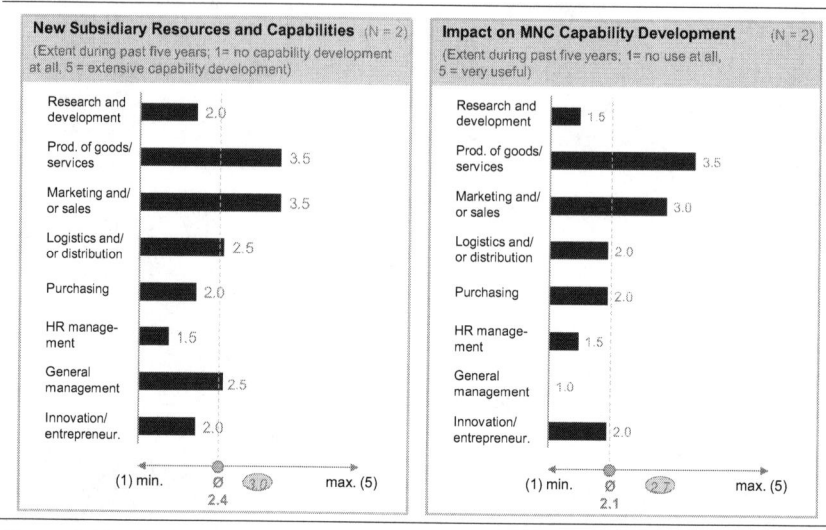

Research and development	2.0
Prod. of goods/services	3.5
Marketing and/or sales	3.5
Logistics and/or distribution	2.5
Purchasing	2.0
HR management	1.5
General management	2.5
Innovation/entrepreneur.	2.0

(1) min. ⌀ 2.4 max. (5)

Impact on MNC Capability Development (N = 2)
(Extent during past five years; 1= no use at all, 5 = very useful)

Research and development	1.5
Prod. of goods/services	3.5
Marketing and/or sales	3.0
Logistics and/or distribution	2.0
Purchasing	2.0
HR management	1.5
General management	1.0
Innovation/entrepreneur.	2.0

(1) min. ⌀ 2.1 max. (5)

Figure 5.111: Survey Results: Greece – New subsidiary resources and impact on MNC capabilities

(3) Further Outcomes

The few entrepreneurial initiatives also positively impacted certain subsidiary performance aspects. For example, the Greek unit achieved small improvements in revenues, market share and profits. Additionally, select facets of the subsidiary role and position were slightly enhanced, such as the product scope and the unit's recognition as a strategically important unit (see Figure 5.112 below). According to local management, the entrepreneurial initiatives helped not only to improve the subsidiary position in the multinational firm but also to prove their capabilities to the corporate center. Consequently, the local unit expects more corporate investment through product trials and pilots in the country:

> "We could show that we have the technical capability to support such kind of a trial. So it was one thing. And the second thing ... the guys from [headquarters] are very confident because Greece has shown that is an appropriate [subsidiary] in order to try this important trial." (I14)

Performance Outcomes (N = 2)
(Extent during past five years; 1 = very limited, 5 = substantial)

Enhanced sales/revenues	2.5
Reduced costs	1.5
Improved market share	2.5
Improved profit	2.5
Improved ROI	2.0
Improved productivity	2.0
Ø	2.1

Subsidiary Role and Position in MNC (N = 2)
(Extent during past five years; 1 = major decline, 3 = no change, 5 = major improvement)

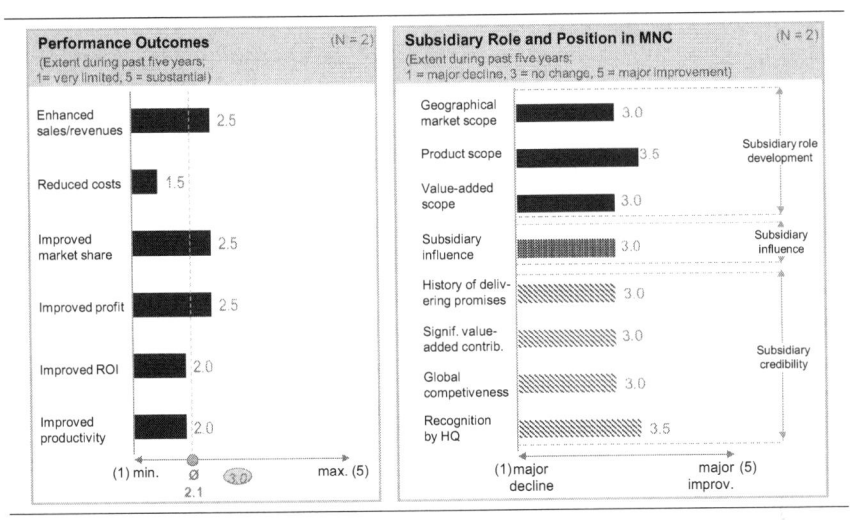

Aspect	Value	Category
Geographical market scope	3.0	Subsidiary role development
Product scope	3.5	Subsidiary role development
Value-added scope	3.0	Subsidiary role development
Subsidiary influence	3.0	Subsidiary influence
History of delivering promises	3.0	Subsidiary credibility
Signif. value-added contrib.	3.0	Subsidiary credibility
Global competitiveness	3.0	Subsidiary credibility
Recognition by HQ	3.5	Subsidiary credibility

Figure 5.112: Survey Results: Greece – Performance outcomes and subsidiary role and position

5.2.6 Romanian Subsidiary

The Romanian subsidiary of Telecomp was first established in the early 1990s. Company B gradually acquired shares in the Romanian units and since the late 2000s has owned a majority and hence held management control over the foreign entity. In 2013, the Romanian subsidiary had close to 8,000 employees and achieved revenues of approximately one billion euros. Among its core services are fixed telephony, internet and television, mobile telephony and internet as well as information and telecommunication solutions in the Romanian market. In addition to these main offerings, the subsidiary also develops and manages value-added services that are bundled with the core services, for instance internet services or internet content. Except for R&D, all main value chain functions are currently carried out at the location, such as service delivery, marketing and sales, purchasing and HR management (A21, I15, S15). With regard to geographical scope, the foreign unit is responsible only for activities within the Romanian market. However, some new services, process approaches or best practices that are developed locally can be and have been shared with other units of the group (I15).

5.2.6.1 Subsidiary Roles

(1) Strategic Market Importance and Subsidiary Competence: Implementer

Within Telecomp, the Romanian subsidiary can be classified as an "Implementer," given the low strategic importance of its market and the low level of subsidiary resources and capabilities (3.0 and 3.1, S15). Regarding the **strategic importance of the subsidiary market**, only the competitive intensity is assessed as high (I15, S15). The main competitors in the Romanian market are considered to be more capable because of, for example, their more advanced network infrastructure and wider network coverage than the Romanian Telecomp unit (I15). The market size and technical dynamism are seen as moderate. The weak economic situations, the entrance of new competitors into the market, and increased price pressure have resulted in an overall shrinking market size in recent years (I15). The level of **subsidiary resources and capabilities** is rated low. Only those in marketing in sales are considered high. All other areas were assessed as moderate or, in the case of purchasing, low. For example, the technical infrastructure and capabilities are, in comparison to the competition, described as weak, with the Romanian unit currently investing aggressively to catch up (I15). Moreover, local purchasing activities are closely integrated with the rest of the MNC with the aim to achieve lower prices through bundling effects (I15).

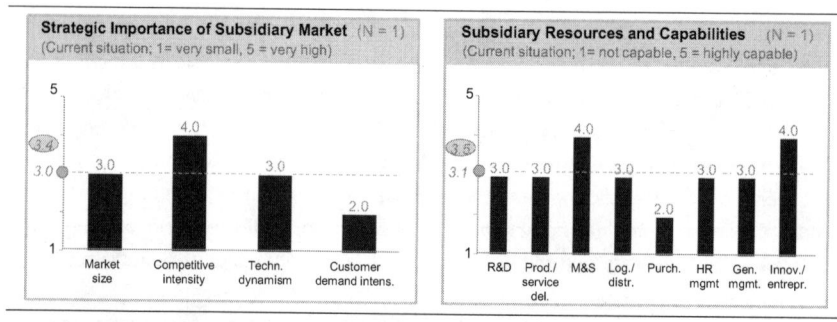

Figure 5.113: Survey Results: ROM – Strategic importance and subsidiary resources/capabilities

(2) Subsidiary Localization and Integration: Quiescent Subsidiary

Based on the assessment by subsidiary managers, the local entity represents a "Quiescent" subsidiary, as both the degree of localization/local responsiveness and the degree of integration were assigned comparatively low average scores. More specifically, the **degree of localization/local responsiveness** was given a mean average score of 3.0 (S15). Only technological dynamism and the immaturity of technology and service delivery sophistication were assessed as high, while all other variables received lower scores. For example, given the low degree of market fragmentation, competitors and their strategies are easily identified by the Romanian unit. According to local management, information on the market distribution and market share of all major players is easily available. Likewise, current competitors' footprints and network structure are relatively easy to identify (I15). The **degree of integration** also received a relatively low score (2.7, S15), as shown in Figure 5.114. Here, most variables indicate low integration of the Romanian unit in the wider MNC, with the exception of purchasing integration and the centralization of technology in the group (both 4.0). However, attempts to integrate purchasing activities more strongly and to centralize technology development were undertaken only very recently by headquarters (I15).

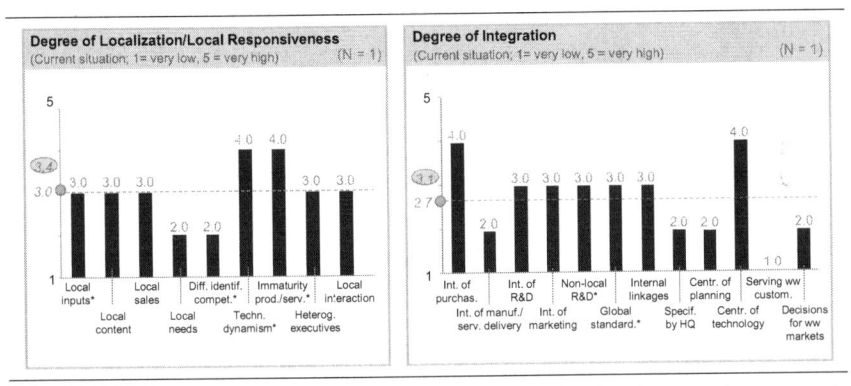

Figure 5.114: Survey Results: ROM – Subsidiary localization/local responsiveness and subsidiary integration

-Making Autonomy

Overall, the Romanian unit has a low degree of decision-making autonomy when compared to other Telecomp subsidiaries (2.9, S15). While it has more leeway for operational decisions, its freedom on the strategic level is much more limited (3.7 vs. 2.3, S15), as shown in Figure 5.115. For example, with regard to new product development, the local organization has some autonomy to partially modify or adapt services to local needs or even to decide the annual product roadmap for Romania (S15). However, when it comes to major product adaptions or projects that require large capital expenditures, then the subsidiary decision-making autonomy is much more restricted, as described by local management:

> "Okay. So we have quite high level of independence in developing and deciding the actual local product growth map. But, of course, what is very under much group control, it's the budget, right?" (I15)

> *"If you have significant investment, of course, you will need to be very well aligned with headquarters. And one of the significant projects is ... very well ... followed-up or closely steered by the headquarters."* (I15)

Subsidiary Autonomy (Current situation; 1= decided centrally by HQ; 5 = decided independently by subsidiary) (N = 1)

◄──── Strategic Decisions: 2.3 ────► ◄──── Operational Decisions: 3.7 ────►

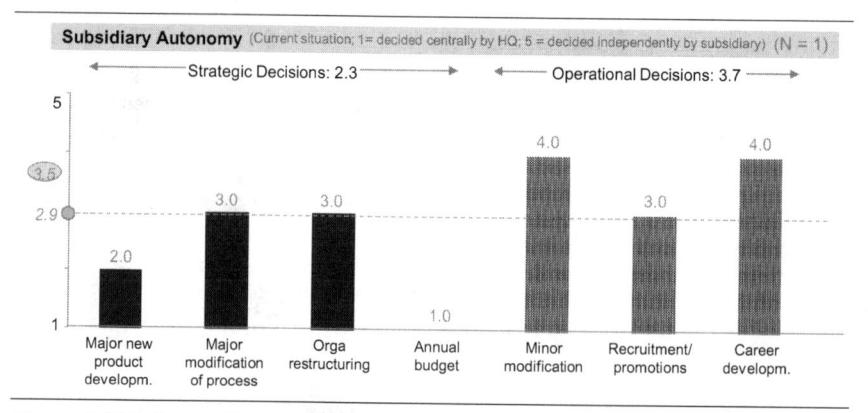

Major new product developm.	2.0
Major modification of process	3.0
Orga restructuring	3.0
Annual budget	1.0
Minor modification	4.0
Recruitment/ promotions	3.0
Career developm.	4.0

Figure 5.115: Survey Results: ROM – Subsidiary decision-making autonomy

5.2.6.2 Subsidiary Initiative-Taking

(1) Entrepreneurial Resource Management

In comparison to the other Telecomp subsidiaries, the Romanian affiliate displayed a low level of new **initiative opportunity identification** during the past five years (2.8, S15). New opportunities were detected internally more often than externally (3.0 vs. 2.5), as shown in Figure 5.116. Internally, the majority of new initiative opportunities were detected within the subsidiary itself, but many were also regularly identified through interactions with other players from within the MNC, such as the center of excellence for with regard to video services in Hungary (I15, S15). Although most new initiative detection occurred internally, interactions with local actors outside the MNC also played an important role. According to Romanian subsidiary management, external partnering is becoming increasingly relevant in the industry, as it helps not only to better identify new trends or opportunities but also to share risks and investments with external parties. Furthermore, only a small fraction of newly identified opportunities make it to realization, as described below:

> *"There is a very – let's say – growing trend of partnering with external players within the technology value chain, because honestly, there's not so much innovation detected internally within [our industry]. ... So the detection of new innovation tends to happen in more technology and internet-oriented companies. [Companies as ours] are partnering with the smaller innovation focused companies and jointly deliver innovations to the actual end users."* (I15)

"There are more, much more [opportunities identified], but they are not necessarily executed. ... I would say that from the actual proposals like 20 percent get done. But you know ... the ideas ... are filtered already ... I don't think it's that high a percentage, because it's not like, we're not like Google trying many ideas and then come up with five percent of them in actual product. We need to be much more efficient because we don't have the luxury of experimenting that much." (I15)

Concerning their **innovativeness**, most new initiative opportunities were characterized as incrementally innovative. Moderately or radically new opportunities were identified less frequently by the Romanian unit, as shown in Figure 5.116.

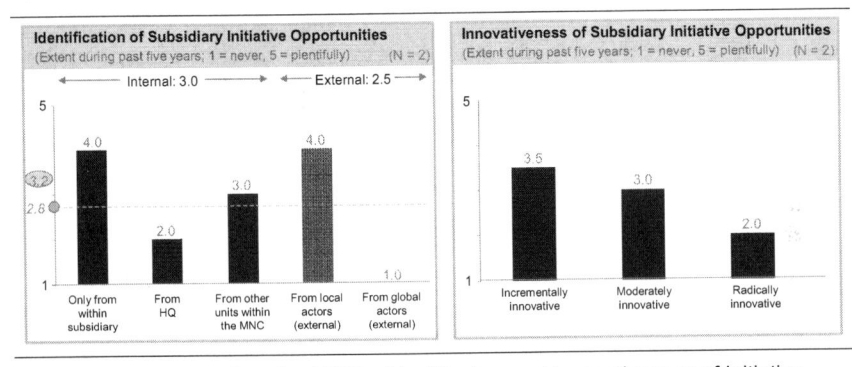

Figure 5.116: Survey Results: ROM – Identification and innovativeness of initiative opportunities

Over the course of realizing initiatives, the Romanian affiliate engaged in a comparatively low level of **resource structuring** (2.4, S15). The foreign subsidiary employed a wider range of internal and external structuring approaches, such as internal and external resource acquisition (both 2.0), as well as resource development within the subsidiary (2.6) or in collaboration with external partners (2.4). Internal resources related to initiative implementation were developed, for example, within the subsidiary's IT department or together with the Telecomp engineering department (I15). Moreover, external collaborations with local actors are frequently used to jointly develop new resources and capabilities when pursuing entrepreneurial projects, as indicated in one example cited below. Subsequently, the various resources were **bundled together** to realize new initiatives. Here, the Romanian affiliate applied only incremental and intermediate bundling (both 3.0), while radical bundling did not take place in the past five years.

"For example, this service, this over-the-top service ... was done in partnership with the technology company that had such an initiative. But they didn't have the right content; they had the technology of delivering the video content via Internet. So we partnered with them and we did it together." (I15)

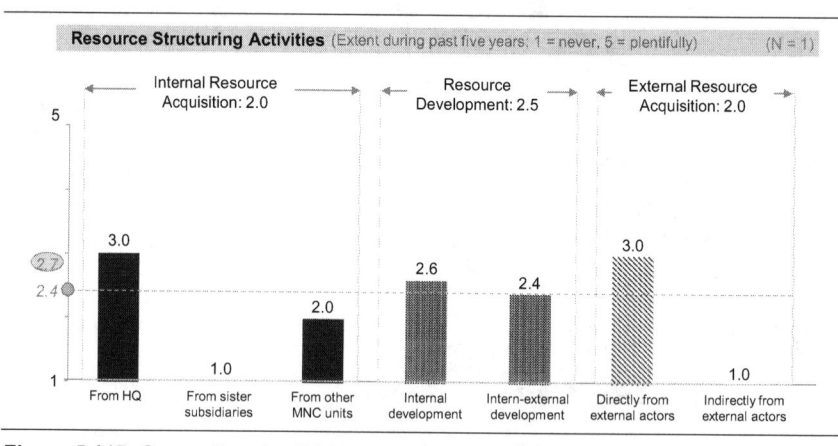

Figure 5.117: Survey Results: ROM – Initiative-related resource structuring activities

Bar chart data:
- Internal Resource Acquisition: 2.0
  - From HQ: 3.0
  - From sister subsidiaries: 1.0
  - From other MNC units: 2.0
- Resource Development: 2.5
  - Internal development: 2.6
  - Intern-external development: 2.4
- External Resource Acquisition: 2.0
  - Directly from external actors: 3.0
  - Indirectly from external actors: 1.0

(Dashed reference line at 2.7 / 2.4)

(2) Headquarters-Subsidiary Alignment

Throughout the initiative-taking activities of the Romanian unit, corporate **headquarters was involved** to a moderate degree (3.3, S15). This involvement often materialized in the form of frequent communication regarding new opportunities and repeated presentations of new initiatives by the subsidiary to the corporate center. For example, new initiatives of a larger scale or with potential relevance for other MNC units were presented in bi-weekly alignment calls with headquarters and other foreign subsidiaries (I15). In other cases, new technology ideas that were identified in Romania were further refined and then presented to the relevant center of excellence as the "*centralizing body that assesses and approves technological developments in the subsidiaries*" (I15).[442] However, headquarters involvement also differed depending on the initiative type. Smaller initiatives, for instance, requiring little investment could be pursued without headquarters involvement or even without their awareness, as described below:

> "If we have product initiatives that don't require significant investments, of course, you will be – let's put it like that, below the radar, right? ... If you have significant investment, of course, you will need to be very well aligned with headquarters." (I15)

> "If you're talking about very important projects that involve many resources and lots of investment, it's only natural that the group deeply is involved. ... This is why ... we're focusing on external partnering and revenue sharing in as many cases as we can." (I15)

---

[442] Before presenting an initiative to the center of excellence, the Romanian subsidiary would commonly first conduct some market research, define the business and marketing requirements, design a basic solution and calculate estimated costs (I15).

The level of **corporate resistance** to initiatives undertaken by the Romanian unit was rated relatively high (3.5, S15). Resistance only seldom took the form of direct rejection by the corporate center, and more commonly occurred as delay of initiatives and requests for greater justification, lobbying and rival initiatives by competing units, and lack of recognition and acceptance by other units in the group (see Figure 5.118).

> "Of course there were cases of resistance. It's not always explicitly stated as such, so you can only guess in some cases what the reasons behind it were. As you can imagine that there are sometimes competing solutions for a specific problem in the group, right?" (I15)

Lastly, the foreign affiliate showed a high level of **subsidiary initiative-selling** activities over the five-year period (3.3, S15). Based on the survey results, this often involved lobbying and selling at the corporate center and attempts to make the corporate center better understand an opportunity. For this purpose, the foreign subsidiary not only determined the resource need and developed the financial business case, but it also tried to highlight and sell the concrete benefits of the initiative to the wider MNC:

> "And for each initiative, you are ... assessing the resources needed, and, of course, build the business case around it – which should be approved. And based on that business case, the budget will be allocated [from headquarters]." (I15)

> "Basically, you don't start with such a deep analysis, right? You have more of a sales pitch. So you're proposing – you're showcasing the product or the solution's highlights and benefits in terms of, I don't know, customer satisfaction potential, sales, retention or maybe savings that you can come up versus other previous technology for solutions, for example. So you're proposing you're showcasing this benefit and then also the business model behind it." (I15)

According to the local management, it was typically more difficult to obtain headquarters approval for radical initiatives, such as the introduction of solutions that were new to the Romanian market or in which the subsidiary was *"first-to-market."* Initiatives that required significant investments were also often harder to sell to the corporate center. In comparison, initiatives that required little investment could be pursued without any major selling and lobbying activities, *"under the radar."* In addition, selling initiatives and obtaining corporate buy-in was argued to work *"best by successfully piloting something with a partner"* and then submitting the successful case to corporate management (I15).

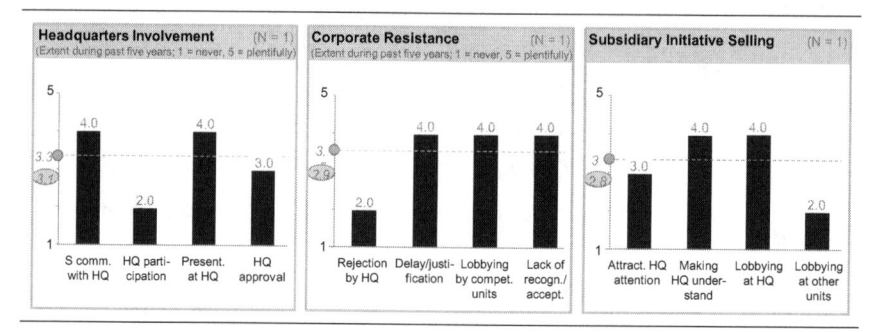

Figure 5.118: Survey Results: ROM – HQ-S alignment and interaction

5.2.6.3 Subsidiary Initiative-Taking Outcome

(1) Extent of Subsidiary Initiative-Taking

Overall, the Romanian affiliate exhibited a low level of subsidiary initiatives during the past five years (1.9, S15), as indicated in Figure 5.119. Although the foreign organization identified a number of initiative opportunities, only about one-fifth were successfully implemented in the end (I15). Of these, internally oriented initiatives were slightly more prevalent than external ones (2.0 vs. 1.8). Internally, global-internal hybrid initiatives were pursued most frequently, with the subsidiary having repeatedly bid successfully for corporate investment. For instance, the Romanian unit was able to convince headquarters to provide funding support for local network infrastructure investments (I15). Externally, the local unit engaged in local market initiatives occasionally (2.0). Examples provided by subsidiary management include the development of a novel marketing approach for IPTV services that was later transferred to sister subsidiaries abroad, and the introduction of a new over-the-top video service in collaboration with a local partner (I15). In addition, a number of "trivial initiatives" were pursued that were more operational in nature and mainly affected the local unit; these included the recent technical changes to some of their locally provided IPTV services and changes of local vendors (I15).

Subsidiary Initiative-Taking (Extent of subsidiary entrepreneurial initiatives within past five years: 1= never, 5 = plentifully) (N = 1)

◄── External initiatives: 1.8 ──► ◄── Internal initiatives: 2.0 ──►

- Global market initiatives: 1.5
- Local market initiatives: 2.0
- Internal market initiatives: 1.5
- Global-Internal hybrid initiatives: 2.5

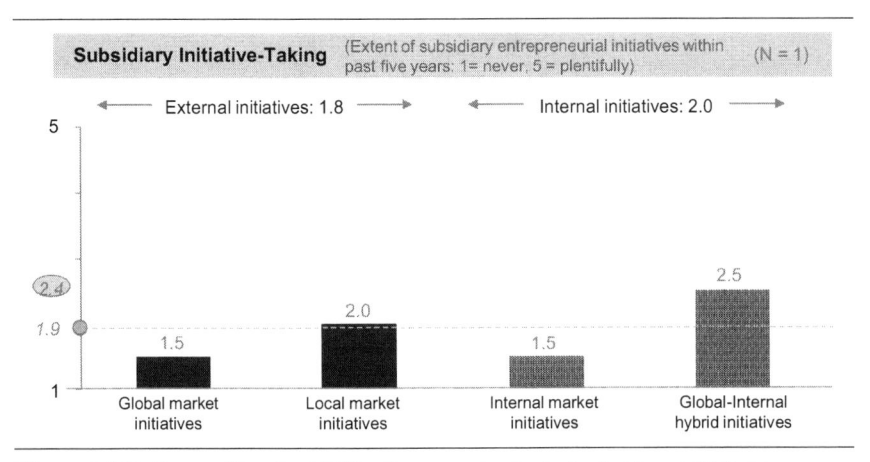

(2.4)
1.9

Figure 5.119: Survey Results: ROM – Types and extent of subsidiary initiatives

(2) Resource-Related Outcomes

The Romanian subsidiary developed a relatively low level of new resources and capabilities from its entrepreneurial initiatives (2.5, S15), as shown in Figure 5.120. With the exception of marketing and sales, no specialized resources were developed in the foreign unit over the past five years. Resources developed in most areas were of little use for other MNC units, but again with the exception of marketing and sales. For example, the novel marketing approach developed locally in Romania could later also be applied in other MNC units, as described in the previous section. However, most new insights and expertise developed locally were shared in the form of "best practices" within the MNC network rather than transferred in the form of new products and services to other locations.

> "So it's been, in my view, the most dynamic field, to couple the over-the-top TV and video services, again a very dynamic area in which best practices can be shared. But if we are talking about developing an actual service that can be then federated across the subsidiaries, this is not the case that often." (I15)

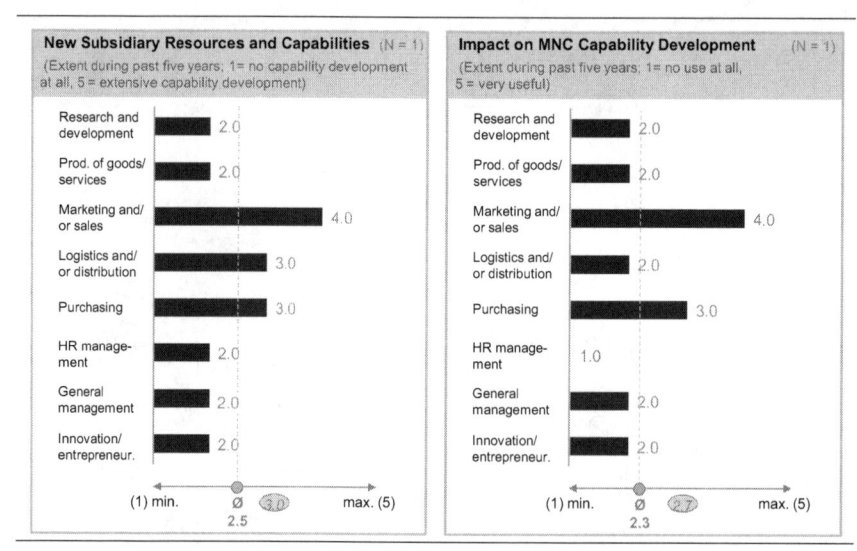

New Subsidiary Resources and Capabilities (N = 1)	Impact on MNC Capability Development (N = 1)
(Extent during past five years; 1= no capability development at all, 5 = extensive capability development)	(Extent during past five years; 1= no use at all, 5 = very useful)

Area	New Subsidiary Resources and Capabilities	Impact on MNC Capability Development
Research and development	2.0	2.0
Prod. of goods/services	2.0	2.0
Marketing and/or sales	4.0	4.0
Logistics and/or distribution	3.0	2.0
Purchasing	3.0	3.0
HR management	2.0	1.0
General management	2.0	2.0
Innovation/entrepreneur.	2.0	2.0
Ø	2.5	2.3

Figure 5.120: Survey Results: ROM – New subsidiary resources and impact on MNC capabilities

(3) Further Outcomes

As to **performance outcomes**, entrepreneurial initiatives mainly led to improvements in sales, market share and costs (see Figure 5.121). With regard to the Romanian **subsidiary's role and position** in the MNC, the foreign entity did advance its product scope and select aspects of its credibility in the wider MNC, as illustrated in Figure 5.121. According to subsidiary management, the entrepreneurial initiatives also helped improve the relationship with the corporate center. Moreover, the stronger collaboration with other units of the MNC led to a better understanding of the subsidiary's roles and responsibilities and brought more transparency on the competencies distributed across the multinational firm (I15).

Performance Outcomes (N = 1)
(Extent during past five years;
1= very limited, 5 = substantial)

- Enhanced sales/revenues: 3.0
- Reduced costs: 3.0
- Improved market share: 3.0
- Improved profit: 2.0
- Improved ROI: 2.0
- Improved productivity: 2.0

(1) min. — Ø 2.5 — max. (5)

Subsidiary Role and Position in MNC (N = 1)
(Extent during past five years;
1 = major decline, 3 = no change, 5 = major improvement)

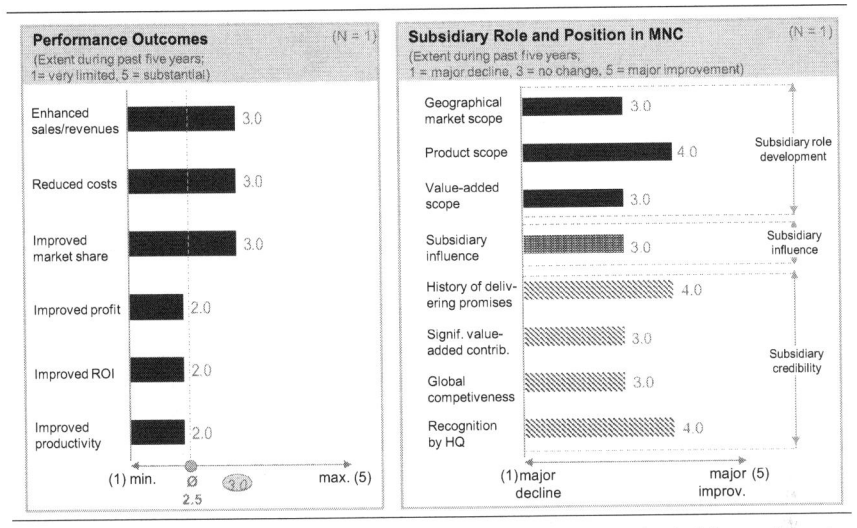

- Geographical market scope: 3.0 — Subsidiary role development
- Product scope: 4.0
- Value-added scope: 3.0
- Subsidiary influence: 3.0 — Subsidiary influence
- History of delivering promises: 4.0
- Signif. value-added contrib.: 3.0 — Subsidiary credibility
- Global competiveness: 3.0
- Recognition by HQ: 4.0

(1) major decline — major (5) improv.

Figure 5.121: Survey Results: ROM – Performance outcomes and subsidiary role and position

5.2.7 Montenegrin Subsidiary

The Montenegrin unit was first established in the late 1990s, and by the mid-2000s company B had obtained full control over the foreign entity by acquiring the majority of shares. With revenues of approximately 100 million Euros and close to 1,000 employees in 2013, the unit is the smallest Telecomp subsidiary in this study. Products offered locally include fixed and mobile telephony, broadband internet and IPTV products and services (A22). Only select value-adding functions are performed locally, such as service delivery, marketing and sales and customer service (S16). With regard to entrepreneurial and innovative activities, the Montenegrin organization is considered to be among the less active in the wider Telecomp organization (I9, I16). However, given declining revenues and increasing regulation in its core business, the subsidiary has been facing increasing pressure to innovate and enter new or adjacent market areas to compensate for the revenue losses (I16). Given its small size, its flexibility and the possibility to implement new initiatives quickly, the subsidiary has also been selected by headquarters as a pilot country to test a new product for the wider multinational group (I16).

5.2.7.1 Subsidiary Roles

(1) Strategic Market Importance and Subsidiary Competence: Implementer

Subsidiary assessment suggests that the Montenegrin unit represents an "Implementer" subsidiary within Telecomp, as both the strategic importance of the subsidiary market and the level of subsidiary resources and capabilities received comparatively low scores (2.5 and 2.6, S16). As concerns the **strategic importance of the subsidiary market**, the local market size in particular is assessed as small, with the local affiliate being responsible only for the small Montenegrin market and as such representing the smallest Telecomp operation in this respect (I16, S16). Furthermore, the customer demand intensity is considered relatively low while the competitive intensity and the technological dynamism are seen as somewhat stronger. Based on subsidiary management's response, the small size and the limited growth potential of the market allow the local unit to drive only limited innovative activities (I16).

The **subsidiary resources and capabilities** were generally assessed at a low level (2.6, S16), especially in R&D, purchasing and HR management, while the remaining value-adding functions are evaluated as moderate. In the interview, the local management furthermore highlighted product development, IT, external partnerships, and the strong brand as areas with higher resources and capabilities (I16).

Strategic Importance of Subsidiary Market (N = 1)
(Current situation; 1= very small, 5 = very high)

- Overall: 2.5
- Market size: 2.0
- Competitive intensity: 3.0
- Techn. dynamism: 3.0
- Customer demand intens.: 2.0

Subsidiary Resources and Capabilities (N = 1)
(Current situation; 1= not capable, 5 = highly capable)

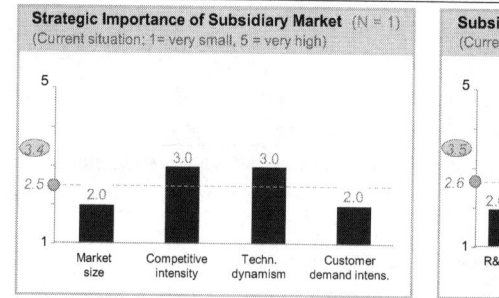

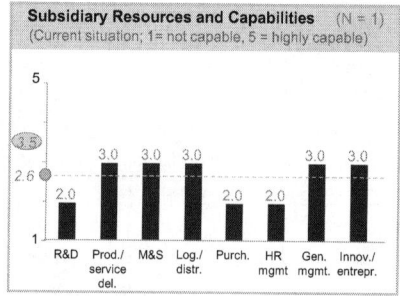

- Overall: 2.6
- R&D: 2.0
- Prod./service del.: 3.0
- M&S: 3.0
- Log./distr.: 3.0
- Purch.: 2.0
- HR mgmt: 2.0
- Gen. mgmt.: 3.0
- Innov./entrepr.: 3.0

Figure 5.122: Survey Results: MON – Strategic importance and subsidiary resources/capabilities

(2) Subsidiary Localization and Integration: Quiescent Subsidiary

Regarding the role dimensions of subsidiary localization/local responsiveness and subsidiary integration, the foreign affiliate in Montenegro can be classified as a "Quiescent Subsidiary" based on the survey results. With an average value of 2.9 (S16), the **degree of localization/local responsiveness** is somewhat low. While local content in locally delivered services, local sales of total sales, and local interactions were assessed as high (all 4.0), the remaining variables indicate moderate or low localization, as shown in Figure 5.123. Similarly, with an average of 2.8, the **degree of subsidiary integration** is also rated rather low (S16). Most variables indicate a low degree of integration, with the exceptions of purchasing activities, non-local R&D input and the centralization of technology.

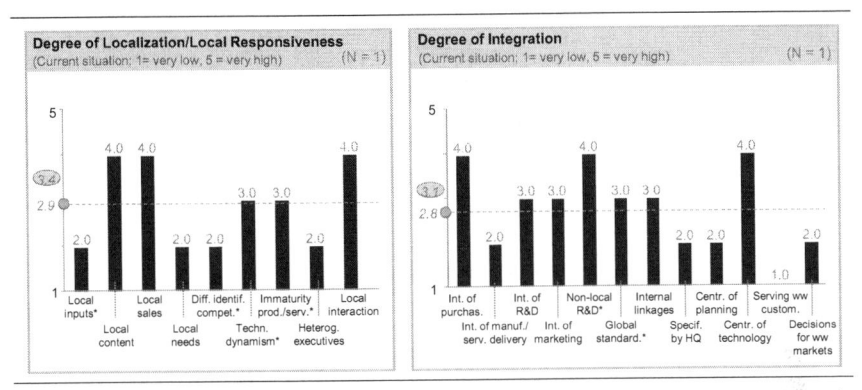

Figure 5.123: Survey Results: MON – Subsidiary localization/local responsiveness and subsidiary integration

(3) Subsidiary Decision-Making Autonomy

The foreign subsidiary in Montenegro has a relatively low level of decision-making autonomy (3.0, S16). However, the local entity can decide largely independently on operational decisions such as minor but significant modifications to existing products or career development plans (see Figure 5.124). In contrast, the foreign unit has much less leeway for strategic decisions (2.3, S16). As was further explained by local management, the overall financial targets and the budget are set centrally by headquarters. Similarly, larger and capital-intense projects are often also managed and steered by the corporate center. In comparison, many decisions on local activities, such as smaller product adaptations or changes to local vendors, can be made locally without headquarters involvement (I16).

> *"Especially, say, for larger capital expense operations, large network or technology investments, this usually needs to be consulted and approved by [headquarters] because of the wider implications ... For partnerships or local innovations, they don't care that ... there we need to consult them less ..."* (I16)

Subsidiary Autonomy (Current situation; 1= decided centrally by HQ; 5 = decided independently by subsidiary) (N = 1)

← Strategic Decisions: 2.3 →   ← Operational Decisions: 4.0 →

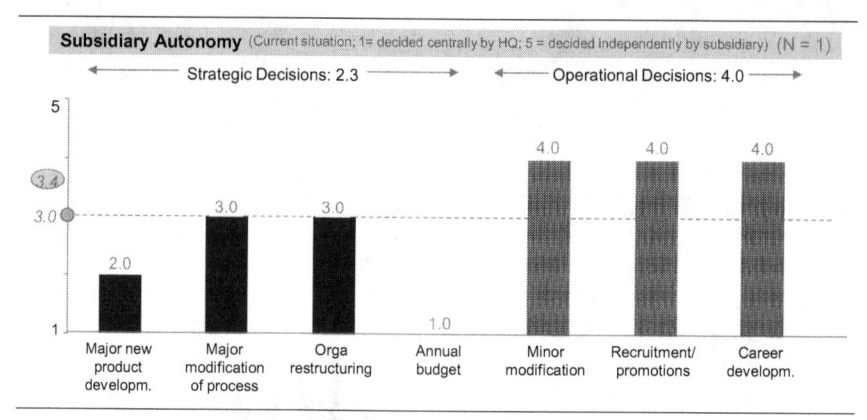

Major new product developm.	2.0
Major modification of process	3.0
Orga restructuring	3.0
Annual budget	1.0
Minor modification	4.0
Recruitment/ promotions	4.0
Career developm.	4.0

(Ø 3.4)

Figure 5.124: Survey Results: MON – Subsidiary decision-making autonomy

5.2.7.2 Subsidiary Initiative-Taking

(1) Entrepreneurial Resource Management

During the past five years, the Montenegrin unit exhibited a low level of new **initiative opportunity identification** (2.6, S16). New opportunities were more frequently identified internally than externally (3.0 vs. 2.0), as presented in Figure 5.125. Internally, most new opportunities were discovered within the foreign unit itself. According to local management, one way of coming up with new ideas was by conducting external market analyses, identifying customer spend and needs and matching this with subsidiary strengths and capabilities. Another way new opportunities were internally discovered was through management meetings on strategic issues that took place once or twice per year. Lastly, some opportunities were identified more ad-hoc and as part of day-to-day operations (I16).

> "Let's say one or two times per year we meet and talk about strategic issues in Romania and develop new ideas. But we also discuss, let's say, these – I would call them smaller strategic initiatives, but that are also important for our organization." (I16)

> "And the other is, I guess, more day-to-day in terms of when we see that there is a potential to quickly do something which would result in a new thing." (I16)

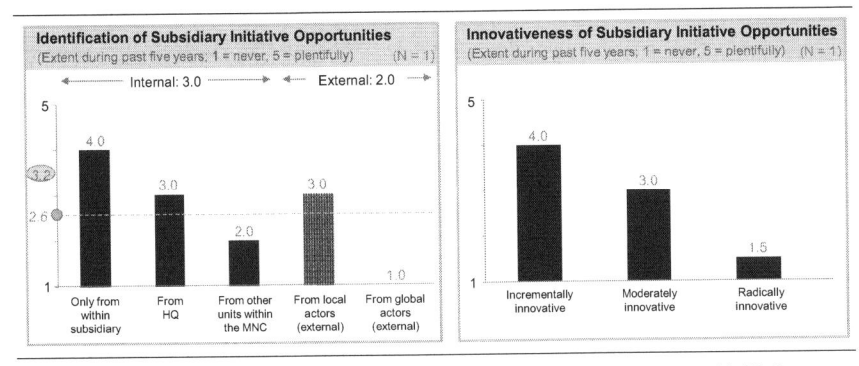

Figure 5.125: Survey Results: MON – Identification and innovativeness of initiative opportunities

As to their **innovativeness,** the majority of newly identified opportunities were incrementally innovative in nature. Less often, new initiative ideas were moderately or, very seldom, radically innovative, as seen in Figure 5.125. Given the maturity of technology and solutions in the core business, opportunities for more radical solutions emerged rarely in this area. Furthermore, given declining market share and revenues in its core business, the local entity attempted to identify new opportunities and adjacent business areas. However, due to its limited experience in these new areas, new ideas often concerned only smaller changes or innovations:

> "Okay, so our core services are not generally the area where there is much innovation or initiatives done. ... So in the core business it is more about smaller changes to existing stuff. You know, to be more in line with market view one cannot invent more fixed minutes in the fixed phone business or improve internet speed over and over. This only happens, let's say, once or twice in a generation." (I16)

> "But most of our initiatives come from these near-core, adjacent areas to classic business .... This is something where we focus our efforts a lot in order to invest in some new stuff. But here were don't have much experience, so often this is not necessarily completely new stuff that was never heard about before in the world; it could just be some new business model or smaller change." (I16)

Overall, the foreign subsidiary in Montenegro engaged only to a low degree in **resource structuring** activities, (2.4, S16). As ways to obtain the resources and capabilities needed to realize initiatives, it primarily used internal resource acquisition from headquarters, internal resource development and resource development in collaboration with external partners (see Figure 5.126). Given the previous experience of headquarters in many areas, the local unit frequently reached out to obtain central support. Resources obtained from the corporate center included, for instance, financial resources or knowledge and expertise or technology in select areas:

"Mostly financial resources, expertise, best practice sharing and something like this. Because not all the stuff that we do is completely new to the world, but it usually has been done somewhere or we have something to gain from inside the father company. So we usually approach them and, okay, you know, there are some things or ideas that we want to -- that we know that are important. So pay TV is a very important area; mobile broad band is a really important area for the entire ... group. And in those areas it is easier to get central resources and support." (I16)

Finally, the various resources and capabilities were **combined** to realize and implement the entrepreneurial initiatives. This regularly took the form of incremental bundling of existing resources and capabilities (4.0). Less often it occurred as intermediate bundling (2.0), and never in the form of radical bundling during the past five years.

Resource Structuring Activities (Extent during past five years; 1 = never, 5 = plentifully)							(N = 1)
Internal Resource Acquisition: 2.3			Resource Development: 2.6		External Resource Acquisition: 1.5		
From HQ	From sister subsidiaries	From other MNC units	Internal development	Intern-external development	Directly from external actors	Indirectly from external actors	
3.0	2.0	2.0	2.9	2.3	2.0	1.0	

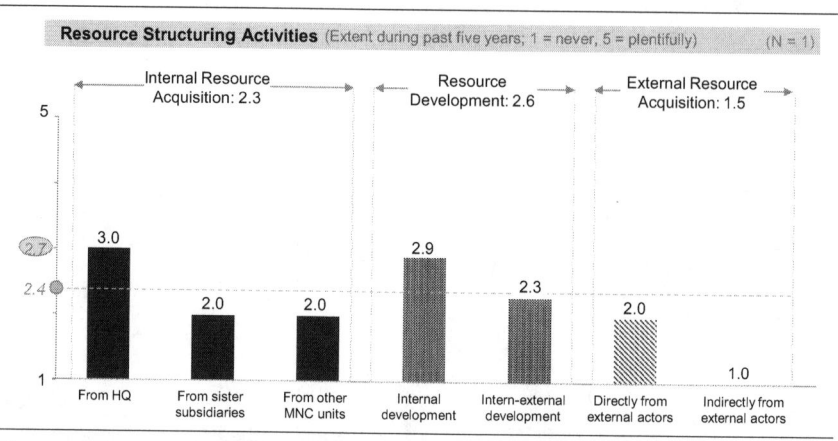

Figure 5.126: Survey Results: ROM – Initiative-related resource structuring activities

(2) Headquarters-Subsidiary Alignment

Overall, the Montenegrin subsidiary experienced a moderate level of **headquarters involvement** (3.3, S16). Although the foreign unit and its entrepreneurial activities were not considered the "*highest priority*" for Telecomp, it nevertheless regularly communicated and presented initiative opportunities to the head office (both 3.0, S16) since it "*want[ed] to be regularly updated*" (I16:107). Moreover, headquarters was repeatedly involved in the refinement of initiatives and their approval was often required. In addition, the foreign entity faced a high level of **corporate resistance** (3.3, S16). This commonly took the form of direct rejection of initiatives or delays and requests for greater justification. For instance, a local initiative aimed at entering a new business field in Montenegro and a number of initiatives related to M&A activities were rejected by headquarters (I16). One of the possible reasons for headquarters' negative response was the distance of the new opportunity from the core business of the foreign unit:

"... Montenegro, because it's so small, usually opportunities for innovation or for partnerships are broader or more far-fetched than in other country units. ... So there is more potential for, let's say, little bit creative ideas and differentiation. So ... this one was not considered very well in the decision body because in Germany this would never fly ... for whatever reasons. But in Montenegro ... at that time, it made perfect sense but it was rejected." (I16)

Finally, the foreign organization exhibited a moderate to high level of **initiative selling** (3.0, S16). Generally, selling was not often required, as the local unit did not frequently pursue larger or more extensive subsidiary initiatives (I16). However, with initiatives that, for example, required higher amounts of financial investment, implied larger changes to the network, or had wider implications for the MNC, selling to headquarters and obtaining its approval was frequently needed (I16).

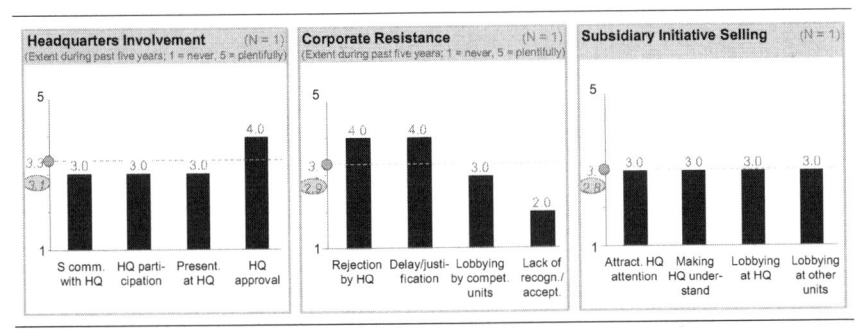

Figure 5.127: Survey Results: MON – Headquarters-subsidiary alignment and interaction

5.2.7.3 Subsidiary Initiative-Taking Outcome

(1) Extent of Subsidiary Initiative-Taking

During the past five years, the Montenegrin subsidiary displayed a low level of successful subsidiary initiatives (1.9, S16). The unit engaged somewhat more in internally than in externally oriented initiatives (2.0 vs. 1.8). Internally, the local affiliate pursued mostly global-internal hybrid initiatives involving the attraction of corporate investment or the reallocation of activities to the subsidiary unit. For instance, the subsidiary convinced headquarters to make Montenegro a pilot country for a new service that combines fixed and mobile broadband access. The piloting activities were then relocated to Montenegro and driven by the local team (A10, I16). Externally, the unit only engaged in local market initiatives that typically represent new products, markets or processes first identified locally and then extended to other units. For example, the subsidiary successfully developed a novel approach to measure media and television usage based on IPTV data. This data is then sold to media and advertising agencies or television stations (I16).

As described previously, many of the subsidiary's entrepreneurial activities were undertaken in non-core or adjacent areas in which the foreign entity hitherto had little experience. These were often trivial initiatives that were of smaller scale, incrementally innovative in nature, and of limited applicability for the wider MNC.[443] As reasons for the lack of larger-scale entrepreneurial initiatives, the local management pointed to the limited amount of personnel resources and restricted local expertise. Certain characteristics of the environment, such as the small and shrinking market, were also mentioned as negative effects on entrepreneurial efforts (I16).

> "You know, our teams are very small so if we want to implement something on [MNC] level; usually the team requires [the innovation hub] and then our central technology teams, technology marketing team or whatever. So there are not a lot of these things that we can say okay, we are now ready for the full [MNC] because for such kind of initiatives we would need to double the size of our department." (I16)

> "But also have in mind Montenegro is the smallest usually, not the biggest member of the biggest market. So usually it is not really the one driving innovation in the [MNC], it's not like that. And as such we are probably not the highest priority for [Company B]." (I16)

Subsidiary Initiative-Taking (Extent of subsidiary entrepreneurial initiatives within past five years; 1= never, 5 = plentifully) (N = 1)

External initiatives: 1.8 | Internal initiatives: 2.0

Global market initiatives	Local market initiatives	Internal market initiatives	Global-Internal hybrid initiatives
1.0	2.5	1.5	2.5

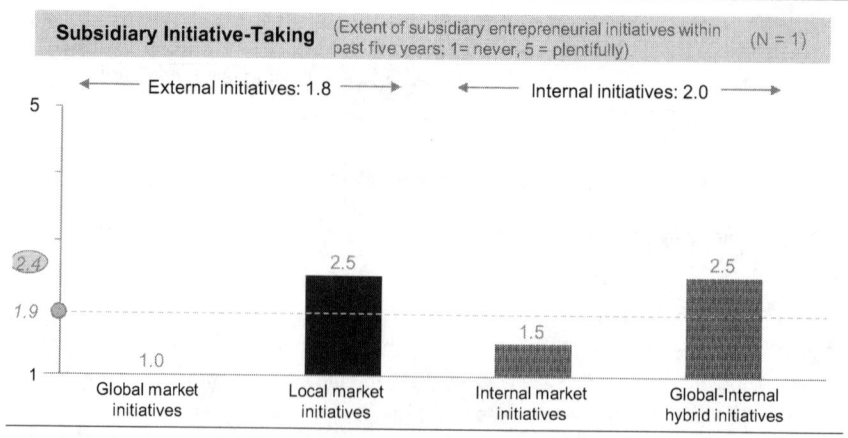

Figure 5.128: Survey Results: MON – Types and extent of subsidiary initiatives

---

[443] According to subsidiary management, of all entrepreneurial activities undertaken in Montenegro, approximately 90% are purely for local application (I16).

(2) Resource-Related Outcomes

Resulting from the entrepreneurial initiatives, the Montenegrin subsidiary was able to develop a limited number of new resources and capabilities (2.4, S16), particularly in the areas of service delivery and innovation/entrepreneurship. As to the applicability for the wider MNC, resources and capabilities from two areas were assessed as useful for other units: marketing and sales and innovation/entrepreneurship, as shown in Figure 5.129.

New Subsidiary Resources and Capabilities (N=1) (Extent during past five years; 1= no capability development at all, 5 = extensive capability development)	Impact on MNC Capability Development (N=1) (Extent during past five years; 1= no use at all, 5 = very useful)
Research and development: 2.0	Research and development: 2.0
Prod. of goods/services: 4.0	Prod. of goods/services: 2.0
Marketing and/or sales: 3.0	Marketing and/or sales: 4.0
Logistics and/or distribution: 2.0	Logistics and/or distribution: 1.0
Purchasing: 2.0	Purchasing: 2.0
HR management: 2.0	HR management: 2.0
General management: 1.0	General management: 1.0
Innovation/entrepreneur.: 3.0	Innovation/entrepreneur.: 4.0
Ø 2.4	Ø 2.3

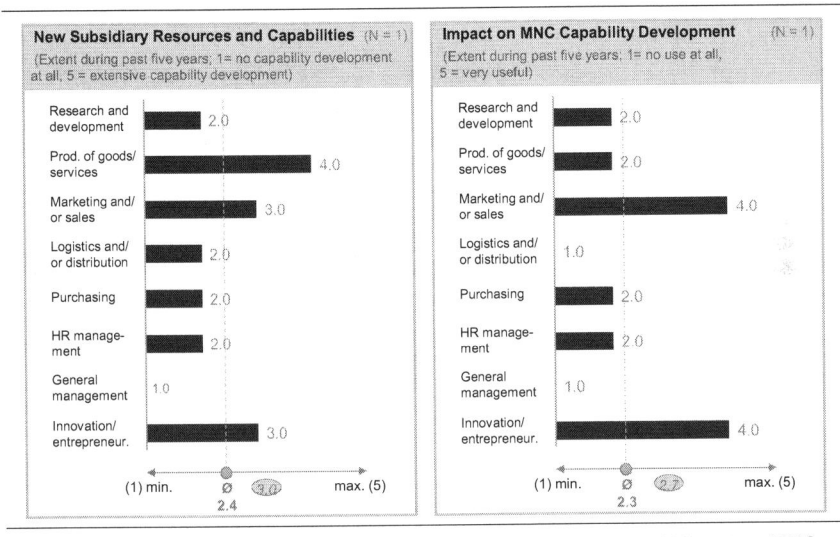

Figure 5.129: Survey Results: MON – New subsidiary resources and impact on MNC capabilities

(3) Further Outcomes

In addition to the creation of new resources and capabilities, subsidiary initiatives also resulted in further **performance outcomes** such as new revenues and cost reductions (I16, S16). With regard to the impact on the **subsidiary's role and position** in the MNC, it remained largely unchanged, with only minor decline in the global competitiveness of the local organization, as illustrated in Figure 5.130.

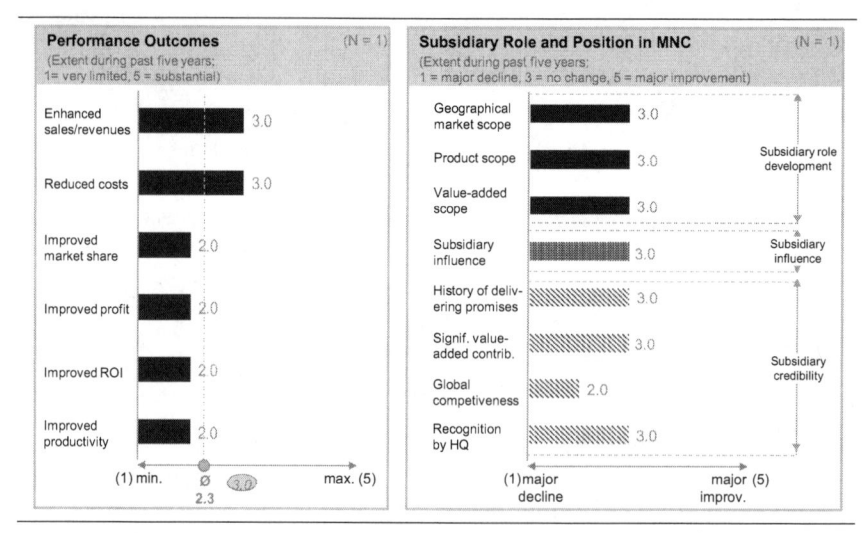

Performance Outcomes (N = 1)	Subsidiary Role and Position in MNC (N = 1)
(Extent during past five years; 1= very limited, 5 = substantial)	(Extent during past five years; 1 = major decline, 3 = no change, 5 = major improvement)
Enhanced sales/revenues — 3.0	Geographical market scope — 3.0 ⎫
Reduced costs — 3.0	Product scope — 3.0 ⎬ Subsidiary role development
	Value-added scope — 3.0 ⎭
Improved market share — 2.0	Subsidiary influence — 3.0 — Subsidiary influence
Improved profit — 2.0	History of delivering promises — 3.0 ⎫
Improved ROI — 2.0	Signif. value-added contrib. — 3.0 ⎬ Subsidiary credibility
	Global competitiveness — 2.0
Improved productivity — 2.0	Recognition by HQ — 3.0 ⎭
(1) min. ø 2.3 max. (5)	(1) major decline major (5) improv.

Figure 5.130: Survey Results: MON – Performance outcomes and changes to subsidiary role and position

5.3 Overview of Findings at Autocomp and Telecomp

As previously outlined in Subsection 4.2.2, consistent findings from multiple cases are not only viewed as more convincing and more robust evidence, but they commonly provide better grounds for generalizing to new cases. Accordingly, this section presents and compares summaries of the empirical results from Autocomp and Telecomp as follows. First, findings on subsidiary roles and subsidiary characteristics are outlined in Subsection 5.3.1. Second, empirical evidence on role-specific subsidiary initiative-taking activities is displayed and compared across cases in Subsection 5.3.2. More specifically, Autocomp and Telecomp findings on entrepreneurial resource management and headquarters-subsidiary alignment sub-processes are presented and discussed (Subsections 5.3.2.1 and 5.3.2.2). Third, empirical evidence on role-specific subsidiary initiative outcomes is shown and then the major findings on role-specific subsidiary initiative-taking are summarized (Subsections 5.3.3 and 5.3.4). Subsection 5.3.5 then concludes with the presentation of additional findings gathered through the empirical study on subsidiary initiative objectives (5.3.5.1), drivers and inhibitors (5.3.5.2), processes (5.3.5.3) and outcomes (5.3.5.4)

5.3.1 Subsidiary Roles

5.3.1.1 Strategic Leader and Active Subsidiary

In total, five subsidiaries represent Strategic Leaders and Active Subsidiaries in both company cases. Given their specific roles, all of these units are located in strategically important markets, and they possess a comparatively high level of subsidiary resources and capabilities. Moreover, they are characterized by relatively high degrees of both localization/local responsiveness and integration (see Table 5.1). As can be expected from these subsidiary role types, all five units enjoy a comparably high degree of decision-making autonomy, not only for operational but also for strategic decisions, including the major development of new product or service offerings and restructuring of the subsidiary organization. Other common characteristics of Strategic Leaders and Active Subsidiaries of this study include the strong external linkages and frequent interactions with local and global stakeholders. Finally, each of these foreign units performs some global function for its parent company or is considered an innovator in the wider multinational firm.

| | Company A – Autocomp ||| Company B – Telecomp |||
Subsidiaries	Germany	Mexico	∅[444]	Hungary	Poland	Croatia	∅[445]
Role Dimensions and Autonomy							
Strategic importance	4.3 (high)	3.8 (high)	3.3	4.0 (high)	4.0 (high)	3.5 (mod)	3.4
Subsidiary resources	4.1 (high)	3.8 (high)	3.4	4.1 (high)	4.0 (high)	3.6 (mod)	3.5
Localization	4.3 (high)	3.9 (high)	3.2	4.0 (high)	3.8 (high)	3.6 (mod)	3.4
Integration	3.8 (high)	3.8 (high)	3.3	3.4 (high)	3.5 (high)	3.3 (mod)	3.1
Autonomy	3.9 (high)	3.3 (high)	3.0	4.0 (high)	3.9 (high)	3.6 (mod-hi)	3.4
Subsidiary Information							
Mode of formation	Greenfield	Acquisition	--	Acquisition	Acquisition	Acquisition	--
Year of foundation	Early 1960s	Early 2000s	--	Early 1990s	Early 2000s	Early 2000s	--
Employees (2013)	~2,500	~3,000	--	~10,000	~5,000	~5,000	--
Other information	Global R&D hub	One of three major R&D hubs worldwide	--	Center of excellence for one service area	Innovation hub for southern and central Europe	One of three innovators	--

Table 5.1: Strategic Leader and Active Subsidiary: Subsidiary role dimensions and other information

5.3.1.2 Contributor and Receptive Subsidiary

In the two companies, a total of three subsidiaries are categorized as both Contributors and Receptive Subsidiaries. According to their role classification they operate in a market environment of relatively low strategic importance but possess a rather high level of subsidiary resources and capabilities. Furthermore, all three entities are characterized by a relatively low degree of localization and a high degree of integration in the MNC. As is common with these role types, their decision-making autonomy is assessed as moderate, with considerably more leeway for operational than for strategic decisions, as shown in Table 5.2 below.

| | Company A – Autocomp ||| Company B – Telecomp ||
Subsidiaries	South Korea	Australia	∅	Slovakia	∅
Role Dimensions and Autonomy					
Strategic importance	3.0 (low to mod)	2.3 (low)	3.3	3.0 (low)	3.4
Subsidiary resources	3.8 (high)	3.7 (mod to high)	3.4	3.9 (high)	3.5
Localization	2.7 (low)	2.4 (low)	3.2	3.1 (low)	3.4
Integration	4.1 (high)	3.3 (mod)	3.3	3.5 (high)	3.1
Autonomy	3.1 (mod)	3.2 (mod to high)	3.0	3.3 (mod)	3.4
Subsidiary Information					
Mode of formation	Acquisition	Greenfield	--	Acquisition	--
Year of foundation	Late 2000s	Late 1950s	--	Late 1990s	--
Employees (2013)	~2,300	~350	--	~4,000	--
Other information	Regional competence center for three areas	Primarily manufacturing location	--	--	--

Table 5.2: Contributor and Receptive Subsidiary: Subsidiary role dimensions and other information

---

[444] This column shows the mean average value of all seven Autocomp subsidiary units.
[445] This column shows the mean average value of all seven Telecomp subsidiary units.

As can be expected from such subsidiary roles, the three foreign units are exposed to comparatively low levels of stimulation in their market environments with, for example, low technical dynamism, high maturity of the life cycle stages of products and services, and easily identifiable competitors and competitor strategies. Although Contributors are often presumed to be older and more established subsidiaries, this holds true only for the Autocomp units, which were first founded in the late 1950s and 1970s and are as such comparatively older. In the case of Telecomp, the Slovakian unit was first established in the late 1990s and hence around the same time as most other Telecomp subsidiaries in this study.

5.3.1.3 Black Hole and Autonomous Subsidiary

In total, two foreign subsidiary units in Autocomp and Telecomp are classified as Black Holes and at the same time as Autonomous Subsidiaries. According to their roles, these local affiliates are located in strategically important market environments, yet they possess only a limited level of resources and capabilities. In addition, the local affiliates are characterized by a high degree of localization and a low degree of integration in the MNC (see Table 5.3). Concerning their relatively high degree of localization, both foreign entities frequently interacted with local actors and locally sold products and services that contained a large amount of local content. Based on the empirical results, the two foreign entities have a comparatively low degree of decision-making autonomy. As such, the findings are in line with the expectations formulated for Black Holes but not for Autonomous Subsidiaries, which were predicted to have more decision-making freedom.[446]

	Company A – Autocomp		Company B – Telecomp	
Subsidiaries	China	Ø	Greece	Ø
Role Dimensions and Autonomy				
Strategic importance	3.5 (mod to high)	3.3	4.1 (high)	3.4
Subsidiary resources	3.0 (low)	3.4	3.1 (low)	3.5
Localization	3.7 (high)	3.2	3.6 (mod to high)	3.4
Integration	2.5 (low)	3.3	2.9 (low to mod)	3.1
Autonomy	2.1 (low)	3.0	3.1 (low to mod)	3.4
Subsidiary Information				
Mode of formation	Greenfield (joint venture)	--	Acquisition	--
Year of foundation	Mid 2000s	--	Late 2000s	--
Employees (2013)	~3,000	--	~10,000	--
Other information	Responsibility for Chinese market only	--	Responsibility for Greece and two other southern European countries	--

Table 5.3: Black Hole and Autonomous Subsidiary: Subsidiary role dimensions and other information

---

[446] See Subsections 3.5.1.3 and 3.5.2.3, which describe the expected levels of subsidiary autonomy for these two role types.

5.3.1.4 Implementer and Quiescent Subsidiary

In total, four foreign units are classified in this research study as both Implementers and Quiescent Subsidiaries. All four subsidiaries were described as operating in markets of little strategic importance and possessing a limited level of subsidiary resources and capabilities. At the same time, all four local affiliates are considered to have a low degree of localization and a low degree of integration. The empirical results indicate that all four units have a relatively low level of decision-making autonomy, as outlined in Table 5.4. Finally, with the exception of the Romanian Autocomp unit, which has the function of a low cost manufacturing location for Eastern Europe, the remaining three foreign subsidiaries hold responsibility only for the limited geographical scope of their respective country market.

Subsidiaries	Company A – Autocomp			Company B – Telecomp		
	Romania	India	Ø	Romania	Montenegro	Ø
Role Dimensions and Autonomy						
Strategic importance	3.1 (low to mod)	2.8 (low)	3.3	3.0 (low)	2.5 (low)	3.4
Subsidiary resources	3.2 (low to mod)	3.0 (low)	3.4	3.1 (low)	2.6 (low)	3.5
Localization	2.7 (low)	2.6 (low)	3.2	3.0 (low)	2.9 (low)	3.4
Integration	2.6 (low)	2.8 (low)	3.3	2.7 (low)	2.8 (low)	3.1
Autonomy	2.7 (low to mod)	2.4 (low)	3.0	2.9 (low)	3.0 (low)	3.4
Subsidiary Information						
Mode of formation	Greenfield	Acquisition	--	Acquisition	Acquisition	--
Year of foundation	Early 2000s	Late 2000s	--	Early 1990s	Late 2000s	--
Employees (2013)	~2,600	~1,700	--	~8,000	~1,000	--
Other information	Low cost manufacturing location for Eastern Europe	Responsibility for Indian market only	--	Responsibility for Romanian market only	Responsibility for Montenegrin market only	--

Table 5.4: Implementer and Quiescent Subsidiary: Subsidiary role dimensions and other information

5.3.2 Subsidiary Initiative-Taking

5.3.2.1 Entrepreneurial Resource Management

(1) Initiative Opportunity Identification

Strategic Leader and Active Subsidiary: In line with the previous predictions, the empirical findings show that these two advanced role types exhibited the highest level of new initiative opportunity identification in the past five years. In both company cases, not only did these subsidiary role types show comparatively high levels of both internal and external identification, but external discovery usually occurred more frequently than in any other role type investigated in this study.[447] Here, the units' strong external network linkages and frequent interactions with external partners helped in the identification of new initiative opportunities. The external partners that supported this were com-

---

[447] One exception is Telecomp's Black Hole/Autonomous subsidiary in Greece, which also showed a high level of external initiative opportunity identification.

monly global or local customers, competitors, or research institutions. In the case of Telecomp, local suppliers and local entrepreneurs also played an important role for initiative discovery. As to the innovativeness of initiative opportunities, Strategic Leaders and Active Subsidiaries discovered radically innovative opportunities more often than any other role type in this study (see Table 5.5).

Contributor and Receptive Subsidiary: In both company cases, Contributors and Receptive Subsidiaries exhibited a moderate level of new initiative discovery in the past five years, as was expected from these two role types. Moreover, given their tighter integration in the MNC and their stronger inward focus, new initiative discoveries most often materialized through sources from within the MNC, such as from within the foreign unit itself or through interactions with the corporate center. In the cases of the subsidiaries in South Korea and Slovakia, new discoveries were supported by existing market insights of employees or through the analytical capabilities of local personnel who investigated market trends and competitive offerings both locally or in other countries as well. Newly identified initiative opportunities were mostly incrementally or moderately innovative while radically innovative initiatives were discovered seldom or even very seldom.

Black Hole and Autonomous Subsidiary: The empirical findings on the two units classified as both Black Holes and Autonomous Subsidiaries showed no cross-case consistency regarding the extent of new initiative discovery in the past five years. While the Greek unit of Telecomp engaged in a low to moderate level of new initiative identification as predicted, the Chinese subsidiary exhibited the lowest level of new initiative discovery of all Autocomp units. It can be assumed that the very limited decision-making autonomy of the Chinese unit and the very high level of headquarters involvement also negatively impacted discovery of new initiative opportunities. However, in both cases, new ideas were more often discovered externally than internally and particularly through interactions with external actors such as local customers or suppliers. Newly discovered opportunities were mostly incrementally or moderately innovative (see Table 5.5).

Implementer and Quiescent Subsidiary: In both Autocomp and Telecomp, all four units classified as both Implementers and Quiescent Subsidiaries displayed comparatively low levels of new initiative opportunity identification in the past five years as expected. New opportunities were also mostly discovered internally, for example within the foreign itself or through interactions with the corporate center. As to their innovativeness, most new opportunities were assessed to be incremental and, less frequently, moderately innovative in nature. Here, entrepreneurial activities often related to replications of existing services and products for use in similar applications, minor changes of existing products or services and improvements of internal processes.

Autocomp	Telecomp	Case Consistency		Fit with Predictions[448]	
		within	across	B/G	J/M
Strategic Leader and Active Subsidiary (n=5)					
High level	Moderate to high level	✓	(✓)	✓	✓
Both internal and external	Both internal and external	(✓)	✓	✗	✓
Often radically innov.	Often radically innov.	✓	✓	n/a	n/a
Contributor and Receptive Subsidiary (n=3)					
Moderate level	Moderate level	✓	✓	✓	✓
Rather internal	Rather internal	✓	✓	✓	✓
Increm./mod. innov.	Increm./mod. innov.	(✓)	✓	n/a	n/a
Black Hole and Autonomous Subsidiary (n=2)					
Low level	Low to moderate level	✓	✗	✗	✗
Rather external	Rather external	✓	✓	✓	✓
Mostly incrementally and moderately innovative	Mostly incrementally and moderately innovative	✓	✓	n/a	n/a
Implementer and Quiescent Subsidiary (n=4)					
Low to moderate level	Low level	(✓)	(✓)	(✓)	(✓)
Rather internal	Rather internal	✓	✓	✓	✓
Increm./mod. innovative	Increm./mod. innovative	✓	✓	n/a	n/a

Table 5.5: Case Comparison: Identification and innovativeness of initiative opportunities

(2) Resource Structuring

Strategic Leader and Active Subsidiary: The empirical results indicate that subsidiaries holding these advanced roles engage in resource structuring activities to a moderate or even high level. Although they can typically utilize their own rich set of existing resources and capabilities, their high levels of initiative-taking activities and their often more radically innovative nature should also necessitate obtaining resources and capabilities to a high degree. In this regard, these advanced role types could be viewed as being in advantageous positions vis-à-vis the other foreign units. For example, their strong internal and external linkages allowed these role types to easily access resources from both the internal and external MNC network. Internal sources included headquarters, central development departments such as engineering, R&D hubs and innovation centers, and sister subsidiaries. External sources that were employed included, among others, global customers, competitors, suppliers and research institutions. In addition to the different sources, a broad array of resource structuring methods was employed by all foreign units of these types, ranging from internal resource development to direct external acquisition from local or even global actors. In comparison to all other role types, the five units classified as Strategic Leaders and Autonomous units

---

[448] The fit of empirical findings with predictions articulated earlier in this thesis is indicated as follows: ✓ = empirical findings are fully or largely consistent with predictions; (✓) = empirical findings are partially consistent with predictions; ✗ = empirical findings are not consistent with predictions.

more frequently utilized external resource acquisition and development than the remaining subsidiaries in this study, as illustrated in Figure 5.6.[449]

Contributor and Receptive Subsidiary: With the exception of the Australian Autocomp unit, Contributor and Receptive subsidiaries performed low to moderate levels of resource structuring activities in the past five years. In the Autocomp case there was no consistency regarding the extent of resource structuring activities between the Australian subsidiary (high level) and the South Korean subsidiary (low level). Potential reasons for the higher than predicted resource structuring activities by the Australian unit could be its lower level of resources coupled with the somewhat higher level of initiatives that it pursued in the past five years, thus possibly necessitating more frequent resource structuring efforts. Concerning the mode of resource structuring, all three units in both Autocomp and Telecomp most frequently engaged in internal resource development when attempting to realize initiatives.

Black Hole and Autonomous Subsidiary: In total, two subsidiary units in Autocomp and Telecomp functioned as a Black Hole and simultaneously an Autonomous Subsidiary. They consistently exhibited an overall low to moderate level of resource structuring activities both within and across cases. However, empirical findings were not completely consistent as to the modes of resource structuring employed in the past five years. While the Autocomp subsidiary in China most frequently acquired the required resources internally from headquarters or other MNC units, the Telecomp affiliate in Greece relied more strongly on external resource acquisition. These discrepancies might be attributed to the differences in decision-making autonomy and headquarters-subsidiary interactions. Given the very limited leeway of the Chinese unit and the very close alignment it needed to have with the corporate center and other MNC entities, it can be assumed that the local entity also often turned to these units when in need of resources or capabilities for its initiatives. In comparison, the Greek Telecomp unit possessed a low to moderate level of decision-making autonomy and needed to align somewhat less often with headquarters or other MNC units when engaging in initiatives. Moreover, the Greek subsidiary needed to realize initiatives in adjacent and new markets and thus required, for example, knowledge and expertise that was perhaps not readily available from inside the multinational firm and therefore frequently turned to actors in the external market.

Implementer and Quiescent Subsidiary: Consistent across both company cases and all four subsidiaries, all units categorized as both Implementer and Quiescent Subsidiary exhibited a low level of resource structuring activities. Moreover, they obtained resources from external sources least often and instead focused mainly on internal

---

[449] One exception is Autocomp's Black Hole/Autonomous subsidiary in China, in which a high level of external resource acquisition also occurred.

resource acquisition and internal development. Given their location in relatively undemanding market environments and their restricted set of resources and capabilities, few new initiatives were pursued in the past five years. Additionally, these were commonly incrementally innovative in nature, thus the need for new resources and capabilities to realize initiatives should have been rather low. Furthermore, the Implementer and Quiescent units were not strongly embedded in internal or external networks, thus making it more difficult to obtain needed resources and capabilities.

Autocomp	Telecomp	Case Consistency		Fit with Predictions	
		within	across	B/G	J/M
Strategic Leader and Active Subsidiary (n=5)					
Moderate to high level	Moderate to high level	(✓)	✓	✓	✓
Various modes	Various modes	(✓)	✓	✗	✓
Contributor and Receptive Subsidiary (n=3)					
Low to high level	Moderate level	✗	✗	✗	✗
Internal development	Internal development	✓	✓	✓	✓
Black Hole and Autonomous Subsidiary (n=2)					
Low to moderate level	Low to moderate level	✓	✓	✓	✗
Int. and ext. acquisition	Rather ext. acquisition	✓	(✓)	(✓)	(✓)
Implementer and Quiescent Subsidiary (n=4)					
Low level	Low level	✓	✓	✓	✓
Int. acquis. and int. devel.	Int. development	(✓)	(✓)	(✓)	(✓)

Table 5.6: Case Comparison: Initiative-related resource structuring activities

(3) Resource Bundling

Strategic Leader and Active Subsidiary: The empirical findings indicate that five local affiliates with these advanced role types consistently engaged in a high level of resource bundling activities during the last five years, as shown in Table 5.7. In addition, radical bundling forms were utilized more frequently than by any other role types, typically involving the extensive combination of completely new resources and capabilities. Given the frequent pursuit of larger-scope entrepreneurial undertakings such as global market initiatives, Strategic Leader and Active Subsidiaries may have needed to combine novel resources and capabilities more extensively in order to realize such forms of subsidiary initiatives.

Contributor and Receptive Subsidiary: All three foreign subsidiaries in the roles of Contributors and Receptive Subsidiaries exhibited low to moderate levels of resource bundling and this was slightly lower than anticipated. However, the local affiliates most frequently employed incremental and intermediate resource combination forms, with some radical bundling having been used only by the Slovakian unit of Telecomp.

Black Hole and Autonomous Subsidiary: The two units in Autocomp and Telecomp in the roles of Black Holes and Autonomous Subsidiaries employed bundling activities to a low extent. Moreover, resource combination efforts predominantly took place as incremental and intermediate bundling. It can be assumed that their low levels of internal resources and capabilities and their limited access to those existing inside or outside the MNC may have impeded their ability to engage in more frequent and more extensive resource combination efforts.

Implementer and Quiescent Subsidiary: All four Autocomp and Telecomp local entities classified as Implementers and Quiescent Subsidiaries exhibited a low to moderate level of resource bundling. Furthermore, these activities predominantly took the form of incremental resource combination. Given the few initiatives that were pursued in the past five years and their often incrementally innovative nature, a small number of new resources and capabilities ultimately needed to be obtained and bundled.

Autocomp	Telecomp	Case Consistency		Fit with Predictions	
		within	across	B/G	J/M
Strategic Leader and Active Subsidiary (n=5)					
High level	High level	✓	✓	✓	✓
More extensive forms	More extensive forms	✓	✓	✓	✓
Contributor and Receptive Subsidiary (n=3)					
Low to moderate level	Moderate level	✗	✗	✗	✗
Incremental/intermediate	Incremental/intermediate	✓	✓	✓	✓
Black Hole and Autonomous Subsidiary (n=2)					
Low level	Low level	✓	✓	✓	✓
Incremental/intermediate	Incremental/intermediate	✓	✓	✓	✗
Implementer and Quiescent Subsidiary (n=4)					
Low to moderate	Low level	(✓)	(✓)	(✓)	(✓)
Mostly incremental	Mostly incremental	✓	✓	✓	✓

Table 5.7: Case Comparison: Initiative-related resource bundling activities

5.3.2.2 Headquarters-Subsidiary Alignment

Strategic Leader and Active Subsidiary: As anticipated, all five foreign affiliates with these more advanced role types enjoyed large degrees of autonomy, and they were able to pursue subsidiary initiatives with little alignment and interaction with headquarters or other MNC units. Likewise, the levels of corporate resistance and initiative selling efforts were assessed lowest among all units abroad (see Table 5.8). Given their relatively extensive freedom, their often large pool of resources and, in some cases, their geographical distance, the more advanced role types could pursue initiatives often without directly involving the corporate center. Moreover, given their strong internal and external network linkages, these subsidiaries could more easily obtain required resources from various sources inside or outside the MNC and thereby limit the need to involve headquarters.

Contributor and Receptive Subsidiary: Empirical findings indicate that foreign affiliates in the roles of both Contributors and Receptive Subsidiaries aligned and interacted with headquarters or other parts of the MNC mostly to a moderate extent. In both company cases, headquarters was involved in initiatives to a moderate degree, with the exception of the South Korean Autocomp unit, which experienced higher levels of participation from the corporate office. Corporate resistance was also evaluated for all three units as low to moderate, frequently materializing in the form of rejections by headquarters or delays of initiatives and/or the request for greater justification by the corporate center. Finally, initiative-selling activities occurred to a low to moderate extent in all three foreign units.

Black Hole and Autonomous Subsidiary: The two units that function as both Black Holes and Autonomous Subsidiaries not only possess low degrees of autonomy, but also experienced comparatively high levels of alignment and interaction with their respective headquarters in Germany when engaging in entrepreneurial initiatives. More specifically, the extent of headquarters involvement was assessed in both units as highest among all foreign subsidiaries in Autocomp and Telecomp. For example, frequent communication with the corporate office and presentations of new opportunities at headquarters were often necessary to obtain approval and resources to continue with initiatives. Similarly, corporate resistance against initiatives was assessed as high. Reasons provided for central opposition against subsidiary initiatives included the existence of suitable and already usable products or solutions in the MNC or the need for market-specific adaptations that were deemed inappropriate or even risky by the corporate office. Lastly, both local organizations engaged in relatively extensive lobbying and selling activities. This included the regular presentation of new initiative opportunities in the wider MNC at regular conference calls or internal conferences.

Implementer and Quiescent Subsidiary: The four subsidiaries in both companies experienced moderate to high levels of headquarters involvement, which was slightly lower than expected. Involvement of the corporate center was particularly necessary when initiatives were of a larger scale, impacted the wider product or service landscape of the MNC or required larger amounts of resources. In addition to headquarters involvement, the four local units all faced high levels of corporate resistance, for example, when requesting further resources or when initiatives were perceived to be competing with other products or solutions in the MNC. Furthermore, the four subsidiaries engaged in moderate to high level of initiative selling activities. Selling and lobbying efforts to convince others in the MNC of the attractiveness of an initiative took place at annual meetings or in the form of regular updates and reports on subsidiary activities, for example. Selling activities were particularly necessary when initiatives were considered to have wider implications for the MNC or when larger financial investments were required.

Autocomp	Telecomp	Case Consistency		Fit with Predictions	
		within	across	B/G	J/M
Strategic Leader and Active Subsidiary (n=5)					
Low level of HQ involv.	Low to mod level of HQ involv.	(✓)	(✓)	(✓)	✓
Low level of corp. resistance	Low level of corp. resistance	✓	✓	✓	✓
Low to mod level of selling	Low to mod level of selling	(✓)	(✓)	✓	✓
Contributor and Receptive Subsidiary (n=3)					
Mod level of HQ involv.	Mod to high level of HQ involv.	✗	✗	✗	✗
Low to mod level of corp. resist.	Moderate level of corp. resist.	✓	(✓)	(✓)	✗
Low to moderate level of selling	Moderate level of selling	(✓)	(✓)	(✓)	✗
Black Hole and Autonomous Subsidiary (n=2)					
High level of HQ involvement	High level of HQ involvement	✓	✓	✓	✗
High level of corp. resistance	High level of corp. resistance	✓	✓	✓	✗
High level of selling	High level of selling	✓	✓	✓	✗
Implementer and Quiescent Subsidiary (n=4)					
Moderate level of HQ involv.	Mod to high level of HQ involv.	✓	(✓)	✗	✓
High level of corp. resistance	High level of corp. resistance	✓	✓	✓	✓
Mod to high level of selling	Mod to high level of selling	(✓)	✓	✓	✓

Table 5.8: Case Comparison: Headquarters-subsidiary alignment and interaction

5.3.3 Subsidiary Initiative Outcome

5.3.3.1 Extent of Subsidiary Initiative-Taking

Strategic Leader and Active Subsidiary: The empirical findings of this study show that all five Strategic Leaders and Active Subsidiaries successfully pursued subsidiary initiatives more often than any of the remaining foreign units. It can be assumed that, among other factors, the stimulating market environment, the high level of resources and the strong internal and external linkages both encouraged and enabled the local entities to engage in entrepreneurial activities. Furthermore, it can be deduced that their strong resource and power positions allowed these advanced role types to pursue initiatives largely independently or, if needed, more easily push them through the socio-political system of the MNC.

Concerning the types of initiatives, externally-oriented entrepreneurial activities such as global and local market initiatives were realized more frequently than internal ones.[450] More specifically, Strategic Leaders and Active Subsidiaries in this study engaged in global market initiatives more often than all other role types. They commonly represented larger scale entrepreneurial efforts for non-local actors such as the development of globally applicable product platforms for global customers. Similarly, all five subsidiaries exhibited the highest level of local market initiatives. Examples included new products or services that first were identified and realized locally and later utilized in other

---

[450] The only exception is the Hungarian unit, which pursued internally and externally-oriented initiatives in the past five years to the same extent.

countries as well. Although not as frequent, internally oriented initiatives were also repeatedly undertaken by these five advanced subsidiary units. In particular, global-internal hybrid initiatives were regularly pursued. Examples of initiatives of this type included convincing headquarters to fund and support the installation of an innovation center in Poland or persuading the central office to select Croatia as a test and pilot site for an innovative internet network structure. Here, the strong internal linkages with other parts of the MNC may have helped with the identification and realization of the global yet internally oriented initiatives.

Contributor and Receptive Subsidiary: All three foreign subsidiaries classified as Contributors and Receptive units exhibited low to moderate levels of entrepreneurial initiatives. As possible reasons for the lower extent of initiatives, subsidiary managers mentioned, for instance, the limited availability of local funding for trial and error activities, the lack of financial support for initiatives from the corporate center and limited headquarters support in general. Furthermore, given these units' low degree of localization, lacking customer proximity and interaction were also brought forward as a potential factor inhibiting entrepreneurial initiatives.

Within Autocomp units, internally oriented initiatives were more prevalent, although at the Telecomp unit in Greece, internally and externally oriented initiatives were undertaken to a similar extent. In both company cases, local market initiatives and global-internal hybrid initiatives occurred most frequently. Initiatives were generally of a smaller scale and often focused on improving or adapting existing products or processes. For example, the Australian subsidiary engaged in initiatives related to developing novel materials for their products, or reducing the costs of its output and manufacturing activities.

Black Hole and Autonomous Subsidiary: The two foreign entities classified as both Black Holes and Autonomous subsidiaries exhibited low and moderate levels of initiative-taking activities. Although both units are located in strategically important markets, their restricted autonomy and their limited set of subsidiary resources and capabilities were seen as factors constraining entrepreneurial activities. Furthermore, Autocomp and Telecomp headquarters showed little willingness to transfer needed resources, such as funding or new technology, to the local organizations, further impeding subsidiary initiatives. Finally, both foreign units experienced high levels of headquarters involvement and corporate resistance against their initiatives, making it more difficult to successfully push new opportunities through the socio-political system of the MNC.

As to initiative types, both units engaged in internally and externally oriented initiatives to a similar extent during the past five years. Of all types, local market initiatives were most prevalent. Examples included the development of new products and services first for local needs and subsequently for use in the wider MNC, as well as the proactive adaption of globally available products to the distinct conditions of the local market. In addition to local market initiatives, global-internal hybrid initiatives were regularly undertaken, typically involving the reallocation of MNC resources or even the shift of value added activities to the foreign subsidiary locations.

Implementer and Quiescent Subsidiary: The four subsidiaries in both companies exhibited low or even the lowest levels of subsidiary initiatives as can be seen in Table 5.9. It can be assumed that their undemanding market environments, their limited set of resources and capabilities as well as their low integration and localization made it difficult for these units to identify and realize entrepreneurial initiatives. Moreover, it can be inferred that high levels of headquarters involvement, strong corporate resistance and, in some instances, misalignments with the corporate center negatively impacted the development and completion of entrepreneurial subsidiary initiatives.

All four subsidiaries categorized as both Implementers and Quiescent units pursued internally oriented initiatives somewhat more frequently than externally oriented ones. While the local organizations of Autocomp engaged more often in local market initiatives, the two Telecomp units pursued global-internal hybrid ones most frequently. The latter commonly involved the attraction of corporate investment, such as the successful bid for a new development center by the Romanian unit of Autocomp or the persuasion of the Telecomp headquarters to make Montenegro the pilot country for a new service offering. In addition to the four "standard" forms of subsidiary initiatives, the Implementer and Quiescent subsidiaries pursued smaller "trivial initiatives" for merely local application, including the improvement of processes and the development of new tools or initiatives to reduce costs.

Autocomp	Telecomp	Case Consistency		Fit with Predictions	
		within	across	B/G	J/M
Strategic Leader and Active Subsidiary (n=5)					
High level of initiatives	High level of initiatives	✓	✓	✓	✓
Mostly external	Mostly ext./int. and ext. alike	(✓)	(✓)	(✓)	(✓)
Contributor and Receptive Subsidiary (n=3)					
Low to mod level of initiatives	Moderate level of initiatives	(✓)	(✓)	✓	✓
Rather internal	Internal and external alike	✓	(✓)	(✓)	(✓)
Black Hole and Autonomous Subsidiary (n=2)					
Moderate level of initiatives	Low level of initiatives	✓	(✓)	✓	✗
Internal and external alike	Rather external	✓	(✓)	(✓)	(✓)
Implementer and Quiescent Subsidiary (n=4)					
Low level of initiatives	Low level of initiatives	✓	✓	✓	✓
Rather internal	Rather internal	✓	✓	✓	✓

Table 5.9: Case Comparison: Types and extent of subsidiary initiatives

5.3.3.2 Resource-Related Outcomes

Strategic Leader and Active Subsidiary: Of all subsidiary role types in this study, Strategic Leaders and Active Subsidiaries in both company cases showed the highest level of specialized resource development as the result of their entrepreneurial subsidiary initiatives (see Table 5.10). Moreover, these newly developed resources were most often of use for other parts of the MNC. Consequently, entrepreneurial initiatives by these advanced role types should have the highest potential for firm-level advantages. It can be assumed that these resources outcomes are at least in part the result of the high level of initiatives undertaken in the past five years and, more specifically, the consequence of the high level of global market initiatives.

Contributor and Receptive Subsidiary: In both company cases, these two role types developed new resources to a low to moderate extent, as seen in Table 5.26 below. New and specialized resources were developed in functional areas such as R&D, production, and innovation/entrepreneurship. However, in both cases the newly developed resources resulting from entrepreneurial initiatives were only of low or moderate use for other parts of the MNC. Consequently, the potential for firm-level advantages can be assumed to be moderate to low as well.

Black Hole and Autonomous Subsidiary: The two foreign entities classified as both Black Holes and Autonomous subsidiaries exhibited somewhat different forms of new resource development in relation to subsidiary initiatives. In the case of Autocomp, the Chinese subsidiary generated a moderate level of new resources, of which some were of use for the wider MNC. In contrast, the Greek Telecomp unit developed a low level of new resources, which were of very limited applicability for other parts of the multinational firm. The difference in resource outcomes can possibly be attributed to the different levels of subsidiary initiative-taking activities. As outlined previously, the Chinese

Autocomp unit engaged in a moderate level of entrepreneurial initiatives and even pursued some global market initiatives. In comparison, the Greek subsidiary of Telecomp exhibited a low degree of initiative-taking and undertook no global market initiatives at all in the past five years.

Implementer and Quiescent Subsidiary: The four foreign units classified as Implementers and Quiescent Subsidiaries all developed only low levels of specialized resources. Moreover, the newly developed resources were assessed as largely location-bound and hence of very limited or no use for other parts of the multinational firms. It can be inferred that the limited resource outcomes are at least in part the result of the very low levels of subsidiary initiative-taking activities by the four foreign entities during the past five years.

Autocomp	Telecomp	Case Consistency		Fit with Predictions	
		within	across	B/G	J/M
Strategic Leader and Active Subsidiary (n=5)					
High level of new resources	High level of new resources	✓	✓	✓	✓
High level of MNC applicability	Mod to high level of MNC applicability	(✓)	(✓)	✓	✓
Contributor and Receptive Subsidiary (n=3)					
Low to mod level of new resources	Low to mod level of new resources	(✓)	✓	✓	✓
Low to mod level of MNC applicability	Mod level of MNC applicability	(✓)	(✓)	(✓)	(✓)
Black Hole and Autonomous Subsidiary (n=2)					
Mod level of new resources	Low level of new resources	✓	✗	✓	✗
Low level of MNC applicability	Low level of MNC applicability	✓	✓	(✓)	✓
Implementer and Quiescent Subsidiary (n=4)					
Low level of new resources	Low level of new resources	✓	✓	✓	✓
Low to mod level of MNC applicability	Low level of MNC applicability	(✓)	(✓)	(✓)	(✓)

Table 5.10: Case Comparison: New subsidiary resources and impact on MNC capabilities

5.3.3.3 Further Outcomes

Strategic Leader and Active Subsidiary: In comparison to the other role types, these two more advanced forms in both company cases were able to improve their role most strongly in the wider MNC as a result of subsidiary initiatives. For example, the two foreign Autocomp entities enhanced their market, product and value-added scope. Likewise, the three Telecomp subsidiaries improved their product and value-added scope. Additionally, all five units abroad were able to strengthen their credibility in their respective multinational organizations while subsidiary power was evaluated to have remained largely unchanged (see Table 5.11 below).

Contributor and Receptive Subsidiary: All three foreign units classified as Contributor and Receptive units showed only minor changes to their roles in the MNC as a result of their low to moderate initiative-taking activities. Concerning subsidiary credibility, the Slovakian subsidiary of Telecomp experienced some advances in the past five years, while the two Autocomp units experienced a slight decrease (Australia) and a stable level of credibility (South Korea).

Black Hole and Autonomous Subsidiary: The two subsidiaries categorized as Black Holes and Autonomous units experienced somewhat different role developments in the past five years. The Chinese Autocomp organization, which engaged a in low to moderate level of initiatives, was able to greatly enhance its value-added scope and to some extent its product scope. In comparison, the Greek entity of Telecomp, which pursued entrepreneurial initiatives to a low extent, kept its role largely unchanged. Furthermore, subsidiary credibility remained mostly stable in both foreign entities.

Implementer and Quiescent Subsidiary: The four foreign units in the roles of Implementers and Quiescent subsidiaries were mostly stable in terms of role development over the past five years. Changes to subsidiary credibility were not consistent within and across cases. They ranged from slight decreases (Indian unit of Autocomp, Montenegrin unit of Telecomp) through stable credibility (Romanian unit of Autocomp) to some moderate improvement (Romanian unit of Telecomp).

Autocomp	Telecomp	Case Consistency		Fit with Predictions	
		within	across	B/G	J/M
Strategic Leader and Active Subsidiary (n=5)					
Positive role development	Positive role development	✓	✓	n/a	n/a
Strong credibility improvement	Mod to strong credibility impr.	(✓)	(✓)	n/a	n/a
Contributor and Receptive Subsidiary (n=3)					
Stable role (minor impr.)	Stable role (minor decline)	✓	✓	n/a	n/a
Slight decline to stable credibility	Slight improvement of credibility	(✓)	✗	n/a	n/a
Black Hole and Autonomous Subsidiary (n=2)					
Positive role development	Stable role (minor impr.)	✓	✗	n/a	n/a
Stable credibility (slight improvement)	Stable credibility (slight improvement)	✓	✓	n/a	n/a
Implementer and Quiescent Subsidiary (n=4)					
Stable role (minor impr.)	Stable role (minor impr.)	✓	✓	n/a	n/a
Slight decline to stable credibility	Slight decline to improvement of credibility	✗	✗	n/a	n/a

Table 5.11: Case Comparison: Further outcomes of subsidiary initiatives

5.3.4 Summary on Role-Specific Initiative-Taking

Strategic Leader and Active Subsidiary: The empirical findings of this research support the view that more advanced subsidiary role types such as Strategic Leaders and Active Subsidiaries commonly function as the entrepreneurial and innovative "spark plugs" in multinational firms (see e.g. Birkinshaw/Fry 1998, Bartlett/Ghoshal 2002, Manolopoulos 2008). In both company cases, these role types exhibited the highest level of entrepreneurial subsidiary initiatives throughout the past five years. None of the other investigated role types pursued global market initiatives more frequently than these two subsidiary forms. As a result of their extensive initiative-taking activities, Strategic Leaders and Active Subsidiaries in this research not only developed high levels of specialized resources and capabilities, but these were also frequently of use for other units in the MNC as well, thereby providing the best grounds for firm-level advantages. As a consequence of their strong subsidiary entrepreneurial activities, these role types were able to strengthen their role and credibility in the multinational network organization more than all other subsidiaries in this research (see Table 5.12).

Certain patterns in the initiative process of Strategic Leaders and Active Subsidiaries also started to emerge in this study. As a result of their strong internal and external embeddedness, their position in strategically important markets and their strong set of resources, these two role types were in an advantageous position to frequently identify new initiative opportunities from both internal and external sources. Furthermore, due to the high level of initiative opportunity identification and its often radically innovative nature, these role types needed to engage in moderate and high levels of resource structuring activities. Similar to the sub-process of initiative identification, needed resources were commonly obtained from various internal and external sources and through different structuring forms. However, external resource acquisition and internal-external resource development were utilized more often than by other role types. The various resources and capabilities were frequently combined through extensive bundling when attempting to accomplish subsidiary initiatives. The empirical findings further indicate that the strong power and resource position of these advanced roles allowed them to pursue initiatives with higher degrees of autonomy and hence with lower headquarters involvement than the other subsidiary types. Likewise, given the strategic importance of these units for the wider MNC and their extensive set of resources, the entities abroad only faced low levels of corporate resistance and needed to engage in only low to moderate levels of initiative-selling activities.

Contributor and Receptive Subsidiary: The findings of the present research show that these three Contributor and Receptive subsidiaries, as expected, engaged in moderate levels of subsidiary initiative-taking. Despite the foreign units' generally strong resources bases, their limited funding – particularly for trial and error activities – and their lacking support from headquarters made it difficult to successfully pursue initiatives of larger scale and higher degrees of innovativeness. For example, newly detected initiative opportunities were commonly incrementally and moderately innovative, and realized initiatives often represented only enhancements or adaptations of existing products and services. In the end, these activities resulted in the development of some specialized resources that were of moderate use for other parts of the MNC. Overall, the Contributor and Receptive units' contribution to firm-level advantages through initiatives was assessed as low to moderate. Owing to their moderate initiative-taking activities, these subsidiaries maintained mostly stable roles in the wider MNC and typically did not further improve their credibility vis-à-vis other units of the multinational firm.

As to the initiative process, these two role types exhibited a moderate level of initiative opportunity identification. Given their tighter integration in the MNC and their stronger inward focus, new initiative discoveries most often materialized through sources from within the MNC, particularly from within the subsidiary units themselves. Due to their strong resource base but lack of headquarters support, required resources were often developed internally within the foreign entities and initiatives were most frequently realized through incremental or intermediate resource bundling activities. As a result of the moderate power position, headquarters involvement was moderate to high and corporate resistance was commonly low to moderate.

Black Hole and Autonomous Subsidiary: The two foreign units identified as Black Holes and Autonomous Subsidiaries exhibited an overall low to moderate level of subsidiary initiatives in the past five years. In particular, local resource constraints and limited subsidiary autonomy appear to represent inhibitors to more frequent initiatives. Headquarters had to be closely involved for central approval and access to the resources necessary to realize entrepreneurial opportunities, for example. The majority of entrepreneurial activities were local market initiatives, such as the development of new services or the adaptation of products originally developed for specific needs in the local countries. Stemming from the limited entrepreneurial activities, the two subsidiaries developed low to moderate levels of new resources, which were of limited use for other MNC units. The small number of initiatives resulted in a stable (Greek unit of Autocomp) to positive subsidiary role development (Chinese unit of Autocomp) and mostly unchanged subsidiary credibility during the past five years.

With regard to the initiative-taking process, these units showed a low to moderate level of initiative identification, and most newly detected opportunities were incrementally and moderately innovative in nature. Due to their high degrees of localization and comparatively low level of integration in the MNC, most new initiative prospects were identified externally through interactions with local market actors. Required resources were obtained in various ways and from different sources. Internal and external resource acquisition forms were both utilized repeatedly in the two company cases. New initiative realization involved a low level of resource combination activities and was commonly achieved through less extensive efforts, such as incremental or intermediate resource bundling. Given their low degrees of autonomy and comparatively weak power positions, headquarters became strongly involved in subsidiary initiatives and local units had to frequently communicate and present them to the corporate center. These role types also usually faced strong corporate resistance and needed to frequently sell initiative ideas due to, for example, the poor strategic fit of initiatives and the lack of trust in the capabilities of the subsidiaries.

Implementer and Quiescent Subsidiary: As expected, the four foreign entities classified as Implementers and Quiescent Subsidiaries played the least important role with regard to entrepreneurial activities (see e.g. Bartlett/Ghoshal 2002). In the present study, these role types exhibited the lowest level of subsidiary initiatives during the past five years. Entrepreneurial efforts were often internally oriented, such as internal market and global-internal hybrid initiatives. Besides the "standard" forms of subsidiary initiatives, these units also repeatedly engaged in "trivial initiatives" for purely local application, including process improvements or local cost reduction measures. In the end, the few subsidiary initiatives produced a limited amount of new resources, which were of very little use for other parts of the MNC. Their contribution to the sustained competitiveness of the MNC should thus be considered lowest of all subsidiary roles studied. As a result, the roles and power positions of Implementer and Quiescent Subsidiaries in their respective MNCs even showed some slight decline.

Concerning the subsidiary initiative process, certain patterns across the four subsidiaries were identified. Due to their location in rather undemanding market environments and their limited resource base, these units detected few new initiative opportunities, and these were most often from within the MNC network. New opportunities were commonly incrementally and moderately innovative and encompassed, for example, replications of existing products or services or internal process improvements. The few required resources for the realization of initiatives were usually obtained from inside the MNC, either through internal development in the subsidiaries or through internal acquisition from other parts of the firm. Given the small number of initiatives and their often incrementally innovative nature, mostly less extensive resource combinations came into play. As a consequence of their limited autonomy and their comparatively weak power position in their MNCs, these role types faced moderate to high levels of headquarters involvement, high levels of corporate resistance and the need to frequently sell their initiatives in the multinational organizations.

		Strategic Leader/Active Subsidiary	Fit with Predictions B/G	Fit with Predictions J/M	Contributor/ Receptive Subsidiary	Fit with Predictions B/G	Fit with Predictions J/M	Black Hole/ Autonomous Subsidiary	Fit with Predictions B/G	Fit with Predictions J/M	Implementer/ Quiescent Subsidiary	Fit with Predictions B/G	Fit with Predictions J/M
(1) Initiative Opportunity Identification		(Moderate to) high level	✓	✓	Moderate level	✓	✓	Low (to mod) level	✗	✓	Low (to mod) level	(✓)	(✓)
		Both int./ ext. identification	✗	✗	Rather internal identification	✓	✓	Rather external identification	✓	✓	Rather internal identification	✓	✗
		Highest level of radically innovative opportunities	n/a	n/a	Mostly increm. and mod. innovative opportunities	n/a	n/a	Mostly increm. and mod. innovative opportunities	n/a	n/a	Mostly increm. and mod. innovative opportunities	n/a	n/a
(2) Resource Structuring		Mod to high level	✓	✓	Low to high level	✓	✓	Low to mod level	✓	✓	Low level	✓	✓
		Various forms (often ext. acquisition and int.-ext. development)	✗	✓	Rather internal development	✓	✓	Ext./int. acquisition	✗	(✓)	Int. development and int. acquisition	✗	(✓)
(3) Resource Bundling		High level	✓	✓	Low to moderate	✗	✗	Low level	✗	✓	Low (to mod) level	✓	✓
		Often more extensive (radical) bundling	✓	✓	Incremental and intermediate	✓	✓	Incremental and intermediate	✓	✗	Mostly incremental bundling	✓	✓
(4) HQ-S Alignment		Low (to mod) level of HQ involvement	(✓)	✓	Mod to high level of HQ involvement	✗	✗	High level of HQ involvement	✗	✗	Mod to high level of HQ involvement	✓	✓
		Low level of corp. resistance	✓	✓	(Low to) mod level of corp. resistance	(✓)	(✓)	High level of corp. resistance	✓	✓	High level of corp. resistance	✓	✓
		Low to mod level of initiative selling	✓	✓	(Low to) mod level of initiative selling	(✓)	✗	High level of initiative selling	✓	✗	Mod to high level of initiative selling	✓	✓
(5) Subsidiary Initiative-Taking		High level of initiatives	✓	✓	(Low to) moderate level of initiatives	✓	✓	Low to moderate level of initiatives	✗	✓	Low level of initiatives	✓	✓
		Often externally-oriented, highest level of global market applicability	(✓)	(✓)	Internal and external, often local market and global-internal hybrid	(✓)	(✓)	Internally and externally-oriented, local market most prevalent	(✓)	(✓)	Rather internally-oriented (internal market and global-internal hybrid)	✓	✓
(6) Resource-Related Outcomes		High level of new resources	✓	✓	(Low to) mod level of new resources	✓	✓	Low to moderate level of new resources	✓	✗	Low level of new resources	✓	✓
		(Mod to) high level of MNC applicability	✓	✓	(Low to) mod level of MNC applicability	✓	(✓)	Low level of MNC applicability	✓	✓	Low to mod level of MNC applicability	✓	✓
(7) Further Outcomes		Positive role development	n/a	n/a	Stable role	n/a	n/a	Stable to positive role development	n/a	n/a	Stable role	n/a	n/a
		(Mod to) strong credibility improv.	n/a	n/a	Stable credibility (slight decline to slight improvement)	n/a	n/a	Stable credibility (slight improvement)	n/a	n/a	Slight decline in credibility	n/a	n/a

Table 5.12: Summary of findings on role-specific subsidiary initiative-taking

5.3.5 Additional Findings on Subsidiary Initiatives

5.3.5.1 Objectives of Subsidiary Initiatives

As outlined in Subsection 2.2.3.2, previous work implies that subsidiary initiatives are pursued with the following objectives: (1) to satisfy the personal needs of local management, (2) to realize new business opportunities, (3) to improve internal business operations, (4) to grow the subsidiary's resource base, and (5) to enhance the subsidiary's position, responsibility and/or autonomy in the MNC. Largely in line with previous suggestions, the following five main objectives of subsidiary initiatives were identified in the present study.[451]

First, entrepreneurial subsidiary initiatives were predominantly undertaken in order to **improve existing business** and/or to **realize new business opportunities** (see Table 5.13 below). Many foreign subsidiary units aimed at responding to specific customer demand for new products or services and attempted to satisfy market needs that were often not recognized elsewhere in the MNC. For example, Autocomp subsidiaries in China, Mexico and India identified needs for specific products in their local markets that were unknown and not yet available in the wider multinational firm. Consequently, some of their initiatives were aimed at developing products and solutions to satisfy particular local market requirements (I3, I6, I8).[452] In other cases, foreign subsidiaries engaged in initiatives to develop new business and increase their revenues. For instance, various Telecomp units outside the home country, Germany, were faced with declining revenues in their core markets and consequently engaged in initiatives geared at developing new products and solutions in adjacent markets to generate new revenues and offset losses in their core business areas (I12, I13, I14, I16).[453] Likewise, some units engaged in entrepreneurial activities to introduce innovative products or solutions in their existing markets to help them further differentiate their offerings and to achieve improved or even leading market positions.[454] Lastly, the Greek subsidiary of Telecomp mentioned the enhancement of existing business by improving customer satisfaction and loyalty (I14).

Second, in certain instances subsidiary initiatives were undertaken with the objective of **improving internal business operations**. For example, in order to maintain or improve

---

[451] It should be noted that foreign subsidiaries in the present study often pursued not only one but multiple objectives at the same time. However, in order to better differentiate and highlight the separate objectives of subsidiary initiatives, they are discussed individually in this subsection.
[452] Aside from these three foreign units, others also engaged in entrepreneurial initiatives to react to local market trends or to meet local customer demand, e.g. the Autocomp subsidiaries in South Korea or Germany (I2, I4).
[453] This was mentioned by, for instance, Telecomp units in Greece, Slovakia, Montenegro and Croatia. Also, a number of managers of Autocomp subsidiaries indicated in the interviews that they pursued initiatives to generate new revenues and profits, e.g. in South Korea, China and Mexico (I3, I4, I6).
[454] This was mentioned by, for example, the Autocomp units from Germany and South Korea (I2, I4) and Telecomp units from Poland or Greece (I11, I14).

competitiveness in their markets, some units focused their entrepreneurial efforts on reducing costs of production or service delivery, such as the Croatian and Greek units of Telecomp (I12, I14) and the German, Australian and Romanian units of Autocomp (I2 I5, I7). Likewise, some units attempted to improve internal processes or make them more efficient (I5, I12).

A third objective identified in the interviews referred to the goal of foreign subsidiaries to **grow their own resources base**. For example, the Chinese Autocomp unit intended to enhance its expertise and capabilities through subsidiary initiatives, particularly in the area of specialized technologies (I6). Likewise, the Romanian subsidiary of the same multinational firm aimed at developing new knowledge and expertise through its entrepreneurial activities (I7).

Fourth, managers of the German Autocomp subsidiary pursued initiatives with the objective of **strengthening the subsidiary's position** in the wider MNC. Given the overall corporate goal of giving increasing responsibilities to its various research and development hubs abroad in the coming years, subsidiary initiative was seen as an opportunity to ensure that the unit remains important in the MNC (I2).

Fifth and last, the findings of the present study suggest that subsidiary initiatives were pursued with the intent of **motivating and retaining employees**. Subsidiary management from the Chinese and Mexican units of Autocomp highlighted the relevance of initiatives for the motivation, satisfaction and pride of local employees and the positive effects on retention of staff. For example, allowing engineering employees to take initiative and work on non-standard and more sophisticated projects was considered an important measure to help retain staff in the subsidiary (I6). Similarly, the Mexican subsidiary management stated that initiatives are pursued at least in part to help attract new engineers and keep existing personnel satisfied. Additionally, successful initiatives that turned from "ideas ... into physical products" were often showcased in the wider MNC and were seen as good tools to improve employee pride (I3).

As the present study shows, subsidiary initiatives were pursued with different objectives (see summary in Table 5.13 below). Most of these appear to be in line with previous scholarly writings. However, one new objective was identified: the attraction, motivation and retention of subsidiary personnel. Interview findings suggest that autonomy to pursue initiatives and the more creative and "non-standard" work related to them has been applied to positively influence subsidiary staff. One objective mentioned in previous writings but not identified in the present research relates to the satisfaction of the personal needs of employee management. Here, possibly the reluctance of local management to share individual and potentially sensitive information with the largely unknown researcher may have prevented the open sharing of this information (see e.g. Easterby-Smith et al. 2012, p. 136; Lindsey 2004, p. 515).

Objectives	Examples from Interviews	Units
(1) Improve existing business and/or develop new business opportunities	- Fulfill customer demand and satisfy market needs - Win new business and generate additional revenues/profits - Introduce innovative products/solutions to better differentiate in existing markets - Enhance customer satisfaction and loyalty	- Autocomp: Germany, Mexico, China, South Korea, India - Telecomp: Croatia, Poland, Slovakia, Greece, Montenegro
(2) Improve internal business operations	- Reduce costs of products and services to maintain/improve competitiveness in the market - Improve internal processes	- Autocomp: Germany, Romania, Australia - Telecomp: Greece, Croatia
(3) Grow subsidiary resource base	- Develop new subsidiary expertise and capabilities (e.g. specific technologies)	- Autocomp: China, Romania
(4) Maintain/ enhance subsidiary position in the MNC	- Remain an important subsidiary vis-à-vis other units of the MNC	- Autocomp: Germany
(5) Motivate, attract and retain employees	- Enhance employee satisfaction - Improve employee pride through wider recognition for entrepreneurial initiatives - Strengthen attraction and retention of subsidiary employees	- Autocomp: Mexico, China

Table 5.13: Identified objectives of subsidiary initiatives

5.3.5.2 Antecedents of Subsidiary Initiatives

Subsection 2.2.4 presented 26 different antecedent groups that were identified through the literature analysis. As described earlier, previous work provides little clarity as to which influencing factors exert the largest influence on subsidiary initiative-taking, and it has not yet investigated in detail what role different antecedents play in the various phases of the initiative process. Therefore, the next two paragraphs describe the empirical findings on (critical) antecedents and their roles throughout the initiative process.

(1) Overview of Antecedents

Based on results of the present research endeavor, five specific antecedent groups appear to play a more critical role in initiative-taking activities than the remaining ones: subsidiary resources and capabilities, subsidiary decision-making autonomy, subsidiary network linkages, external market context, and entrepreneurial attitude and mindset of subsidiary management.

In the subsidiary units investigated, the level of **subsidiary resources and capabilities** appear to play a critical, perhaps the most critical, role for subsidiary entrepreneurial initiatives.[455] More specifically, two resource forms were repeatedly noted by subsidiary managers in the interviews as highly relevant for entrepreneurial activities: specialized resources and capabilities as well as slack resources. Specialized resources such as market knowledge and the technical expertise of local employees were considered important drivers for entrepreneurial subsidiary activities by all advanced role types. Having a sound understanding of the market environment, the latest market trends and developments and of customer demand was viewed as an important prerequisite for identifying and exploiting subsidiary initiative opportunities. Likewise, highly qualified personnel with the necessary experience and technical or project management knowledge, for example, was seen as important for generating new ideas and for pushing initiatives toward completion (e.g. I2, I3, I10, I11, I12). In addition, slack resources in the form of, for instance, excess financial or personnel resources, were identified as critical drivers of entrepreneurial activities since they allowed the foreign units to engage in such trial-and-error activities without approaching or involving other parts of the MNC (I2, I12). For example, the Mexican subsidiary of Autocomp was able to leverage excess budget and R&D personnel to form a local innovation team with the intent of driving local entrepreneurial and innovative activities (I3).

In line with previous research (e.g. Birkinshaw 1995, Birkinshaw/Hood 1997, Birkinshaw et al. 1998, Zahra et al. 2000), **subsidiary decision-making autonomy** was frequently specified as a critical driver of subsidiary initiatives, particularly in the case of the more advanced role types, as shown in Figure 5.131. According to subsidiary management, autonomy allowed these units to freely decide which entrepreneurial activities to pursue and how to manage them without having to ask for permission or to align with the corporate center (e.g. I2, I3, I10, I12). As a consequence, more new initiative opportunities were not only identified but also realized in the end by these foreign entities. In contrast, subsidiary initiatives were often inhibited in less advanced role types due to their lack of autonomy. For example, the Indian unit of Autocomp did not have the freedom to decide on any small or large changes in the organization. Consequently, no major initiatives were developed in the past five years by this entity (I8).

Concurrent with findings of other scholars, the present research indicates that **external and internal network linkages** and close interactions with internal and external network actors helped stimulate and further develop subsidiary initiatives (see e.g. Andersson et al. 2001a, Lou 2001, Andersson 2003, Tseng et al. 2004, Holm et al. 2005 for similar findings).[456] Concerning external network linkages, particularly close proximity and interactions with customers not only supported the identification of new initiative

---

[455] Subsidiary resources and capabilities were mentioned as either drivers or inhibitors to subsidiary initiative in all 14 subsidiary manager interviews.
[456] Internal and/or external subsidiary network linkages were mentioned as either drivers or inhibitors to subsidiary initiative in 12 out of the 14 subsidiary manager interviews.

opportunities but also drove their validation and refinement as they progressed and developed (e.g. I2, I4, I6, I10). In addition to close interactions with customers, collaboration with competitors, external research institutions and governmental organizations also strengthened the identification and realization of subsidiary initiatives. Finally, cooperation and joint initiatives with local suppliers and business partners helped better identify new ideas and aided in gaining access to resources needed for the realization of initiatives (e.g. I2, I3, I11, I12). For example, the Croatian Telecomp subsidiary identified numerous new initiative opportunities through close relationships with its local suppliers and through its cooperation with a local technical university (I12). Likewise, the Mexican unit of Autocomp benefited from its connection to a local university through creation of new initiative ideas, and from its relationship with a local partner to obtain technology and resources needed for the implementation of initiatives (I3). Similar to external network linkages, those within the MNC seemed advantageous for subsidiary entrepreneurial initiatives. The empirical results of this study show that close relationships and interactions with headquarters, internal service providers, R&D centers or other MNC units helped with identifying new market trends, detecting new initiative opportunities and obtaining access to internal resources and capabilities (e.g. I2, I3, I4, I5). For instance, the German and Mexican Autocomp units utilized their relationships with the central development departments to obtain needed resources and funding to develop and drive initiatives (I2, I3). Similarly, the Polish, Hungarian and Croatian subsidiaries of Telecomp identified new ideas or obtained resources needed for the realization of initiatives through internal linkages with sister subsidiaries and the corporate center (I10, I11, I12).

Another antecedent group mentioned as a driver or inhibitor in each subsidiary interview is the **external market context**.[457] Factors such as local market dynamism, competitive intensity, customer demand intensity and market size were mentioned as critically affecting subsidiary initiative-taking activities.[458] For example, the dynamic and emerging market environment of the Mexican Autocomp subsidiary was described as highly beneficial for innovative and entrepreneurial activities as it helped to "*boost innovation and creativity*" (I3). Relatedly, the declining core business of many foreign Telecomp subsidiaries such as those in Hungary, Croatia or Greece forced the foreign units to explore new growth opportunities in adjacent markets and stimulated the development of new entrepreneurial initiatives (I10, I12, I14). Strong competitive pressure also impacted the entrepreneurial activities of the foreign entities and provoked them to

---

[457] The external market context was mentioned as either a driver or inhibitor of subsidiary initiative in 13 out of the 14 subsidiary manager interviews.
[458] It should be noted that the four factors that comprise the external market context are identical with the four indicators used for the operationalization of the role dimension "strategic importance of the subsidiary's market environment" (see Subsection 4.3.1.1). However, as these factors were mentioned often individually in the interviews, it was decided to select a broader term for the antecedent group.

engage in initiatives geared towards, for example, stronger market differentiation or cost reduction (e.g. I2, I11, I12). Moreover, intense customer demand for such things as innovative or low cost solutions was suggested as a driver of entrepreneurial subsidiary behavior in various foreign entities (e.g. I2, I12). Finally, the size of the subsidiary market was mentioned as an element of the market context that influenced subsidiary initiatives. For instance, smaller and, in some cases, shrinking market environments such as those of the Montenegrin and Romanian Telecomp units or the Australian and Indian subsidiaries of Autocomp were brought up as factors inhibiting entrepreneurial initiatives. In such environments, the range of opportunities for innovative and entrepreneurial activities was described as limited and, consequently, the levels of realized initiatives were comparatively low (I5, I8, I15, I16).

Furthermore, the empirical results indicate that an **entrepreneurial attitude and mindset** on the part of subsidiary managers, and their efforts to promote an entrepreneurial atmosphere, played an important role for subsidiary initiatives in a number of the units investigated (for similar arguments see e.g. Birkinshaw et al. 1998, Birkinshaw 1999).[459] The findings suggest that the creation of an entrepreneurial and risk-taking atmosphere helped with the identification and development of initiatives. For example, in the Mexican Autocomp subsidiary, the characteristics and attitudes of the local subsidiary team were described as "*young, very ambitious, very motivated, very excited*" and at the same time "*creative and not set in a certain way of thinking,*" thereby making it a "*good place for innovation*" (I3). Moreover, local subsidiary management over time created an entrepreneurial atmosphere and "*lit a fire ... on innovation ... and established a culture of innovation and product development*" (I3). This resulted in a high level of subsidiary initiatives. Similarly, in the Hungarian subsidiary of Telecomp, the local CEO and executives brought in own ideas on new entrepreneurial opportunities, encouraged initiative-taking activities and often provided immediate support for new ideas (I10). Moreover, a risk-taking attitude, with the local subsidiary management team "*never being afraid of trying out new things or models,*" has helped the Croatian unit come to be considered "*one of the innovators and templates for new products and new innovations in the Group*" (I12).

Lastly, three further antecedent groups were repeatedly stated in the interviews. First, the often **complex and competitive approval and resource allocation** processes in the MNCs were cited as inhibitors to entrepreneurial initiative. Corporate bureaucracy and lengthy alignment processes with headquarters were said to slow down initiative

---

[459] Entrepreneurial attitude and mindset are understood as the subsidiary management's orientation towards proactive, risk-taking and innovative behavior and their support to create an atmosphere in which entrepreneurial initiative-taking is fostered (see e.g. e.g. Miller 1983, Covin/Slevin 1991, Zahra/Covin 1995, Lumpkin/Dess 1996, Covin/Miles 1999). Entrepreneurial attitude and mindset were mentioned as either a driver or inhibitor to subsidiary initiative in 5 out of the 14 subsidiary manager interviews.

progress or, in some instances, even bring it to a complete stop. Given the usually scarce resources in the MNCs for entrepreneurial initiatives, most subsidiaries needed to engage in a complex corporate approval process aimed at obtaining the headquarters sanctioning and resources needed to realize their initiatives (e.g. I3, I4, I7, I10, I14, I15, I16). Furthermore, **headquarters-subsidiary communication and relationships** were more frequently brought up as inhibitors rather than drivers of entrepreneurial subsidiary initiative (I3, I4, I13). For example, the sparse communication between the South Korean unit of Autocomp and headquarters resulted in an insufficient understanding of local circumstances and local market needs at the corporate center. As a result, headquarters' willingness to support and fund entrepreneurial initiatives was limited and priority was often given to other subsidiary locations (I4). Likewise, in the case of the Slovakian Telecomp subsidiary, the subsidiary manager had a weak relationship with managers at headquarters. Consequently, several communication attempts to bring new initiative opportunities to the attention of the corporate center failed and many were ignored (I13). In comparison, the strong headquarters-subsidiary communication and relationship of the Mexican Autocomp unit helped with the progression of various initiatives. Here, frequent communication and strong collaboration with headquarters not only strengthened the credibility of the foreign unit over time but also helped the Mexican entity better understand *"how to package ... ideas in order to get approval, to get budget"* (I3). Finally, **corporate direction or even pressure** to engage in entrepreneurial and innovative activities appeared to have a positive effect on subsidiary initiatives (e.g. I3, I10, I14). Specific innovation targets and incentive schemes were repeatedly mentioned as drivers to entrepreneurial and innovative subsidiary activities. Particularly in the case of Telecomp, headquarters often set particular innovation targets for different subsidiary locations (e.g. Montenegro, Slovakia), which led to increased entrepreneurial activities in those units (I3, I6, I13).

As indicated above, the findings indicate that drivers and inhibitors played various parts in specific subsidiary role settings. In the case of **Strategic Leaders/Active Subsidiaries**, it can be assumed that the simultaneous presence of numerous drivers helped facilitate entrepreneurial initiatives. For example, in the present study these units were required to frequently engage in initiatives due to their demanding market context with such factors as high market dynamism, intense competitive intensity and strong customer demand intensity. In this type of market context, customers commonly require complex and sophisticated solutions, innovations are often fast-paced and existing competitive advantages are not sustainable for a long periods, thereby stimulating entrepreneurial subsidiary behavior.[460] Furthermore, their rich endowment with subsidiary resources and capabilities not only helped with the identification and realization of

---

[460] See Subsection 3.5.1.1 for a detailed discussion on the potential impact of market context on subsidiary initiatives.

initiatives but also facilitated the interaction and alignment process with other corporate entities, including headquarters. Likewise, high degrees of autonomy and strong internal and external network linkages helped with the pursuit of entrepreneurial activities in these advanced role types. Finally, the entrepreneurial attitude and mindset of subsidiary management proved beneficial to the creation of subsidiary initiatives in these units (see Figure 5.131). Taken together, the presence of these various drivers may help further explain why the more advanced role types showed the highest level of initiatives in the end.

In comparison to Strategic Leaders/Active Subsidiaries, foreign units in the roles of **Contributors/Receptive Subsidiaries** benefited from fewer drivers and they faced a higher number of inhibiting factors to entrepreneurial initiatives. For example, their subsidiary resources and capabilities, moderate degrees of autonomy and strong internal network linkages were mentioned as factors that positively influenced subsidiary initiatives. In contrast, the limited size and growth of the markets in which these units operated, weak headquarters-subsidiary communication and relationships and limited subsidiary resources and autonomy apparently constrained entrepreneurial activities in these foreign entities. It can be assumed that, given the less supportive context, all three subsidiaries in the role of Contributors/Receptive subsidiaries exhibited only low to moderate levels of subsidiary initiatives.

Despite their often encouraging market context and their strong external market linkages, **Black Holes/Autonomous Subsidiaries** were also confronted with a number of obstacles to entrepreneurial activities. For instance, limited autonomy, scarce subsidiary resources and capabilities and weak headquarters-subsidiary relations were cited as subsidiary-level context factors that often restricted the foreign unit's ability to engage in entrepreneurial initiatives. Likewise, complex and competitive resource allocation processes, as well as limited internal network linkages, presented obstacles to successful entrepreneurial activities by foreign units in the roles of Black Holes/Autonomous subsidiaries. It can be presumed that, as a consequence, these units exhibited low and moderate levels of subsidiary initiatives.

Strategic Leader & Active Subsidiary

Drivers

- **Environmental Level Context**
  - Market context (dynamism, competitive intensity, customer demand intensity)
- **Corporate Level Context**
  - Subsidiary autonomy
- **Subsidiary Level Context**
  - Subsidiary resources and capabilities
  - External and internal network linkages
- **Individual Level Context**
  - Entrepreneurial attitude and mindset

Inhibitors

- **Corporate Level Context**
  - Complex and competitive resource allocation/approval

Contributor & Receptive Subsidiary

Drivers

- **Environmental Level Context**
  - …
- **Corporate Level Context**
  - Some subsidiary autonomy
- **Subsidiary Level Context**
  - Some subsidiary resources and capabilities
  - Internal network linkages
- **Individual Level Context**
  - …

Inhibitors

- **Environmental Level Context**
  - Limited market size/growth
- **Corporate Level Context**
  - Complex and competitive resource allocation/approval
- **Subsidiary Level Context**
  - Limited subsidiary autonomy
  - Weak HQ-S communication and relationship
  - Limited subsidiary resources and capabilities
  - Lacking external network linkages

Black Hole & Autonomous Subsidiary

Drivers

- **Environmental Level Context**
  - Market context (dynamism, competitive intensity)
- **Corporate Level Context**
  - …
- **Subsidiary Level Context**
  - External network linkages
- **Individual Level Context**
  - …

Inhibitors

- **Corporate Level Context**
  - Complex and competitive resource allocation/approval
  - Internal network linkages
- **Subsidiary Level Context**
  - Weak HQ-S communication and relationship
  - Limited subsidiary resources and capabilities

Implementer & Quiescent Subsidiary

Drivers

- **Environmental Level Context**
  - Market context (dynamism, competitive intensity)
- **Corporate Level Context**
  - …
- **Subsidiary Level Context**
  - …
- **Individual Level Context**
  - …

Inhibitors

- **Environmental Level Context**
  - Limited market size/growth
- **Corporate Level Context**
  - Complex and competitive resource allocation/approval
- **Subsidiary Level Context**
  - Limited subsidiary autonomy
  - Weak HQ-S communication and relationship
  - Limited subsidiary resources and capabilities
  - Lacking external network linkages
- **Individual Level Context**
  - Lacking entrepreneurial attitude and mindset

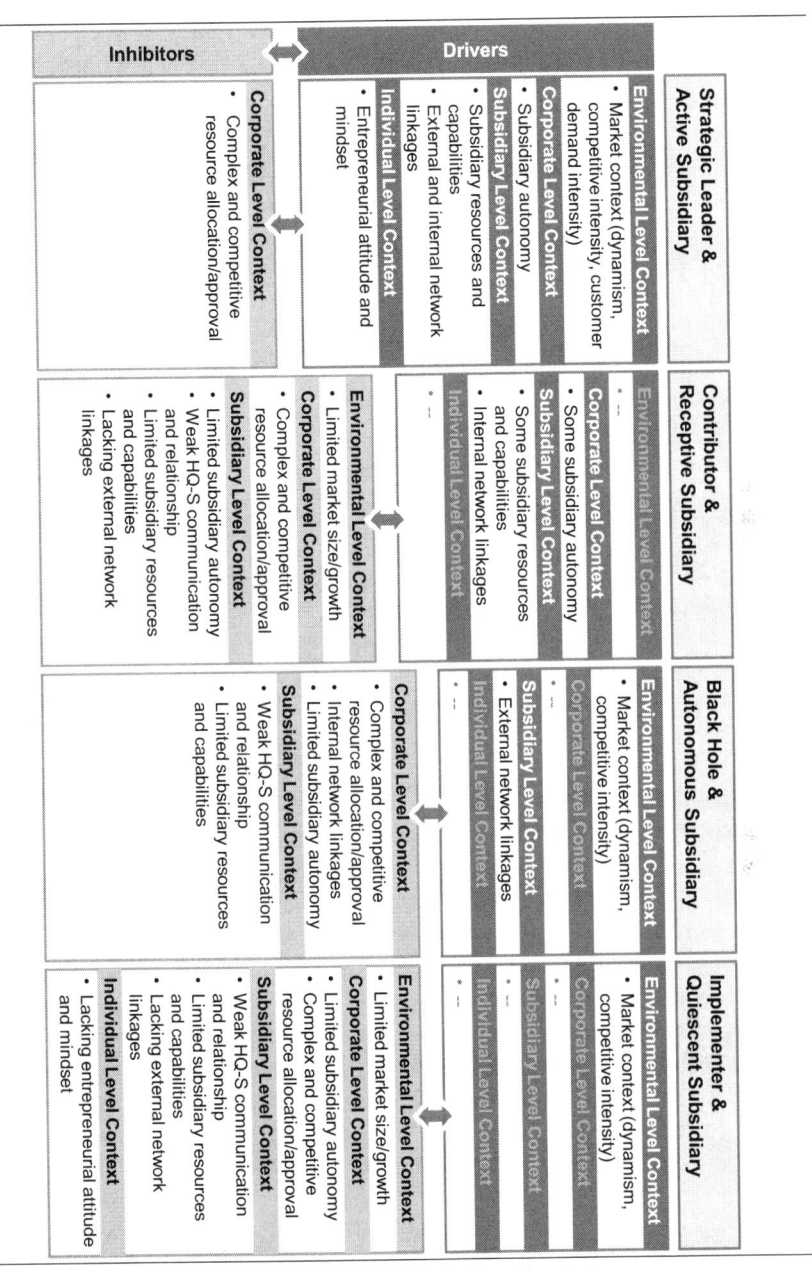

Figure 5.131: Main antecedents of subsidiary initiatives by role types

Finally, **Implementers/Quiescent Subsidiaries** operated in the least favorable context of all role types, with numerous factors hindering entrepreneurial initiatives. In the present study, inhibitors were observed at all context levels, that is, the environmental, corporate, subsidiary and individual level contexts, as shown in Figure 5.131 above. For instance, the relevant subsidiary markets were typically assessed as small and stagnant or even shrinking in size and they were often unimportant for the wider MNC. In such environments, it can be assumed that fewer initiative opportunities arise and subsidiaries do not need to be particularly proactive or aggressive to remain competitive in these market contexts.[461] Additionally, the Implementers/Quiescent Subsidiaries in this study commonly possessed few resources and capabilities and limited autonomy and they lacked external network linkages. This in turn restricted their ability to independently identify and drive initiatives towards completion.

5.3.5.3 Subsidiary Initiative Process

The qualitative findings from the 18 interviews provide additional valuable insights into the initiative process that has not been systematically and purposefully researched.[462] Although the present study was unable to fully and comprehensively investigate the complex processes of all subsidiary initiatives, the empirical results at least seem to further support the different sub-processes which were presented as part of research framework in Sections 3.2 and 3.4. Hence, findings on subsidiary initiative identification, resource structuring and headquarters-subsidiary alignment will be discussed subsequently and are summarized in Figure 5.132.[463]

Subsidiary initiative identification: In Subsection 3.4.2.1, it was articulated that subsidiary initiatives can be identified either externally through interactions with global and local network partners or internally through interactions with actors from within the corporate system. These considerations could not only be further supported but also augmented by the findings in this study. *External* initiative identification commonly took place through contacts with global or local network actors such as global customers, local customers, competitors, technology partners or universities. *Internal* identification often occurred within the subsidiary itself or through interactions with sister subsidiaries and/or headquarters. Inside the foreign units, new initiative opportunities were, for instance, detected through discussions in team meetings or local workshops.[464] Similarly, conference calls and meetings or information exchanges with representatives

---
[461] See Subsection 3.5.1.1 for a detailed discussion on the potential impact of the subsidiary market environment on initiative-taking activities.
[462] See, for example, Sections 1.2 and 3.1 for further details on research gaps related to entrepreneurial processes.
[463] Initiative-related resource bundling activities (see Subsection 3.4.2.3) were not explicitly discussed in the interviews and hence no additional findings are outlined in this section of the thesis.
[464] Local workshops to identify initiative opportunities were mentioned by the Autocomp units in Romania (I7) and Australia (I5), among others.

from sister subsidiaries helped with the detection of new initiative possibilities. Lastly, communication with headquarters and other central units aided in finding opportunities for new entrepreneurial initiatives.[465] *External context factors* supporting subsidiary identification included network linkages and interactions with global and local actors outside the MNC or pressures and opportunities arising from the external market context. Among the *internal factors* supporting the detection of new initiatives were subsidiary resources and capabilities in the form of creative and knowledgeable staff. For instance, the local staff's market knowledge and sound understanding of the latest trends and developments, as well as their ability to appropriately interpret and utilize information, were seen as important aspects.[466] Moreover, internal network linkages with other MNC units, as well as subsidiary autonomy to freely choose and pursue entrepreneurial opportunities, appear to positively influence initiative identification.

Resource structuring: Subsection 3.4.2.2 describes four principal resource structuring approaches to obtain resources needed for the realization of subsidiary initiatives: internal and external resource acquisition, and internal and internal-external resource accumulation. In the present study, all resource structuring approaches were identified and the relevant findings are described below. *Internal resource acquisition* commonly meant obtaining specialized resources such as advanced knowledge, core technologies or special engineering equipment from headquarters, from global or regional R&D hubs and from sister subsidiaries. Acquiring such resources from other parts of the MNC often proved difficult for the foreign units given the resource scarcity in the multinational firm and the fear of external knowledge drain to local competition or product piracy, for example. In a similar vein, resources and capabilities were *acquired externally* from suppliers, vendors or partners outside the boundaries of the multination firm. One example included the acquisition of consulting services and expertise in order to help develop value propositions, product specifications and "go-to-market strategies" when entering new and adjacent markets (I14). In addition to acquiring resources, required resources and capabilities were *developed internally* in the foreign subsidiaries[467] or in collaboration with external actors. Examples of internal resource accumulation for initiatives included research and development efforts (in engineering or IT), knowledge transfer through expatriates, local training of staff or sharing of best practices among MNC units. Finally, some resources were developed in collaboration with external partners such as global customers, technology providers, research institutions or even competitors. For instance, the German Autocomp unit collaborated with research institutions and competitors to develop technologies needed for a new product initiative.

---

[465] The term "other central units" refers to entities such as global R&D centers or product and innovation units.
[466] Local staff knowledge and expertise was mentioned as a critical driver for initiative identification by, among others, the Autocomp units from Germany and Mexico and the Telecomp subsidiaries from Hungary, Poland and Croatia.
[467] In some cases resources were developed in collaboration with other MNC units as well.

Among the factors influencing resource structuring activities were external and internal network linkages. In the present study, it appeared beneficial to have long-term relationships with both internal and external network partners, as this helped with access to their resource pools. Aside from network linkages, existing resources and capabilities in the foreign subsidiaries also supported resource development efforts. For instance, the extensive product development expertise and the strong R&D force of the South Korean and Mexican Autocomp units helped with the advancement of technologies and the adaptation of products.

Headquarters-subsidiary alignment: Subsection 3.4.3 outlined three different sub-processes related to the alignment between headquarters and the foreign subsidiary as part of initiative-taking activities: headquarters involvement, corporate resistance and subsidiary initiative selling. In addition to these three sub-processes, further details could be identified with regard to subsidiary initiative evaluation and approval. The findings are outlined below.

When explaining *headquarters involvement*, subsidiary management often referred to their leeway for innovative and entrepreneurial activities and the need for alignment and interaction. According to the interview findings, the extent of headquarters involvement was often dependent on the type of subsidiary initiatives and, relatedly, the amount of resources needed for their realization. For example, subsidiary managers stated that they often possessed some autonomy for smaller scale activities such as purely local initiatives and smaller product adaptations or initiatives geared towards improving costs. As these initiatives commonly required only limited capital expenditures, they did not need to be aligned with the corporate center or were deliberately pursued "under the radar" without involving the corporate center.[468] In contrast, more expansive initiatives with large investment needs had to be aligned with and approved by headquarters, and consequently the involvement of the corporate center was much more frequent (e.g. I5, I7, I8, I13, I16). Furthermore, the level of existing subsidiary resources and the foreign units' ability to obtain additional resources played an important role for headquarters involvement. It was suggested that, in particular, those units that did not possess sufficient resources to realize initiative opportunities on their own or that were unable to obtain them elsewhere had to approach headquarters or other MNC units, thereby increasing initiative awareness and interaction within the wider multinational firm (e.g. I8, I15).

---

[468] Likewise, the initial phases of subsidiary initiatives could in some cases be completed locally without involving headquarters, including idea generation, concept development and the production of prototypes. However, activities beyond these steps then required headquarters involvement through, for example, making proposals and asking for further funding (I3).

5 – Empirical Findings

	Influencing Factors	Process Elements/Details
Entrepreneurial Resource Management		
Subsidiary Initiative Identification	• External and internal network linkages • Subsidiary resources/capabilities (e.g. creative and knowledgeable staff) • External market context (e.g. market dynamism and pressures) • Subsidiary autonomy	**External Identification** – via • Global network actors (e.g. customers, competitors) • Local network actors (e.g. customers, competitors, partners, vendors, research institutions) **Internal Identification** – via • Headquarters • Sister subsidiaries or other MNC units • The local subsidiary
Resource Structuring	• External and internal network linkages • Subsidiary resources/capabilities (e.g. level of own specialized resources; slack resources for trial and error)	**Resource Acquisition** • Internal acquisition from inside the MNC (e.g. HQ, sister subsidiaries or other MNC units) • External acquisition from outside the MNC • Local network actors (e.g. suppliers, vendors, partners) **Resource Accumulation/Development** • Internal resource development (e.g. in subsidiary or in collaboration with other MNC units) • Intern-external development (e.g. technology partners, customers, competitors and research institutions)
HQ-S Alignment	• Subsidiary resources/capabilities (e.g. level of own specialized resources; slack resources for trial and error; access to resources outside MNC, ability to package and sell initiatives) • Initiative type (e.g. associated risk and resource need; fit with corporate priorities) • HQ-S relationship (e.g. communication, subsidiary importance to HQ) • Subsidiary reputation and credibility (e.g. track record of successful initiatives)	**Headquarters Involvement** • Autonomy w/rgds to entrepreneurial activities • Interaction/alignment with HQ • Initiative evaluation and approval **Initiative Selling** • Formal selling • Informal selling **Corporate Resistance** • Initiative rejection • Lack of interest and support • Lack of understanding and request for further clarification/justification

Figure 5.132: Additional findings on subsidiary initiative sub-processes

Partially linked to headquarters involvement are the sub-processes and activities related to *subsidiary initiative evaluation and approval*. In both company cases, larger scale initiative opportunities commonly had to follow standardized alignment processes with the corporate center. According to both headquarters and subsidiary management, this was to ensure uniformity in product development activities and strategic fit of entrepreneurial and innovative activities with corporate objectives (I1, I8, I10). In both companies, central decision-making bodies were in place with responsibility for assessing and approving new subsidiary initiative proposals and for granting needed resources such as funding or personnel (I1, I2, I6, I10).[469] Among other criteria, new initiative ideas were assessed based on their fit with market and customer needs, financial benefits such as revenue and profit potential, cost saving opportunities and required resources and time for their realization (I6, I14, I15, I16). In addition to the characteristics of the initiatives themselves, the strategic priority of markets and the subsidiaries therein for headquarters also appear to play a certain role (I4). Before being brought to the attention to decision-making bodies at the corporate center, some initiatives also underwent evaluation and approval steps within the foreign unit itself (I7, I13).

Certain subsidiary initiative-taking activities also encountered *resistance from other parts of the MNC*. Resistance manifested itself, among other forms, as direct initiative rejection, lack of interest and willingness to support, limited understanding and request for further clarification and justification (I3, I5, I6, I11, I13). In addition to the foreign subsidiaries' roles and power positions, it appears that corporate resistance was also influenced by the type of initiative, its commercial viability, the perceived fit with the wider strategy of the MNC and the match with the subsidiary's role and capabilities. For example, initiatives of large scale and scope and with high investment needs were said to face resistance more frequently than those with smaller financial needs, especially in situations of scarce resources in the wider MNC (I4, I7, I15). Similarly, initiative opportunities were often rejected if they did not demonstrate commercial benefits such as increased revenues, profits or costs reductions (I8). New initiative ideas also often faced corporate resistance when they did not correspond to corporate priorities and strategic objectives. For instance, low-cost and lower-quality product proposals by the Chinese and Mexican units of Autocomp were rejected because of headquarters' concern about negative impacts on wider brand perception (I3, I6). In some cases it was argued that headquarters also did not understand the particular situations and specific needs in local markets and therefore showed resistance against some local initiatives, although they made "perfect sense" locally (I3, I5, I6). Finally, the subsidiary's role and perceived ability to realize proposed initiatives also seem to have impacted corporate resistance.

---

[469] For instance, within Autocomp, a central innovation steering board consisting of members from different business units, segments and functional areas were responsible for the evaluation, selection and approval of entrepreneurial and innovative projects coming from foreign subsidiaries (I2).

Less advanced subsidiary types, such as Implementers and Quiescent Subsidiaries, often did not have the experience and necessary capabilities in the eyes of the corporate center to successfully realize certain initiatives, which resulted in their rejection (I8).[470]

The subsidiary units in this study employed a wide variety of *selling and lobbying efforts* to help bring their entrepreneurial initiatives toward approval and realization. However, it appears that two approaches in particular were frequently employed: formal initiative proposals to headquarters in line with corporate evaluation and approval processes, and more informal selling efforts and tactics.

The formal initiative-selling to headquarters at Autocomp commonly involved the preparation of presentations, outlining, for example, the new initiative opportunity, the related market need and the potential added value for customers. For more advanced initiatives, in-person presentations of initiative concepts and even the showcasing of product samples at the corporate center were applied (I3, I4). Similarly, at Telecomp, foreign subsidiaries made "sales pitches" in the form of presentations showcasing the opportunity and highlighting the revenue and profit potential or benefits, such as enhanced customer satisfaction and retention (I15). Less formal initiative-selling occurred in both company cases, for instance, in regular alignment calls with headquarters and other foreign units or in international workshops and functional exchange forums in which new ideas, technologies or solutions were discussed by participants. For example, Autocomp hosted an annual engineering conference where participating managers from different functional areas "showcased" new initiative ideas in attempt to sell them to other colleagues (I5, I6, I7, I10, I11).[471]

It appears that, in addition to the subsidiary role context, other factors exerted some influence on the subsidiary initiative-selling sub-process. Among these is the type of initiative. For example, initiatives of a larger scale and scope, more radical ones and those that need more extensive resourcing seem to require more extensive selling efforts by subsidiaries (I13, I15, I16). Also, the strategic fit of proposed initiatives with objectives of the MNC appears to play a role. It was suggested that initiatives are more difficult to sell when similar products, services or solutions already exist in the MNC or when they did not correspond with the wider goals of the multinational firm (I3, I6, I14, I16). Similarly, the ability to appropriately package, present and sell initiative opportunities to decision makers at Headquarters was seen as beneficial (I3, I4). Another influencing factor mentioned by a number of subsidiary interviewees relates to the relationship of headquarters and foreign subsidiaries. It was mentioned that close

---

[470] See also Subsection 5.3.2.2 herein for further details on role-specific resistance.
[471] In some cases, local selling to subsidiary management was also required before being able to bring the initiative to the attention of the corporate center (I3, I7, I13, I15).

relationships, frequent communication and alignment made it easier to reach decision-makers and convince them of the value of proposed initiatives (I3, I4, I6, I13). Finally, subsidiary credibility and the perceived ability to realize initiatives (e.g. through a proven track record) was considered to facilitate initiative selling activities (I3, I8).

5.3.5.4 Subsidiary Initiative Outcomes

As outlined above, subsidiary initiatives may bring with them not only benefits but also certain risks at the environmental, organizational and individual levels. As presented in Subsection 5.3.3, subsidiary initiatives deliver resource-related outcomes and can result in changes to the subsidiary role, power and credibility vis-à-vis headquarters. In addition, they can positively impact further performance outcomes such as subsidiary revenues, costs, profit, market share and productivity. Further findings were obtained through the headquarters and subsidiary interviews and are briefly summarized below and in Table 5.14.

Environmental level: Although previous research has highlighted various environmental level benefits of subsidiary initiatives,[472] no beneficial outcomes were brought up in the interviews conducted as part of this study. However, the risk of losing proprietary know-how to other market players was mentioned in relation to the Chinese Autocomp subsidiary. Both subsidiary and headquarters managers stated that technical knowledge transferred from the corporate center to the local subsidiary for the realization of initiatives was, at times, shared with competitors or other local market players.[473]

Organizational level: At the *corporate level*, one specific benefit of subsidiary initiatives that was repeatedly mentioned was the development of new or improved products or solutions that were subsequently applicable for other locations of the MNC as well (I1, I3, I10, I11, I12, I13, I14). In addition, certain risks were perceived to possibly occur at the corporate level. First, some initiatives were seen as unfit or even conflicting with the strategic priorities of the MNC. Although they may appear useful from a local perspective, they were not always in line with the wider objectives of the multinational firm (I3, I6).[474] Second, some initiatives were assessed as redundant as similar activities were already being pursued elsewhere or had been attempted before in the multinational company. Such entrepreneurial efforts were thus seen as creating inefficiencies, dupli-

---

[472] See Subsection 2.2.4.1 herein for further details on environmental-level consequences of subsidiary initiatives.
[473] While this might be perceived as a risk from the standpoint of the multinational firm, this form of knowledge transfer could also be a benefit from a country-level view, as it can support the host country's economic development.
[474] For example, one initiative by the Mexican Autocomp subsidiary aimed at delivering a low-cost product for the local market. Yet this was seen as a risk by headquarters since it did not mesh with the global brand positioning of a high-quality provider and it was believed to negatively influence brand perception (I3). In a similar vein, the Chinese subsidiary manager argued *"Das Problem ist allerdings, dass aus europäischer Sicht viele Lösungsvorschläge aufgrund des hohen Standards, den man in Europa gewohnt ist, absurd erscheinen"* (I6).

cating work and resulting in additional costs for the MNC (I2, I3, I10).[475] Lastly, some entrepreneurial activities of subsidiaries were said to have increased competition within the MNC, with internally competing solutions and rivalry for scarce resources (I10, I15).

At the *subsidiary level*, multiple benefits were articulated by interviewees. Initiatives were said to potentially lead to enhanced competitive position in subsidiary markets (I2, I4), to new or improved products or services and to the extension of local product portfolios (I2, I3, I10). In many cases they also resulted in financial benefits for the local units, such as increased revenues and profits or reduced costs (I3, I4, I5, I6, I16). Other benefits include improved subsidiary resources in the form of new or enhanced technical know-how, additional employees in R&D or new or enhanced relationships with external partnerships (I6, I7, I10, I14). In certain cases, initiatives also positively influenced the role and position of foreign subsidiaries within the multinational firm leading to, for example, new subsidiary responsibilities or a broadened scope of products and activities.[476] Furthermore, as positive outcome, subsidiary initiatives were said to have improved the relationship between headquarters and the foreign units, including a better understanding of headquarters' needs, better attention and recognition from the corporate center as important units, enhanced trust and credibility and closer collaboration within the home base and other MNC units (I3, I6, I10, I14, I15). Aside from the various benefits, three potential risks at the subsidiary level were also identified. First, it was argued that initiatives increase the complexity of subsidiary operations as they may result in additional products and services or an extended scope of subsidiary activities (I2). Second, while initiatives may (positively) impact headquarters' attention, they may also lead to increased headquarters involvement and centralization of decision-making (I15). Third, it was stated that successful initiatives not only positively influence subsidiary recognition as important units, but may also lead to higher performance expectations for the future (I12).

Individual level: While previous research does not appear to have identified individual-level outcomes of subsidiary initiatives, the present research detected two potential benefits and one possible risk. Several interviews noted that entrepreneurial subsidiary activities positively impacted employee motivation and pride, as well as employee retention. For instance, the Mexican subsidiary manager at Autocomp stated *"... the impact it had on this team and the motivation and the sense of pride ... is probably more valuable than it finally turning into a product."* In a similar vein, the Romanian manager remarked that *"people feel good when they have an idea and when they see that this idea is taken*

---

[475] For instance, the Mexican unit of Autocomp decided to engage in an initiative to develop a new product that allowed control of automotive interior systems by hand gestures. As it later turned out, headquarters was already engaged in a very similar product development activity using slightly different technology (I3).

[476] The Mexican Autocomp unit was able, for example, to grow its R&D activities and attract significant investment from headquarters (I1, A5), the German unit was able to expand its scope of products (I2) and the Greek Telecomp subsidiary was selected as the global lead for piloting two new service offerings (I14).

into consideration" (I3, I6, I7). As potential risks, it was mentioned that certain initiatives that are not aligned with headquarters may also result in difficulties with superiors or with the corporate office. Accordingly the Mexican subsidiary manager explained: "*Of course I've had my bosses and my bosses' bosses ... complain about some of the ideas. ... Do I get a bad reputation or do I get in trouble with my boss a bit? Yeah, but in the end ... it's a very acceptable risk.*" (I3).

Level	Perceived Benefits	Perceived Risks
Environmental		
	• n/a	• External knowledge drain
Organizational (Corporate)		
	• New/improved products/services developed locally and of use elsewhere in the MNC	• Misfit with corporate priorities • Inefficiencies and additional costs • Subsidiary competition
Organizational (Subsidiary)		
	• Competitive market position • New/improved products/services • Subsidiary financial performance • Subsidiary resources/capabilities • Subsidiary role & position • HQ-S relationship • Collaboration within MNC • Collaboration with external partners	• Subsidiary management complexity • HQ involvement • Higher performance expectations
Individual		
	• Employee motivation/retention • Entrepreneurial spirit/drive	• Difficulties with superiors/corporate office

Table 5.14: Perceived risks and benefits of subsidiary initiatives

5.3.6 Conclusion

The present research was undertaken with the aim to more comprehensively investigate the potential relationship between (a) the different roles of foreign subsidiaries in MNCs, (b) their initiative-taking behavior and (c) initiative outcomes.[477] This subsection briefly summarizes the key results obtained through this study.

(a) As outlined throughout this chapter, the empirical findings of this research strengthen the view that the subsidiary role context influences entrepreneurial activities and their outcomes in foreign units of MNCs. The present study provides additional evidence that the more advanced subsidiary role types such as Strategic Leaders and Active Subsidiaries seem to function as entrepreneurial "spark plugs" and thereby represent important contributors to firm-level advantages in the MNC. In both company cases, these role types exhibited the highest level of entrepreneurial subsidiary initiatives. It appears that the simultaneous occurrence of numerous context drivers strongly facilitated entrepreneurial initiatives. For example, these units typically operated in highly demanding market contexts, they were well endowed with subsidiary resources and capabilities, they possessed high degrees of autonomy and they had strong internal and external network linkages.[478] In contrast, Implementer and Quiescent Subsidiaries played the least important role with regard to entrepreneurial activities. In the present research, these role types exhibited low levels of subsidiary initiatives. It is assumed that their undemanding market environments, their limited set of resources and capabilities and their low levels of integration and localization made it difficult for these units to identify and realize entrepreneurial initiatives.[479]

The empirical findings further indicate that, aside from the subsidiary role setting consisting of environmental and organizational level factors, individual-level variables also play a critical role for subsidiary initiatives. In particular, the entrepreneurial attitude and mindset of subsidiary managers appear to further support entrepreneurial activities in foreign units of MNCs (see Figure 5.133). These findings are in line with previous entrepreneurship writings suggesting that the interplay of (1) external environmental conditions, (2) organizational ability and (3) individual entrepreneurial motivation and ability is important when it comes to entrepreneurial outcomes and performance (see e.g. Lumpkin/Dess 1996, Bird 1999, Hostager/Neil 1998, Shane et al. 2003, Ireland et al. 2009). However, the precise way in which these aspects interact could not be ascertained in this research and should be investigated further in future research.

---

[477] See Section 1.2 for details on the research objectives and research questions.
[478] See Subsection 5.3.5.2 for details on role-specific antecedents.
[479] Moreover, it appears that high levels of headquarters involvement, strong corporate resistance and – in some instances – misalignments with the corporate center negatively impacted the development and completion of entrepreneurial subsidiary initiatives.

```
┌─────────────────────────────────┐
│ Environmental Opportunity       │
│ • Strategic importance of       │
│   subsidiary's environment      │
└─────────────────────────────────┘
┌─────────────────────────────────┐
│ Organizational Ability          │
│ • Subsidiary resources/         │      ┌──────────────┐      ┌──────────────┐
│   capabilities                  │      │  Subsidiary  │      │  Subsidiary  │
│ • Subsidiary decision-making    │ ───▶ │  Initiative- │ ───▶ │  Initiative  │
│   autonomy                      │      │    Taking    │      │   Outcome    │
│ • Subsidiary external and       │      └──────────────┘      └──────────────┘
│   internal network linkages     │
└─────────────────────────────────┘
┌─────────────────────────────────┐
│ Individual Motivation           │
│ • Subsidiary manager            │
│   motivation and attitude       │
└─────────────────────────────────┘
```

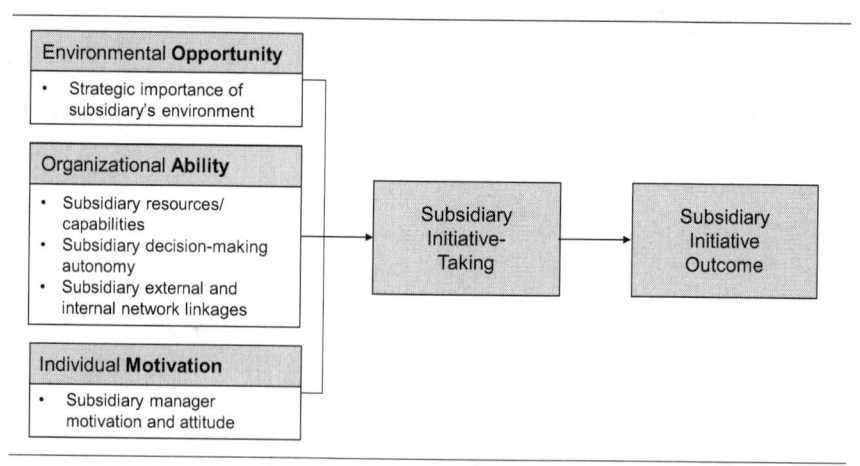

Figure 5.133: Key antecedents of entrepreneurial subsidiary initiatives

(b) Moreover, this research also developed new insights into the (sub)processes of subsidiary initiative-taking and further details as to how it differs among different subsidiary roles. While the initiative-taking process and related activities seem, at least at first sight, highly diverse and difficult to predict, the theoretically derived (sub)processes of the research framework received additional backing by the empirical findings. It appears that subsidiary initiative-taking commonly involves activities related to initiative opportunity identification, resource structuring and bundling, as well as interaction and alignment with other parts of the MNC.[480]

Certain role-specific patterns also emerged in this study. For instance, Strategic Leader and Active Subsidiaries exhibited the highest level of external initiative identification, they most frequently engaged in resource structuring activities from internal and external sources and they encountered the lowest level of headquarters involvement and corporate resistance. In comparison, Implementer and Quiescent Subsidiaries displayed comparatively low levels of new initiative opportunity identification and these were mostly from internal sources. They also obtained few new resources for initiative realization, which were from primarily internal MNC sources, and they faced moderate to high levels of headquarters involvement and high levels of corporate resistance. They frequently faced the need to sell their initiatives in the multinational organizations.[481] These role-specific patterns are, at least to a large extent, in line with the theoretically derived predictions presented in Section 3.5. Hence, further evidence was generated not only as to how the subsidiary role context may affect entrepreneurial outcomes of

---
[480] See also Figure 5.132 in this chapter for a summary view of subsidiary initiative (sub)processes.
[481] See also Table 5.12 in this chapter for a summary view on role-specific findings of subsidiary initiative (sub)processes.

foreign units in general, but also as to how it may impact different (sub)processes of subsidiary initiative-taking and also lead to different outcomes in the end.

(c) This study identifies a wide variety of initiative consequences across the environmental, organizational and even individual levels. As shown above, outcomes were largely beneficial to foreign subsidiaries and in certain cases for the wider MNC. Initiative outcomes could in part also be linked to subsidiary role context, as predicted in Section 3.5. For instance, of all role types, Strategic Leaders and Active Subsidiaries most frequently pursued global market initiatives. Likewise, these role types most often developed new or improved resource bundles in the form of products or services that were of use for the wider MNC. Consequently, entrepreneurial initiatives by these advanced role types should have the highest potential for firm-level advantages. Other benefits of entrepreneurial activities at the subsidiary level include, for example, new or enhanced subsidiary resources and capabilities, stronger financial performance and an improved subsidiary role and position in the MNC. Interestingly, subsidiary initiatives were also said to positively influence employee motivation and retention as well as the entrepreneurial "mood" of staff in foreign units. Nevertheless, it could also be shown that outcomes of subsidiary entrepreneurial activities are not purely beneficial, but that there are potential risks such as, for example, misfit with corporate priorities, inefficiencies and additional costs for the MNC and enhanced complexity or higher performance expectations for the subsidiary.

6 Contributions, Limitations and the Road Ahead

6.1 Implications for International Business Research

The objective of the present research was to more comprehensively and holistically investigate the potential relations between the role a foreign subsidiary holds in the MNC, its entrepreneurial initiative-taking behavior and the resulting outcomes.[482] For this purpose, a contingent and resource-oriented research framework was developed, and an empirical investigation in the form of a multiple case study design was performed. The findings provide answers to all three research questions formulated at the beginning of this thesis.

First, new empirical evidence was gathered, supporting the notion that the extent and types of subsidiary initiatives are at least in part dependent upon the role a foreign units holds in the MNC. Second, the results suggest that subsidiary roles impact initiative-taking behavior and the way related activities unfold in foreign units. Although it has been stated previously that the initiative process may take various forms and is difficult to predict, certain role-specific patterns were identified relating to initiative identification, resource structuring and bundling as well as to headquarters-subsidiary alignment. Third, it was shown that due to variations in types of initiatives and initiative activities, the outcomes also varied by subsidiary role type. Consequently, this dissertation makes several contributions relating to IB research on (1) subsidiary roles, (2) subsidiary initiatives and (3) headquarters-subsidiary relationships. In addition, contributions are made to (4) organizational theories and (5) methodological approaches. These are summarized below.

(1) This research further enhances our understanding of subsidiary role types and their capacity for entrepreneurial undertakings in multinational firms. Previous literature has only generally stated that the role a foreign subsidiary holds should impact its ability for innovative and entrepreneurial behavior.[483] However, more detailed studies linking subsidiary roles to the innovative and entrepreneurial activities of foreign units were lacking. In this regard, the present study was able to go beyond merely substantiating the notion that more advanced role types, such as Strategic Leaders and Active Subsidiaries, commonly function as the entrepreneurial "spark plugs" in the MNC. In more depth, it provided new evidence as to *why different role types engage in entrepreneurial initiatives* to varying degrees and often in distinctive ways, thereby producing specific initiative outcomes in the end.[484]

---

[482] See Section 1.2 herein for a summary of the main objectives.
[483] See Sections 1.2 and 3.1 and Subsection 3.2.1.3 herein for additional details.
[484] For instance, it was shown that the more advanced role types commonly operate in a highly beneficial subsidiary context in which numerous drivers positively influence the identification and realization of entrepreneurial activities at the same time. Furthermore, their strong resource-based power facilitated alignment and interaction with the

In addition to the four predefined role dimensions, this research identified various other characteristics of subsidiary role types. Thus not only was a *rich description of different role types* provided, but *additional commonalities* were also identified. For instance, it was shown that all advanced role types in this research enjoyed high degrees of subsidiary autonomy and fulfilled some special function for the wider MNC such as a global or regional innovation hub.[485] Moreover, the research confirms the *complexity and ambiguity* that was voiced by other scholars concerning *subsidiary role allocation*. For instance, it was revealed that strongly entrepreneurial subsidiary units differ in various dimensions from those that are rarely entrepreneurial, signaling the need for a multidimensional role differentiation using more than the two or three dimensions commonly applied in the field (see e.g. Schmid 2004, p. 247, Rugman et al 2011, p. 257).[486] Moreover, this study identified some cases in which there were differing perceptions of subsidiary roles between headquarters and subsidiaries. The research hence underlined the usefulness of a more differentiated role assessment viewed from various angles (see e.g. Schmid/Daniel 2010, p. 259).[487]

(2) This research also enriches our understanding of the subsidiary initiative phenomenon in multiple ways. While previous work mostly focused on individual aspects such as initiative antecedents, processes or outcomes, the present work *represents a more holistic approach* by investigating the topic from an "end-to-end" perspective. By linking distinct antecedents to central aspects of initiative-taking behavior and outcomes in an empirically tested framework, it provides a more comprehensive view and helps better explain how role context impacts entrepreneurial activities and produces different end results both at the subsidiary level and firm level.[488]

The empirical findings further suggest that the phenomenon of subsidiary initiatives consists not only of entrepreneurial activities with implications for the wider MNC as originally proposed (see e.g. Birkinshaw/Ridderstråle 1999). This research shows that foreign subsidiaries also regularly pursue entrepreneurial endeavors that are more

---

corporate center and improved the chances that their initiatives would make it through the socio-political system of the MNC. In contrast, the least advanced types (Implementers/Quiescent Subsidiaries) face a much less favorable context for entrepreneurial initiatives to occur and succeed, thereby producing fewer subsidiary initiatives and less specialized and MNC-relevant resources in the end. See Subsection 5.3.4 herein for a summary of role-specific initiative-taking.

[485] Additional characteristics assessed in the empirical study were e.g. subsidiary autonomy, mode and year of formation, size in terms of employees, and execution of special roles/functions in the MNC, such as Center of Excellence. See Subsection 4.3.4 for an overview of additional control measures, and Subsection 5.3.1 for additional findings on subsidiary role types.

[486] See Subsection 3.2.1.1 for an overview of certain shortcomings in the subsidiary role literature.

[487] For example, there were significant deviations in role assessment between headquarters and subsidiaries for two Autocomp subsidiaries and five Telecomp subsidiaries. As a result, these seven units were excluded from the present study. See Subsection 4.2.2.3 herein for further details.

[488] For example, it was shown that the resource-related context of the more advanced subsidiary role types, for example the possession of specialized market knowledge or technical expertise, helped with the identification and realization of (often more advanced) entrepreneurial initiatives. For more detail on key antecedents and their impact on subsidiary initiatives see Subsection 5.3.5.2 herein.

incremental and operational in nature, such as efforts to improve local processes, to develop new technical tools or to reduce costs. Consequently, the concept of subsidiary *entrepreneurial initiative should be viewed more comprehensively* to also include such "trivial initiatives" as well.

In addition, this study provides *novel insights into the distinct contextual settings* that facilitate entrepreneurial subsidiary initiatives. Whereas earlier work identified more than 50 antecedents, the present study helped clarify which ones are potentially more important than others and how these affect various elements of initiative-taking behavior and outcomes. Concerning the subsidiary role context, it was shown that the strategic importance of the subsidiary market environment, subsidiary resources and capabilities, subsidiary autonomy, and internal and external network linkages can be viewed as critically important. Aside from the subsidiary role context, the empirical findings further highlight the *important function of entrepreneurial attitude and mindset* of subsidiary management for the identification and realization of entrepreneurial opportunities. Especially when these different drivers are in place simultaneously, more (extensive forms of) entrepreneurial subsidiary activities are likely to occur. Moreover, detailed insights were gained into *how specific factors from the role context impact various (sub)processes* of subsidiary entrepreneurial initiatives. For example, it was shown not only that subsidiary resources and capabilities play a critical role for subsidiary initiatives, but also how different types of resources and capabilities affect different initiative (sub)processes and hence lead to more or less advantageous outcomes in the end.

This study also includes a *systematic investigation of the subsidiary initiative-taking process*. It thereby not only confirmed central elements of initiative-taking behavior further, but it also revealed certain commonalities across selected subsidiary role types.[489] In addition, rich and novel insights into the process activities were provided through the empirical investigation of entrepreneurial initiatives in 14 foreign subsidiaries. This not only shed further light onto the initiative process "black box," but also helped better explain how foreign affiliates use and expand resources and capabilities and potentially contribute to firm-level advantages.[490]

Finally, new findings were presented with regard to *antecedents, objectives and outcomes*. For instance, it was shown that, at least in this study, initiatives seem to positively affect employee motivation and entrepreneurial spirit and drive in the foreign organizations.

---

[489] For instance, it could be shown that more advanced role types in this study more frequently identified new initiative opportunities than all other role types. They frequently obtained and extensively bundled needed resources, and they faced low headquarters involvement, low corporate resistance and relatively rarely engaged in selling activities. See Subsection 5.3.4 herein for a summary view of role specific initiative-taking behavior.

[490] See Subsection 5.3.5.3 herein for additional findings on the subsidiary initiative process.

(3) Certain findings also contribute to research on headquarters-subsidiary relationships. This work delivered new insights into the *interaction and alignment between headquarters and foreign subsidiaries*, particularly as concerns entrepreneurial initiative-taking. It was further substantiated empirically that the role a foreign subsidiary holds influences, at least to a certain degree, headquarters-subsidiary alignment. Furthermore, some common *patterns were identified for specific subsidiary roles types*, and initial hypotheses were developed as to why this might be the case.[491] Furthermore, certain processes elements, such as headquarters involvement, headquarters resistance and initiative selling were given additional validation and described in more depth through the empirical study. Overall, this helped to shed further light onto how and why different types of subsidiaries manage to push initiatives through the socio-political system better than others. Finally, new findings were generated as to *how initiatives impact headquarters-subsidiary relations*. The empirical results suggest that they, for instance, enhance headquarters trust and credibility in the foreign unit, strengthen subsidiary recognition as a strategically important unit, and lead to closer collaboration with the corporate center.

(4) The research framework applied in this thesis also provides some enhancement to organizational theories. In comparison to previous writings, the present publication includes a *more extensive discussion of the different theoretical approaches* in the subsidiary initiative field and their applicability for this specific study. Consequently, a model was presented for role-specific initiative-taking that rests, among other theoretical foundations, on the more recent dynamic and process-oriented strands of the RBV to help explain how foreign affiliates create subsidiary-level and even firm-level advantages. It thereby represents a *novel approach to applying the RBV at the subsidiary level* and helps to shed further light onto the "process black box" of how foreign units may obtain, develop and utilize resources to create value through entrepreneurial initiatives. Additionally, contingency theory came into play to help explain how the resource management process may differ across contextual settings. As such, it responded to calls from other scholars who had suggested that for the resource-based view, linking context factors, process characteristics and process outcomes could yield important contributions and help better understand how resource-based advantages develop (e.g. Brush/Artz 1999, p. 246, Helfat et al. 2007, p. 43, Crook et al. 2008, p. 1153, Sirmon/Hitt 2009, p. 1392).[492]

---

[491] For instance, the more advanced roles were usually able to pursue subsidiary initiatives more autonomously, they faced less corporate resistance and they engaged in less frequent initiative selling activities than all other role types. See Subsection 5.3.2.2 herein for details.

[492] Some scholars have criticized the traditional RBV, among other aspects, for being rather static in nature and insufficiently addressing the process through which firms obtain different resources and capabilities to create competitive advantage and how this is impacted by the firm's context. See Subsection 3.3.2 herein for further details.

(5) Lastly, some methodological contributions of this study are highlighted. First, different *elements of the process-oriented RBV* and resource-related outcomes were *operationalized and empirically tested* – a task that has been said to be an ongoing struggle for researchers (see e.g. Barney et al. 2001, p. 636, Barney et al. 2011, p. 1311). Second, while previous work often explored subsidiary role differentiation in different MNCs, the present study focused on two multinational firms in order to achieve a better understanding of *role settings within the intra-organizational network of specific MNCs*.[493] Moreover, most previous studies have examined subsidiary initiatives only from a subsidiary-level perspective. In order to investigate the topic more comprehensively and to ensure accurate measurement of the phenomenon, both *headquarters and subsidiary perspectives* were included in this research.

6.2 Implications for Management Practice

This dissertation also produced insights that are highly relevant for management practice. The findings underline the broad value of entrepreneurial initiatives for both the MNC and individual subsidiaries abroad. It was shown that such initiatives can result in, for instance, new or enhanced products or services for local and firm-wide application, improved financial performance, stronger competitive positions in local markets and even greater employee motivation and retention. In addition, this study further clarified in which subsidiary contexts different forms of initiatives thrive and which factors might act as inhibitors to subsidiary entrepreneurship. This should give managers of multinational companies guidance on how to better organize for decentralized entrepreneurial activities in their firms and how to best leverage different subsidiary units based on their individual contextual settings. The findings of the present research also have certain managerial implications for both head-office and subsidiary managers. Based on the results of this study, headquarters is encouraged to (1) actively manage and shape its portfolio of foreign subsidiaries and (2) centrally optimize for subsidiary initiatives. Moreover, subsidiary management can take additional measures to (3) locally optimize for entrepreneurial initiatives. These recommendations are described in more detail below.

(1) Managing the portfolio of foreign subsidiaries: The empirical findings support the view that subsidiary role matters and, at least to some degree, influences the extent and types of subsidiary initiatives undertaken in foreign units of MNCs. Consequently, corporate managers of multinational firms wishing to better understand and influence decentralized entrepreneurial activities in their foreign subsidiaries should (a) ensure they have sufficient transparency on the differentiated subsidiary roles in their multinational network and (b) actively manage their subsidiary portfolio in a strategic manner.

---

[493] For an overview of the criticism of subsidiary role literature and research, see Subsection 3.2.1.1 herein.

(a) Having clear *transparency on the current subsidiary roles* in the MNC network will help corporate managers better understand the capacity of their foreign units for the different forms of entrepreneurial initiative. While there are indications in this study that the headquarters of both multinational firms were aware of some differences among their foreign subsidiaries, a more in-depth assessment and understanding of their strategic roles and their entrepreneurial capability for the wider MNC appeared lacking.[494] Hence, a regular evaluation of units abroad, perhaps through a methodology similar to the one applied in this dissertation, should be useful not only to determine roles and likelihood of initiatives, but also to improve headquarters' understanding of the unique contexts in which the foreign entities operate.

(b) Once a clear view on the differentiated subsidiary roles in the network of the multinational firm is established, corporate management can, at least in part, *actively shape the subsidiary portfolio to optimize for decentralized entrepreneurship* across the MNC. For instance, some of the often scarce resources and capabilities of the wider MNC could be purposefully channeled to Black Hole subsidiaries to help them engage in more (external market) initiatives.[495] Alternatively, the geographical scope of a Contributor subsidiary could be expanded to include strategically more important markets, or the localization of a Receptive Subsidiary could be strengthened to increase the chances for external market initiatives. However, optimizing the subsidiary portfolio for decentralized entrepreneurship must be done within the context of the different strategic priorities and constraints of the MNC. It should be seen as a longer-term effort that can only be influenced by headquarters to a certain extent as, for instance, resources are commonly scarce in an organization and cannot always be easily transferred to other locations of the MNC.[496]

(2) Centrally optimizing for subsidiary initiatives: Besides adjusting (parts of) the subsidiary role portfolio to the entrepreneurial needs of the wider MNC, corporate managers can take further measures to encourage and enable decentralized initiatives in their foreign affiliates. Here, it is headquarters managers' critical task to optimally balance between promoting autonomous initiative at the subsidiary level and, at the same time, limiting potential risks such as organizational inefficiency or lack of focus. This requires, among other aspects, openness of the corporate center for decentralized

---

[494] For example, Telecomp broadly divided their foreign subsidiaries into four categories ranging from less advanced to very advanced units depending on their scope of operations and market position. Autocomp classified their locations into, e.g., "best-cost countries" such as India and Australia, and competence center locations such as Romania.

[495] In the present study, for example, the Chinese unit of Autocomp, categorized as a Black Hole, was hindered in the realization of some external market initiatives due to the lack of resources in the form of advanced technological know-how that was present in the MNC but that headquarters did not want to transfer to the foreign entity.

[496] Moreover, subsidiary role development is not only influenced by headquarters but also driven by the local environment and the subsidiary itself, as described in subsection 3.2.1.2.

entrepreneurship in the MNC and mechanisms to encourage, steer and support the development of initiatives that are aligned with the needs of the wider MNC, as explained in more detailed below.

First of all, corporate managers should keep an *open mind about entrepreneurial activities that arise from the periphery* of their organizations. Initiatives should not be immediately viewed as threats or risks to the MNC that need to be challenged or even rejected, but should rather be understood as potential drivers of subsidiary-level or even firm-level advantages. This may require a change in headquarters' attitude towards a more geocentric view of the MNC and implies a higher tolerance for failure, as many initiative opportunities will not be successful in the end. Such a change could be supported by, for example, temporary transfers of headquarters managers to foreign affiliates and *vice versa*, the use of global business teams and increased collaborative efforts between the corporate office and subsidiary units. Moreover, headquarters managers should create an MNC-wide climate that motivates calculated risk-taking and encourages subsidiary managers to bring forward new initiative ideas for further assessment and evaluation.

Second, as outlined in this study, one of the biggest perceived risks was that subsidiary initiatives might not fit corporate priorities and support divergent interests of the foreign affiliates. Hence, headquarters should clearly *formulate and communicate its strategy, goals and values to its foreign subsidiaries* to ensure that entrepreneurial initiatives are aligned with them. This can be facilitated by, for instance, strengthening normative integration and creating shared values. Possible measures to achieve this include extensive travel and transfers of managers between headquarters and subsidiaries, joint work teams, task forces or committees and extensive socialization and communication with the units abroad (Ghoshal/Bartlett 1988, p. 371-373, Nohria/Ghoshal 1994, p. 493-494).

Third, the corporate center can *set up structured programs to help encourage and steer the flow of subsidiary initiatives* in a more organized way. Elements of such a program could include an incentive and reward system for new initiative ideas, a clear initiative application and evaluation process, an initiative assessment and selection committee, a central pool of resources available for new initiative ideas and a well-defined resource allocation mechanism. Such a structured steering system could have many advantages. Headquarters would gain early transparency on initiative ideas, and benefits and risks could be assessed in a consistent manner and compared to both subsidiary and corporate needs. In addition, subsidiary units would not only be rewarded for generating ideas, but they would have a clear path to socialize and legitimize their initiatives and a well-defined way to obtain needed resources for their realization.

Fourth, the study demonstrates that successful initiative-taking activities seem to be driven by a favorable role context combined with entrepreneurial motivation and drive at the subsidiary level. Consequently, corporate headquarters should be able to further strengthen subsidiary initiatives by *selecting and placing entrepreneurial-minded managers in foreign affiliates*, especially in units that represent more advanced role types such as Strategic Leaders or Active Subsidiaries.[497] Furthermore, headquarters should put in place appropriate incentive and reward schemes to encourage subsidiary management to develop and drive autonomous entrepreneurial activities that are in line with the strategy, objectives and values of the wider MNC.

Fifth, it was shown that resources and capabilities play a key role for the identification and realization of subsidiary initiatives. Hence, headquarters management could *facilitate access to needed external and internal resources, capabilities or funds*. This could mean, for example, headquarters support with connecting their foreign entities to global partners, (such as technology providers), implementing a central resource pool for initiatives, or facilitating collaboration and resource exchanges between different units of the MNC.

(3) Locally optimizing for subsidiary initiatives: A number of implications can be drawn for subsidiary management as well. The study's findings underline the critical role of local managers in fostering entrepreneurial activities and successfully maneuvering them through the socio-political landscape of the MNC. This means that subsidiary managers must understand, among other facets, their unit's role in the wider MNC and its capacity for specific forms of entrepreneurial activities. Furthermore, they can act as internal entrepreneurs to encourage and facilitate initiatives that are appropriate for their subsidiary context. Finally, they can function as internal promoters and actively sell their initiatives in the wider MNC, as described below in more detail.

First, subsidiary managers should, just as at the corporate level, have a *clear view of their unit's role and position* in the multinational network and its *ability to realize initiatives of different types*. For instance, managers of Implementer or Quiescent Subsidiaries should be aware that the limited opportunity space in their market environment, their restricted capabilities and weak power position in the MNC are likely to impede the chances for successful initiative-taking, especially for those activities of larger scope or more radical in nature. Consequently, subsidiary management should find and promote the right opportunities to pursue, that is, initiatives that are close to the strengths and capability profile of their organization and considered realistically achievable. Moreover, initiative opportunities should be more or less proportional to the perceived role and

---

[497] It is assumed that in less advanced subsidiary role types, fewer initiative opportunities will arise and foreign units will have limited abilities to realize them. Hence placing entrepreneurial managers in more advanced units should be of more use to the MNC.

position of the subsidiary in the MNC to enhance their chances of making it through the headquarters-subsidiary alignment process (Birkinshaw/Fry 1998, p. 60, Birkinshaw/Hood 1998c, p. 792).

Second, subsidiary managers wishing to foster initiative-taking activities in their organizations should take an active role as internal entrepreneurs themselves and *promote a climate and culture that encourages proactive, risk-taking and innovative behavior* among their local teams as well. This could imply, for example, that local management does not merely conduct "business as usual" and as prescribed by the corporate center but continuously challenges the status quo and seeks out new ways to exploit and expand their resource base through entrepreneurial activities. Initiative needs to come from subsidiary management whose responsibility it is to be entrepreneurial and to seek out new opportunities. Country managers must therefore act as "opportunity sensors" with a sound view of external industry and market trends and of the internal MNC landscape if they wish to identify and respond to emerging opportunities in both arenas. Moreover, subsidiary management should place a strong emphasis on creating an entrepreneurial subsidiary climate and culture that fosters idea contribution from employees, encourages calculated risk-taking and has a reasonable tolerance for failure. Some measures to help achieve this might be to attract, retain and develop more entrepreneurial-minded employees in the subsidiary or to implement structures or programs that locally incentivize and reward initiative-taking rather than immediately penalizing failed attempts (Delany 2000, p. 241, Bartlett/Ghoshal 2002, p. 239-240, Scott et al. 2009, p. 46).

Third, a key function of subsidiary management is to help initiatives move through the socio-political system of the MNC so that they can be approved and implemented in the end. Correspondingly, foreign management must both *effectively promote and sell initiative opportunities* in the short term, but also appropriately manage the headquarters-subsidiary relationship in the long term. As identified in this study, initiatives can be promoted via formal proposals or more informal selling efforts and tactics. For formal initiative proposals, it is important that subsidiary managers understand how to optimally package and sell initiative ideas to headquarters. This could, for example, relate to the optimal timing of when initiative ideas should be communicated, the information that needs to be provided and the presentation format, or the relevant forums and audiences for initiative proposals.[498] Here, repeated and close collaboration with headquarters or the transfer of managers between headquarters and subsidiaries could prove useful, as this would help foreign units better understand what is expected from the corporate center. In addition, it is critical that local management understand and, ideally, anticipate

---
[498] When selling and promoting initiatives, it is also advisable not only to highlight the benefits for the subsidiary location, but also to specify potential (economic) benefits for the MNC as a whole and ideally link these to the strategy and priorities of the wider MNC.

reasons for potential resistance from the corporate office beforehand so these can be appropriately managed and mitigated.[499]

Fourth and last, the empirical findings suggest that, especially for less advanced roles, weak headquarters-subsidiary relationships and communication can represent an inhibitor to successful initiative-taking. Hence, it is recommended that subsidiary management also *actively manage the long term relationship with the parent company* so that trust and credibility in the foreign unit can be improved and additional leeway can be gained for autonomous activities over time. Possible measures to instill confidence might include regular alignment and interaction with headquarters and displaying to them that the subsidiary complies, at least most of the time, with central guidelines and requests. In addition, local management should develop a good understanding of the political landscape and power structures in the corporate office and build a network of relationships with actors that are of relevance for supporting or approving initiative proposals. A further measure to strengthen confidence in the foreign organization endeavors is to develop and communicate a clear subsidiary strategy and to explain how different entrepreneurial initiatives fit into this "bigger picture," how they relate to MNC priorities, and how they will contribute to subsidiary-level and firm-level advantages. Doing so should reduce the risk of initiatives appearing as isolated or even opportunistic activities pursued for merely local needs or benefits. This also demonstrates to headquarters that the local organization has a clear plan for the road ahead and well-defined way to add value not only locally but for the multinational firm as a whole.

6.3 Limitations

As highlighted in the subsection before, the present study provided many new insights for both IB research and management practice. However, as with all research, it does not come without limitations relating to both conceptual and methodological aspects. This section is devoted to outlining these limitations.

Conceptual Limitations: A number of restrictions are linked to the conceptual framework applied for the present research, namely (a) the focus on select subsidiary initiative antecedents as independent variables, (b) the inclusion of a simplified initiative process view and (c) the concentration on specific outcome measures only at the subsidiary level.

(a) A deliberate choice was made to focus on two subsidiary role typologies with a total of four role dimensions as the independent variables in the research framework.[500] As

---

[499] Such reasons might include lacking trust by headquarters or poor credibility of the unit abroad, the complexity or uniqueness of the initiative idea and the related proposal or the limited fit of the initiative with the MNC strategy

outlined in Subsection 3.2.1.1, employing such two-dimensional role typologies could result in an *oversimplification of reality*, as subsidiary units commonly differ along multiple dimensions and even across functions or value chain activities (Schmid 2004, p. 247, Rugman et al. 2011, p. 253). Many other influencing factors have been suggested in previous writings that were explicitly excluded here.[501] However, through the case analyses additional influencing factors surfaced that also appear to be of importance and should be further investigated. Of particular interest could be the *function of local managers* and their role in identifying, enacting and promoting subsidiary initiatives. As argued in Subsection 3.4.5, the subsidiary role context should not mechanistically and unidirectionally regulate initiative-taking behavior. Instead, subsidiary managers should have some strategic choice on how to deal with initiative opportunities in different contextual settings.

(b) Based on previous research and theoretical considerations, different (sub)processes of subsidiary initiative-taking were incorporated in the research framework to allow for a structured and systematic investigation of the phenomenon. While the process elements were generally supported by the empirical results, it must be acknowledged that this represents a *simplified and technocratic process view on entrepreneurial initiative-taking*. As such, it likely does not adequately address the dynamic and emergent nature of initiatives and it does not cover all process elements and activities that are possible in reality. For instance, the detailed case analyses revealed aspects such as initiative evaluation, selling activities in the local unit, headquarters resource commitment and initiative implementation, none of which were explicitly included in the initial framework.

(c) Guided by resource-based considerations and literature on subsidiary and firm-level advantages (e.g. Birkinshaw et al. 1998, Rugman/Verbeke 2001), the present study *focused on resource-related outcomes of initiatives at the subsidiary level*. While some further control measures were included, such as subsidiary financial performance and subsidiary role development, many other potential outcomes were not considered. These include country, industry or individual-level outcomes such as host country economic development, impact on industry offerings and structure or changes to the individual career progression of subsidiary managers. Furthermore, this research did not investigate how the newly generated and specialized resource bundles are further transferred and utilized by other MNC units to create firm-level advantages. Instead, it only assessed the general applicability for wider multinational firm and as such can only give indications for how subsidiary initiatives can benefit the MNC as a whole. It would therefore be interesting to further investigate how the newly developed resource bundles are further diffused and adapted by other units of the MNC.

---

[500] For a detailed description of the selection of subsidiary role typologies for this study see Subsection 3.2.1.4.
[501] For an overview of the previously identified antecedents see Subsection 2.2.4.

Methodological Limitations: This study also suffers from certain methodological limitations related to (a) the generalizability of findings, (b) the selected geographical scope, (c) the focus on subsidiary respondents and (d) the conceptualization and measurement of resource-related constructs.

(a) As is common with case study design, this research provides *limited grounds for statistical generalization* for the following reasons. First, only two company cases were analyzed, which had been selected for particular reasons and by using specified selection criteria. The cases represent large multinational companies from transnational industries that conduct significant business outside their home markets.[502] Second, the two cases represent companies only from the automotive and telecommunications industries. Third, subsidiaries from a total of 12 different country locations were investigated and analyzed, so many other countries remain uncovered. Consequently, it has to be questioned to what extent the results can be transferred to other MNCs, for example, from different industries or with different geographical footprints. Although statistical generalization was neither intended nor deemed possible, a number of theoretically derived propositions were replicated both within and across the cases, thereby providing grounds for analytical generalization.

(b) This research also contains *limitations in regard to its geographical scope and* its lack of consideration for *cultural effects* on initiative-taking activities. First, only MNCs with headquarters in Germany were considered in order to facilitate personal contacts and visits to the home bases. Second, as mentioned above, while subsidiary units from 12 different countries are investigated, this leaves many other countries uncovered. Aside from the limited geographical scope, this research did not further investigate the potential impact of country culture on entrepreneurial initiatives in the foreign affiliates of MNCs. For example, it would be interesting to find out how aspects such as risk avoidance, future orientation or performance orientation in different countries influence entrepreneurial activities, since these constitute proactive, risk-taking and innovative activities that might progress or flourish differently depending on the cultural environment.

(c) In comparison to many earlier works, one advantage of this study is that it collected data from both headquarters and subsidiary management and included secondary sources. This was done to obtain a comprehensive view on subsidiary initiative-taking behavior from various perspectives. Nevertheless, the *majority of both survey and interview data was still collected from subsidiary managers* and only two respondents were included from the corporate office. While results from both levels were largely congruent, the empirical findings might nevertheless be skewed towards the subsidiary perspective. Another possible limitation is concerned with the nature of entrepreneurial

---

[502] See Subsection 4.2.2.3 for a description of the case selection.

initiatives, which are often pursued autonomously and without initial headquarters sanctioning or even awareness. Since this research utilized the support of headquarters managers to gain access to foreign subsidiaries, it cannot be completely ruled out that some local managers provided responses that they deemed socially desirable in the wider MNC. While subsidiary respondents were assured of the confidentiality of their interview contributions, the question remains as to what extent they openly and freely shared all details on subsidiary initiatives, particularly those realized without headquarters' knowledge or that were not successful in the end.

(d) Lastly, some limitations must be mentioned with regard to the *operationalization and measurement of certain constructs* that were used in the empirical study. First, while it was possible in the questionnaire to rely on previously applied measurements of subsidiary initiatives, investigating the phenomenon through interviews proved more difficult. In some instances it appeared difficult for respondents to differentiate between regular innovation activities and autonomously driven initiatives of the subsidiary that were also proactive and risk-taking in nature. The study attempted to mitigate the issue by clearly outlining the phenomenon under investigation in the beginning of the interviews, by regularly referring to the survey responses obtained beforehand and by asking clarifying questions on described initiatives throughout the interview. Similarly, given the scope of the study and the investigation of the various initiative-related facets, different resources and capabilities that were obtained and bundled could not be investigated in depth. For instance, it was not possible to analyze in detail what type of distinct resources and capabilities were actually acquired or developed from the various internal or external sources and how they, individually or jointly, contributed to subsidiary-level or even firm-level advantages in the end.

6.4   Avenues for Further Research

The present study was able to address a number of the research gaps described in Section 2.3. Nevertheless, not all of these could be addressed and new avenues for future research emerged through this study as well. These relate to conceptual and methodological research opportunities, as outlined in more depth below.

Conceptual Research Opportunities: With regard to antecedents, this work further underlines the importance of subsidiary roles and their impact on subsidiary initiative-taking activities and outcomes. Beyond the role context, it was shown that entrepreneurial subsidiary managers and their local teams have a vital role to play as well. Since they are the ones that identify and enact initiative opportunities, more emphasis should be placed in future research on better understanding the *role, motivation and the key attributes of subsidiary managers* and how this links to entrepreneurial initiatives abroad. Moreover, it would be interesting to investigate if and how different contextual settings benefit from different types of internal entrepreneurs. For instance, does a Contributor subsidiary require or benefit from a different type of entrepreneur to enable and drive internally oriented initiatives, versus a Strategic Leader subsidiary that commonly pursues externally oriented ones that are often more radical in nature? While some work has started to explore these questions in more depth (e.g. Dörrenbächer/ Geppert 2009, 2010), the subsidiary initiative field would likely benefit from further research in this area.

The results of this study further suggest that critical elements for the successful pursuit of entrepreneurial initiatives include the existence of (internal and external) market opportunities, the subsidiary's (and individual's) ability to identify and realize them, and the motivation and drive of local entrepreneurs.[503] However, it remains unclear how these different factors interact and *how opportunity, ability and motivation are precisely linked*. Are these factors fully or partially complementary? Can a subsidiary market environment rich in entrepreneurial opportunities, at least in part, compensate for limited subsidiary entrepreneurial ability represented by, for instance, a narrow set of resources and capabilities or lacking internal and external network linkages? Can a strong entrepreneurial motivation and drive of local management partially offset restricted subsidiary resources and capabilities? Future research could prove valuable so that the relationships between these factors and their impact on subsidiary initiatives and outcomes can be better understood.

Another area worthy of further investigation is the *subsidiary initiative process*. While the present work has already helped to illuminate the "initiative process black box," more detailed studies are needed in order to examine the individual development processes of separate initiatives over time, the related activities and the actors involved. For instance, the sub-processes of initiative identification, resource structuring and resource bundling should be analyzed in more detail. This could help answer such questions as how new opportunities are identified by different subsidiary actors, or which types and what amounts of resources are obtained from various sources, and how they are further developed and bundled in order to realize initiatives. Likewise, a more in-depth look at the evaluation and approval activities both within the foreign units and at headquarters would certainly broaden our understanding.

This research has largely focused on entrepreneurial initiatives that originate in foreign affiliates of MNCs. However, the empirical findings indicate that some entrepreneurial initiatives are also triggered or even driven centrally by headquarters with the objective

---

[503] For a similar line of thinking underlining the importance of motivation and ability to enact entrepreneurial opportunities see e.g. Stevenson and Jarillo (1990), Gnyawali and Fogel (1994), Hostager et al. (1998), Shane (2003) or Shane et al. (2003).

of diffusing them across multiple units of the MNC (see e.g. Williams 2009). Accordingly, another avenue for research is to examine the *relationship between entrepreneurship at the corporate and at the subsidiary level.* This could help us better comprehend how they are linked and perhaps are complementary or even contradictory. With regard to headquarters involvement, it would also be valuable to take a closer look at the broader variety of different actors that are engaged from a central perspective. This study's findings suggest that central actors may include, for example, approval committees, central innovation managers, global R&D heads or engineers. It would be interesting to better understand what role they play and what impact they have on the initiative process.

Lastly, *subsidiary initiative outcomes* could benefit from further research. While it was shown that initiatives can result in, for example, new and specialized resources and capabilities even for wider application in the MNC, many questions remain unanswered. For example, how are these new resource bundles further diffused and utilized elsewhere in the multinational firm? How do different resource outcomes impact subsidiary role development? How do they affect competition or collaboration between different units of the MNC? In addition, much of existing work focuses more on organizational than on environmental or individual-level outcomes. In particular, the findings of this study indicate that they may positively influence employee motivation and retention, or, on the other hand, negatively impact individual relations with superiors or the corporate office. Accordingly, it would be worthwhile to further explore both individual-level and environmental-level consequences of initiatives. Finally, existing research has given much attention to the benefits of subsidiary initiatives. As outlined in this dissertation, initiatives are also perceived to carry various risks for the MNC, such as misalignment with corporate priorities, added management complexities or additional costs. In order to fully and comprehensively understand the value of subsidiary initiatives for the MNC as a whole, more research would certainly be beneficial (see also Boojihawon 2007, Verbeke et al. 2007, Strutzenberger/Ambos 2014).

Methodological Research Opportunities: This dissertation presents and tests a conceptual framework of role-specific initiative-taking in two company cases with a total of 14 foreign subsidiary units. Given the limited generalizability of the findings, a *large scale test* of the framework and the propositions is advised. Further value is also expected from *additional case studies* with MNCs that are headquartered outside of Germany and have a different geographical footprint from that of the firms included in this work. This could provide additional insight with regard to the transferability of our empirical results.

Aside from additional case studies or even large-scale empirical tests, the subsidiary initiative process must be studied in more depth. It is recommended that detailed case studies be conducted with the entrepreneurial process as the unit of analysis, ideally in a longitudinal manner to better analyze the dynamic and emergent nature of subsidiary initiatives. Furthermore, given that subsidiary initiative-taking is a multi-level phenomenon, such a detailed process investigation should span multiple levels, including the individual entrepreneur and local teams, the subsidiary, the MNC and the business environment as a whole.

Appendix

Appendix A: Overview of Questionnaires

No.	Format	Respondent (Unit, Location)
Autocomp – Questionnaires		
S1	Paper-based	Global Innovation Manager (Headquarters, Germany)
S2	Online	Head of Production Operations (Subsidiary, Germany)
S3	Online	Head of R&D (Subsidiary, Mexico)
S4	Online	Head of R&D (Subsidiary, South Korea)
S5a	Online	Head of R&D (Subsidiary, Australia)
S5b	Online	Vice President Sales and Engineering (Subsidiary, Australia)
S6	Online	Country Manager (Subsidiary, China)
S7a	Online	Head of R&D (Subsidiary, Romania)
S7b	Online	Senior Director R&D (Subsidiary, Romania)
S8	Online	Head of Product Engineering and Sales (Subsidiary, India)
Telecomp – Questionnaires		
S9	Paper-based	Head of Product Marketing Europe (Headquarters, Germany)
S10	Online	Head of Product Development (Subsidiary, Hungary)
S11	Online	Senior Director Product Management (Subsidiary, Poland)
S12	Online	Director Product Development (Subsidiary, Croatia)
S13	Online	Head of Product Development (Subsidiary, Slovak Republic)
S14a	Online	Director Product Development and New Business (Subsidiary, Greece)
S14b	Online	Senior Strategic Project Manager (Subsidiary, Greece)
S15	Online	General Manager Products and Product Development (Subsidiary, Romania)
S16	Online	Director Product Development (Subsidiary, Montenegro)

Appendix B: Overview of Interviews

No.	Format	Interviewee (Unit, Location)
Autocomp – Interviews		
I1	Face-to-face interview	Global Innovation Manager (Headquarters, Germany)
I2	Telephone interview	Head of Production Operations (Subsidiary, Germany)
I3	Telephone interview	Head of R&D (Subsidiary, Mexico)
I4	Telephone interview	Head of R&D (Subsidiary, South Korea)
I5	Telephone interview	Vice President Sales and Engineering (Subsidiary, Australia)
I6	Telephone interview	Country Manager (Subsidiary, China)
I7	Telephone interview	Head of R&D (Subsidiary, Romania)
I8	Telephone interview	Head of Product Engineering and Sales (Subsidiary, India)
Telecomp – Interviews		
I9	Face-to-face interview	Head of Product Marketing Europe (Headquarters, Germany)
I10	Telephone interview	Head of Product Development (Subsidiary, Hungary)
I11	Telephone interview	Senior Director Product Management (Subsidiary, Poland)
I12	Telephone interview	Director Product Development (Subsidiary, Croatia)
I13	Telephone interview	Head of Product Development (Subsidiary, Slovak Republic)
I14	Telephone interview	Director Product Development (Subsidiary, Greece)
I15	Telephone interview	General Manager Products and Development (Subsidiary, Romania)
I16	Telephone interview	Director Product Development (Subsidiary, Montenegro)

Appendix C: Overview of Archival and Secondary Data

No.	Document	Source	Retrieval Date
Autocomp – Archival and Secondary Data			
A1	Company A – fact book 2013	Company A	April 2014
A2	Company A – fact book 2012	Company A	April 2013
A3	Autocomp – facts & figures 2012	Company A	April 2013
A4	Overview subsidiary locations of Autocomp	Company A	May 2012
A5	Report on Mexican R&D center	Company A	May 2013
A6	Overview presentation subsidiary Romania	Company A	June 2012
A7	Report on R&D investment subsidiary Romania	Company A	June 2012
A8	Overview subsidiary India	Company A	November 2012
Telecomp – Archival and Secondary Data			
A9	Company B – company report 2014	Company B	May 2015
A10	Company B – company report 2013	Company B	April 2014
A11	Overview Telecomp subsidiary Hungary	Company B	October 2014
A12	Company B public presentation 2015	Company B	March 2015
A13	Overview Telecomp subsidiary Poland	Company B	October 2014
A14	Overview innovation center subsidiary Poland	Company B	April 2015
A15	Overview initiative subsidiary Poland	Company B	April 2015
A16	Public presentation subsidiary Croatia 2013	Company B	April 2015
A17	Overview Telecomp subsidiary Croatia	Company B	April 2015
A18	Overview initiative subsidiary Croatia 2013	Company B	April 2015
A19	Overview Telecomp subsidiary Slovak Republic	Company B	April 2015
A20	Overview Telecomp subsidiary Greece	Company B	April 2015
A21	Overview Telecomp subsidiary Romania	Company B	April 2015
A22	Overview Telecomp subsidiary Montenegro	Company B	April 2015

Appendix D: Subsidiary Questionnaire

Please return the questionnaire to:
Prof. Dr. Stefan Schmid
Chair for International Management and Strategic Management
ESCP Europe Campus Berlin
Topic: *Subsidiary Entrepreneurship*
Heubnerweg 8-10
14059 Berlin, Germany

Fax: +49 (0)30 405 405 44
E-Mail: lars.dzedek@escpeurope.de

In case of questions, please contact:
Lars R. Dzedek
Doctoral Candiate
Phone: +49 (0)30 22398 062
Fax: +49 (0)30 405 405 44
E-Mail: lars.dzedek@escpeurope.de

Survey on:

Entrepreneurial Activities by Foreign Subsidiaries of Multinational Corporations

Brief Background on the Survey:

- The following survey is conducted by **ESCP Europe Business School** as part of research project that investigates entrepreneurial activities by foreign subsidiaries of multinational corporations in the automotive supplier industry.
- **Your company's headquarters** have kindly agreed to participate in this study and **identified you** as a senior executive that is knowledgeable about the entrepreneurial and innovative efforts that your subsidiary has engaged in over the past five years.
- Should you be aware of **any other suitable senior executive** at your subsidiary that is, in addition to you, also well-informed about entrepreneurial and innovative activities in your subsidiary, please feel free to forward this questionnaire and/or the link to the online survey listed below.
- Should you have any further questions, please contact Lars R. Dzedek, key responsible for this research project, using the details provided above.

Information on the Completion of the Questionnaire:

- You may also **complete this survey online** using the following link: http://ww2.unipark.de/uc/ESCP_Europe/
- The completion of the questionnaire will take **approximately 25-30 minutes**.
- The questionnaire will **not ask** you to provide **any direct financial or performance figures** or any specific details of previous entrepreneurial activities of your subsidiary, such as technical information of new products and/or services.
- As agreed with your corporate headquarters, your responses will be handled **strictly confidential** and will not be shared with anyone outside your company.
- You may **return the completed questionnaire** until [date] by email, fax or regular mail using the contact details displayed at the top of this page.

Next Steps:

- Following the analysis of this questionnaire, we **will contact you shortly** to arrange for a follow-up interview by telephone to discuss selected aspects in more detail.
- If desired, we will be happy to provide you with a **management report** that outlines the key findings of this study in the end.

Thank you very much for your participation!

Appendix

Basic Information on Subsidiary and Respondent

1. Please provide the following **general information** about yourself and your subsidiary:

Your name (last, first): _____

Your position and title: _____

Your email address: _____

Location of subsidiary
(region, country, city): _____

Year of subsidiary's
establishment: _____

2. Please indicate how your subsidiary was originally **established**:

Subsidiary was **newly founded** by parent company (greenfield investment)...............	☐	Subsidiary was **taken-over** by parent company from another organization (acquisition/brownfield investment).........	☐

3. Please indicate the **functional activities** that are currently performed by your subsidiary:

Research and/or development..................	☐	Marketing and/or sales.....................	☐	Purchasing.................	☐
Production of goods and/or services...............	☐	Logistics and/or distribution.....................	☐	HR Management...........	☐
Customer service and/or after sales..............	☐	Other (please specify)..................	☐	_____	

1. Evaluation of the Subsidiary Role Dimensions

1. Strategic Importance of the Subsidiary Environment

The following questions will assess your opinion about different characteristics of your **current subsidiary's market environment.**

Please indicate for each characteristic listed below to what extent it applies to the market environment for which your subsidiary is responsible at the moment.

	Very small 1	2	3	4	Very high 5
Market size (e.g. sales value/volume, number of customers)	☐	☐	☐	☐	☐
Competitive intensity (e.g. number of major customers, quality and sophistication of competitive products/services)	☐	☐	☐	☐	☐
Technological dynamism (e.g. number of innovations and patents developed in the market each year)	☐	☐	☐	☐	☐
Customer demand intensity (e.g. sophistication and complexity of products/services demanded by customers)	☐	☐	☐	☐	☐

2. Subsidiary Resources and Capabilities

The following questions will assess your opinion about different **capabilities or competencies of your subsidiary** in comparison to all other subsidiaries of your company.

Please indicate for each activity listed below the relative level of capabilities or competencies your subsidiary currently possesses.

	Not capable 1	2	3	4	Highly capable 5
Research and development	☐	☐	☐	☐	☐
Production of goods and/or services	☐	☐	☐	☐	☐
Marketing and/or sales	☐	☐	☐	☐	☐
Logistics and/or distribution	☐	☐	☐	☐	☐
Purchasing	☐	☐	☐	☐	☐
HR management	☐	☐	☐	☐	☐
General management	☐	☐	☐	☐	☐
Innovation and/or entrepreneurship	☐	☐	☐	☐	☐

3. Subsidiary Localization and Local Responsiveness

The following questions will assess your opinion about some **further characteristics** of your subsidiary, such as local engagement or local adaptations of products and/or services.

Please indicate for each characteristic listed below to what extent it applies to your subsidiary at the moment.

	Very low 1	2	3	4	Very high 5
Extent of **inputs** that subsidiary receives **from other units** of your company	☐	☐	☐	☐	☐
Extent of **local content** in locally produced **goods or services**	☐	☐	☐	☐	☐
Share of sales (from total sales of subsidiary) that comes **from goods or services** that are produced at your **subsidiary location**	☐	☐	☐	☐	☐
Extent to which subsidiary's **customers and their needs differ** from those of other units of your company	☐	☐	☐	☐	☐
Extent to which subsidiary's **competitors and their strategies are easily identified**	☐	☐	☐	☐	☐
Stability of technology and level of **manufacturing/service delivery sophistication** in subsidiary's market environment	☐	☐	☐	☐	☐
Maturity of life cycle stage of product/service line(s) and manufacturing processes	☐	☐	☐	☐	☐
Extent to which subsidiary **interacts with local actors** (e.g. other firms, government or research institutions)	☐	☐	☐	☐	☐
Heterogeneity of **subsidiary executive** group (e.g. differences in backgrounds, nationality)	☐	☐	☐	☐	☐

4. Subsidiary Integration

The following questions will assess your opinion about different aspects concerning the **integration of your subsidiary in the company's network**. Please indicate for each aspect listed below to what extent it applies to your subsidiary at the moment.

	Very low				Very high
	1	2	3	4	5
Extent to which subsidiary's **purchasing activities** are integrated with the rest of your company.............	☐	☐	☐	☐	☐
Extent to which subsidiary's **manufacturing process/service delivery process** is integrated with the rest of your company........	☐	☐	☐	☐	☐
Extent to which subsidiary's **R&D activities** are integrated with the rest of your company.............	☐	☐	☐	☐	☐
Extent to which subsidiary's **marketing activities** are integrated with the rest of your company.............	☐	☐	☐	☐	☐
Extent to which **products/services are adapted** to local market needs.............	☐	☐	☐	☐	☐
Proportion of local R&D (from total R&D) incorporated in the **products/services** sold by your subsidiary.............	☐	☐	☐	☐	☐
Extent to which **manufacturing/service delivery decisions** are linked to world-wide market areas (rather than the local market).............	☐	☐	☐	☐	☐
Extent to which **quality specifications for product/service** are developed **by headquarters** (rather than by the subsidiary).........	☐	☐	☐	☐	☐
Extent to which **subsidiary serves** its MNC's customers worldwide.............	☐	☐	☐	☐	☐
Extent to which **technology development is centralized** and shared within the internal company network.............	☐	☐	☐	☐	☐
Extent to which **subsidiary depends on linkages within your company's network**.............	☐	☐	☐	☐	☐
Extent to which **planning of product/service delivery, inventory and quality control is centralized**.............	☐	☐	☐	☐	☐

5. Subsidiary Autonomy

The following questions will assess your opinion about the **level of influence** your subsidiary has on a number of different strategic and operational decisions. Please indicate for each decision listed below to what extent it is made centrally by headquarters or independently by your subsidiary at the moment.

	Decided centrally by head-quarters				Decided independ-ently by subsidiary
	1	2	3	4	5
Major development of a new product/service.............	☐	☐	☐	☐	☐
Minor but significant modification of an existing product/service.............	☐	☐	☐	☐	☐
Major modification of a production and/or service delivery process.............	☐	☐	☐	☐	☐
Restructuring of the subsidiary organization involving the creation or abolition of departments.............	☐	☐	☐	☐	☐
Recruitment and promotion to positions just below that of the subsidiary's general manager.............	☐	☐	☐	☐	☐
Career development plans for departmental managers.............	☐	☐	☐	☐	☐
Formulating and approving your subsidiary's annual budgets.............	☐	☐	☐	☐	☐

2. Evaluation of the Subsidiary Initiative Process

2.1 Initiative Opportunity Identification

6. Identification of Subsidiary Initiative Opportunities

The following questions will assess your opinion about the **identification of new entrepreneurial opportunities** by your subsidiary during the **past five years** (even if they were not implemented/realized in the end).

Please indicate to what extent new entrepreneurial opportunities emerged through the sources listed below.

Note: The term "entrepreneurial opportunity" refers to all opportunities for entrepreneurial activities ranging from smaller internal improvement efforts (e.g. efficiency improvements, rationalization activities) to the pursuit of more extensive and/or radical endeavors (e.g. highly innovative products and/or services).

	Never 1	2	3	4	Plentifully 5
Internally, **solely from within the subsidiary** (e.g. by subsidiary employees or subsidiary management)	☐	☐	☐	☐	☐
Internally, through any type of interaction with **sister subsidiaries** or **other units** of your company (e.g. internal R&D units of your company)	☐	☐	☐	☐	☐
Internally, through any type of interaction with **corporate headquarters**	☐	☐	☐	☐	☐
Externally, through any type of interaction with **local actors outside the subsidiary** (e.g. local customers, suppliers, business partners, consultants, research or governmental institutions)	☐	☐	☐	☐	☐
Externally, through any type of interaction with **global actors outside the company** (e.g. global customers, suppliers, consultants, research or governmental institutions)	☐	☐	☐	☐	☐

2.2 Innovativeness of Opportunities

7. Innovativeness of Identified Subsidiary Initiative Opportunities

The following questions will assess your opinion about the **innovativeness of the new entrepreneurial opportunities** that were identified by your subsidiary during the **past five years** (even if they were not implemented/realized in the end).

Please indicate to what extent the new entrepreneurial opportunities belong to the classifications listed below.

	Never 1	2	3	4	Plentifully 5
Replication of existing product/service or process to be used in similar applications	☐	☐	☐	☐	☐
New application for existing product/service or process with little or no modifications at all	☐	☐	☐	☐	☐
Minor changes in existing product/service or process	☐	☐	☐	☐	☐
Significant changes in existing product/service or process	☐	☐	☐	☐	☐
Combination of two or more existing products/services into one unique product/service	☐	☐	☐	☐	☐
Product/service or process that was "new to the world"	☐	☐	☐	☐	☐

2.3 Resource Structuring and Bundling

8. Resource Structuring Efforts

The following questions will assess your opinion about the **acquisition and/or development of new resources and capabilities** that were required to further pursue and eventually implement the new entrepreneurial opportunities that were identified by your subsidiary during the past five years.

Please indicate to what extent your subsidiary engaged in the following activities when further pursuing these new entrepreneurial opportunities.

Note: The term "acquisition" refers to buying existing resources or capabilities "off-the-shelf" that are – more or less – directly available for purchase from different internal or external sources. In contrast, the term "development" represents the gradual accumulation of resources and capabilities within the subsidiary itself (e.g. through research and development activities or learning efforts by the subsidiary).

Resources and capabilities can include both tangible assets (e.g. physical assets such as plant, equipment, machines; financial assets such as equity capital; or human capital such as experienced employees) and intangible assets (e.g. operational, technological or managerial know-how or brand assets).

	Never 1	2	3	4	Plentifully 5
Extent to which new opportunities could be realized **only with the existing** resources and capabilities of the subsidiary *(i.e. no additional resources and capabilities had to be acquired and/or developed in order to realize the opportunity)*	☐	☐	☐	☐	☐
Extent to which new opportunities required to both **use existing resources and capabilities** and to also **acquire and/or develop new ones**	☐	☐	☐	☐	☐
Extent to which new opportunities were realized **only with newly acquired and/or developed resources and capabilities** *(i.e. no existing capabilities were used)*	☐	☐	☐	☐	☐

9. Acquisition of Resources and Capabilities

The following questions will assess your opinion **only** about the **acquisition** of new resources and/or capabilities that were required to further pursue and eventually implement the new entrepreneurial opportunities that were identified by your subsidiary during the past five years.

Please indicate for the different internal and external sources to what extent they were used to acquire resources and/or capabilities when further pursuing the entrepreneurial opportunities.

Note: "Acquisition" refers to buying existing resources or capabilities "off-the-shelf" that are – more or less – directly available for purchase from different internal or external sources.

*Resources and capabilities were acquired **internally** from the following sources within the company...*

	Never				Plentifully
Corporate headquarters *(e.g. buying equipment, machinery, brand assets or technology from headquarters)*	☐	☐	☐	☐	☐
Sister subsidiaries	☐	☐	☐	☐	☐
Other units of this company besides headquarters and sister subsidiaries *(e.g. internal R& units)*	☐	☐	☐	☐	☐

*Resources and capabilities were acquired **externally** from the following sources outside the company...*

	Never				Plentifully
Directly from external actors in the local or global market *(e.g. buying equipment, machinery, brand assets or technology from external suppliers, competitors or research institutions)*	☐	☐	☐	☐	☐
Indirectly through merging with or acquiring another firm/organization in the local or global market *(e.g. acquiring or merging with a competitor to gain access to know-how, technology or brand assets that could otherwise not be accessed)*	☐	☐	☐	☐	☐

Appendix

10. Internal Development of Resources and Capabilities within the Subsidiary

The following questions will assess your opinion **only** about the **internal development** of new resources and capabilities within your subsidiary that were required to further pursue and eventually implement the new entrepreneurial opportunities that were identified by your subsidiary during the past five years.

Please indicate for each activity listed below the level of investments your subsidiary made in order to internally develop the needed resources and/or capabilities.

Note: "Internal development" refers to the gradual accumulation of resources and capabilities within the subsidiary itself *without* any type of interaction with external actors from outside the company (e.g. through research and development activities or learning efforts by the subsidiary alone).

	Very limited				Substantial
	1	2	3	4	5
Research and/or development (e.g. development of new technology)	☐	☐	☐	☐	☐
Production (e.g. enhancement of production capabilities)	☐	☐	☐	☐	☐
Marketing and/or sales (e.g. improvement of brand image, training of sales force)	☐	☐	☐	☐	☐
Logistics and/or distribution (e.g. optimization of logistics processes)	☐	☐	☐	☐	☐
Purchasing (e.g. optimization of procurement process)	☐	☐	☐	☐	☐
HR management (e.g. improvement of personnel recruiting capabilities)	☐	☐	☐	☐	☐
General management (e.g. enhancement of managerial know-how)	☐	☐	☐	☐	☐

11. Internal-External Resource Development

The following questions will assess your opinion **only** about the **development** of new resources and capabilities **in collaboration with external partners** that were required to further pursue and eventually implement the new entrepreneurial opportunities that were identified by your subsidiary during the past five years.

Please indicate for each activity listed below to what extent your subsidiary developed new resources or capabilities together with external partners (e.g. in strategic alliances, joint ventures or partnerships in more general).

	Never				Plentifully
	1	2	3	4	5
Research and/or development (e.g. joint development of new technology with external partner)	☐	☐	☐	☐	☐
Production (e.g. adoption of new manufacturing capabilities from external partner)	☐	☐	☐	☐	☐
Marketing and/or sales (e.g. adoption of marketing and sales tactics from external partner)	☐	☐	☐	☐	☐
Logistics and/or distribution (e.g. learning from joint execution of logistics process with external partner)	☐	☐	☐	☐	☐
Purchasing (e.g. joint development of optimized procurement process)	☐	☐	☐	☐	☐
HR management (e.g. learning new recruitment capabilities from external partner)	☐	☐	☐	☐	☐
General management (e.g. transfer of management best practice from external partner)	☐	☐	☐	☐	☐

12. Bundling of Resources and Capabilities by the Subsidiary

The following questions will assess your opinion about the **integration and combination of resources and capabilities** that your subsidiary obtained from the different internal and external sources in order to further pursue and eventually implement the new entrepreneurial opportunities that were identified during the past five years.

Please indicate to what extent your subsidiary needed to engage in the following resource and capability combination activities during this timeframe.

	Never				Plentifully
	1	2	3	4	5
New opportunities required some minor combination of **already existing resources** and capabilities of the subsidiary......	☐	☐	☐	☐	☐
New opportunities required the combination of **newly obtained resources** and capabilities **with already existing ones** in the subsidiary..	☐	☐	☐	☐	☐
New opportunities required the extensive combination of **completely new resources** and capabilities that were newly obtained	☐	☐	☐	☐	☐

2.4 Headquarters-Subsidiary Alignment

13. Headquarters' Involvement

The following questions will assess your opinion about the degree to which **headquarters were involved** in the entrepreneurial activities that your subsidiary engaged in during the past five years.

Please indicate for each of activity listed below to what the extent headquarters were involved.

Note: *The term "headquarters" refers to corporate headquarters as well as to regional/divisional headquarters, if applicable.*

	Never				Plentifully
	1	2	3	4	5
Extent to which subsidiary managers **communicated with** counterparts in **headquarters** concerning the new opportunities...	☐	☐	☐	☐	☐
Extent to which **headquarters participated closely in the refinement and development** of the new opportunities......	☐	☐	☐	☐	☐
Extent to which subsidiary **communicated and/or presented** new opportunities **at headquarters** (e.g. in the form of business plans, project proposals).........................	☐	☐	☐	☐	☐
Extent to which **headquarters' approval** was required for the continuation and/or implementation of the new opportunities...	☐	☐	☐	☐	☐

14. Resistance from Headquarters and other MNC Units

The following questions will assess your opinion about **difficulties or resistance** your subsidiary encountered from other units of your company when engaging in entrepreneurial activities during the past five years.

Please indicate for each aspect listed below to what extent it applies to your subsidiary.

Note: The term "headquarters" refers to both corporate headquarters as well as regional headquarters, if applicable.

	Never 1	2	3	4	Plentifully 5
Rejection of entrepreneurial activity by headquarters.................	☐	☐	☐	☐	☐
Delay of entrepreneurial activity and/or request for **greater justification** by headquarters...................	☐	☐	☐	☐	☐
Lobbying and rival activities by competing divisions or other units of your company......................	☐	☐	☐	☐	☐
Lack of recognition and/or **acceptance** by other units of your company.................................	☐	☐	☐	☐	☐

15. Subsidiary Initiative Selling

The following questions will assess your opinion about your subsidiary's efforts aimed at **lobbying and selling** the new entrepreneurial opportunities within your company during the past five years.

Please indicate for each activity listed below to what extent it applies to your subsidiary.

Note: The term "headquarters" refers to both corporate headquarters as well as regional headquarters, if applicable.

	Never 1	2	3	4	Plentifully 5
Attracting headquarters' attention to a new opportunity...	☐	☐	☐	☐	☐
Making headquarters understand a new opportunity...	☐	☐	☐	☐	☐
Lobbying and/or selling efforts at headquarters to get support for a new opportunity.........................	☐	☐	☐	☐	☐
Lobbying and/or selling efforts at <u>sister subsidiaries</u> or <u>other units</u> of your company to get support for a new opportunity...	☐	☐	☐	☐	☐

3. Subsidiary Initiative Outcomes

3.1 Successful Initiatives

16. Level of Successful Subsidiary Initiatives (per type)

The following questions will assess your opinion about the characteristics of **"successful" entrepreneurial opportunities pursued by your subsidiary** that were finally approved and/or implemented during the past five years.

Please indicate to what extent the successfully approved and/or implemented entrepreneurial opportunities related to the following characteristics.

Note: For the following questions please also consider those entrepreneurial opportunities that are currently being implemented or that will be implemented in the near future.

	Never 1	2	3	4	Plentifully 5
Significant extensions to existing international responsibilities..	☐	☐	☐	☐	☐
Enhancement to product and/or service lines which are already **sold internationally**....................................	☐	☐	☐	☐	☐
New international business activities that were first **started locally**..	☐	☐	☐	☐	☐
New products and/or services developed locally and sold internationally...	☐	☐	☐	☐	☐
Proposals to transfer manufacturing to subsidiary location from elsewhere in the corporation.................................	☐	☐	☐	☐	☐
Reconfiguring of local subsidiary operations from domestic to international orientation......................................	☐	☐	☐	☐	☐
Successful bids for **corporate investment** in subsidiary location..	☐	☐	☐	☐	☐
New corporate investment in R&D or manufacturing attracted by local subsidiary management...............................	☐	☐	☐	☐	☐

Appendix

3.2 Resources and Capabilities Resulting from Initiatives

17. Development of Specialized Subsidiary Resources and Capabilities

The following questions will assess your opinion about the overall **enhancement of your subsidiary's capabilities or competencies** as the result of the entrepreneurial activities pursued by your subsidiary during the past five years.

Please indicate to what extent your subsidiary developed new capabilities or competencies for each of the activities listed below.

	No capability development at all				Extensive capability development
	1	2	3	4	5
Research and/or development	☐	☐	☐	☐	☐
Production of goods and/or services	☐	☐	☐	☐	☐
Marketing and/or sales	☐	☐	☐	☐	☐
Logistics and/or distribution	☐	☐	☐	☐	☐
Purchasing	☐	☐	☐	☐	☐
HR management	☐	☐	☐	☐	☐
General management	☐	☐	☐	☐	☐
Innovation and/or entrepreneurship	☐	☐	☐	☐	☐

18. Subsidiary Initiative-Taking Impact on MNC Capability Development/Subsidiary Importance

The following questions will assess your opinion about the **contribution** of the newly developed subsidiary's capabilities or competencies **to the overall competencies of your company**.

Please indicate to what extent these new subsidiary capabilities or competencies are also of use for other units of your company for each of the activities listed below.

	No use at all				Very useful
	1	2	3	4	5
Research and/or development	☐	☐	☐	☐	☐
Production of goods and/or services	☐	☐	☐	☐	☐
Marketing and/or sales	☐	☐	☐	☐	☐
Logistics and/or distribution	☐	☐	☐	☐	☐
Purchasing	☐	☐	☐	☐	☐
HR management	☐	☐	☐	☐	☐
General management	☐	☐	☐	☐	☐
Innovation and/or entrepreneurship	☐	☐	☐	☐	☐

3.2 Performance Measures

19. Subsidiary Initiative Performance Outcomes

The following questions will assess your opinion about the **performance outcomes** of the entrepreneurial activities pursued by your subsidiary during the past five years.

Please indicate to what extent the entrepreneurial activities resulted in the following performance outcomes for your subsidiary.

	Very limited				Substantial
	1	2	3	4	5
Enhanced sales or revenues	☐	☐	☐	☐	☐
Reduced costs	☐	☐	☐	☐	☐
Improved market share	☐	☐	☐	☐	☐
Improved profit	☐	☐	☐	☐	☐
Improved return on investment	☐	☐	☐	☐	☐
Improved productivity	☐	☐	☐	☐	☐

3.3 Additional Outcome Measures

20. Further Subsidiary Initiative Outcomes

The following questions will assess your opinion about the **impact on different subsidiary characteristics** as the result of the entrepreneurial activities pursued by your subsidiary during the past five years.

Please indicate to what extent the entrepreneurial activities resulted in changes to the following subsidiary characteristics.

	Major decline		No change		Major improvement
	1	2	3	4	5
Subsidiary's geographical market scope	☐	☐	☐	☐	☐
Subsidiary's product scope	☐	☐	☐	☐	☐
Subsidiary's value-added scope	☐	☐	☐	☐	☐
Subsidiary influence on the outcomes/performance of other subsidiaries	☐	☐	☐	☐	☐
Subsidiary history of delivering what it has promised to headquarters	☐	☐	☐	☐	☐
Significant value-added contribution the subsidiary makes to the company	☐	☐	☐	☐	☐
Global competitiveness of the subsidiary in its market environment	☐	☐	☐	☐	☐
Recognition of subsidiary by headquarters as strategically important unit	☐	☐	☐	☐	☐

Appendix E: Subsidiary Interview Guide

Subsidiary Initiative-Taking in MNCs: **Subsidiary** Interview Guideline
Prerequisites (to be completed before interview)
Questionnaire completed by subsidiary manager in advance... ☐   Perception of subsidiary role by HQ and subsidiary (largely) identical... ☐   Subsidiary indicated (at least some) initiative-taking activity in questionnaire................................ ☐   Interviewee is expected to be knowledgeable about initiative-taking activities of subsidiary........ ☐   Findings from questionnaire incorporated in interview guideline .... ☐
Basic Information on Subsidiary and Interviewee (to be completed before interview)
Name of interviewee: _____   Position/title of interviewee: _____   Number of years in current position/in company: _____   Location of subsidiary (region, country, city): _____   Number of employees in subsidiary: _____   Year when subsidiary was established: _____   Mode of establishment (greenfield/acquisition/other): _____   Date and time of interview: _____   Interview mode (face to face/telephone/other): _____
Introduction to the Interview

- Brief introduction of interviewee and interviewer
 - Brief presentation of study objectives and of interview objectives
 - Explanation of timeframe
 - Explanation of interview structure
   ○ Basic characteristics of the subsidiary
   ○ Changes in environmental and organizational conditions over past five years
   ○ Entrepreneurial activities of subsidiary – in general – over past five years
   ○ Development process of entrepreneurial activities/projects
   ○ Outcomes of entrepreneurial activities/projects for subsidiary and wider MNC

1. Basic Subsidiary Characteristics

I would like to first start with discussing some basic characteristics of your subsidiary.

[Remark: Questions will only be asked on subsidiary characteristics for which no information could be obtained from alternative sources, such as HQ or secondary data]

PRODUCT/MARKET/VALUE-ADDING SCOPE
- Which important value-adding activities are currently performed by your subsidiary?
- For which main product/business/service lines is your subsidiary responsible at the moment?
- For which geographical market area(s) is your subsidiary responsible at the moment?

2. Development of Environmental and Subsidiary Characteristics

I would like to continue with the changes in environmental and subsidiary conditions that occurred over the past five years. You have indicated that your subsidiary ...

(a) ... operates in a market that is of [high/medium/low] **strategic importance** *(market size, competitive intensity, technological dynamism, customer demand intensity).*
- How did these market conditions change over the past five years?
- How did this affect the entrepreneurial activities of your subsidiary?

(b) ... possesses a [high/medium/low level] of **capabilities or competencies** *(in R&D, production of goods/services, marketing/sales, logistics/distribution, purchasing, HR management, general management, innovation/entrepreneurship).*
- How did these subsidiary capabilities/competencies change over the past five years?
- How did this affect the entrepreneurial activities of your subsidiary?

(c) ... pursues [many/some/few] **activities locally** *(e.g. inputs from other units, extent of local content) and shows a [high/medium/low]* **local market orientation** *(e.g. interaction with local actors).*
- How did the local engagement and local orientation change over the past five years?
- How did this affect the entrepreneurial activities of your subsidiary?

(d) ...shows [high/medium/low] **integration** *in your company's network.*
- How did the degree of subsidiary integration change over the past five years?
- How did this affect the entrepreneurial activities of your subsidiary?

3. Subsidiary Initiatives : Entrepreneurial Activities in General

I would now like to discuss – in general – the entrepreneurial activities of your subsidiary during the past five years. You have indicated that your subsidiary has been [heavily/moderately/only little] engaged in entrepreneurial activities during this timeframe.

INITIATVE DETAILS
- Cold you estimate the amount of entrepreneurial activities/projects your subsidiary has initiated during this timeframe – even if they were not approved and/or implemented in the end?
- How many (or what percentage) of these entrepreneurial activities/projects were finally approved?
- Could you briefly describe <u>the three most important</u> entrepreneurial activities/projects of your subsidiary that were approved for implementation during the past five years?

DRIVERS/INHIBITORS
Besides the environmental and organizational conditions mentioned before:
- What other important factors facilitated or inhibited entrepreneurial activities in your subsidiary? In which manner?

4. Subsidiary Initiative Process: Resource Management

4.1 Initiative Opportunity Identification

I would now like to discuss the identification of entrepreneurial opportunities by your subsidiary during the past five years. You have indicated that opportunities for new entrepreneurial activities/projects were frequently identified through [source(s) x,y, ...].

> [Remark: If identification of different entrepreneurial opportunities varies too widely, have respondent refer to three most important initiatives/projects mentioned above.]

PROCESS DETAILS
- How were new entrepreneurial opportunities identified from [source(s) x, y, ...]?
- Who was typically involved from within your subsidiary?

DRIVERS/INHIBITORS
- Could you explain to me the reasons for the identification through [source(s) x, y, ...]?
- What important factors facilitated or inhibited the identification of new opportunities by your subsidiary? How?

4.2 Resource Structuring

I would now like to discuss your activities concerned with obtaining resources and capabilities that were necessary to further pursue and eventually implement the entrepreneurial opportunities.

> [Remark: If structuring of different entrepreneurial opportunities varies too widely, have respondent refer to three most important initiatives/projects mentioned above.]

You have indicated ...

(a) ... *that the entrepreneurial activities frequently required the internal/external* **acquisition** *of new resources/capabilities from [source(s) x,y,...].*

PROCESS DETAILS
- How were resources/capabilities acquired from these specific sources?
- From which internal/external actors in particular were these resources/capabilities acquired?
- Could you provide examples of key resources and/or capabilities that were acquired?

DRIVERS/INHIBITORS
- Could you explain why it was decided to acquire new resources/capabilities from this/these particular source(s)?
- What important factors facilitated or inhibited the acquisition of new resources/capabilities by your subsidiary?

(b) ... *that the entrepreneurial activities frequently required the internal/internal-external* **development** *of new resources/capabilities in [functional area(s) x, y, ...].*

PROCESS DETAILS
- How were resources/capabilities developed by your subsidiary? Can you give examples?
- Could you specify the kind of resources and/or capabilities that were developed?
- [Remark: If internal-external development:]
  With which external actor(s) did you cooperate when developing new resources/capabilities?

DRIVERS/INHIBITORS
- Could you explain why it was decided to develop new resources in this/these manner(s)?

What other important factors facilitated or inhibited the development of new resources/capabilities by your subsidiary?

4.3 Resource Bundling

You have indicated that your entrepreneurial initiatives frequently involved [minor combinations of existing resources/combinations of new and existing resources/combinations of completely new resources].

> [Remark: If bundling of different entrepreneurial opportunities varies too widely, have respondent refer to three most important initiatives/projects mentioned above.]

PROCESS DETAILS
- How were resources/capabilities from the different sources integrated in order to realize entrepreneurial opportunities? Can you give examples?

DRIVERS/INHIBITORS
- Could you explain why your entrepreneurial activities required [minor combination of existing resources/combination of new and existing resources/combination of completely new resources]?
- What important factors facilitated or inhibited the integration and combination of resources/capabilities by your subsidiary?

5. Subsidiary Initiative Process: HQ-S Alignment

I would now like to discuss the alignment and interaction of your subsidiary with headquarters and other units of your company during the entrepreneurial activities.

5.1 Headquarters Involvement

You have indicated that headquarters were [heavily/moderately/only little] involved in your entrepreneurial activities.

> [Remark: If HQ involvement for different entrepreneurial opportunities varies too widely, have respondent refer to three most important initiatives/projects mentioned above.]

PROCESS DETAILS
- Could you describe the interactions between HQ and subsidiary throughout the pursuit of entrepreneurial activities (e.g. form and frequency of interaction)?
- Who was typically involved from (a) HQ side and (b) subsidiary side?
- How was HQ involved in during your entrepreneurial activities?
- Were there cases when your subsidiary decided not to involve headquarters? If so, when and why?

DRIVERS/INHIBITORS
- Could you explain why headquarters were [heavily/moderately/only little] involved?
- What important factors facilitated or inhibited HQ involvement?

5.2 Corporate Resistance

You have indicated that headquarters and other units of your company showed a [high/medium/low level] of resistance towards the entrepreneurial activities of your subsidiary.

> [Remark: If corporate resistance for different entrepreneurial opportunities varies too widely, have respondent refer to three most important initiatives/projects mentioned above.]

PROCESS DETAILS
- Can you describe the resistance that your subsidiary encountered?

DRIVERS/INHIBITORS
- What do you believe were the reasons for [high/medium/low] resistance?
- Which role did – in particular – subsidiary influence and subsidiary power play in this process?
  [Remark: 1 = no relevance at all; 5 = very important]
- What important factors facilitated or inhibited resistance against your subsidiary's entrepreneurial activities?

5.3 Subsidiary Initiative Selling

You have indicated that your subsidiary engaged in a [high/medium/low level] of lobbying and selling activities within your company.

> [Remark: If subsidiary selling for different entrepreneurial opportunities varies too widely, have respondent refer to three most important initiatives/projects mentioned above.]

PROCESS DETAILS
- Can you describe your subsidiary's activities related to lobbying/selling at HQ or other units of your company?
- Who was typically involved from (a) HQ side and (b) subsidiary side or (c) other units of your company?
- Through which channels did the lobbying/selling take place?
- To what extent did your subsidiary's lobbying/selling activities help to overcome resistance and push entrepreneurial opportunities towards implementation?

DRIVERS/INHIBITORS
- What do you believe were the reasons for [high/medium/low] lobbying and selling activities?
- What other important factors facilitated or inhibited resistance against your subsidiary's entrepreneurial activities?

6. Subsidiary Initiative: Outcomes

As a last point, I would now like to discuss – in more detail – the outcomes and consequences of entrepreneurial activities that were eventually approved and/or implemented during the past five years.

> [Remark: If subsidiary initiative outcomes for different entrepreneurial opportunities vary too widely, have respondent refer to three most important initiatives/projects mentioned above.]

GENERAL OUTCOMES
- What were the **key benefits** resulting from the approved entrepreneurial activities for ...
  (a) ... the subsidiary
  (b) ... the company as a whole
  (c) ... or even the market environment of your subsidiary?

- What were the associated **costs and/or risks** associated with the approved entrepreneurial activities for ...
  (a) ... the subsidiary
  (b) ... the company as a whole
  (c) ... or even the market environment of your subsidiary?

OUTCOMES AND MNC COMPETENCE DEVELOPMENT (INTERNAL)

You have indicated that your subsidiary has – as the result of its entrepreneurial activities during the past five years – developed [many/some/few] new specialized capabilities/competencies particularly in [functional area(s) x, y, ...].

- Can you give examples of new capabilities/competencies developed in [functional area(s) x, y, ...]?
- Can you further explain to what extent these new capabilities/competencies ...
  - ... are superior to those that exist elsewhere in your company?
    [Remark: 1 = equal to others; 5 = highly superior]
  - ... could be transferred to other locations and/or other units of your company?
    [Remark: 1 = not transferable at all; 5 = easily transferable]

SUBSIDIARY ROLE DEVELOPMENT

You have indicated that your subsidiary's (a) geographical market scope and/or (b) product scope and/or (c) value-added scope have – as the result of its entrepreneurial activities during the past five years – [greatly improved/not changed/weakened].

- How in particular did ...
  (a) ... the geographical market scope
- (b) ... the product scope
- (c) ... the value-added scope
  ... change as a result of the entrepreneurial activities?
- How did the overall position and standing of your subsidiary vis-à-vis HQ change as a result of the entrepreneurial activities?

Closing/Wrap-Up of Interview

- Is there anything else that we have not discussed that you think is important?
- *Thank you very much for your time and your valuable input*
- *Explanation of next steps and good-bye*

Appendix F: Headquarters Interview Guide

Subsidiary Initiative-Taking in MNCs: Headquarters Interview Guideline

Introduction to the Interview
- *Introduction of interviewee and interviewer*
- *Presentation of research project, objectives and approach*
- *Explanation of interview structure*

1. Role of HQ Manager and Information on MNC and Division
- What is your specific role and responsibilities in the organization?
- How is the overall organization structured (e.g. divisions/business units, geographical presence)?
- What are the basic facts and figures of your division (e.g. number of employees, annual turnover)?
- What are the main products/services of your division?
- What is your involvement in entrepreneurial activities that take place in foreign subsidiaries?

2. Overview of Foreign Subsidiaries and Interaction with HQ
- How many foreign subsidiaries does your division have in total?
- In which countries are they located?
- What role do the foreign subsidiaries play with regard to innovation and entrepreneurship in the wider division?
- How are their entrepreneurial activities managed and steered from headquarters (e.g. highly centralized/decentralized management, type of approval process)?
- How and (if so) why does this differ across the foreign subsidiaries?

3. Selection of Units for Research and Subsidiary Role Assessment

Subsidiary Selection
- Can you specify those foreign subsidiary units that fulfill the following criteria:
    - Are fully owned by your company (i.e. parent company has >50% ownership)
    - Are 5 years of age or older
    - Perform both manufacturing/service delivery and R&D/engineering activities

Subsidiary Role Assessment

Remark: Application of HQ questionnaire to assess the four subsidiary role dimensions for each foreign unit that fulfills the three criteria above

4. Details on Selected Subsidiaries Remark: Questions to be asked for each of the selected subsidiaries
- What are the basic facts & figures of the subsidiary (e.g. number of employees, annual turnover)?
- What role does the subsidiary currently have (e.g. low cost manufacturing unit, competence center)?
- What specific capabilities/expertise does the subsidiary possess at the moment?
- What does the local market environment look like at the moment (e.g. market size, market dynamism)?
- How entrepreneurially active has the subsidiary been in the past five years (e.g. 1 very low, 5 very high)?
- Can you provide examples of entrepreneurial activities the subsidiary undertook in the past five years?

Closing/Wrap-Up of Interview
- Is there anything else that we have not discussed that you think is important?
- *Thank you very much for your time and your valuable input*
- *Alignment on next steps and good-bye*

References

Adner, Ron/Helfat, Constance E. (2003): Corporate Effects and Dynamic Managerial Capabilities. In: Strategic Management Journal, Vol. 24, No. 10, 2003, pp. 1011-1025.

Aharoni, Yair (1993): In Search for the Unique: Can Firm-Specific Advantages be Evaluated? In: Journal of Management Studies, Vol. 30, No. 1, 1993, pp. 31-49.

Ahokangas, Petri/Juho, Anita/Haapanen, Lauri (2010): Toward the Theory of Temporary Competitive Advantage in Internationalization. In: Sanchez, Ron/Heene, Aimé (Eds., 2010): Enhancing Competences for Competitive Advantage. Emerald Group Publishing, Bingley, 2010, pp. 121-144.

Ahuja, Gautam/Katila, Riitta (2004): Where Do Resources Come From? The Role of Idiosyncratic Situations. In: Strategic Management Journal, Vol. 25, No. 8/9, 2004, pp. 887-907.

Almeida, Paul/Phene, Anupama (2004): Subsidiaries and Knowledge Creation: The Influence of the MNC and Host Country on Innovation. In: Strategic Management Journal, Vol. 25, No. 8-9, 2004, pp. 847-864.

Almeida, Paul/Phene, Anupama/Grant, Robert M. (2003): Innovation and Knowledge Management: Scanning, Sourcing, and Integration. In: Easterby-Smith, Mark/Lyles, Marjorie A. (Eds., 2003): The Blackwell Handbook of Organizational Learning and Knowledge Management. Blackwell, Malden et al., 2003, pp. 356-371.

Alvarez, Sharon A./Agarwal, Rajshree/Sorenson, Olav (Eds., 2005): Handbook of Entrepreneurship Research: Disciplinary Perspectives. Springer, New York, 2005.

Alvarez, Sharon A./Barney, Jay B. (2002): Resource-Based Theory and the Entrepreneurial Firm. In: Hitt, Michael A./Ireland, R. Duane/Camp, S. Michael/Sexton, Donald L. (Eds., 2002): Strategic Entrepreneurship: Creating a New Mindset. Blackwell, Oxford, 2002, pp. 89-105.

Alvarez, Sharon A./Barney, Jay B. (2005): How Do Entrepreneurs Organize Firms Under Conditions of Uncertainty? In: Journal of Management, Vol. 31, No. 5, 2005, pp. 776-793.

Alvarez, Sharon A./Barney, Jay B. (2010): Entrepreneurship and Epistemology: The Philosophical Underpinnings of the Study of Entrepreneurial Opportunities. In: Academy of Management Annals, Vol. 4, No. 1, 2010, pp. 557-583.

Alvarez, Sharon A./Busenitz, Lowell W. (2001): The Entrepreneurship of Resource-Based Theory. In: Journal of Management, Vol. 27, No. 6, 2001, pp. 755-557.

Ambos, Björn/Schlegelmilch, Bodo B. (2005): In Search for Global Advantage. In: European Business Forum, Spring, Vol. 21, 2005, pp. 23-24.

Ambos, Björn/Schlegelmilch, Bodo B. (2007): Innovation and Control in the Multinational Firm: A Comparison of Political and Contingency Approaches. In: Strategic Management Journal, Vol. 28, No. 5, 2007, pp. 473-486.

Ambos, Tina C./Ambos, Björn/Schlegelmilch, Bodo B. (2006): Learning from Foreign Subsidiaries: An Empirical Investigation of Headquarters' Benefits from Reverse Knowledge Transfers. In: International Business Review, Vol. 15, No. 3, 2006, pp. 294-312.

Ambos, Tina C./Andersson, Ulf/Birkinshaw, Julian (2010): What Are the Consequences of Initiative-Taking in Multinational Subsidiaries? In: Journal of International Business Studies, Vol. 41, No. 7, 2010, pp. 1099-1118.

Ambos, Tina C./Birkinshaw, Julian (2010): Headquarters' Attention and Its Effect on Subsidiary Performance. In: Management International Review, Vol. 50, No. 4, 2010, pp. 449-469.

Ambrosini, Véronique/Bowman, Cliff (2009): What Are Dynamic Capabilities and Are They a Useful Construct in Strategic Management? In: International Journal of Management Reviews, Vol. 11, No. 1, 2009, pp. 29-49.

Ambrosini, Véronique/Bowman, Cliff/Collier, Nardine (2009): Dynamic Capabilities: An Exploration of How Firms Renew their Resource Base. In: British Journal of Management, Vol. 20, 2009, pp. S9-S24.

Amit, Raphael/Schoemaker, Paul J. H. (1993): Strategic Assets and Organizational Rent. In: Strategic Management Journal, Vol. 14, No. 1, 1993, pp. 33-46.

Anderson, Erin/Coughlan, Anne T. (1987): International Market Entry and Expansion via Independent or Integrated Channels of Distribution. In: Journal of Marketing, Vol. 51, No. 1, 1987, pp. 71-82.

Anderson, Erin/Gatignon, Hubert (1986): Modes of Foreign Entry: A Transaction Cost Analysis and Propositions. In: Journal of International Business Studies, Vol. 17, No. 3, 1986, pp. 1-26.

Andersson, Ulf (2003): Managing the Transfer of Capabilities within Multinational Corporations: The Dual Role of the Subsidiary. In: Scandinavian Journal of Management, Vol. 19, No. 4, 2003, pp. 425-442.

Andersson, Ulf/Björkman, Ingmar/Forsgren, Mats (2005): Managing Subsidiary Knowledge Creation: The Effect of Control Mechanisms on Subsidiary Local Embeddedness. In: International Business Review, Vol. 14, No. 5, 2005, pp. 521-538.

Andersson, Ulf/Forsgren, Mats (1994): Degree of Integration in some Swedish MNCs. Working Paper No. 4/1994. Uppsala University, Department of Business Studies, 1994.

Andersson, Ulf/Forsgren, Mats (1996): Subsidiary Embeddedness and Control in the Multinational Corporation. In: International Business Review, Vol. 5, No. 5, 1996, pp. 487-508.

Andersson, Ulf/Forsgren, Mats (2000): In Search of Centre of Excellence: Network Embeddedness and Subsidiary Roles in Multinational Corporations. In: Management International Review, Vol. 40, No. 4, 2000, pp. 329-350.

Andersson, Ulf/Forsgren, Mats/Holm, Ulf (2001a): Subsidiary Embeddedness and Competence Development in MNCs – A Multi-Level Analysis. In: Organization Studies, Vol. 22, No. 6, 2001, pp. 1013-1034.

Andersson, Ulf/Forsgren, Mats/Pedersen, Torben (2001b): Subsidiary Performance in Multinational Corporations: The Importance of Technology Embeddedness. In: International Business Review, Vol. 10, No. 1, 2001, pp. 3-23.

Andersson, Ulf/Björkman, Ingmar/Furu, Patrick (2002a): Subsidiary Absorptive Capacity, MNC Headquarters´ Control Strategies and Transfer of Subsidiary Competences. In: Lundan, Sarianna M. (Ed., 2002): Network Knowledge in International Business. Edward Elgar, Cheltenham, Northampton, 2002, pp. 115-136.

Andersson, Ulf/Forsgren, Mats/Holm, Ulf (2002b): The Strategic Impact of External Networks: Subsidiary Performance and Competence Development in the Multinational Corporation. In: Strategic Management Journal, Vol. 23, No. 11, 2002, pp. 979-996.

Andersson, Ulf/Forsgren, Mats/Holm, Ulf (2007): Balancing Subsidiary Influence in the Federative MNC: A Business Network View. In: Journal of International Business Studies, Vol. 38, No. 5, 2007, pp. 802-818.

Andersson, Ulf/Pahlberg, Cecilia (1997): Subsidiary Influence on Strategic Behaviour in MNCs: An Empirical Study. In: International Business Review, Vol. 6, No. 3, 1997, pp. 319-334.

Aragón-Correa, Alberto J./Sharma, Sanjay (2003): A Contingent Resource-Based View of Proactive Corporate Environmental Strategy. In: Academy of Management Review, Vol. 28, No. 1, 2003, pp. 71-88.

Ardichvili, Alexander/Cardozo, Richard/Ray, Sourav (2003): A Theory of Entrepreneurial Opportunity Identification and Development. In: Journal of Business Venturing, Vol. 18, No. 1, 2003, pp. 105-123.

Astley, W. Graham/Sachdeva, Paramjit S. (1984): Structural Sources of Intraorganizational Power: A Theoretical Synthesis. In: The Academy of Management Review, Vol. 9, No. 1, 1984, pp. 104-113.

Astley, W. Graham/Van De Ven, Andrew H. (1983): Central Perspectives and Debates in Organization Theory. In: Administrative Science Quarterly, Vol. 28, No. 2, 1983, pp. 245-273.

Astley, W. Graham/Zajac, Edward J. (1991): Intraorganizational Power and Organizational Design: Reconciling Rational and Coalitional Models of Organization. In: Organization Science, Vol. 2, No. 4, 1991, pp. 399-411.

Astley, W. Graham/Zammuto, Raymond F. (1992): Organization Science, Managers, and Language Games. In: Organization Science, Vol. 3, No. 4, 1992, pp. 443-460.

Bain, Joe S. (1956): Barriers to Competition. Harvard University Press, Cambridge, 1956.

Banalieva, Elitsa R./Sarathy, Ravi (2011): A Contingency Theory of Internationalization. In: Management International Review (MIR), Vol. 51, No. 5, 2011, pp. 593-634.

Barney, Jay B. (1986a): Strategic Factor Markets: Expectations, Luck, and Business Strategy. In: Management Science, Vol. 32, No. 10, 1986, pp. 1231-1241.

Barney, Jay B. (1986b): Types of Competition and the Theory of Strategy: Toward an Integrative Framework. In: The Academy of Management Review, Vol. 11, No. 4, 1986, pp. 791-800.

Barney, Jay B. (1991): Firm Resources and Sustained Competitive Advantage. In: Journal of Management, Vol. 17, No. 1, 1991, pp. 99-120.

Barney, Jay B. (2001a): Is the Resource-Based "View" a Useful Perspective for Strategic Management Research? Yes. In: Academy of Management Review, Vol. 26, No. 1, 2001, pp. 41-56.

Barney, Jay B. (2001b): Resource-Based Theories of Competitive Advantage: A Ten-Year Retrospective on the Resource-Based View. In: Journal of Management, Vol. 27, No. 6, 2001, pp. 643-650.

Barney, Jay B./Arikan, Asli M. (2001): The Resource-Based View: Origins and Implications. In: Hitt, Michael A./Freeman, R. Edward/Harrison, Jeffrey S. (Eds., 2001): The Blackwell Handbook of Strategic Management. Blackwell Publishers, Oxford, 2001, pp. 124-188.

Barney, Jay B./Clark, Delwyn N. (2007): Resource-Based Theory – Creating and Sustaining Competitive Advantage. Oxford University Press, Oxford, New York, 2007.

Barney, Jay B./Ketchen, David J./Wright, Mike (2011): The Future of Resource-Based Theory: Revitalization or Decline? In: Journal of Management, Vol. 37, No. 5, 2011, pp. 1299-1315.

Barney, Jay B./Wright, Mike/Ketchen Jr, David J. (2001): The Resource-Based View of the Firm: Ten Years after 1991. In: Journal of Management, Vol. 27, No. 6, 2001, pp. 625-641.

Baron, Robert A. (2007): Entrepreneurship: A Process Perspective. In: Baum, Robert J./Frese, Michael/Baron, Robert A. (Eds., 2007): The Psychology of Entrepreneurship. Lawrence Erlbaum Associates, Mahwaw, 2007, pp. 19-39.

Baron, Robert A./Ensley, Michael D. (2006): Opportunity Recognition as the Detection of Meaningful Patterns: Evidence from Comparisons of Novice and Experienced Entrepreneurs. In: Management Science, Vol. 52, No. 9, 2006, pp. 1331-1344.

Barringer, Bruce R./Bluedorn, Allen C. (1999): The Relationship between Corporate Entrepreneurship and Strategic Management. In: Strategic Management Journal, Vol. 20, No. 5, 1999, pp. 421-444.

Bartlett, Christopher A. (1986): Building and Managing the Transnational: The New Organizational Challenge. In: Porter, Michael E. (Ed., 1986): Competition in Global Industries. Harvard Business School Press, Boston, 1986, pp. 367-401.

Bartlett, Christopher A./Ghoshal, Sumantra (1986): Tap Your Subsidiaries for Global Reach. In: Harvard Business Review, Vol. 64, No. 6, 1986, pp. 87-94.

Bartlett, Christopher A./Ghoshal, Sumantra (1989): Managing Across Borders: The Transnational Solution. Harvard Business School Press, Boston, 1989.

Bartlett, Christopher A./Ghoshal, Sumantra (1991): Global Strategic Management: Impact on the New Frontiers of Strategy Research. In: Strategic Management Journal, Vol. 12, Special Issue: Global Strategy, 1991, pp. 5-16.

Bartlett, Christopher A./Ghoshal, Sumantra (2002): Managing Across Borders: The Transnational Solution. 2nd edition, Harvard Business School Press, Boston, 2002.

Beach, Lee Roy/Mitchell, Terence R. (1978): A Contingency Model for the Selection of Decision Strategies. In: The Academy of Management Review, Vol. 3, No. 3, 1978, pp. 439-449.

Bechara, John/Van De Ven, Andrew H. (2011): Triangulating Philosophies of Science to Understand Complex Organizational and Managerial Problems. In: Tsoukas, Haridimos/Chia, Robert (Eds., 2011): Philosophy and Organization Theory (Research in the Sociology of Organizations, Volume 32). Emerald, Bingley, 2011.

Becker-Ritterspach, Florian/Dörrenbächer, Christoph (2009): Intrafirm Competition in Multinational Corporations: Towards a Political Framework. In: Competition & Change, Vol. 13, No. 3, 2009, pp. 199-213.

Becker-Ritterspach, Florian/Dörrenbächer, Christoph (2011): Konzerninterner Wettbewerb in Multinationalen Unternehmen: Eine organisationspolitische Skizze. In: Schmid, Stefan (Ed., 2011): Internationale Unternehmen und das Management ausländischer Tochtergesellschaften. Gabler, Wiesbaden, 2011, pp. 27-52.

Benito, Gabriel R./Grøgaard, Brigitte/Narula, Rajneesh (2003): Environmental Influences on MNE Subsidiary Roles: Economic Integration and the Nordic Countries. In: Journal of International Business Studies, Vol. 34, No. 5, 2003, pp. 443-456.

Benito, Gabriel R./Tomassen, Sverre/Bonache-Pérez, Jaime/Pla-Barber, José (2005): A Transaction Cost Analysis of Staffing Decisions in International Operations. In: Scandinavian Journal of Management, Vol. 21, No. 1, 2005, pp. 101-126.

Berger, Ulrike/Bernhard-Mehlich, Isolde (2006): Die Verhaltenswissenschaftliche Entscheidungstheorie. In: Kieser, Alfred/Ebers, Mark (Eds., 2006): Organisationstheorien. 6th edition. Kohlhammer, Stuttgart, 2006, pp. 170-214.

Bettis, Richard A./Prahalad, Coimbatore K. (1995): The Dominant Logic: Retrospective and Extension. In: Strategic Management Journal, Vol. 16, No. 1, 1995, pp. 5-14.

Bhave, Mahesh P. (1994): A Process Model of Entrepreneurial Venture Creation. In: Journal of Business Venturing, Vol. 9, No. 3, 1994, pp. 223-242.

Birkinshaw, Julian (1995): Encouraging Entrepreneurial Activity in Multinational Corporations. In: Business Horizons, May/June, 1995, pp. 32-38.

Birkinshaw, Julian (1996): How Multinational Subsidiary Mandates Are Gained and Lost. In: Journal of International Business Studies, Vol. 27, No. 3, 1996, pp. 467-495.

Birkinshaw, Julian (1997): Entrepreneurship in Multinational Corporations: The Characteristics of Subsidiary Initiatives. In: Strategic Management Journal, Vol. 18, No. 3, 1997, pp. 207-229.

Birkinshaw, Julian (1998): Foreign-Owned Subsidiaries and Regional Development: The Case of Sweden. In: Birkinshaw, Julian/Hood, Neil (Eds., 1998): Multinational Corporate Evolution and Subsidiary Development. Macmillan, Houndmills et al., 1998, pp. 268-298.

Birkinshaw, Julian (1998a): Corporate Entrepreneurship in Network Organizations: How Subsidiary Initiative Drives Internal Market Efficiency. In: European Management Journal, Vol. 16, No. 3, 1998, pp. 355-364.

Birkinshaw, Julian (1998b): Foreign-Owned Subsidiaries and Regional Development: The Case of Sweden. In: Birkinshaw, Julian/Hood, Neil (Eds., 1998): Multinational Corporate Evolution and Subsidiary Development. Macmillan, Houndmills et al., 1998, pp. 268-298.

Birkinshaw, Julian (1999): The Determinants and Consequences of Subsidiary Initiative in Multinational Corporations. In: Entrepreneurship: Theory & Practice, Vol. 24, No. 1, 1999, pp. 9-36.

Birkinshaw, Julian (2000): Entrepreneurship in the Global Firm. Sage, London et al., 2000.

Birkinshaw, Julian (2001): Strategy and Management in MNE Subsidiaries. In: Rugman, Alan M./Brewer, Thomas (Eds., 2001): The Oxford Handbook of International Business. Oxford University Press, New York, 2001, pp. 380-401.

Birkinshaw, Julian (2004): Publishing Qualitative Research in International Business. In: Marschan-Piekkari, Rebecca/Welch, Catherine (Eds., 2004): Handbook of Qualitative Research Methods for International Business. Edward Elgar, Cheltenham, Northampton, 2004, pp. 570-587.

Birkinshaw, Julian/Morrison, Allen J. (1995): Configurations of Strategy and Structure in Subsidiaries of Multinational Corporations. In: Journal of International Business Studies, Vol. 26, No. 4, 1995, pp. 729-753.

Birkinshaw, Julian/Fry, Nick (1998): Subsidiary Initiatives to Develop New Markets. In: Sloan Management Review, Vol. 39, No. 3, 1998, pp. 51-61.

Birkinshaw, Julian/Holm, Ulf/Thilenius, Peter/Arvidsson, Niklas (2000): Consequences of Perception Gaps in the Headquarters-Subsidiary Relationship. In: International Business Review, Vol. 9, No. 3, 2000, pp. 321-344.

Birkinshaw, Julian/Hood, Neil (1997): An Empirical Study of Development Processes in Foreign-Owned Subsidiaries in Canada and Scotland. In: Management International Review, Vol. 37, No. 4, 1997, pp. 339-364.

Birkinshaw, Julian/Hood, Neil (1998a): Introduction and Overview. In: Birkinshaw, Julian/Hood, Neil (Eds., 1998): Multinational Corporate Evolution and Subsidiary Development. Macmillan, Houndmills et al., 1998, pp. 1-19.

Birkinshaw, Julian/Hood, Neil (1998b): Micro-Politics and Conflicts in Multinational Corporations. In: Journal of International Management, Vol. 12, No. 3, 1998, pp. 266-283.

Birkinshaw, Julian/Hood, Neil (1998c): Multinational Corporate Evolution and Subsidiary Development. Macmillan, Houndmills et al., 1998.

Birkinshaw, Julian/Hood, Neil (1998d): Multinational Subsidiary Evolution: Capability and Charter Change in Foreign-Owned Subsidiary Companies. In: Academy of Management Review, Vol. 23, No. 4, 1998d, pp. 773-795.

Birkinshaw, Julian/Hood, Neil/Jonsson, Stefan (1998): Building Firm-Specific Advantages in Multinational Corporations: The Role of Subsidiary Initiative. In: Strategic Management Journal, Vol. 19, No. 3, 1998, pp. 221-241.

Birkinshaw, Julian/Hood, Neil/Young, Stephen (2005): Subsidiary Entrepreneurship, Internal and External Competitive Forces, and Subsidiary Performance. In: International Business Review, Vol. 14, No. 2, 2005, pp. 227-248.

Birkinshaw, Julian/Morrison, Allen/Hulland, John (1995): Structural and Competitive Determinants of a Global Integration Strategy. In: Strategic Management Journal, Vol. 16, No. 8, 1995, pp. 637-655.

Birkinshaw, Julian/Nobel, Robert/Ridderstråle, Jonas (2002): Knowledge as a Contingency Variable: Do the Characteristics of Knowledge Predict Organization Structure? In: Organization Science, Vol. 13, No. 3, 2002, pp. 274-289.

Birkinshaw, Julian/Pedersen, Torben (2009): Strategy and Management in MNE Subsidiaries. In: Rugman, Alan M. (Ed., 2009): The Oxford Handbook of International Business. 2nd edition. Oxford University Press, Oxford, 2009, pp. 367-388.

Birkinshaw, Julian/Ridderstråle, Jonas (1999): Fighting the Corporate Immune System: A Process Study of Subsidiary Initiatives in Multinational Corporations. In: International Business Review, Vol. 8, No. 2, 1999, pp. 149-180.

Birkinshaw, Julian/Toulan, Omar/Arnold, David (2001): Global Account Management in Multinational Corporations: Theory and Evidence. In: Journal of International Business Studies, Vol. 32, No. 2, 2001, pp. 231-248.

Blau, Peter M. (1964): Exchange and Power in Social Life. Wiley, New York, 1964.

Blau, Peter M. (1970): A Formal Theory of Differentiation in Organizations. In: American Sociological Review, Vol. 35, No. 2, 1970, pp. 201-218.

Blau, Peter M./Schoenherr, Richard A. (1971): The Structure of Organizations. Basic Books, New York, 1971.

Blazejewski, Susanne (2009): Normative Control in MNC. In: Feldman, Maryann P./Santangelo, Grazia D. (Eds., 2009): New Perspectives in International Business Research (Progress in International Business Research, Volume 3). Emerald Group Publishing, Bingley, 2009, pp. 83-111.

Blazejewski, Susanne/Becker-Ritterspach, Florian (2011): Conflicts in Headquarters-Subsidiary Relations: A Critical Literature Review and New Directions. In: Dörrenbächer, Christoph/ Geppert, Mike (Eds., 2011): Power and Politics in the Multinational Corporation. The Role of Institutions, Interests and Identities. Cambridge University Press, Cambridge et al., 2011, pp. 147-189.

Blumentritt, Timothy P./Nigh, Douglas (2002): The Integration of Subsidiary Political Activities in Multinational Corporations. In: Journal of International Business Studies, Vol. 33, No. 1, 2002, pp. 57-77.

Blundel, Richard (2007): Critical Realism: A Suitable Vehicle for Entrepreneurship. In: Neergaard, Helle/Ulhøi, John P. (Eds., 2007): Handbook of Qualitative Research Methods in Entrepreneurship. Edward Elgar, Cheltenham, 2007, pp. 75-96.

Boccardelli, Paolo/Magnusson, Mats G. (2006): Dynamic Capabilities in Early-Phase Entrepreneurship. In: Knowledge and Process Management, Vol. 13, No. 3, 2006, pp. 162-174.

Bøllingtoft, Anna (2007): A Critical Realist Approach to Quality in Observation Studies. In: Neergaard, Helle/Ulhøi, John P. (Eds., 2007): Handbook of Qualitative Research Methods in Entrepreneurship. Edward Elgar, Cheltenham, 2007, pp. 406-433.

Bonoma, Thomas V. (1985): Case Research in Marketing: Opportunities, Problem, and a Process. In: Journal of Marketing Research, Vol. 22, No. 2, 1985, pp. 199-208.

Boojihawon, Dev Kumar/Dimitratos, Pavlos/Young, Stephen (2007): Characteristics and Influences of Multinational Subsidiary Entrepreneurial Culture: The Case of the Advertising Sector. In: International Business Review, Vol. 16, No. 5, 2007, pp. 549-572.

Borini, Felipe Mendes/Fleury, Maria Tereza Leme/Fleury, Afonso (2009a): Corporate Competences in Subsidiaries of Brazilian Multinationals. In: Latin American Business Review, Vol. 10, No. 2/3, 2009, pp. 161-185.

Borini, Felipe Mendes/Leme Fleury, Maria Tereza/Corrêa Fleury, Afonso Carlos/Oliveira Junior, Moacir de Miranda (2009b): The Relevance of Subsidiary Initiatives for Brazilian Multinationals. In: Revista de Administração de Empresas (RAE), Vol. 49, No. 3, 2009, pp. 253-265.

Bortz, Jürgen/Döring, Nicola (2006): Forschungsmethoden und Evaluation für Human- und Sozialwissenschaftler. 4th edition, Springer, Heidelberg, 2006.

Bouquet, Cyril/Birkinshaw, Julian (2008a): Managing Power in the Multinational Corporation: How Low-Power Actors Gain Influence. In: Journal of Management, Vol. 34, No. 3, 2008, pp. 477-508.

Bouquet, Cyril/Birkinshaw, Julian (2008b): Weight versus Voice: How Foreign Subsidiaries Gain Attention from Corporate Headquarters. In: Academy of Management Journal, Vol. 51, No. 3, 2008b, pp. 577-601.

Bower, Joseph, L. (1970): Managing the Resource Allocation Process: A Study of Corporate Planning and Investment. Harvard Business School Press, Boston, 1970.

Bowman, Cliff/Ambrosini, Veronique (2003): How the Resource-Based and the Dynamic Capability Views of the Firm Inform Corporate-Level Strategy. In: British Journal of Management, Vol. 14, No. 4, 2003, pp. 289-303.

Bowman, Cliff/Collier, Nardine (2006): A Contingency Approach to Resource-Creation Processes. In: International Journal of Management Reviews, Vol. 8, No. 4, 2006, pp. 191-211.

Bowman, Edward H./Hurry, Dileep (1993): Strategy through the Option Lens: An Integrated View of Resource Investments and the Incremental-Choice Process. In: The Academy of Management Review, Vol. 18, No. 4, 1993, pp. 760-782.

Brühl, Rolf/Horch, Nils/Orth, Matthias (2008): Der Resource-Based View als Theorie des Strategischen Managements – Empirische Befunde und Methodologische Anmerkungen. ESCP-EAP Working Paper No. 44, ESCP-EAP European School of Management, 2008.

Brunner, Markus (2009): Resource-Dependence-Ansatz. In: Schwaiger, Manfred/Meyer, Anton (Eds., 2009): Theorien und Methoden der Betriebswirtschaft. Verlag Franz Vahlen, München, 2009, pp. 29-40.

Brush, Candida G./Greene, Patricia G./Hart, Myra M. (2001): From Initial Idea to Unique Advantage: The Entrepreneurial Challenge of Constructing a Resource Base. In: Academy of Management Executive, Vol. 15, No. 1, 2001, pp. 64-78.

Brush, Thomas H./Artz, Kendall W. (1999): Toward a Contingent Resource-Based Theory: The Impact of Information Asymmetry on the Value of Capabilities in Veterinary Medicine. In: Strategic Management Journal, Vol. 20, No. 3, 1999, p. 223.

Bryson, John M./Bromiley, Philip (1993): Critical Factors Affecting the Planning and Implementation of Major Projects. In: Strategic Management Journal, Vol. 14, No. 5, 1993, pp. 319-337.

Buckley, Peter J./Casson, Mark (1976): The Future of the Multinational Enterprise. 2nd edition, Macmillan, London, 1976.

Burgelman, Robert A. (1983a): Corporate Entrepreneurship and Strategic Management: Insights from a Process Study. In: Management Science, Vol. 29, No. 12, 1983, pp. 1349-1364.

Burgelman, Robert A. (1983b): A Process Model of Internal Corporate Venturing in the Diversified Major Firm. In: Administrative Science Quarterly, Vol. 28, No. 2, 1983, pp. 223-244.

Burgelman, Robert A. (1984): Designs for Corporate Entrepreneurship in Established Firms. In: California Management Review, Vol. 26, No. 3, 1984, pp. 154-166.

Burgelman, Robert A. (2011): Bridging History and Reductionism: A Key Role for Longitudinal Qualitative Research. In: Journal of International Business Studies, Vol. 42, No. 5, 2011, pp. 591-601.

Burns, Tom (1961): Micropolitics: Mechanisms of Institutional Change. In: Administrative Science Quarterly, Vol. 6, No. 3, 1961, pp. 257-281.

Burns, Tom/Stalker, George M. (1961): The Management of Innovation. Tavistock, London, 1961.

Burrell, Gibson/Morgan, Gareth (1979): Sociological Paradigms and Organisational Analysis: Elements of the Sociology of Corporate Life. Heinemann, London, 1979.

Business Monitor (2013): Australia – Autos Report Q1 2014. Business Monitor International, London, 2013.

Cantwell, John/Mudambi, Ram (2005): MNE Competence-Creating Subsidiary Mandates. In: Strategic Management Journal, Vol. 26, No. 12, 2005, pp. 1109-1128.

Capron, Laurence/Shen, Jung-Chin (2007): Acquisitions of Private vs. Public Firms: Private Information, Target Selection, and Acquirer Returns. In: Strategic Management Journal, Vol. 28, No. 9, 2007, pp. 891-911.

Carlson, John R./Zmud, Robert W. (1999): Channel Expansion Theory and the Experiential Nature of Media Richness Perceptions. In: Academy of Management Journal, Vol. 42, No. 2, 1999, pp. 153-170.

Castrogiovanni, Gary J. (1991): Environmental Munificence: A Theoretical Assessment. In: The Academy of Management Review, Vol. 16, No. 3, 1991, pp. 542-565.

Cavanagh, Andrew/Freeman, Susan (2012): The Development of Subsidiary Roles in the Motor Vehicle Manufacturing Industry. In: International Business Review, Vol. 21, No. 4, 2012, pp. 602-617.

Chandler, Alfred D. (1962): Strategy and Structure. Chapters in the History of the Industrial Enterprise. MIT Press, Cambridge, 1962.

Chandler, Gaylen N./Hanks, Steven H. (1994): Market Attractiveness, Resource-Based Capabilities, Venture Strategies, and Venture Performance. In: Journal of Business Venturing, Vol. 9, No. 4, 1994, pp. 331-349.

Chang, Eunmi/Taylor, M. Susan (1999): Control in Multinational Corporations (MNCs): The Case of Korean Manufacturing Subsidiaries. In: Journal of Management, Vol. 25, No. 4, 1999, pp. 541-565.

Chen, Tain-Jy/Chen, Homin/Ku, Ying-Hua (2012): Resource Dependency and Parent-Subsidiary Capability Transfers. In: Journal of World Business, Vol. 47, No. 2, 2012, pp. 259-266.

Chetty, Sylvie K./Wilson, Heather I. M. (2003): Collaborating with Competitors to Acquire Resources. In: International Business Review, Vol. 12, No. 1, 2003, pp. 61-81.

Child, John (1972): Organizational Structure, Environment and Performance: The Role of Strategic Choice. In: Sociology, Vol. 6, No. 1, 1972, pp. 1-22.

Child, John (1975): Managerial and Organizational Factors Associated with Company Performance – Part 2: A Contingency Analysis. In: Journal of Management Studies, Vol. 12, No. 1-2, 1975, pp. 12-27.

Child, John (1997): Strategic Choice in the Analysis of Action, Structure, Organizations and Environment: Retrospect and Prospect. In: Organization Studies, Vol. 18, No. 1, 1997, pp. 43-76.

Chiles, Todd H./Vultee, Denise M./Gupta, Vishal K./Greening, Daniel W./Tuggle, Christopher S. (2010): The Philosophical Foundation of a Radical Austrian Approach to Entrepreneurship. In: Journal of Management Inquiry, Vol. 19, No. 2, 2010, pp. 138-164.

Christmann, Petra/Day, Diana/Yip, George S. (1999): The Relative Influence of Country Conditions, Industry Structure, and Business Strategy on Multinational Corporation Subsidiary Performance. In: Journal of International Management, Vol. 5, No. 4, 1999, pp. 241-265.

Chung, Lai Hong/Gibbons, Patrick T./Schoch, Herbert P. (2000): The Influence of Subsidiary Context and Head Office Strategic Management Style on Control of MNCs: The Experience in Australia. In: Accounting, Auditing & Accountability Journal, Vol. 13, No. 5, 2000, pp. 647-666.

Ciabuschi, Francesco/Dellestrand, Henrik/Kappen, Philip (2011): Exploring the Effects of Vertical and Lateral Mechanisms in International Knowledge Transfer Projects. In: Management International Review, Vol. 51, No. 2, 2011, pp. 129-155.

Ciabuschi, Francesco/Forsgren, Mats/Martín, Oscar M. (2012): Headquarters Involvement and Efficiency of Innovation Development and Transfer in Multinationals: A Matter of Sheer Ignorance? In: International Business Review, Vol. 21, No. 2, 2012, pp. 130-144.

Ciabuschi, Francesco/Martín, Oscar M. (2010): Determinants of HQ's Involvement in Innovation Transfer. In: Andersson, Ulf/Holm, Ulf (Eds., 2010): Managing the Contemporary Multinational. Edward Elgar, Cheltenham, Northampton, 2010, pp. 182-210.

Ciabuschi, Francesco/Martín, Oscar M./Ståhl, Benjamin (2010): Headquarters' Influence on Knowledge Transfer Performance. In: Management International Review, Vol. 50, No. 4, 2010, pp. 471-491.

Coff, Russell W. (2002): Human Capital, Shared Expertise, and the Likelihood of Impasse in Corporate Acquisitions. In: Journal of Management, Vol. 28, No. 1, 2002, pp. 107-128.

Cohen, Wesley M./Levinthal, Daniel A. (1990): Absorptive Capacity: A New Perspective on Learning and Innovation. In: Administrative Science Quarterly, Vol. 35, No. 1, 1990, pp. 128-152.

Collinson, Simon C./Pettigrew, Andrew M. (2009): Comparative International Business Research Methods: Pitfalls and Practicalities. In: Rugman, Alan M. (Ed., 2009): The Oxford Handbook of International Business. 2nd edition. Oxford University Press, Oxford, 2009, pp. 765-796.

Collis, David J. (1994): Research Note: How Valuable Are Organizational Capabilities? In: Strategic Management Journal, Vol. 15, No. 8, 1994, pp. 143-152.

Collis, Jill/Hussey, Roger (2009): Business Research. A Practical Guide for Undergraduate and Postgraduate Students. Palgrave MacMillan, New York, 2009.

Conner, Kathleen R./Prahalad, Coimbatore K. (1996): A Resource-Based Theory of the Firm: Knowledge versus Opportunism. In: Organization Science, Vol. 7, No. 5, 1996, pp. 477-501.

Couto, João P./Vieira, José C./Borges-Tiago, Maria T. (2005): Determinants of the Establishment of Marketing Activities by Subsidiaries of MNCs. In: Journal of American Academy of Business, Cambridge, Vol. 6, No. 2, 2005, pp. 305-313.

Covin, Jeffrey G. (1991): Entrepreneurial versus Conservative Firms: A Comparison of Strategies and Performance. In: Journal of Management Studies, Vol. 28, No. 5, 1991, pp. 439-462.

Covin, Jeffrey G./Covin, Teresa Joyce (1990): Competitive Aggressiveness, Environmental Context, and Small Firm Performance. In: Entrepreneurship: Theory & Practice, Vol. 14, No. 4, 1990, pp. 35-50.

Covin, Jeffrey G./Miles, Morgan, P. (1999): Corporate Entrepreneurship and the Pursuit of Competitive Advantage. In: Entrepreneurship: Theory & Practice, Vol. 23, No. 3, 1999, pp. 47-63.

Covin, Jeffrey G./Slevin, Dennis P. (1989): Strategic Management of Small Firms in Hostile and Benign Environments. In: Strategic Management Journal, Vol. 10, No. 1, 1989, pp. 75-87.

Covin, Jeffrey G./Slevin, Dennis P. (1991): A Conceptual Model of Entrepreneurship as Firm Behavior. In: Entrepreneurship: Theory & Practice, Vol. 16, No. 1, 1991, pp. 7-25.

Creswell, John W. (2003): Research Design: Qualitative, Quantitative, and Mixed Method Approaches. 2nd edition, Sage, Thousand Oaks, 2003.

Cronin, Patricia/Ryan, Frances/Coughlan, Michael (2008): Undertaking a Literature Review: A Step-by-Step Approach. In: British Journal of Nursing, Vol. 17, No. 1, 2008, pp. 38-43.

Crook, T. Russell/Ketchen Jr, David J./Combs, James G./Todd, Samuel Y. (2008): Strategic Resources and Performance: A Meta-Analysis. In: Strategic Management Journal, Vol. 29, No. 11, 2008, pp. 1141-1154.

Cuervo, Álvaro/Ribeiro, Domingo/Roig, Salvador (Eds., 2007): Entrepreneurship: Concepts, Theory and Perspective. Springer, Berlin et al., 2007.

Cui, Anna Shaojie/Griffith, David A./Cavusgil, S. Tamer (2005): The Influence of Competitive Intensity and Market Dynamism on Knowledge Management Capabilities of Multinational Corporation Subsidiaries. In: Journal of International Marketing, Vol. 13, No. 3, 2005, pp. 32-53.

Cui, Anna Shaojie/Griffith, David A./Cavusgil, S. Tamer/Dabic, Marina (2006): The Influence of Market and Cultural Environmental Factors on Technology Transfer between Foreign MNCs and Local Subsidiaries: A Croatian Illustration. In: Journal of World Business, Vol. 41, No. 2, 2006, pp. 100-111.

Cyert, Richard M./March, James G. (1963): A Behavioral Theory of the Firm. Prentice Hall, Englewood Cliffs, 1963.

Daft, Richard L./Lengel, Robert H. (1986): Organizational Information Requirements, Media Richness and Structural Design. In: Management Science, Vol. 32, No. 5, 1986, pp. 554-571.

Damanpour, Fariborz (1991): Organizational Innovation: A Meta-Analysis of Effects of Determinants and Moderators. In: The Academy of Management Journal, Vol. 34, No. 3, 1991, pp. 555-590.

Damanpour, Fariborz (1996): Organizational Complexity and Innovation: Developing and Testing Multiple Contingency Models. In: Management Science, Vol. 42, No. 5, 1996, pp. 693-716.

Daniel, Andrea (2010): Perception Gaps between Headquarters and Subsidiary Managers: Differing Perspectives on Subsidiary Roles and their Implications. Gabler (mir-Edition), Wiesbaden, 2010.

Daniels, John D./Cannice, Mark V. (2004): Interview Studies in International Business Research. In: Marschan-Piekkari, Rebecca/Welch, Catherine (Eds., 2004): Handbook of Qualitative Research Methods for International Business. Edward Elgar, Cheltenham, Northampton, 2004, pp. 185-206.

Das, T. K./Teng, Bing-Sheng (2000): A Resource-Based Theory of Strategic Alliances. In: Journal of Management, Vol. 26, No. 1, 2000, pp. 31-62.

Daub, Matthias (2009): Coordination of Service Offshoring Subsidiaries in Multinational Corporations. Gabler (mir-Edition), Wiesbaden, 2009.

Davidsson, Per/Wiklund, Johan (2007): Level of Analysis in Entrepreneurship Research: Current Research Practice and Suggestions for the Future. In: Cuervo, Álvaro/Ribeiro, Domingo/Roig, Salvador (Eds., 2007): Entrepreneurship: Concepts, Theory and Perspective. Springer, Berlin et al., 2007, pp. 245-266.

Davis, Lee N./Meyer, Klaus E. (2004): Subsidiary Research and Development, and the Local Environment. In: International Business Review, Vol. 13, No. 3, 2004, p. 359-382.

Dawes, John (2008): Do Data Characteristics Change According to the Number of Scale Points Used? An Experiment Using 5-Point, 7-Point and 10-Point Scales. In: International Journal of Market Research, Vol. 50, No. 1, 2008, pp. 61-77.

D'Cruz, Joseph (1986): Strategic Management of Subsidiaries. In: Etemad, Hamid/Dulude, Louise Séguin (Eds., 1986): Managing the Multinational Subsidiary. Response to Environmental Changes and to Host Nations R&D Policies. Croom Helm, London, Sydney, 1986, pp. 75-89.

De Beule, Filip (2011): Subsidiary Strategic Evolution in China. In: Verbeke, Alain/Tavaes Lehmann, Ana T./Van Tulder, Rob (Eds., 2011): Entrepreneurship in the Global Firm. Emerald, Bingley, 2011, pp. 199-222.

De Clercq, Dirk/Castañer, Xavier/Belausteguigoitia, Imanol (2011): Entrepreneurial Initiative Selling within Organizations: Towards a More Comprehensive Motivational Framework. In: Journal of Management Studies, Vol. 48, No. 6, 2011, pp. 1269-1290.

Deci, Edward L./Ryan, Richard M. (1985): Intrinsic Motivation and Self-Determination in Human Behavior. Plenum, New York, 1985.

Deci, Edward L./Ryan, Richard M. (2002a): Handbook of Self-Determination Research. The University of Rochester Press, Rochester, 2002.

Deci, Edward L./Ryan, Richard M. (2002b): Overview of Self-Determination Theory: An Organismic Dialectical Perspective. In: Deci, Edward L./Ryan, Richard M. (Eds., 2002): Handbook of Self-Determination Research. The University of Rochester Press, Rochester, 2002, pp. 3-33.

Delany, Ed (1998): Strategic Development of Multinational Subsidiaries in Ireland. In: Birkinshaw, Julian/Hood, Neil (Eds., 1998): Multinational Corporate Evolution and Subsidiary Development. Macmillan, Houndmills et al., 1998, pp. 239-265.

Delany, Ed (2000): Strategic Development of the Multinational Subsidiary through Subsidiary Initiative-Taking. In: Long Range Planning, Vol. 33, No. 2, 2000, pp. 220-244.

Dellestrand, Henrik (2011): Subsidiary Embeddedness as a Determinant of Divisional Headquarters Involvement in Innovation Transfer Processes. In: Journal of International Management, Vol. 17, No. 3, 2011, pp. 229-242.

Denrell, Jerker/Fang, Christina/Winter, Sidney G. (2003): The Economics of Strategic Opportunity. In: Strategic Management Journal, Vol. 24, No. 10, 2003, pp. 977-990.

Dess, Gregory G./Lumpkin, G. T. (2005): Research Edge: The Role of Entrepreneurial Orientation in Stimulating Effective Corporate Entrepreneurship. In: The Academy of Management Executive, Vol. 19, No. 1, 2005, pp. 147-156.

Dess, Gregory G./Lumpkin, G. T./Covin, Jeffrey G. (1997): Entrepreneurial Strategy Making and Firm Performance: Tests of Contingency and Configuration Models. In: Strategic Management Journal, Vol. 18, No. 9, 1997, pp. 677-695.

DeTienne, Dawn R./Chandler, Gaylen N. (2004): Opportunity Identification and Its Role in the Entrepreneurial Classroom: A Pedagogical Approach and Empirical Test. In: Academy of Management Learning & Education, Vol. 3, No. 3, 2004, pp. 242-257.

DeTienne, Dawn R./Chandler, Gaylen N. (2007): The Role of Gender in Opportunity Identification. In: Entrepreneurship: Theory & Practice, Vol. 31, No. 3, 2007, pp. 365-386.

DeTienne, Dawn R./Shepherd, Dean A./De Castro, Julio O. (2008): The Fallacy of "Only the Strong Survive: The Effects of Extrinsic Motivation on the Persistence Decisions for Under-Performing Firms. In: Journal of Business Venturing, Vol. 23, No. 5, 2008, pp. 528-546.

Dierickx, Ingemar/Cool, Karel (1989): Asset Stock Accumulation and the Sustainability of Competitive Advantage. In: Management Science, Vol. 35, No. 12, 1989, pp. 1504-1511.

Dimitratos, Pavlos/Jones, Marian V. (2005): Future Directions for International Entrepreneurship Research. In: International Business Review, Vol. 14, No. 2, 2005, pp. 119-128.

Dimitratos, Pavlos/Liouka, Ioanna/Ross, Duncan/Young, Stephen (2009a): The Multinational Enterprise and Subsidiary Evolution: Scotland since 1945. In: Business History, Vol. 51, No. 3, 2009, pp. 401-425.

Dimitratos, Pavlos/Liouka, Ioanna/Young, Stephen (2009b): Regional Location of Multinational Corporation Subsidiaries and Economic Development Contribution: Evidence from the UK. In: Journal of World Business, Vol. 44, No. 2, 2009, pp. 180-191.

Donaldson, Lex (1995): American Anti-Management Theories of Organizations: A Critique of Paradigm Proliferation. Cambridge University Press, New York, Melbourne, 1995.

Donaldson, Lex (2001): The Contingency Theory of Organizations. Sage, Thousand Oaks et al., 2001.

Dörrenbächer, Christoph/Gammelgaard, Jens (2006): Subsidiary Role Development: The Effect of Micro-Political Headquarters-Subsidiary Negotiations on the Product, Market and Value-Added Scope of Foreign-Owned Subsidiaries. In: Journal of International Management, Vol. 12, No. 3, 2006, pp. 266-283.

Dörrenbächer, Christoph/Gammelgaard, Jens (2011): Subsidiary Power in Multinational Corporations: The Subtle Role of Micro-Political Bargaining Power. In: Critical Perspectives on International Business, Vol. 7, No. 1, 2011, pp. 30-47.

Dörrenbächer, Christoph/Geppert, Mike (2006): Micro-Politics and Conflicts in Multinational Corporations: Current Debates, Re-Framing, and Contributions of this Special Issue. In: Journal of International Management, Vol. 12, No. 3, 2006, pp. 251-265.

Dörrenbächer, Christoph/Geppert, Mike (2009): A Micro-Political Perspective on Subsidiary Initiative-Taking: Evidence from German-Owned Subsidiaries in France. In: European Management Journal, Vol. 27, No. 2, 2009, pp. 100-112.

Dörrenbächer, Christoph/Geppert, Mike (2010): Subsidiary Staffing and Initiative-Taking in Multi-national Corporations – A Socio-Political Perspective. In: Personnel Review, Vol. 39, No. 5, 2010, pp. 600-621.

Dörrenbächer, Christoph/Geppert, Mike (Eds., 2011): Politics and Power in the Multinational Corporation. The Role of Institutions, Interests and Identities. Cambridge University Press, Cambridge et al., 2011.

Dougherty, Deborah (1992): Interpretative Barriers to Successful Product Innovation in Large Firms. In: Organization Science, Vol. 3, No. 2, 1992, pp. 179-202.

Doz, Yves L./Prahalad, Coimbatore K. (1981): Headquarters Influence and Strategic Control in MNCs. In: Sloan Management Review, Vol. 23, No. 1, 1981, pp. 15-29.

Doz, Yves L./Prahalad, Coimbatore K. (1984): Patterns of Strategic Control within Multinational Corporations. In: Journal of International Business Studies, Vol. 15, No. 2, 1984, pp. 55-72.

Doz, Yves L./Prahalad, Coimbatore K. (1986): Controlled Variety: A Challenge for Human Resource Management in the MNC. In: Human Resource Management, Vol. 25, No. 1, 1986, pp. 55-71.

Doz, Yves L./Prahalad, Coimbatore K. (1991): Managing DMNCs: A Search for a New Paradigm. In: Strategic Management Journal, Vol. 12, Special Issue, 1991, pp. 145-164.

Doz, Yves. L. (2011): Qualitative Research for International Business. In: Journal of International Business Studies, Vol. 42, No. 5, 2011, pp. 582-590.

Dunning, John H. (1977): Trade, Location of Economic Activity and the MNE: A Search for an Eclectic Approach. In: Ohlin, Bertil G./Hesselborn, Per-Ove/Wijkan, Per M. (Eds., 1977): The International Allocation of Economic Activity. MacMillan, London, 1977, pp. 395-418.

Dunning, John H. (1998): Location and the Multinational Enterprise. In: Journal of International Business Studies, Vol. 29, No. 1, 1998, pp. 45-66.

Dunning, John H. (2008): Multinational Enterprises and the Global Economy. 2nd edition, Edward Elgar, Cheltenham, Massachusetts, 2008.

Dutton, Jane E./Ashford, Susan J. (1993): Selling Issues to Top Management. In: Academy of Management Review, Vol. 18, No. 3, 1993, pp. 397-428.

Dyer, Jeffrey H./Singh, Harbir (1998): The Relational View: Cooperative Strategy and Sources of Interorganizational Competitive Advantage. In: The Academy of Management Review, Vol. 23, No. 4, 1998, pp. 660-679.

Easterby-Smith, Mark/Lyles, Marjorie A./Peteraf, Margaret A. (2009): Dynamic Capabilities: Current Debates and Future Directions. In: British Journal of Management, Vol. 20, 2009, pp. S1-S8.

Easterby-Smith, Mark/Lyles, Marjorie A./Tsang, Eric W. K. (2008): Inter-Organizational Knowledge Transfer: Current Themes and Future Prospects. In: Journal of Management Studies, Vol. 45, No. 4, 2008, pp. 677-690.

Easterby-Smith, Mark/Thorpe, Richard/Jackson, Paul (Eds., 2012): Management Research. 4th edition, Sage, London et al., 2012.

Easton, Geoff (2002): Marketing: A Critical Realist Approach. In: Journal of Business Research, Vol. 55, No. 2, 2002, pp. 103-109.

Easton, Geoff (2010): Critical Realism in Case Study Research. In: Industrial Marketing Management, Vol. 39, No. 1, 2010, pp. 118-128.

Ebers, Mark/Gotsch, Wilfried (2006): Institutionenökonomische Theorien der Organisation. In: Kieser, Alfred/Ebers, Mark (Eds., 2006): Organisationstheorien. 6th edition. Kohlhammer, Stuttgart, 2006, pp. 247-308.

Egelhoff, William G. (1988): Strategy and Structure in Multinational Corporations: A Revision of the Stopford and Wells Model. In: Strategic Management Journal, Vol. 9, No. 1, 1988, pp. 1-14.

Eisenhardt, Kathleen M. (1989a): Agency Theory: An Assessment and Review. In: The Academy of Management Review, Vol. 14, No. 1, 1989, pp. 57-74.

Eisenhardt, Kathleen M. (1989b): Building Theories from Case Study Research. In: Academy of Management Review, Vol. 14, No. 4, 1989, pp. 532-550.

Eisenhardt, Kathleen M./Graebner, Melissa E. (2007): Theory Building from Cases: Opportunities and Challenges. In: Academy of Management Journal, Vol. 50, No. 1, 2007, pp. 25-32.

Eisenhardt, Kathleen M./Martin, Jeffrey A. (2000): Dynamic Capabilities: What Are They? In: Strategic Management Journal, Vol. 21, No. 10/11, 2000, pp. 1105-1121.

Eisenhardt, Kathleen M./Schoonhoven, Claudia Bird (1996): Resource-Based View of Strategic Alliance Formation: Strategic and Social Effects in Entrepreneurial Firms. In: Organization Science, Vol. 7, No. 2, 1996, pp. 136-150.

Emerson, Richard M. (1962): Power-Dependence Relations. In: American Sociological Review, Vol. 21, No. 1, 1962, pp. 31-40.

Enright, Michael J./Subramanian, Venkat (2007): An Organizing Framework for MNC Subsidiary Typologies. In: Management International Review (MIR), Vol. 47, No. 6, 2007, pp. 895-924.

Erramilli, M. Krishna/Agarwal, Sanjeev/Kim, Seong-Soo (1997): Are Firm-Specific Advantages Location-Specific Too? In: Journal of International Business Studies, Vol. 28, No. 4, 1997, pp. 735-757.

Fahy, John (2000): The Resource-Based View of the Firm: Some Stumbling-Blocks on the Road to Understanding Sustainable Competitive Advantage. In: Journal of European Industrial Training, Vol. 24, No. 2-4, 2000, pp. 99-104.

Fahy, John (2002): A Resource-Based Analysis of Sustainable Competitive Advantage in a Global Environment. In: International Business Review, Vol. 11, No. 1, 2002, pp. 57-77.

Fahy, John/Hooley, Graham (2002): Sustainable Competitive Advantage in Electronic Business: Towards a Contingency Perspective on the Resource-Based View. In: Journal of Strategic Marketing, Vol. 10, No. 4, 2002, pp. 241-253.

Fama, Eugene F./Jensen, Michael C. (1983): Separation of Ownership and Control. In: Journal of Law and Economics, Vol. 26, No. 2, 1983, pp. 301-325.

Ferdows, Kasra (1989): Mapping International Factory Networks. In: Ferdows, Kasra (Ed., 1989): Managing International Manufacturing. North-Holland/Elsevier, Amsterdam et al., 1989, pp. 3-21.

Ferdows, Kasra (1997): Making the Most of Foreign Factories. In: Harvard Business Review, Vol. 75, No. 2, 1997, pp. 73-88.

Ferris, Gerald R./Treadway, Darren C. (2012): Politics in Organizations: History, Construct Specification, and Research Directions. In: Ferris, Gerald R./Treadway, Darren C. (Eds., 2012): Politics in Organizations. Theory and Research Considerations. Routledge, New York, Hove, 2012, pp. 3-26.

Fink, Arlene (2009): How to Conduct Surveys – A Step-by-Step Guide. 4th edition, Sage, Thousand Oaks et al., 2009.

Fink, Arlene (2010): Conducting Research Literature Reviews: From the Internet to Paper. 3rd edition, Sage, Thousand Oaks et al., 2010.

Fladmoe-Lindquist, Karin/Tallman, Stephen (1994): Resource-Based Strategy and Competitive Advantage among Multinationals. In: Shrivastava, Paul/Huff, Anne S./Dutton, Jane E. (Eds., 1994): Resource-based View of the Firm. Jai Press, Greenwich, 1994, pp. 45-72.

Fletcher, Margaret/Plakoyiannaki, Emmanuella (Eds., 2011): Rethinking Case Study in International Business and Management Research. Edward Elgar, Cheltenham, Northampton, 2011.

Fletcher, Margaret/Plakoyiannaki, Emmanuella (2001): Case Selection in International Business: Key Issues and Common Misconceptions. In: Piekkari, Rebecca/Welch, Catherine (Eds., 2001): Rethinking the Case Study in International Business and Management Research. Edward Elgar, Cheltenham, Northampton, 2001, pp. 171-191.

Flick, Uwe (2004): Design and Process in Qualitative Research. In: Flick, Uwe/von Kardoff, Ernst/Steinke, Ines (Eds., 2004): A Companion to Qualitative Research. Sage, London et al., 2004, pp. 146-152.

Flick, Uwe (2009): An Introduction to Qualitative Research. 4th edition, Sage, London et al., 2009.

Flick, Uwe (2014): An Introduction to Qualitative Research. 5th edition, Sage, London et al., 2014.

Forsgren, Mats (2008): Theories of the Multinational Firm. Edward Elgar, Cheltenham, Northampton, 2008.

Forsgren, Mats/Holm, Ulf (2010): MNC Headquarters' Role in Subsidiaries' Value-Creating Activities: A Problem of Rationality or Radical Uncertainty. In: Scandinavian Journal of Management, Vol. 26, No. 4, 2010, pp. 421-430.

Forsgren, Mats/Holm, Ulf/Johanson, Jan (2005): Managing the Embedded Multinational: A Business Network View. Edward Elgar, Cheltenham, Northampton, 2005.

Forsgren, Mats/Johanson, Jan/Sharma, Deo (2000): Development of MNC Centres of Excellence. In: Holm, Ulf/Pedersen, Torben (Eds., 2000): The Emergence and Impact of MNC Centres of Excellence. A Subsidiary Perspective. Macmillan, St. Martin's Press, Houndmills, London, New York, 2000, pp. 45-67.

Forsgren, Mats/Pedersen, Torben (1997): Centres of Excellence in Multinational Companies: The Case of Denmark. Working Paper No. 2, Institute of International Economics and Management, Copenhagen Business School, 1997.

Forsgren, Mats/Pedersen, Torben (1998): Centres of Excellence in Multinational Companies: The Case of Denmark. In: Birkinshaw, Julian/Hood, Neil (Eds., 1998): Multinational Corporate Evolution and Subsidiary Development. Macmillan, Houndmills et al., 1998, pp. 141-161.

Forsgren, Mats/Pedersen, Torben (2000): Subsidiary Influence and Corporate Learning – Centres of Excellence in Danish Foreign-Owned Firms. In: Holm, Ulf/Pedersen, Torben (Eds., 2000): The Emergence and Impact of MNC Centres of Excellence. A Subsidiary Perspective. Macmillan, St. Martin's Press, Houndmills et al., 2000, pp. 68-78.

Forsgren, Mats/Pedersen, Torben/Foss, Nicolai J. (1999): Accounting for the Strengths of MNC Subsidiaries: The Case of Foreign-Owned Firms in Denmark. In: International Business Review, Vol. 8, No. 2, 1999, pp. 181-196.

Foss, Kirsten/Foss, Nicolai J./Nell, Phillip C. (2012): MNC Organizational Form and Subsidiary Motivation Problems: Controlling Intervention Hazards in the Network MNC. In: Journal of International Management, Vol. 18, No. 3, 2012, pp. 247-259.

Foss, Nicolai J. (1997): The Boundary School. Working Paper 97-5. Copenhagen Business School, 1997.

Foss, Nicolai J. (1998): The Resource-Based Perspective: An Assessment and Diagnosis of Problems. In: Scandinavian Journal of Management, Vol. 14, No. 3, 1998, pp. 133-149.

Foss, Nicolai J. (2003): Bounded Rationality in the Economics of Organization: "Much Cited and Little Used". In: Journal of Economics Psychology, Vol. 24, No. 2, 2003, pp. 245-264.

Foss, Nicolai J./Ishikawa, Ibuki (2006): Towards a Dynamic Resource-Based View: Insights from Austrian Capital and Entrepreneurship Theory. SMG Working Paper No. 6/2006. Center for Strategic Management and Globalization at Copenhagen Business School, Frederiksberg, 2006.

Foss, Nicolai J./Klein, Peter G./Kor, Yasemin Y./Mahoney, Joseph T. (2008): Entrepreneurship, Subjectivism, and the Resource-Based View: Toward a New Synthesis. In: Strategic Entrepreneurship Journal, Vol. 2, No. 1, 2008, pp. 73-94.

Foss, Nicolai J./Pedersen, Torben (2002): Transferring Knowledge in MNCs: The Role of Sources of Subsidiary Knowledge and Organizational Context. In: Journal of International Management, Vol. 8, No. 1, 2002, pp. 49-67.

Freiling, Jörg (2008): RBV and the Road to the Control of External Organizations. In: Management Revue, Vol. 19, No. 1/2, 2008, pp. 33-52.

Frost, Tony S. (2001): The Geographic Sources of Foreign Subsidiaries' Innovations. In: Strategic Management Journal, Vol. 22, No. 2, 2001, pp. 101-123.

Furu, Patrick (2001): Drivers of Competence Development in Different Types of Multinational Subsidiaries. In: Scandinavian Journal of Management, Vol. 17, No. 1, 2001, pp. 133-149.

Gagné, Marylène/Deci, Edward L. (2005): Self-Determination Theory and Work Motivation. In: Journal of Organizational Behavior, Vol. 26, No. 4, 2005, pp. 331-362.

Galunic, D. Charles/Eisenhardt, Kathleen M. (1996): The Evolution of Intracorporate Domains: Divisional Charter Losses in High-Technology, Multidivisional Corporations. In: Organization Science, Vol. 7, No. 3, 1996, pp. 255-282.

Gammelgaard, Jens (2009): Issue Selling and Bargaining Power in Intrafirm Competition: The Differentiating Impact of the Subsidiary Management Composition. In: Competition & Change, Vol. 13, No. 3, 2009, pp. 214-228.

Gammelgaard, Jens/Pedersen, Torben (2003): Internal versus External Knowledge Sourcing of Subsidiaries: An Organizational Trade-Off. CKG Working Paper No 8/2003. Copenhagen Business School, 2003.

Garbuio, Massimo/King, Adelaide W./Lovallo, Dan (2011): Looking Inside: Psychological Influences on Structuring a Firm's Portfolio of Resources. In: Journal of Management, Vol. 37, No. 5, 2011, pp. 1444-1463.

Geh, Eugene (2011): Understanding Strategic Alliances from the Effectual Entrepreneurial Firm's Perspective – An Organization Theory Perspective. In: SAM Advanced Management Journal (07497075), Vol. 76, No. 4, 2011, pp. 27-36.

Geppert, Mike/Dörrenbächer, Christoph (2011): Politics and Power in the Multinational Corporation: An Introduction. In: Dörrenbächer, Christoph/Geppert, Mike (Eds., 2011): Politics and Power in the Multinational Corporation. The Role of Institutions, Interests and Identities. Cambridge University Press, Cambridge et al., 2011, pp. 3-40.

Gerring, John (2007): Case Study Research. Principles and Practices. Cambridge University Press, Cambridge et al., 2007.

Ghauri, Pervez N. (2004): Designing and Conducting Studies in International Business Research. In: Marschan-Piekkari, Rebecca/Welch, Catherine (Eds., 2004): Handbook of Qualitative Research Methods for International Business. Edward Elgar, Cheltenham, Northampton, 2004, pp. 109-124.

Ghauri, Pervez N./Grønhaug, Kjell (2005): Research Methods in Business Studies. A Practical Guide. 3rd edition, Prentice Hall, Harlow et al., 2005.

Ghoshal, Sumantra (1986): The Innovative Multinational: A Differentiated Network of Organizational Roles and Management Roles. Graduate School of Business Administration. Harvard University, Cambridge. Dissertation, 1986.

Ghoshal, Sumantra/Bartlett, Christopher A. (1988): Creation, Adoption, and Diffusion of Innovations by Subsidiaries of Multinational Corporations. In: Journal of International Business Studies, Vol. 19, No. 3, 1988, pp. 365-388.

Ghoshal, Sumantra/Bartlett, Christopher A. (1990): The Multinational Corporation as an Interorganizational Network. In: Academy of Management Review, Vol. 15, No. 4, 1990, pp. 603-625.

Ghoshal, Sumantra/Bartlett, Christopher A. (1994): Linking Organizational Context and Managerial Action: The Dimensions of Quality of Management. In: Strategic Management Journal, Vol. 15, Issue Supplement S2, 1994, pp. 91-112.

Ghoshal, Sumantra/Moran, Peter (1996): Bad for Practice: A Critique of the Transaction Cost Theory. In: The Academy of Management Review, Vol. 21, No. 1, 1996, pp. 13-47.

Ghoshal, Sumantra/Nohria, Nitin (1986): Multinational Corporations as Differentiated Networks. Working Paper No. 1789-86. Sloan School of Management, Massachusetts Institute of Technology, 1986.

Ghoshal, Sumantra/Nohria, Nitin (1989): Internal Differentiation within Multinational Corporations. In: Strategic Management Journal, Vol. 10, No. 4, 1989, pp. 323-337.

Gibbert, Michael/Ruigrok, Winfried/Wicki, Barbara (2008): What Passes as a Rigorous Case Study? In: Strategic Management Journal, Vol. 29, No. 13, 2008, pp. 1465-1474.

Gibbs, Graham R. (2007): Analyzing Qualitative Data. Sage, London et al., 2007.

Ginsberg, Ari/Venkatraman, N. (1985): Contingency Perspectives of Organizational Strategy: A Critical Review of the Empirical Research. In: The Academy of Management Review, Vol. 10, No. 3, 1985, pp. 421-434.

Giroud, Axèle/Scott-Kennel, Joanna (2009): MNE Linkages in International Business: A Framework for Analysis. In: International Business Review, Vol. 18, No. 6, 2009, pp. 555-566.

Glaser, Barney G. (1978): Theoretical Sensitivity. Advances in the Methodology of Grounded Theory. Sociology Press, Mill Valley, 1978.

Glaser, Barney G./Strauss, Anselm, L. (1967): The Discovery of Grounded Theory: Strategies for Qualitative Research. Aline de Gruyter, New York, 1967.

Gnyawali, Devi R./Fogel, Daniel S. (1994): Environments for Entrepreneurship Development: Key Dimensions and Research Implications. Vol. 18, No. 4, 1994, pp. 43-62.

Göbel, Fabian (2009): Case Study Approach. In: Schwaiger, Manfred/Meyer, Anton (Eds., 2009): Theorien und Methoden der Betriebswirtschaft. Handbuch für Wissenschaftler und Studierende. Vahlen, München, 2009, pp. 359-376.

Godfrey, Paul C./Gregersen, Hal B. (1999): Where Do Resources Come From? A Model of Resource Generation. In: Journal of High Technology Management Research, Vol. 10, No. 1, 1999, p. 37.

Golden, Brian R. (1992): The Past Is the Past – Or Is It? The Use of Retrospective Accounts as Indicators of Past Strategy. In: Academy of Management Journal, Vol. 35, No. 4, 1992, pp. 848-860.

Grant, Robert M. (1991): The Resource-Based Theory of Competitive Advantage: Implications for Strategy Formulation. In: California Management Review, Vol. 33, No. 3, 1991, pp. 114-135.

Greene, Patricia O./Brush, Candida G./Hart, Myra M. (1999): The Corporate Venture Champion: A Resource-Based Approach to Role and Process. In: Entrepreneurship: Theory & Practice, Vol. 23, No. 3, 1999, pp. 103-122.

Greening, Daniel W./Gray, Barbara (1994): Testing a Model of Organizational Response to Social and Political Issues. In: Academy of Management Journal, Vol. 37, No. 3, 1994, pp. 467-498.

Grohmann, Janine (2010): An Integration-Responsiveness Perspective on Subsidiary Entrepreneurship in Diversified Firms. School of Economics and Management. Technische Universität Berlin. Dissertation, 2010.

Guba, Egon G. (1990): The Alternative Paradigm Dialog. In: Guba, Egon G. (Ed., 1990): The Paradigm Dialog. Sage, Newbury Park et al., 1990, pp. 17-30.

Guba, Egon G./Lincoln, Yvonne S. (1994): Competing Paradigms in Qualitative Research. In: 1994): Handbook of Qualitative Research. Sage, Thousand Oaks et al., 1994.

Gummesson, Evert (2000): Qualitative Methods in Management Research. 2nd edition, Sage, Thousand Oaks et al., 2000.

Gupta, Anil K./Govindarajan, Vijay (1991): Knowledge Flow Patterns, Subsidiary Strategic Roles, and Strategic Control within MNCs. Academy of Management Best Papers Proceedings, 1991/08, Academy of Management, 1991, pp. 21-25.

Gupta, Anil K./Govindarajan, Vijay (1991): Knowledge Flows and the Structure of Control within Multinational Corporations. In: Academy of Management Review, Vol. 16, No. 4, 1991, pp. 768-792.

Gupta, Anil K./Govindarajan, Vijay (1994): Organizing for Knowledge Flows within MNCs. In: International Business Review, Vol. 3, No. 4, 1994, pp. 443-457.

Gupta, Anil K./Govindarajan, Vijay (2000): Knowledge Flows within Multinational Corporations. In: Strategic Management Journal, Vol. 21, No. 4, 2000, pp. 473-496.

Hagan, Christine M. (1996): The Core Competence Organization: Implications for Human Resource Practices. In: Human Resource Management Review, Vol. 6, No. 2, 1996, pp. 147-164.

Håkanson, Lars/Nobel, Robert (2000): Technology Characteristics and Reverse Technology Transfer. In: International Management of Technology: Theory, Evidence and Policy, Vol. 40, No. 1, 2000, pp. 29-48.

Håkanson, Lars/Nobel, Robert (2001): Organizational Characteristics and Reverse Technology Transfer. In: Management International Review, Vol. 41, No. 4, 2001, pp. 395-420.

Håkansson, Håkan/Snehota, Ivan (1989): No Business is an Island: The Network Concept of Business Strategy. In: Scandinavian Journal of Management, Vol. 5, No. 3, 1989, pp. 187-200.

Håkansson, Håkan/Snehota, Ivan (1995): Developing Relationships in Business Networks. Routledge, London, New York, 1995.

Hansen, David J./Shrader, Rodney/Monllor, Javier (2011): Defragmenting Definitions of Entrepreneurial Opportunity. In: Journal of Small Business Management, Vol. 49, No. 2, 2011, pp. 283-304.

Hansen, Morten T. (1999): The Search-Transfer Problem: The Role of Weak Ties in Sharing Knowledge across Organization Subunits. In: Administrative Science Quarterly, Vol. 44, No. 1, 1999, pp. 82-111.

Harpaz, Itzhak/Meshoulam, Ilan (1997): Intraorganizational Power in High Technology Organizations. In: The Journal of High Technology Management Research, Vol. 8, No. 1, 1997, pp. 107-128.

Hart, Chris (2003): Doing a Literature Review: Releasing the Social Science Research Imagination. 7th edition, Sage, London et al., 2003.

Hart, Stuart L. (1995): A Natural-Resource-Based View of the Firm. In: The Academy of Management Review, Vol. 20, No. 4, 1995, pp. 986-1014.

Hartmann, Swantje (2011): External Embeddedness of Subsidiaries. Influences on Product Innovation in MNCs. Josef Eul, Lohmar, 2011.

Harzing, Anne-Wil (2000): An Empirical Analysis and Extension of the Bartlett and Ghoshal Typology of Multinational Companies. In: Journal of International Business Studies, Vol. 31, No. 1, 2000, pp. 101-120.

Harzing, Anne-Wil K./van der Wal, Ron (2008): Google Scholar as a New Source for Citation Analysis. In: Ethics in Science and Environmental Politics, Vol. 8, No. 1, 2008, pp. 61-73.

Harzing, Anne-Wil/Noorderhaven, Niels (2006): Knowledge Flows in MNCs: An Empirical Test and Extension of Gupta and Govindarajan's Typology of Subsidiary Roles. In: International Business Review, Vol. 15, No. 3, 2006, pp. 195-214.

Harzing, Anne-Wil/Sorge, Arndt/Paauwe, Jaap (2002): HQ-Subsidiary Relationships in Multinational Companies: A British-German Comparison. In: Geppert, Mike/Matten, Dirk/ Williams, Karren (Eds., 2002): Challenges for European Management in a Global Context. Springer, New York, 2002.

Haugland, Sven A. (2010): The Integration-Responsiveness Framework and Subsidiary Management: A Commentary. In: Journal of Business Research, Vol. 63, No. 1, 2010, pp. 94-96.

Hauschild, Stefan/zu Knyphausen-Aufseß, Dodo/Rahmel, Martin (2011): Measuring Industry Dynamics: Towards a Comprehensive Concept. In: Schmalenbach Business Review, Vol. 63, No. 4, 2011, pp. 416-454.

Haynie, J. Michael/Shepherd, Dean A./McMullen, Jeffrey S. (2009): An Opportunity for Me? The Role of Resources in Opportunity Evaluation Decisions. In: Journal of Management Studies, Vol. 46, No. 3, 2009, pp. 337-361.

He, Xinming/Wei, Yingqi (2011): Linking Market Orientation to International Market Selection and International Performance. In: International Business Review, Vol. 20, No. 5, 2011, pp. 535-546.

Healy, Marilyn/Perry, Chad (2000): Comprehensive Criteria to Judge Validity and Reliability of Qualitative Research within the Realism Paradigm. In: Qualitative Market Research, Vol. 3, No. 3, 2000, pp. 118-126.

Hedlund, Gunnar (1981): Autonomy of Subsidiaries and Formalization of Headquarters Subsidiary Relationships in Swedish MNCS. St. Martin, New York, 1981.

Hedlund, Gunnar (1986): The Hypermodern MNC – A Heterarchy? In: Human Resource Management, Vol. 25, No. 1, 1986, pp. 9-35.

Helfat, Constance E. (1997): Know-How and Asset Complementarity and Dynamic Capability Accumulation: The Case of R&D. In: Strategic Management Journal, Vol. 18, No. 5, 1997, pp. 339-360.

Helfat, Constance E./Finkelstein, Sydney/Mitchell, Will/Peteraf, Margaret A./Singh, Harbir/ Teece, David J./Winter, Sidney G. (2007): Dynamic Capabilities: Understanding Strategic Change in Organizations., Blackwell, Malden, 2007.

Helfat, Constance E./Peteraf, Margaret A. (2003): The Dynamic Resource-Based View: Capability Lifecycles. In: Strategic Management Journal, Vol. 24, No. 10, 2003, pp. 997-1010.

Hickson, D. J./Hinings, C. R./Lee, C. A./Schneck, R. E./Pennings, J. M. (1971): A Strategic Contingencies' Theory of Intraorganizational Power. In: Administrative Science Quarterly, Vol. 16, No. 2, 1971, pp. 216-229.

Hillman, Amy J./Withers, Michael C./Collins, Brian J. (2009): Resource Dependence Theory: A Review. In: Journal of Management, Vol. 35, No. 6, 2009, pp. 1404-1427.

Hitt, Michael A./Ireland, R. Duane/Camp, S. Michael/Sexton, Donald L. (2001): Strategic Entrepreneurship: Entrepreneurial Strategies for Wealth Creation. In: Strategic Management Journal, Vol. 22, No. 6-7, 2001, pp. 479-491.

Hitt, Michael A./Ireland, R. Duane/Camp, S. Michael/Sexton, Donald L. (2002): Strategic Entrepreneurship: Integrating Entrepreneurial and Strategic Management Perspectives. In: Hitt, Michael A./Ireland, R. Duane/Camp, S. Michael/Sexton, Donald L. (Eds., 2002): Strategic Entrepreneurship: Creating a New Mindset. Blackwell, Oxford, 2002, pp. 1-16.

Hitt, Michael A./Ireland, R. Duane/Hoskisson, Robert E. (2007): Strategic Management: Competitiveness and Globalization. 7th edition, Thomson South-Western, Cincinnati, 2007.

Hitt, Michael A./Ireland, R. Duane/Sirmon, David G./Trahms, Cheryl A. (2011): Strategic Entrepreneurship: Creating Value for Individuals, Organizations, and Society. In: Academy of Management Perspectives, Vol. 25, No. 2, 2011, pp. 57-75.

Hjorth, Daniel/Jones, Campbell/Gartner, William B. (2008): Introduction for 'Recreating/ Recontextualising Entrepreneurship'. In: Scandinavian Journal of Management, Vol. 24, No. 2, 2008, pp. 81-84.

Hofer, Charles W. (1975): Toward a Contingency Theory of Business Strategy. In: The Academy of Management Journal, Vol. 18, No. 4, 1975, pp. 784-810.

Hoffman, Richard C. (1994): Generic Strategies for Subsidiaries of Multinational Corporations. In: Journal of Management Issues, Vol. 6, No. 1, 1994, pp. 69-87.

Höhne, Elisabeth (2009): Kontingenztheorie. In: Schwaiger, Manfred/Meyer, Anton (Eds., 2009): Theorien und Methoden der Betriebswirtschaft. Verlag Franz Vahlen, München, 2009, pp. 85-92.

Holm, Ulf/Holmström, Christine/Sharma, Deo (2005): Competence Development through Business Relationships or Competitive Environment? – Subsidiary Impact on MNC Competitive Advantage. In: Management International Review, Vol. 45, No. 2, 2005, pp. 197-218.

Holm, Ulf/Pedersen, Torben (2000a): The Centres of Excellence Project: Methods and some Empirical Findings. In: Holm, Ulf/Pedersen, Torben (Eds., 2000): The Emergence and Impact of MNC Centres of Excellence. A Subsidiary Perspective. Macmillan, Houndmills et al., 2000, pp. 23-41.

Holm, Ulf/Pedersen, Torben (2000b): Introduction and Overview. In: Holm, Ulf/Pedersen, Torben (Eds., 2000): The Emergence and Impact of MNC Centres of Excellence. A Subsidiary Perspective. Macmillan, Houndmills et al., 2000, pp. 1-20.

Hoskisson, Robert E./Covin, Jeffrey G./Volberda, Henk W./Johnson, Richard A. (2011): Revitalizing Entrepreneurship: The Search for New Research Opportunities. In: Journal of Management Studies, Vol. 48, No. 6, 2011, pp. 1141-1168.

Hoskisson, Robert E./Hitt, Michael A./Wan, William P./Yiu, Daphne (1999): Theory and Research in Strategic Management: Swings of a Pendulum. In: Journal of Management, Vol. 25, No. 3, 1999, pp. 417-456.

Hostager, Todd J./Neil, Thomas C./Decker, Ronald L./Lorentz, Richard D. (1998): See Environmental Opportunities: Effects of Intrapreneurial Ability, Efficacy, Motivation and Desirability. In: Journal of Organizational Change Management, Vol. 11, No. 1, 1998, pp. 11-25.

Hymer, Stephen H. (1976): The International Operations of National Firms: A Study of Direct Foreign Investment. MIT Press, Cambridge, London, 1976.

Inkpen, Andrew C. (1996): Creating Knowledge through Collaboration. In: California Management Review, Vol. 39, No. 1, 1996, pp. 123-140.

Inkpen, Andrew C. (1998): Learning and Knowledge Acquisition through International Strategic Alliances. In: The Academy of Management Executive (1993-2005), Vol. 12, No. 4, 1998, pp. 69-80.

Inkpen, Andrew C. (2005): Learning through Alliances: General Motors and NUMMI. In: California Management Review, Vol. 47, No. 4, 2005, pp. 114-136.

Inkpen, Andrew C./Beamish, Paul W. (1997): Knowledge, Bargaining Power, and the Instability of International Joint Ventures. In: The Academy of Management Review, Vol. 22, No. 1, 1997, pp. 177-202.

Ireland, R. Duane/Hitt, Michael A./Camp, S. Michael/Sexton, Donald L. (2001): Integrating Entrepreneurship and Strategic Management Actions to Create Firm Wealth. In: The Academy of Management Executive (1993-2005), Vol. 15, No. 1, 2001, pp. 49-63.

Ireland, R. Duane/Hitt, Michael A./Sirmon, David G. (2003): A Model of Strategic Entrepreneurship: The Construct and its Dimensions. In: Journal of Management, Vol. 29, No. 6, 2003, pp. 963-989.

Ireland, R. Duane/Webb, Justin W. (2006): International Entrepreneurship in Emerging Economies: A Resource-Based Perspective. In: Cooper, Arnold C./Alvarez, Sharon A./Carrera, Alejandro A./Mesquita, Luiz F./Vassolo, Roberto S. (Eds., 2006): Entrepreneurial Strategies: New Technologies and Emerging Markets. Blackwell, Malden et al., 2006, pp. 47-70.

Jarillo, Carlos J./Martinez, Jon I. (1990): Different Roles for Subsidiaries: The Case of Multinational Corporations in Spain. In: Strategic Management Journal, Vol. 11, No. 7, 1990, pp. 501-512.

Järvensivu, Timo/Törnroos, Jan-Åke (2010): Case Study Research with Moderate Constructionism: Conceptualization and Practical Illustration. In: Industrial Marketing Management, Vol. 39, No. 1, 2010, pp. 100-108.

Jennings, Peter L./Perren, Lew/Carter, Sara (2005): Guest Editors' Introduction: Alternative Perspectives on Entrepreneurship Research. In: Entrepreneurship Theory and Practice, Vol. 29, No. 2, 2005, pp. 145-152.

Jensen, Michael C./Meckling, William H. (1976): Theory of the Firm: Managerial Behavior, Agency Costs and Ownership Structure. In: Journal of Financial Economics, Vol. 3, No. 4, 1976, pp. 305-360.

Jenssen, Jan Inge/Jørgensen, Geir (2004): How Do Corporate Champions Promote Innovations? In: International Journal of Innovation Management, Vol. 8, No. 1, 2004, pp. 63-86.

Jindra, Björn (2005): A Strategy View on Knowledge in the MNE – Integrating Subsidiary Roles and Knowledge Flows. In: Journal of Economics and Business, Vol. 8, No. 1 and 2, 2005, pp. 43-72.

Jindra, Björn/Giroud, Axèle/Scott-Kennel, Joanna (2009): Subsidiary Roles, Vertical Linkages and Economic Development: Lessons from Transition Economies. In: Journal of World Business, Vol. 44, No. 2, 2009, pp. 167-179.

Johanson, Jan/Vahlne, Jan-Erik (1977): The Internationalization Process of the Firm – A Model of Knowledge Development and Increasing Foreign Market Commitments. In: Journal of International Business Studies, Vol. 8, No. 1, 1977, pp. 25-34.

Johnson, Julius H. Jr. (1995): An Empirical Analysis of the Integration-Responsiveness Framework: U.S. Construction Equipment Industry Firms in Global Competition. In: Journal of International Business Studies, Vol. 26, No. 3, 1995, pp. 621-635.

Johnson, William A./Medcof, John W. (2002): Entrepreneurial Behavior in the MNC: An Extended Agency Theory Analysis of the Parent-Subsidiary Relationship and Subsidiary Initiative. In: International Journal of Entrepreneurship and Innovation Management, Vol. 2, No. 2/3, 2002, pp. 186-203.

Johnson, William A./Medcof, John W. (2007): Motivating Proactive Subsidiary Innovation: Agent-Based Theory and Socialization Models in Global R&D. In: Journal of International Management, Vol. 13, No. 4, 2007, pp. 472-487.

Johnston, Stewart/Menguc, Bulent (2007): Subsidiary Size and the Level of Subsidiary Autonomy in Multinational Corporations: A Quadratic Model Investigation of Australian Subsidiaries. In: Journal of International Business Studies, Vol. 38, No. 5, 2007, pp. 787-801.

Jones, Marian V./Coviello, Nicole/Tang, Yee K. (2011): International Entrepreneurship Research (1989-2009): A Domain Ontology and Thematic Analysis. In: Journal of Business Venturing, Vol. 26, No. 6, 2011, pp. 632-659.

Jones, Marian V./Dimitratos, Pavlos (Eds., 2004): Emerging Paradigms in International Entrepreneurship. Edward Elgar, Cheltenham, Northampton, 2004.

Kelle, Udo/Erzberger, Christian (2004): Qualitative and Quantitative Methods: Not in Opposition. In: Flick, Uwe/von Kardoff, Ernst/Steinke, Ines (Eds., 2004): A Companion to Qualitative Research. Sage, London et al., 2004, pp. 172-177.

Kerr, Steven/Schriesheim, Chester A./Murphy, Charles J./Stogdill, Ralph M. (1974): Toward a Contingency Theory of Leadership Based upon the Consideration and Initiating Structure Literature. In: Organizational Behavior and Human Performance, Vol. 12, No. 1, 1974, pp. 62-82.

Keupp, Marcus M. (2008): Subsidiary Initiatives in International Research and Development: A Survival Analysis. Graduate School of Business Administration, Economics, Law and Social Sciences. University of St. Gallen, Dissertation, 2008.

Keupp, Marcus M./Gassmann, Oliver (2009a): International Innovation and Strategic Initiatives: A Research Agenda. In: Research in International Business and Finance, Vol. 23, No. 2, 2009a, pp. 193-205.

Keupp, Marcus Matthias/Gassmann, Oliver (2009b): The Past and the Future of International Entrepreneurship: A Review and Suggestions for Developing the Field. In: Journal of Management, Vol. 35, No. 3, 2009b, pp. 600-633.

Kieser, Alfred (2006): Der Situative Ansatz. In: Kieser, Alfred/Ebers, Mark (Eds., 2006): Organisationstheorien. 6th edition. Kohlhammer, Stuttgart, 2006, pp. 215-245.

Kieser, Alfred/Ebers, Mark (Eds., 2006): Organisationstheorien. 6th edition, Kohlhammer, Stuttgart, 2006.

Kieser, Alfred/Kubicek, Herbert (1992): Organisation. 3rd edition, Walter de Gruyter, Berli, New York, 1992.

Kieser, Alfred/Walgenbach, Peter (2010): Organisation. 6th edition, Schäffer-Poeschel, Stuttgart, 2010.

Kirzner, Israel M. (1973): Competition and Entrepreneurship. University of Chicago, Chicago, London, 1973.

Knott, Anne Marie (2003): The Organizational Routines Factor Market Paradox. In: Strategic Management Journal, Vol. 24, No. 10, 2003, pp. 929-943.

Knott, Anne Marie/Bryce, David J./Posen, Hart E. (2003): On the Strategic Accumulation of Intangible Assets. In: Organization Science, Vol. 14, No. 2, 2003, pp. 192-207.

Kogut, Bruce/Zander, Udo (1992): Knowledge of the Firm, Combinative Capabilities, and the Replication of Technology. In: Organization Science, Vol. 3, No. 3, 1992, pp. 383-397.

Kogut, Bruce/Zander, Udo (1993): Knowledge of the Firm and the Evolutionary Theory of the Multinational Corporation. In: Journal of International Business Studies, Vol. 24, No. 4, 1993, pp. 625-645.

Kor, Yasemin Y./Mahoney, Joseph T. (2004): Edith Penrose's (1959) Contributions to the Resource-Based View of Strategic Management. In: Journal of Management Studies. pp. 183-191.

Kraaijenbrink, Jeroen/Spender, J.-C. /Groen, Aard J. (2010): The Resource-Based View: A Review and Assessment of Its Critiques. In: Journal of Management, Vol. 36, No. 1, 2010, pp. 349-372.

Kretschmer, Katharina (2008): Performance Evaluation of Foreign Subsidiaries. Gabler (mir-Edition), Wiesbaden, 2008.

Krishnan, Rishikesha T. (2006): Subsidiary Initiative in Indian Software Subsidiaries of MNCs. In: Vikalpa: The Journal for Decision Makers, Vol. 31, No. 1, 2006, pp. 61-71.

Kuckartz, Udo (2010): Einführung in die Computergestützte Analyse Qualitativer Daten. 3rd edition, VS Verlag für Sozialwissenschaften, Wiesbaden, 2010.

Kuratko, Donald F. (Ed., 2009): Entrepreneurship: Theory, Process, and Practice. 8th edition, South-Western, Mason, 2009.

Kuratko, Donald F./Ireland, R. Duane/Covin, Jeffrey G./Hornsby, Jeffrey S. (2005): A Model of Middle-Level Managers' Entrepreneurial Behavior. In: Entrepreneurship: Theory & Practice, Vol. 29, No. 6, 2005, pp. 699-716.

Kutschker, Michael/Schmid, Stefan (2011): Internationales Management. 7th edition, Oldenbourg, München, 2011.

Lado, Augustine A./Boyd, Nancy G./Wright, Peter/Kroll, Mark (2006): Paradox and Theorizing within the Resource-Based View. In: Academy of Management Review, Vol. 31, No. 1, 2006, pp. 115-131.

Lane, Peter J./Lubatkin, Michael (1998): Relative Absorptive Capacity and Interorganizational Learning. In: Strategic Management Journal, Vol. 19, No. 5, 1998, p. 461.

Lawrence, Paul R./Lorsch, Jay W. (1967): Organization and Environment. Managing Differentiation and Integration. Harvard University Press, Cambridge, MA, 1967.

Lechner, Christoph/Kreutzer, Markus (2010): Strategic Initiatives: Past, Present and Future. In: Mazzola, Pietro/Kellermanns, Franz W. (Eds., 2010): Handbook of Research on Strategy Process. Edward Elgar, Cheltenham, Northampton, 2010, pp. 283-303.

Lee, Ji-Ren/Chen, Jen-Shyang (2003): Internationalization, Local Adaptation, and Subsidiary's Entrepreneurship: An Exploratory Study on Taiwanese Manufacturing Firms in Indonesia and Malaysia. In: Asia Pacific Journal of Management, Vol. 20, No. 1, 2003, pp. 51-72.

Lee, Nick/Lings, Ian (2008): Doing Business Research. A Guide to Theory and Practice. Sage, London et al., 2008.

Lee, Soo Hee/Williams, Christopher (2005): Political Heterarchy and Dispersed Entrepreneurship in the MNC. JIBS/AIB/CIBER Frontiers Conference, 2005.

Lee, Thomas W. (1999): Using Qualitative Methods in Organizational Research. Sage, Thousand Oaks et al., 1999.

Lepisto, Douglas A./Pratt, Michael G. (2012): Politics in Perspectives: On the Theoretical Challenges and Opportunities in Studying Organizational Politics. In: Ferris, Gerarld R./Treadway, Darren C. (Eds., 2012): Politics in Organizations. Theory and Research Considerations. Routledge, New York, Hove, 2012, pp. 67-98.

Lichtenstein, Benyamin M. /Brush, Candida G. (2001): How Do "Resource Bundles" Develop and Change in New Ventures? A Dynamic Model and Longitudinal Exploration. In: Entrepreneurship: Theory & Practice, Vol. 25, No. 3, 2001, pp. 37-58.

Lin, Shao-Lung/Hsieh, An-Tien (2010): The Integration-Responsiveness Framework and Subsidiary Management: A Response. In: Journal of Business Research, Vol. 63, No. 8, 2010, pp. 911-913.

Lindsay, Valerie (2004): Computer-assisted Qualitative Data Analysis: Application in an Export Study. In: Marschan-Piekkari, Rebecca/Welch, Catherine (Eds. 2004): Handbook of Qualitative Research Methods for International Business. Edward Elgar, Cheltenham, Northampton, 2004, pp.486-52

Lindsay, William M./Rue, Leslie W. (1980): Impact of the Organization Environment on the Long-Range Planning Process: A Contingency View. In: The Academy of Management Journal, Vol. 23, No. 3, 1980, pp. 385-404.

Ling, Yan/Floyd, Steven W./Baldridge, David C. (2005): Toward a Model of Issue-Selling by Subsidiary Managers in Multinational Organizations. In: Journal of International Business Studies, Vol. 36, No. 6, 2005, pp. 637-654.

Liouka, Ioanna (2007): Opportunity Identification in MNC Subsidiaries: Context and Performance Implications. Department of Management. University of Glasgow, Dissertation, 2007.

Lockett, Andy/Thompson, Steve/Morgenstern, Uta (2009): The Development of the Resource-Based View of the Firm: A Critical Appraisal. In: International Journal of Management Reviews, Vol. 11, No. 1, 2009, pp. 9-28.

Lorsch, Jay W./Lawrence, Paul R. (1965): Organizing for Product Innovation. In: Harvard Business Review, Vol. 43, No. 1, 1965, pp. 109-122.

Low, Murray B./MacMillan, Ian C. (1988): Entrepreneurship: Past Research and Future Challenges. In: Journal of Management, Vol. 14, No. 2, 1988, pp. 139-161.

Lumpkin, G. T./Dess, Gregory G. (1996): Clarifying the Entrepreneurial Orientation Construct and Linking It to Performance. In: Academy of Management Review, Vol. 21, No. 1, 1996, pp. 135-172.

Luo, Yadong (1999): The Structure-Performance Relationship in a Transitional Economy: An Empirical Study of Multinational Alliances in China. In: Journal of Business Research, Vol. 46, No. 1, 1999, pp. 15-30.

Luo, Yadong (2001): Determinants of Local Responsiveness: Perspectives from Foreign Subsidiaries in an Emerging Market. In: Journal of Management, Vol. 27, No. 4, 2001, pp. 451-477.

Luo, Yadong (2002): Organizational Dynamics and Global Integration: A Perspective from Subsidiary Managers. In: Journal of International Management, Vol. 8, No. 2, 2002, pp. 189-215.

Luo, Yadong (2003): Market-Seeking MNEs in an Emerging Market: How Parent-Subsidiary Links Shape Overseas Success. In: Journal of International Business Studies, Vol. 34, No. 3, 2003, pp. 290-309.

Luo, Yadong/Peng, Mike W. (1999): Learning to Compete in a Transition Economy: Experience, Environment, and Performance. In: Journal of International Business Studies, Vol. 30, No. 2, 1999, pp. 269-295.

Luo, Yadong/Tan, J. Justin (1997): How Much does Industry Structure Impact Foreign Direct Investment in China? In: International Business Review, Vol. 6, No. 4, 1997, pp. 337-359.

Lyles, Marjorie A./Salk, Jane E. (2007): Knowledge Acquisition from Foreign Parents in International Joint Ventures: An Empirical Examination in the Hungarian Context. In: Journal of International Business Studies, Vol. 38, No. 1, 2007, pp. 3-18.

Lyly-Yrjänäinen, Jouni/Suomala, Petri/Uusitalo, Olavi (2008): Global Key Account as a Vehicle for Diffusing Subsidiary Initiatives in Multinational Corporations. Paper presented at the 3rd International Conference on Business Market Management, St. Gallen, 2008.

Macharzina, Klaus (2003): Neue Theorien der Multinationalen Unternehmung. In: Holtbrügge, Dirk (Ed., 2003): Management Multinationaler Unternehmungen. Festschrift zum 60. Geburtstag von Martin K. Welge. Physica-Verlag, Heidelberg, 2003, pp. 25-40.

Machulik, Mario (2010): Das EPRG-Konzept von Howard V. Perlmutter: Eine umfassende Rekonstruktion und eine empirische Analyse im Spannungsfeld von Archetypen und Hybridformen internationaler Unternehmungen. Verlag Dr. Kovač, Hamburg, 2010.

Madhok, Anoop/Phene, Anupama (2001): The Co-Evolutional Advantage: Strategic Management Theory and the Eclectic Paradigm. In: International Journal of the Economics of Business, Vol. 8, No. 2, 2001, pp. 243-256.

Mahnke, Volker/Venzin, Markus/Zahra, Shaker A. (2007): Governing Entrepreneurial Opportunity Recognition in MNEs: Aligning Interests and Cognition under Uncertainty. In: Journal of Management Studies, Vol. 44, No. 7, 2007, pp. 1278-1298.

Mahoney, Joseph T. (1995): The Management of Resources and the Resource of Management. In: Journal of Business Research, Vol. 33, No. 2, 1995, pp. 91-101.

Mahoney, Joseph T./Pandian, Rajendran J. (1992): The Resource-Based View within the Conversation of Strategic Management. In: Strategic Management Journal, Vol. 13, No. 5, 1992, pp. 363-380.

Maitland, Elizabeth/Sammartino, André (2009): Subsidiaries in Motion: Assessing the Impact of Sunk versus Flexible Assets. In: Cheng, Joseph L./Maitland, Elizabeth/Nicholas, Stephen (Eds., 2009): Managing Subsidiary Dynamics: Headquarters Role, Capability Development, and China Strategy. Vol. 22. Emerald, Bingley, 2009, pp. 55-83.

Makadok, Richard (2001): Toward a Synthesis of the Resource-Based and Dynamic Capability Views of Rent Creation. In: Strategic Management Journal, Vol. 22, No. 5, 2001, p. 387.

Manolopoulos, Dimitris (2008): A Systematic Review of the Literature and Theoretical Analysis of Subsidiary Roles. In: Journal of Transnational Management, Vol. 13, No. 1, 2008, pp. 23-57.

Marcati, Alberto (1989): Configuration and Coordination – The Role of U.S. Subsidiaries in the International Network of Italian Multinationals. In: Management International Review, Vol. 29, No. 3, 1989, pp. 35-50.

March, James G. (1962): The Business Firm as a Political Coalition. In: The Journal of Politics, Vol. 24, No. 4, 1962, pp. 662-678.

March, James G. (1991): Exploration and Exploitation in Organizational Learning. In: Organization Science, Vol. 2, 1991, pp. 71-87.

March, James G./Simon, Herbert A. (1958): Organizations. Wiley, New York, 1958.

Maritan, Catherine A./Peteraf, Margaret A. (2011): Building a Bridge Between Resource Acquisition and Resource Accumulation. In: Journal of Management, Vol. 37, No. 5, 2011, pp. 1374-1389.

Marschan-Piekkari, Rebecca/Welch, Catherine (2004a): Handbook of Qualitative Research Methods for International Business. Edward Elgar, Cheltenham, Northampton, 2004.

Marschan-Piekkari, Rebecca/Welch, Catherine (2004b): Research Methods in International Business: The State of the Art. In: Marschan-Piekkari, Rebecca/Welch, Catherine (Eds., 2004): Handbook of Qualitative Research Methods for International Business. Edward Elgar, Cheltenham, Northampton, 2004, pp. 5-24.

Marschan-Piekkari, Rebecca/Welch, Catherine/Penttinen, Heli/Tahvanainen, Marja (2004): Interviewing in the Multinational Corporation: Challenges of the Organizational Context. In: Marschan-Piekkari, Rebecca/Welch, Catherine (Eds., 2004): Handbook of Qualitative Research Methods for International Business. Edward Elgar, Cheltenham, Northampton, 2004, pp. 244-263.

Martinez, Jon I./Jarillo, Carlos J. (1991): Coordination Demands of International Strategies. In: Journal of International Business Studies, Vol. 22, No. 3, 1991, pp. 429-444.

Mason, Edward S. (1939): Price and Production Policies of Large-Scale Enterprise. In: The American Economic Review, Vol. 29, No. 1, 1939, pp. 61-74.

Maurer, Julia (2011): Relationships between Foreign Subsidiaries: Competition and Cooperation in Multinational Plant Engineering Companies. Gabler (mir-Edition), Wiesbaden, 2011.

Mayring, Philipp (2002): Einführung in die Qualitative Sozialforschung. Beltz, Weinheim, Basel, 2002.

Mayring, Philipp (2010): Qualitative Inhaltsanalyse – Grundlagen und Techniken. 11th edition, Beltz, Weinheim, Basel, 2010.

McDougall, Patricia Phillips/Oviatt, Benjamin M. (2000): International Entrepreneurship: The Intersection of Two Research Paths. In: Academy of Management Journal, Vol. 43, No. 5, 2000, pp. 902-906.

McEvily, Bill/Zaheer, Akbar (1999): Bridging Ties: A Source of Firm Heterogeneity in Competitive Capabilities. In: Strategic Management Journal, Vol. 20, No. 12, 1999, pp. 1133-1156.

Medcof, John W. (1997): A Taxonomy of Internationally Dispersed Technology Units and its Application to Management Issues. In: R&D Management, Vol. 27, No. 4, 1997, pp. 301-318.

Medcof, John W. (2001): Resource-Based Strategy and Managerial Power in Networks of Internationally Dispersed Technology Units. In: Strategic Management Journal, Vol. 22, No. 11, 2001, pp. 999-1012.

Medcof, John W. (2007): Subsidiary Technology Upgrading and International Technology Transfer, with Reference to China. In: Asia Pacific Business Review, Vol. 13, No. 3, 2007, pp. 451-469.

Meyer, Klaus E./Mudambi, Ram/Narula, Rajneesh (2011): Multinational Enterprises and Local Contexts: The Opportunities and Challenges of Multiple Embeddedness. In: Journal of Management Studies, Vol. 48, No. 2, 2011, pp. 235-252.

Miles, Matthew B./Huberman, A. Michael (1994): Qualitative Data Analysis. 2nd edition, Sage, Thousand Oaks et al., 1994.

Miles, Matthew B./Huberman, A. Michael/Saldaña, Johnny (2007): Qualitative Data Analysis. A Methods Sourcebook. 3rd edition, Sage, Thousand Oaks et al., 2007.

Miller, Danny (1983): The Correlates of Entrepreneurship in Three Types of Firms. In: Management Science, Vol. 29, No. 7, 1983, pp. 770-791.

Miller, Danny/Shamsie, Jamal (1996): The Resource-Based View of the Firm in Two Environments: The Hollywood Film Studios from 1936 to 1965. In: The Academy of Management Journal, Vol. 39, No. 3, 1996, pp. 519-543.

Minbaeva, Dana B. (2008): HRM Practices Affecting Extrinsic and Intrinsic Motivation of Knowledge Receivers and Their Effect on Intra-MNC Knowledge Transfer. In: International Business Review, Vol. 17, No. 6, 2008, pp. 703-713.

Mintzberg, Henry (1983): Power in and around Organizations. Prentice Hall, New York, 1983.

Mintzberg, Henry (1985): The Organization as Political Arena. In: Journal of Management Studies, Vol. 22, No. 2, 1985, pp. 133-154.

Mintzberg, Henry/Waters, James A. (1985): Of Strategies, Deliberate and Emergent. In: Strategic Management Journal, Vol. 6, 1985, pp. 257-272.

Mole, Kevin F./Mole, Miranda (2010): Entrepreneurship as the Structuration of Individual and Opportunity: A Response Using a Critical Realist Perspective: Comment on Sarason, Dean and Dillard. In: Journal of Business Venturing, Vol. 25, No. 2, 2010, pp. 230-237.

Moliterno, Thomas P./Wiersema, Margarethe F. (2007): Firm Performance, Rent Appropriation, and the Strategic Resource Divestment Capability. In: Strategic Management Journal, Vol. 28, No. 11, 2007, pp. 1065-1087.

Moore, Karl J. (2001): A Strategy for Subsidiaries: Centres of Excellences to Build Subsidiary Specific Advantages. In: Management International Review, Vol. 41, No. 3, 2001, pp. 275-290.

Moore, Karl J./Heeler, Roger (1998): A Globalization Strategy for Subsidiaries – Subsidiary Specific Advantages. In: Muchielli, Jean-Louis/Buckley, Peter J./Cordell, Victor V. (Eds., 1998): Globalization and Reionalization. Strategies, Policies and Economic Environments. International Business Press, Binghampton, 1998, pp. 1-14.

Moran, Peter/Ghoshal, Sumantra (1997): Value Creation by Firms. Working Paper No. 97/19/SM, INSEAD, Fontainebleau, 1997.

Morgan, Gareth/Smircich, Linda (1980): The Case for Qualitative Research. In: Academy of Management Review, Vol. 5, No. 4, 1980, pp. 491-500.

Morrow, J.L./Sirmon, David G./Hitt, Michael A./Holcomb, Tim R. (2007): Creating Value in the Face of Declining Performance: Firm Strategies and Organizational Recovery. In: Strategic Management Journal, Vol. 28, No. 3, 2007, pp. 271-283.

Mothe, Caroline/Quelin, Bertrand V. (2001): Resource Creation and Partnership in R&D Consortia. In: Journal of High Technology Management Research, Vol. 12, No. 1, 2001, p. 113-138.

Mowery, David C./Oxley, Joanne E./Silverman, Brian S. (1996): Strategic Alliances and Interfirm Knowledge Transfer. In: Strategic Management Journal, Vol. 17, 1996, pp. 77-91.

Mowery, David C./Oxley, Joanne E./Silverman, Brian S. (2002): The Two Face of Partner-Specific Absorptive Capacity: Learning and Cospecialization in Strategic Alliances. In: Contractor, Farok J./Lorange, Peter (Eds., 2002): Cooperative Strategies and Alliances. Elsevier, Oxford, 2002, pp. 291-320.

Mu, Shaohua/Gnyawali, Devi, R./Hatfield, Donald, E. (2007): Foreign Subsidiaries' Learning from Local Environments: An Empirical Test. In: Management International Review, Vol. 47, No. 1, 2007, pp. 79-102.

Mudambi, Ram (1999): MNE Internal Capital Markets and Subsidiary Strategic Independence. In: International Business Review, Vol. 8, No. 2, 1999, pp. 197-211.

Mudambi, Ram/Mudambi, Susan M./Navarra, Pietro (2007): Global Innovation in MNCs: The Effects of Subsidiary Self-Determination and Teamwork. In: Journal of Product Innovation Management, Vol. 24, No. 5, 2007, pp. 442-455.

Mudambi, Ram/Navarra, Pietro (2004): Is Knowledge Power? Knowledge Flows, Subsidiary Power and Rent-Seeking within MNCs. In: Journal of International Business Studies, Vol. 35, No. 5, 2004, pp. 385-406.

Mudambi, Ram/Pedersen, Torben (2007): Agency Theory and Resource Dependency Theory: Complementary Explanations for Subsidiary Power in Multinational Corporations. SMG Working Paper No. 05/2007. Copenhagen Business School, 2007.

Neergaard, Helle (2004): Sampling in Entrepreneurial Settings. In: Marschan-Piekkari, Rebecca/ Welch, Catherine (Eds., 2004): Handbook of Qualitative Research Methods for International Business. Edward Elgar, Cheltenham, Northampton, 2004, pp. 253-278.

Nelson, Richard R./Winter, Sidney G. (1982): An Evolutionary Theory of Economic Change. Belknap Press, Cambridge, 1982.

Nienhüser, Werner (2004): Die Resource-Dependence-Theorie – Wie (gut) erklärt sie Unternehmensverhalten? In: Festing, Marion/Martin, Albert/Mayrhofer, Wolfgang/Nienhüser, Werner (Eds., 2004): Personaltheorie als Beitrag zur Theorie der Unternehmung – Festschrift für Prof. Dr. Wolfgang Weber zum 65. Geburtstag. Rainer Hampp Verlag, München, Mering, 2004.

Nienhüser, Werner (2008): Resource Dependence Theory – How Well Does It Explain Behavior of Organizations? In: Management Revue, Vol. 19, No. 1/2, 2008, pp. 9-32.

Nobel, Robert/Birkinshaw, Julian (1998): Innovation in Multinational Corporations: Control and Communication Patterns in International R&D. In: Strategic Management Journal, Vol. 19, No. 5, 1998, pp. 479-496.

Nohria, Nitin/Ghoshal, Sumantra (1994): Differentiated Fit and Share Values: Alternatives for Managing Headquarters-Subsidiary Relations. In: Strategic Management Journal, Vol. 15, No. 6, 1994, pp. 491-502.

Nohria, Nitin/Gulati, Ranjay (1996): Is Slack Good or Bad for Innovation? In: The Academy of Management Journal, Vol. 39, No. 5, 1996, pp. 1245-1264.

O'Donnell, Sharon W. (2000): Managing Foreign Subsidiaries: Agents of Headquarters, or an Independent Network? In: Strategic Management Journal, Vol. 21, No. 5, 2000, p. 525-548.

Oviatt, Benjamin M./McDougall, Patricia P. (2005): Defining International Entrepreneurship and Modeling the Speed of Internationalization. In: Entrepreneurship: Theory & Practice, Vol. 29, No. 5, 2005, pp. 537-553.

Özsomer, Ayşegül/Gençtürk, Esra (2003): A Resource-Based Model of Market Learning in the Subsidiary: The Capabilities of Exploration and Exploitation. In: Journal of International Marketing, Vol. 11, No. 3, 2003, pp. 1-29.

Pacheco-de-Almeida, Gonçalo/Henderson, James E./Cool, Karel O. (2008): Resolving the Commitment versus Flexibility Trade-Off: The Role of Resource Accumulation Lags. In: Academy of Management Journal, Vol. 51, No. 3, 2008, pp. 517-536.

Pacheco-de-Almeida, Gonçalo/Zemsky, Peter (2007): The Timing of Resource Development and Sustainable Competitive Advantage. In: Management Science, Vol. 53, No. 4, 2007, pp. 651-666.

Parhankangas, Annaleena/Arenius, Pia (2003): From a Corporate Venture to an Independent Company: A Base for a Taxonomy for Corporate Spin-Off Firms. In: Research Policy, Vol. 32, No. 3, 2003, pp. 463-481.

Paterson, S. L./Brock, David. M. (2002): The Development of Subsidiary-Management Research: Review and Theoretical Analysis. In: International Business Review, Vol. 11, No. 2, 2002, pp. 139-163.

Patton, Michael Q. (2002): Qualitative Research and Evaluation Methods. Sage, Thousand Oaks et al., 2002.

Pearce, Robert (1999): The Evolution of Technology in Multinational Enterprises: The Role of Creative Subsidiaries. In: International Business Review, Vol. 8, No. 2, 1999, pp. 125-148.

Peng, Mike W (2001): The Resource-Based View and International Business. In: Journal of Management, Vol. 27, No. 6, 2001, pp. 803-829.

Penrose, Edith T. (1959): The Theory of the Growth of the Firm. Basil Blackwell, Oxford, 1959.

Perlmutter, Howard V. (1969): The Tortuous Evolution of the Multinational Corporation. In: Columbia Journal of World Business, Vol. 4, No. 1, 1969, pp. 9-18.

Perren, Lew/Ram, Monder (2004): Case-Study Method in Small Business and Entrepreneurial Research: Mapping Boundaries and Perspectives. In: International Small Business Journal, Vol. 22, No. 1, 2004, pp. 83-101.

Perry, Chad (1998): Process of a Case Study Methodology for Postgraduate Research in Marketing. In: European Journal of Marketing, Vol. 32, No. 9/10, 1998, pp. 785-802.

Pertusa-Ortega, Eva M./Molina-Azorin José F./Claver-Cortés Enrique (2010): Competitive Strategy, Structure and Firm Performance. A Comparison of the Resource-Based View and the Contingency Approach. In: Management Decision, Vol. 48, No. 8, 2010, pp. 1282-1303.

Peterson, Richard B. (2004): Empirical Research in International Management: A Critique and Future Agenda. In: Marschan-Piekkari, Rebecca/Welch, Catherine (Eds., 2004): Handbook of Qualitative Research Methods for International Business. Edward Elgar, Cheltenham, Northampton, 2004, pp. 25-55.

Pfeffer, Jeffrey (1981): Power in Organizations. Pitman, Marshfield, 1981.

Pfeffer, Jeffrey (1992): Managing with Power: Politics and Influence in Organizations. Harvard Business School Press, Boston, 1992.

Pfeffer, Jeffrey/Salancik, Gerald R. (1978): The External Control of Organizations: A Resource Dependence Perspective. Harper & Row, New York, 1978.

Phene, Anupama/Almeida, Paul (2003): How Do Firms Evolve? The Patterns of Technological Evolution of Semiconductor Subsidiaries. In: International Business Review, Vol. 12, No. 3, 2003, pp. 349-367.

Phene, Anupama/Almeida, Paul (2008): Innovation in Multinational Subsidiaries: The Role of Knowledge Assimilation and Subsidiary Capabilities. In: Journal of International Business Studies, Vol. 39, No. 5, 2008, pp. 901-919.

Piekkari, Rebecca/Welch, Catherine/Paavilainen, Eriikka (2009): The Case Study as Disciplinary Convention: Evidence From International Business Journals. In: Organizational Research Methods, Vol. 12, No. 3, 2009, pp. 567-589.

Poppo, Laura/Weigelt, Keith (2000): A Test of the Resource-Based Model Using Baseball Free Agents. In: Journal of Economics & Management Strategy, Vol. 9, No. 4, 2000, pp. 585-614.

Porter, Michael E. (1980): Competitive Strategy. The Free Press, New York, 1980.

Porter, Michael E. (1981): The Contributions of Industrial Organization to Strategic Management. In: The Academy of Management Review, Vol. 6, No. 4, 1981, pp. 609-620.

Porter, Michael E. (1985): Competitive Advantage. Free Press, New York, 1985.

Porter, Michael E. (1986): Competition in Global Industries. A Conceptual Framework. In: Porter, Michael E. (Ed., 1986): Competition in Global Industries. Harvard Business School Press, Boston, 1986, pp. 15-60.

Porter, Michael E. (1990): The Competitive Advantage of Nations. The Free Press, New York,

Prahalad, Coimbatore K./Bettis, Richard A. (1986): The Dominant Logic: A New Linkage between Diversity and Performance. In: Strategic Management Journal, Vol. 7, No. 6, 1986, pp. 485-501.

Prahalad, Coimbatore K./Doz, Yves. L. (1981): An Approach to Strategic Control in MNCs. In: Sloan Management Review, Vol. 22, No. 4, 1981, pp. 5-13.

Prahalad, Coimbatore K./Doz, Yves L. (1987): The Multinational Mission. Balancing Local Demands and Global Vision. The Free Press/Macmillan, New York, London, 1987.

Prescott, John E. (1986): Environments as Moderators of the Relationship between Strategy and Performance. In: The Academy of Management Journal, Vol. 29, No. 2, 1986, pp. 329-346.

Priem, Richard L./Butler, John E. (2001): Is the Resource-Based "View" A Useful Perspective for Strategic Management Research? In: Academy of Management Journal, Vol. 26, No. 1, 2001, pp. 22-40.

Pugh, D. S./Hickson, D. J./Hinings, C. R./Turner, C. (1969): The Context of Organization Structures. In: Administrative Science Quarterly, Vol. 14, No. 1, 1969, pp. 91-114.

Pugh, Derek S./Hickson, David J. (1968): Eine dimensionale Analyse bürokratischer Strukturen. In: Mayntz, Renate (Ed., 1968): Bürokratische Organisation. Kiepenheuer & Witsch, Köln, Berlin, 1968.

Pugh, Derek S./Hickson, David J./Hinings, C. R. /Turner, Christopher (1968): Dimensions of Organization Structure. In: Administrative Science Quarterly, Vol. 13, No. 1, 1968, pp. 65-105.

Pugh, Derek S./Hickson, David. J. (1976): Organizational Structure in its Context. The Aston Program I. Ashgate Publishing, Westmead, 1976.

Qu, Riliang (2007): The Role of Market Orientation in the Business Success of MNCs' UK Subsidiaries. In: Management Decision, Vol. 45, No. 7, 2007, pp. 1181-1192.

Rabbiosi, Larissa (2011): Subsidiary Roles and Reverse Knowledge Transfer: An Investigation of the Effects of Coordination Mechanisms. In: Journal of International Management, Vol. 17, No. 2, 2011, pp. 97-113.

Rall, Wilhelm (2002): Der Netzwerkansatz als Alternative zum zentralen und hierarchisch gestützten Management der Mutter-Tochter-Beziehungen. In: Macharzina, Klaus/Oesterle, Michael-Jörg (Eds., 2002): Handbuch Internationales Management. Grundlagen – Instrumente – Perspektiven. 2nd edition. Gabler, Wiesbaden, 2002, pp. 759-775.

Randøy, Trond/Li, Jiatao (1998): Global Resource Flow and MNE Network Integration. In: Birkinshaw, Julian/Hood, Neil (Eds., 1998): Multinational Corporate Evolution and Subsidiary Development. Macmillan, Houndmills et al., 1998, pp. 76-101.

Raţiu, Cătălin/Molz, Rick (2010): Multinationals and Corporate Environmental Strategies: Fostering Subsidiary Initiative. In: Molz, Rick/Raţiu, Cătălin/Taleb, Ali (Eds., 2010): The Multinational Enterprise in Developing Countries. Routledge, Oxon, New York, 2010, pp. 179-193.

Renz, Timo (1998): Management in internationalen Unternehmensnetzwerken. Gabler, Wiesbaden, 1998.

Rosenzweig, Philip M./Singh, Jitendra V. (1991): Organizational Environments and the Multinational Enterprise. In: The Academy of Management Review, Vol. 16, No. 2, 1991, pp. 340-361.

Roth, Kendall (1995): Managing International Interdependence: CEO Characteristics in a Resource-Based Framework. In: The Academy of Management Journal, Vol. 38, No. 1, 1995, pp. 200-231.

Roth, Kendall/Morrison, Allen J. (1990): An Empirical Analysis of the Integration-Responsiveness Framework in Global Industries. In: Journal of International Business Studies, Vol. 21, No. 4, 1990, pp. 541-564.

Roth, Kendall/Morrison, Allen J. (1992): Implementing Global Strategy: Characteristics of Global Subsidiary Mandates. In: Journal of International Business Studies, Vol. 23, No. 4, 1992, pp. 715-735.

Roth, Kendall/Nigh, Douglas (1992): The Effectiveness of Headquarters-Subsidiary Relationships: The Role of Coordination, Control, and Conflict. In: Journal of Business Research, Vol. 25, No. 4, 1992, pp. 277-301.

Roth, Kendall/O'Donnell, Sharon (1996): Foreign Subsidiary Compensation Strategy: An Agency Theory Perspective. In: The Academy of Management Journal, Vol. 39, No. 3, 1996, pp. 678-703.

Rubin, Rebecca B./Rubin, Alan M./Haridakis, Paul M./Piele, Linda J. (2010): Communication Research: Strategies and Sources. 7th edition, Wadsworth, Boston, 2010.

Rugman, Alan M./Verbeke, Alain (1992): A Note on the Transnational Solution and the Transaction Cost Theory of Multinational Strategic Management. In: Journal of International Business Studies, Vol. 23, No. 4, 1992, pp. 761-771.

Rugman, Alan M./Verbeke, Alain (2001): Subsidiary-Specific Advantages in Multinational Enterprises. In: Strategic Management Journal, Vol. 22, No. 3, 2001, pp. 237-250.

Rugman, Alan M./Verbeke, Alain (2002): Edith Penrose's Contribution to the Resource-Based View of Strategic Management. In: Strategic Management Journal, Vol. 23, No. 8, 2002, pp. 769-780.

Rugman, Alan M./Verbeke, Alain (2003): Extending the Theory of The Multinational Enterprise: Internalization and Strategic Management Perspectives. In: Journal of International Business Studies, Vol. 34, No. 2, 2003, pp. 125-137.

Rugman, Alan M./Verbeke, Alain/Nguyen, Quyen T. K. (2011a): Fifty Years of International Business Theory and Beyond. In: Management International Review, Vol. 51, No. 6, 2011, pp. 755-786.

Rugman, Alan M./Verbeke, Alain/Yuan, Wenlong (2011b): Re-conceptualizing Bartlett and Ghoshal's Classification of National Subsidiary Roles in the Multinational Enterprise. In: Journal of Management Studies, Vol. 48, No. 2, 2011, pp. 253-277.

Sargent, John/Matthews, Linda (2006): The Drivers of Evolution/Upgrading in Mexico's Maquiladoras: How Important Is Subsidiary Initiative? In: Journal of World Business, Vol. 41, No. 3, 2006, pp. 233-246.

Saunders, Mark/Lewis, Philip/Thornhill, Adrian (2012): Research Methods for Business Students. 6th edition, Pearson, Essex, 2012.

Scherer, Andreas G. (2006): Kritik der Organisation oder Organisation der Kritik? Wissenschaftstheoretische Bemerkungen zum Umgang mit Organisationstheorien. In: Kieser, Alfred/Ebers, Mark (Eds., 2006): Organisationstheorien. 6th edition. Kohlhammer, Stuttgart, 2006, pp. 19-62.

Scherm, Ewald/Pietsch, Gotthard (2007): Organisation. Oldenbourg, München, 2007.

Schmid, Stefan (1994): Orthodoxer Positivismus und Symbolismus im Internationalen Management – Eine kritische Reflexion situativer und interpretativer Ansätze. Discussion Paper No. 49. Catholic University Eichstätt, Ingolstadt, 1994.

Schmid, Stefan (1996): Multikulturalität in der internationalen Unternehmung: Konzepte – Reflexionen – Implikationen. Gabler, Wiesbaden, 1996.

Schmid, Stefan (2003): How Multinational Corporations Can Upgrade Foreign Subsidiaries: A Case Study from Central and Eastern Europe. In: Stüting, Heinz-Jürgen/Dorow, Wolfgang/Claassen, Frank/Blazejewski, Susanne (Eds., 2003): Change Management in Transition Economies: Integrating Corporate Strategy, Structure and Culture. Palgrave/Macmillan, Houndmills et al., 2003, pp. 273-290.

Schmid, Stefan (2004): The Roles of Foreign Subsidiaries in Network MNCs – A Critical Review of the Literature and Some Directions for Future Research. In: Larimo, Jorma/Rumpunen, Sami (Eds., 2004): European Research on Foreign Direct Investment and International Human Resource Management. Vol. 112. Vaasan Yliopiston Julkaisuja, Vaasa, 2004, pp. 237-255.

Schmid, Stefan (2005): Kooperation: Erklärungsperspektiven interaktionstheoretischer Ansätze. In: Zentes, Joachim/Swoboda, Bernhard/Morschett, Dirk (Eds., 2005): Kooperationen, Allianzen und Netzwerke: Grundlagen – Ansätze – Perspektiven. Gabler, Wiesbaden, 2005.

Schmid, Stefan/Bäurle, Iris/Kutschker, Michael (1998): Tochtergesellschaften in international tätigen Unternehmungen – Ein "State-of-the-Art" unterschiedlicher Rollentypologien. Discussion Paper No. 104. Catholic University Eichstätt, Ingolstadt, 1998.

Schmid, Stefan/Daniel, Andrea (2010): Headquarters-Subsidiary Relationships from a Social Psychological Perspective: How Perception Gaps Concerning the Subsidiary's Role May Lead to Conflict. In: Dörrenbächer, Christoph/Geppert, Mike (Eds., 2010): Politics and Power in the Multinational Corporation: The Role of Institutions, Interests and Identities. Cambridge University Press, Cambridge et al., 2010, pp. 255-280.

Schmid, Stefan/Daub, Matthias (2005): Service Offshoring Subsidiaries – Towards a Typology. Working Paper No. 12, ESCP-EAP European School of Management Berlin, 2005.

Schmid, Stefan/Dzedek, Lars R. (2011): Subsidiary Initiatives in Multinational Corporations: What Do We Know About Them, Their Antecedents And Their Consequences? ESCP Europe Working Paper No. 59. ESCP European School of Management, Berlin, 2011.

Schmid, Stefan/Dzedek, Lars R./Lehrer, Mark (2014): From Rocking the Boat to Wagging the Dog: A Literature Review of Subsidiary Initiative Research and Integrative Framework. In: Journal of International Management, Vol. 20, No. 2, 2014, pp. 201-218.

Schmid, Stefan/Hartmann, Swantje (2011): Product Innovation Processes in Foreign Subsidiaries – The Influence of Local Stakeholders. In: Schmid, Stefan (Ed., 2011): Internationale Unternehmungen und das Management ausländischer Tochtergesellschaften. Gabler, Wiesbaden, 2011, pp. 258-291.

Schmid, Stefan/Kretschmer, Katharina (2010): Performance Evaluation of Foreign Subsidiaries: A Review of the Literature and a Contingency Framework. In: International Journal of Management Reviews, Vol. 12, No. 3, 2010, pp. 219-258.

Schmid, Stefan/Kutschker, Michael (2003): Rollentypologien für ausländische Tochtergesellschaften in Multinationalen Unternehmungen. In: Holtbrügge, Dirk (Ed., 2003): Management Multinationaler Unternehmungen. Festschrift zum 60. Geburtstag von Martin K. Welge. Physika/Springer, Heidelberg, 2003, pp. 161-182.

Schmid, Stefan/Machulik, Mario (2006): What Has Perlmutter Really Written? A Comprehensive Analysis of the EPRG Concept. ESCP-EAP Working Paper No. 16. ESCP-EAP European School of Management, Berlin, 2006.

Schmid, Stefan/Maurer, Julia (2011): Relationships Between MNC Subsidiaries – Opening a Black Box in the International Business Field. In: Schmid, Stefan (Ed., 2011): Internationale Unternehmungen und das Management ausländischer Tochtergesellschaften. Gabler, Wiesbaden, 2011, pp. 53-83.

Schmid, Stefan/Oesterle, Michael-Jörg (2009): Internationales Management als Wissenschaft – Herausforderungen und Zukunftsperspektiven. In: Oesterle, Michael-Jörg/Schmid, Stefan (Eds., 2009): Internationales Management. Forschung, Lehre, Praxis. Schäffer-Poeschel, Stuttgart, 2009, pp. 3-36.

Schmid, Stefan/Schurig, Andreas (2003): The Development of Critical Capabilities in Foreign Subsidiaries: Disentangling the Role of the Subsidiary's Business Network. In: International Business Review, Vol. 12, No. 6, 2003, pp. 755-782.

Schmid, Stefan/Schurig, Andreas/Kutschker, Michael (2002): The MNC as a Network – A Closer Look at Intra-Organizational Flows. In: Lundan, Sarianna M. (Ed., 2002): Network Knowledge in International Business. Edward Elgar, Cheltenham, 2002, pp. 45-72.

Schotter, Andreas/Beamish, Paul W. (2011): Performance Effects of MNC Headquarters-Subsidiary Conflict and the Role of Boundary Spanners: The Case of Headquarter Initiative Rejection. In: Journal of International Management, Vol. 17, No. 3, 2011, pp. 243-259.

Schotter, Andreas/Bontis, Nick (2009): Intra-Organizational Knowledge Exchange: An Examination of Reverse Capability Transfer in Multinational Corporations. In: Journal of Intellectual Capital, Vol. 10, No. 1, 2009, pp. 149-164.

Schreyögg, Georg (1997): Kommentar: Theorien organisatorischer Ressourcen. In: Ortmann, Günther/Jörg, Sydow./Türk, Klaus (Eds., 1997): Theorien der Organisation: Die Rückkehr der Gesellschaft. Westdeutscher Verlag, Wiesbaden, 1997, pp. 481-486.

Schreyögg, Georg (1999): Organisation. 3rd edition, Gabler, Wiesbaden, 1999.

Schreyögg, Georg (2012): Grundlagen der Organisation. Basiswissen für Studium und Praxis. Springer Gabler, Wiesbaden, 2012.

Schumpeter, Joseph A. (1934): The Theory of Economic Development. Harvard University Press, Cambridge, 1934.

Schwenk, Charles R. (1988): The Cognitive Perspective on Strategic Decision Making. In: Journal of Management Studies, Vol. 25, No. 1, 1988, pp. 41-55.

Scott, Pamela Sharkey/Gibbons, Patrick T. (2009): How Subsidiaries Are Battling to Survive and Grow. In: Strategy & Leadership, Vol. 37, No. 4, 2009, pp. 43-47.

Scott, Pamela/Gibbons, Patrick/Coughlan, Joseph (2010): Developing Subsidiary Contribution to the MNC – Subsidiary Entrepreneurship and Strategy Creativity. In: Journal of International Management, Vol. 16, No. 4, 2010, pp. 328-339.

Selznick, Philip (1957): Leadership in Administration. A Sociological Interpretation. University of California Press, Berkely, Los Angeles, 1957.

Shane, Scott (2000): Prior Knowledge and the Discovery of Entrepreneurial Opportunities. In: Organization Science, Vol. 11, No. 4, 2000, pp. 448-469.

Shane, Scott (2003): A General Theory of Entrepreneurship. Edward Elgar, Cheltenham, Northampton, 2003.

Shane, Scott/Locke, Edwin A./Collins, Christopher J. (2003): Entrepreneurial Motivation. In: Human Resource Management, Vol. 13, No. 2, 2003, pp. 257-279.

Shane, Scott/Venkataraman, Sankaran (2000): The Promise of Entrepreneurship as a Field of Research. In: Academy of Management Review, Vol. 25, No. 1, 2000, pp. 217-226.

Shelanski, Howard A./Klein, Peter G. (1995): Empirical Research in Transaction Cost Economics: A Review and Assessment. In: Journal of Law, Economic, & Organization, Vol. 11, No. 2, 1995, pp. 335-361.

Shepherd, Dean A./DeTienne, Dawn R. (2005): Prior Knowledge, Potential Financial Reward, and Opportunity Identification. In: Entrepreneurship: Theory & Practice, Vol. 29, No. 1, 2005, pp. 91-112.

Shuy, Roger W. (2001): In-Person versus Telephone Interviewing. In: Gubrium, Jaber F./Holstein, James A. (Eds., 2001): Handbook of Interview Research. Context & Method. Thousand Oaks, London, New Delhi, 2001, pp. 537-555.

Siggelkow, Nicolaj (2007): Persuasion with Case Studies. In: Academy of Management Journal, Vol. 50, No. 1, 2007, pp. 20-24.

Simon, Herbert A. (1976): Administrative Behavior. A Study of Decision-Making Processes in Administrative Organization. 3rd edition, Free Press, New York, 1976.

Simonin, Bernard L. (2004): An Empirical Investigation of the Process of Knowledge Transfer in International Strategic Alliances. In: Journal of International Business Studies, Vol. 35, No. 5, 2004, pp. 407-427.

Sinkovics, Rudolf R./Penz, Elfriede/Ghauri, Pervez N. (2008): Enhancing the Trustworthiness of Qualitative Research in International Business. In: Management International Review, Vol. 48, No. 6, 2008, pp. 689-714.

Sirmon, David G./Gove, Steve/Hitt, Michael A. (2008): Resource Management in Dyadic Competitive Rivalry: The Effects of Resource Bundling and Deployment. In: Academy of Management Journal, Vol. 51, No. 5, 2008, pp. 919-935.

Sirmon, David G./Hitt, Michael A. (2003): Managing Resources: Linking Unique Resources, Management, and Wealth Creation in Family Firms. In: Entrepreneurship Theory and Practice, Vol. 27, No. 4, 2003, pp. 339-358.

Sirmon, David G./Hitt, Michael A. (2009): Contingencies within Dynamic Managerial Capabilities: Interdependent Effects of Resource Investment and Deployment on Firm Performance. In: Strategic Management Journal, Vol. 30, No. 13, 2009, pp. 1375-1394.

Sirmon, David G./Hitt, Michael A./Arregle, Jean-Luc/Tochman Campbell, Joanna (2010): The Dynamic Interplay of Capability Strengths and Weaknesses: Investigating The Bases of Temporary Competitive Advantage. In: Strategic Management Journal, Vol. 31, No. 13, 2010, pp. 1386-1409.

Sirmon, David G./Hitt, Michael A./Ireland, R. Duane (2007): Managing Firm Resources in Dynamic Environments to Create Value: Looking Inside the Black Box. In: Academy of Management Review, Vol. 32, No. 1, 2007, pp. 273-292.

Sirmon, David G./Hitt, Michael A./Ireland, R. Duane/Gilbert, Brett Anitra (2011): Resource Orchestration to Create Competitive Advantage: Breadth, Depth, and Life Cycle Effects. In: Journal of Management, Vol. 37, No. 5, 2011, pp. 1390-1412.

Sohail, M. S./Ayadurai, S. (2007): The Effects of Environmental Turbulence on Multinational Subsidiaries Performance and Entrepreneurial Behavior: Evidence from a Developing Nation. In: Journal of International Marketing & Marketing Research, Vol. 32, No. 1, 2007, pp. 41-55.

Sohail, Sadiq M./Ayadurai, Selvamalar (2004): Entrepreneurship in Multinational Subsidiaries: Perspectives from a Developing Nation. In: Journal of Management & World Business Research, Vol. 1, No. 1, 2004, pp. 45-57.

Sohail, Sadiq M./Ayadurai, Selvamalar (2007): The Effects of Environmental Turbulence on Multinational Subsidiaries Performance and Entrepreneurial Behavior: Evidence from a Developing Nation. In: Journal of International Marketing & Marketing Research, Vol. 32, No. 1, 2007, pp. 41-55.

Sousa, Filipe J. (2010): Metatheories in Research: Positivism, Postmodernism, and Critical Realism. In: Woodside, Arch G. (Ed., 2010): Organizational Culture, Business-to-Business Relationships, and Interfirm Neworks (Advances in Business Marketing and Purchasing, Volume 16). Emerald, Bingley, 2010, pp. 455-503.

Spanos, Yiannis E./Lioukas, Spyros (2001): An Examination into the Causal Logic of Rent Generation: Contrasting Porter's Competitive Strategy Framework and the Resource-Based Perspective. In: Strategic Management Journal, Vol. 22, No. 10, 2001, p. 907.

Stake, Robert E. (1995): The Art of Case Study Research. Sage, Thousand Oaks et al., 1995.

Steensma, H. Kevin/Marino, Louis/Weaver, K. Mark/Dickson, Pat H. (2000): The Influence of National Culture on the Formation of Technology Alliances by Entrepreneurial Firms. In: The Academy of Management Journal, Vol. 43, No. 5, 2000, pp. 951-973.

Stevenson, Howard H./Jarillo, J. Carlos (1990): A Paradigm of Entrepreneurship: Entrepreneurial Management. In: Strategic Management Journal, Vol. 11, Special Issue on Corporate Entrepreneurship, 1990, pp. 17-27.

Stone, Dan N./Deci, Edward L./Ryan, Richard M. (2009): Beyond Talk: Creating Autonomous Motivation through Self-Determination Theory. In: Journal of General Management, Vol. 34, No. 3, 2009, pp. 75-91.

Stonehouse, George/Snowdown, Brian (2007): Competitive Advantage Revisited: Michael Porter on Strategy and Competitiveness. In: Journal of Management Inquiry, Vol. 16, No. 3, 2007, pp. 256-273.

Stopford, John M./Wells, Louis T. (1972): Managing the Multinational Enterprise. Organization of the Firm and Ownership of the Subsidiaries. Basic Books, New York, 1972.

Strutzenberger, Anna/Ambos, Tina C. (2014): Unraveling the Subsidiary Initiative Process. In: International Journal of Management Reviews, Vol. 16, No. 3, 2014, pp. 314-339.

Surlemont, Bernard (1998): A Typology of Centres within Multinational Corporations: An Empirical Investigation. In: Birkinshaw, Julian/Hood, Neil (Eds., 1998): Multinational Corporate Evolution and Subsidiary Development. Macmillan, Houndmills et al., 1998, pp. 162-188.

Sydow, Jörg (2006): Management von Netzwerkorganisationen – Zum Stand der Forschung. In: Sydow, Jörg (Ed., 2006): Management von Netzwerkorganisationen. Beiträge aus der Managementforschung. 4th edition. Gabler, Wiesbaden, 2006, pp. 387-472.

Szulanski, Gabriel (1996): Exploring Internal Stickiness: Impediments to the Transfer of Best Practice within the Firm. In: Strategic Management Journal, Vol. 17, Winter Special Issue, 1996, pp. 27-43.

Szulanski, Gabriel (2000): The Process of Knowledge Transfer: A Diachronic Analysis of Stickiness. In: Organizational Behavior & Human Decision Processes, Vol. 82, No. 1, 2000, pp. 9-27.

Taggart, James H. (1997a): Autonomy and Procedural Justice: A Framework for Evaluating Subsidiary Strategy. In: Journal of International Business Studies, Vol. 28, No. 1, 1997, pp. 51-76.

Taggart, James H. (1997b): An Evaluation of the Integration-Responsiveness Framework: MNC Manufacturing Subsidiaries in the UK. In: Management International Review, Vol. 37, No. 4, 1997, pp. 295-318.

Taggart, James H. (1998): Identification and Development of Strategy at Subsidiary Level. In: Birkinshaw, Julian/Hood, Neil (Eds., 1998): Multinational Corporate Evolution and Subsidiary Development. Macmillan, Houndmills et al., 1998, pp. 23-49.

Tan, Danchi/Mahoney, Joseph T. (2006): Why a Multinational Firm Chooses Expatriates: Integrating Resource-Based, Agency and Transaction Costs Perspectives. In: Journal of Management Studies, Vol. 43, No. 3, 2006, pp. 457-484.

Teece, David J./Pisano, Gary/Shuen, Amy (1990): Firm Capabilities, Resources and the Concept of Strategy. Economic Analysis and Policy Working Paper EAP-38, Institute of Management, Innovation and Organization, University of California, Berkeley, 1990.

Teece, David J./Pisano, Gary/Shuen, Amy (1997): Dynamic Capabilities and Strategic Management. In: Strategic Management Journal, Vol. 18, No. 7, 1997, pp. 509-533.

Teng, Bing-Sheng (2007): Corporate Entrepreneurship Activities through Strategic Alliances: A Resource-Based Approach toward Competitive Advantage. In: Journal of Management Studies, Vol. 44, No. 1, 2007, pp. 119-142.

Thomke, Stefan/Kuemmerle, Walter (2002): Asset Accumulation, Interdependence and Technological Change: Evidence from Pharmaceutical Drug Discovery. In: Strategic Management Journal, Vol. 23, No. 7, 2002, pp. 619-635.

Thompson, James D. (1967): Organizations in Action. McGraw-Hill, New York et al., 1967.

Tiwana, Amrit (2008): Do Bridging Ties Complement Strong Ties? An Empirical Examination of Alliance Ambidexterity. In: Strategic Management Journal, Vol. 29, No. 3, 2008, pp. 251-272.

Tsai, Ming-Ten/Yu, Ming-Chu/Lee, Kuo-Wei (2006): Relationships between Subsidiary Strategic Roles and Organizational Configuration: The Case of Taiwanese Multinational Companies. In: International Journal of Commerce and Management, Vol. 16, No. 1, 2006, pp. 3-14.

Tsai, Wenpin (2001): Knowledge Transfer in Intraorganizational Networks: Effects of Network Position and Absorptive Capacity on Business Unit Innovation and Performance. In: Academy of Management Journal, Vol. 44, No. 5, 2001, pp. 996-1004.

Tsai, Wenpin/Ghoshal, Sumantra (1998): Social Capital and Value Creation: The Role of Intrafirm Networks. In: Academy of Management Journal, Vol. 41, No. 4, 1998, pp. 464-476.

Tsang, Eric W. K. (1998): Motives for Strategic Alliance: A Resource-Based Perspective. In: Scandinavian Journal of Management, Vol. 14, No. 3, 1998, pp. 207-221.

Tseng, Cher-Hung/Fong, Cher-Min/Su, Kuo-Hsien (2004): The Determinants of MNC Subsidiary Initiatives: Implications for Small Business. In: International Journal Globalisation and Small Business, Vol. 1, No. 1, 2004, pp. 92-114.

Ulrich, David/Barney, Jay B. (1984): Perspectives in Organizations: Resource Dependence, Efficiency, and Population. In: The Academy of Management Review, Vol. 9, No. 3, 1984, pp. 471-481.

Utterback, James M./Abernathy, William J. (1975): A Dynamic Model of Process and Product Innovation. In: Omega, The International Journal of Management Science, Vol. 3, No. 6, 1975, pp. 639-656.

Van De Ven, Andrew H./Poole, Marshall S. (1995): Explaining Development and Change in Organizations. In: Academy of Management Review, Vol. 20, No. 3, 1995, pp. 510-540.

Venaik, Sunil/Midgley, David F./Devinney, Timothey M. (2002): A New Perspective on the Integration-Responsiveness Pressures Confronting Multinational Firms. Working Paper 2002/93/MKT, INSEAD, 2002.

Verbeke, Alain/Chrisman, James J./Yuan, Wenlong (2007): A Note on Strategic Renewal and Corporate Venturing in the Subsidiaries of Multinational Enterprises. In: Entrepreneurship: Theory & Practice, Vol. 31, No. 4, 2007, pp. 585-600.

Verbeke, Alain/Yuan, Wenlong (2005): Subsidiary Autonomous Activities in Multinational Enterprises: A Transaction Cost Perspective. In: Management International Review, Special Issue No. 2, 2005, pp. 31-52.

Vernon, Raymond (1966): International Investments and International Trade in The Product Cycle. In: Quarterly Journal of Economics, Vol. 80, No. 2, 1966, pp. 190-207.

Vigoda, Eran (2003): Developments in Organizational Politics. Edward Elgar, Cheltenham, Northampton, 2003.

Vigoda-Gadot, Eran/Drory, Amos (Eds., 2006): Handbook of Organizational Politics. Edward Elgar, Cheltenham, Northampton, 2006.

Volkmann, Christine K./Tokarski, Kim O./Grünhagen, Marc (2010): Entrepreneurship in a European Perspective: Concepts for the Creation and Growth of New Ventures. Gabler, Wiesbaden, 2010.

Vroom, Victor H./Yetton, Phillip W. (1973): Leadership and Decision-Making. University of Pittsburgh, Pittsburgh, 1973.

Wang, Heli/Chen, Wei-Ru (2010): Is Firm-Specific Innovation Associated with Greater Value Appropriation? The Roles of Environmental Dynamism and Technological Diversity. In: Research Policy, Vol. 39, No. 1, 2010, pp. 141-154.

Welch, Catherine/Marschan-Piekkari, Rebecca/Penttinen, Heli/Tahvanainen, Marja (2002): Corporate Elites as Informants in Qualitative International Business Research. In: International Business Review, Vol. 11, No. 5, 2002, pp. 611-628.

Welch, Catherine/Piekkari, Rebecca/Plakoyiannaki, Emmaunella/Paavilainen-Mäntymäki, Eriikka (2011): Theorising from Case Studies: Towards a Pluralist Future for International Business Research. In: Journal of International Business Studies, Vol. 42, No. 5, 2011, pp. 740-762.

Welge, Martin K. (1987): Unternehmungsführung. Band 2: Organisation. C.E Poeschel, Stuttgart, 1987.

Wernerfelt, Birger (1984): A Resource-Based View of the Firm. In: Strategic Management Journal, Vol. 5, No. 2, 1984, pp. 171-180.

Wernerfelt, Birger (2011): The Use of Resources in Resource Acquisition. In: Journal of Management, Vol. 37, No. 5, 2011, pp. 1369-1373.

Westney, Eleanor D./Zaheer, Srilata (2003): The Multinational Enterprise as an Organization. In: Rugman, Alan M. (Ed., 2003): The Oxford Handbook of International Business. Oxford University Press, Oxford, 2003, pp. 349-379.

White, Roderick E./Poynter, Thomas E. (1984): Strategies for Foreign-Owned Subsidiaries in Canada. In: Business Quarterly, Summer, 1984, pp. 59-69.

White, Roderick E./Poynter, Thomas E. (1989): Achieving Worldwide Advantage with the Horizontal Organization. In: Business Quarterly, Vol. 54, No. 2, 1989, pp. 55-60.

Whittington, Richard (1988): Environmental Structure and Theories of Strategic Choice. In: Journal of Management Studies, Vol. 25, No. 6, 1988, pp. 521-536.

Wiklund, Johan/Shepherd, Dean A. (2009): The Effectiveness of Alliances and Acquisitions: The Role of Resource Combination Activities. In: Entrepreneurship: Theory & Practice, Vol. 33, No. 1, 2009, pp. 193-212.

Williams, Christopher (2009): Subsidiary-Level Determinants of Global Initiatives in Multinational Corporations. In: Journal of International Management, Vol. 15, No. 1, 2009, pp. 92-104.

Williams, Christopher/Lee, Soo Hee (2009): International Management, Political Arena and Dispersed Entrepreneurship in the MNC. In: Journal of World Business, Vol. 44, No. 3, 2009, pp. 287-299.

Williams, Christopher/Lee, Soo Hee (2011a): Entrepreneurial Contexts and Knowledge Creation within the Multinational Corporation. In: Journal of World Business, Vol. 46, No. 2, 2011, pp. 253-264.

Williams, Christopher/Lee, Soo Hee (2011b): Political Heterarchy and Dispersed Entrepreneurship in the MNC. In: Journal of Management Studies, Vol. 48, No. 6, 2011, pp. 1243-1268.

Williamson, Oliver E. (1975): Markets and Hierarchies – Analysis and Antitrust Implications. Free Press, New York, 1975.

Wilson, Jonathan (2010): Essentials of Business Research – A Guide to Doing Your Research Project. Sage, London, 2010.

Woodward, Joan (1965): Industrial Organization: Theory and Practise. Oxford University Press, London, 1965.

Worthington, William J. (2007): Resource Portfolio Management: Bundling Process. Department of Management. Texas A&M University. Dissertation, 2007.

Wright, Peter (1987): A Refinement of Porter's Strategies. In: Strategic Management Journal, Vol. 8, No. 1, 1987, pp. 93-101.

Wrona, Thomas (2005): Die Fallstudienanalyse als wissenschaftliche Forschungsmethode. Working Paper No. 10, ESCP-EAP European School of Management, 2005.

Yamin, Mo/Andersson, Ulf (2011): Subsidiary Importance in the MNC: What Role Does Internal Embeddedness Play? In: International Business Review, Vol. 20, No. 2, 2011, pp. 151-162.

Yamin, Mo/Hsin-Ju Stephie, Tsai/Holm, Ulf (2011): The Performance Effects of Headquarters' Involvement in Lateral Innovation Transfers in Multinational Corporations. In: Management International Review (MIR), Vol. 51, No. 2, 2011, pp. 157-177.

Yamin, Mo/Sinkovics, Rudolf R. (2010): ICT Deployment and Resource-Based Power in Multinational Enterprise Futures. In: Futures, Vol. 42, No. 9, 2010, pp. 952-959.

Yamin, Mohammad (2002): Subsidiary Entrepreneurship and the Advantage of Multinationality. In: Havila, Virpi/Forsgren, Mats/Hakansson, Hakan (Eds., 2002): Critical Perspectives on Internationalisation. Pergamon Press, Oxford, 2002, pp. 133-150.

Yamin, Mohammad (2005): Subsidiary Business Networks and Opportunity Development in Multinational Enterprises: A Comparison of the Influences of Internal and External Business Networks. In: Ghauri, Pervez N./Hadjikhani, Amjad/Johanson, Jan (Eds., 2005): Managing Business Opportunity Development in Business Networks. Palgrave Macmillan, Houndmills et al., 2005, pp. 91-109.

Yin, Robert K. (2009): Case Study Research. 4th edition, Sage, Thousand Oaks et al., 2009.

Yli-Renko, Helena/Autio, Erkko/Sapienza, Harry J. (2001): Social Capital, Knowledge Acquisition, and Knowledge Exploitation in Young Technology-Based Firms. In: Strategic Management Journal, Vol. 22, No. 6-7, 2001, pp. 587-613.

Young, Stephen/Dimitratos, Pavlos/Dana, Léo-Paul (2003): International Entrepreneurship Research: What Scope for International Business Theories? In: Journal of International Entrepreneurship, Vol. 1, No. 1, 2003, pp. 31-42.

Young, Stephen/Tavares, Ana T. (2004): Centralization and Autonomy: Back to the Future. In: International Business Review, Vol. 13, No. 2, 2004, pp. 215-237.

Zaefarian, Ghasem/Henneberg, Stephan C./Naudé, Peter (2011): Resource Acquisition Strategies in Business Relationships. In: Industrial Marketing Management, Vol. 40, No. 6, 2011, pp. 862-874.

Zahra, Shaker A. (1993): A Conceptual Model of Entrepreneurship as Firm Behavior: A Critique and Extension. In: Entrepreneurship: Theory & Practice, Vol. 17, No. 4, 1993, pp. 5-21.

Zahra, Shaker A. (1995): Corporate Entrepreneurship and Financial Performance: The Case of Management Leveraged Buyouts. In: Journal of Business Venturing, Vol. 10, No. 3, 1995, pp. 225-247.

Zahra, Shaker A. (1996): Governance, Ownership, and Corporate Entrepreneurship: The Moderating Impact of Industry Technological Opportunities. In: The Academy of Management Journal, Vol. 39, No. 6, 1996, pp. 1713-1735.

Zahra, Shaker A./Covin, Jeffrey G. (1995): Contextual Influences on the Corporate Entrepreneurship-Performance Relationship: A Longitudinal Analysis. In: Journal of Business Venturing, Vol. 10, No. 1, 1995, pp. 43-58.

Zahra, Shaker A./Dharwadkar, Ravi/George, Gerard (2000): Entrepreneurship in Multinational Subsidiaries: The Effects of Corporate and Local Environment Contexts. CIBER Working Paper No. 99/00-027, Georgia Institute of Technology, Atlanta, 2000.

Zahra, Shaker A./George, Gerard (2002): Absorptive Capacity: A Review, Reconceptualization, and Extension. In: Academy of Management Review, Vol. 27, No. 2, 2002, pp. 185-203.

Zahra, Shaker A./Jennings, Daniel F./Kuratko, Donald F. (1999): The Antecedents and Consequences of Firm-Level Entrepreneurship: The State of the Field. In: Entrepreneurship: Theory & Practice, Vol. 24, No. 2, 1999, pp. 47-67.

Zahra, Shaker A./Sapienza, Harry J./Davidsson, Per (2006): Entrepreneurship and Dynamic Capabilities: A Review, Model and Research Agenda. In: Journal of Management Studies, Vol. 43, No. 4, 2006, pp. 917-955.

Zahra, Shaker A./Wright, Mike (2011): Entrepreneurship's Next Act. In: Academy of Management Perspectives, Vol. 25, No. 4, 2011, pp. 67-83.

Zalan, Tatiana/Lewis, Geoffrey (2004): Writing about Methods in Qualitative Research: Towards a More Transparent Approach. In: Marschan-Piekkari, Rebecca/Welch, Catherine (Eds., 2004): Handbook of Qualitative Research Methods for International Business. Edward Elgar, Cheltenham, Northampton, 2004, pp. 507-526.

Zollo, Maurizio/Winter, Sidney G. (2002): Deliberate Learning and the Evolution of Dynamic Capabilities. In: Organization Science, Vol. 13, No. 3, 2002, pp. 339-351.

Zou, Shaoming/Cavusgil, S. Tamer (1996): Global Strategy: A Review and an Integrated Conceptual Framework. In: European Journal of Marketing, Vol. 30, No. 1, 1996, pp. 52-69.

zu Knyphausen-Aufseß, Dodo (1997): Auf dem Weg zu einem Ressourcenoritierten Paradigma? Resource Dependence-Theorie der Organisation und Resource-Based View des Strategischen Managements im Vergleich. In: Ortmann, Günther/Jörg, Sydow./Türk, Klaus (Eds., 1997): Theorien der Organisation: Die Rückkehr der Gesellschaft. Westdeutscher Verlag, Wiesbaden, 1997, pp. 452-480.

Zucchella, Antonella/Maccarini, Maurizio E./Scabini, Paolo (2007): Entrepreneurial Capabilities in MNE Subsidiaries: The Case of the Dialysis Industry. In: International Journal of Entrepreneurship and Small Business, Vol. 4, No. 3, 2007, pp. 305-324.

Zucchella, Antonella/Scabini, Paolo (2007): International Entrepreneurship: Theoretical Foundations and Practices: Theoretical Foundations and Empirical Analysis. Palgrave/Macmillan, Basingstoke, 2007.